Classical Literature on Screen

Martin M. Winkler argues for a new approach to various creative affinities between ancient verbal and modern visual narratives. He examines screen adaptations of classical epic, tragedy, comedy, myth, and history, exploring, for example, how ancient rhetorical principles regarding the emotions apply to moving images and how Aristotle's perspective on thrilling plot-turns can recur on screen. He also interprets several popular films, such as *300* and *Nero*, and analyzes works by international directors, among them Pier Paolo Pasolini (*Oedipus Rex, Medea*), Jean Cocteau (*The Testament of Orpheus*), Mai Zetterling (*The Girls*), Lars von Trier (*Medea*), Arturo Ripstein (*Such Is Life*), John Ford (Westerns), Alfred Hitchcock (*Psycho*), and Spike Lee (*Chi-Raq*). This book demonstrates the undiminished vitality of classical myth and literature in our visual media, as with screen portrayals of Helen of Troy. It is important for all classicists and for scholars and students of film, literature, and history.

MARTIN M. WINKLER is University Professor and Professor of Classics at George Mason University. His most recent books are *Cinema and Classical Texts: Apollo's New Light* (Cambridge, 2009), *The Roman Salute: Cinema, History, Ideology* (2009), and *Arminius the Liberator: Myth and Ideology* (2015). He has also published numerous articles, book chapters, and reviews, and edited several essay collections on classical antiquity and film.

Classical Literature on Screen

Affinities of Imagination

MARTIN M. WINKLER

CAMBRIDGE
UNIVERSITY PRESS

CAMBRIDGE
UNIVERSITY PRESS

University Printing House, Cambridge CB2 8BS, United Kingdom

One Liberty Plaza, 20th Floor, New York, NY 10006, USA

477 Williamstown Road, Port Melbourne, VIC 3207, Australia

314-321, 3rd Floor, Plot 3, Splendor Forum, Jasola District Centre, New Delhi - 110025, India

79 Anson Road, #06-04/06, Singapore 079906

Cambridge University Press is part of the University of Cambridge.

It furthers the University's mission by disseminating knowledge in the pursuit of education, learning and research at the highest international levels of excellence.

www.cambridge.org
Information on this title: www.cambridge.org/9781107191280
DOI: 10.1017/9781108123358

First published 2017

A catalogue record for this publication is available from the British Library

Library of Congress Cataloging in Publication data
Names: Winkler, Martin M., author.
Title: Classical literature on screen : affinities of imagination / Martin M. Winkler.
Description: New York : Cambridge University Press, 2017. | Includes bibliographical
references and index.
Identifiers: LCCN 2017026504 | ISBN 9781107191280
Subjects: LCSH: Classical literature – History and criticism. | Motion pictures and literature.
Classification: LCC PA3009 .W56 2017 | DDC 880.09–dc23
LC record available at https://lccn.loc.gov/2017026504

ISBN 978-1-107-19128-0 Hardback
ISBN 978-1-316-64187-3 Paperback

Contents

List of Illustrations

Images are either screenshots, in the public domain, or from the William Knight Zewadski Collection, the Jerry Murbach Collection, and the author's collection. High-resolution reproductions of all illustrations, many in color, may be found under the Resources tab at http://www.cambridge.org/9781107191280.

Acknowledgments

I am primarily indebted to Maria Cecília de Miranda Nogueira Coelho, who has been most helpful and supportive in various ways, not least through her friendship and hospitality. Frederick Ahl, Josef Früchtl, Sue Matheson, Mae Smethurst, and Alejandro Valverde García alerted me to certain important details or provided valuable advice. Wolfgang Haase originally granted me the equally pleasing and necessary leeway to be extensively Aristophanic. The Japanese Ku Na'uka Theatre Company furnished me with digital versions of their productions of Greek drama. Jocy de Oliveira supplied me with answers, via e-mail, to specific questions about *Kseni*. With his customary generosity, William Knight Zewadski granted me access to his unique collection of film stills. I am also grateful to Jerry Murbach for permission to use images from his collection of stills. At the press, Michael Sharp once again provided editorial expertise and support. In Washington, DC, the aptly named and extraordinarily secret (*scire nefas*) League of Extraordinary Gentlemen has for many years supplied me with intellectual and other nourishment (*vina liques*) through Thomas Mann, its founder, convener, and genial host.

Preliminary versions of four chapters were published in disparate international venues and have been revised and brought up to date here.[1] The present book is a companion to *Cinema and Classical Texts: Apollo's New Light*, which had been dedicated to the god of light and enlightenment.[2] Apollo was also the leader of the nine Muses, the Greek and Roman patron goddesses of arts and sciences, hence of all creative and intellectual endeavors. Poet and filmmaker Jean Cocteau on several occasions referred to the cinema as the tenth Muse.[3] It is therefore appropriate that I should pay homage to the classical ladies in this "sequel" to the Apollo book. I list, however, not nine but eighteen of their most remarkable

---

[1] Chapter 4: Winkler 2014b; Chapter 5: Winkler 2014a; Chapter 9: Winkler 2013; Chapter 10: Winkler 2016. – I cite secondary works in my notes by author's or editor's last name and date of publication. Full references are in my Bibliography. In cases when a last name can refer to more than one person, I include the first name in my note references to avoid ambiguity. However, I refer to my own publications by last name only, as here.

[2] Winkler 2009a.   [3] References in Winkler 2009a: 41 note 53.

screen incarnations by combining their Greek and Italic ancestries: the Olympian Muses of Hesiod and the *Camenae* of Livius Andronicus. Horace provides me with a precedent for doing so.[4] In naming my eighteen, I am being entirely subjective. All affinities of passion are.

---

[4] Hesiod, *Theogony* 75–79; Livius Andronicus, *Odusia* 1.1; Horace, *Odes* 2.16.38. On the *Camenae* see now Alex Hardie 2016.

ΤΑΙΣ ΤΟΥ Μαρτινου Μουσαισ κινηματογραφικαισ

ΤΑΙΣ ΝΥΝ Ολυμπιαισ

ΑΙ ΕΙΣΙΝ

Μαργαριτησ Χορταξια – νεα Τερψιχορη

Βοδιλ Κιηρ – νεα Πολυμνια

Κλαυδεττη Κολβηρ – νεα Κλειω

Λουισα Μικροποταμοι – νεα Ερατω

Φρανσοαση Δορληακη – νεα Ουρανια

Χαρισ Κελλια – νεα Ευτερπη

Σιμωνη Σιμων – νεα Θαλεια

Καπυσινη – νεα Καλλιοπη

Αυδρια Επκαιουσα – νεα Μελπομενη

ΙΕΡΑ ΗΔΕ Η ΒΙΒΛΟΣ

CAMENIS MARTINI CINEMATOGRAPHICIS

NOSTRI AEVI

QVAE SVNT

DANIELA DARIOEA

MARGARITA GARBO

LILIANA GIS

IOANNA HARLO

VERONICA LACVS

CAROLA LONGOBARDA

LORETTA NOVELLA

SILVIA SIDNIA

NORMA TONSTRIX

SACER HIC LIBER

Introduction

"The classical literatures provide us with prototypes of virtually all later narrative forms and with paradigms of the processes which govern their interaction and evolution." So wrote, in 1966, Robert Scholes and Robert Kellogg in their influential study *The Nature of Narrative*.[1] The statement may seem a truism but is worth our attention, both in regard to the prominence of studies in the classical tradition – or classical reception, as it is now called – and in connection with the wide range of narrative media in word and image, usually in combination. "The raw material of human existence remains ever the same, the molds by which it is given significance and recognizable shape are forever being recreated," Scholes and Kellogg observed later on.[2] This, too, is an accurate if basic statement. But it is important because of a major shift in the way stories have come to be told.

1   Narrative from Text to Image

Verbal narratives – in Greece and Rome, an oral tradition that became the literature of epic, drama, historiography, and the novel – have by now yielded their primacy to visual narratives. Scholes and Kellogg were well aware of this change:

The most powerful influence on contemporary narrative art is not esthetic or even cultural in any broad sense … [There is now] a technological change which may leave a mark on the narrative tradition as profound as the invention of letters itself. We refer to the invention of the motion-picture film with its attendant devices of synchronous sound track and videotape, and with its flexible means of presentation in theater or home.[3]

At their time, Scholes and Kellogg could still call this a "glance in the direction of the future."[4] Half a century later, that future has arrived. It is

[1] Quoted from Scholes, Phelan, and Kellogg 2006: 57. Original edition: Scholes and Kellogg 1966. Phelan is the author of an additional chapter outlining narrative theory since the book's original publication. I quote from the new edition but name only the authors of the quotations I adduce.
[2] Scholes, Phelan, and Kellogg 2006: 156.   [3] Scholes, Phelan, and Kellogg 2006: 279–280.
[4] Scholes, Phelan, and Kellogg 2006: 279.

our present and even has begun to turn into our past. Videotape, for instance, which was looming on the horizon in 1966, is a dead technology in the twenty-first century.

Scholes and Kellogg next argue, correctly, for film as a form of narrative rather than dramatic art, especially regarding the importance of point of view for all narratives. An "acceleration of tradition," they continue, "is an open invitation [to artists] in the field of cinema." But those working on visual narratives only continue doing what literary artists have always done:

> Whether the poet of the film plunders the older forms to feed his new medium . . . or simply allows this new technique to generate new kinds of story . . ., the new form offers open doors where the old has little left but mirrored walls . . . . book and [stage] play are lambs co-existing with a lion cub that is just beginning to find its strength.

This strength they connect with the emergence of European art cinema that had begun around 1960. The films of Ingmar Bergman, Alain Resnais, and Michelangelo Antonioni, whom Scholes and Kellogg name, were decisive, among others, to convince even obstinate naysayers that the cinema was now the equal of all other art forms. (Similar debates had occurred during the silent era.) Cinema as art of visual narrative threatens to eclipse the art of written narrative: "The monuments of the past will remain, as Homeric epic remains, to remind us of a vanished literary medium . . . But the main impetus of narrative art may well pass from the book to the cinema, even as it passed from the oral poet to the book-writer long ago. Truly, all things flow."[5]

This Heraclitean nature of narrative, at least in regard to classical narrative as it returns on our screens, is the *raison d'être* of the present book. Previously I advanced and applied a first theory of the study of classics and cinema: *classical film philology*.[6] Here I pursue a comparable approach to the ways in which the cinema has turned to classical antiquity throughout its history, but from a different perspective. I examine works by the poets of the film, as Scholes and Kellogg elegantly call the great cinema artists, and works by those who plunder: not so much older forms as ancient plots and characters. I can, of course, only pursue a small number of possible subjects, but I hope that these will illuminate, by force of example, the daunting amount of potential themes. Affinities with antiquity, and not only narrative

---

[5] The preceding quotations are from Scholes, Phelan, and Kellogg 2006: 281. Currie 2010 bears out such a perspective by prominently including filmic narrative in his analyses.

[6] Winkler 2009a: 57–69.

ones, are persistent in our culture, and nowhere more so than in the cinema and its later offspring, television and digital media. These visions and modernizations of the past may occasionally produce blurred or distorted images, but they may also offer new insights into well-known works. The chapters in this book contain examples of both kinds. Some deal with works that exhibit, whether intentionally or not, surprising affinities with classical models and enhance our appreciation of, even our sense of awe before, their complexity. Others examine productions that use or abuse antiquity for commercial or political purposes.

I use the term *affinity* rather than *adaptation* or any of its synonyms and terminological relatives. It encompasses all of the latter's varieties while also accommodating yet other reworkings, and it saves us from theoretical agonies over what exactly visual adaptations of literary texts are. Scholars have by now produced a veritable terminological jungle, in which the following growths, as it were, have been thriving: "translation, actualization, reading, critique, dialogization, cannibalization, transmutation, transfiguration, incarnation, transmogrification, transcoding, performance, signifying, rewriting, detournement."[7] Or, more succinctly but still rather nebulously: "Borrowing, Intersecting, and Transforming Sources."[8]

All such procedures are part and parcel of any reception of an earlier culture by a later one. Here the sensible words written by a formerly influential American educator are worth remembering. Almost a century ago John Erskine instituted the Great Books curriculum in higher education. In the opening essay of a collection titled *The Delight of Great Books*, which first appeared in 1928, Erskine came to the heart of the matter on his first page. The great and immortal authors, he maintained, "wrote to be read by the general public, and they assumed in their readers an experience of life and an interest in human nature, nothing more." Just previously Erskine had observed, with characteristic vividness, that "the men who wrote these books would have been horrified if they had known that you and I might think of them only as matter for school and college courses."[9] Erskine was also a popular novelist and a much sought-after public intellectual. He knew that general readers – and now viewers – are as important for literature as any kind of scholar or intellectual. A reader can become a writer; today, readers can easily become screenwriters or filmmakers. All things flow. Adaptations of any kind and on any level of quality are

---

[7] Quoted from Stam 2005: 4 (in section titled "Beyond 'Fidelity'"). Cf. further MacCabe, Murray, and Warner 2011.

[8] Quoted from Andrew 1984: 98 (title of a section in chapter "Adaptation").

[9] Erskine 1935b: 11.

therefore not only to be expected but also unavoidable. Erskine has sensible and humorous things to say about this aspect of great works later in his essay. He mentions a few representative examples of authors whose familiar and beloved creations were reworked by others: Homer by Virgil, Chaucer by Shakespeare, Shakespeare by Shaw, Malory by Tennyson, Malory and Tennyson by Edwin Arlington Robinson.[10]

If such creative reworkings of classical prototypes and paradigms, to quote Scholes and Kellogg's terms, occur on the highest level, how much more often will they occur in popular culture? Here are two revealing answers to this question, one classical and one modern. Roman epic poet Manilius said about Homer: "Posterity has led all the springs flowing from his mouth into its own poetry and so has dared to distribute [one] stream into [many] clear rivers, made fertile by one man's gifts."[11] All literature in the history of Western culture derives from Homer, regardless of the artistic or technological medium involved. Wolfgang Petersen, director of the epic film *Troy* (2004), once adduced another nature image to characterize Homer, the *Iliad*, and its tradition, to which his own film belongs: "If there is something like a tree of storytelling, on which each book, each film, is a tiny leaf, then Homer is its trunk."[12]

I have adduced Scholes and Kellogg and Erskine at some length to point out that my book is intended as a small contribution to a long flow of tradition. It is also part of an ongoing process that carries my studies of the presence of the classical cultures in our visual media into areas that have remained unexamined or mentioned only briefly. As before, I address specific mythical, historical, or mythic-historical aspects of classical literature and their reappearances on screen.

2 Tiresias' Memory: From Homer to Film Studies

The Quarrel of the Ancients and the Moderns, which I adduce in Chapter 2, may prompt at least some of my readers to ask, in the terms made familiar by Harold Bloom, whether there does not exist a certain anxiety of influence – a concept in principle applicable not only to poets but to artists in other creative media as well – between ancient authors and

[10] Erskine 1935b: 18–20.
[11] Manilius, *Astronomica* 2.8–11: *cuiusque ex ore profusos / omnis posteritas latices in carmina duxit / amnemque in tenuis ausa est deducere rivos / unius fecunda bonis.* Here and throughout, translations from non-English sources are my own unless otherwise indicated.
[12] Quoted from Kniebe 2004.

their modern adaptors. This question may be too large for me to answer; it should be posed and answered in connection with specific modern works that exhibit affinities with specific classical models or precursors. Instead, I would here like to discuss one related but different sort of influence that seems to me both symptomatic and dangerous. It is the misleading, indeed false, influence deriving from a misinformed postulate of affinity. A particularly revealing example will illustrate what I have in mind. It also shows why classical philologists ought to engage in cinema studies.

Emigré Russian film scholar Mikhail Iampolski began a monograph on intertextuality and film with a famous episode of the *Odyssey* and accordingly called his book *The Memory of Tiresias*.[13] Why he should have chosen this title is of interest. On three of his four pages of "Introduction" Iampolski prominently discusses Tiresias, as readers would expect him to do. What he tells them, however, is something wholly unexpected for those who have come across Tiresias in classical literature. It is therefore necessary for me to quote Iampolski's take on Tiresias and his memory at some length.

Iampolski prepares his argument by introducing Mnemosyne, the divine personification of memory and the mother of the Muses. Her function is this:

Mnemosyne seems to draw the poet she endows with superior memory into another world, the world of oblivion and the past, identified with death. Lethe, the river of oblivion that flows through Hades, annihilates the memory of the deceased: indeed, it is this very act that renders them dead.[14]

To classical mythologists, the operative term here is *seems*. Mnemosyne was a daughter of the sky god Uranus and the earth goddess Gaia and thus a Titan goddess herself. Her association with the Underworld is far-fetched at best and seems to hinge on Hesiod's statement that Mnemosyne can provide forgetting (*lêsmosynê*) of cares and rest from cares.[15] The statement about Lethe, the River of Forgetting, is unobjectionable, but the juxtaposition of Mnemosyne and Lethe is merely willful. On Iampolski's next page we meet Tiresias:

Among the prophets whose memory the gods preserved after their death, there is one, named Tiresias, who stands out. While still a young man Tiresias happened to sight the goddess Athena bathing in the fountain of Hippocrene. For this he was blinded but at the same time granted the gift of foresight. Later, while wandering

---

[13] Iampolski 1998. The original appeared in Russian in 1993.   [14] Iampolski 1998: 1.
[15] Hesiod, *Theogony* 54–55.

along the slopes of Mount Cyllene he happened to see two snakes copulating and was turned into a woman for many years. The blind androgyne Tiresias was chosen by the gods to bear forever a memory that would not fade.[16]

The version of the myth in which Athena blinds Tiresias and then grants him the gift of understanding bird song – not quite the same as foresight – is attested.[17] But it is not the best-known one. That is the one on which Iampolski reports only in part. He omits Tiresias wounding or killing one of the snakes copulating and being turned into a woman and then, years later, again either wounding one of the same snakes copulating or killing one of another couple of snakes during their copulation and being turned back into a man. When Zeus and Hera call on him to tell them whether men or women receive greater pleasure from sexual intercourse, Tiresias, having the requisite experience, decides in favor of women. An angry Hera strikes him blind, a delighted Zeus grants him second sight.[18]

But this is not the worst misinformation. Nowhere in ancient sources is Tiresias an androgyne: simultaneously male and female. Rather, the story of the snakes and Zeus and Hera's quarrel works only if Tiresias is first of the one and then of the other sex. Forgetting this logical point, Iampolski instead blindly follows modern poetry. Perhaps best known is T. S. Eliot's Tiresias from "The Fire Sermon" in *The Waste Land*. Here are the lines in question:

> I Tiresias, though blind, throbbing between two lives,
> Old man with wrinkled female breasts . . . .
> I Tiresias, old man with wrinkled dugs . . . .
> (And I Tiresias have foresuffered all
> Enacted on this same divan or bed;
> I who have sat by Thebes below the wall
> And walked among the lowest of the dead.)[19]

---

[16] Iampolski 1998: 2.

[17] Pherecydes in Apollodorus, *Library* 3.6.7; Callimachus, *Hymn to Athena – Bath of Pallas* 57–131. Frazer 1921: 361–367 collects the references and discusses the myth's variants in the ancient sources. On Callimachus' hymn see now Stephens 2015: 233–262.

[18] Hesiod, *Melampodia*, Fragment 275 (Merkelbach-West) = 211a–b (Most); easily accessible in Most 2007: 286–289 (Greek and English). The source of the fragment is an ancient commentary (*scholion*) on Homer, *Odyssey* 10.494. The ancient Greek and Latin texts concerning Tiresias are conveniently collected and translated (into French) in Brisson 1976; the book also contains iconographic information. Readers need not be structuralists to profit from Brisson's study. See now also Torres 2014. The *Lexicon Iconographicum Mythologiae Classicae*, 8 Suppl., 1188–1191 (s. v. "Teiresias"), shows no image of either a female or a hermaphroditic Tiresias.

[19] T. S. Eliot, *The Waste Land*: III. "The Fire Sermon" 218–219, 228, and 243–246; quoted from Rainey 2005: 64.

In his note on line 218 Eliot quotes, *in toto*, Ovid's retelling of Tiresias, the snakes, and the gods' quarrel.[20] Eliot observes:

Tiresias, although a mere spectator and not indeed a "character," is yet the most important personage in the poem, uniting all the rest .... all the women are one woman, and the two sexes meet in Tiresias. What Tiresias *sees*, in fact, is the substance of the poem. The whole passage from Ovid is of great anthropological interest.

Eliot did not impute androgyny to Ovid's Tiresias. It seems likely that he took this feature from Guillaume Apollinaire's play *The Breasts of Tiresias*. A feminist scholar explains:

The breasts of Tiresias had made a slightly earlier and even more startling appearance in Guillaume Apollinaire's surrealist play of that name, begun in 1903 but not staged until 1917 – a play that Eliot, with his interest in French avant-garde literature, must almost surely have known.[21]

Iampolski's statement that Tiresias possessed an unfailing memory, however, is on firmer ground. Circe tells Odysseus that Persephone, the queen of the Underworld, had granted only Tiresias the powers of thought and awareness after his death.[22]

But what about Tiresias' memory? Since he is a prophet, the future, not the past, is more important for Tiresias as indeed it is for Odysseus, whose sole reason to descend to the realm of the dead is to obtain information about his return – not to be reminded of something that already occurred. So Iampolski tells us next:

The blind Tiresias would later meet Odysseus in the underworld. Recognizing Odysseus, Tiresias foretells his future. Alongside the seer Odysseus encounters his own mother, who sees him but fails to recognize him. The blind man, it turns out, can see better, for his blindness has retained the past and its images in the dark. To recognize is to place what you see alongside what you know, alongside what has already been. Odysseus's mother, bereft of her memory, cannot "see" her son. Sight without memory is blind.[23]

Only the first two sentences above are correct. Yes, Odysseus encounters the shade of his mother, but he encounters quite a number of other shades

[20] Eliot quotes Ovid, *Metamorphoses* 3.320–338 in Latin. The following quotation is from Rainey 2005: 72–73.
[21] Garber 2000: 158 (in chapter titled "The Secret of Tiresias"). Garber's book first appeared as Garber 1995. Iampolski 1998: 3 has a few things to say about Apollinaire and Eliot.
[22] Homer, *Odyssey* 10.492–495. Heubeck, in Heubeck and Hoekstra 1989: 69, gives a concise explanation.
[23] Iampolski 1998: 2.

as well and converses with them.[24] It is wrong to assert that Anticleia does not recognize her son or that she preserves no memory either of him or of her own life. On the contrary, mother and son have a moving encounter, and Anticleia explains to Odysseus the kind of existence the shades are leading and reveals that she had died of grief over his long absence from home. The reunion of dead mother and living son extends over more than seventy lines.[25] It is even longer than Odysseus' meeting with Tiresias, which immediately preceded it.[26] Iampolski neglects to inform his readers about the importance of the blood of sacrificial animals, which the shades drink. Homer's Tiresias, but not Iampolski's, explains this to Odysseus. Here are the decisive lines in their exchange. Tiresias to Odysseus:

> Now draw back from the pit, and hold your sharp sword away from me,
> so that I can drink from the blood and speak the truth to you.

Odysseus to Tiresias:

> I see before me now the soul of my perished mother,
> but she sits beside the blood in silence, and has not yet deigned
> to look directly at her own son and speak a word to me.
> Tell me, lord, what will make her know me, and know my presence?

Tiresias' reply:

> Easily I will tell you and put it in your understanding.
> Any one of the perished dead you allow to come up
> to the blood will give you a true answer, but if you begrudge this
> to any one, he will return to the place where he came from.

The result, as Odysseus states, is in accordance with this: "I / waited steadily where I was standing, until my mother / came and drank the dark-gurgling blood, and at once she knew me."[27]

Odysseus' mother, then, is *not* bereft of her memory and *can* see her son. And what about Tiresias, whose memory, Iampolski says, has retained the past? Tiresias provides Odysseus with only one piece of information about the past; everything else he tells him is about the future.[28] The past is not

---

[24] Altogether, Odysseus meets twenty-six shades (*Odyssey* 11.51–332 and 385–630): his companion Elpenor, Tiresias, Anticleia; fourteen heroines; three heroes from the Trojan War (Agamemnon, Achilles, Ajax); and six heroes from a more distant past.
[25] Homer, *Odyssey* 11.152–225.   [26] Homer, *Odyssey* 11.90–151.
[27] The preceding quotations are Homer, *Odyssey* 11.95–96, 141–144, 146–149, and 151–153; quoted from Lattimore 1967: 170–172. See further Heubeck in Heubeck and Hoekstra 1989: 80–81 (on *Odyssey* 11.51–54) and 86 (on 11.144–149).
[28] Tiresias mentions the reason why Poseidon is persecuting Odysseus (Homer, *Odyssey* 11. 101–103).

the point when we consult a prophet or seer (unless we are Oedipus); the future is. And that is what prophets usually tell us about, for they "speak ahead," as the very term *pro-phet* (from Greek *prophêtês*) tells us. More importantly, Iampolski does not consider Circe, the sorceress and prophetess who gives Odysseus information and sends him to meet Tiresias: "What Tiresias tells Odysseus could equally well have been relayed by Circe."[29]

Has Iampolski actually read Homer? If so, he has seriously misunderstood him. The result is predictable in its vagueness and assertion by authorial fiat:

Vision, sight, seeing, and looking are all concepts connected with spectacle. Many texts confront us culturally as mobile pictures. In the twentieth century, cinema has come to embody this cultural tendency to cultivate spectacle. But the story Homer tells us also serves to remind us that seeing without remembering means not understanding. The memory of Tiresias turns out to be a better spectator than the clouded gaze of Odysseus's mother. A spectacle that is not immersed in memory, that has not been granted access to the sources of Mnemosyne, remains a meaningless collection of disjointed fragments. The memory of culture, the memory of Tiresias must be linked up to the individual text for the desired "union of beginning and end" to take place and for history to emerge.[30]

At least as far as its Homeric aspects are concerned, the preceding carries not a shred of conviction. The rest is obfuscation. So we may be forgiven if we dissent from Iampolski's conclusion: "The blind androgyne Tiresias has come out of antiquity to our own time."[31] The concluding paragraph in Iampolski's introduction is then intended to justify all the heavy weather about Homer and Tiresias. I quote it without further comment:

The memory of Tiresias gives us our bearings; it is the guiding thread that keeps us, however illusory its effects may be, from losing ourselves in the chaos of texts and the chaos of being .... The memory of Tiresias, it seems to me, might well serve as a symbol for cultural theory today, which is also called upon to unite, juxtapose, and make sense of things.[32]

To look to the Homeric epics for a foundation, or foundational symbol, of cultural theory is laudable. But Homer's Tiresias hardly fits the bill. On the last text page of his book Iampolski asserts, with the finality of one speaking *ex cathedra*: "The memory of the blind man – Tiresias – becomes the sign,

---

[29] Heubeck in Heubeck and Hoekstra 1989: 76.   [30] Iampolski 1998: 2.
[31] Iampolski 1998: 3. The sentence is followed by mentions of Apollinaire and Eliot.
[32] Iampolski 1998: 4.

as it were, of intertextuality."[33] We know that it does not and cannot become such a sign. But we may realize something else. Are not the memory and the cleverness of Odysseus, who is not only an accomplished narrator and rhetorical strategist but also a hero who does not lose himself in the chaos of texts or being, far more suitable to provide Iampolski with his bearings on his own journey through intertextuality and cinema? Odysseus' mother virtually makes the point when she observes to him: "All this is hard for the living to look on."[34] Odysseus looks, understands, and later tells about it. In Iampolski's words, he makes sense of things. Moreover, Odysseus' descent to the Underworld is itself a miracle of intertextuality, although perhaps not of the kind Iampolski has in mind: "Consideration of the episode as a whole leads ... to the conclusion that the poet has succeeded admirably in combining motifs from religious practice, folk-tale and saga, and subordinating each to the overall concept of the poem."[35]

My goal with the preceding was not to show up Iampolski as an ignoramus about antiquity or to set him up as a convenient straw man to be knocked down. Rather, Iampolski's misguided discussion of Tiresias provides me with a revealing justification for my book. *The Memory of Tiresias* has been extremely well received by film scholars; one of them has even listed it second among his choice of the five most inspirational books on cinema ever written. His reason is this:

a dazzling demonstration of how, when, where and why films quote other films (and other media) and why we should care. A book so far ahead of its time we haven't caught up with it.[36]

---

[33] Iampolski 1998: 253. This is the last page of his "Conclusion" (245–253), followed by endnotes and back matter. He quotes (235) from Apollodorus that Athena granted Tiresias the power to understand the sounds of birds and gave him a staff to walk with. Iampolski's context is a "series of sketches on the theme of blindness" (234) by Sergei Eisenstein; they include a *Belisarius* and a *Tiresias* of 1941 and 1944. "Both depict blind men of antiquity" (234), which is not strictly true. The story of the historical Belisarius' blindness is a medieval legend that became popular in literature and painting. Iampolski mentions a few of the latter (234). Tiresias appears again when Iampolski deals with modern intertextual theories and Eisenstein (242): "For Eisenstein, text and intertext could not be correlated unless an invisible text could be extrapolated from them, which could then bring their correlation into effect ... For Eisenstein this [i.e. "a structural invariable," after Michael Riffaterre] becomes a 'third text,' a speculative, almost mystical interpretant, existing in the Platonic sphere of pure ideas, which only the blind Tiresias is able to divine." All clear?

[34] Homer, *Odyssey* 11.156; quoted from Lattimore 1967: 172.

[35] Heubeck in Heubeck and Hoekstra 1989: 76–77.

[36] Australian critic Adrian Martin, quoted from James 2010: 24. He had earlier called Iampolski's book "the most significant text in the field of film studies over the past fifteen years" (Adrian Martin 2008: 61).

No word, however, about Tiresias. It seems to have escaped all and sundry film scholars what foundation the dazzling demonstration is built on. Therein lies another reason why we should care.

Classicists who deal with the cinema and related media are sometimes upbraided for being trespassers, as it were, upon the territory that is considered to belong to film scholars more or less exclusively, while any field of literary and narrative studies, and any historical era, is to be included in cinema studies as a matter of course. Iampolski's Tiresias demonstrates – conclusively, I think – that classical scholars today are as good as required to be familiar with films, film history, and film scholarship, if only to keep track of, and whenever possible to refute, the most egregious errors about Greece and Rome or the superficial and glib affirmations concerning the ancient cultures that tend to occur.

Here are two further instances, minor but amusing. Athena – Minerva to Romans – was closely associated with an owl. But a distinguished philosopher and film scholar twice speaks of "the owl Minerva," as if the goddess were her own bird.[37] The first of these two occurrences is worth quoting in its context for its anachronistic mixed metaphor: "cinema began to invite philosophical inquiry, serving as a runway off which the owl Minerva could take flight." Neither owls nor classical gods would know what to do with runways.

Another instance involves the suspenseful moment in Alfred Hitchcock's *Strangers on a Train* (1951), when the main character encounters a menacing dog in his persecutor's home. The animal turns out to be harmless. A philosophical film scholar associates it with the Cerberus of Hesiod's *Theogony*.[38] After quoting the lines that report Cerberus' trick of letting someone in but not out again (because he devours him), the author wonders about Hitchcock's hero: "Why does the dog allow him exit [*sic*]?" The obvious answer – that the dog in the film is not a Cerberus – does not occur to the philosopher. Instead, he speculates about protagonist and antagonist as "if not co-rulers of the kingdom of death, at least king and vice regent."[39] Comment seems superfluous. In such wrong assertions that find their way to gullible readers, I confess, lies my own anxiety over any merely supposed affinities or influences of the Ancients on the Moderns.

A distinguished film director once addressed the matter of affinity between antiquity and cinema. Abel Gance frequently referred to classical authors and topics, especially Homer, in his writings on film. In a 1973

---

[37] Carroll 2013: 2 and 162.   [38] Hesiod, *Theogony* 767–773.
[39] Both quotations from Yanal 2005: 109.

interview Gance said about his understanding of the cinema: "It's the Epic ... One must rise to the level of the heroes one wants to depict." He is best remembered today for his stupendous silent epic *Napoleon* (1927), probably still the greatest film made about its subject. Gance defined epic with these words: "It's total drama of a kind which only the cinema, in my opinion, could give us today."[40]

3   Chapter Sequence

My book consists of ten chapters in five parts. Each part deals with a different kind of the cinema's affinity with classical models. Part I ("Creative Affinities") seeks to demonstrate the essential unities between classical and cinematic narratives across time and media. Chapter 1 outlines the concept of visualization (*enargeia*) from the perspective of classical rhetoric, especially by means of Quintilian's *Institutio oratoria* (*Handbook of Rhetoric*) as a *summa* of ancient theory and practice. The chapter also provides a bridge, as it were, from Homer's epics, our earliest classical narratives, to film. The inherently visual nature of Homeric and later classical epic has recently received much attention; I hope to broaden our understanding of it by pointing to some significant details hitherto overlooked. Chapter 2 adduces the Quarrel of the Ancients and the Moderns as a frame of reference for the ways in which Jean Cocteau and Pier Paolo Pasolini, two acknowledged poets of the film, have approached the Oedipus myth. Here I hope to make evident that there was and is no need for the kind of anxiety that Scholes and Kellogg were still harboring in spite of their openness to the importance of visual technology. Their apprehension about cinema and its relatives as animals of prey that threaten to devour the art of textual narrative has not become a reality and is unlikely ever to become one. Erskine's measured and anxiety-free perspective is more sensible, and it is closer to the actual state of things today. Part I thus lays a theoretical, but in part also practical, foundation for what is to follow.

Part II, on "Elective Affinities," deals with one tragic and one comic Greek heroine. Chapter 3 demonstrates the hold of an ancient myth on the modern imagination in one particular aspect. Medea's infanticide occurred

---

[40] Both quotations are from Kramer and Welsh 1978: 168 and 167 (in chapter titled "Gance on Gance: Film as Incantation," 161–170). This chapter was first published as Kramer and Welsh 1974. To the latter statement, Gance immediately added a qualifier: "if there weren't imbeciles running it." On Gance and antiquity see my comments, with quotations, in Winkler 2009a: 4–5.

off the stage in Euripides' play and on the stage in Seneca's; modern stage and film adaptations follow either model. This chapter thus presents a kind of close-up – actually, a wide range of close-ups – on a specific moment in the two classical tragedies. It also addresses, more briefly, comparable moments in thematically related fictional and historical stories: post-classical and modern Medeas. By contrast, Chapter 4 offers a panoramic overview – an extreme long shot – of the unexpected variety of screen appearances that Aristophanes' most famous play, and to a smaller degree its author, can be made to undertake. The affinities between Euripides' and Seneca's *Medea* and Aristophanes' *Lysistrata* on the one hand and their screen adaptations on the other are generally by choice on the part of the latters' creators (hence my term *elective*), even if some modern versions may veer far from their source. But all attest to the endless variability and resilience of the originals.

Chapter 4 also traces an ideological and a political development. Classical scholars are right to point out that Aristophanes and his fictional heroine were neither pacifists nor proto-feminists, although a common modern understanding of the play has turned both into exactly that. In the early years of the twenty-first century, the play achieved global impact. The more important therefore it is for us to increase our awareness of the reach of modern mass media when classical history and literature are concerned.

By contrast, Part III ("Non-elective Affinities") presents a kind of oppo-site approach to cinematic survivals of classical themes and, once again, offers one close-up and one long shot. Chapter 5 examines a specific narrative twist and the emotional impact that it can have on readers and viewers. My starting point is Aristotle's term *ekplêktikôteron* ("more strik-ing") in his *Poetics*. I apply this concept to the two most complex Greek novels that have survived complete, *Leucippe and Clitophon* and *An Ethiopian Tale*. Both can be regarded as precursors of modern mystery stories or thrillers. In part, they prefigure the most famous film thriller of all time: *Psycho*.

Dorothy Sayers demonstrated long ago that Aristotle's *Poetics* can use-fully be applied to modern mystery plots. But authors of mystery fiction and screenwriters or directors of thrillers are not, as a rule, concerned with their classical precursors even in the rare cases that they are aware of them. Alfred Hitchcock was not trying to be Aristotelian in *Psycho* and presum-ably had never heard of Achilles Tatius or Heliodorus. The emotional impact of Hitchcockian and ancient Greek shock and suspense on viewers and readers is virtually identical when it comes to the fate of a major

character whom readers or viewers would never expect to be killed off.
Aristotle explains the close affinity of our Greek authors to the Master of
Suspense. Statements from classic detective fiction by Edgar Allan Poe and
John Dickson Carr support my case.

If Hitchcock, well educated as he was, did not see himself as part of the
classical tradition, the same may be said about John Ford. Even so, Ford's
body of work may well be the closest in spirit to that of Virgil in modern
culture. This is the subject of Chapter 6. Ford's affinities with Virgil are
evident but wholly unintended. Virgil and Ford were poets of their respective civilizations, in particular of their countries' early history and ascent to
world empire. Thematic similarities and a certain melancholia in their epic
presentations of early history prompt the question: *What price empire?*
In the early twenty-first century, issues of empire and power have come to
haunt Americans, not only politicians, journalists, and popular historians,
and have provoked the question: *Are We Rome?*[41] The affinities between
Virgil and Ford have today taken on greater poignancy. Virgil's greatness
arose from his historical situation after a long civil war; Ford's mature work
came after World War II. Both are strikingly close to each other across
time, especially in their portrayals of heroes. Accordingly my focus is on
Virgil's *Aeneid* and Ford's Westerns.

Part IV ("Counter-Affinities") is on distortions of history by political
ideology and on what we might call counter-history. Chapter 7 examines
the extent to which Fascism, not quite as discredited or dead and buried as
is commonly assumed, permeates *300*, a giant blockbuster about the Battle
of Thermopylae. It is a cliché that historical fiction and films are at least as
much about the time and culture in which they were produced as they are
about the past.[42] *Historia ... magistra vitae*: If Cicero's definition of the
importance of the past for the present is valid, then this side of history,
historiography, and historical fiction on page and screen deserves close
attention.[43] The cinema has, from its earliest days, turned to recreations of
classical and biblical history.[44] And it has influenced popular perceptions
of the past to an extent far greater than scholars and teachers of history
could hope to do. Film has radically changed our understanding of history

---

[41] I allude here to the title of Murphy 2007. Several comparable and sometimes anguished
questions have been raised since September 11, 2001. For an example involving film see Harty
2014.

[42] A brief recent restatement of such presentism, as academic jargon calls it, is in Richards
2014: 20.

[43] The quotation ("history ... is the teacher of life") is from Cicero, *On the Orator* 2.9.36.

[44] On early narrative films (about the passion of Jesus) see my brief comments in Winkler 2009b:
77–78.

with its power to influence us either intentionally (e.g. as propaganda) or subliminally. *300* furnishes us with a remarkable illustration of both the importance and the critical neglect of the ideological nature of historical cinema. An event from long ago is imbued with a modern worldview and makes a contemporary political and military situation appear defensible by emphasizing patriotism, sacrifice for the homeland, and gory heroic death. The fact that the film's closeness to fascist ideology is unintentional only enhances its political and educational importance. The more astonishing it is, then, that classical scholars and historians were ready to point out predictable inaccuracies and inventions in *300* but turned a blind eye to its blatantly fascist nature. My chapter demonstrates what the English title of Mikhail Romm's anti-Fascist documentary from 1965 spells out: We are dealing with *Ordinary Fascism*.

Chapter 8 turns to a major character from Roman history. Hitchcock, master of aphoristic wit, is widely credited with the adage that a film is only as good as its villain. If we apply this to the past – history being only as fascinating as its villains – then it is readily apparent that the bad guys of yesteryear make for the most thrilling baddies on screen today. Hence the appeal of evil Roman emperors: Caligula, the screaming madman of *The Robe* (1953) and *Demetrius and the Gladiators* (1954); the perverted Caligula of *Caligula* (1979) and its various exploitation rip-offs; the sophisticated megalomaniac Commodus of *The Fall of the Roman Empire* (1964); the pathologically creepy Commodus of *Gladiator* (2000). But the baddest of all is Nero. It is not difficult to see why he has been a staple of cinema since the silent era. His most remarkable screen portrayals came with Charles Laughton's Nero in *The Sign of the Cross* (1932) and Peter Ustinov's in *Quo Vadis* (1951). But the *good* Nero of *Imperium: Nero* is a victim of circumstances, a youngster who means well but is mistaken in his belief that a good end justifies evil means. Even if the historical Nero did not fiddle while Rome burned and was not as abysmally bad as Hollywood has liked to portray him, the whitewashing of Nero in the television film analyzed in this chapter is astonishing. But why does this film portray such an unhistorical and, for popular culture, unusual Nero? The chapter points to a sixteenth-century precursor and to a particular narrative impulse as an answer. Both chapters of Part IV have wider ramifications and so are in the nature of medium long shots.

The book closes with Part V ("Aesthetic Affinities"), which is meant to provide a measure of relief from the serious aspects of previous chapters, especially those on history. My closing chapters pay tribute to a few of the most beautiful ladies in classical myth and literature and to the actresses who played them on the screen. Chapter 9 deals with Franco Rossi, the only director to film two of the most prestigious and influential three ancient epics, the *Odyssey* and the *Aeneid*. Extraordinary actresses portray Homer's and Virgil's royal ladies. Rossi's films are without equal as serious attempts faithfully to adapt Homer and Virgil in ways that remain fully cinematic. His achievements, unknown to all but a handful of aficionados, are milestones in the history of transformations of classical texts to the screen. Unfortunately Rossi could not film a version of the *Iliad*, as he had planned to do for a number of years.

Chapter 10 demonstrates the affinities of word and image in a way that is different from the one followed in all preceding chapters. Here texts support illustrations, for the images constitute a major part of my argument. Helen of Troy, the most beautiful mortal woman, has been portrayed on large and small screens by a series of attractive actresses. Helen's variety is not, strictly speaking, infinite, but it is quite surprising. This chapter also complements an earlier one on Helen.[45] In Edgar Allan Poe's poem "To Helen" (1845), the lady's beauty triggers in the speaker a reminiscence and, we may conclude, an awareness of the greatness of all antiquity. So Helen may be a fitting representative of "the glory that was Greece" and "the grandeur that was Rome" with whom to conclude this book. Poe saw Helen standing "statue-like" "in yon brilliant window-niche."[46] So can we, for instance in museums, but we can also see her moving on our brilliant screens that, themselves window-shaped, provide us with views of the classical and our own cultures.

This book can be approached in two ways. Readers can either progress from chapter to chapter, or they can selectively turn to individual topics. Such duality, I believe, is an advantage. The subject of classics and cinema – including television and later digital media – has become one of the chief areas in reception studies on antiquity. Teachers and scholars on various levels and in various areas of higher education will be able to use the book as a whole, for instance in developing new courses, or to assign individual chapters in existing courses on Greek or Roman topics. They can also turn to a particular chapter for purposes of their own, such as further research and publication. Moreover, those in non-classical fields will be able to use my chapters as well, e.g. those on Medea and Lysistrata (theater, women's studies) or the one on *300* (political science, cultural studies). These are

---

[45] Winkler 2009a: 210–250.

[46] The words quoted are in lines 9, 10, 12, and 11 of the poem's revised version, here taken from Poe 1984a: 62. The original 1831 version had "the beauty of fair Greece" and "the grandeur of old Rome" while its Helen stood "in that little window-niche." The improvements are obvious.

only a few possibilities among several. Needless to say, I hope that the book has something to offer colleagues in film and media studies, too. The thematic progression among the different kinds of affinity that the book addresses in the sequence of its chapters is expressed in the headings of its five parts and needs no further elaboration here.

The different length of my chapters, however, deserves a brief comment. This variety is intentional. It demonstrates that certain circumscribed topics which are dealt with in the shorter chapters but which belong within a wider area of reception – e.g. Medea's infanticide vs. the Medea myth as a whole; good Nero vs. evil Nero – deserve a kind of critical "close-up," an examination that can throw the larger topic into greater relief. By contrast, the two longest chapters, on *Lysistrata* and *300*, demonstrate wider implications and connections, and not only literary, historical, or cinematic ones. In the former case (Chapter 4) I present an extensive set of data on Lysistrata and related female figures on our screens, which can serve as a convenient basis for work by others on future screen adaptations of Aristophanes' play. The 2015 release of *Chi-Raq* indicates that the long and varied tradition of Lysistrata striking on our screens is certain to continue. The latter case (Chapter 7) shows how and why a convincing argument about the ideological aspect of a film which has elicited extensive comments and which may have reached larger audiences worldwide than any other ever made about ancient Greece has to be developed carefully and on different levels. The case for the presence of what Umberto Eco has called a "fascist nebula" in *300* must be argued in detail and in connection with cultural contexts both past (e.g. Nazism and Italian Futurism) and present (e.g. CGI technology).

I am aware that I have not exhausted all possibilities, but I hope that the chapters will stimulate further thought. Concerning transliterations of Greek names, readers should not expect complete consistency. I usually follow common practice (Latinized spellings), but not always. I preserve, of course, the spellings found in passages by others that I quote.

4   Ancients and Moderns: Author's Confession

I close this introduction with a lover's confession. I borrow this Latin term from John Gower's fourteenth-century *Confessio Amantis*, which was indirectly addressed to Venus, the most beautiful goddess. My own confession is not of an erotic nature, but it is still meant as one of a double passion, that for classical antiquity (the Ancients) and for stories told in images (by the Moderns). A comparable confession by someone who was involved in the Quarrel of the Ancients and the Moderns in eighteenth-century France expresses – *mutatis mutandis* – my own sentiments better than I could voice them myself. So I will let him speak for me here.

In 1756, Anne Claude Philippe Comte de Caylus, whose official name is much longer and even more impressive, published the second volume of his *Recueil d'Antiquités egyptiennes, etrusques, grecques et romaines* ("Collection of Egyptian, Etruscan, Greek, and Roman Antiquities"). In his *Avertissement* ("Preface") he had this to say about the antiquarian:

> The moment of discovery is to him a lively pleasure. He examines these ancient Monuments; he compares them with those that are already known; he investigates their differences or similarities; he reflects; he debates; he puts down conjectures that the distance of time and the silence of Authors have rendered necessary. If one of these pieces presents him with ideas about how Art operates in a manner neglected, lost, or rejected by the Moderns, the pleasure of experimenting with them and of describing them encourages and enlivens him and flatters his taste. But nothing is comparable to the satisfaction of anticipating some usefulness for the public. This idea pervades him; it touches his heart; and the happiness of succeeding amply compensates him for all his cares and all his troubles. Here they are, I declare: the stimuli that have seduced me.[47]

I invite my readers to apply this declaration to the pages that follow. Whatever changes and differences may separate the Ancients from the Moderns of the eighteenth century and from those of the twenty-first are not essential. They are differences of form – media and technology – but not of creative impulses. Discoveries of affinities, either similarities or differences, even across millennia provide lively pleasures. Here, I declare, are some of the many stimuli that have seduced me.

---

[47] Quoted from Comte de Caylus 1756: ii.

PART I

Creative Affinities

Ancient Texts and Modern Images

1 | The Classical Sense of Cinema and the Cinema's Sense of Antiquity

Since the arrival of photography and cinematography – which really is cinematophotography, the photography of movement – ways of seeing and reading have changed fundamentally.[1] Analyses of moving-picture narratives have considerably influenced and advanced interpretations of modern literature and other arts. Critic James Bridle even speaks of a New Aesthetic, according to which literary and artistic creations reflect the visual media that are now pre-eminent.[2] Visually oriented analysis has also begun to influence Classical Studies, an area of scholarship concerned primarily with texts, not images. But a coherent appreciation of the visual qualities of ancient narrative that goes beyond then-existing art forms like painting, sculpture, and theater has largely been neglected. The same is true for those narrative qualities inherent in Greek and Roman visual media, static as they are, that go beyond forms of expression that existed in classical literature. This chapter attempts an introduction to the affinities between ancient narrative texts and modern visual narratives. It provides a theoretical basis for the individual topics addressed in subsequent chapters.[3]

The continuity of ancient literature and modern cinema is the main subject of this book. For this reason I begin with classical rhetorical theory about the imagination, the visual effect of words on the mind, in connection with ancient views of the affinities between verbal and visual arts. I then turn to a brief survey of how certain filmmakers have regarded the Greeks, especially Homer, as precursors of their new medium.

1 Quintilian on Emotions: Rhetoric and Imagination

Only fragments survive of the tragedies of the early Roman poet Pacuvius. One is a revealing summary of the importance of rhetoric in the classical cultures. A character in Pacuvius' *Hermione* exclaims that rhetoric "bends

---

[1] On the topic see, e.g., Berger 1972.
[2] An initial bibliography is in Berry et al. 2012: 64–71. This short e-book is partly outdated already. The Wikipedia article "New Aesthetics" may be the best starting point for an up-to-date orientation.
[3] Cf. the introductory outline of this topic in Winkler 2015a.

the soul" and is "the queen of all things."[4] The idea goes back to Euripides and is a commonplace.[5]

Pacuvius' line was preserved by Cicero, one of the greatest masters of Roman rhetoric during the last phase of the Roman Republic. Cicero has Marcus Antonius, grandfather of Mark Antony and one of the greatest orators of *his* time, quote Pacuvius in the context of the decisive importance of his listeners' emotional response for an orator's success.[6] But Pacuvius' memorable statement casts a much longer shadow. At the height of the early Roman Empire, Quintilian, the last great Roman orator and teacher of rhetoric, returned to Pacuvius on two occasions in his treatise.[7] On either occasion Quintilian did not quote but only alluded to and summarized Pacuvius, whom he did not name but whom he called a famous tragic poet. This is sufficient testimony for the close familiarity with Pacuvius that could still be expected in educated Roman circles.

Why is this line by Pacuvius important for our subject? The reason becomes clear when we consider its contexts, both in Cicero and in Quintilian. Cicero's Antonius quotes Pacuvius after emphasizing that one of the orator's principal tasks is to incite in his listeners suitable emotional reactions to what they are hearing. By such reactions they are meant to be influenced toward agreement with the speaker.[8] Quintilian goes into much greater detail when he turns to the same side of an orator's responsibilities. The fact that he adduces specific visual terminology to make his case in a practical handbook on the successful orator's education is significant.

Earlier, Quintilian had stressed that the very beginning of a speech should set the stage for the listeners coming around to the speaker's and not to his opposition's point of view on the matter being discussed.[9] Influencing or, in blunter terms, manipulating the listener is the orator's chief task besides, or perhaps even more than, presenting facts or evidence.[10] The listeners' emotions are the target of this manipulation.

---

[4] Pacuvius, Fragment 187 (Warmington): *flexanima atque omnium regina rerum.* On the play and for its surviving fragments see Schierl 2006: 280–311, especially 309–310 on this fragment.
[5] Euripides, *Hecuba* 816. Schierl 2006: 19 (with notes 94–95) and 310 examines the Euripidean background of Pacuvius' line.
[6] Cicero, *On the Orator* 2.187. Cicero, *Tusculan Disputations* 2.47 (with *ratio* ["reason"] for *oratio*), may also allude to Pacuvius' verse.
[7] Quintilian, *Handbook of Rhetoric* 1.12.18 and 6.2.4. Otto 2009: 108–127 gives a systematic analysis of the pertinent central passages in Quintilian.
[8] Cicero, *On the Orator* 2.185–187.   [9] Quintilian, *Handbook of Rhetoric* 4.1.
[10] So recently Serafim 2015: 96, on judicial rhetoric: "By instructing the audience as to how and what to think, imagine and remember, orators seek to engage the audience, elicit their verbal or non-verbal reaction in the law court, create a certain disposition in them towards the litigants,

Quintilian devotes an entire chapter to the listeners' emotional responses that the speaker wishes to evoke.[11] It is not by accident – nothing in Quintilian ever is – that near the climax of his analysis the master includes an explicit analogy to actors on the stage.[12] Nothing, he had observed before, can impart greater power to a speech than the hearers' emotional reactions.[13] Not the facts but the emotional effect they have when presented in the right manner decide a case. Quintilian is quite blunt about this:

Arguments almost always derive from the nature of the case itself, and there are always more that favor the better side. So the side that wins because of them knows only that his [the orator's] counsel has not failed him. But when it is necessary to put pressure on the jury and to turn their minds away from a consideration of the truth: this is where the speaker's fundamental task lies. No litigant teaches him this; this is not to be found in any [preparatory] trial notes. Evidentiary proofs may indeed lead the jury to believe that our case is the better one. But their emotions [as evoked by our appeals] make them want to believe so, too. And what they *want* to believe they *will* believe.[14]

This passage follows immediately on Quintilian's allusion to Pacuvius. It was prompted by Quintilian's observation that an orator who succeeds in stirring up and sweeping along his listeners and in putting them into any mood he might want, even to the degree that they begin to weep or become angry under the spell of his words, has always been a rare phenomenon. Nevertheless, Quintilian then adds, this is exactly what the power of eloquence rules over: *haec eloquentia regnat.*[15] The author of the Greek treatise *On the Sublime*, traditionally attributed to one Longinus and variously dated from the first to the third century AD, goes even further: "Now what is rhetorical imagery able to accomplish? ... it not only persuades the audience, it also enslaves it."[16]

But how exactly is it possible to influence others' emotions when, as Quintilian later observes, humans are by no means masters even of their own feelings? His answer to this question is important, for here Quintilian adduces a number of Greek and Latin terms that connect the verbal – a speech – with the visual – what we see in our minds:

stir up and manipulate their emotions, and thus affect their verdict." Konstan 2007 gives a concise introduction to the topic.

[11] Quintilian, *Handbook of Rhetoric* 6.2.   [12] Quintilian, *Handbook of Rhetoric* 6.2.35.
[13] Quintilian, *Handbook of Rhetoric* 6.2.2.   [14] Quintilian, *Handbook of Rhetoric* 6.2.4–5.
[15] Quintilian, *Handbook of Rhetoric* 6.2.3–4.
[16] *On the Sublime* 15.8; quoted from Arieti and Crossett 1985: 94. Cf. the translators' note on the verbs in the second sentence quoted (94–95).

What the Greeks call phantasies [*phantasiai*] – we [Romans] might call them visions [*visiones*] – through which images of absent things are represented in our minds [*repraesentantur animo*] in such a way that we seem to make them out with our eyes and to have them present – whoever perceives these right will have the greatest power of expressing emotions. Some say a person who can imagine things, voices, and actions most realistically is endowed with rich imagination [*euphantasiôtos*], and we can easily succeed in this if we only want to.[17]

We readily give ourselves over to idle fantasies and daydreams, Quintilian continues, and imagine ourselves on a journey on land or sea, in battle, addressing a crowd, and disposing of wealth we do not possess – as if all this were reality. So we can use such powers of imagination (*hae ... imagines*) purposefully in a speech. Quintilian is primarily concerned with judiciary speeches and, from a first-person perspective, gives as an example a murder case. A killer suddenly attacks; his victim turns pale with fear, screams, and begs for mercy or tries to run away; the killer strikes; the victim collapses; his blood, his deathly pallor, his dying groans, and his final sigh of agony – all this the speaker sees (*in oculis habebo*) although it occurs only in his mind (*animo insidet*).[18] Earlier, Quintilian stated that "a credible image of things, one that appears to take listeners practically into the presence of something," can be of great advantage to a speaker when added to the bare facts.[19]

According to Quintilian, we understand, listeners become emotionally involved in just the way the speaker wishes if they begin to visualize the very situations or people they are being told about. Their mental vision of the words they are hearing is decisive. Mentally listeners translate, as it were, the words they hear into images. Just as the speaker's words tell the story of the case or argument under deliberation, so the listeners' imagination follows the speaker with the pictures created in their mind's eye.[20]

How does this process of imagination work? The very term is revealing. It derives from *imago* ("image, picture"; cf. *hae ... imagines* above) and denotes or connotes a process of creative visualization. What we do not actually see we see in our minds. The absent becomes present. Hence *representation*, the English derivative of *repraesentatio*, which refers to

---

[17] Quintilian, *Handbook of Rhetoric* 6.2.29–30.

[18] The passage summarized is Quintilian, *Handbook of Rhetoric* 6.2.30–31.

[19] Quintilian, *Handbook of Rhetoric* 4.2.123: *adiecta veris credibilis rerum imago, quae velut in rem praesentem perducere audientes videtur.* An extremely vivid example follows immediately.

[20] A related phenomenon is the Evil Eye, as when Medea casts deadly images at the bronze giant Talos in Book 4 of Apollonius' *Argonautica*. On this see Dickie 1990, with detailed references. Dickie 1990: 287 note 2 decides in favor of "deadly" rather than "invisible" or "unclear" as appropriate meaning of Apollonius' (four-syllabic) adjective *aidêlos*.

the act (*-atio*) of bringing something that is not there back (*re-*) and thus making it present (*-praesent-*). In this way people long dead or deeds carried out long ago come back to new life. They become contemporaneous with ourselves. In Quintilian's words, quoted above: *repraesentantur animo* – they are brought back to the present in our minds. For this reason the present tense of verbs in such parts of a speech is the most common and most appropriate.[21]

2   Visualization: *Enargeia* and *Phantasia*

Immediately after his murder example, Quintilian speaks of what Greeks called *enargeia* ("clarity, vividness, clear view"). Its Latin equivalents, he adds with reference to Cicero, are *inlustratio* (= *illustratio*, "illustration") and *evidentia*.[22] The Ciceronian terms are synonymous with *repraesentatio*.[23] They are worth brief etymological explanations. Both belong to the realm of the visual. *Illustratio* is the process of bringing something into (*in-*, *il-*) the light (*lu-*, the root of such words as *lux* and *lumen*: "light") so that it can be seen. *Evidentia* refers to the same process, although in reverse: It is the result of bringing something out (*e-*) so that one can see (*vide-*) it. Thus *evidentia* is the effect of *phantasiai*, the mental images mentioned above, which are important for the orator first to evoke in himself in order then to impart their effect on his audience.[24] In this way, Quintilian explains, *enargeia* turns speech into a vivid because innately visual demonstration, which works on our emotions as if we were present at what is being told us. The orator Julius

---

[21] Lausberg 2008: 405 (§ 814) collects the ancient evidence. In general see, among numerous other studies, Phelan 1996 and especially Booth 1983. A particularly vivid example of the affect of words heard on the mind's imaginative powers from late classical literature occurs in Heliodorus' *An Ethiopian Story* 3.1–3, which I quote and examine in Winkler 2009a: 5.

[22] Lausberg 2008: 399–407 (§§ 810–819) collects all major Greek and Roman text passages on *evidentia* and examines them systematically. There is no need to do so again here. On *enargeia* see G. Zanker 1981, a good starting point.

[23] Quintilian, *Handbook of Rhetoric* 8.3.61; cf. 4.2.63–64.

[24] Quintilian, *Handbook of Rhetoric* 6.2.36. Lausberg 2008: 401–402 (§ 811) provides the ancient text passages on *phantasiai*. Grethlein 2013: 16–19 offers a list of ancient rhetorical passages on *enargeia* and *phantasia*, with quotations, interpretive comments, and extensive references to modern scholarship. See also Plett 2012, especially 7–21 (chapter titled "Classical Sources and Their Humanist Reception"), 135–182 (chapter "Enargeia in Theory and Practice of the Visual and Verbal Arts"), and 199–216 (bibliography for *enargeia* and related terms, in particular *ecphrasis*); Otto 2009, particularly important; Bussels 2013: 57–80 and 178–183 (notes; chapter titled "*Enargeia* as Epistemological Requirement and Rhetorical Virtue: Quintilian on Vividness"). Webb 1997, 2016a, and 2016b are fundamental for the wider context, with extensive references to classical texts and modern scholarship.

Rufinianus accordingly defined *enargeia* as "the imagination that places a fact [or deed] before incorporeal eyes."[25] Greek rhetorical treatises evince the same understanding: *enargeia* is "an expression which brings the object signified under our eyes."[26]

Demonstration (in Latin, *demonstratio*) is itself a visual term, deriving from the verb *monstrare* ("to show"), and appears in various rhetorical contexts.[27] The inherently visual nature of what is meant by *enargeia, demonstratio*, and their synonyms is fundamental. Quintilian adduces several vivid examples from Virgil's *Aeneid* to bring home this point.[28] After all, the human sense of sight is the sharpest of all, as Cicero had Lucius Licinius Crassus, his own teacher of rhetoric and the greatest orator of *his* time, memorably put it on one occasion.[29] Cicero himself, in a fictitious dialogue with his son on the divisions – i.e. classifications – of rhetoric, contrasted the brilliant style (*oratio illustris*) with the clear style (*oratio dilucida*):

> it is this department of oratory which almost sets the fact before the eyes – for it is the sense of sight that is most appealed to .... brilliance is worth considerably more than the clearness above mentioned. The one helps us to understand what is said, but the other makes us feel that we actually see it before our eyes [*ut videre videamur*].[30]

Cicero's terms for the emotional kind of speech (*illustris*) and for the intellectual kind (*dilucida*) are both formed on the root *lu-*: "light." They are visual terms. A recent scholar is therefore wholly justified to speak of Cicero's "judicial theater."[31] Indeed, a term such as *oratorical theater* might be appropriate to describe classical rhetorical performances. Cicero,

---

[25] Julius Rufinianus, *De schematis dianoeas* 1: *imaginatio quae actum incorporeis oculis subicit.* Rufinianus may not have been the author of this treatise.

[26] *Anonymus Seguierianus* 95.111: *logos hyp' opsin agôn to dêloumenon.* The translation is from Russell 2001: 60 note 12 (on Quintilian, *Handbook of Rhetoric* 6.2.32). Cf. *To Herennius* 4.68. For comparable modern perspectives on the Roman context see, e.g., the essays collected in Elsner and Meyer 2014.

[27] Festive and ornate speeches, especially eulogies, belonged to the *genus demonstrativum*, one of the three kinds of speeches in classical rhetoric. Its Greek equivalent was the *epideiktikon*, a term that also referred to visualization (*epideiknynai* = "to show"). On epic *deixis*, the act or process of pointing out or showing, see Bakker 2005.

[28] Quintilian, *Handbook of Rhetoric* 6.2.32–33. The passage begins: *Insequitur* enargeia ... *quae non tam dicere videtur quam ostendere* ("There follows *enargeia* ... which seems not so much to tell as to show").

[29] Cicero, *On the Orator* 3.40.160: *oculorum, qui est sensus acerrimus.*

[30] Cicero, *The Divisions of Oratory* 6.20; quoted from Rackham 1942: 327. As the Latin shows, the master orator reinforces his point with a pleasing wordplay.

[31] Jon Hall 2014. This book contains useful basic information on Roman rhetorical practice, not only Cicero's.

Quintilian, and all public orators before and after them belong within this tradition. Only incompetent speakers are an exception.

As the last teacher of oratory in classical antiquity, Quintilian could look back on centuries of Greek and Roman rhetorical theory and practice. His work offers a comprehensive synthesis of everything that preceded it and for this reason is our best guide. But others, Greeks as well as Romans, had been specific about the matter that concerns us here. The author of the rhetorical treatise addressed to Herennius, traditionally ascribed to Cicero but probably not his work, put the matter in almost cinematic language when he defined the rhetorical term *demonstratio* by referring to a sequence of events:

"Demonstration" is the verbal expression of a situation in such a way that a certain activity appears to be in the process of being conducted and the matter seems to lie before our eyes. This will be the case if we understand everything that happens before, afterwards, and at the moment of action itself and do not deviate from any of its consequences or accompanying circumstances.[32]

Cicero and Quintilian are equally clear about what they call *subiectio sub oculos* or *sub oculos subiectio*: putting – literally, and more dramatically: throwing – something before someone else's eyes.[33] Variants occur elsewhere. The expression has a long history; it appears, for example, in Aristotle's *Rhetoric*.[34]

The treatise *On the Sublime* devotes a chapter to visualization. Its author observes about the effective speaker: "it has now become the vogue to use the word ['image'] whenever, as a result of enthusiasm and emotion, you think you are gazing at what you are describing and you set it in the sight of those who hear you." Examples from the tragedians and one from Homer vividly illustrate the point.[35]

---

[32] *To Herennius* 4.55.68. The original deserves quoting: *Demonstratio est, cum ita verbis res exprimitur ut geri negotium et res ante oculos esse videatur. Id fieri poterit si, quae ante et post et in ipsa re facta erunt, comprehendemus aut a rebus consequentibus aut circumstantibus non recedemus.*

[33] Cicero, *Orator* 40.139: *rem dicendo subiciet oculis*, with which cf. Quintilian, *Handbook of Rhetoric* 9.2.40: *illa vero, ut ait Cicero, sub oculos subiectio*; Cicero, *On the Orator* 3.53.202: *rerum ... sub aspectum paene subiectio*. The phrase is *ponere ante oculos* ("to place something before someone's eyes") in *To Herennius* 4.48.61 (with a list of suitable objects) and in Quintilian, *Handbook of Rhetoric* 10.2.26.

[34] Aristotle, *Rhetoric* 3.11.1 (1411b23): *pro ommatôn poiein*. Aristotle here also emphasizes the idea of action or activity in the context of a listener's mental visualization. The equivalent Greek term is *hypotypôsis* ("sketch"); variant: *diatypôsis*.

[35] *On the Sublime* 15.1; quoted from Arieti and Crossett 1985: 87. They point out in their commentary on the same page that the author follows Aristotle, *Poetics* 1455a22.

All the chief rhetorical terms examined above refer to the visual or imply it; they express and anticipate what narratives in moving images do as a matter of course.[36] Listeners perceive what a speaker places before their eyes not literally but mentally. The process presupposes the concept of the mind's eye, attested in Plato and a major aspect of Neo-Platonic and later philosophy.[37] Just as listeners perceive what they hear, so, by analogy, readers imagine what they read on the page.[38] A speaker's or writer's detailed verbal descriptions incite the listener or reader toward mental visualization:

vivid descriptions are produced not so much by describing as by noting the particulars of scenes. Though auditory details as well as details that appeal to senses other than sight are sometimes used, most details appeal to sight. Rhetoricians promote visualization by noting forceful actions, particularizing actions with objects, and contrasting features of the scene – particularly light and darkness. Details are selected for their ability not only to promote visualization but also to heighten an emotional response and suggest plausibility.[39]

Quintilian explains how this works. Citing a particular example from Cicero, he asks – rhetorically, of course: "is anybody so far removed from mentally creating images of things being described [*procul a concipiendis imaginibus rerum*] that he does not ... seem to be looking at the people and their surroundings and clothing and, moreover, himself fills in further details

[36] The ancient *loci* are collected and discussed in Lausberg 2008; see § 1244 (s. vv. *demonstratio, evidentia, illustratio, imaginatio, imago, oculus, repraesentare, repraesentatio*) and § 1245 (s. vv. *enargeia, phantasia, hypotypôsis*) for indices. Modern studies, with additional references, include Sheppard 2014, especially 2–10 and 19–46 (chapter titled "Visualization, Vividness [*Enargeia*] and Realism") on Greek sources, with numerous quotations pertinent to the present topic, and Walker 1993. See also Spina 2005.

[37] E.g. Plato, *Republic* 7.533d2 (*to tês psychês omma*: "the eye of the soul"). On Greek scientific theories of viewing and seeing see, e.g., van Hoorn 1972: 42–71 (on pre-Aristotelians), 73–107 (Aristotle and related authors), and 236–244 (Democritus, Aristotle, and early moderns). See also Vernant 1991c. This essay, originally published in 1975, contains a section titled "Spoken Images" and is immediately followed by one titled "Phantasia" (171–173, 173–174). For later Latin references to *oculus mentis* ("the mind's eye") and related expressions see, e.g., van Fleteren 1999; Law 1989. In general see Collins 1991. For the cinema see, e.g., Hochberg and Brooks 1996, with illuminating illustrations and further references.

[38] A summary appears in Esrock 1994: 178–205 and 233–236 (notes; concluding chapter titled "The Reader's Visual Response"). Her chapter's section headings may be listed here: "Imaging Affects Memory," "Imaging Helps Make a Fictional World Concrete," "Imaging Evokes the Psychodynamics of Vision," "Imaging Positions the Reader Within a Text," and "Imaging Is a Means of Establishing a Formal Contrast." Related to this context is the formulaic term *videres* or *aspiceres* ("you could have seen") in both ecphrastic and vivid historiography and epic; on this see, e.g., Woodman 1989: 139–140 (= 2012: 159–160), and especially Gilmartin 1975.

[39] Quoted from Innocenti 1994: 374.

[*sibi ipse adstruat*] what is not even being expressed in words?"[40] The answer is self-evident. So we can only agree with Portuguese film director Manoel de Oliveira, who observed about the reader: "He reads, he meditates, and, when he reads, he makes his film" of what he reads.[41] The vividness (*enargeia*) in an author's verbal description (*ecphrasis*) produces moving images in the mind of the reader. The *ecphrases* of paintings in the *Eikones* ("Images") of Philostratus the Elder and Philostratus the Younger are convincing demonstrations of this circumstance, for the pictures they describe often contain actions or movements.[42] The matter could not have been expressed more concisely or more elegantly than de Oliveira put it.[43] Like the Greeks and Romans, de Oliveira and many other filmmakers know that narratives reach or extend across what we today call verbal and visual media.[44] Storytelling, whether ancient or modern, transcends any one means of artistic expression.

3   In the Beginning, Homer

Not only rhetoricians were aware of the close affinities between the verbal and the visual. Greek poet Simonides of Keos famously held that painting is silent poetry while poetry is painting that speaks. Today we would speak of *literature* rather than *poetry*. Horace's *ut pictura poesis* is one of the most famous and influential restatements of Simonides.[45] Greek biographer and essayist Plutarch reports on Simonides' view as follows, adding a telling example:

Simonides . . . calls painting inarticulate poetry and poetry articulate painting: for the actions which painters portray as taking place at the moment literature narrates and records after they have taken place. Even though artists with colour and design,

---

[40] Quintilian, *Handbook of Rhetoric* 8.3.64. His quotation from Cicero, *Against Verres* 5.33.86, has been omitted here.

[41] The quotation is from an interview with Manoel de Oliveira conducted in French in 2008 and included on the American DVD release of de Oliveira's *Belle toujours* (2006). De Oliveira's words quoted near the end of this chapter are from the same interview.

[42] Both of the ancient authors' works carry the same title. On the earlier see Baumann 2011 and Plett 2012: 37–50.

[43] Related to all this, but too large a subject for inclusion, are cognitive science, philosophy, psychology, and studies of the imagination, especially in connection with the cinema. Good starting points – there are many others in these constantly evolving fields – are Bordwell 1989; Currie 1995; Plantinga 1997; Plantinga and Smith 1999; Currie and Ravenscroft 2004: 185–204 ("Emotions in Imagination"); Plantinga 2009. All provide extensive further references.

[44] I allude here to the titles of Ryan 2004; Ryan and Thon 2014. A number of the essays collected in these volumes pertain to the topic at hand.

[45] Horace, *Art of Poetry* 361. I discuss the matter in greater detail and adduce further references in Winkler 2009a: 22–26. Scholarship on the connections between text and image in Greek and Roman culture is now extensive. A recent addition is Giuliani 2013.

and writers with words and phrases, represent the same subjects, they differ in the material and the manner of their imitation; and yet the underlying end and aim of both is one and the same; the most effective historian is he who, by a vivid representation of emotions and characters, makes his narration like a painting. Assuredly Thucydides is always striving for this vividness [*enargeia*] in his writing, since it is his desire to make the reader a spectator, as it were, and to produce vividly in the minds of those who peruse his narrative the emotions of amazement and consternation which were experienced by those who beheld them.[46]

In the second century A D the Sophist Lucian observed that Homer was "the best of painters."[47] The first Homeric word painting is, appropriately, of Zeus and his lightning bolt.[48] In the century before Lucian, Greek orator Dio Chrysostom ("Goldmouth," a well-deserved honorific) had none other than Phidias, one of the greatest sculptors of antiquity, state that Homer showed his listeners or readers beautiful images of all the gods.[49] Phidias himself made the statues of Athena in the Parthenon and of Zeus at Olympia. As a result of his art, Dio's Phidias had said a little earlier, Homer could put any emotion he wished into his listeners' or readers' hearts.[50] We can imagine Quintilian nodding assent. Centuries before, Plato had Socrates define poetry as a kind of public speaking (*dêmêgoria*), which is to say, as a form of rhetoric.[51]

On the Life and Poetry of Homer, an appreciation of Homer that has come down to us under Plutarch's name but is apocryphal, concludes with a eulogy of Homer's *enargeia*. The author even cites Simonides' famous saying about poetry and painting:

If one were to say that Homer was a teacher of painting as well [as an epic poet], this would be no exaggeration, for as one of the sages said, "Poetry is painting which speaks and painting is silent poetry." Who before, or who better than Homer displayed for the mind's eye [*tê phantasia tôn noêmatôn*] gods, men, places, and various deeds, or ornamented them with the euphony of verse? He sculpted in the medium of language . . . . Hephaestus, making the shield of Achilles and sculpting in gold the earth, the heavens, the sea, even the mass of the sun and the beauty of the moon, the swarm of stars that crowns the universe, cities of various sorts and fortunes, and moving, speaking creatures [*zôa kinoumena kai phthengomena*] – what practitioner of arts of this sort can you find to excel him?[52]

---

[46] Plutarch, *On the Fame of the Athenians* 3.1 (= *Moralia* 346f–347a); quoted from Babbitt 1936: 501.

[47] Lucian, *Imagines* 8. On Lucian see, e.g., Cistaro 2009.   [48] Homer, *Iliad* 2.150–153.

[49] Dio Chrysostom, *Discourse 12 (Olympic)*, 73.

[50] Dio Chrysostom, *Discourse 12 (Olympic)*, 69.   [51] Plato, *Gorgias* 502c.

[52] Pseudo-Plutarch, *On the Life and Poetry of Homer* 216; quoted from Keaney and Lamberton 1996: 307 and 309. They provide a textual edition and facing translation, together with much other information.

The shield of Achilles, described in Book 18 of the *Iliad*, is a case in point: a verbal description (*ecphrasis*) of a series of static images, many of which are so intricate as to tell mini-narratives. They present *verbal motion pictures* in the literal sense of these words.[53] As Greeks and Romans realized, the very beginning of classical literature is highly visual. Not least for this reason, scenes from the Homeric epics were depicted in Greek and Roman visual arts again and again.[54] From our own perspective we can now add that the beginning of classical literature is also inherently cinematic.

The author of our essay next adduces, and quotes from, a passage in the *Odyssey*, the moment in which Odysseus' nurse Eurycleia discovers his scar and realizes his true identity.[55] This is a pivotal moment, deservedly famous. Our essayist introduces the passage in the following manner: "Let us examine another of the many examples that show that his creations are such that we seem to see them rather than hear them." He comments on the lines he quotes with these words: "Here, while everything that can be displayed to the eye is presented as if in a painting, there is still more – things that the eye cannot grasp, but only the mind." He concludes about Homeric epic in general: "Many other things are described in the same graphic manner by the poet, as one can see simply from reading him."[56]

Dio Chrysostom and our unknown essayist were by no means the only ancient writers to consider Homeric epic in visual terms. Maximus of Tyre is a later one. One of his *Orations* is titled "Homer the Philosopher" and contains this appreciation:

Homer's poetry can be envisaged in the following manner. Think of a philosophically educated painter, a Polygnotus or a Zeuxis, who paints with deliberation . . . His artistic skill allows him to preserve an accurate image of reality in the shapes and contours he portrays; his virtue ensures that it is true beauty he imitates as he arranges his lines into a satisfying pattern.[57]

---

[53] I have examined *ecphrases* on the shield in "The *Iliad* and the Cinema," in Winkler 2006b: 57–63. For a variety of approaches to visual aspects of classical epic see Lovatt 2013, especially 17–21; Lovatt and Vout 2013. Both have extensive references.

[54] Examples are too numerous to list. A case in point, which has received much recent attention, are the *Tabulae Iliacae*, which show episodes from the Trojan War. On these see especially Squire 2011 and Petrain 2014, both with detailed references to other scholarship on this and related topics. On Pompeiian wall images of the Trojan War see Heslin 2015: 51–100.

[55] Homer, *Odyssey* 19.467–477.

[56] Pseudo-Plutarch, *On the Life and Poetry of Homer* 217; quoted from Keaney and Lamberton 1996: 309. The translators' word choice *examine* rather misses the impact of the original's *idômen* ("let us look at").

[57] Maximus of Tyre, *Orations* 26.5; quoted from Trapp 1997: 218. Trapp, xcvii–xcviii, lists alternative numbering systems. Pollitt 1974: 148–149 examines this passage's philosophical side.

Phidias, Polygnotus, Zeuxis: Homer the visual artist could not be in better company.

As one can see simply from reading: When we listen to a story or read one, we see it in our minds. Since the time of Homer, plot-driven narratives have inevitably been turned into their readers' mental motion pictures.[58] The verbal and the visual are inseparable, and not only where static situations (in a text) or images (paintings, statues) are concerned. The prologue to Longus' *Daphnis and Chloe* elegantly demonstrates Simonides' point.[59] Long before Longus, Apollonius of Rhodes did the same in his portrayal of Medea's initial infatuation with Jason. Medea sees, in her mind's eye, Jason's handsome figure and mentally hears his words: "Everything appeared again before her eyes."[60] Apollonius' description of Phrixus and the ram with the golden fleece on Jason's cloak is another case in point. Phrixus seems to be listening to what the ram is telling him, and anyone looking at the cloak might well wish to preserve silence in order to be able to hear what is being said.[61] Nearly two-and-a-half millennia later, Patricia Highsmith, author of highly complex psychological novels, unconsciously agreed with Simonides: "painting is the art most closely related to writing."[62] Hence the adaptability of any kind of narrative literature to the screen. Narrative films are visual texts. Consequently, both modes of storytelling are highly suitable for, and capable of, interpretive analyses.

Sculpture is closely related to writing as well. The baroque *enargeia* with which Apuleius has the narrator of *The Golden Ass* describe the effect that a statue of Diana, the goddess of the hunt, has once had on him is a telling example. The description begins with a visual exhortation and emphasizes the motions that this unmoving image implies:

Look [*ecce*] – Diana, sculpted from Parian marble, takes up the exact middle of the whole room, a perfectly splendid statue; with her dress puffed out, with a lively forward movement [*procursu*] toward those entering and demanding veneration through the deity's sheer majesty. Dogs surround and protect the goddess on all sides. These are marble as well, but their eyes are menacing; they prick up their ears, flare their nostrils, and bare their fangs. If sounds of barking were to reach

---

[58] The late-fifth-century A D Greek poet Colluthus provides an end point to this development, if only as far as classical antiquity is concerned. On his fragmentary epyllion (short epic) *Abduction of Helen* see now Cadau 2015: 135–221 (chapter titled "Colluthus' Visual Epyllion").

[59] On this passage see Winkler 2009a: 22–24. Roman mythological and landscape paintings provide a visual analogy to Longus' passage.

[60] Apollonius of Rhodes, *Argonautica* 3.453–456.

[61] Apollonius of Rhodes, *Argonautica* 1.763–767.

[62] The immediately following sentence reads: "Painters are accustomed to using their eyes, and it is good for a writer to do the same." Both quotations are from Highsmith 1966: 8.

a viewer from somewhere outside, he would assume that they are coming from the jaws of these dogs. And not just that, but the master sculptor achieved the absolute apex of his art in this: The dogs' chests are rising steeply; their hind legs press against the ground, their front legs are running away![63]

The text continues with an elaborate description of the rocky grotto behind the statue, the water basin at Diana's feet in which she is about to bathe, and Actaeon, the Peeping Tom whom she changes into a stag.[64] Actaeon is, in fact, in the middle of his metamorphosis; the ferocious dogs will pounce on him any moment. The astonishing *enargeia* both in the verbal account of this sculpture group and in the work itself is there for a reason. Text and sculpture both tell a gruesome story in the most gripping way possible. Readers of Apuleius may regret that the sculpture of Diana, Actaeon (half human, half stag), the dogs, and all the peaceful and pleasant natural surroundings never really existed. It should have.

We may briefly juxtapose a comparable perspective on the emotional power of dramatic statuary, this time in regard to an actual work. In 1770, British composer and music historian Charles Burney observed, in his travel journal, about the equestrian bronze statue of Emperor Marcus Aurelius on the Campidoglio in Rome: "The horse moves and the emperor speaks."[65] Who could disagree?

4   From Homer to Cinema

Roman epic poet Manilius and film director Wolfgang Petersen, both quoted in my Introduction, paid tribute to Homer as *fons et origo* of all our narrative traditions. One reason for Homer's importance and perhaps his greatest asset is his sense of *enargeia*. Art historian Paul Barolsky has this to say on the matter:

Homer is exceptionally vivid when, for example, he pictures the palace of Menelaos ... [or] the palace of Alcinous .... even if Homer's descriptions do not permit us to reconstruct his great palaces, his evocations of color, materials, scale, and light incite us to imagine these magnificent dwelling spaces.[66]

For our purposes, the last of these qualities may be the most important. Barolsky observes:

---

[63] Apuleius, *The Golden Ass* 2.4.3–5.   [64] Apuleius, *The Golden Ass* 2.4.6–10.
[65] Quoted from Burney 1969: 137 (under the date of September 28, 1770).
[66] Barolsky 2009: 23–24. The inconsistent spellings of the Greek names are Barolsky's.
    The Homeric passages in question appear in Books 4 and 7 of the *Odyssey*.

Light ..., whether flooding interior spaces, reflecting from polished stone and polished wooden furniture, or reflected by armor, is a crucial aesthetic phenomenon in the Homeric poems .... Homer's sense of light as atmosphere and enhancement captures not only the splendor of the art, but also the total sense of life ... that such art suggests.[67]

Film directors and their cinematographers can only agree. The affinity of their art to Homer's is undeniable.

Exceptionally vivid: Listeners or readers may not be able to reconstruct Homeric settings even if they can imagine them, but the cinema can reconstruct practically anything. Whenever a filmmaker tells a story, that story's settings have to be displayed on the screen. In films of literature, verbal *enargeia* becomes visual *enargeia*. Enrico Guazzoni, one of the greatest among the Italian directors of historical spectacles in the silent era, once described the matter in convincing terms. "No subject could better attract and excite an artist," he stated in an interview, than that of *Antony and Cleopatra*, his epic of 1914. Guazzoni's explanation reminds us of such ancient terms as *enargeia* or *sub oculos subiectio* and of the emotional effect that results:

It presented above all the opportunity of parading before the spectators' eyes the most characteristic sites of ancient Rome and Egypt, each of which was imprinted in their minds as they were sitting on their school benches, but which they have never seen and which they could never really see even if they spent the treasures of Croesus. So it offered the possibility to reconstruct landings and battles that remain among the most memorable of those times and that can be seen reproduced on the cinema screen only with trembling emotion. And finally the love of Antony and Cleopatra, besides being itself one of the most passionate subjects of history, magnificently lent itself to a reconstruction of life as led in the court of the Ptolemies with all its pomp, but also with scenes of intimacy full of fascination for their luxurious display.

The chief attraction of history, Guazzoni reveals, lies in its spectacle and emotional appeal: pomp and romance. A filmmaker's visual sense is therefore the indispensable basis on which to build, literally and figuratively, everything. Guazzoni continued:

I studied each part of this reconstruction with great scrupulousness: on its sites, in museums, in libraries. A legion of craftsmen and workers from Cines completed this research, themselves ready for the patient work of rebuilding whole quarters of cities, palaces, monuments, halls, living rooms, fountains, pools, furniture,

---

[67] Barolsky 2009: 24–25.

weapons and costumes, in such a way that everything corresponds to the most absolute historical truth.[68]

Historical experts who cast a critical eye over Guazzoni's films will notice that his ideal of authenticity is conspicuously not in evidence. But no matter. Visual rhetoric, that is to say, the *enargeia* of every detail, counts; the facts do not, or at least not decisively. In an article published in 1918, Guazzoni, looking back on his work, explained why this is the case:

the cinema, very much differently from the theater, will permit us to encompass and to present visions of the vastest grounds; it will be able to eschew any limitations, breaking, for example, the traditional shackles of the unity of time and place; it will be able, through aesthetic and representational moments, to reconstruct great figures and the environment in which they moved – in sum, a whole world.

Guazzoni directed many historical epics and brought several such worlds – Roman, Egyptian, biblical, medieval – before his viewers' amazed eyes. His films ranged from comparatively short ones (*Agrippina, Brutus*; both 1911) to a gigantic super-production like *Quo Vadis?* (1913). About his approach to historical spectacle Guazzoni went on to observe:

Research into particular details – because the cinema is a cruel document to convict those who do not take care of the particular, even the smallest one – is altogether a battle unleashed in the soul of a film director who carries out a most delicate mission with compunction and devotion. And because of these details I must consult entire libraries on the customs of the era I want to revive, consult ancient texts, visit museums, rummage through antiquarian shops, design weapons and tools with the guidance of historical documents, track down rites and ceremonies, discover examples of hairstyles, and after all this prepare drawings and sketches and look after their execution by supervising huge teams of designers, carpenters, tailors, prop men, and so on.[69]

Such cinematic *enargeia* is a Herculean labor. It helped that Guazzoni had received training as a painter.[70] Often he was his own designer of sets, costumes, and more; his own art director, screenwriter, and editor. Now undeservedly neglected, Guazzoni is a prime example of what we might call the Quintilianic nature of filmmaking.

---

[68] The two quotations are from Prolo 1951: 55. The interview appeared in the *Giornale d'Italia* of November 4, 1913. Cines, the studio for which Guazzoni was working, was one of the leading production companies in Italy during the silent era.

[69] These two passages are from Guazzoni 1918: 55 and 56.

[70] The title of the only monograph to attempt a detailed appreciation of his work is therefore telling. Bernardini, Martinelli, and Tortora 2005 call him "director-painter."

Long before Quintilian or the cinema, the Sophist Gorgias, after whom Plato named one of his best-known dialogues, had defined speech in a vivid near-personification as a ruler of great power (*logos dynastês megas estin*), "for it is capable of stopping fear, taking away sorrow, working up pleasure, and increasing pity" in its audiences. (Cf. Pacuvius' "queen of all things.") Poetry, which Gorgias defines as metrical speech, evokes strong emotions in listeners and, we may add, readers:

Into those who hear it there enters fearsome fright, tearful pity, and mournful longing; because of speeches their mind undergoes its own suffering at the successes and failures of others' deeds and persons.[71]

Gorgias' points equally apply to visual poetry.[72] The following words by Colin McGinn, a modern philosopher of the mind who is also an occasional novelist and a dedicated film viewer, provide an apposite parallel concerning film viewing:

It is not that we just passively observe things; we actively construct an interpretation of what we are seeing. It is as if the movie itself really took place in our minds, with the images on the screen acting as mere stimuli. Movie watching is inherently an imaginative act . . . . The pleasure of movies is partly the pleasure of integrating what we bring from the inside with what the world imposes on our senses.[73]

No ancient or modern rhetorician, poet, or poetic filmmaker is likely to dissent.

In his 1897 preface to *The Nigger of the "Narcissus"* Joseph Conrad observed: "All art . . . appeals primarily to the senses." So does literature, "if its high desire is to reach the secret spring of responsive emotions. It must strenuously aspire to the plasticity of sculpture, to the colour of painting, and to the magic suggestiveness of music." Writing not so much about himself as on behalf of each "worker in prose," Conrad famously stated:

My task which I am trying to achieve is, by the power of the written word, to make you hear, to make you feel – it is, before all, to make you *see*! That – and no more: and it is everything![74]

---

[71] Gorgias, *Encomium of Helen* 8–9. Cf. Segal 1962.

[72] Neill 1996 observes in passing (193 note 1) that it all began with Gorgias. Barnes 1982: 462–466 outlines Gorgias' poetics in connection with other Sophists'.

[73] McGinn 2005: 53–54.

[74] Conrad 1979: 145–148; quotations at 146 and 147. The preface originally appeared as afterword to the novel's serial publication.

Ancient orators – and not only these – could only agree. So did D. W. Griffith, the great pioneer to whom the cinema owes much of its language: grammar and style of narration in moving images. He is reported to have repeated Conrad's dictum as characterization of his own work virtually verbatim: "The task I'm trying to achieve is above all to make you see."[75]

Conrad, Griffith, and any other artist in the realm of verbal-and-visual storytelling are in excellent company: Shakespeare's. In *Henry V* the figure of the Chorus serves as prologue and epilogue to the play and provides helpful transitions between acts. In the prologue he rhetorically asks the spectators: "Can this cockpit [of the stage] hold / The vasty fields of France?" Or the "two mighty monarchies" that will be at war? Or the Battle of Agincourt? The Chorus urges viewers fully to envision the mighty story with its countless humans and animals that are only hinted at: "let us, ciphers to this great account, / On your imaginary forces work." More importantly:

> Piece out our imperfections with your thoughts.
> Into a thousand parts divide one man
> And make imaginary puissance.
> Think, when we talk of horses, that you see them
> Printing their proud hoofs i'th' receiving earth.
> For 'tis your thoughts that now must deck our kings,
> Carry them here and there, jumping o'er times,
> Turning th'accomplishment of many years
> Into an hour-glass.[76]

Not each of the Chorus' exhortations to imagine a grander scale of things need be quoted here, but the one that opens Act 3 is significant for our topic. Here are the most important lines:

> Thus with imagined wings our swift scene flies
> In motion of no less celerity
> Than that of thought . . . .
> Play with your fancies, and in them behold

---

[75] Quoted from Jacobs 1939: 119 (no source reference provided). Griffith's restatement of Conrad is usually dated to 1913, when Griffith was on the verge of an epic breakthrough with his multi-story *Intolerance* (1916), and has been adduced innumerable times; occasionally it has been considered apocryphal. If he really did not say it, he should have – and easily could have. On the subject see McFarlane 1996: 3–5 (section titled "Conrad, Griffith, and 'Seeing'"), with further references.

[76] William Shakespeare, *King Henry V*, Prologue 11–12, 20, 18–19, and 23–31. All quotations from and references to this play are based on Craik 1995.

> Upon the hempen tackle ship-boys climbing;
> Hear the shrill whistle . . .;
>   . . . behold the threaden sails . . . .
>   O do but think
> You stand upon the rivage and behold
> A city on th'inconstant billows dancing . . . .
>   Follow, follow!
> Grapple your minds to sternage of this navy,
> And leave your England . . . .
> Work, work your thoughts, and therein see a siege;
> Behold the ordnance on their carriages . . . .
> And eke out our performance with your mind.[77]

Verbs like *see* and *behold* occur frequently in these passages and point out what is actually not being seen or beheld; evidently, viewers need not be directed to look at something that is right before their eyes. The epilogue then summarizes the Chorus' presentation of the play's great theme. I quote only its beginning and its final line:

> Thus far, with rough and all-unable pen,
> Our bending author hath pursued the story,
> In little room confining mighty men . . . .
> In your fair minds let this acceptance take.[78]

The case for the importance of the mind's eye, for thoughtful and emotional visualization of what is not there even in a visual context, could not be made more convincingly.

We may now attempt a summation of the preceding argument, one that ties together antiquity, theater, narrative prose, and narrative cinema. Here a statement, simultaneously concise and elegant, by the great French film scholar André Bazin is apropos. He observed in 1956: "Despite all its technological attractions, cinema is decidedly and primarily an art born from theater and the novel, an art of man and his destiny."[79] If the *logos* is a *dynastês megas*, so is any *logos eikonikos*, as we might call a film in homage to Gorgias and ancient rhetoricians. Any story told, and told well, in moving images that are also emotionally moving are stories about human destiny.

Manoel de Oliveira, one of the most articulate of artistic filmmakers, once described the structure of the cinematic work of art in relation to the other major arts. Demonstrating his own sense of *enargeia* and echoing Conrad, although doubtless unconsciously, de Oliveira said this about

---

[77] *King Henry V*, 3.0.1–3, 7–10, 13–15, 17–19, 25–26, and 35.
[78] *King Henry V*, Epilogue 1–3 and 14.   [79] Bazin 2014b: 259.

what he termed "the cinematographic monument" as a visual and aural structure:

It's a Greek monument, which consists of four columns: the first is the image, the second is the word, the third is the sound, and the fourth is music . . . The image is the visible, the structure of the visible. Word and sound remain like [*restent comme*] the image . . . . the image is always present, the image is present in everything . . . Each [element] has its place and its very force in the equilibrium of expression.[80]

Greek director Theodore Angelopoulos, who engaged with ancient myth, literature, and history in most, perhaps in all, of his films, evinced a comparable perspective. In an interview he put the matter of the mutual interactions between past and present, between antiquity and cinema, as succinctly as we could wish:

If we recall the Greek classics, we notice that most of them work with myths referring to much older periods, and in this context history is used as a continuous backdrop, independent of any thematic concerns. My attachment to our history derives from the fact that I am Greek, from the overall relationship of history with Greek art and specifically with literature, and in this century, with Greek cinema.[81]

In another interview Angelopoulos observed what might well serve as an epigraph to the present book: "You see, I have a soft spot for the ancient writings. There really is nothing new. We are all just revising and reconsidering ideas that the ancients first treated!"[82] French director Jacques Rivette was of the same opinion; nor were he and Angelopoulos the only ones:

As [Jean] Cocteau and others have said, you have to imitate . . .[Jean] Renoir said it, too. Follow the example of the classic writers [*les époques classiques*]. They all took the same subject and did something different with it, putting their own mark on it. Whereas now we're trying to do something original, and everything is the same.[83]

Rivette did not specifically refer to classical authors. Still, he said these words in an interview concerning his mammoth film *Out 1* (1971), which

---

[80] Cf. with this passage the one by Abel Gance at Winkler 2001b: 15. It is another vivid and affectionate restatement of the affinities between and among the arts.

[81] O'Grady 2001: 70.   [82] Horton 2001: 88.

[83] Quoted from the documentary *The Mysteries of Paris: Jacques Rivette's* Out 1 *Revisited* (2015). The subtitles, here quoted, do not exactly reproduce Rivette's words (from 1990).

pays homage to, and derives from, works by one classical and one classic author: Aeschylus and Balzac.[84]

We may agree, then, with the following assessment by an American film scholar, screenwriter, and teacher of screenwriting: "'Homer was the best screenwriter ever,' I like to say whenever I teach screenwriting. True, Homer was blind and never saw a film in his life. But what I then point out is that Homer gave us all we need to know in creative cinematic narrative in terms of life as a journey towards our own Ithacas after our own Trojan Wars and adventures and misadventures."[85]

---

[84] Aeschylus' plays in *Out 1*, which is almost thirteen hours long, are *Prometheus Bound* and *The Seven Against Thebes*.

[85] Horton 2016: 62 (beginning of review of Alexander 2013, a textbook in which the *Odyssey* plays a prominent part).

2 | Pasolini's and Cocteau's Oedipus
No Quarrel of the Ancients and the Moderns in the Cinema Age

The Quarrel of the Ancients and the Moderns – *la Quérelle des Anciens et des Modernes* or the Battle of the Books – is a late-seventeenth- to early-eighteenth-century French and European phenomenon, but it had precursors in classical antiquity.[1] In *Frogs*, his comedy of 405 BC, Aristophanes pitted the tragic dramatists Aeschylus, dead for about fifty years, against the recently deceased Euripides in a literary contest held in the Underworld. Aeschylus, the older, wins out over Euripides, the modern. In his commentary on the play, Kenneth Dover summarized the contest with the pithy phrase "old ways good, new ways bad."[2] In the following century, Alexandrian scholar-poets reacted against the Homeric model of long epic composition; Callimachus in particular is still famous for the maxim that a big book is a big bad thing.[3] Several Roman poets in the Late Republic, especially Catullus, were inspired by the Alexandrians but came under attack from traditionalists. Cicero, for example, called them *neôteroi* ("the youngsters") and *poetae novi* ("new poets"); neither of these expressions was meant as a compliment.[4] More contemptuously, Cicero also called them *cantores Euphorionis* ("Euphorion's parrots").[5] Ironically, a younger Cicero had himself belonged among these same

---

[1] Lecoq 2001 is a handy anthology of sources and provides a list of seventeenth- and eighteenth-century publications (including Jonathan Swift and Alexander Pope), a chronology of events, and a bibliography. The volume's opening essay – Fumaroli 2001 – is a book-length introduction. On the earlier background, especially the *Querelle du Cicéronianisme*, see Fumaroli 1980. In view of my argument in Chapter 1 it is worth noting that Fumaroli 1980 also examines sixteenth- and early-seventeenth-century debates concerning classical rhetoric and its applicability to contemporary painting. See further Burlingame 1920; Jones 1936; Norman 2011; Levine 1991 and 1999. The Augustan age in the title of Levine 1991 refers to British, not Roman, culture.

[2] Dover 1993: 69. He continues: "The heroic ideals of Aeschylean tragedy will preserve the city, the unsettling realism of Euripidean tragedy will subvert it." On the contest between the two poets in Aristophanes see Dover 1993: 10–37, especially 22–23.

[3] This is usually quoted as *mega biblion, mega kakon*, but the actual text is *to mega biblion ison . . . tô megalô kakô* (Fragment 465 [Pfeiffer]).

[4] Cicero, *Letters to Atticus* 7.2.1; *Orator* 48.161.

[5] Cicero, *Tusculan Disputations* 3.45. The phrase literally means "chanters of Euphorion," i.e. of Euphorion's kind of poetry. The Euphorionic tag loses much if rendered literally. (This works better, e.g., in German, with *Absinger* or *Nachbeter* for *cantores*.) Euphorion of Chalkis was a third-century Greek poet and grammarian.

Neoterics.[6] The arguments outlined here went in either direction: for and against the old or the new.

1   Horace on the Ancients and the Moderns

In early imperial Rome we find traces of another debate about the Greeks and the Romans. Horace examines the issue in *Epistles* 2.1, an open letter about poetry and literature addressed to Emperor Augustus. He states that those who disdain recent adaptations of works by revered and usually long-dead authors, especially Homer, and judge nothing to be comparable to the old masters are in serious error. Their judgment is wrong because it is no more than a prejudice against anything modern. "I find it offensive," says Horace, "that something is criticized ... merely because it is new."[7] Blind reverence to everything ancient ("so sacred is each and every ancient poem") and quick condemnation of everything modern only denies the great authors of the past one of their most important achievements, the creation of a never-ending tradition of influence.[8] Horace later asks rhetorically: "If the Greeks had hated anything modern as much as we do now, what would now be ancient?"[9] He has previously observed that the earliest works of the Greeks are the greatest of all, so the attitude with which he takes issue, had it prevailed, would have stopped any literary creativity since the time of Homer dead in its tracks.

That such was not the case is due to two main factors. One is the flexibility and adaptability of myth, the earliest and perhaps greatest source of subject matter in the ancient literary and visual arts. This flexibility derives from the oral tradition that preserved and embellished heroic tales for centuries before the invention of writing. The other factor is the Greek and Roman view of artistic creativity, which is best described in the Latin terms *imitatio* and *aemulatio*. Poets' creative imitation of their predecessors and their intellectual competition with them ("emulation") ensure the continuing presence of the Ancients among the Moderns.

Keepers of the classical flame, guardians of the Ivory Tower, dwellers among the dreamy spires of academe, and self-appointed Beckmessers and

---

[6]   A large amount of scholarship exists on this subject. A useful introduction, with references to the major works, appears in Conte 1994: 136–154 (a chapter titled "Neoteric Poetry and Catullus").

[7]   Horace, *Epistles* 2.1.76–77: *indignor quicquam reprehendi ... quia nuper.*

[8]   The quotation in my parenthesis is from Horace, *Epistles* 2.1.54: *adeo sanctum est vetus omne poema.* Cf. also 2.1.64 and 86–89, an especially vivid and witty passage.

[9]   Horace, *Epistles* 2.1.90–91: *quodsi tam Graecis novitas invisa fuisset / quam nobis, quid nunc esset vetus?*

Pecksniffs may regard much of what has been outlined here with predictable scorn. In the words of Horace, someone like this "despises and hates everything except what he sees long removed from the face of the earth, dead and done with at his own time."[10] Such a person Horace calls a *fautor veterum*: a fanatic worshiper of the ancients.[11] His descendants in our time still turn up their delicate noses at the contamination of ancient classics by modern mass media. The former they find, like Horace's fan, perfect; the latter they find, almost by definition and still like Horace's fan, vulgar.[12] And commercial to boot. They conveniently forget that ancient bards and poets, whether fictional like Homer's Demodocus and Phemius, or real like Pindar, Horace, Virgil, and countless others, made their living with their art.

In retrospect across the centuries, it is evident that Horace had the best kind of understanding of the nature of influence and the importance of the Ancients for the Moderns. The views of two English-language poet-critics, one from the eighteenth century and one from the twentieth, are sufficient to reinforce Horace's verdict. In *An Essay on Criticism*, first published in 1711, Alexander Pope stated unequivocally and with his typical Horatian wit and elegance:

> Some *foreign* Writers, some our *own* despise;
> The *Ancients* only, or the *Moderns* prize:
> (Thus *Wit*, like *Faith*, by each Man is apply'd
> To *one small Sect*, and All are *damn'd beside*.)
> Meanly they seek the Blessing to confine,
> And force *that Sun* but on a *Part* to Shine;
> Which not alone the *Southern Wit* sublimes,
> But ripens Spirits in cold *Northern Climes*;
> Which from the first has shone on *Ages past*,
> Enlights the *present*, and shall warm the *last*:
> (Tho' *each* may feel *Increases* and *Decays*,
> And see now *clearer* and now *darker Days*)
> Regard not then if Wit be *Old* or *New*,
> But blame the *False*, and value still the *True*.[13]

---

[10] Horace, *Epistles* 2.1.21–22: *nisi quae terris semota suisque / temporibus defuncta videt fastidit et odit.*

[11] Horace, *Epistles* 2.1.23.

[12] Cf. the *perfecti veteres* and the *viles atque novi* at Horace, *Epistles* 2.1.37–38. A modern example may be found at Winkler 2015c: 3.

[13] Alexander Pope, *An Essay on Criticism* 394–407; quoted from Butt 1961: 285–287. The annotations to these lines are valuable for my context, not least the textual variant "the *French* Writers" in line 394.

T. S. Eliot concisely restated Pope's and Horace's positions in his influential essay "Tradition and the Individual Talent." There he observed:

No poet, no artist of any art, has his complete meaning alone. His significance, his appreciation is the appreciation of his relation to the dead poets and artists . . . . what happens when a new work of art is created is something that happens simultaneously to all the works of art which preceded it. The existing monuments form an ideal order among themselves, which is modified by the introduction of the new (the really new) work of art among them. The existing order is complete before the new work arrives; for order to persist after the supervention of novelty, the *whole* existing order must be, if ever so slightly, altered; and so the relations, proportions, values of each work of art toward the whole are readjusted; and this is conformity between the old and the new. Whoever has approved this idea of order . . . will not find it preposterous that the past should be altered by the present as much as the present is directed by the past.[14]

Artist of any art: Eliot includes the visual arts. In 1919, when his essay was first published, the art of the moving image was still developing toward full maturity. This, more than anything else, was to become the really new. The mutual interaction of Ancients and Moderns, not only in poetry and prose but also across different media, especially verbal and visual ones, received a major impulse. This development became especially important when poets or playwrights became filmmakers and, with their literary and cinematic works, became classics after their deaths. As a great classical poet, Horace is to us an Ancient rather than a Modern, but in his *Epistle* (and not only there), he revealed a decidedly modern outlook. Like Horace (and others), modern artists of page and screen were first Moderns and then became Ancients. They turned into classics. We will encounter two of them shortly.

2   Charles Perrault against Antiquity

Horace was outspoken in his attack on the self-appointed guardians of tradition. He anticipated at least some of the *Querelle des Anciens et des Modernes*, the debate about the relative virtues of the Old Masters vis-à-vis those of contemporaries that was conducted in France, Italy, the United Kingdom, and elsewhere. But the shade of Horace, could it have known French, might have been astonished at a programmatic statement made by Charles Perrault in his 1687 poem *Le siècle de Louis le Grand*.[15] The king is

---

[14] Eliot 1950b: 49–50.   [15] Fumaroli 2001: 18–24 gives an introduction to the work.

Louis XIV, the Sun King. One couplet in the poem, which runs to well over 500 lines, is sufficient illustration of Perrault's perspective on the ancient and the modern. In lines 70–71 he observed:

> *La docte Antiquité dans toute sa durée*
> *A l'égal de nos jours ne fut point éclairée.*
>
> Learned Antiquity, for as long as it lasted,
> Was never enlightened to equal our times.[16]

Horace and Perrault numbered themselves among the Moderns, but unlike Perrault Horace was not in the least disdainful of the Ancients and did not deny them their high standing. Virtually all of Horace's works, most famously his *Odes*, demonstrate how sensible his position was in balancing the old and the new and in finding praiseworthy qualities in both. Horace's view on "the folly of archaism," as C. O. Brink has called it, applies not only to poetry but also to all creative endeavors in literature and the visual arts.[17] After all, Horace is the author of the famous phrase *ut pictura poesis*, one of the most influential statements about the affinities between text and image. (I mentioned it in Chapter 1.) As the terms *imitatio* and *aemulatio* reveal, Greeks and Romans prized creative and intellectual competition with artistic models much more highly than originality. Such an approach was predestined, as it were, by the flexibility of myth already referred to. Ancient Greeks and Romans were noticeably un-neurotic about towering father figures and rarely suffered from what Harold Bloom has famously called "the anxiety of influence."[18] Classicist D. S. Carne-Ross once observed about the importance of *imitatio* and *aemulatio* for literature and visual arts after the end of antiquity:

the relations between Greek and Latin and the various literatures and cultures they have influenced, that dialogue, or *agon*, with antiquity (taking the form of admiring emulation or of fierce rejection) . . . has been the most constant feature of Western civilization for the last two thousand years and is still active today.[19]

The word *agôn* ("contest, competition") and Carne-Ross's expression *fierce rejection* may remind us of Perrault, if in a somewhat different sense.

---

[16] Perrault 1692. The original was in four volumes (1692–1697). I quote from the one-volume reprint of 1971. The original prints the poem with separate pagination (1–25), following the last page (252) of the *Parallèle des Anciens et des Modernes*; in the reprint, which has continuous pagination across all volumes, the poem is on pages 79–85; my quotation is at 80. (I have deleted the comma originally printed at the end of line 70.) The poem can also be found in Lecoq 2001: 256–273.

[17] Brink 1982: 74.   [18] Bloom 1997.   [19] Carne-Ross 1969: 194.

3 Oedipus from Sophocles to Pasolini

To employ the analogy by Manilius mentioned in my Introduction, few ancient rivers have become as mighty a stream as the myth of Oedipus. The spring of this story is Homer, for Oedipus is mentioned by name in the *Iliad* and the myth is briefly retold in the *Odyssey*.[20] This myth has provided a sheer endless flow of both ancient and modern imitations and emulations, including any number of Modernizers. Sophocles' tragedy *Oedipus the King* (or *Oedipus Rex*), probably dating to after 430 B C, gave this river its canonical flow. A few examples of the varieties of ancient and modern adaptations may be instructive as an answer to the Horatian question "What would now be old?" Sophocles, who was from a district in Attica near Athens called Colonus, made a Theban myth Athenian in his tragedy *Oedipus at Colonus*.[21] We also know of several other Greek and Roman *Oedipus* plays, now lost, including one by Julius Caesar. Lines 981–982 in Sophocles' *Oedipus the King*, in which Jocasta tells Oedipus not to worry about sleeping with his mother because sons often do so in their dreams, anticipates Freud's theory of the Oedipus complex. So the Oedipus story, with its nearly endless retellings in drama, epic, other poetic genres, painting, opera, cinema, and psychoanalysis – even in the counter-psychoanalysis plus philosophy of the *Anti-Oedipus* by Gilles Deleuze and Félix Guattari from 1972, with a foreword by Jacques Derrida – may well be the best example to illustrate Horace's and Manilius' perspective, if no doubt extending far beyond their wildest imaginations.[22]

Beginning in the early twentieth century and independently of the concurrent preoccupation with Oedipus in psychoanalysis, the new medium of cinema turned to Oedipus numerous times, beginning in its earliest years.[23] In the mighty Oedipal river since Homer and Sophocles, one particular twentieth-century tributary stands out: that of Italian poet, dramatist, essayist, novelist, journalist, screenwriter, and film director Pier Paolo Pasolini, who made *Oedipus Rex* in 1967. His film is a landmark of *auteur* cinema, unlikely ever to be eclipsed.[24] Pasolini, to modernize the well-known

---

[20] Homer, *Iliad* 23.679 and *Odyssey* 11.271–280.

[21] Cf. Richardson 1993: 243 (on *Iliad* 23.679–680): "The story that he [Oedipus] died at Athens seems to be an Athenian innovation, and the location at Colonus may be Sophocles' own invention."

[22] Its English version is Deleuze and Guattari 1977.

[23] I outline the history of Oedipus on the screen in Winkler 2009a: 122–153, on which some of the following is based. Solomon 2015 examines Oedipus and related aspects of Greek drama on screen, with additional references.

[24] On the *auteur* concept as continuation of classical views of authorship see Winkler 2009a: 34–50.

Hellenistic and Roman concept of the *poeta doctus*, "the learned poet," was a *poeta doctus cinematographicus*.

Oedipus Rex is the most poetic retelling of the Oedipus myth as both *imitatio*, this time in the medium of moving images, and *aemulatio*, the latter by means of direct recourse to Sophocles, whose text Pasolini himself translated. The film's very structure eloquently links the Ancient and the Modern. *Oedipus Rex* begins and ends in modern Italy. The infancy of Oedipus is patterned on Pasolini's own childhood in the 1920s; the final wanderings of blind Oedipus take place in the 1960s and are contemporary with the filming process itself. In between comes the long main part, the story of Oedipus from his exposure to his self-exile from Thebes, filmed on Moroccan locations of archaic appearance as an indication of the time-lessness of myth. The settings which frame the main story and the chronology from the 1920s to the 1960s show that Pasolini saw himself in Oedipus. Laius and Jocasta are patterned on Pasolini's parents down to their clothing and the décor of their home. As Pasolini said: "The baby in the prologue is I, his father is my father, an infantry officer, and the mother, a schoolmistress, is my mother."[25] Pasolini also said that his relationship with his father had been distant and problematic and that he was always closer to his mother.[26]

The goal Pasolini pursued with his film reveals his understanding of Greek myth and psychoanalysis. In his own words:

I had two objectives: first to make a kind of complete metaphoric – and therefore mythicized – autobiography; and second to confront both the problem of psychoanalysis and the problem of the myth. But instead of projecting the myth onto psychoanalysis, I re-projected psychoanalysis on the myth. This was the fundamental operation in *Oedipus [Rex]*.[27]

Pasolini combines an archetypal story with a modern comment on the human condition. He made the story contemporary and at the same time uncovered its archaic roots. *Oedipus Rex* effectively illustrates Pasolini's concept of *il cinema di poesia*, "the cinema of poetry."[28] Through psychoanalysis and cinema, Pasolini's Oedipus is equally ancient and modern, an Everyman and thus the kind of individual who had been the foundation for Sophocles' Oedipus.

---

[25] Quoted from Schwartz 1992: 509.   [26] Cf., e.g., Schwartz 1992: 512.

[27] Quoted from Schwartz 1992: 506. Cf. Stack 1970: 126–127.

[28] I have attempted a brief explanation of this concept, in Pasolini and beyond, in Winkler 2009a: 50–57, with further references.

The film's ending is indebted to *Oedipus at Colonus*, Sophocles' play about Oedipus' reconciliation with the gods just before his death. Pasolini's Oedipus wanders through a modern city. (Pasolini filmed this part in Bologna.) Then he returns to the meadow where we had first seen him as a newborn baby in the film's prologue. "Life ends where it began," says blind Oedipus. This is Pasolini's variant on T. S. Eliot's "In my beginning is my end" and "In my end is my beginning," respectively the opening and closing lines of "East Coker" in *Four Quartets*. In another creative parallel to Pasolini, Oedipus has now become a musician-poet. As Pasolini said: "Once Oedipus has blinded himself, he re-enters society by sublimating all his faults. One of the forms of sublimation is poetry. He plays the pipe, which means, metaphorically, he is a poet."[29]

A young man called Angelo is blind Oedipus' guide instead of Antigone. Angelo ("Messenger") meets Oedipus when the latter is approaching Thebes, and he leads Oedipus to the Sphinx. The first indication that we receive of the Sphinx's presence is not visual but aural: We hear a strange chant whose source we do not know. In Greek and Roman visual arts and ever after, the Sphinx has been portrayed as a theriomorphous female monster. Pasolini has none of this, for his Sphinx is something altogether different, a creature of bizarre appearance. And it seems to be male (Figure 2.1). Even more astonishing is the fact that the Sphinx does not pose any riddle for Oedipus to solve but informs him that the riddle is Oedipus himself: "Your life is a riddle. But which?" "I don't know," Oedipus replies. "I don't want to know." We could never imagine Sophocles' Oedipus saying that. "It's useless, my son," the Sphinx continues as Oedipus attacks it. We could never imagine this in Sophocles' play, either. "The abyss into which you throw me is inside yourself," the Sphinx concludes. But *this* we *can* understand, provided we think of the complexities of Sophocles' entire subject of knowledge and ignorance, of vision and blindness, and of blindness and insight in connection with both Oedipus and the Sphinx.

The Sphinx was originally a monster to be defeated; only later did she acquire her riddle, not least as a means to demonstrate Oedipus' intelligence.[30] The mythical Sphinx, of course, knows the answer to her riddle, and so, alone, does Oedipus. Pasolini's Sphinx does not know what the riddle of Oedipus' existence is, and neither does he. The Sphinx presumably would like to know; Oedipus does not. But when Oedipus kills the

---

[29] Quoted from Stack 1970: 129.

[30] On this see Edmunds 1995, especially 159–161 (section titled "The Riddle of the Sphinx"); also Davies 2014.

Figure 2.1 A strange Sphinx in Pier Paolo Pasolini's *Oedipus Rex*.

Sphinx in an impulsive charge, one that reminds us of his fit of rage when he killed his father at the crossroads, we can perhaps better understand the tangle of fate, of action undertaken knowingly or impulsively, and of the result, for we could redistribute the dialogue just quoted. Is not the Sphinx, at least in the Sophoclean and all later versions, itself a riddle? And if so, which? In other words, what is the purpose of such a creature's existence, apart from being a mythical monster to be undone by someone who happens to come along and answers a rather obvious question? Could Pasolini's Sphinx apply the question *Your life is a riddle, but which?* to itself and answer it? Would the Sphinx not have to say, simply, *I don't know?* Would such a Sphinx, or any Sphinx, even want to know? All this, of course, is not to imply that Pasolini's Sphinx is Oedipus or that Oedipus is the Sphinx.

Still, Pasolini's metaphor of the abyss which unites the two points us to the fundamental aspect of all existence, human or otherwise: its precariousness and the fact that we could never escape from this very precariousness. Oedipus, as every reader or viewer of Sophocles' play understands, cannot avoid his fate. Equally the Sphinx in the myth cannot escape her destiny of eventually encountering someone with the answer to her question, for the very concept of a riddle presupposes the concept of a solution; that is to say, the existence of that solution. So answers to riddling questions are inescapable. Pasolini's Sphinx accepts Oedipus' arrival and his attack without doing anything about it, such as defending itself. Is it tired of being a Sphinx or accepting the inevitable? Is the Sphinx's own abyss in Oedipus? Is this what we could call, after Henry James, the turn of the existential or philosophical screw that eventually stops grasping anything? Or is this the famous *mise en abîme* that postmodern scholars are frequently enamored of? Is it the abyss that each of us faces at some point? Is that why Sophocles' play about knowledge and ignorance and about fate and guilt or responsibility and about the meaning or futility of existence has become so fascinating, with all its modern ramifications from Freud to film? One more question: Should I stop asking such questions?

Let me then approach the subject of "Sophocles the Ancient versus Pasolini the Modern" in a different way. Greek writer-director Michael Cacoyannis once described *Oedipus Rex* and Pasolini's second film based on Greek tragedy, his *Medea* of 1969, in the following terms:

> Pasolini did not make [films of] Greek tragedy. He made very striking films about the myths on which tragedy is based .... Pasolini's Oedipus is set in a very primitive society. And absolutely no inner torment of Oedipus is suggested .... he was aiming at something totally different. It has nothing to do with Greek tragedy. It has to do with mythology.[31]

These are valuable observations, but Cacoyannis is not entirely right. Yes, the archaic society of Pasolini's "Afro-Greeks," as they have been called, points to the origins and early phases of human culture, one that is still far from being near any classical or even pre-classical greatness.[32] Pasolini's Delphi, a tiny desert oasis, is a case in point. So the world of *Oedipus Rex* shows us a society in which the foundations of classicism are only beginning to be laid. As Cacoyannis said, this has to do with mythology – a lot, in fact. But it also has more than a little to do with tragedy, for Pasolini's Oedipus does show inner torment. One particular instant is yet another unexpected deviation from the myth and from Sophocles. Oedipus, having just found out that his wife Jocasta is also his mother, has intercourse with her one more time; shortly after, she hangs herself. This is not just a kinky twist added to a tale already chock-full of hair-raising elements. Rather, it underlines, in a psychologically convincing way, the despair and loneliness of someone who feels hopelessly abandoned: one who has left Polybus and Merope, the couple who raised him as their child; one who knows that he has killed his father; one who knows who his wife really is and who knows that he cannot continue living with her even if she were not to kill herself; and, finally, one who, upon finding his real mother, cannot simply be her

---

[31] Quoted from McDonald and Winkler 2001: 81–82.
[32] The term quoted is from Todini 1985.

son. This Oedipus has no one left, for there is no Antigone to take pity on him, only an Angelo, who is not one of the brightest. Small wonder that Oedipus, fully in the know, takes a desperate last plunge into the abyss.

In *Oedipus Rex* we have not a case of Ancient versus Modern but a case of Ancient and Modern existing side by side in a strange and eccentric but also highly poetic work, in which the Ancient is being illuminated by the Modern and vice versa. The film's ending in the meadow bears this out, because it exerts an unusually powerful grip on viewers' emotions. The film's settings and its divergences from the canonical version of the Oedipus story throw the classical sophistication of fifth-century drama into greater relief than has ever been the case on screen.

4   Cocteau's Orphic Oedipus

Pasolini was one of the greatest poetic filmmakers who turned to classical antiquity. Jean Cocteau was probably the greatest poet of the cinema to do so a generation earlier. Cocteau was often referred to simply as "the Poet" (*le Poète*). He wrote the libretto for the opera-oratorio *Oedipus Rex*, with music by Igor Stravinsky, that premiered in 1927, and he adapted Sophocles' play into his own modernized version, *The Infernal Machine* of 1934. It followed on his earlier "contraction," as Cocteau called it, of Sophocles' *Antigone* from 1922. As classically influenced filmmaker, however, Cocteau is most famous for what is unofficially called his Orphic Trilogy: *Blood of a Poet* (1930), *Orphée* (1950; coming after his 1925 play of the same title), and *The Testament of Orpheus* (1960). The second film in this trilogy is a particularly profound masterpiece.[33] The third might as well be called *The Testament of Cocteau*. *The Testament of Orpheus* revisits themes, scenes, and characters from *Orphée*. Both *Blood of a Poet* and *The Testament of Orpheus* feature archetypal – and, of course, Orphic – poets, played by Cocteau himself in the latter film. Cocteau had also turned to fairy tale and medieval legend, as in *Beauty and the Beast* (1946), based on Perrault, and *The Eternal Return* (1943), a modernization of the tale of Tristan and Isolde. An Yseult makes a brief appearance in *The Testament of Orpheus*. Cocteau did not direct *The Eternal Return* but clearly was its guiding spirit.

In *The Testament of Orpheus* the Poet, a time traveler, is killed more than once. He descends to the Underworld and returns. His last death happens when a statue of the goddess Minerva comes alive and throws a spear into

---

[33]   I have written about it in Winkler 2009a: 281–294 ("Princess Death").

Figure 2.2 Poet and Sphinx in Jean Cocteau's *The Testament of Orpheus.*

his back. But he is resurrected because poets never die. It is poignant to remember that Cocteau died about three years after making this film. The Poet's death and resurrection have a direct link to the Oedipus myth, because the Poet encounters first a fantastic Sphinx (Figure 2.2) and then blind Oedipus and his guide Antigone. The latter pass him by silently. Oedipus is here being played, in a cameo, by Jean Marais, who had been Cocteau's Orpheus in *Orphée* and the Tristan figure in *The Eternal Return*. So there is a multiple eternal return here: that of Orpheus and *Orphée* and that of Cocteau as the Poet and, by extension, of all poets. The fate of this poet and of all others is part of what Cocteau calls "phoenixology" (*la phénixologie*), a term borrowed from Salvador Dalí. In retrospect and without slighting Dalí, we could now say that Cocteau made the concept wholly his own. He dedicated a poem titled *Phénixologie* to photographer Lucien Clergue, who accompanied the filming of *The Testament of Orpheus* and later published his images in a book of photographs.[34] In response to an interviewer's question about the scene of the poet's resurrection, Cocteau defined the concept like this:

<hr />

[34] Clergue 2003. Cocteau's poem is at Clergue 2003: 11; it is dated 1959 and makes no mention of Dalí. An English-language edition of the book (Clergue 2001) is less attractive and does not contain Cocteau's poem.

Figure 2.3 The Poet before a painting of Oedipus in Jean Cocteau's *The Testament of Orpheus*.

That is to say that poets die and live again. Dalí invented a very beautiful science: phoenixology. Phoenixology, that means that people die often to be reborn. It is the rebirth of the phoenix. Burn, burn to change into ashes, and in their turn the ashes become oneself. One becomes oneself through this phenomenon of phoenixology.[35]

Such death and rebirth depend on the artist's achievement: "Naturally, works of art create themselves and dream of killing their creators," Cocteau explains in *The Testament of Orpheus*, not entirely logically. He also states about the innate quality of art works: "Of course they exist before the artist discovers them. But it's always Orpheus, always Oedipus ...." A large painting by Cocteau of blind Oedipus and his two daughters appears on screen (Figure 2.3), followed by a portrait of Orpheus.[36]

---

[35] The original can be found at http://alpha-risk.net/blog/wp-content/uploads/970103-Radio-Archives-Journal-du-testament-dOrphée2.mp3. Cocteau said: "C'est à dire que les poètes meurent et revivent. Dalí a inventé une science très belle: la phénixologie. La phénixologie, cela veut dire que les personnes meurent souvent pour renaître. C'est la renaissance du phénix. Brûle, brûle pour se changer en cendres, et à leur tour les cendres se changent en soi-même. On devient soi-même à travers ce phénomène de la phénixologie."

[36] The Oedipus of *The Testament of Orpheus* is also in Clergue 2003: 60 (Clergue's photograph of Cocteau and the painting here mentioned) and 166–172. The Sphinx is even more prominent (Clergue, frontispiece and 158–165). The images have captions by Cocteau.

5   From Horace and Perrault to Cinema

A particular aphorism of Cocteau's about the cinema is therefore apropos here: "In short," he once said (actually, more than once), "it is an admirable vehicle for poetry."[37] Many of the Ancients, foremost among them Simonides, could well assent, providing they could have heard Cocteau and understood the medium of moving images that we Moderns now take for granted.

Cocteau and Pasolini, two great filmmaker-poets, created the most profound renditions of Greek myths (Orpheus, Oedipus) ever achieved in the cinema, the modern medium that is best suited for mythical story-telling. One of the most learned and most influential scholars of cinema, André Bazin, once summarized the matter in a concise and elegant way: "Fiction and filmmaking do not engage in mutual imitation; they only adopt common purposes, they fulfill the same aims, without copying each other."[38] Simonides already knew about the common purposes of text and image. But why, in particular, the cinema? An attractive explanation, frequently repeated, has been credited to Bazin, although it was neither by him nor put in the same words. The (mis)quotation can be heard, most famously, in the arresting beginning of Jean-Luc Godard's film *Contempt* (1963). It is this: "The cinema, said André Bazin, substitutes to our gaze an alternate world, which conforms to our desires."[39] This insight also fits the ancient cultures if we replace the word *cinema* with the broader term *visual narrative*.

One other great poetic filmmaker has addressed the same matter. Manoel de Oliveira, whom we might call the cinema's Nestor since he was still active at age 105, rejected all die-hard Modernists in 2010:

Nowadays there is a frequent confusion about the word *modern*, as if it designated a new and improved morality, signifying, in and of itself, something *good,*
better, as if that which is older were, in and of itself, something *bad, undesirable*,
and that which is *modern* something *good*, in life as well as in the arts. In a certain

---

[37] From Clergue 2003: 13: "Bref, c'est un admirable véhicule de poésie." Cocteau's text containing this quotation is not in Clergue 2001.

[38] Bazin 1997b: 237. The original essay had appeared in 1947.

[39] Compare the following two French versions: 1. Mourlet 1959: 34: "le cinéma est un regard qui se substitue au nôtre pour nous donner un monde accordé à nos désirs." 2. The statement heard in *Contempt*: "Le cinéma, disait André Bazin, substitue à notre regard un monde qui s'accorde à nos désirs." Mourlet's article has been republished several times. On Mourlet, Bazin, and Godard's misattribution see de Baecque 2003: 216–217 and Paige 2004: especially 21 note 14 (on Mourlet's "genuinely fascist overtones").

sense, we are losing fairness in criteria in a movement towards abstraction of the authentic values, thereby equating *modern* and *good* in an absolute sense.

De Oliveira takes up a stance that contradicts Perrault's and sounds virtually like a Horace of our own time when he says a little later:

> There is no *old* without *modern*, because the latter generates the *old*, and everything *old* was, in its own time, *modern. Old* or *modern* are made up of good and bad parts, and tradition is like sifting wheat, separating it from the chaff, time being the greater judge.[40]

We may now adapt Perrault's claim about learned antiquity to the topic at hand. In antiquity's end is our beginning, so let us no longer say, with Perrault:

> *La docte Antiquité dans toute sa durée*
> *A l'égal de nos jours ne fut point éclairée.*

Rather, let us affirm *this*, even if it contains a certain measure of hyperbole:

> *La docte Antiquité dans toute sa durée*
> *A l'égal de nos films est toute éclairée.*

We can, however, take this modernization of Perrault one step further. In accordance with Bazin, we might conclude:

> *Le docte cinéma dans toute sa durée*
> *A l'égal d'Antiquité a tout éclairé.*

Classical antiquity, primarily its literature, can help prepare us for anything in life. So can the cinema. Modernist visual poet Alain Resnais made the point in his film *Wild Grass* (2009). Its narrator states that, when you come out of the film theater, nothing surprises you any more. And that is just as it should be, equally for what is Ancient (Learned Antiquity) and for what is Modern (the cinema) and for the persistent affinities that exist between them.

My observations in this chapter may not have convinced each and every die-hard *fautor veterum* among my readers. But they – and I – might take one particular and humane exhortation by Horace into consideration: "Let some limit prevent excessive quarrels." Horace, of course, put it much more concisely and far more elegantly: *excludat iurgia finis.*[41]

---

[40] Both quotations are from *Absoluto* ("[The] Absolute"), a long conversation, recorded on video, with writer-director Manoel de Oliveira about his work and philosophy of life and of cinema. Its release version, edited to appear more like a monologue than an interview, is available on the American DVD of his film *The Strange Case of Angélica* (2010). My quotations are based on the subtitles provided on the DVD, with slight adjustments. De Oliveira was born in 1908 and died in 2015.

[41] Horace, *Epistles* 2.1.38.

PART II

Elective Affinities

Tragedy and Comedy

3 | Medea's Infanticide
How to Present the Unimaginable

"She was a vicious character; she was a murderess . . . . Medea killed her children." With these words Homer Thrace, a fictional character whom we will get to know better later on, expressed the standard view of Medea. In antiquity, we find an even briefer summary in Quintilian's handbook on rhetoric. He refers to Medea on no more than two occasions; the second has only two words: *atrox Medea* ("horrible Medea").[1] This view of Medea derives from Euripides' play of 431 BC, which has overshadowed all other versions of the Medea myth:

Because of the success of Eur.'s play, the figure of Medea came to be identified most of all with the act of infanticide: the high point in the play, when she resists her maternal feelings and insists on the violent act, became crystallized in the popular mind as the essence of Medea's life and character. Concentration on this deed entailed ever increasing emphasis . . . on Medea's passionate emotions and violence.[2]

Before Euripides, Medea did not murder her children, although she was blamed for their deaths or inadvertently caused them.[3] After Euripides, it was impossible to rescue Medea from the reputation that Homer Thrace was familiar with. Seneca, in his play, has Medea put the matter most concisely: *Medea fiam* ("I will *become* Medea" or, more colloquially, "I'll turn myself into the real Medea") and *Medea nunc sum* ("now I *am* Medea").[4] Seneca's Medea knows that the essential Medea is Euripides'. "She has the mother instinct of Medea," a wife tells her husband about his ex-wife, whom she detests, in Richard Linklater's film *Before Midnight* (2013). "A woman killing her kids to punish her ex-husband." Media may change; Medea does not, at least not in popular memory. With some exceptions, the post-classical Medea has been perceived as emotionally unhinged, psychopathic, or immoral. In the words of

---

[1] Quintilian, *Handbook of Rhetoric* 11.3.73.
[2] Mastronarde 2002: 15 (at beginning of section titled "Medea's Motivations and Decisions").
[3] Schwinge 2004 is a recent survey of the ancient tradition. See also Page 1938: 21–25; Mastronarde 2002: 50 and 52–53; Tedeschi 2010, especially 5–7 ("Varianti del mito") and 8–35 ("Fortuna di Medea"). On the *Medea* of Neophron, of which only fragments survive, and the possibility that it may have antedated Euripides' play and anticipated Euripides' innovations of the myth see Mastronarde 2002: 57–64. On Medea and child murder see further Corti 1998.
[4] Seneca, *Medea* 171 and 910.

Ovid's Medea: "I understand and approve of what is right; I do what is wrong."[5] Medea utters this as part of an interior monologue long before she commits any wrong and years before she ever contemplates infanticide. Her words have been adduced, outside their immediate context, as characteristic of her entire personality. Clearly she appears as wholly evil. But great characters in great literature never are.[6]

How can as horrendous an act as child murder be explained? In Euripides, Medea's development from rational abhorrence to emotional self-persuasion, replete with wavering indecision and a process of argument and counter-argument, convincingly shows us someone driven to the abyss. Stagecraft and rhetoric express Medea's inner state, her *mentalité*. They help explain her acts but do not absolve her. To understand all is certainly *not* to forgive all. Herein, at least in part, lies the eerie fascination that Medea compels.

As its name tells us, a theater – in Greek, *theatron* – is a "viewing space," a place in which we watch as we listen. But acts of violence in the Greek theater took place off stage. How then could the playwrights ensure that climactic violence exerts its greatest emotional grip on the spectators? For this there existed, appropriately enough, a combination of the verbal and the visual. The verbal aspects are speeches reporting what has occurred off stage, as by a messenger or even a perpetrator (e.g. Clytemnestra in Aeschylus' *Agamemnon*); in addition, audiences may hear the death screams of someone being killed. The visual side is the use of the *ekkyklêma*, the wheeled platform that displays *tableaux vivants* of the dead and possibly their killers. Both ways often occur together. The result is the greatest possible emotional impact from climactic violence. Greek visual artists, such as vase painters, often took their inspiration from literature, primarily from epic and tragedy as the two pre-eminent genres which retold famous myths. So a few Greek vases depict a Euripidean Medea: in the act of infanticide.[7]

---

[5] Ovid, *Metamorphoses* 7.20–21: *video meliora proboque, / deteriora sequor*. Ovid's tragedy *Medea* is lost.

[6] Gill 1996: 154–174 and 216–226 (chapter sections titled "Euripides' *Medea*: The Case for Infanticide" and "Medea's Self-Mastering Anger") examines in detail how Euripides develops Medea's revenge strategy and gives extensive references. On Medea in general cf., e.g., the contributions in Clauss and Johnston 1997.

[7] A full account appears in *Lexicon Iconographicum Mythologiae Classicae*, 6.1–2 (1992), s. v. "Medeia," where see section B on Medea and infanticide, especially B.2.29–33a (the act of murder) and 30–31 (Medea with the apron customarily worn during sacrificial rites). See further Guiraud 1996 and Galasso 2013, with illustrations and bibliographies. Galasso's final three images, from Campanian and Apulian vases, show Medea in the act of killing one child or both her children. Vout 2012 examines Medea in Roman paintings, Buchanan 2012 on Roman sarcophagi. Both provide illustrations.

The Greek stage tradition changed in Roman times, when tragedy could put horrendous slaughter and other acts of mayhem before the spectators' eyes. The plays of Seneca are our best evidence. From them derived the graphic violence in medieval and in Elizabethan and Jacobean drama.[8] The tradition of what we might call, with Sir Philip Sidney, "the sweet violence of a tragedy" culminated in Antonin Artaud's theater of cruelty and, beyond this, in the cinema.[9] Film is probably the most powerful medium to combine the verbal and the visual as means of excitement; hence, at least in part, its penchant for violence.[10]

I now turn to the depiction of Medea's infanticide as presented on screen.[11] Film scholar Ian Christie has observed that few films showing Medea as murderess, especially child murderess, could exist before "the permissive and experimental sixties" because a "conventionally 'cine-matic' Medea would show us precisely what we don't want to see ... above all, the killing of the children." This matter, he concludes, "remains deeply troubling and fundamentally taboo."[12] Since then, filmmakers have been able to choose whether to show Medea's infanticide on screen or to omit the act after carefully setting up viewers' anticipation of it. So we could speak of a Euripidean strand and of a Senecan one. Although there are no rigid divisions, examples of both exist. This chapter will examine particularly well-known or important instances, even though it does not attempt to be all-inclusive. Since Medea's victims tend to get short shrift, I devote one section of this chapter to her children. The topic demands that I devote much of this chapter to detailed analytical descrip-tions of the scenes in question. I omit controversial Dutch director Theo van Gogh's five-hour television (TV) series *Medea* (2005), his last film, which sets the story in circles of contemporary high finance, business, and politics but in which the infanticide is dealt with only briefly and does

---

[8] On the medieval tradition see especially Enders 1999, with frequent recourse to Greek and Roman rhetoric. The later traditions are too well known to need documentation here. For Medea see Morse 1996; on the later Medea, Heavey 2015. On tragedy and violent cinema see Simkin 2006.

[9] The quotation is from Sidney 2002: 98. The phrase, which furnished the title of Eagleton 2003, derives from Aristotle's concept of tragic pleasure as outlined in his *Poetics*. Butcher 1907: 267 speaks of "a noble emotional satisfaction" in the spectator.

[10] Cf., for just one example, the title of Bazin 1982.

[11] Dumont 2009: 139–145 lists and briefly describes the different screen appearances of Medea. See also Kyriakos 2013: 4, 13, and 15, especially brief mentions of little-known Greek adaptations. On the three most prominent films (by Pasolini, von Trier, and Dassin, all examined below) see in particular Christie 2000. See also Mimoso-Ruiz 1996 (in a thematic journal issue titled *Médée et la violence*); Rodighiero 2009, especially 581–586 on Medea. Stephan 2006 includes several detailed studies of films, with extensive references.

[12] Christie 2000: 145–146.

not appear on screen.[13] Also omitted is Tonino De Bernardi's *Médée Miracle* (2007), with Isabelle Huppert in the Medea part, in which the modern Medea loses – but does not kill – her children and ultimately turns her revenge against herself. This may be regarded as a variant on an earlier, in this case Brazilian, version: Oduvaldo Viana Filho's *Caso Especial – Medéia* ("Special Case – Medea"), a 1973 TV film, excluded as well. In it, Medea abandons her plan to kill her children, leaves them in Jason's care, and kills herself. As one scholar comments: "It is an ending that is neither tragic nor heroic, because Medéia does not assume responsibility for her actions and their terrible consequences."[14]

1 Pier Paolo Pasolini's *Medea*

In the Euripidean strand, directors follow, no doubt unwittingly, Horace, who was firm about the artistic principle of *not* showing: "do not drag onto the stage what should happen inside," he says in the *Art of Poetry* and then specifically mentions four examples, the first of them this: "Medea should not slaughter her boys in front of the audience." He concludes: "Whatever of this sort you show me, I disbelieve and detest."[15]

   With this perspective, poet, playwright, and filmmaker Pier Paolo Pasolini might well have agreed. His 1969 film of *Medea*, with a commanding Maria Callas in her only film appearance, is a loose and idiosyncratic re-creation of Euripides.[16] Pasolini could never have shown the excesses that six years later appeared in *Salò; or, The 120 Days of Sodom*, his last film. Even so, his *Medea* includes a graphic human sacrifice. Pasolini showed the victim's death on screen and, more discreetly, his dismemberment. Medea as Colchian priestess presided over it all; as a result, her infanticides will take on aspects of ritual sacrifice as well.[17]

   Pasolini's film culminates in a long and intense infanticide sequence. Medea tenderly bathes the younger boy and then, reclining on a couch in the children's bedroom, holds him on her lap, rocking and soothing

---

[13] The film was shown after its right-wing director had fallen victim to a political assassination the year before. On this see Buruma 2006a (= 2006b).

[14] Quoted from Coelho 2013a: 366. Her section on the film (363–366) is my source here.

[15] Horace, *Art of Poetry* 182–183, 185, and 188. Boyle 2014 adduces these lines and their context in his discussion of "Seneca's Theatre of Violence" (xlix–liii) and observes: "Seneca's *Medea* breaks these prescriptions" (xlix). On the topic see further Rodighiero 2003. On depictions of violence in Greek culture generally see Seidensticker and Vöhler 2006.

[16] On Callas and Medea see especially the chapter in Stephan 2006: 182–193 and 292–295 (notes).

[17] So argued by Kvistad 2010.

Figure 3.1 Medea before her infanticides in Pier Paolo Pasolini's *Medea*.

him (Figure 3.1). Colchian music and wordless singing on the sound-track that drown out the gentle music of the children's tutor prepare us for what comes next. Medea looks off into the distance, and Pasolini cuts to a medium close-up on a dagger lying on the ground near her. When Medea emerges from the bedroom, a slightly shaky camera shows her, in long shot, fetching her other son, and we suspect what she has just done. The camera's unsteadiness indicates Medea's inner turmoil; the fact that it is minimal and may easily be overlooked points to her enormous self-control. She appears wholly undisturbed, but we know that she is not.

Medea now bathes and cuddles her older child, and Pasolini draws everything out more. Medea talks to him, smiles at him, rocks him; he, in her arms, smiles back at her in not one but two extreme and heartbreaking close-ups. The tutor's music continues. Medea reaches down, and a different close-up on her dagger, now stained with blood, confirms for us what has happened to the younger child and will now happen to the older. These close-ups might be regarded as the visual – i.e. cinematic – equivalents of the verbal in Euripides: the children's screams. In his play they die together.

The tutor goes on playing, then he falls asleep. The end of the music and a close-up on the peacefully sleeping tutor reveal what Medea is doing off screen. When we see her next, she is putting her son on his bed and gently straightening his clothing. From a high angle we see both boys lying on their backs, as if they were asleep and at peace. But theirs is the sleep of death. Our view of their dead bodies, which Medea has lovingly laid to rest, is the filmic equivalent of the ancient *ekkyklêma*. There is no trace of blood anywhere on the children's bodies or on their spotless white clothing. They remain clean and pure, literally after their baths and, more importantly, symbolically. The deaths of these angelic children were painless. The cinema generally, although not always, presents Medea's children as little lambs in order to increase viewers' emotional involvement. Our sympathy is with the innocent sufferers.

Pasolini developed a theory of "the cinema of poetry," a hallmark of his work.[18] The infanticide sequence is one of the best illustrations of this concept because it is extremely powerful and moving. Everything is restful and quiet, as if we were witnessing an idyllic family scene that is free of any turmoil or anguish. Subdued colors reinforce an overall atmosphere of drowsiness and calm. From such a perspective it makes sense that Pasolini, following Callas's request, removed a lullaby that Medea sings to her younger son: "He asked ... that she sing a short lullaby, in Greek, to Medea's baby son. She agreed but asked that it be omitted when she saw the rushes with sound track."[19] In view of the often-noted fact that one of the world's greatest singers does not get to sing in her only film appearance, this circumstance deserves to be more widely known. Medea's smaller son, however, is no longer a baby. To viewers who are experiencing pity and fear (*eleos* and *phobos*), the two chief emotions evoked by tragedy according to Aristotle, the inclusion of the lullaby might have been overwhelming.

Only if we look very closely do we see that a trickle of blood has seeped from the corner of the smaller boy's mouth when Pasolini shows each of them stretched out on their beds for the last time. Pasolini thus avoids showing what Horace would have detested. His Medea is regal, calm (but not always), and stoical (but not always). In an interview conducted during filming Callas spoke out against Medea's aggressiveness as alien to herself and stated her belief that she succeeded in making Medea live "with a rich humanity" (*con una umanità ricca*) in the spectators' minds.[20] Pasolini said

---

[18] Cf. above, Chapter 2.

[19] Schwartz 1992: 555. Pasolini's treatment for the film ("Visioni della Medea") is reproduced in Pasolini 1991: 477–540; its scene 95 (535–538) is a highly poetic rendition of what will appear on screen and includes Medea's song to her older (!) son (537). Pasolini emphasizes the religious nature of the scene. The volume also reprints an interview with Callas (Gambetti 1991) and Pasolini's poem "Callas" (585–586), composed during filming in June, 1968.

[20] Gambetti 1991: 476. Scholarship on Pasolini's *Medea* is extensive; a recent study by a classicist is Shapiro 2013.

about his Medea: "Here is a woman, in one sense the most modern of women, but there lives in her an ancient woman – strange, mysterious, magical, with terrible inner conflicts." And about Callas: "[She] comes out of a peasant world, Greek, antique, and then had a bourgeois formation. Thus in a certain sense, I tried to concentrate in her character that which she is, in her total complexity."[21] Maria Callas may be the cinema's greatest Medea.

2   Arturo Ripstein's *Such Is Life*

In his book *Greek Tragedy into Film*, Kenneth MacKinnon adopts three categories of film adaptations of stage plays from Jack Jorgens's book *Shakespeare on Film* but introduces a final category of his own: *meta-tragedy*.[22] Meta-tragic films focus on a combination of visual poetry along with reflections on the very nature of the medium of cinema. MacKinnon did not know Mexican director Arturo Ripstein's *Such Is Life* of 2000, based on Seneca, which belongs into this category.[23] Ripstein worked in collaboration with his wife, screenwriter Paz Alicia Garciadiego; their film presents a feminist retelling set in contemporary Mexico City. The story takes place in a working-class milieu, filmed at least in part on existing locations. Julia, the modern Medea, lives in a cluttered apartment in a lower-class development. Accordingly, the murder sequence looks utterly realistic and far removed from that tranquility we saw in Pasolini's *Medea*.

It begins when the camera, presumably handheld, moves toward the partly open door of the bathroom. The effect is like an intrusion: as if the camera, and we with it, were surreptitiously watching something we are not meant to see. Julia, her back to us, is bathing her two children, a little boy and a slightly older girl. She is breathing intensely, an ominous sign. Julia turns around and looks directly into the camera and at us before turning back to the children.

When Julia gets her knife, Ripstein makes much more of this than Pasolini had done, even raising the sound of cutlery clattering in a drawer

---

[21] Both quotations are from Schwartz 1992: 554; source references at 719 notes 26 and 27.

[22] MacKinnon 1986: 126–164; Jorgens 1977. A more recent and more detailed study is Michelakis 2013. On Medea: MacKinnon, 146–161; Michelakis, 64–78 and 173–189. MacKinnon 2016 gives a very brief overview.

[23] On this film see Vita 2011, Danese 2013, and especially Tovar Paz 2002. The latter discusses the classical myth, Medea in film, Latin-American culture and cinema, and Ripstein's approach to filmmaking; he provides extensive references as well.

to a jarring level. The children's beds and a playpen are nearby. Constantly breathing loudly and emitting anguished sounds, Julia briefly puts the knife into a bowl of water that also contains an assortment of coins. She goes back to the bathroom but turns around, looks at us, and closes the door in our faces. Ripstein thus makes us, and Julia as well, aware of the very medium that tells her story. Strangely but powerfully, this only heightens the realism of what follows.

Now the infanticide sequence turns deadly serious. With a long and intricate traveling shot through the apartment, Ripstein increases the level of horror and shock when Julia opens the door again. She is holding the knife in one hand and her little boy, now dressed, by the other. She practically forces him to run with her through the apartment and back into the bathroom. She treats the child quite roughly, even pushing him down into the tub as if to drown him. But she turns and sees her daughter, who has come to the bathroom door in innocent curiosity. Julia runs out, pushes the girl away, and bangs the door shut with such force that it partly opens again. Together with the uncomprehending but clearly frightened girl, we hear the mother's anguished breathing and the sound of the water running into the tub. Unlike the girl we know what is about to happen. And we can look into the bathroom, where Julia has raised the knife beside her head and then brings it down. The moment passes so quickly that it is easily missed.

Immediately afterwards, everything gets yet more intense. Julia's loud and breathy sounds raise our terror. She comes out with the dead child in her arms and the bloody knife in her hand. The boy's body is wrapped in a bloodstained white sheet. Julia walks through the apartment and goes outside. The girl clings to her mother but is pushed away again. Still she follows her. In a manner of speaking, she imitates her mother by picking up her teddy bear. Now we begin to fear for her life, not least when Julia puts down the boy and, knife still in hand, turns to the girl. Most viewers will want to warn her: *Keep far away from your mother!* But mercifully the daughter is safe. Then the father arrives.

In the film's final scene, Julia leaves in a taxi, which then appears on the TV screen in the apartment. But the TV set is not where we have seen it before. It now stands in the corridor, where it cannot serve any realistic function or purpose. Here Ripstein is particularly meta-tragic. He integrates this medium of mass communication, an offspring of the cinema, into the story on several occasions. One has occurred when Julia and her husband made love for the last time. The TV set was near their bed and was turned on, showing a sports event. Later that set will show the two on their bed during their moments of intimacy. There is no longer a separation of the story and the medium that tells it.[24] In a particularly revealing moment, Ripstein and his camera crew had been briefly reflected in a mirror as they were filming in Julia's apartment. What we have seen as a realistic world – such is life – is turned into a screen world or, better, into a screened world. What postmodern scholars like to call "self-referentiality" has rarely been achieved more powerfully or to better purpose than in *Such Is Life*. As Ripstein stated the year before his Medea film was released: "people in states of desperation, people at the end of their rope, sinners in the broadest aspect, and people who bear guilt in suffering and in despair … make for wonderful, dark storytelling … Great sufferers are ambiguous and mysterious, and that is what art should ultimately be."[25] Euripides and Seneca might agree.

3   Jocy de Oliveira's *Kseni*

A comparable strategy was incorporated into Brazilian multimedia artist Jocy de Oliveira's modern opera *Kseni* ("The Stranger") in its theatrical and video versions of 2005 and 2006. The stage productions, performed first in Germany and then in Brazil, incorporated filmic images; their video records seamlessly fused both media. *Kseni* is a political and strongly feminist work. Although de Oliveira took Euripides' play as her inspiration, this Medea is both modern and timeless: a "universal and atemporal myth … to encourage reflection on a more human [read: *humane*], integrated society."[26] As a result, de Oliveira's Medea appears on stage, hence also on screen, in a dual incarnation:

I decided to unravel Medea's personage with the addition of her double. The spoken words in *Sprechgesang* style were interpreted by [an] actress … and the demanding singing part by [a] soprano …. I believed the complexity of the personage demanded this to enhance our scenic vision.

As we will see, a separation of Medea's character into two performers had already occurred a few years earlier on the Japanese stage. De Oliveira's perspective – "I chose a symbolic venue to express my concept of *Kseni*" – also throws a different light on Medea's infanticide:

---

[24] Cf. Tovar Paz 2002: 190–192.   [25] Quoted from de la Mora 1999: 9.
[26] Quoted from the description of *Kseni* in the bilingual booklet accompanying the *Coleção Jocy de Oliveira* (DVD boxed set), 48–49; quotations at 49.

In my understanding Medea did not kill her children, she liberated them from a world that excluded her as a barbarian: foreigner, transgressor, immigrant. She preferred to take her children's souls with her rather than abandoning them in this inhospitable world. The importance of this concept led me to the vision of Medea carrying her children in her chariot of fire as a transforming element of purification.[27]

De Oliveira emphasized water and blood to a greater extent than either Pasolini or Ripstein had done:

She [Medea] speaks the words "No civilized woman would do this" [the title of one the opera's five acts] in many languages[,] thus bringing the figure of Medea closer to that of other women. This echo becomes stronger when the actress and singer appears in the film wearing only a loose robe. Following on from this scene, the audience see her naked body. Medea throws the bloody water that has collected in a sandy puddle on the beach over herself, while images of the two children are superimposed onto that of her own. At that very moment her body unclothed by any garment that could identify her as belonging to a particular culture comes to symbolize the body not of an individual woman, but of everywoman.[28]

4   Jules Dassin's *A Dream of Passion*

The most complex meta-tragedy of Medea, produced and filmed in Greece, appeared in 1978. Its working title had been *I alli Mideia* ("The Other Medea"). Its eventual release title, *Kravgi gynaikôn* ("Cry of Women"), was translated literally for a few foreign releases, such as *Cri de femmes* in France. Today the film is generally known by its international title, *A Dream of Passion* (Figure 3.2). It is taken from Shakespeare's *Hamlet*, Act 2 Scene 2, when Hamlet muses about the player king's ability to imagine the various characters he may play "in a fiction, in a dream of passion."[29] Writer-director Jules Dassin was inspired by an actual case of infanticide by the wife of an American navy officer stationed in Athens. Dassin's wife, Greek actress and singer Melina Mercouri, had played Euripides' Medea

---

[27] The preceding quotations are taken, in slightly edited form, from an e-mail communication by de Oliveira.

[28] Quoted from Coelho 2013a: 377.

[29] Shakespeare, *Hamlet* 2.2.546; quoted from Harold Jenkins 1982: 269. Shakespeare's phrase, which appears on screen at the beginning, is also the title of Strasberg 1987 on Method acting.

Figure 3.2 Poster for Jules Dassin's *A Dream of Passion*.

on stage in 1976.[30] Her "interpretation was praised for its humanity and emotional power."[31] Critics were not that kind to *A Dream of Passion*.[32]

Maya, the actress Mercouri plays, is in rehearsal for Euripides' *Medea* and visits Brenda, the murderous American mother, in prison in order to learn what may have caused such an act. Eventually Maya becomes drawn ever more deeply into Brenda's world and mind. At one point Maya and her theatrical company are watching Ingmar Bergman's *Persona* (1966), in which the personalities of a stage actress who had a nervous breakdown while playing Electra and her nurse are fused; for a time it is as if they become one. Maya also confesses to having had an abortion and to having taken a friend's man away from her, both echoes of aspects in the Medea myth.

---

[30] Stehlíková 2012: 145 note 5 provides some background information on this production.
[31] Quoted from Mavromoustakos 2000: 172.
[32] The assessments by Christie 2000: 161–162 and Shelley 2011: 227–234 (with excerpts from contemporary reviews) are later instances of critical disdain. Stehlíková 2012 bravely attempts to rehabilitate Dassin but wrongly asserts (146) that *A Dream of Passion* was awarded the Golden Palm at the 1978 Cannes Film Festival. It was nominated but did not win. Decades of neglect are the more regrettable because Dassin was working with Giorgos Arvanitis, the remarkable cinematographer of Michael Cacoyannis's *Iphigenia*, released the year before.

In the film's most powerful sequence Maya visits the house, now deserted, in which the crime had occurred, and Dassin combines several narrative layers. He is realistic in the horror being shown and meta-tragic – indeed, meta-cinematic – in the manner in which he presents it. Maya's visit is fused with Brenda's remembrance of that night, with Maya imagining herself as witness of the murders and, for one moment, even becoming Brenda. All this is eventually fused with a rehearsal of Euripides' play. Such complexity justifies a detailed description.

Maya first listens to Brenda telling her the beginning of her story, then leaves the prison and arrives at Brenda's former home. Dassin films Maya's way out of the prison and her approach to the house from her point of view; at the same time the camera is noticeably unsteady while dissonant music is on the soundtrack. This combination of image and sound indicates to us the emotional impact of Brenda's tale on Maya and prepares us for the revelation of what had happened, which is shown both objectively and subjectively. Inside the dark house, and as if from Maya's perspective, the camera approaches Brenda kneeling and praying before a crucifix. We already know that she is extremely pious, even fanatical about her religion. She turns around, almost as if she were noticing Maya. From a close-up on her face Dassin cuts to her three little children frolicking in the bathtub. Brenda's reminiscences continue in voice-over: "The night was gold, their little heads were gold . . . ." A cut back to an anguished Brenda shows her at the bathroom door: "And I said: 'I don't have the strength. My heart will break before I take a knife in my hand.'" The music has now become plangent. But then Brenda remembers "the horror and the Antichrist" and tells her God: "I'll bring them to you."

Another unsteady but continuous tracking shot, taken from her point of view, brings Brenda through parts of the house and into the kitchen, where she opens a cutlery drawer. Several large knives are conspicuous. Her intense praying continues in voice-over. It is a long and somewhat rambling monologue directed at God. A medium shot of her while she reaches into the drawer also reveals Maya, who is staring at Brenda from the shadows. Here different narrative levels begin to fuse. A shock cut brings the knife drawer into extreme close-up. There is a sharp metal sound as Brenda takes one of the largest knives. She holds the gleaming blade up before her face as if she were praying to it. Maya, in a closer shot, keeps watching. The women's faces are lit as if they were in a horror film. Cut. Unexpectedly, we now see and hear the chorus of Euripides' *Medea*, dressed in black, in rehearsal at the ancient theater of Delphi. That outdoor scene is as dark as the one in Brenda's house.

Another cut, and we are in the two smaller children's bedroom. They are now sleeping peacefully. Ominously, the door slowly opens in one corner of the screen, and a dark figure holding a knife enters and approaches. Brenda's voice and mournful instrumental music are on the soundtrack while Dassin shows us several of the pictures on the bedroom wall, made by the children. These are followed by an image of the Madonna and Child. More shots of the sleeping children. One of them, a girl, is lying on her back, her arms folded across her chest as if she were already dead. Her mother hovers above her. Brenda turns around, the camera unsteadily circling her. A close-up on a Greek icon of Mary and little Jesus, decorated in silver, looks as if the divine mother were watching the scene as well and giving Brenda her blessing. That shot is followed, shockingly, by an extreme close-up on the bloodstained face of an adult Jesus on the cross. Cut. A different icon of Mary and her son now appears in a medium shot on a wall in the background. From below the frame, Brenda's hand holding the knife rises, in the extreme foreground, before the religious image and ascends out of the frame. Now the voices of the women in Euripides' chorus are heard again; after a second or two they appear on screen, their arms raised high. Another cut. Now Maya is observing Brenda in a close-up so extreme that only half her face is visible. She watches as if in speechless horror.

Cut. Brenda now enters the bedroom next door, in which her eldest child, a boy, is sleeping. As before, Brenda hesitates on the threshold. The close-up shot on her profile is similar to the earlier one, but everything now has become much more intense. When she looks over at her son, the camera moves into a close-up on him. His glasses are on his chest, and a small book is open by his hand. The shot itself radiates domestic and familial happiness. The boy seems to feel his mother's presence and drowsily opens his eyes while we hear Brenda breathing heavily. The child begins to smile at his mother. A close-up on Brenda's face from his point of view tells him that all may not be well. Cut back to the boy. In one of the most gripping shots in the film, his smile vanishes. The boy looks down. We do not see the bloodied knife in his mother's hand, but he does. Brenda now moves into the room, her face momentarily going out of focus. Cut to the boy. In terror, he jumps out of bed and runs off. Dassin now cuts to the Greek chorus and back into the house. In long shot, Brenda is struggling in the doorway with her son, who is desperately trying to escape from her. A quick insert on Maya's face, again in extreme close-up, reminds us that she is still there, silently watching. Next comes the most powerful moment in the fusions of narrative levels: It is not

Brenda but Maya who is wrestling with the doomed child. The reason why Dassin included *Persona* is now clear: Brenda and Maya have become one, at least in Maya's mind. Maya understands Brenda and can now become Euripides' Medea. The dream of passion has become an affinity of imagination while also turning into a tragic nightmare.

Another insert with Euripides' chorus; then we are in the backyard of Brenda's house. The boy has managed to free himself. His mother pursues him. As she does, we hear the voices of the chorus. Brenda approaches her son, walking into a close-up on her hand holding the bloody knife in another horror-film shot. Cut to the chorus, with a rapid back-and-forth panning shot on the women's faces. The next cut takes us back to Brenda. She is sitting at the kitchen table and writing a Father's Day card. Somewhere nearby water is running. A medium close-up on Brenda, with the sign HOME SWEET HOME on the wall behind her, shows us that she has taken a bath or shower, presumably cleansing herself spiritually after her triple bloodshed. We realize that the boy could not escape his mother. A close-up on the kitchen sink reveals the knife blade being rinsed; bloody water is swirling. Another cut to the stage. Jason has found out about his children's deaths: "Monster! Pestilence to gods and men. To mutilate the flesh of her children." He is first seen in medium close-up, then in extreme long shot from above. We pity him in his loneliness and abandonment. Maya appears on the side of the stage. She is dressed in the same clothes we saw her wearing in Brenda's home.

Like Pasolini before and Ripstein after him, Dassin strives to present the child-murder sequence as intensely as possible. But the three adopt radically different ways of doing so. Pasolini resorted to a high level of visual poetry, which permeates as peaceful and quiet an atmosphere as can be imagined for an archaically simple home. Medea's children do not suffer any emotional or physical pain. With Julia and Brenda, this can no longer be the case. Everything is much more realistic. Julia lives in a drab apartment, so a sense of squalor is palpable. Brenda has lived in a middle- or upper-middle-class suburb, and the children's rooms are cozy and comfortable: HOME SWEET HOME. Dassin undermines this harmonious appearance with his horror-film effects and, most of all, by intercutting the different narrative and temporal levels. Viewers may understand or even forgive Pasolini's Medea and Ripstein's Julia, but Dassin's Brenda can hardly claim a strong hold on their sympathies. Her Christian belief brings her a measure of consolation: "even though the children were dead, they would live." This is in strong contrast to what we will then hear Jason tell Medea in Euripides' play: "My sons will live to torture you forever."

Dassin's achievement, however, comes at a price. Despite all the anguish she undergoes, Brenda is almost eerie in her murderous determination. Her religious obsession ("The words of God are pure, purified seven times") is a notable weakness in Dassin's screenplay. Brenda's fixation on God does not result from her turmoil over her husband's adultery but predates it; it appears to be a contributing factor to his desertion. We know from Brenda's reminiscences that he had become nauseated by her incessantly paraded holier-than-thou attitude and sermonizing. (Her words just quoted had been directed at him.) The conclusion is unavoidable that the wife's religious mania drove the husband away. But extreme religiosity, especially when it is misguided, is a handy, indeed too easy, explanation for the inexplicable. This mother kills her children out of religious self-righteousness: *God wants me to bring their innocent souls from this wicked world to Him in Paradise* or, more simply: *God told me to, so I have to do the right thing.* From a dramatic point of view, this amounts to a lack of creative imagination and psychological insight on a writer-director's part. Dassin, I suspect, may have been aware of this shortcoming and tried to make up for it by cinematic trickery: horror-type lighting and editing, intercutting of different layers. Alternatively, one might argue, Dassin intended Brenda's Christian belief as a modern, and readily comprehensible, substitute for the religious and supernatural aspects of his classical source. In ancient myth, Medea is a granddaughter of the sun god Helios, with whom Pasolini's Medea was in close emotional and intellectual contact. Such was possible because Pasolini did not tell a contemporary story. So Dassin's answer to a question about Brenda's fanaticism is appropriate but, from a dramatic point of view, less than convincing:

That's a reflection of Euripides, when Medea calls upon the gods to witness that an oath is broken. It's a parallel. And it's true that many women need these kinds of crutches.[33]

Brenda was played by American actress Ellen Burstyn, who had played the mother of a little girl possessed by the devil in William Friedkin's supernatural-religious thriller *The Exorcist* five years earlier and was experienced with working within a strong aura of Christianity in a horror-type environment.[34] And in 1976 there had been another supernatural horror-thriller, written and directed by Larry Cohen. Its title: *God Told Me To.*

---

[33] Quoted from Georgakas and Anastasopoulos 1978: 22.
[34] As Dassin stated: "It was Ellen Burstyn I had in mind every time I wrote of Brenda." Quoted from Georgakas and Anastasopoulos 1978: 21.

"You don't love God the way I do," says a husband and father of two little children to the investigating police officer after killing his family. Still, analogies between and among these films should not be pushed too far.

In the three cinema films about Medea discussed so far, we do not see the child murders being committed, although close-ups on knives before or after (or both) leave no doubt about what the mothers did. The two close-ups in *Medea* are poetic and intense by virtue of being brief. The kitchen knife in *Such Is Life* is shown realistically, but without blood. The one in *A Dream of Passion* is presented much more graphically, and Dassin's shot of the knife lying in the sink may have been held for too long. But even if Dassin's version of the Medea story may fall short in certain ways, its very shortcomings offer food for thought.

I next examine two adaptations in which the actual infanticides occur on screen, although both versions are based on Euripides, not Seneca. In addition, both show novel plot twists. Again I proceed against chronology but in ascending order of complexity.

5   Satoshi Miyagi's *Medea*

Dassin had combined aspects of theater and cinema in *A Dream of Passion*, and so does, although markedly differently, the video version of a particularly compelling Japanese stage production. This is the *Medea* by Satoshi Miyagi, first produced in 1999. Miyagi has also staged *Antigone*, *Electra* (after Sophocles via German playwright Hugo von Hofmannsthal), *The Trojan Women*, and *Phèdre* (Racine after Euripides). He has summarized the dramaturgical principles of his method, called Kunauku, as follows:

The Kunauka system is mostly the same as that of the puppet theatre . . . . Kunauka divides one part between a "narrating actor" and a "moving actor." The "narrating actor" must firstly listen to the music and then ensure that the dialogue is delivered in conjunction with the music as calculated. With this, the foundation of the auditory part is made, and the "moving actor" must then create movement to go with it.

In such situations, the audience will also gradually . . . transform reality into a dream. Perhaps you could say the audience purifies their conception of reality . . . While the spectators watch . . . they look upon the irredeemable reality as though it were a dream, and through this, experience physically pleasurable sensations.[35]

---

[35]   Quoted from http://www.kunauka.or.jp/en/miyagi/dramaturgy02.htm. *Kunauka* is frequently transliterated as *Ku Na'uka*.

Miyagi has said that he found ancient plays especially suitable for the division of a dramatic character into two separate bodies, one static as speaker or narrator and the other moving but silent, a method derived from Japanese Bunraku puppet theater:

It took a good bit of searching and experimenting before I found plays that provided material for what I wanted to express with the "two actors, one role" method. What I found was that, rather than the plays of Shakespeare, the "father of modern theater," or later masters like Chekhov, it is the so-called classical trage-dies, like *Medea* with protagonists possessed by clearly recognizable passions such as love or hate and aware of their state, as are the other characters. Seeing glimpses of the divide or the lapses between word and movement through these works shows how much the two long for each other. From the moment human beings acquired language, they became separated from the world in one sense. Using theater to search for ways to repair and come to peace with that schism has been a theme in my creative work from the beginning and remains so today as well.[36]

Miyagi's *Medea* is set in a "luxury traditional restaurant" in late-nineteenth-century Japan: "Several gentlemen who seem to be civil servants or judges visit to dine there and make [the] maids play 'MEDEA' for entertainment."[37] As a result, all the moving actors are women. They perform in a large central space, while the speaking or narrating actors, all males, are placed on the periphery. These function, in part, as the voices of the characters in the play and as a kind of modernized Greek chorus, reacting to what they are witnessing. A highly stylized infanticide takes place on stage and thus on screen as well. Miyagi has concluded about the effect of this kind of tragedy:

Theatre is an art that revolves around words (speech) and the group ... The moments in which theatre arts excel over TV or film in terms of expressive strength result from the fact that the constraints of reality are heavily placed upon it. The reason why a real actor/human being takes on the role as "mover" instead of a puppet when a part is divided between the "speaker" and the "mover" undoubt-edly lies here. The actor who has been forbidden to speak, and the actor who has been forbidden to move, mirror the state of the members of our information-obsessed society in which the logos and pathos, the words and the body of the people have been torn apart.[38]

---

[36] Quoted from a 2012 interview with Miyagi published by The Japan Foundation: Performing Arts Network Japan, at http://www.performingarts.jp/E/art_interview/1209/1.html. See further Smethurst 2014.

[37] The two quotations are taken from the introductory summary of the production's video version on DVD.

[38] Quoted from http://www.kunauka.or.jp/en/miyagi/dramaturgy02.htm.

"Miyagi," it has been observed, "thinks that the suppressed energy of both roles [the silent and the moving actor] creates dynamism beyond reality."[39]

The child-murder sequence in this *Medea* is particularly gripping. Medea has only one child, a son played by a young adult woman. Her long ponytail and dress do not look incongruous but enhance the viewers' sense of pathos, of pity and fear. A male speaker in the background utters Medea's thoughts:

Arm yourself, my heart: the thing that you must do is fearful, yet inevitable. Why wait, then? My accursed hand, come, take the sword, take it and forward to the frontier of your despair. No cowardice; no tender memories; forget that you once loved him, that of your body he was born. For one short day forget your son; afterwards weep.[40]

Medea, alone in the performance space, reveals a knife. Her son enters reading, and Medea attacks him. He tries to escape at first, then stands immobile and awaits his mother's approach. In this way he becomes complicit in his own death. Miyagi draws out the moment almost beyond a viewer's endurance. There is total silence. From a distance, the camera moves close to mother and child, who are facing each other. Unexpectedly Medea drops down to her knees before her son, takes the knife's handle into her mouth, and reaches up. She loosens his scarf. The camera moves yet closer. In medium close-up her son reaches out and gently wipes the tears off Medea's face as she looks up at him. The camera recedes, showing us a full view of both, with the men watching in the dark background. Quick and subdued but insistent percussion is now audible. The child opens his arms wide, Medea seizes them, and vigorously pulls him to her. In this way she impales him on her knife's blade (Figure 3.3). With extreme and stylized slowness, the child sinks down across Medea's shoulders and collapses. The percussion continues, but now there are loud rhythmic accents. Medea rises, her dead child over her shoulder and the knife still in her mouth. The camera moves into a rapid close-up on her, staring straight ahead to screen right. As if in slow motion, Medea turns and faces the camera and the viewers. Fade-out.

While Miyagi is primarily an artist for the stage, the video records of his productions incorporate, as they must, cinematic principles such as camera movements and editing. The moment of infanticide is mesmerizing, not least because it combines filmic techniques with the complete silence of the

---

[39] Smethurst 2014: 843.

[40] These words render Euripides, *Medea* 1242–1249. My quotations from the production are taken from the English-language subtitles of the company's DVD.

Figure 3.3 The infanticide in Satoshi Miyagi's *Medea*.

moving actors. All this enhances the social criticism in Miyagi's *Medea*. As a theater scholar has said: "With Medea ... as a Korean woman who lived in Japan, [the production] evoked the pain of the colonized woman, forced into division from her language and body, with the former suppressed and the latter exploited sexually."[41] A classical scholar concurs but then takes the matter a step further: "In *Medea* Miyagi effectively placed the men in control with his technique of separating each role into two parts ... At the finale these male voices died at the hands of the female actors."[42]

6   Lars von Trier's *Medea*

The most haunting, and most difficult to watch, re-enactment of Medea's infanticide ever put on screen occurs in Lars von Trier's *Medea* of 1988. Made in Denmark for public TV, it was based on a screenplay co-written by Carl Theodor Dreyer, who is von Trier's acknowledged model:

---

[41]   Anan 2006: 408.
[42]   Smethurst 2014: 845–846. She also reports: "Miyagi maintained that Euripides disliked women" (845). Such a view is regrettable.

"I respect him for always going against the flow of the age."[43] Long before the advent of feminism or even the coinage of the term, Dreyer was one of the cinema's greatest spokesmen for women and their exploitation and suffering at the hands of male-dominated societies, whether medieval (*The Passion of Joan of Arc*, 1928), pre-modern (*Day of Wrath*, 1943), or modern (*The President*, 1919, Dreyer's first film; *Master of the House*, literally: "Thou Shalt Honor Thy Wife," 1925), and culminating in *Gertrud* (1964), his final film. The main female characters in Dreyer's body of work are strong-willed individuals, so Medea seems to have been a logical choice to follow Gertrud. Dreyer died before he could make *Medea*, which was intended to be his first film in color. Dreyer had also wanted Maria Callas to play Medea.[44] Later, when she was playing Pasolini's Medea, she called him "an exceptional man."[45] The screenplay for Dreyer's version became the basis for von Trier's, although this film is at least as much von Trier's as Dreyer's.[46] Dreyer, writing in collaboration with Preben Thomsen, began with the following statement:

This screenplay is not directly based on the tragedy of Euripides, but it is inspired by his play. At the same time the film is an attempt to tell the true story that may have inspired the great greek [*sic*] poet.[47]

There was no true story, but this statement can still impress us with how seriously Dreyer, one of the cinema's greatest humanists, must have taken his subject.

Dreyer had his Medea, on screen, gently singing to her children while poisoning them under the pretext of giving them medicine. The scene, had it been filmed, might have been close to Pasolini's in spirit and atmosphere and in its murderous tenderness: "I shall kill my children out of love," says Medea.[48] The script tells us what would have appeared on screen. Medea first fetches some of her medicines, then sits on the children's bed. She takes her younger son by the hands, kisses the other's mouth, and speaks soothingly to both. Then she induces the older son to drink his medicine:

---

[43] Quoted from Thomsen 2003: 111.

[44] On this see, e.g., Berthelius and Narbonne 2003: 47. Other film scholars have stated the same. Dreyer's Jason was originally to be played by Peter O'Toole; cf. Mimoso-Ruiz 1981: 332.

[45] Quoted from Gambetti 1991: 475.

[46] On von Trier, Dreyer's influence on him, and the *Medea* film see especially Björkman 2003: 111–121 (this book's title presumably derives from the fact that the director's name originally was simply Trier, not von Trier) and Bainbridge 2007: 14–16. See further Mimoso-Ruiz 1981.

[47] My quotations are from the English-language version of Dreyer's script, published on the Dreyer Internet site by the Danish Film Institute (http://english.carlthdreyer.dk/Service/Drey er_News/2011/Dreyers-Medea-script-online.aspx); here Dreyer, *Medea*: 2.

[48] Dreyer, *Medea*: 34 (scene 26).

"If you are good and take it, / You will grow big and strong – ". The boy replies "Like father!" and drinks. The younger boy resists ("Phew!") but drinks. Then he asks Medea for a lullaby. She complies:

> I'm rocking you
> Into the gentle sleep,
> May the night's hands stroke
> Your forehead tenderly
> As mine now.
> When the dark gently falls,
> The day loses its color,
> As your little face now.

Medea stops singing. She then continues:

> Oh, darkness,
> Whose deepest terror we do not know,
> I surrender to rest
> In the terrible lap of death
> The easy, intractable death.

There follow some brief stage directions. Then: "The boys are asleep now." Shortly after: "The nurse enters, going over to the dead boys." That is all we are told.[49] And that is all that Dreyer would have shown. The short lines and the capital letters at their beginnings tell us that this is to be understood as poetry. Dreyer's visual poetry would have matched it: The scene would have been tender and peaceful. Parallels to Pasolini's poetic sequence are obvious. Maria Callas had originally sung a lullaby in his *Medea* as well.

Von Trier radically changed all this. His settings achieve an effect of timelessness. Buildings and clothing, tools and weapons could come from the Dark or early Middle Ages. Von Trier has called this a Viking look and stated: "I tried to give the film an almost archaic character."[50] All this makes for an austere style. *Medea* was recorded on videotape and only later transferred to film stock; footage was further treated in the lab to achieve extremely desaturated colors.[51]

For the setting of the child murders, von Trier takes Medea and her two little sons out into the countryside. A vast empty plain suggests all-encompassing desolation. A dead tree emerging from this sea of grass and with two branches extending from opposite sides of the trunk in a manner

[49] Dreyer, *Medea*: 35–36 (Scene 27); quotations at 36.
[50] Quoted from Tapper 2003: 78. See also Björkman 2003: 114–118 and cf. Baertschi 2013.
[51] On the complex process see Björkman 2003: 119, on the film's visual style Christie 2000: 159.

suggesting a cross provides an obvious but powerful symbol. The tree functions as a kind of *nature morte* or *memento mori*: a being that could not save itself from death.

The summary by Ian Christie of this sequence is perceptive and incisive. I quote it here to spare the reader – and myself – a harrowing description in such detail as was necessary for *A Dream of Passion*. Medea

sets out in the dawn half-light with her children. She pushes the younger in a cart that seems part-perambulator and part-tumbril . . . Soon it is bright daylight over an open landscape . . . . the setting subliminally evokes a *via dolorosa* leading to Calvary, as the barren heath rises to a hill, on which stands a tree . . .

The children . . . are not the hapless innocents of most versions: the older boy is a saddened, knowing spectator of his mother's disgrace. He realizes that he and his brother must die in order to complete her revenge on their faithless father, telling her, "I know what's to happen." When the younger boy playfully runs away as Medea struggles with the rope she has brought, his brother chases him and helps her hang him. As Medea kneels, traumatized by this first killing, the older boy gently prompts her, "Help me, mother." He then arranges his own noose and she holds him aloft until her strength fails.[52]

The death tree was prominently featured on advertising posters for von Trier's film. Christie adds: "The fact that [this] *Medea* shows the older child as complicit . . . is perhaps the single most horrifying moment in all reworkings of *Medea*."[53] We might delete the word *perhaps*. As would be the case again in Miyagi's staging, Medea's child is complicit in his own death – here also in his brother's.

In strong contrast to the devastating events we witness is the pleasant birdsong that we hear throughout the sequence. Far from having a reassuring effect, however, it serves to increase our fear and terror. And it appears to be artificial. The bird sounds never change; a short recording of chirps and tweets is repeated again and again in a sheer endless loop. First- or one-time spectators are unlikely to notice this. The birdsong, the plain, and the tree all indicate man's abandonment in an implacable and unconcerned world, not only Medea's. Ultimately, von Trier's is an existentialist tragedy. About the child-murder sequence he has observed:

Dreyer wanted to give them poison. He thought it was too violent to have them knifed, which is what happens in the classical drama. He thought that was too bloody. He just wanted them to die in their sleep. I chose to make it more dramatic. I think there's more edge to my version as a whole. I thought it was better to hang the children. And more consequential. Either you kill them or you don't.

[52] Christie 2000: 156–157.   [53] Christie 2000: 163.

The action ought to be presented as it is. There's no reason to tidy it up and make it look more innocent than it is.[54]

More dramatic: It certainly is that. *The action ought to be presented*: It is, harrowingly so. The most intense moments are the one boy helping his brother to die faster and then putting the noose around his own neck. It is unlikely that Dreyer would have approved. Neither would Horace or Aristotle or perhaps any Greek. So a female critic may be justified to speak of this Medea's "sadistic intensity and bottomless grief" and to conclude about *Medea* in regard to von Trier's later work: "*Antichrist* [2009] returns to the trajectory of *Medea* and *Dogville* [2003] in which a gifted woman struggling against a repressive culture epitomized in a male antagonist avenges the crimes against her – with the revenge as unimaginable and apocalyptic as her powers have been suppressed."[55]

Still, von Trier's version is not bloody. And that makes it the more gripping. We may contrast the blood-stained children, their throats cut by their mother, in Martin Scorsese's neo-*noir* thriller *Shutter Island* (2010), a moment that may remind us of the spirits of the dead girls killed by their father in Stanley Kubrick's *The Shining* (1980). As it later turns out, the vision of the protagonist in *Shutter Island* is a nightmare that contrasts with his reality – but *is* it his reality? In a later scene a flashback reveals that his wife, mentally unstable, had drowned their three small children and was in turn killed by her grief-stricken husband. This second scene with the dead children is much longer than the first and thus much more intense, but their deaths, unlike their mother's, are wholly bloodless. Scorsese links the horror of intra-familiar killings with that of the Holocaust. But it is all rather overdone. *Shutter Island* is not among this director's great works.

In antiquity not even Seneca, who is notorious among many for his gruesome scenes, was as explicit as he could have been. A recent commentator on his *Medea* explains:

The narrated violence [in Senecan drama] is generally graphic and extensive .... Medea ... slashes her arm and kills two sons onstage; but none of these events is accompanied by the kind of graphic verbal detail we find in the narrated violence of other plays .... Seneca's theatrical violence seems in no sense an attempt to cater to what he depicts in the prose works as a decadent appetite ... By controlling the representation of violent death on the stage Seneca is able to shape the perception

---

[54] Quoted from Björkman 2003: 118.

[55] Badley 2010: 47 and 146. She links this development to the influence of Japanese horror films on von Trier (146–147). We can now expand this brief list of von Trier's films to include the two-part *Nymphomaniac* of 2013. The typographical error stating that his *Medea* is fifty-seven minutes long (Badley 2010: 47) is easily corrected by a reversal of the numerical digits.

and evaluation of it . . . . Seneca humanizes the sufferers and the suffering, controls what the audience sees and how they see it in the theatre, and furnishes them with a conceptual framework with which to judge it.[56]

With certain obvious adjustments, this summary seems to fit von Trier's *Medea* scene. Yes, it is graphic and detailed, but it does not cater to decadent sensibilities; quite the contrary. Von Trier shapes our perception and evaluation, as indeed any artist will do or attempt to do. And he humanizes the sufferers, who are agents at the same time. Who could not be overwhelmed by their fate?

7   Natalia Kuznetsova's *Medea*

A special case among film adaptations of the Medea tragedies is the Russian *Medea* of 2009. It was produced, written, and directed by Natalia Kuznetsova, who also was behind the camera and composed the music for her film. It is an independent and low-budget production but contains computer graphics and 3-D animation. Although it was probably unknown to Kuznetsova, Jocy de Oliveira's *Kseni* may be regarded as exhibiting a parallel approach, given its highly stylized visuals and a pre-eminence on music. Kuznetsova composed her score long before filming began. Her *Medea* is based on Seneca's, which Kuznetsova had first read as a theater student and which made a lasting impression on her. The film represents what Kuznetsova calls *rhythmodrama*: "The atmosphere would be created by music."[57] As a result, music is audible for all but two of the film's sixty-six minutes. Kuznetsova has characterized her film in these terms: "We aimed for minimalism . . . so that the decorations and bright details didn't distract the acting . . . The actors had to understand text written in complicated poetic language two thousand years ago. Rehearsals went in studio method and under music that gave the unity of atmosphere." About the part of Medea she reports: "Role of Medea took special atten-tion. As a result, Lilian Navrozashvili (a usually smiling and charming woman) got so into her role, that a colleague of hers, who met us in the

---

[56] Quoted from Boyle 2014: l–lii (in section titled "Seneca's Theatre of Violence"). Decades after Seneca, Quintilian had apposite words to say about the power of the imagination on our emotions and the dangers of explicit or graphic displays as well; see especially *Handbook of Rhetoric* 6.1.30–32 and 6.2.31–32.

[57] My information and subsequent quotations come from the film's Internet page: http://www .medea.harryhotterfilm.ru/english/about_film.htm. They are left unedited and uncorrected to preserve Kuznetsova's original English, which is often charmingly unidiomatic.

theatre after rehearsals, saw her face and asked me, 'What have you done with her?'"[58]

There is no natural sound of actors reciting their lines; rather, we hear them in voice-over (in Russian). The film preserves many of Seneca's key lines and expressions, including *Medea fiam* and *Medea nunc sum*. On its home-video release, subtitles – at crucial moments in red – are unfortunately taken from an archaic and stilted-sounding English translation, which detracts from the power of the images. Since mythical Colchis, Medea's homeland, is in modern Georgia, Navrozashvili's Medea resorts to modern Georgian.

The way Kuznetsova presents Medea's infanticides is remarkable, even if it does not achieve the poetry of Pasolini's or the intensity of von Trier's versions. Medea has a vision of the Furies and of her dead brother Apsyrtus, whom she had killed during her and the Argonauts' escape from Colchis. In medium close-up she pulls a large dagger from her white and red robes and approaches her older son, who is on the beach. Extremely unsteady camera movements, a crashing wave, and rising water levels prepare us – no, not for the murder, which Kuznetsova does not show, but for a poetic visualization of it: A large white jar, standing upright before a black background, is overflowing with a dark red liquid. Soon after, the dead boy's hand, protruding from a cloak, tells us what has happened. Back at home an exhausted Medea, in slow motion, drops her bloody dagger to the ground. Soon, however, she hears Jason and the Corinthians approaching. She rallies and gets ready for her next deed. In a medium close-up she picks up her dagger. Her small son approaches; Medea gently kisses him on the forehead. He looks up, smiling.

The second infanticide occurs after a shot of the older boy's hand, but this time it is from Jason's point of view, as a zoom-in to an extreme close-up of the hand tells us. Jason and Medea are outside. She looks down on him from a high balustrade. This is an existing location rather than a constructed set. The blade of her dagger shines in the sunlight and receives a special close-up. To Jason's horror, the other boy walks into the shot, approaching his mother. While Jason vainly pleads with Medea and offers his own life, she hoists the child up into her arms. Extreme close-ups, rather unsteady, on the two heighten our apprehension, as does insistent percussive music. Then Medea's hand holding the dagger appears in the frame. Several close-ups follow: one on Jason screaming; one on the

---

[58] Kuznetsova's term "studio method" seems to mean rehearsals in a studio, not Method acting. A ten-minute interview with Kuznetsova at the 2010 Cyprus Film Festival can be seen at https://www.youtube.com/watch?v=Vfz5Nng9b58. About her film's subject she says there: "*Medea* is for educated people."

dagger: raised, then descending; and three on the white jar overflowing with its red liquid. But this time it is first seen from above. It has been tilted and, in staggered slow motion, falls on its side. An extreme close-up on part of its opening and the spilling liquid drive home Medea's deed. A final shot from a little further back shows us a composition as elegant as it is expressive: The jar, now lying on its side, is spilling its remaining contents. We see it from the side, its white material surrounded by utter darkness; its opening equally dark but with some of its liquid still inside. Its level slowly decreases. Intentionally, the composition is not quite symmetrical. Kuznetsova holds this shot for an almost unbearably long time. It symbolizes the slow draining of blood from the boy's body and the ebbing away of his life. A cut returns us to Medea on the balustrade and Jason below her. We see the jar one last time as it is lying, empty and deserted, on the beach. Kuznetsova's sense of visual poetry makes the sequence of Medea's second infanticide particularly memorable.

8   Post-Classical Medeas

The emotions that Dreyer intended to evoke in viewers may be deduced from a later film with a medieval setting, Ridley Scott's *Kingdom of Heaven* (2005). The historical Princess Sibylla was the mother of young Baldwin V, King of Jerusalem, who died of leprosy in 1186 at age nine. In the film Sibylla kills him with poison to spare him the fate of her brother, King Baldwin IV, who had died of the same disease after several years of great suffering. "How did my boy deserve it?" Sibylla exclaims. "No kingdom is worth my son's life in Hell. I'll go to Hell instead." The sequence of her infanticide is emotionally involving, but it seems unrealistic. Sibylla gently chants to the child on her lap, then pours the poison into his ear. Viewers may be reminded of the death of Hamlet's father. Subdued requiem-like choral music and then a solo soprano voice are heard on the soundtrack. This kitschy effect undermines the scene's intensity. By contrast, a far more realistic study of the mercy killing of a young child by his mother appears in French writer-director Philippe Claudel's modern drama *I've Loved You So Long* (2008). A mother, a physician, is returning from a fifteen-year prison sentence. The story gradually reveals that she had killed her six-year-old son with a lethal injection to spare him the suffering that would inevitably have come with his incurable disease.[59]

---

[59]   On the subject in connection with Medea see in particular Pucci 1980.

Poisoning one's children can look quite different from the sanitized version shown in *Kingdom of Heaven*. A horrendous actual case from 1945 appears in Oliver Hirschbiegel's film *Downfall* (2004). It deals with the fate of Hitler and those in his bunker during the fall of Berlin and is based primarily on the recollections of Hitler's private secretary, who survived, and on the work of historian Joachim Fest, especially his book from which the film took its title.[60] Joseph Goebbels's wife Magda brings her six young children into the bunker in order to kill them before her and her husband's murder-suicide. Hers is a kind of perverted mercy killing. This is her reasoning as reported by Fest:

A longtime ardent admirer of Hitler, she had resolved, if the worst came to pass, that she would kill her children before committing suicide. All efforts to dissuade her had been unsuccessful and she had even stubbornly said no when Hitler urged her to reconsider. She could not let her husband die alone, she said, and if she was going to join him in death, then their children must die too.[61]

In a letter to her son by an earlier marriage Magda Goebbels wrote: "After the Führer and National Socialism, the world won't be worth living in, and that is why I have brought the children here. They are too good for the life that will come after us, and merciful God will understand if I myself give them deliverance."[62] A perverse sense of religiosity is evident.

The recollections of Albert Speer, Hitler's chief architect, who was in the bunker when the children arrived, give us further information. As Fest reports, Speer considered Magda Goebbels "an emotionally strong woman with an occasional tendency to sentimentality, for whom her own children were everything." Speer continued, in Fest's account:

it soon became clear that the children had been brought there to die. That required a coldness and callousness that he [Speer] had never attributed to her. No one with whom he later discussed it was able to understand it either .... almost everyone from Hitler's inner circle tried to get her to change her mind ... But Magda Goebbels had remained firm ..., and as time went by her refusal to take the children away became visibly more impatient and finally even curt. Eva Braun ended her remarks about Magda Goebbels with the words: "What on earth got into her? Or have we all become so unfeeling and inhuman?"[63]

---

[60] Junge 2002 and 2011; Fest 2002b and 2004. Fest and Eichinger 2004 is a reissue of Fest 2002b and includes the screenplay, film stills, and interviews. Eichinger was the film's producer and screenwriter.

[61] Fest 2004: 114.   [62] Fest 2004: 143. The addressee survived the fall of Berlin.

[63] Fest 2007: 152–153.

Downfall shows a hell on earth. The children's deaths are its strongest condemnation of the inhuman regime that was Nazism. The infanticide sequence has to be experienced firsthand and in context. No verbal description could convey its power. *Downfall* follows the actual events as reconstructed and reported by Fest quite accurately, if not in every detail.[64] Here is Fest's account:

> On the evening of May 1, Magda Goebbels put her children to bed, having first given them a sleeping potion; they may also have been given a morphine injection. Then, in the presence of Dr. Stumpfegger [Hitler's personal physician], with someone holding the children's mouths open, she put drops of hydrogen cyanide down their throats. Only her oldest daughter, Helga, who in the last few days had been anxiously asking what would become of them all, appeared to have resisted. The bruises on the body of the twelve-year-old girl seemed to indicate that the poison was not administered without the use of force. Magda Goebbels, ashen-faced, came back to the deep bunker where her husband was waiting for her. "It is done," she said. Together they went to his living room, and there, weeping, she played a game of solitaire.[65]

In the film, the mother herself forces some of the sleeping children's mouths open. Afterwards she does not weep, and she says nothing to her husband. She plays her game of solitaire in view not only of him but also of others. All this makes her appear cold and callous. But these changes hint at her immense power of self-control. The astonishing performance by actress Corinna Harfouch makes us realize that this mother may have been inhuman, that she was horribly misguided in her ideology and about the future that was still possible for her children, but also that she was not unfeeling. The very iciness of her appearance indicates the opposite underneath.

In retrospect, the extreme but justifiable realism of *Downfall* makes it understandable that an earlier German film, *Reason Asleep* (1984), a modernized version of the Medea story by feminist writer-director Ula Stöckl, shows the modern Medea's infanticide but leaves it ambiguous.[66] Stöckl herself refused to believe that a mother could bring herself to committing such a deed. In an interview she stated that she "could not imagine that

---

[64] See Fest 2004: 143–144.

[65] Fest 2004: 143–144. On the following page Fest provides a photograph of the parents and all their children (alive). There is also a photographic record of the children's corpses.

[66] The original title is *Der Schlaf der Vernunft* ("The Sleep of Reason") and refers to the well-known engraving by Francisco Goya. On the film see especially the chapter in Stephan 2006: 182–193 and 292–295 (notes). Stöckl had previously co-written and co-directed *The Golden Thing* (*Das goldene Ding*, 1971), in which the story of Jason and the Golden Fleece is being acted by twelve- to sixteen-year-old children.

a woman should kill the dearest she has, her children, for revenge on her husband." Stöckl linked this conclusion to her own views about feminism, father-son and mother-daughter relations, and feminist mothers. She also reported that she included the infanticide "not at all realistically" in her film.[67] She explained:

Dream or reality? This implies that it is left to the spectator to decide what to do with the images. From my perspective it was quite clearly intended that the daughters, just as the husband, had long separated themselves emotionally from Dea [Stöckl's modern Medea] and that it is Dea's great task – and this can be done only under great pain – to separate herself from something that has already separated itself from her. And the most definitive form of this is death. At the same time I thought, if I stage this realistically, my Medea or my Dea will land in a lunatic asylum or in prison, because I could not include, in my modern version, the ending in which she climbs into a mythological sun chariot and floats off and away. Hence I thought it's a very courageous undertaking if she can summon the powers of her imagination to envision how these daughters and [her husband's] lover might die.[68]

Stöckl's film contains several dream sequences; the one about Dea's children's deaths is remarkable because the second daughter kills herself upon seeing her sister dead.[69] Stöckl here anticipates, in part, von Trier's version of the children's deaths, although in her film the daughters die separately. Stöckl also foreshadows Ripstein's meta-tragic use of the TV set. When asked why on several occasions in her film TV appears as an independent medium within the medium of film, Stöckl replied: "This gave me the opportunity to stage a kind of chorus via the TV set. Everything you see there has been staged in advance ... And once I even include the ending of *Das goldene Ding*."[70] In spite of all this, Stöckl's Dea is closer to Dassin's Maya, for the sleep of reason may well be a dream of passion. In Stöckl's own arresting words: "By dreaming it, Dea really kills her husband, the children, and her rival."[71]

---

[67] Both quotations from Stephan 2006: 233; source references at 309 notes 68 and 69. In this context Stöckl reports that, much later, she found corroboration of her understanding of Medea in the work of Karl Kerényi. Apparently she had read Kerényi 1944.

[68] Stephan 2006: 234; source reference at 309 note 70.

[69] Stephan 2006: 236–237 describes this dream sequence and summarizes the others.

[70] Stephan 2006: 310 note 79 (with source reference). Stephan here also speculates that the inclusion of the earlier film indicates Stöckl's self-ironic use of media and her own history as a filmmaker.

[71] Quoted from Stöckl's conversation with journalist Christa Maerker, now available at http://www.ula-stoeckl.com/Film-Seiten/17_Der_Schlaf_der_Vernunft.html. The same Internet page provides a plot summary and the film's credits.

We may contrast the imaginative case of infanticide shown in *Reason Asleep* and the actual case in *Downfall* with a fictional one that deals not only with one family but also with an imminent worldwide apocalypse: the nuclear annihilation of the human race. In Stanley Kramer's 1959 film of Nevil Shute's novel *On the Beach*, a young naval officer about to leave on an assignment attempts to convince his wife to administer a poison capsule ("a special kind of sleeping pill") to their little daughter and herself. He wants to spare them the pain resulting from radioactive fallout and describes the disease's symptoms to her. The mother, inexperienced, is hopeful ("this cures it"); he is frank: "Darling, you know nothing [so far has] cured it. This ends it." When the implications dawn on her, the mother reacts in horror: "You're not trying to tell me you want me to kill Jennifer!" The husband feels guilty and later asks: "How do you tell the woman you love she has to kill herself and her baby? How do you do it?" The couple's final scene together ("Now it's all over, isn't it?") shows us their love for each other and their peaceful deaths. We understand that they have administered the poison to their daughter and themselves. "God, God forgive us," the mother says.

But nuclear annihilation did not occur in the twentieth century, and the bleak prospect that Kramer manages to sustain for almost all of his film's length would have been too depressing for viewers and too risky for its performance at the box office. So the film has to negate its very premise. Rather unconvincingly, a ray of hope is introduced at the last moment. Mankind will probably survive. But this circumstance throws a melancholic light on the family's fate. Their deaths may have been unnecessary.

As we have seen, some of the child murders are mercy killings. Another instance occurs in Jonathan Demme's *Beloved* (1998), an adaptation of Toni Morrison's novel set in the nineteenth-century American South. A black slave cuts her oldest daughter's throat and attempts to kill her other children to spare them the misery and inhumanity of slavery.[72] Then there is the case of the mother who is forced to choose between life for one of her children and death for the other in Alan J. Pakula's *Sophie's Choice* (1982), an adaptation of the novel by William Styron. The titular situation is set in a Nazi concentration camp. Another example appears in Chinese director Xiaogang Feng's *Aftershock* (2010), based on a novel that deals with the 1976 earthquake in the city of Tangshan. In both of these films, the

---

[72] On Morrison, *Medea*, and the wider cultural context see, e.g., Haley 1995; Fikes 2002; Wetmore 2013.

mother has a son and a daughter and chooses the former over the latter. In *Sophie's Choice* the son did not survive; in *Aftershock* the daughter did.

9   Medea's Children

What about Medea's children? And what about the feelings of the young actors who play them? Usually they are preteens or young teenagers. Do they have any idea of what kind of scene they are acting in, even if, one hopes, they cannot fully comprehend what is being filmed? Although they may not be aware of their characters' violent fate, sometimes, it seems, they are to a certain degree. Jocy de Oliveira has reported about the boy actors in *Kseni*:

In Brazil ... I interviewed several children. They were kids from poor suburban areas of Rio [de Janeiro]. I chose two boys. They were trained to perform without being too much aware of the infanticide myth. Obviously, they saw the special-effects preparation to create blood filling a pond. They did not question, since they came from violent communities (slums), where death is somehow routine.

This is a telling comment on the universal nature of the Medea story that de Oliveira wants to present. Separately from these actors, there was also a singing performer. Here, she says, another approach was necessary:

With the boy singer, it was different. He was prepared, and participated in rehearsals, for months ... It was a difficult task since he was brought up in a religious family ... However, he did not ask too many questions. Kids are used to the playful world of fantasy.[73]

On stage and screen, child actors are usually extraordinary. The young actors playing the Goebbels children in *Downfall* may provide the best example of all. Another is the actor who played Medea's younger son for Kuznetsova. The director has been full of praise for him on several occasions:

In one glance I realized that I saw the star of world cinema! :-) So as a real star, 5-year old Bogdan showed his tongue to the director; after half-hourly shooting he told he was tired and wanted to go home; he refused to repeat episodes (maybe he thought he did everything ideally, but forgot that others were not as genius as him) .... the role of the Younger son, brilliantly played by Bogdan Rubanov, is one of the best in the film.

---

[73] Quotations, as before, from e-mail communication by de Oliveira.

This testimony may stand as a tribute to all of Medea's screen and stage children, whether in adaptations of Euripides and Seneca or in tales of modern Medeas.[74]

Occasionally the cinema affords us a glimpse into the hearts of children threatened by infanticide. Insights, of course, come from adults: their screenwriters and directors. In Neil Jordan's *Byzantium* (2012), a teenage daughter who barely survived death at her mother's hands immediately after birth states, in a voice-over that explains to us the images of a pre- and even hyper-Dickensian milieu: "It is still a fact that the day you are born is the day you are most likely to be murdered. More human souls are killed by mothers' hands than by the hands of strangers." The fact that *Byzantium* is a gory and ghoulish vampire thriller does not detract from the power of its scene, set in 1804, or from the truth of the girl's statement. Her voice-over adds: "My mother tried to murder me, but love confounded her." Not all children are as lucky.

The anguish of a mother who has killed her child or children can be felt or understood, whereas the emotions of the children about to be killed can never be known. But stage and screen can prompt us to reflect by showing us Medea's children after their deaths. Here, in chronological order, are four examples. Two involve the classical Medea, two modern Medeas. Isabelle Huppert played Euripides' Medea at the Festival of Avignon in 2000. The production was directed by Jacques Lassalle and preserved in a highly cinematic video version. The fate of Medea's children is especially powerful. Moments of great emotional intensity between a weeping mother and her two uncomprehending little boys occur shortly before the murders. Medea smothers them with her embraces and kisses, effectively rendered in close-ups. Theater audiences could not have had such a view. All this, together with Medea's anguished words, heightens our sense of apprehension and horror. Then she says, echoing Euripides: "I can't look at you any more."[75] The nurse leads them into a kind of cave. There Jason discovers their dead bodies. We do not see his shock at the moment of discovery, but we still get an unexpected emotional jolt. The stage is now drenched in gloomy blue light. The boys, followed by Medea, slowly emerge from the cave and advance toward their father. All three are wearing white or nearly white clothes. The children's hair is bleached, and their faces reveal

---

[74] A related example may be found in Toubiana and Strauss 2001: 61–62. Here Theodore Angelopoulos speaks about *Landscape in the Mist* (1988), in which a five-and-a-half-year-old boy and a teenage girl have harrowing experiences searching for their father. The young actors were evidently in great distress, especially the girl, who had to act in a rape scene.

[75] Euripides, *Medea* 1076–1077.

Figure 3.4 Medea and her dead children in Jacques Lasalle's stage production of *Medea*.

a ghastly and ghostly paleness as they stand silent in front of their mother. When they first appear, their large dark eyes are especially noticeable. The overall effect is that of living corpses (Figure 3.4). This unusual and chilling staging of the aftermath of their deaths speaks volumes.

As mentioned, in some versions of her myth Medea inadvertently kills her children. A comparable modern example occurs in Simon Wincer's *Quigley Down Under* (1990), a quasi-Western set in nineteenth-century Australia. The titular hero, an American sharpshooter, protects a prostitute called Crazy Cora upon his arrival in Australia. He later learns from her why and how she left her native Texas:

Roy was hunting sage hens when the Comanches came. I grabbed the baby and a pistol, and I hid in the root cellar out back. The Indians tore up our sod house. I was real quiet, but then the baby started crying. I tried to shush him and suckle him, but he just wouldn't stop. One Comanche, I remember, he acted real drunk and wore my green apron. He must have heard something. He started hollering and coming closer. So I put my hand gentle-like over my baby's mouth. "Don't cry. Daddy'll be home soon." The Indians found us, but they just laughed. They was drunk, didn't wanna hurt anybody, and rode away. At sundown, Roy came home, but I was still afraid to come out of the cellar. I was afraid of what he'd do when he saw I'd smothered our son . . . He just buried the baby, put me in the wagon, and we went 70 miles to Galveston without stopping. He never said a word. Put me on the first ship he found. It was headed to Australia. Then he said, "Don't want no woman that would kill my son to save herself." And he turned and he walked away, and he never looked back. I know, 'cause I watched to see if he would.

Wincer does not include a flashback; we only hear Cora's words just as Quigley does. But the effect is the more powerful. Like Jason in the myth, the husband in the film does not cut a very good figure even if we can understand his misunderstanding of Cora's desperate situation.

In Spanish writer-director Alejandro Amenábar's supernatural thriller *The Others*, released one year later, the spirits of a mother and her little son and daughter revisit the moments of the children's deaths.[76] *The Others* is a psychological horror film indebted to Henry James's classics ghost story *The Turn of the Screw*. In a gripping reversal at the film's climax it turns out that the titular others are the mother and her children. Her husband had been killed in war, and she, feeling hopelessly abandoned and forlorn, had killed them. She had acted, it appears, as if in a trance. Now she explains:

At first I couldn't understand what the pillow was doing in my hand or why you didn't move. But then I knew. It had happened. I had killed my children. I got the rifle. I put it to my forehead. Then I pulled the trigger. Nothing. Then I heard your laughter in the bedroom. [*Relieved:*] Ahh. You were playing with the pillows as if nothing had happened. And I thought the Lord in His great mercy . . . was giving me another chance . . . telling me: "Don't give up. Be strong. Be a good mother. For them." But now – now – what does all this mean? Where are we?

The scene is very dark, and subdued strings are on the soundtrack. The mother speaks only hesitantly, as if her remembrance were as much for herself as for her children. She holds them in her arms, their heads just below hers; the effect is that of a *pietà*-like composition. When the children ask about their father and the state of limbo that, she had told them, comes after death, the mother confesses: "I don't know if there even is a limbo. I'm no wiser than you are. But I do know that I love you. I've always loved you." We understand that she will continue to love them just as they will always love her. The little boy then speaks for all of them: "Mummy, look. It doesn't hurt any more." The dead children are reconciled with their killer.

The outcome is significantly different in the Canadian-British TV series *Olympus* (2015). This film is the brainchild of Nick Willing, who had directed the American TV film *Jason and the Argonauts* of 2000. *Olympus* radically rewrites and re-imagines the myths about gods and about Minos and Ariadne, Daedalus and Icarus, Aegeus and his sons, and Medea. Medea is now the wife of King Aegeus of Athens. This she was in the myth after she had

---

[76] On this film see Torrance 2010.

Figure 3.5 Dead Alcimenes in *Olympus*.

escaped from Corinth, the city in which her revenge on Jason had taken place. As in her myth, this Medea is a kind of witch or sorceress. Aegeus has children, but his most famous son, Theseus, is nowhere seen or mentioned. Medea's backstory is introduced rather late when she encounters her dead sons. Apparently the most famous part of her myth could not be ignored. The first appearance of her children is quite a surprise, both to Medea and to viewers. Medea has just defeated a monstrous enemy but is left lying unconscious on the ground. The camera pans along her body and then tilts up, revealing a young boy standing beside her. His throat has been cut; streaks of dried blood are still visible (Figure 3.5). "Why are you helping her?" he asks someone we have not yet seen. Then a smaller boy is revealed, kneeling by Medea's head. He, too, has had his throat cut. "She's our mother," he replies. "I think she's in trouble." His name is Tisander, as we find out a little later. The older boy's reaction: "Good!" For viewers puzzled by the appearance and identity of these children, the older one provides an explanation: "She cut our throats and left us to die." Tisander rebukes him: "Stop it, Alcimenes. You know she had to." "She didn't *have* to," the other counters. Tisander gives viewers astonished at the boys' their appearance the full explanation: "She just wanted to hurt our father Jason, after he's left her." Medea, regaining consciousness, has heard their exchange: "I'm sorry," she tells them. Tisander immediately adds: "See, she's sorry." Alcimenes: "She didn't love us." "Yes, she did!" his brother exclaims. Clearly Tisander has forgiven her; Alcimenes has not, for he adds: "I am going to sit and watch her die." Medea says: "I loved you." "See, she loved us very much," Tisander exclaims. "If that were true," Alcimenes retorts, "she wouldn't have *killed* us." Then, since the main plot has to continue, the children have to leave their mother. Tisander gently kisses her on the cheek. "Good-bye, mother. I miss you." "Don't go," Medea pleads. Alcimenes has one final word for her: "You dropped us." Medea's last utterance to them is "I'm so sorry." The children are led away. "I'm sorry," she repeats to herself.

This is the first of several scenes between Medea and her murdered children. Alcimenes remains unforgiving, even slapping Medea's face later; Tisander is more understanding. This is the only part of *Olympus* that is emotionally involving to viewers who know about Medea. The images of little children who look, talk, and act as if they were alive but who have had their throats cut are able to evoke at least some measure of pity and terror. As a result, the aftermath of the violence perpetrated on them, violence that we never see, makes the doses of graphic violence elsewhere in *Olympus* rather questionable. In particular, this is the case in an earlier scene in which Medea's sister Chalciope, a ruthless Amazon-type killer as she is not in myth, brutally kills a child (not her own) for no discernible reason.

Even in an age of widespread ignorance about the classical cultures, it seems, the general public can be assumed to know about Medea's infanticide. Homer Thrace's words about Medea, quoted at the beginning of this chapter, have already told us as much. It is also remarkable that Medea's children in *Olympus* bear the Latinized names preserved by Greek historian Diodorus.[77]

10 Happy Ending?

But let us not dwell any longer on such dark matters. Instead, let us contemplate the really unimaginable: the Medea story with an apparently happy ending. For this, we have Jules Dassin's best-known film with Melina Mercouri, the romantic comedy *Never on Sunday* (1960). Dassin

---

[77] Diodorus Siculus, *Library of History* 4.54.1. Diodorus also mentions (4.55.2) another son, Thessalus, who survived Medea's attempt on his life so he could become ancestor of the Thessalians. Medea's sons, according to other sources, are Mermerus and Pheres (Apollodorus, *Library* 1.9.28); Polyxenus or Medus, said by most to be Medea's son by Aegeus (so Apollodorus, *Library* 1.9.28; Diodorus, *Library of History* 4.55.5, who also reports an Asian king as father at 4.55.7; Pausanias, *Description of Greece* 2.3.8, who also reports his name as Polyxenus and his father as Jason, following Hellanicus). There is also a daughter Eriopis and a son Argus. Elsewhere Medea has seven sons and seven daughters. Cf. Mastronarde 2002: 49–51.

wrote the script and played American tourist Homer Thrace. Homer is on his first trip to Greece. He has had an average education in classical culture, but he lacks any deeper understanding. His name, a clever choice on Dassin's part, is fully appropriate. It combines the names of the first and greatest Greek poet and of an area of Greece known in antiquity for its backwardness. Homer Thrace makes friends with various people in Piraeus. In particular, he meets the irrepressible and irresistible Illya, a self-employed working girl with the proverbial heart of gold.[78] Illya loves Greek tragedy. On her birthday she is prevailed upon to tell the story of Euripides' *Medea* and Sophocles' *Oedipus the King*. Here is the part of the dialogue that sets up Illya's tale of Medea:

HOMER THRACE: Illya, what's playing tomorrow?
ILLYA: *Medea.*
THE CAPTAIN: Illya, how many times have you seen it?
ILLYA: Fifteen.
HOMER [*to the captain*]: That's extraordinary.
THE CAPTAIN [*to Homer*]: Especially when she has no idea what the play is about. Whatever in the play is unpleasant, she changes.
HOMER: But how?
THE CAPTAIN: In her head. She just rejects anything that to her is ugly . . . . I'll get her to tell the story of *Medea* as Illya sees it.

So he does. Illya's summary, made the more charming by her unidiomatic English, begins like this:

Medea is a beautiful play, but for you men is not much compliment. The play is about what a woman suffers for a man. Once upon a time there was a princess from far away. Her name is Medea – with beautiful long black hair. A Greek, he comes; right away Medea crazy for him. She will listen to nobody; she wants *him*. She fights with her father, her whole country; eh, Medea was very sweet, but sometimes she has a bad temper.

At this moment Homer, aside to the captain, utters the first part of his comment about Medea quoted at the beginning. Illya continues:

Anyhow, she goes to Greece to marry this man. He's a prince. His name is [*she makes a spitting sound*] Jason. She's good to him. She gives him two beautiful children. But he, right away with a blond princess in Athens [*she clicks her tongue, indicating lust*] you know what! This Jason is not even a gentleman to tell Medea lies. No! He says

---

[78] Her name is often given as Ilia or Illia as well. On the spelling Illya see Mercouri 1971: 137. Horton 1984: 28–29 sees Aristophanes and *Lysistrata* behind the comedy in the film. Alexis Salomos, the actor playing the film's villain, had directed a stage production of *Assemblywomen* in Paris in 1958, with music by Manos Hadjidakis, the composer of *Never on Sunday*.

right to her face that he wants that other blonde because he's a prince. Medea cries and says: "I am a princess, too." Beautiful, how she cries! Everything she does for Jason. Even she gives presents to the blonde. [*Homer, shocked, comments that these were poisoned.*] But everybody says bad things about her. They say she's a witch. There are twelve rich ladies in beautiful dresses, but they say bad things about her, too. [*Homer knows that these are the Greek chorus.*] And Medea cries. I tell you, she breaks your heart. She's afraid. She takes the children and she hides them. But in the end Jason sees how much Medea loves him, and they get a wonderful chariot, and she gets the children – and they all go to the seashore!

Now Homer is really shocked: "No! The Greek tragedy! She gives it a happy ending! She doesn't even say Medea killed her children!" The word *even* is telling: This, Homer implies, is what *everybody* knows about Medea! The captain tries to calm him down: "Illya is happy. She worked out a way of living. Let her alone." But Homer is unconvinced: "No, it's impossible. A whore can't be happy." Soon he will be smitten with her, but at the moment he imagines himself as her intellectual savior: "I'd like to reach her mind." Reason and morality are his goals: "I've got to educate her. To transform her." Then he finds out that *Oedipus Rex* also has a happy ending: "And they all go to the seashore?" he asks incredulously. The captain confirms: "They *always* go to the seashore."

 This surprising happy ending is, however, not as outrageous as it may appear to Homer Thrace or most of us today. According to the *Philippic Histories* of the Roman historian Pompeius Trogus, which are lost but preserved, indirectly, in their *Epitome* by Justin, Jason and Medea get divorced and Medea is exiled. But out of compassion for her, Jason undertakes a second voyage to Colchis – where husband and wife are reconciled! And there is no mention of any infanticide.[79] Pompeius belongs to the age of Emperor Augustus, Justin to the second century AD. Dassin may not have been familiar with this particular ancient variant.

 The scene in his film is as charming as it is witty, but it does not lack a serious undertone. What makes Homer so superior to Illya – his greater and, he thinks, accurate knowledge of myth and literature? He seems not to have noticed that Jason did not fall for a blonde *in Athens*. Or is this a slip on writer Dassin's part? Ironically, Dassin was to turn into a dedicated Hellenophile while Mercouri, later his wife and his Medea in *A Dream of Passion*, came to be something like the incarnation of the eternal spirit of classical Greece. Homer, in the scene discussed, calls Illya "an idea." Dassin probably saw such an idea in Mercouri. But Homer's idea of Greece is no

---

[79] Justin, *Epitome* 42.2.12.

more than a garden-variety one. As Dassin, a former communist and refuge from McCarthyism, said in an interview:

most people never saw the political point of that film which was very important to me. I've always been concerned about the movement of the U.S. to impose its political policies, attitudes, and ways of thinking on other people – a light way of saying imperialism. NEVER ON SUNDAY is the story of a guy who came to tell the Greeks how to live, how to act, how to uncorrupt themselves. The very nature of his project unites him with the dictators of the country. In our film, these were the exploiters of the Piraeus prostitutes. We always find ourselves in bed with the dictators.[80]

Dassin had said much the same in an earlier interview, in which he also calls Homer Thrace "this rather idiotic boy-scout character" and refers to "the very falseness of his position."[81] This Homer was in fact the starting point of Dassin's film. Mercouri reports him announcing it in these words:

I have an idea for a movie. It's about a man who tries to make people think as he does . . . He's a guy who can walk into the happiest environment and by the time he leaves, succeeds in making everyone miserable. He screws everything up . . . He's not a bad guy. He's just dangerously naïve . . . She's so happy he can't stand it.[82]

So Homer embarks on his course of education, causing Illya nothing but misery. But he cannot convince her that Medea killed her children. The two attend a performance of Euripides' *Medea* in the theater of Herod Atticus on the slope of the Acropolis, and Dassin intercuts moments from the play with the audience's reactions. The performance is standard-issue tragedy, meant to express the eternal classical. Fake-ancient costumes and make-up, pompous declamations, and all-around seriousness of purpose are intended to impress Greek (in the theater) and international audiences (of the film) with a stereotypical presentation of the glorious culture that was Greece. Illya is wholly involved: She cries, she laughs, but always at the wrong moments and in contrast to the reactions of the other spectators. A scary Medea, her face distorted, clutches and raises her dagger. The audience is crying or terrified; Illya is laughing. But her inappropriate reactions amount to a facile ploy on Dassin's part. He makes rather too simplistic fun of Illya.

Then comes the pay-off, and here Dassin succeeds admirably. A dissolve takes us to the end of the performance. The viewers are applauding, the

---

[80] Quoted from Georgakas and Anastasopoulos 1978: 24. Dassin adds that he did not emphasize this side "strikingly enough."

[81] Gow 1970: 68.

[82] Mercouri 1971: 135. Dassin here also refers to the American way of life and calls Homer a "boy scout."

actors are taking their bows. As the Medea actress comes on stage, Homer shouts to Illya over the general din: "But I tell you that Medea killed her children!" Illya knows better: "Homer, don't be stupid!" She points toward the stage – and there they are: The child actors now also take their bows. Q.E.D. Illya was right all along, as anybody can see. She smiles in happy triumph. All's well that ends well, including this tragedy of Medea. It is much better to go to the seashore than to be a vicious character and a murderess.

11   Endings: Possible and Impossible

Ula Stöckl once addressed the subject of myth, tragedy, and cinema in the following terms: "Every tragedy contains its own special archetype of human behavior. The story, the legend around it, is the myth ... Today's greatest myth, I dare say, is cinema." About presentations of myth on screen, she added: "There is never just one story or one response. There are lots of stories, responses, and interests." Myths are especially complex: "Each character has his very special, very own, very justifiable reasons for being and/or acting so and so." After addressing the importance of death in human life she concluded, speaking from her own filmmaking experience:

I decided that *death* in cinema is as real as your thoughts, and as unreal as cinema. Cinema is just the image of a certain kind of death imagined. And if you dare imagining, for example, an end of relationship with a beloved person .... just give it the image you choose to be the right one for you.

The result: "You just created a new space for new possibilities." Stöckl's immediately following sentence may serve as an appropriate epilogue to this chapter's topic: "Myth always is the story of a bitter ending."[83] As far as Medea is concerned, only Illya is likely to disagree.

The final words spoken by the Medea characters in two films contradict each other. Pasolini's Medea exclaims to Jason: "Nothing is now possible anymore" (*Niente è più possibile, ormai*). Stöckl's Dea, surprised, whispers to herself: "Everything is possible" (*Alles ist möglich*). In their different ways, both Medea and Dea are right, not only about their own stories but also about the extremes which the cinema can reach in its retelling of complex myths. It always provides new space for new possibilities. One of these might even include the seashore.

---

[83] Stöckl 1985: 47–49 and 51.

4 | Striking Beauties
Aristophanes' Lysistrata

In 1903 Georges Méliès, the first wizard of cinema, made one of the earliest comedies with a classical setting: *Jupiter's Thunderballs*. This burlesque of myth, in which Méliès himself played the father of gods and men, is still funny today. Its original title, *Le tonnerre de Jupiter*, contains a wordplay (and is more accurate than the English title). Comic antiquity has had a long history in the cinema. The slapstick, byword for early screen comedy, had most likely been in use as comic prop on the ancient stage.[1]

Films based on ancient comedies, however, are a different matter. The Roman playwright Plautus is best represented, via Molière and Heinrich von Kleist, by *Amphitryon – Happiness from the Clouds* (1935), made in Nazi Germany by partly Jewish writer-director Reinhold Schünzel in the teeth of Nazi censorship, and by the better-known *A Funny Thing Happened on the Way to the Forum*. But Greek comedy? Here the screen does not have much to offer, with the one exception that is the subject of this chapter. Old Comedy survives only in the plays of Aristophanes and is too obscure in its topical political attacks and until recently has been too explicit or obscene for the cinema. Conversely, the few later comedies, like those by Menander, may have been too gentle to have attracted filmmakers.[2] So the cinema seems to have missed out on a golden opportunity. Fortunately, the screen history of Aristophanes' *Lysistrata*, his raciest and most influential play, absolves the cinema from charges of comic negligence. Films of *Lysistrata* additionally offer us an entertaining and instructive opportunity to trace various thematic ramifications of plot and character across film genres and continents.

Since it would be absurd to deal with one of the funniest and raciest comedies ever written in a pedantic or schoolmasterly manner, I have tried to pay homage to the spirit of Aristophanes by permitting myself greater Aristophanaughty leeway – the kind ancient Greeks called *parrhêsia* ("freedom of expression") – than might be customary in an academic publication.

---

[1] On the Greek slapstick (*baktêria*) and its later development, especially in the *commedia dell'arte*, see the brief but instructive comments in Griffith 2015, with references.

[2] His *Dyskolos* (The Grouch") was updated for the big screen in 1965 with the Greek *O parthenos* ("The Male Virgin"). A few television adaptations also exist.

Certain of my wordplays may strike the prim and prissy as inappropriate. Believers in political correctness may therefore wish to skip this chapter to spare themselves such punishment.

1   Comedy and Theory: No Funny Business

"I do not intend to enter the swamp of abstract debate on the nature of comedy and the comic, for that is a quicksand out of which many never climb." With this sensible if metaphorically mixed declaration Gerald Mast, one of the most perceptive American critics of literature and film, began *The Comic Mind*, his fundamental study of film comedy.[3] Comedy, even more than satire, is a genre so large and varied as to be resistant to theory. Nevertheless, in the first of his book's five sections, entitled "Assumptions, Definitions, and Categories," Mast bravely enters the swampy quicksand of theory. In his opening chapter ("Comic Structures") he identifies eight basic plots, beginning with ancient Greece. The first is "the familiar plot of New Comedy" with its Roman continuations in Plautus and Terence. The next three plots are "distillations of elements that were combined in Aristophanic Old Comedy." One is "intentional parody or burlesque," like Aristophanes' parody of Euripides. Another one presents a "*reductio ad absurdum*," in which a "simple human mistake or social question is magnified, reducing the action to chaos and the social question to absurdity," with or without obvious didacticism:

Aristophanes used it by taking a proposition (if you want peace, if you want a utopian community, if you want to speculate abstractly) and then reducing the proposition to nonsense – thereby implying some more sensible alternative.

Then there is "an investigation of the workings of a particular society, comparing the responses of one social group or class with those of another, contrasting people's different responses to the same stimuli and similar responses to different stimuli."[4]

This and much more is outlined with good sense and illustrated by numerous examples. Still, it all remains rather dry, if not as dry as things were to become twelve years later in *Comedy/Cinema/Theory*, a collection of scholarly essays. The editor's "Introduction" has a quotation from

---

[3] Mast 1979: 3. Groundbreaking works on comedy include Bergson 1913 (originally published in French in 1911 and often reprinted) and, from a literary-archetypal perspective, Frye 1957, especially 43–52 and 163–186. Cf. Weitz 2009, which opens with an indirect tribute to cinema as today's chief comic medium. Bermel 1982 is still useful. Schechter 1994 has a few things to say about cinema, too (Chaplin).

[4] The quotations are from Mast 1979: 4–6.

Aristophanes (*Assemblywomen* 1155–1156) for its first epigraph and refers to Aristophanes several times.[5] A contribution in this book by William Paul on Charles Chaplin's *City Lights* (1931) bears a title exciting to academics but yawn-inducing to all others: "Charles Chaplin and the Annals of Anality." Its learned author analizes rather than analyzes *City Lights* by taking Aristophanes' verbal vulgarity as its theoretical starting point.[6] The first insight about Aristophanes is this: "Three of his eleven extant plays use names of animals for their titles (*Wasps; Birds; Frogs*) and appropriately so because the plays are filled with a sense of animality."[7] "Thoughtful cogitators!" we may be tempted to exclaim with Aristophanes' Strepsiades about the providers of such perspicacity. "Lord Zeus, what subtlety of mind!"[8] Subtle cogitators will deduce that Aristophanes' other plays must be filled with a parallel sense of ecclesiality, thesmophoriality, Acharniality, and a few other *-alities*. The anal scholar then turns to Aristophanes' obscenity and adduces two quotations from the first edition of the now classic work on the subject, Jeffrey Henderson's *The Maculate Muse*.[9] He – the analist, not Henderson – reaches the following accurate conclusion before turning to specific scenes in Chaplin's film:

As with Aristophanes, the vulgarity is often acknowledged in order to be dismissed. Chaplin is most often praised for his abilities as a mime, his pathos, his subtlety of expression, his humanism, and … his satire. As far as I know, no one has ever thought to praise him for the anality of his humor.[10]

There must be a reason for such lack of praise. Even if Prof. Paul does not appall us, we may be better off if we forget gray theory and turn to Chaplin's films directly. They redound with Aristophanic moments, plot elements, characters, scenes, and more; the subject deserves a separate analysis (but not analisis). The anarchic subversion of social order and conventions is already present in the earliest short films that introduce the Little Tramp and continues, despite certain elements of sentimentality introduced later, up to *A King in New York* (1957), the last film Chaplin both directed and starred in. *A King in New York* targets pop culture and its vulgarities (television),

---

[5] Horton 1991b: 1, 10–11, and 16–17 quotes or mentions Aristophanes.   [6] Paul 1991.

[7] Paul 1991: 114.

[8] Aristophanes, *Clouds* 101 (*merimnophrontistai*) and 153. The translations are by Henderson 1998: 21 and 27.

[9] Henderson 1991. The first edition appeared in 1975. Robson 2006 is a recent if less thorough examination of the subject. Amusingly in this Aristophanic context, the name of his highly respectable German publishing house (Narr) means "Fool" or "Jester." Detailed information on all matters Aristophanic is now available in Olson 2014.

[10] Paul 1991: 114–115; quotation at 115.

plastic surgery, fake progressivism, the chase after the dollar, and, most importantly, political intolerance and hypocrisy (McCarthyism). Chaplin was at that time exiled from the US and made the film in England.

Many Aristophanic and Plautine things happened on the way from antiquity to our own time. *A Funny Thing Happened on the Way to the Forum* may be the best proof.[11] This Broadway musical, written by Burt Shevelove and Larry Gelbart and with music and song lyrics by Stephen Sondheim, is a loose adaptation of plot elements taken from Plautus. It had won Tony Awards in 1963 and was filmed by Richard Lester in 1966. The film version is especially effective. Lester reinforces the words by cleverly filling the screen with his visual trademarks, slapstick and sight gags, in particular extreme close-ups in distorting wide-angle shots and, where warranted, extremely rapid cutting. The clever slave Pseudolus, supported by an off-screen chorus, introduces us to the plot and to the essence of comedy by directly addressing the viewers. This amounts to a brief if misplaced Aristophanic *parabasis*, the elaborate ode in the middle of a play in which the chorus chants to the audience. In defense of the quasi-parabatic opening of *A Funny Thing Happened on the Way to the Forum* we might remember that decades ago several leading classical scholars, including such big swords as Ulrich von Wilamowitz-Moellendorff and Eduard Fraenkel, had speculated that the *parabasis* belonged at the beginning of Aristophanes' plays.[12]

Shevelove may well have had Aristophanes at the back of his mind when he was working on Plautus.[13] As early as 1941, while still an undergraduate at Yale University, he had adapted *Frogs*. His and Sondheim's musical of Aristophanes' play was revived for Broadway in a revised and expanded version in 2004, on which actor-singer Nathan Lane had collaborated. *Frogs* contained topical references to then President George W. Bush but did not meet with the success of *A Funny Thing Happened on the Way to the Forum*. Shakespeare and George Bernard Shaw replace Aeschylus and Euripides in the contest for the title of best poet.[14]

Inspired by Chaplin and Lester, let us leave the anti-Aristophanic Thinkery of theory, the prison house of comedy and a useless Cloudcuckooland or Aristophanes' *nephelokokkygia*. After all: "Theories of comedy are ultimately rationalizations for whatever the theorist happens to think is funny."[15] Instead,

---

[11] Information on the play and film now in Sondheim 2010: 79–109.

[12] There is no evidence, however, to support this view. See Hubbard 1991.

[13] Cicero, *On Duties* 1.29.104, makes it clear that Plautus can justifiably be adduced in connection with Aristophanes. Cf. Duckworth 1992: 379 and 394, quoting earlier scholarship.

[14] Gamel 2007 surveys the history and fortunes of this adaptation. See further Given 2011, with additional references.

[15] Quoted from Corliss 1974: 88.

let us proceed with our topic, Aristophanes' presence in the cinema, in the manner in which comic and satiric artists and even the personified Better Argument and Worse Argument in Aristophanes' *Clouds* proceed: by force of example. Such a procedure will readily demonstrate Aristophanes' importance for the screen. It is also intended to have a seductive effect on readers: to make them want to find additional instances on their own. Gabriel Pascal's classy 1941 adaptation of Shaw's *Major Barbara*, to which Shaw himself contributed the scenario and dialogue, provides a handy guide to such an undertaking. A quotation from *Frogs* that was not in Shaw's stage version is heard early in the film. A letter by Shaw addressing the viewer as "Friend" appears immediately after the credits. Here Shaw reassures us that the story, although "a PARABLE" in which we may all recognize ourselves, is nothing to be afraid of; on the contrary, "you will not be bored by it . . . If you do not enjoy every word of it, we shall both be equally disappointed. Well, friend: have I ever disappointed you?" Of course not. Shaw echoes Apuleius' exhortation to his readers: *Lector, intende: laetaberis!* ("Reader, pay attention, and you will have a good time!")[16] So we may take a Shavian perspective on our topic: Cineaste, pay attention, and you will have a good time finding Aristophanes here, there, and everywhere! To put our motto in classy Apuleian terminology: *Spectator, intende: laetaberis Aristophanem passim inveniens!* Pseudo-parabatic aside from author to reader: If you, friend, do not enjoy every word of this chapter, or at least most words, we shall both be equally disappointed. But has Aristophanes ever disappointed us? Of course not.

As mentioned, the most important of Aristophanes' plays in film history is *Lysistrata*.[17] Most of this chapter will deal with its adaptations to the silver screen, modernized and more or less loose (in only one sense of the word) as these are. A brief consideration of films that exhibit the spirit of Aristophanic comedy will round off our survey. My main focus will be on the cinema, although television and, on occasion, the stage will play supporting parts. On occasion I include some other Aristophanic antics that warrant our attention.

2   Battleground of Emotions

In 1965 maverick American writer-director Samuel Fuller left Hollywood because of increasing difficulties with the studio system, which was in the

---

[16] Apuleius, *The Golden Ass* 1.1.6.

[17] Henderson 1980 provides a detailed introduction to the play. For modern textual editions, with commentary or translation, see Henderson 1987 (text and commentary) and 2000 (text and unbowdlerized translation).

process of breaking up. Two enterprising Frenchmen hoping to become producers had lured Fuller to France, promising to finance a film to be called *Flowers of Evil*, an adaptation not of Baudelaire but of *Lysistrata*. Judging the treatment he had been given "very bad," Fuller wrote an original screenplay, a "semi-science fiction" that was "zany" enough, he thought, to fit Aristophanes' original.[18] The film was

about a secret society of beautiful women of all nations – the Flowers of Evil – who use violence, science and sex in a plot to stop all wars. The opening scene involves a ballerina pirouetting from the stage to the street as she flees a homicidal all-female motorcycle gang; the final scene is set in outer space with the leading lady abandoned, revolving endlessly into the darkness. "I thought that was a hell of an ending."[19]

A critic concludes: "*Flowers of Evil* reflects Fuller's delight in turning genre conventions on their ear, as it takes the James Bond international spy genre … and turns its sexy temptresses into peacenik protagonists."[20] Financing never materialized, however, and the project was abandoned.

By this time the New Wave had become dominant in French cinema and was a strong intellectual force in the country's culture at large. Several New Wave filmmakers had started out as critics and reviewers, writing primarily for the journal *Cahiers du cinéma*. They particularly extolled the artistry of American directors who had been either looked down upon by the critical establishment in their own country or at best had been taken for granted. Fuller was one of them. While in France, he was invited by his *Cahiers du cinéma* champion Jean-Luc Godard, now a major if controversial director, to appear in Godard's *Pierrot le fou* and to play himself. Fuller agreed. In an early scene the main character observes to Fuller, who spoke no French, via an interpreter that he has always wanted to know what exactly the cinema is. Fuller's reply, unscripted and unprompted by Godard, was: "The film is like a battleground – there's love, hate, action, violence, death – in one word, emotions."[21]

Fuller's spontaneous and now famous definition of cinema fits his own body of work, but it also describes most narrative cinema and any other narrative art form. But was it only a clever *aperçu*? Or was Fuller, in France for a specific purpose, thinking of his own film? The interpreter renders *le cinéma* in the question put to Fuller as "this movie," and Fuller replies accordingly:

[18] Fuller is quoted from Server 1994: 144. See further Brody 2008: 245–246.
[19] Quoted from Server 1994: 144; the last sentence is Fuller's. Cf. Fuller's brief recollection in Fuller with Lang Fuller and Rudes 2002: 429–430.
[20] Dombrowski 2008: 175.
[21] On this see Server 1994: 49, Brody 2008: 245–246, and Fuller's own words in Fuller, Lang Fuller, and Rudes 2002: 431–432.

"The film" rather than, more generally, "Film" or "The cinema." More specifically, his answer fits *Lysistrata*. Action (i.e. war), violence, death: These are the surroundings in which Lysistrata proposes her plan and the situation in which and for which Aristophanes wrote the play. Love is one of its central concerns. Hate is its corollary – women's hatred of a seemingly endless war. These feelings come together in an explosive mix in a play unlikely ever to have left an audience cold. In one word: emotions.

But there is more. One of the most striking ancient portraits of poets, orators, philosophers, and other intellectuals is a bronze head now commonly but not exclusively identified as representing Aristophanes. It was earlier believed to show Seneca, the Stoic philosopher, statesman, and tragic playwright.[22] It is from the Villa of the Papyri near Herculaneum and now on display in the National Archaeological Museum in Naples. The head is a copy of that of a seated bronze statue, now lost, which dates to around 180 BC. The face exhibits a mixture of emotions that Fuller could have related to: "power of movement," "features meaningful but difficult to penetrate," and especially "fire, intoxication, affliction, and [an] edge of verbal expression." "The head is turned, in a sudden lateral movement, as if it were a spy's ... [with] the mouth slightly opened as if for the thrust of a clever utterance." It reveals an "ingenious and pointed perception of character as man's destiny."[23] In other words, a battleground of emotions.

More than forty marble copies of the head survive in addition to this bronze one. Modern copies, most likely in plaster made to look like marble, unexpectedly appear in films. Raoul Walsh's *The World in His Arms* (1952) is a rollicking adventure-romance-comedy. The plot is historical hokum involving the Alaska Purchase of 1867. At its climax the hero's beloved is about to be married off to the sadistic villain but is rescued at the last moment by her sweetheart and his friends. The ensuing melee works both as an action setpiece and as a not-too-serious general fracas. And Aristophanes is

---

[22] This is the reason why the bust is still referred to as Pseudo-Seneca. For additional information, including photographs, see Paul Zanker 1995: 150–154 and 369 notes 4–5 (additional references); Schefold 1997: 266–269 (with ills. 149 and 150) and 521–522 (review of scholarship). Schefold makes it clear that its identification as Aristophanes' head suits this bronze better than any other ancient character proposed by scholars, among them the archaic Greek poet Hesiod. Even so, a copy of this bust still appears on the cover of a recent book on Seneca (Bartsch and Schiesaro 2015). And major museums still provide misinformation as well. Labels for a herm in the Capitoline Museum in Rome (MC 514) and for a marble version from the second century AD in Rome's National Museum both call the head Pseudo-Seneca; the latter mentions a couple of other identifications but does not name Aristophanes. These are just two random instances.

[23] Quotations from Schefold 1997: 266 and 268. He is fully justified in waxing rhapsodic in his appreciation and interpretation of this unforgettable work.

witnessing it all, with rather a bemused detachment on his face. But what is he doing here? No one in the film has mentioned him, and no one as much as casts a passing glance at or takes the slightest notice of the head. The camera ignores it as well, for there is neither a close-up nor anything else to emphasize its presence. Aristophanes is simply there, a decorative piece among many other classy furnishings. And that seems to be the very point. If Fuller was right to define cinema as emotional battleground in the context of his own *Lysistrata* project, then Walsh's set decorator had been intuitively right to put Aristophanes in the thick of such a Hollywood battleground. In retrospect, the presence of Aristophanes indicates the common ground between his boisterous comedy on the one hand and plot-driven cinema on the other. The very inattention that the marble head receives shows the ignorance of this affinity among filmmakers, viewers, and critics, but it also tells us that we need not make a big deal about it. To those who recognize the bust, the point is self-evident. A comparable case can be seen, but only by alert viewers and on a large screen, in George Sidney's *Scaramouche* (1952), the glossy M-G-M remake of a perennial swashbuckler. The same head of Aristophanes appears briefly in the background during one scene and serves no function at all. It is just there.[24]

The hero of *The World in His Arms* is played by handsome Hollywood star Gregory Peck, who was to have another encounter with our Aristophanes in *Mirage* (1965), a thriller directed by Edward Dmytryk and adapted from a novel by Howard Fast. Caught in a bewildering concatenation of strange

---

[24] Aristophanes himself appears as a character on screen in adaptations of Plato's *Symposium*: in Marco Ferreri's French television film *Le banquet* (1989), with Irene Papas as Diotima, and, sort of, in Michael Wurth's American *The Symposium* (2003), in which modern characters take on the roles of the participants; Aristophanes' part is taken by a woman. Edvin Tiemroth's *En sjael efter døden* ("A Soul After Death"), a 1963 Danish television film, includes Aristophanes. Coky Giedroyc's *Aristophanes: The Gods Are Laughing* (1995) is a fictional biography of the poet as founder of political satire and considers his continuing influence on the modern stage. It contains, of course, an anti-war message. This Aristophanes regrets his satire of Socrates in the *Clouds*, believing that it contributed to Socrates' trial and condemnation (cf. Plato, *Apology* 19c). Rosalie Crutchley, the Acte of Mervyn LeRoy's *Quo Vadis* (1951), is here Aristophanes' mother. Aristophanes' speech in the *Symposium* is translated into an animated cartoon and song ("The Origin of Love") in John Cameron Mitchell's *Hedwig and the Angry Inch* (2001), adapted from an Off-Broadway musical whose sexual and political grotesqueries and anti-authoritarianism Aristophanes might have appreciated; cf., most recently, Garcia 2015. Writer-director Tim Blake Nelson incorporated Aristophanes' speech into his comedy-drama *Leaves of Grass* (2009). Gunning 2005 adduces Aristophanes' speech in connection with Alfred Hitchcock's *Vertigo* (1958) and the independent short film *The Geography of the Body* (1943), directed by experimental filmmaker, poet, and future academic Willard Maas. The main title of Gunning's article, although without its pun, is Aristophanes' definition of love (*Symposium* 192e) and so quoted in Maas's film. In *Symposium* (1973), directed by Dimitris Kollatos, passages from *Lysistrata* are being recited; cf. Kyriakos 2013: 202 note 19.

Figure 4.1 Aristophanes as spectator in Edward Dmytryk's *Mirage*.

incidents, a solid Manhattan businessman thinks he has lost his mind and memory, meets an alluring but mysterious brunette, and gets entangled in a labyrinthine intrigue that threatens his life. At one point he visits a self-styled "consulting psychiatrist, not an analyst," who is also, he confesses, a "genius." The good doctor admits to having once collaborated with "a Freudian" on a "foolish book" called *The Dark Side of the Mind*. The head shrink has the same head of Aristophanes displayed on a stand between his bookshelf and the door to his office (Figure 4.1). Its fate is the same as that in *The World in His Arms*: to be ignored. Presumably it is there only to give patients a reassuring message: *Yes, your shrink has a classical education, but no need to worry about Oedipal complexities. No dark side of the mind here!* By now, viewers will not be surprised about the neglect that the bust meets with: It is standard Hollywood operating procedure. Even in *noir* cinema, which focuses on the dark side of the mind and of society at large, the head appears in the usual manner. In Roy William Neill's little-known *Black Angel* (1946), a plaster copy sits on a doctor's desk in the Los Angeles County Hospital. Although it is prominent on screen, it remains ignored.

The same head, gleaming white, is noticeable among the dark clutter in the den of the titular character of Robert Siodmak's *noir* thriller *The Strange Affair of Uncle Harry* (1945). The good uncle, intriguingly played by sometimes suave, sometimes caddish George Sanders, is a superannuated bachelor. He is under the thumb of his hypochondriac sister, who has an unhealthy obsession with him. Then he meets an attractive young lady and healthily falls in love. Then his jealous sister gets busy. Then he gets away with murder. Then comes a final twist. As usual, Aristophanes has nothing whatever to do with any of this. But then, in a manner of speaking, he does. His bust is firmly associated with the cinema, as may be seen in a *LIFE* magazine photograph from 1962 that was taken in the Louvre. Greek actress Melina Mercouri, beloved star of *Never on Sunday* (1960), *Phaedra* (1962), and *A Dream of Passion* (1978), all directed by Jules Dassin, her husband since 1966, is laughing uproariously in front of our Aristophanes. Ironically, the caption only identifies the head as an "ancient Greek bust."[25] *O tempora, o ignorantia!*

Aristophanes' head had fared slightly better in one of Hollywood's classic sophisticated comedies, George Cukor's *The Philadelphia Story* (1940), based on the Broadway hit by Philip Barry. Various post- and premarital romantic entanglements are played out among the high-society set in the City of Brotherly Love, except that things are not all that brotherly or loving. At one point the unforgettably named C. K. Dexter Haven, played by suave Cary Grant, plots with a low-class reporter, played by James Stewart, against a vulgar media mogul who is also a blackmailer. The setting, Haven's cottage, has Aristophanes for part of its décor. The reporter absentmindedly pets him in passing. This *must* have been the reason why Stewart received an Academy Award!

But we need not despair as long as we remember that even Fred Astaire was a friend of Aristophanes, if not of his head, at least as far as the screenwriters of Charles Walters' *Easter Parade* (1948) made him out to be. In this glossy and classy M-G-M musical, set before World War I and co-starring Judy Garland, Fred plays a famous dancer who has just learned that his female partner is ready for a career without him. He goes to a bar to drown his sorrows. Fortunately Mike the sympathetic bartender, who has seen it all, is there to advise him about blondes and brunettes: "I can boil down trouble into two classifications." What might these be? The answer is easy: "Women and their mothers." How does Mike know? That answer is easy, too: He has never been married. "Meet my friend Mike," the character played by Astaire will say soon after; "he's a disciple of Aristophanes." In due course, of course, he will run into Judy.

Back to *Pierrot le fou*. The film in which Fuller utters his memorable words is itself a story of everything Fuller mentions. It tells of a young

---

[25] The image can be viewed on the LIFE Internet site. In the caption to another photo taken on the same occasion, Demosthenes does not suffer the indignity of such anonymity.

husband and father who spontaneously runs off with a former lover when they meet again after many years. Action, violence, and death mark their flight from society and civilization. The woman, played by Anna Karina, Godard's ex-wife, eventually leaves him, and he kills first her and then himself. The battle of the sexes in *Pierrot le fou* does not even loosely match that in *Lysistrata*, but the film shows and comments on the difficulties of a couple when a female partner displays a powerful personality and a stronger will than the male. The film is poignant to viewers who are aware of Godard's own emotional turmoil over the wife who had left him for another man and with whom he was still obsessively in love. Godard had made Karina a star, and to him she personified his creative energies. A contemporary journalist perceptively observed: "*Pierrot le fou* has come to scream in my face that a fairly young man whom I know ... named Jean-Luc Godard, died ... because he loved a woman madly, and because this woman left him."[26] French philosopher Bernard-Henri Lévy said about the film almost four decades later: "*Pierrot le fou* taught me love .... I loved women more because of Godard's film. He pulled the struts out from under foolishness."[27]

In its own way *Pierrot le fou* achieves a kind of twisted Aristophanic moment in a line scripted by Godard that was his "purest, most vulgar moment of wish-fulfillment."[28] But it also appears to be a *cri de coeur* of utter anguish that fuses most, perhaps all, of the emotions Fuller had enumerated. It is made the more unforgettable because Godard assigned the words in question to the woman. I quote them without translation: "Baise moi."

Godard's next film, *Masculine Feminine* (1966), reworked themes from *Pierrot le fou* and has male and female protagonists again modeled on himself and Karina. A recent study of Godard summarizes the male character in *Masculine Feminine* in terms that fit the one in *Pierrot le fou* and Godard himself equally well: "he is hopelessly and uncalculatingly, romantically and impractically in love with a woman who guilelessly and calmly pulls him in and pushes him away, caresses him and insults him, makes love to him and betrays him, a woman whose sense of art and life are utterly remote from his own."[29] The two films in turn led to another round of love, marriage, and divorce for Godard. Eighteen-year-old actress Anne Wiazemsky watched *Pierrot le fou* – "It struck me like an artistic thunderbolt (*coup de foudre*)" – and then *Masculine Feminine* and immediately fell in love with their creator: "It was as if it [*Masculine Feminine*] were a letter written to me. I loved the film because I loved the man who was behind the

---

[26] Quoted from Brody 2008: 250; source reference at 651 note 32.
[27] Quoted from Brody 2008: 250–251; source reference at 651 note 36.   [28] Brody 2008: 248.
[29] Brody 2008: 267.

film .... then I did one of the craziest things that I've ever done: I wrote a love letter to Godard, I told him that I loved the film because I loved him."[30]

If any one classical author can be said to have pulled the struts out from under male foolishness, it is Aristophanes even more than the later Roman satirists (Horace, Juvenal), epigrammatists (Catullus, Martial), or novelists (Petronius, Apuleius). As Fuller's abandoned project exemplifies, Aristophanes in general and *Lysistrata* in particular are naturals for the cinema, even if the verbal fireworks and explicit sexual humor of the original could not be reproduced on screen in anything like an unadulterated fashion until recently. Matters are different in the era of *South Park*, the Farrelly Brothers, and Judd Apatow (e.g. *The 40-Year-Old Virgin*, 2005; no, a male virgin!). Even so, Aristophanes' comedy-satire of a Greek wives' sex strike has made it onto the screen several times. Decades ago, a distinguished filmmaker and, yes, theoretician of the cinema explained why. Sergei Eisenstein wrote in a short 1933 reply to a questionnaire, published under the title "Cinema and the Classics":

As well as working with contemporary authors it is very important for filmmakers to pay attention to the literary classics. However, work on the classics must not be organised along the lines of superficial borrowing but as a matter of studying all the elements that constitute their specificity. We must interpret their signs and observe how a particular element should develop into a new one, passing through different stages in time and class. This applies equally to the technique of depicting characters and to the means and methods of embodying them ... Without [such] alteration *Lysistrata* would scarcely produce the dramatic elaboration of the scenes of women's rebellions that regularly break out in our scripts.[31]

Two things are noteworthy. By "the classics" Eisenstein does not primarily mean the ancient Greeks or Romans; he uses the phrase in a general sense. With the one exception quoted above, his examples of classics are Balzac and Shakespeare. But that one exception is the other telling aspect. Not epic or tragedy but comedy, if with a social and serious dimension. Aristophanic cinephiles can only be grateful to Eisenstein for singling out their favorite.

3   Lysistrata in the Silent and Early Sound Eras

The charming title of the first film adaptation of Aristophanes' play, made by Louis Feuillade in France in 1910 as a one-reeler, is revealing: *Lysistrata*

---

[30] Quotations from Brody 2008: 271 and 272.
[31] Eisenstein 1988: 276; source reference in Taylor 1988: 325 note 41.

ou La grève des baisers (literally: "Lysistrata or The Strike of Kisses"). Apparently this title was meant to reassure the good citizens that they could watch the film without being unduly scandalized.[32] The subtitle seems to derive from French playwright Maurice Donnay's version of *Lysistrata*, directed by Paul Porel at the Grand Théâtre in Paris in 1892.[33] Feuillade was the right man to introduce Aristophanes to the new medium of film. When he died in 1925 at age fifty-three, he was one of the most prolific and versatile writer-directors in cinema history. Between 1906 and 1924 he directed well over six hundred films in all genres and had become artistic director of the Gaumont studio the year after he began making films. Feuillade made numerous short comedies about the adventures of Bébé, Bout-de-zan, and other sassy urchins. In his six-and-a-half-hour thriller serial *Les vampires* (1915) he also introduced the anagrammatically named Irma Vep as the screen's first vamp, dressed in a black catsuit. The titular vampires are not nocturnal bloodsuckers but a secret crime organization masterminded by Irma Vep. In several of his early films Feuillade turned to noble subjects from Greek and Roman history, literature, and myth and introduced an approach to filmmaking that he called *le film esthétique*: aesthetic cinema. His film of Aristophanes is an example.

Since Feuillade championed aestheticism, it is doubtful that he would have enjoyed the next appearance of Lysistrata. *Coontown Suffragettes*, a short film made on location in Florida around 1914, is a crude comedy about racial stereotypes in which a black woman does not know her place. The film, which featured Hattie McDaniel, is presumed lost, a circumstance that not even Aristophanes might lament. Under the heading "The Mammy," one of the terms for stereotypical female blacks, a historian describes the film as follows:

Mammy is distinguished ... by her ... fierce independence. She is usually big, fat, and cantankerous ... The comedy ... dealt with a group of bossy mammy washerwomen who organize a militant movement to keep their good-for-nothing husbands at home. Aristophanes would no doubt have risen from his grave with righteous indignation. But the militancy of the washerwomen served as a primer for the mammy roles Hattie MacDaniel [*sic*] was to perfect in the 1930s.[34]

---

[32] A (very) faint echo of this circumstance will recur in 1991 on German television. The comedy series *Die lieben Verwandten* ("Those Dear Relatives") contained an episode called "Wie damals bei Lysistrata" ("Just Like Back Then With Lysistrata") in which a modern Lissy (or Lizzy) encourages a wife who refuses to cook to go on strike against her husband.

[33] Cf. Lacour 1903, where the phrase *la grève des baisers* appears at 380.

[34] Bogle 2001: 9. Hattie McDaniel is best known for her portrayal of Mammy in Victor Fleming's *Gone with the Wind* (1939), a part for which she was the first black performer to be nominated for and to win an Academy Award.

This film was in strong contrast to the near-contemporary *Et huskors* (1914 or 1915), whose informal English title is "Enough of It" and which had both *Lysistrata* and *Lysten styret* ("Lust-Driven," a pun on "Lysistrata") as alternate titles. Directed in Denmark by Holger-Madsen – he had added a hyphen to his name a few years before – from a script by Harriet Bloch, the film tells a story about contemporary upper-class society. Earlier, Bloch had written the short comedy *Love or Money* (1912; also known as *Outwitted*), in which a wealthy single mother, ardently pursued by three suitors, concocts a plan with a female friend to test the men's intentions. In the process the women enjoy themselves immensely at the men's expense.

An actress who unfortunately never made it to the screen in *Lysistrata*, although she had been a memorable Lysistrata on the Russian stage in 1923, is Olga Baclanova (originally Baklanova). She toured the US with the Moscow Art Theatre in 1925–1926. When she decided to stay, Paramount promoted her by drawing attention to her past stardom, for example with a 1929 publicity photo of her as a rather stern-looking Lysistrata. After she had appeared prominently in a few silent films, Baclanova's Russian accent cut short her American career upon the introduction of sound. Still, she remains memorable as Cleopatra – no, not the ancient queen but the unscrupulous villainess and blond mantrap in Todd Browning's cult shocker *Freaks* (1932).

Sound came to the screen in 1929.[35] A year later, Aristophanes, although by name only, made a brief appearance in the Our Gang short *Shivering Shakespeare*. Here the kids are forced to act (if that is the word) in a wild and silly abbreviation of *Quo Vadis?* It is called "The Gladiator's Dilemma," written and directed by one Mrs. Funston Evergreen Kennedy, whose Aristophanic name is perhaps the best thing about the film. She is called Kennedy because her husband is played by stalwart comic actor Edgar Kennedy. A playbill informs the internal and external audiences that the authorial lady is indebted, among others, to Shakespeare, Aristophanes, Bacon, Cervantes, and American humorist Irvin S. Cobb, all distinguished evergreens, albeit to varying degrees of funstonness. Such high-class debts do not protect the good Mrs. from getting lots of pies in the face at the film's climax.

Charles Riesner's *Politics* of the following year is set in an average (and fictional) mid-sized American town during Prohibition. The local women

---

[35] A serendipitous detail from late in the silent era that is worth mentioning is the moment in Walter (or Walther) Ruttmann's poetic documentary *Berlin: Symphony of a Great City* (1927), in which the camera passes a *Litfaßsäule* (advertising column) showing a poster for a stage production of *Lysistrata*.

take up a battle against gangsters and corrupt politicians: "Now it's *our* turn!" A title card reveals the impact of their revolt on the local males, especially husbands: "For the first time in history, women had men worried." Viewers may well believe this, not least since there is no mention of Lysistrata. But there *is* a strike. The women's candidate for mayor, played by formidable comedienne Marie Dressler, proclaims: "We'll stop everything." Predictably, a pretty young thing, married only the day before, asks the crucial question: "Everything?" The answer: "Yes, darling: parlor, bedroom, and bath." This comes as close to mentioning the unmentionable as may have been possible at that time. A text card after the initial credits had informed viewers what was at stake: "This story is dedicated to women – who have been fighting for their rights ever since Adam and Eve started the loose-leaf system."

4   Triumphs of Love

The first sound feature of *Lysistrata* appeared in Austria shortly after the end of World War II. *Triumph der Liebe* ("Triumph of Love," 1947; called *Lysistrata* in the US) was made by prolific and versatile, if not especially distinguished, director Alfred Stöger. The screenplay added a number of contemporary overtones to the film's ancient settings and costumes (Figure 4.2). It featured a cast as popular as it was distinguished and even put Aristophanes and Diogenes on screen. Aristophanes was played by German stage actor, director, and impresario Erich Ziegel, who had launched the careers of a number of famous actors, among them Gustav Gründgens and Fritz Kortner, the latter of whom we will encounter again. Josef Meinrad was Cinesias; handsome leading man O. W. Fischer played a non-Aristophanic Agathos ("Good Guy"; Figure 4.3). Comedian Paul Kemp, who had played Sosias and Mercury in *Amphitryon – Happiness from the Clouds*, here, is one Damon. Still other non-Aristophanic names occur. The film's star is Judith Holzmeister, an actress with a special interest in ancient drama who was at home more in the theater than in the film studio. Holzmeister had opposed the Nazi regime, known a number of resistance fighters personally, and helped hide a Jewish woman. This and her physical beauty and commanding presence made her an ideal Lysistrata. When the film premiered in New York City, Bosley Crowther, the influential film critic of *The New York Times*, was impressed by her but not by the film (and possibly not by her name):

Distinguished Films, Inc. Presents Aristophanes Famous Comedy "LYSISTRATA"

Figure 4.2 American lobby card for Alfred Stöger's *Triumph der Liebe*.

With all due allowance for the difficulties under which an Austrian company must have worked in making a motion-picture version of "Lysistrata" in Vienna right after the war, it must be admitted that its effort . . . is a heavy and tedious rendition of the comedy of Aristophanes. The settings and costumes are surprisingly the most commendable features of the show – saving, perhaps, the classic beauty of Judith Helzmeister [*sic*] in the title role. As the bold Athenian lady who persuades the members of her sex to boycott their husbands' advances in order to put a stop to war, Miss Helzmeister makes it thoroughly obvious why the gentlemen found it

Figure 4.3 Lysistrata and Agathos in Alfred Stöger's *Triumph der Liebe.*

impossible to resist. And she also acts with nice decorum in a much abbreviated role. But an incompleted endeavor to turn this ancient comedy into a comic operetta is evidenced painfully. And the general direction and editing are stiff and amateurish to a fault. Very poor English subtitles and apparent censor cuts in many scenes render this film a doubtful item for American audiences.[36]

Thus spake, *ex cathedra Novi Eburaci*, the powerful *proboulos kinêmato-graphikos* to the demes of America and probably kept quite a number of people from watching the film. Today it deserves a fresh look, not least because of its leading lady.

The French-Italian *Destinées* or *Destini di donne* (1953) deserves a fresh look as well, not least because of its bevy of beautiful leading ladies. The film was released in the US as *Daughters of Destiny* and in the UK as *Love, Soldiers and Women.* Its Dutch title is telling as well: *De grootheid der vrouw* ("The Greatness of Woman"; Figure 4.4). The silhouette of a male figure representing Destiny introduces and comments on three unrelated tales

---

[36] Quoted from http://movies.nytimes.com/movie/review?res=9A05E0DF1438EE3BBC4152DF B0668383659EDE (June 19, 1948).

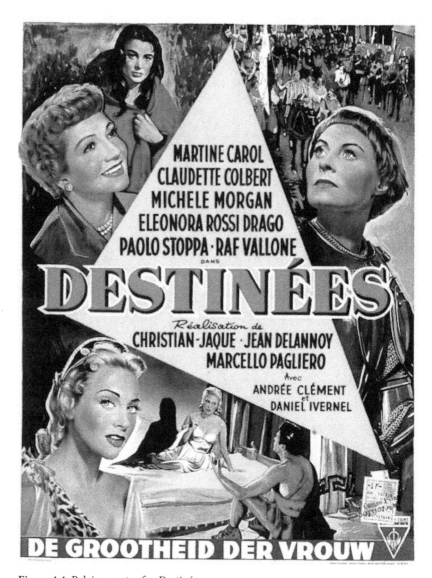

Figure 4.4 Belgian poster for *Destinées*.

about women's experiences with war. The first is a modern story. An American widow, played by elegant Claudette Colbert, travels to Italy, where her husband had fought in World War II, and discovers his affair with an Italian farmgirl (Eleonora Rossi Drago), who has borne him a child. The second episode is about Jeanne d'Arc, played by Michèle Morgan. The final segment, about thirty-five minutes long, is "Lysistrata," directed by Christian-Jaque and starring a vivacious Martine Carol. The first woman,

Destiny says, is a victim of war; the second wanted war; the third won it. Destiny calls Lysistrata "frivolous" and her story "amusing."[37] So it is, for this is a lighthearted romp through Aristophanes' play, with slapstick-type gags, fake beards, and uniforms that could come from some operetta. A film historian comments:

Christian-Jaque made this episode, freely inspired by Aristophanes, with ... star Martine Carol, then vamp number one of French cinema ... dressed to reveal her anatomy. Anna Magnani and Silvana Mangano had at first wanted this part, but the more popular French actress landed it. Since the prudish censorship of the 1950s forbade the off-color language Aristophanes had his characters utter, [screenwriter] Henri Jeanson ... sprinkled his dialogues and sarcastic repartees with all-too-contemporary allusions. He made fun of the backwoods language and the electioneering lies of politicians and of [Marshal] Pétain during the Fourth Republic ("we will win because we are the stronger," "we are not withdrawing, we are moving back") ... [This was a] sketch spiced with rather nice eroticism (in fact, the chastest of Martine Carol's films), made at Cinecittà.[38]

Lysistrata is married to Callias, the Athenians' most important general. In the assembly the demagogue Nicéphore (i.e. Nikêphoros: "Bearer of Victory"), an import into the play alongside several others, argues that the war against Sparta ought to go on even after their recent victory, which could end it. The war has already lasted for sixty years. The general mood among males is contained in this exclamation: "Peace? What peace? What an idea!" But the women have what Lysistrata calls a secret weapon, one stronger than any men's. They occupy the assembly, momentarily becoming pseudo-Aristophanic *ekklêsiazousai*, and proclaim their strike. They do so by snappily raising and extending their right arms in a familiar gesture. "La loi, c'est moi!" Lysistrata proclaims, outdoing with her pleasant rhyme the Sun King's famous *mot* about *l'état*. A comic battle between the women, led by Lysistrata, and the men, led by Callias, ensues in the city square. The men are defeated by a group of women armed with fruit and vegetables, and Callias gets tied up by his wife. At the end, he has made his peace with peace: "To die for Athens but to live for Lysistrata!" He asks her what he should do now that the war is over. She has just the right piece of advice: "Do the same as all the generals: politics!"

---

[37] On the episode see Coelho 2008 and Duarte 2011. The latter, a translator of Aristophanes, adduces the Brazilian film *Carnaval Atlântida* (1952), directed by José Carlos Burle, for its Aristophanic overtones. In this film, producer Cecílio B. de Milho (!) wants to make an epic about Helen of Troy and hires Xenofontes, a professor of Greek history, as a consultant, but the eventual results are a modern musical. Duarte briefly mentions a few other films as well.

[38] Dumont 2009: 230.

Before this genial ending occurs, Lysistrata has arranged for an alliance with the Spartan women. As the Athenian strikers are close to giving up, an Athenian carrier pigeon arrives from Sparta with the message that the Spartan women are making common cause with them. This pigeon is called Pericles. When several smaller pigeons arrive soon after, Lysistrata concludes that Pericles has made his own peace in Sparta and got married there. Peace and family values! "Long live the peace! Long live the birds!" Lysistrata exclaims, alluding to the titles of two other plays by the author who invented her. The women's rebellion does not change anybody's political or social status; rather, the episode affirms the standard male view of them as lovers and wives. This becomes clear at the end, when couples are strolling along with their little children. The story thus conforms to La Rochefoucauld's Maxim 466, which we could read at its opening: "Of all the violent passions the one that becomes a woman best is love" (*De toutes les passions violentes celle qui sied le moins mal aux femmes, c'est l'amour*). It also bears out a quotation by Voltaire that had appeared at the very beginning of the film: "All the reasonings of men are not worth one sentiment of one woman" (*Tous les raisonnements des hommes ne valent pas un sentiment d'une femme*). *Vive la paix! Vive l'amour! Vivent les femmes!*

This Lysistrata story is an amusing caprice. And it is fitting that its titular lady should have been played by Martine Carol. In 1951 she had been the eponymous lady of *Caroline chérie*, a role she reprised in a sequel: *Une caprice de Caroline chérie* (1953). Carol was the most popular sex symbol in French cinema before Brigitte Bardot. She had just appeared in René Clair's charming romantic comedy *Beauties of the Night* (1952) and as the title character of the colorful romance-adventure *Lucrezia Borgia* (1953) and was to play the titular seductresses of *Madame du Barry* (1954) and *Nana* (1955), all three directed by Christian-Jaque, whom she married in 1954.[39] Carol achieved her cinematic apotheosis as the titular *grande horizontale* of Max Ophüls' *Lola Montès* (1955). Christian-Jaque directed a variety of then daringly erotic costume and melodramas. He was sometimes regarded as France's answer to Cecil B. DeMille, although his films, attractive as they are, could not be made on DeMille's colossal scale. Christian-Jaque is today best known for the classic swashbuckler *Fanfan la Tulipe* (1952), starring an irresistible Gérard Philipe.

By contrast, Jean Negulesco's *Jessica* (1962) is a fluffy romantic comedy set, and filmed, in a small village on Sicily. The title character, played by

---

[39] On Carol and Christian-Jaque see Chapuy 2001. He pays due attention to the on-screen attractions of Carol's well-rounded personality.

sexy Angie Dickinson, is an American midwife, whose presence completely discombobulates the local husbands, even those with very pretty wives. The wives believe that Jessica has used her "Devil-inspired body" to seduce their men. But their frustrated husbands, who get nowhere with Jessica, have begun to pay much more and closer attention to their wives – yes, with their eyes closed during lovemaking. As some of the wives despair of ever being able to get rid of Jessica, the prettiest of them suddenly breaks into laughter. She remembers something: "I was thinking of something funny . . . It's a story called *Lysistrata*, about a group of women who lived a long time ago. Their husbands kept going off to war, and they didn't want them to. So they decided to deny themselves to their husbands, and pretty soon the husbands stayed home." The wives are astonished: "This couldn't happen here, in Sicily – never!" "But this happened in Greece," they are informed. "They had a strike, a kind of sit-up strike." The wives now reason that such a strike is just the thing to get rid of Jessica: no sex, no births, no need for midwives. "We must all stand together!" (Yes, the pun is intended.) After some hesitation ("But it's Saturday!") they vote. They strike.

Not all the wives stick to the sit-up situation but lay down their arms and backs. Jessica finds her own romance with the local *marchese*, and harmony is restored throughout. She even sets the women straight, telling one of them: "Aren't you women ever going to understand that I'm not the one to be afraid of? It's yourselves." There will be plenty to do for Jessica a few months later.

5   Ridin' High; or, How the West Was Fun

The first full-scale American updating of Aristophanes was George Marshall's *The Second Greatest Sex* (1955), a little-known musical-comedy Western in color and CinemaScope. The *AFI* [American Film Institute] *Catalog* summarizes its plot as follows:

In 1880, Osawkie, Kansas, is engaged in a feud with neighbor towns Mandaroon and Jones City over which town should be the county seat, a position marked by the possession of the safe containing local citizens' records. While the men fight in the hills, the women of Osawkie mourn their long absence [in the film's opening number, "What Good Is a Woman Without a Man?"]. The announcement that the men are returning with the safe causes the women to celebrate, but they grow doubly angry when their husbands and boyfriends show up too exhausted for a proper homecoming. The next day Matt Davis helps build the town courthouse and commiserates with Sheriff Joe McClure about why Joe's daughter Liza will not set a date to marry him. As Joe explains that Liza feels that

Matt is more interested in the town than in her, the stagecoach bearing the satin for Liza's wedding gown arrives. The townswomen, including spinster [and self-described "old-maid schoolteacher"] Cassie Slater, rough Cousin Emmy, and coquette Birdie Snyder, tease Liza, who spurns Matt's attentions until he charms her into kissing him. She almost agrees to set the date, but when Matt is distracted by a commotion at the courthouse, she leaves in a huff. Meanwhile traveling salesman and ladies' man Roscoe Dobbs arrives, causing Cassie to faint after he kisses her. At night Matt serenades Liza outside her house, and the whole family is pleased to witness her run into his arms, although Joe struggles to explain to his curious teenaged son Newt why love and sex cause so many problems. The wedding follows soon after, and the highlight of the reception occurs when Cassie drinks spiked punch and tries to lasso Roscoe. [She succeeds quite easily, at least in a literal sense.] Later Matt carries Liza over the threshold, but, as soon as she readies for bed, he learns that the Mandaroons have stolen the safe back and infuriates her by racing to town to form a posse. Osawkie's men immediately take off again to Mandaroon, only to find that the Jones City men now have the safe. They join the fracas underway in Jones City, but are waylaid by a bout of mumps that has taken over the town. Three weeks later the men are still recovering and send a note to the women explaining that they now must return to Mandaroon. Upon reading the note, the women gather in town to discuss how they can settle the feud. Meanwhile the men appropriate the safe but quickly come to an impassible river. There Matt sends Newt with another message, and, when Liza reads that the men still are not returning, she seizes on Cassie's recollection of the Greek women of Aristophanes' play *Lysistrata*, who went "on strike" against their husbands to end a war. By the time the men come home, the women have barricaded themselves in an abandoned fort, and although the men storm the fort, the women remain resolute. After drinking at the saloon all night, the men want to give in, but Matt convinces them that to do so would be to give up all control over their wives. Just then Newt arrives to announce that the water level in the river has fallen, exposing the safe, and the men rush out to defend it. At the river a fight among the three rival towns commences but ends when the safe falls into a bed of quicksand and is lost forever. Osawkie's men travel straight to the fort, but there Liza informs them that a truce must be signed between the cities before they will unlock the gate, and just then the other towns' men arrive, looking for their women. When their wives are revealed to be in the fort, too, the leaders of the three towns agree [to Liza's suggestion] to found a new, neutral site as the shared county seat, and the ladies open the gate. By the time the joyous crowd disperses, Birdie and Reverend Maxwell are holding hands while Roscoe and Cassie plan to marry, and Newt, after receiving his first kiss, finally understands what the big deal is all about.[40]

---

[40] Quoted from http://www.afi.com/members/catalog/DetailView.aspx?s=&Movie=51646.

Reading this, we finally understand that clear plot summary is not a big deal for all film scholars. My parenthetic additions try to help out a bit, as do a few corrections of spelling errors and adjustments of punctuation. Still, the story's absurdity is just right as a disguise of the marital contest between Aristophanes' men and women, which is far too explicit to make it onto the Puritan screen of the 1950s unchanged.[41] Marshall, versatile veteran of many genres but especially at home in Westerns and comedies, had previously directed *Destry Rides Again* (1939), a milestone of comedy Westerns. It featured the most famous catfight in film history, with Marlene Dietrich and Una Merkel slugging it out over a young James Stewart. After the stylish Western-and-musical spoof *Red Garters* (1954), Marshall was a good choice for this new *Lysistrata*. Attractive as it is in color and widescreen, with vigorous dancing and plenty of feminine eye candy, the film is overall too sweet and unsophisticated to be fully Aristophanic in spirit, something it could not have been in 1950s America. Even the war is made harmless: Nobody carries a gun, no shot is fired, and warfare, if that is the right word, is restricted to fisticuffs. Verbally, too, the film is tame. The only daring word ever uttered is *sex*, first coming out of the mouth of teenage Newt, who mistakes it for a plural. "What are sex?" he asks his embarrassed father. But the word is not all that dangerous since the film's title had prepared viewers, although there it has a different meaning.

The moments in the film that directly deal with Aristophanes are clever and amusing. They contain the film's witty highlight, the song "Lysistrata." Much of the verbal humor in the rest of the film is sophomoric. The Aristophanic background comes to the fore when Cousin Emmy, played by popular hillbilly singer Cynthia May Carver (aka Cousin Emmy), expresses her disdain for men: "They've been gone off to war for thousands of years, and ain't nothin' women can do to stop 'em." But Cassie the schoolteacher demurs: "There *was* – once, in ancient Greece, or rather a play about ancient Greece, by Aristophanes." The following dialogue ensues:

[41] Klein 2014: 63–86 devotes a chapter to the film although her book is on theater. Ridin' high at low noon on the Theory Far-Go stage from Thinkery City, Klein, guns blazing, attacks the film with such killer ammo as "normative masculinity," "performative surrogacy," and "gender normativity" before squeezing off this final salvo to put Marshall & Co. out of her misery (86): "While any inquisitive viewer can certainly weigh the information presented in Marshall's film, it takes an oppositional reading like the kind championed by feminist critics ... to dismantle the film's fairly unified Cold War code of patriarchal but domesticated imperialism." Aristophanes, trapped in the PC Corral, bites the dust, as do his deputies Wit and Humor.

COUSIN EMMY: You can be proud of your book learnin', Miss Slater, but it won't bring the men home. Men love a good scrape, almost as much as they love a good woman. Or a bad one.

LIZA: Just how did the women of Greece stop *their* men, Cassie?

CASSIE: It's only a play: *Lysistrata*. It didn't really happen.

LIZA'S MOTHER: *Lysistrata*? I remember reading that in high school.

CASSIE: Oh, you did?

MOTHER: Wasn't that the one that – Newt, put your fingers in your ears.

NEWT: Oh, I know; you're gonna talk about –

MOTHER: *Newt!*

In order to work as humor, this exchange presupposes audience familiarity with the plot of *Lysistrata*. And indeed no explanation of the play is given. We only see and hear the women huddling together, chattering indistinctly and giggling. One good lady's short high-pitched scream of surprise-delight-shock informs us that the facts of marital life have been imparted to those who did not know Aristophanes; then the scene fades out. That girls in the mid-nineteenth century are said to have read *Lysistrata* in high school is an intentional anachronism. Cassie is right to be surprised. When Liza later asks Cassie how the Greek women kept their men from going to war, Cassie only tells her that they went on a strike but does not reveal what kind of strike this was. Even so, this information provides Liza with the spark she needs. But nothing is spelled out either to her or to the cinema audience, which included minors.

Liza calls the women to assembly in the saloon and proposes the strike (Figure 4.5). Katy, one of the prettiest, comments: "Liza's right. If the men *can't* win this county war and *won't* make peace, then it's up to us, just as it was to the women in Athens." Here, too, the dialogue plays on some audience awareness of classical literature because only Greece and not Athens had been named before. The women's big song number follows. Liza is now fully in the picture about the past:

LIZA:
I can give you all the data
on the gal named Lysistrata,
so you know what a riot she began.
When the menfolk kept a-fightin',
Lysistrata saw the light 'n'
so she sat right down and figured herself
a most ingenious plan.

ALL [*vigorously, as every following time*]:
Lysistrata, Lysistrata!

Figure 4.5 The assemblywomen about to strike in George Marshall's *The Second Greatest Sex*.

LIZA:
– sat right down and figured herself a plan.

CASSIE:
It was so ingenious –

ALL:
Lysistrata, Lysistrata!

LIZA:
She was young and lusty
but was slowly gettin' rusty,
'cause for years she had a-waited
for the man that she had mated
to return to her before she got too old.
All she got from him were promises,
and what good are those promises?

KATY:
They ain't gonna keep your feet warm –

BIRDIE:
And they ain't gonna keep your bed warm –

CASSIE [*in correct English*]:
And they aren't going to keep just anyone warm at all.

ALL:
Oh no, not warm at all. Oh no, not warm at all.
[*To Cassie:*] Oh, tell us what she did.

The women's request to know what happened in antiquity rather contradicts the earlier scene in which apparently either Cassie or Liza's mother had already told them what Lysistrata had done. But the current scene works better this way, for now the repressed spinster can let the pussycat out of the bag, sort of. She does so in a way completely unobjectionable to anyone in the audience:

CASSIE:
Well, she told her friend Lampito,
if they gave their men the veto,
that like as not they soon would call a truce.
So they captured the Acropolis
and turned that whole metropolis
right upside down,
inside out,
and every which way but loose.

ALL:
Lysistrata, Lysistrata!

CASSIE:
– turned that whole metropolis upside down.

ALL:
It was so ingenious!
Lysistrata, Lysistrata!

LIZA:
It was mighty darin',
but she had those women swearin'
that there'd be no bill-'n'-cooing –

BIRDIE [*alarmed*]:
No more pitch-'n'-wooing?

LIZA:
– till the menfolk said
their fightin' days were through.
It was quite an ultimatum –

KATY:
Did that ultimatum got 'um?

LIZA:
Yes; in twenty-one years
they came back home
and raised a family.

ALL:
They raised a family.
They raised a family.
Oh why, oh why can't we?

KATY:
Do we follow Lysistrata?

ALL:
Oh yes, oh yes, we gotta.

TWO OLDER AND RATHER AMPLE WOMEN:
'Cause in twenty-one years we'll be too thin and frail.

Twenty-one years? Since the Peloponnesian War began in 431 BC and *Lysistrata* was performed in 411, Liza's chronology is pretty accurate. But it presupposes the historicity of something that, as Cassie had already told everybody, never happened. How were contemporary viewers to understand this? Or did it not matter? After all, *The Second Greatest Sex* was not meant for ancient historians or for dour Aristarchuses, petty Pecksniffs, and other dry-as-dust denizens of Thinkeries. And therein lies part of its charm.

Cousin Emmy, taking a dim view of men and women alike, now interrupts:

Well, in all my life I never did see
sich downright plain stupidity,
snifflin' and a-wailin' for
a pack of ornery males.

Cousin Emmy is herself a bit on the ornery side. But no matter. The women remain undaunted:

ALL:
Lysistrata, Lysistrata!

KATY:
Do we swear to follow her all the way?

ALL [*raising their right hands*]:
Yes, oh yes, we swear it.
Lysistrata, Lysistrata!

LIZA:
You know what you've sworn to do,
so now I'm only warnin' you:
you've made a solemn promise!

KATY:
Are we stickin' to that promise?

ALL:
Oh yes, oh yes, till our men come home for good.

LIZA:
Well, girls, I'm mighty proud of you;
we're doin' what we've been forced to do.

ALL:
We ain't gonna let 'em hug us,
we ain't gonna let 'em kiss us,
we're just gonna let 'em miss us, never fear.
They'll miss us, never fear.
They'll miss us, never fear.

THE TWO OLDER WOMEN:
We wish that they were here!

ALL [*filing out*]:
Lysistrata, Lysistrata!
If it worked for her,
it'll work for us
if we stick together.
Lysistrata, Lysistrata!
Hope it works for us!

The text gives no more than a faint impression of this upbeat three-minute number. Marshall rightly keeps it visually unremarkable, with a static camera and minimal and unobtrusive editing in order to concentrate completely on the lyrics. The music is simple and repetitive, but its tempi are snappy and its rhythms jazzy. Small wonder: It is by Henry Mancini. All this is just right for the turning point of the plot.

"Liza McClure" is an appropriate name for our heroine, played by alluring Jeanne Crain. "Birdie Snyder" is equally fitting for the character who sports the most outstanding physical attributes. Was "Birdie" chosen for its common slang meaning, especially in regard to all the great birds in Aristophanes' *Lysistrata*? Birdie was played by buxom blonde Mamie Van Doren, Universal's answer to Twentieth Century-Fox's Marilyn Monroe. ("Mamie" is a nickname taken from Mrs. Eisenhower.) Birdie is "cosseted

Figure 4.6 Liza (l.) and Birdie (ctr.) in George Marshall's *The Second Greatest Sex.*

and corseted from neck to ankle in 'period' costumes flatteringly and eye-poppingly designed" for her (Figure 4.6). "Mamie," a wise scholar has observed, "is, once again, in dumb blonde mode, although she has a number of good lines."[42] Here are a few. Looking at Liza's wedding dress, Birdie innocently confesses: "Oh, if I had a white satin wedding dress, I'd never take it off. Well, hardly ever." When she later learns that the men have raised a pair of bloomers as their flag of truce, Birdie says: "I wondered what had happened to them." But she is not entirely uneducated. Liza rejoices in the success of the women's strategy ("It worked for the women of Greece, why wouldn't it work for the women of Kansas?"), and Birdie is reassured: "For a while I was losing my faith in history."

But why dwell on Birdie the broad-chested bimbo? Not only because most male viewers in the theater will have closely watched this Birdie just as they were meant to but also because she is a near reincarnation of Aristophanes' Spartan Lampito, as the following lines from *Lysistrata* indicate. When Lampito first appears on stage, Lysistrata comments on her beauty: "What rosy cheeks, what firmness of physique!" Calonice, however, comes straight

---

[42] Both quotations are from Lowe 2008: 85. Lowe, 82–90 provides credits, a brief summary, comments, and visual evidence of Miss Mamie's sex appeal.

to the points: "And what a fine set of tits you've got!" Lampito's reaction ("Hey, you're feeling me up like a beast for sacrifice!") leaves no doubt as to the exact manner in which Calonice pays tribute to the firmness of Lampito's physique.[43] In his commentary on the play Jeffrey Henderson observes: "The beauty of Spartan women was legendary" and "the (conventionally) small-breasted Attic wives express their admiration of their buxom colleague."[44] *Plus ça change, plus c'est la même chose*: Male attitudes to women's curvaceously curving curvatures have not changed all that much in the course of time between Lampito in Athens and Birdie the bosomy broad in Hollywood.[45] In the well-rounded personality of Mamie Van Doren, *The Second Greatest Sex* can boast a fine set of assets. Size does matter, so thanks for the Mamieries! An early female feminist film critic even coined the term "Mammary Woman" to describe the phenomenal phenomenon.[46] With its tone of astonished resignation, the German release title of *The Second Greatest Sex* may have put the case best: *Das gibt es nur in Kansas* ("Only in Kansas")!

Academically parabatic aside: Is it too much to speculate that the name Lampito may contain a naughty pun on *lampas* ("torch, light, lamp") even if there is no etymological connection? Probably, but the point is worth bringing up, if not to scholars then to cinephiles. In Raoul Walsh's *They Drive by Night* (1940), a *film noir* set in the milieu of truckers, a driver observes about a new truck-stop waitress: "Classy chassis." Further banter follows between her and the men, but she has the last line: "You couldn't even pay for the headlights." The waitress is played by sassy Ann Sheridan, Hollywood's Oomph Girl, a serendipitous fact that only heightens the innuendo. In the British farce *Carry On Cabby* (1963) a novice female driver is concerned about how to attract male customers and receives this piece of advice: "Just flash your headlamps at them." The popular front wins.

Readers whom all this strikes as vulgar – correctly, of course – may wish to remember that neither Hollywood nor Aristophanes ever had the slightest intention to appeal only to sophisticates. The pectoral obsession

---

[43] Aristophanes, *Lysistrata* 80 and 83–84. The translations are from Henderson 2000: 279.
It behooves me to report that this moment is boldly recreated in the Greek comedy *I gynaikokratia*. On this film see below.

[44] Henderson 1987: 77, on *Lysistrata* 79 (with quotation of Homer, *Odyssey* 13.412) and 83, with additional comment on *to khrêma* as Calonice's "emotional reaction to something strange, extraordinary, sizeable or numerous of its kind" in this line. For a well-rounded view of this matter see Gerber 1978.

[45] Cartledge 1990: 39 calls Diallage, the personification of Athenian and Spartan reconciliation, "the literal ancient equivalent of a modern 'sex-goddess' like Marilyn Monroe."

[46] Rosen 1973: 281, in chapter titled "Mammary Madness" (267–282 and 385 [notes]).

of American males – *O mammaries, o mores!* – is best expressed in the cinema by the entire *oeuvre* of Russ Meyer, simultaneously worshipped and exploited in the person of Jane Russell in *The Outlaw* (1943), and spectacularly satirized in writer-director Frank Tashlin's *The Girl Can't Help It* (1956) with the help of pneumatic girl Jayne Mansfield.

The comments on Jayne's pectoral abundance by two of her directors are, well, revealing. Tashlin said about American men: "The immaturity of the American Male – this breast fetish ... Imagine a statue with breasts like Mansfield's. Imagine *that* in marble. We ... make an idol of a woman because she's deformed in the breasts. There's nothin' more hysterical to me than big-breasted women – like walking leaning towers."[47] Andrew Marton was practically at a loss for words concerning *It Happened in Athens* (1962): "she was immense. I mean her bosom was just – you wouldn't believe it in a caricature ... We tried to minimize them, but how can you minimize a mountain?"[48]

Jane Russell may be a comparable case. Her film *The Outlaw*, produced and partly directed by eccentric Howard Hughes, was entangled in censorship battles for years. "'What are the two great reasons for Jane Russell's rise to stardom?' asked one of the slogans for *The Outlaw* in February 1946, answering the question with a picture of the lady with her reasons highlighted."[49] Hughes even designed a cantilevered brassiere to show off his star's globular qualities, but apparently she never wore it.

Aristophanes never lost sight of the political in his comedies. Tashlin's Jayne is a well-appointed modern case in point. *The Girl Can't Help It* involves several layers of satire on contemporary society and its males. Richard Corliss has put this particular case quite convincingly:

In Jayne Mansfield, Tashlin found the ultimate image of everything fifties capitalism cherished: quantity over quality, shallowness over style, the machine over the individual, the immediate over the sublime. Not that Tashlin rejected these values. His was a satire that epitomized its subject rather than eviscerating it ... Mansfield embodied Tashlin's bracingly gross vision of the monster only a fifties culture could create.

But the satirist is not immune from satire himself. Corliss again:

After all, it was Tashlin who had the breast fixation ... When he has Mansfield hold two quart bottles of milk against her breasts, and then say, "Everybody thinks of me as a sexpot – nobody thinks of me as equipped for motherhood," he is defining his own obsessions as well as those of the consumer culture.[50]

---

[47] Quoted from Cameron 1969: 76; cf. further the observations, with illustrations, at 75–81.
[48] Quoted from D'Antonio 1991: 357.   [49] Quoted from Cameron 1969: 113.
[50] Corliss 1974: 83–84.

We can never know if Aristophanes had the same obsession. But his women are no mere objects of satire, and neither are Tashlin's. Corliss comments on the latter in terms that may make us think of *Lysistrata*:

The subject of his non-Lewis films was usually the bourgeois, suburban man's image of voluptuous womankind, and his blond heroines – Jayne Mansfield [and others] – were sweet, gentle, often intelligent women who had to pretend to be sexy and brash in order to fulfill the image their men had of them. Tashlin gives these women a sympathetic ribbing, and saves his ridicule for the weak-chinned men . . . whose breast fixation Tashlin simultaneously shares and deplores.[51]

Buxom blondes who are intelligent may have been too much for any weak-chinned male to have contemplated. Beauty may be skin-deep or chest-high, but true attractiveness is a different matter.

After this doubly hemispherical excursus, back to *The Second Greatest Sex*. As always in history, the men are worried about who is wearing the pants and who the panties (or bloomers). Liza's husband explains why: "If we give in to them now, the war won't be the only thing that's finished around here. We'll be finished as far as any claim to self-respecting manhood is concerned, and any time they snap their fingers we're going to have to jump and like it." Altogether, then, we can assent to a contemporary reviewer's verdict: "What Aristophanes started 2,400 odd years ago with *Lysistrata*, Universal has now finished in grand style in its *The Second Greatest Sex*."[52]

But *which* is the second greatest sex? Women, as we might expect in patriarchal America? Are the men *El sexo fuerte*, as the film's Spanish release title puts it? Not this time. The song following "Lysistrata" makes it all clear. Liza's father, the henpecked sheriff, tells it as it is to the other men after the women's strike has begun to show its effect: "*We're* just the second greatest sex, the unimportant sex, to women." Sheriffs are authority figures in serious Westerns, but rarely in comedy Westerns. The fact that this easily cowed sheriff is played by old-time vaudevillian Bert Lahr, best known to filmgoers as the Cowardly Lion in Victor Fleming's *The Wizard of Oz* (1939), adds an amusing detail. In 1966 Lahr would appear as Peisetaerus in a successful stage version of *Birds*.

Only in Kansas, though? Actually, in other states, too, at least sort of. In Andrew V. MacLaglen's comedy Western *The Ballad of Josie* (1967),

[51] Corliss 1974: 87. Tashlin made a number of comedies with Jerry Lewis and Dean Martin. Readers with an interest in Mansfield similar to Tashlin's may wish to consult, e.g., Jordan 2009: 145–188 and 209–211 (notes; chapter titled "Sex as Cinematic Eroticism: Jayne Mansfield's Breasts" and naturally illustrated). This book provides references to further Mansfieldiana.
[52] *Variety* (October 5, 1955); quoted from Lowe 2008: 90.

Doris Day plays the titular widow who gets entangled in a Wyoming range war with cattlemen. She is independent-minded enough to face all male opponents and the first to wear pants and a pair of men's boots, and she incites the local women to revolt. Wives begin to fight with their husbands in their bedroom, Josie reports. A classical parallel is now at hand, but the screenwriters rather miss their chance. Josie is compared not to Lysistrata but to someone else. "You're worse than that Greek gal that caused all the fightin' twixt her folks and the Trojans," her chief male enemy tells her, moments before he throws in the towel. Josie has won, but on her wedding day she burns her jeans. All the data on the gal named Josie make clear that she is not really a Lysistrata.

In Volker Vogeler's *Valley of the Dancing Widows* (1975), a German-Spanish Western comedy, the wives of a small Texas town learn to be completely independent of their husbands and much better off without them. Against their wives' wishes, the men had marched off to fight in the Civil War. When they return four years later and expect to take up their former male and marital prerogatives again, the women resist them, both with a sex strike and to the point of turning themselves into the kind of ladies announced in the film's title. A supplementary title expresses the matter concisely: "A German Film Idyll Laced with Arsenic."[53] Writer-director Vogeler explained that he was reacting to personal experiences:

> I heard about this story [of Hungarian wives] and remembered it when, in my private life, I got into difficulties in my marriage, which did not exclusively result from my own personality, and for this very reason awakened a certain feeling of inferiority in me. I think that after 10,000 years of concrete male-dominated culture a kind of changing of the guard is something normal, right, and logical; that men, at least for a time, will perish before something new develops.[54]

Even when they present us with outrageous and in-your-face zaniness, the greatest comedies deliver food for thought together with laughter. In Aristophanes or, for that matter, in the dark comedies of Plautus, Shakespeare, Ionesco, or Beckett, the very seriousness underlying the plot reinforces a play's power. Comedy, as our next two films show, does not solve actual problems.

---

[53] The text continues with the information that the plot is based on a true story: Hungarian wives resorted to poison in order to get rid of their husbands returning from World War I. This and other information is taken from Hembus 1995: 627–628 and Weisser 1992: 342.

[54] Quoted from Hembus 1995: 628. The names of one male and one female who appear in Vogeler's film are worth mentioning: Crazy Butch and Scarlett O'Hara.

6 (Trans-)Mission Accomplished?

"One of the giants of Weimar and post-World War II German speaking theatre as an actor and director."[55] This is an accurate assessment of the stage career of Fritz Kortner, whose adaptation of *Lysistrata* is our next subject. Kortner is best known to cinephiles from G. W. Pabst's *Pandora's Box* (1929), an adaptation of two plays by Frank Wedekind: *Erdgeist* ("Earth Spirit") and *Die Büchse der Pandora*. Kortner played the upper-class newspaper publisher who ruins himself for and is eventually killed by Lulu, the modern Pandora with whom he is sexually obsessed. The part of Lulu is the cinematic apotheosis of American actress Louise Brooks, who personified the independent-minded woman of the Jazz Age in her personal life and in her films, at least as far as producers or directors allowed her. Kortner, who was Jewish and had been born as Fritz Nathan Kohn, was attacked and vilified in the Nazi press on several occasions.[56] In 1933 he emigrated with his family to England and, in 1937, to America. He returned to the Federal Republic of Germany in 1947.

Kortner made his debut as a television director with *Die Sendung der Lysistrata* (1961) from his own script. The title contains a wordplay: it means both "The Mission of Lysistrata" and "The Transmission [*or* Broadcast] of *Lysistrata*." It was produced in Hamburg by Norddeutscher Rundfunk, one of the public German television stations, and shot on 35mm film stock. It tells parallel modern and ancient stories (Figure 4.7). As Kortner put it: "The road from 400 BC to 1960 A D is only a brief dolly shot."[57] A promotional brochure provides this plot summary:

Several interested parties have gathered at the home of Dr. Salbach, a physicist, to enjoy, or to get irritated by, a television production of Aristophanes' comedy *Lysistrata*. Two actresses who perform in the play are present among them: Mrs. Salbach, who plays Lysistrata, is the wife of the host. He has received an academic job offer as nuclear scientist in the U.S.A., but this evening he is beginning to doubt whether to accept or not. The other is capricious Uschi Hellwig, wife of an attorney, also present, and the play's Myrrhine. Furthermore Dr. Kienast, another physicist, and his wife. Kienast is a political opportunist who, with fanatical obstinacy, has always taken the stronger side or at least what he took to

---

[55] Bock 2009: 256.

[56] In his memoirs Kortner mentions several instances: Kortner 1969: 245–246, 261–266, and 272.

[57] Kortner's statement and the following summary are taken from *Illustrierte Film-Bühne* no. 05602. The Hamburg television museum (*Fernsehmuseum Hamburg*) has published a number of photographs taken on the set at http://www.fernsehmuseum-hamburg.de/bilder galerievondendreharbeiten.html.

Figure 4.7 The two stories of Fritz Kortner's *Die Sendung der Lysistrata. Illustrierte Film-Bühne.*

be the stronger side. The spark for a highly explosive ignition within this company is provided by Ellinger, a journalist recently fired, gruff, aggressive, and embittered.

The play begins. *Lysistrata* by Aristophanes is on the screen. Lysistrata, the beautiful Athenian woman, is determined to end, once and for all, the man-killing slaughter, the nearly endless Peloponnesian War of brother against brother. She assembles the women of Athens and a female ambassador of Sparta, the enemy, before the Acropolis to describe her plan to end the war by feminine ways and means. She persuades the women, who at first are outraged, to refuse themselves to their husbands until these declare their readiness for honest peace negotiations. The marital strike is successful – in the play.

Meanwhile, in front of the television screen, a "war" fought with sharpened intellectual weapons is in full swing. At issue are problems of our own time. No agreement is reached.

This text only hints at the main issue Kortner tackled in the modern story: pacifism vs. rearmament, a hot topic in 1950s Germany, and, beyond this, nuclear armament. Salbach's wife, the Lysistrata in the play, is terrified of a nuclear apocalypse: "To destroy more and more, that's what's at stake." She tells her husband, who believes in deterrence as justification of his research: "Whatever you work on, fertilizer or fuel or whatever, it turns into bombs." Whereas Salbach eventually declines the American offer, Kienast, who is ignorant about Aristophanes' play, considers all talk about pacifism to be "un-German" and "anti-American intrigues." Kortner also referred to the Holocaust and added the possibility of continuing anti-Semitism, another sensitive topic. Kortner is firmly against the establishment. Kienast, Salbach's boss, and his wife are upper-middle-class right-wingers and do not cut very good figures. Before the broadcast Mrs. Kienast asks: "Who is it by?" When she is told "Aristophanes," she immediately draws the conclusion: "A left-winger [*Ein Linker*]." Ellinger informs her about political history: "In 411 BC, they didn't exist yet." But she pays him no heed.

Kortner's film is barely known today, although at the time it caused a scandal throughout the country and led to extensive discussion in the media. At that time Germany had only public television channels. Program oversight was in the hands of regional administrations within the *Bundesländer*, the individual German states; their common programming was broadcast nationwide. Several states at first refused to show Kortner's film after an internal preview but relented when he agreed to make cuts. Still, the ultra-conservative Free State of Bavaria and four others with conservative governments prevented the film from being shown. In response, the producer opened it in cinema theaters in these states on the very evening of its television broadcast.[58] The German film industry's voluntary self-censorship board (*Freiwillige Selbstkontrolle der Filmwirtschaft*), which determines the minimum age for admission to all films and can refuse approval of a commercially more attractive lower age unless cuts are made, allowed Kortner's film to be released theatrically without any cuts to viewers eighteen and older. His text was published as a

---

[58] See "*Lysistrata*: Südlich der Gürtellinie." Like this one, many, if not most, of the articles and reviews published in *Der Spiegel* at that time were unsigned. Kortner's film was broadcast on a Tuesday (January 17, 1961) at 10:15 p.m., not exactly a prime slot. Programming run by the different public stations in common had already ended.

book, and by a Bavarian publisher at that.[59] Kortner himself was the subject of a long article on the film and his career in the left-leaning newsweekly *Der Spiegel* and was featured on its cover.[60]

It is worth recalling, even today, some of the reactions to Kortner's film that were published in *Der Spiegel*; in the *Frankfurter Allgemeine Zeitung*, a leading centrist daily; in *Der Stern*, a general news, culture, and gossip glossy and self-styled muckraking weekly; and in *Hör Zu*, the country's largest radio and television weekly published by a huge and influential right-wing conglomerate.[61] The main point of criticism was that the film dealt too openly with sexuality. Although its producer protested his best intentions ("I would never produce anything that would make me feel embarrassed in front of my children"), the director of one public television station confessed: "I would not want to watch this television film together with my wife. Nor with my nineteen-year-old son." Another one said: "I cannot broadcast 'Lysistrata'; it would violate the [federal] broadcasting law. I consider the film to be aesthetically below the limit, morally offensive, and politically one-sided."[62] Dr. Clemens Münster, who as boss of German television in Bavaria had caused the whole scandal about the film, remained firm in his opposition:

Münster did not find the Kortner product simply bad ("A term I consciously avoided") and not immoral, either; no, with all the obstinacy he could muster he found it violated the viewers' moral sensibility.[63]

More to the point, Münster objected to Kortner's portrayal of those in favor of nuclear armament "in a manner that is simply unfair."[64] But things got even worse. Unintentionally revealing his own discomfort and his insecure

---

[59] Kortner 1961.
[60] "Kortner: Na sowas." "Na sowas" (colloquial German for, roughly, "Well, I declare!") are the film's final words. The article's author, generally critical of Kortner, calls the film "boring" and states that Kortner availed himself of an opportunity to make himself ridiculous.
[61] I here summarize and quote from the account provided by Pundt 2002: 262–265 (section entitled "Die paternalistische Entscheidung über die Moral: *Die Sendung der Lysistrata*"). Quotations without specific source references are from Pundt.
[62] The three quotations are from "Lysistrata: Ehestreik gegen Atomtod": 84. My translation "below the limit" is a literal rendition of *unter der Grenze*, a phrase that means, more idiomatically, "beyond the limit" and implies "below the belt."
[63] Telemann 1961. His title puns on the common meaning of *Münster* ("Cathedral"). Bavaria was (and is) a bulwark of Catholicism. Telemann reports that Münster had once hoped to adapt *Lysistrata* himself but had abandoned the plan as impossible. On Telemann's views of Kortner's film, which he considered an unqualified artistic failure, and on his defense of its broadcast and his sarcasm concerning the public-television bosses see also Telemann 1960.
[64] "Lysistrata: Ehestreik gegen Atomtod": 84; also quoted in "*Lysistrata*: Südlich der Gürtellinie": 58.

grasp of the entire matter, a columnist for *Der Stern* wondered about the wives' non-compliance with what at that time was commonly referred to as their marital duties:

How can people who recommend the refusal of such fundamental private rights in order to enforce political points of view refuse superintendents of public broad-casting the right to reject an affair with Mr. Kortner on behalf of their political points of view? Measured against the wives' love strike, the pre-emption of Kortner's "Lysistrata" [on television] is truly a humane and downright harmless weapon of destruction.

Got that? What was he thinking? To judge by his style, probably not much. His convoluted sentence structure and vagueness of expression hide a tortured logic that would not be out of place in the Thinkery of Aristophanes' *Clouds*. But the critic's imagery – "affair" and "weapon of destruction" (in the original, *Vernichtungswaffe*) – is something else alto-gether. Humane destruction? Censorship as a kind of V-2? Perhaps this is an instance of what psychoanalysts call the return of the repressed. What a columnist in *Hör Zu* could muster is less offensive but still feeble, although expressed in forced-humor mode:

So immoral, so public-enemy-like, so pernicious as one might have expected it really wasn't after all; but unfortunately the artistic mastering of the task Kortner had set himself was imperfect. So rest in peace, Lysistrata!

The case for the defense seems to have been made rather half-heartedly. *Die Welt*, another widely read right-wing daily, concluded, wearily as if tired by something *infra dig*, that "things more *dégoutant* [had] been shown on television than women denying themselves to their men in order that these end their wars." Evidently, patriarchal blinkers were still firmly in place. The *Frankfurter Allgemeine Zeitung*, however, rose to make the case for Kortner, if not for Aristophanes:

The filmic image does not contain any erotic derailments. If the television stations that originally wanted to refrain from broadcasting [the film] thought they could not offer their public certain instances of lasciviousness, then this reservation must have been based on Aristophanes' original text that, translated into German, the television broadcast largely utilizes.

Well over half a century later, much of this is either depressing or hilarious, depending on one's disposition. But there is more. *Der Spiegel* had on its staff a satirical television reviewer who wrote under the pseudonym "Telemann." As classical-music lovers know, Telemann is a regular German name, but here it is meant as a pun: "TV Man." Under his professional name Martin Morlock, also a pseudonym, Telemann was a writer, a journalist, a contributor to satirical journals and to Germany's most popular cabaret troupes, and the author of television serials. His scoffing columns (*Glossen*) became popular nationwide.[65] Telemann turned to the Kortner scandal on two occasions, satirizing and attacking primarily Kortner and Münster. Telemann set himself up as the ultimate artistic arbiter of the film, referring to himself in the third person and confessing in a tone of world-weary satiety: "Both times [watching it in a theater and at home], before his eyelids became heavy, he could feel no stirring of the senses that would not have occurred during a ball given by the nobility."[66] The arbiter also distinguished ancient Greek vocabulary of measurement (in translation) from contemporary German: "one should examine what difference it makes whether our maturing youths in the theater or in the living room are trying to figure out what actually an 'eight-inch comforter' might be." The phrase, not all that mysterious even to those used only to metrical measures, was cut by Kortner himself before the broadcast.[67]

Telemann ended his first *Lysistrata* column with a witty broadside against Münster and Bavaria, exposing the philistinism that had been on plentiful display all around. He adopted Bavarian dialect and the persona of Josef (or Jozef) Filser, a satirical creation of the late popular Bavarian author and satirist Ludwig Thoma. Filser is a bigot who reveals his parochialism in his utterances. Telemann presented his Filser *redivivus* as a reactionary member of the Bavarian parliament who – guess why – went to see the film in a Munich theater. This Filser draws attention to the callipygian asset of Kortner's most beautiful actress: "Romy Schneider wagged her hind quarters a few times so you'd be led to think that she's right horny. But, the Devil take it, there warn't nuttin' to see."[68]

Kortner changed the play's ending. As peace negotiations between Athens and Sparta are under way, Kortner's Proboulos sees an opportunity to attack the Spartans unawares. He also intends to "liquidate" Lysistrata, which causes Ellinger in the modern story to interject: "One victim … ridiculous. We were used to quite different numbers." The Proboulos,

[65] They have been collected in Bartz and Ruchatz 2006.   [66] Telemann 1961.
[67] Telemann 1960. The expression is Aristophanes' (*Lysistrata* 109); Kortner had transferred it from Lysistrata to Myrrhine.
[68] This is worth quoting in its inimitable original, whose spelling expresses the broad Bavarian backwoods brogue: "Die Romy Schneider hat ein bar Mahl mit dem Hinterkwardier gewakelt, damit man meinte, daß sie recht lüstern ist. Aber g'sehn hast ums Verrecken nix" (Telemann 1961). Not so! Pundt 2005: 167 reports that Schneider's low-cut dress momentarily exposed a nipple. Careful autopsy confirms – barely and only from very large image projection.

foiled, then pretends to go along with Lysistrata's plan and even offers to put up a statue to her in Athens, but only in order to get his hands on the money stored on the Acropolis, which the women still occupy. Lysistrata, however, sees through his slimy scheme. Kortner's casting for the Proboulos may have given some viewers a jolt. Suabian Willy Reichert had been popular on the stage as a regional comic and successfully continued his career in the 1950s and 1960s on radio and television, mainly as a jovial and cuddly type.

At the end Kortner's Lysistrata appears on her marital bed and caresses its linen, then apostrophizes both in rather a maudlin effusion of poetry that is worth quoting even though its tone is impossible to reproduce in translation:

Bedstead, thou framework of begetting love, for all our lifetime you grant a hidden refuge to our nocturnal bodies, until body and love grow cold and we breathe out our strength. Bedsheet, witness closest to our skins and discrete sufferer of our nightly activities, thou flag of life, be hoisted, since now man and woman are reconciled and man and man have united against the banner of death. Wave in its stead, thou white sheet of life. Wave in all directions under the sky ... [69]

Such solemnity may have struck viewers as rather bizarre, even kitschy, and we can imagine the shade of Aristophanes scoffing. But it is just possible that Kortner was influenced by some lines in Euripides' *Alcestis*, a tragedy about a devoted wife who voluntarily dies for her husband. A servant woman reports that a weeping Alcestis took her last farewell from her marriage bed by repeatedly kissing it and by addressing it as the place where she had given up her virginity for the sake of the man for whom she is now giving up her life.[70]

Kortner's film has a remarkable cast, among whom Romy Schneider, a blond Myrrhine, is the internationally best-known member. Schneider had become famous in a series of popular costume romances in the 1950s as the young Bavarian princess Sissi, the future empress Elizabeth of Austria, and was eager to shed her image as a saccharine cutie. Myrrhine

---

[69] The original: "Bettstatt, du Gerüst zeugender Liebe, / lebenslang bietest du Unterschlupf / unseren nächtlichen Leibern, / bis erkaltet Leib und Lieb / und wir verhauchen unsere Kraft. / Bettuch, hautnächster Zeuge / und verschwiegener Dulder / unseres nächtlichen Tuns, / du Fahne des Lebens, sei gehißt, / da versöhnt Mann und Frau / und Mann und Mann vereint sich haben / gegen die Flagge des Todes. / Wehe statt ihrer, du weißes Tuch des Lebens. / Wehe in allen Richtungen unter dem Himmel ...." The text is slightly different but even more poetic at Kortner 1961: 85.

[70] Euripides, *Alcestis* 175–188. Alcestis also imagines her husband in the same bed with a new wife.

was just right for this. Schneider, as the actress who plays her, tells her husband: "I play a very lascivious woman, seductive, largely coquettish, and wearing far too little." The last of these descriptors applies only to Myrrhine's scene with Cinesias, in which the disclosing disclothure referred to above occurs.

Schneider's career was at this point in a slump, but it would take off again in 1962. In writer-director Luchino Visconti's "Il lavoro," a segment of the episodic film *Boccaccio '70*, Schneider played an aristocrat's wife who demands payment for conjugal sex when she finds out that her husband pays call girls for the same sort of thing. Schneider later acted in a few erotic and controversial French films, including Jacques Deray's *The Swimming Pool* (1969) and Andrzej Zulawski's *That Most Important Thing: Love* (1975).

Barbara Rütting, Kortner's dark-haired Lysistrata, was appearing in mainstream commercial cinema. After giving up her acting career, she became involved in politics on behalf of human and animal rights and the environment and was briefly arrested in 1984 when protesting American missiles in Germany. In 2003 and 2008 she was elected to the Bavarian Parliament (*Landtag*) for the Green Party (*Bündnis 90 / Die Grünen*) and, being the oldest member, opened its sessions as its *Alterspräsidentin*. She left the party in 2009, not least because of its support for the presence of German troops in Afghanistan. After retiring from politics, she continued to be engaged in peace and related activities. This erstwhile Lysistrata reminds us of Aristophanes' *Assemblywomen*, for she became a *Lysistratê ekklêsiazousa* and head of her own *ekklêsia*, if only briefly and in a nominal capacity.

Aristophanes' Lysistrata successfully accomplished her mission. So did Kortner's. So, perhaps, did the modern equivalent of his Lysistrata, Salbach's wife. Still, the modern story of Kortner's film does not have the happy ending contemporary viewers may have expected. But then, during neither Aristophanes' nor Kortner's time were conflicts or wars ever stopped by art. Kortner later characterized his film as "primarily pacifist but not successful."[71] Still, it seems to have influenced the 1962 Spanish

---

[71] Kortner 1971: 137. This book, the continuation of Kortner 1969, was published posthumously and edited by Kortner's widow. In 1975 West German television broadcast an adaptation of left-wing playwright Rolf Hochhuth's *Lysistrata und die NATO*, set on a Greek island on which the US intends to install a missile site against the Soviet Union. The local wives, fearing a retaliatory attack and urged on by Dr. Lysistrate Soulidis, a member of parliament, go on strike against their husbands, who are ready to sell the necessary plots to the Americans. East German television, wholly state-controlled, had broadcast adaptations in 1955 (*Lysistrata*) and 1959 (*Lysistrata oder der Bettstreik der Athenerinnen* ["Lysistrata or the Athenian Women's Bed Strike"]). *Unternehmen Ölzweig* ("Operation Olive Branch"), the East German stage adaptation of British playwright Ewan MacColl's 1947 version of *Lysistrata* by that title, was broadcast on television in 1961; it was also broadcast as a radio play. The latter's description, available at

production *Escuela de seductoras* ("School of Seductresses"), directed by León Klimovsky.[72]

About eight years later, Kortner found an unexpected ally, although it is unlikely that he ever became aware of this ally's existence. A spirited, dedicated, and smart filmmaker took up Lysistrata's banner and defended her against entrenched male sexism in politics and society. For the first time in film history, this was a woman. Her film about *Lysistrata* was not as scandalous as Kortner's, but it, too, met with initial incomprehension. Unlike Kortner, she found a measure of cultural and artistic vindication.

7   Lysistrata the Feminist: Zetterling and Her Girls

Contemporary social, political, and cultural concerns fed directly into Aristophanes' work.[73] In the case of *Lysistrata*, Henderson's commentary demonstrates this on many a page. But if Aristophanes was politically concerned, and if he put unforgettable women on the Acropolis, in the assembly, and elsewhere, was he also a proto-feminist? Modern (female) feminists tend to think so, and some classical scholars have attempted to make a case for this view, if not without awareness of the differences between then and now. In the preface to her book on what she calls Aristophanes' "woman plays," one of them writes:

http://www.ddr-hoerspiele.net/lp/unternehmen-oelzweig.html, begins by calling Lysistrata "the brave, beautiful Greek woman" and ends like this: "The people of our republic, for whom the daily struggle for peace and socialism has become the content of their lives [*Lebensinhalt*], recognized in Lysistrata and her friends courageous pathbreakers from ancient times."

[72] Several other versions followed. They include Carl Mesterton's *Lysistrate* (1963) for Finnish television; a 1964 *Lysistrata* directed by Prudence Fitzgerald for the BBC-television series *Festival*; Dimitris Spentzos's short *Lysistrati '67* (1967); the French *Lysistrata* (1973), directed for television by Georges Folgoas from a stage production directed by Robert Manuel; the Belgian *Lysistrata* (1976), directed by Ludo Mich and with a cast performing naked to emphasize Aristophanes' anarchic attitude (and presumably in imitation of Kenneth Tynan's *Oh! Calcutta!*); Vito Molinari's Italian television film *Mai di sabato, signora Lisistrata* ("Never on Saturday, Mrs. Lysistrata," 1979), a version of the musical comedy *Un trapezio per Lisistrata* ("A Trapezoid for Lysistrata," 1958), set during the Cold War and with a title that perhaps pays tribute to Jules Dassin's *Never on Sunday*; Inger Åby's Swedish-television *Lysistrate* (1982), with Lena Nyman in the title role; Dimitris Tzelas's video *I Lysistrati ap' to Thiseio* ("Lysistrata from the Theseion," 1986); the Russian *Komediya o Lisistrate* ("Comedy About Lysistrata," 1989), directed by Valeri Rubinchik; and the French-Hungarian *La grève de l'amour* ("Love Strike," 1991), directed by Nino Monti as a segment (twenty-five minutes) of the "Série rose" of late-night erotica and featuring one Euripides. The partial echo of the title of Feuillade's film seems wholly accidental. Cinephiles at least hope so.

[73] Sidwell 2009 is one recent scholarly study of this.

all [these plays] appear to speak quite eloquently to contemporary concerns about women's rights and interests, the value of women's work, and the relationships between women and war, women and literary representation, and women and politics .... if we strive to understand these works more accurately, then both the cultural distance and the cultural proximity of late fifth-century Athens to late twentieth-century America will become clearer .... I try to retrieve what ... the plays meant within that culture ... [and] the value of these plays for a late twentieth-century reader, specifically a female reader, and suggest ways of evaluating their current and future cultural relevance.[74]

This sounds laudable, if a bit idealistic. More realistic, at least about Aristophanes' most famous woman play, are the following comments by Henderson:

The remarkable feature of Lysistrata's success is the degree to which it depends on fantasy and wishful thinking ... Since these are comic characters in a comic situation, they offer the spectators only comic choices. Whether or not Ar. held the same views in life as his sympathetic characters hold onstage, we may be certain that he would not have argued his views as a citizen with anything like the methods employed by his characters ... It was the comic poet who gave communal expression to the social currents running beneath the surface of public discourse .... Lysistrata reminds the spectators of the blessings of peace and denounces the evils of the present war (not all war: 1133–4) in terms with which none of the spectators would quarrel ... None [of the women] questions her ordinary role or seeks in any way to change it. On the contrary, the women want only to return to their normal lives.

About Lysistrata herself Henderson concludes: "she is not merely a representative of her own sex but also an advocate of traditional values for all Greeks male and female."[75] Another scholar concurs:

Both the proto-feminist and the pacifist readings of the play are demonstrably wrong. But this is not where classicists can, or should, stop. When contemporary audiences are reading something into the play which is either not there (feminism) or not quite there (pacifism), they ... are projecting something onto the ancient play which helps, or perhaps enables them in the first place, to interact with it in ways that are meaningful to them. This kind of productive misreading ... is a necessary part of making the ancient text "ours."[76]

Yet another scholar is even more severe: "I would suggest that in each of the women's plays something closely approximating to the normal order of things (including a satisfyingly superior position for the men) is restored at

---

[74] Taaffe 1993: x; the expression "woman plays" appears at 9.
[75] Henderson 1987: xix, xxx–xxxii, and xxxvii.   [76] Revermann 2010: 71–72.

the end ... Restoration of normality means the return of the male to power."[77]

Feminists have on occasion claimed Lysistrata as a sort of patron saint. In 1972, for instance, Germaine Greer adapted Aristophanes for a stage play called *Lysistrata: The Sex Strike*.[78] To Greer, Lysistrata is anything but a female eunuch. Lysistrata exemplifies women's opposition to male dominance and can provide inspiration to her modern sisters.[79]

Some years before *Valley of the Dancing Widows*, a male feminist's film with echoes of Aristophanes, Lysistrata's feminist apotheosis had come with *The Girls* (*Flickorna*, 1968). This Swedish film was directed by actress-turned-director Mai Zetterling and co-written by her and her husband, British novelist David Hughes.[80] Zetterling described her interest in *Lysistrata* in a memoir. Without being completely wrong, she reveals more about the modern understanding of the play than about the culture in which it was produced:

> Aristophanes' *Lysistrata* ... had created such a furore when it had first been played in Greece. Here were all the ingredients that I was so fond of: humour, sensuality, even downright bawdiness. Yet it was at the same time a critical look at the stage of things in society. It was most certainly anti-war and its heroines were strong, thoughtful and plucky ... The film was to be set in Sweden. On tour with the play *Lysistrata*, three actresses, whose own lives are in a mess, begin to realise that the play is a tragedy after all, and become totally involved with the light-hearted way in which Aristophanes treats serious matters – so much so that their own destinies are affected.[81]

The actresses who tour a wintry Sweden in the film are played by three internationally famous Swedish actresses: Bibi Andersson ("Liz Lindstrand"), Harriet Andersson, and Gunnel Lindblom (Figure 4.8). The women's interactions with the men in their lives and with male-dominated society are

---

[77] Rutherford 2015: 63–64.   [78] Greer 2000.

[79] A PBS documentary called *Lysistrata: Female Power and Democracy: From Comedy to Reality* offers insights from Jane Fonda, other feminists, and stage experts. Macmillan Films, an educational video production company, offers this video alongside *Lysistrata: Beyond Sex*. As the company informs us: "To help us tell our story, we've researched an all-star lineup of Greek scholars including ... Jeffrey Henderson (the author of the only compiled translation of Aristophanes' woman's plays)." No dates or director information are provided. It does not detract from Henderson's all-star status to mention that he is not the *only* compiled translator of Aristophanes. The company also has a feature-length film of the play, which it advertises thus: "Immerse yourself in Aristophanes' shocking ancient Greek comic masterpiece." Both quotations are from the company's Internet pages concerning *Lysistrata*.

[80] Sloan 2008 attempts a brief assessment of the film and lists some further references. Her misspelling *Flikorna* occurs throughout.

[81] Zetterling 1985: 195–196.

Figure 4.8 Harriet Andersson (l.), Bibi Andersson (ctr.), and Gunnel Lindblom (r.) in Mai Zetterling's *The Girls*.

influenced by their experiences with the play. "We can't get involved in politics. Our duty is to look after our home and husband and children and husband," one of them has said early on; the repetition of *husband* is revealing. Their social, marital, and political self-awareness is raised, but can the three overcome all-pervasive traditional prejudices? Or will they relapse into the structures and strictures they have lived under all along once the run of their play is over? After one particular performance in the boondocks Liz vainly attempts to engage the audience, and not only the women, in a discussion; her words express the position feminists have assumed about Aristophanes' play:

Can we change ourselves? That's why Aristophanes wrote this play. To get things moving, to make people care . . . to stop us sitting around, believing we can do nothing. There *are* things we can do. Above all, he wants us to stop thinking that we're so marvelous. You're sitting here now, completely satisfied with yourselves. What you've just seen was a trifle. A comedy, nothing to take seriously. A real classic, scholarly and nice, but nothing you give a thought [to] . . . Don't you see? We *have* to talk . . . People have to be able to talk. Don't you understand that it's *we* who make the world what it is?

Liz meets a silence uncomfortable for both sides. The actor who plays the Proboulos – a fascinating character study of a man who is decent enough on the whole but blind to all the stereotypes of women and prejudices against them that a male-dominated society has ever held – attempts to defuse the awkward situation with humor: "What? Another revolt among the women?" He leads Liz, now in tears, off the stage. Her words might as well be Zetterling's own in regard to her film. *The Girls* is Zetterling's call for understanding between men and women and among people in general. But will anyone heed it? Kortner's pessimistic perspective is here taken up again by a female filmmaker, but it goes further: more serious, more realistic. As Zetterling remembered:

When *The Girls* opened in Stockholm in 1968, it was a resounding flop. Swedish audiences seemed unable to grasp the ironical nature of the film, and at the time, we could hardly take comfort from the fact that when it was shown again, some six years later, audiences all over the world were to shout and applaud throughout.

Zetterling went on to quote from a Paris newspaper article about the film, written by Simone de Beauvoir: "All the images have multiple dimensions, the theatrical scenes reflect real life . . . Ironic and comic, this film moves us by the beauty of its landscapes, its poetry and above all its subtle tenderness." According to Zetterling, de Beauvoir was "so impressed that she asked me to make a film of her novel [*sic*] *The Second Sex*."[82] Zetterling concluded:

It was a joy to be appreciated after all the rejections I had had and it was also important to meet other women who were trying to direct films . . . . I had always liked women with guts but I didn't like to see them behave like steam-rollers, without the slightest trace of humour.[83]

De Beauvoir was enthusiastic about Zetterling, *The Girls*, and the film they were planning together. She described the project in an interview:

I have a really big project, making a film based on *The Second Sex* with a Swedish director named Mai Zetterling, who's done some excellent feminist films. She did a film called "The Girls." You haven't seen it? Well, it's really beautiful. So, we're going . . . to try to look at different aspects of the condition of woman. I'm really interested in it. We're going to collaborate on it and I'm really looking forward to it, since film, if it's done well, has a very strong impact on people. It can make women aware of a lot of things, more than books can, and it can easily reach workers' wives, wives of employees, since everybody has TV nowadays. It's a way of speaking to all women; one can do this more effectively through film and television than one can do in a book that they're not going to read. Reaching them through books is a bit too difficult. I'll be busy with this through the coming year, maybe even two years

---

[82] The preceding two quotations are from Zetterling 1985: 204.   [83] Zetterling 1985: 218.

because it will take a long time to make, since *The Second Sex* covers the entire condition of women.[84]

In a manner of speaking, *The Second Sex* is to meet *The Second Greatest Sex* via *The Girls*. But de Beauvoir and Zetterling never made their film, which was too ambitious to become reality. If they had pulled off this Herculean labor, the result might have been something unique in the history of cinema, in the history of feminism, and indirectly in the reception history of Aristophanes.

In the scene of *The Girls* described above, Liz does not behave like a steamroller. Quite the contrary. But she shows no trace of humor. Shortly after, she is asked about her impromptu call for discussion and action during a press conference: "Do you really believe in Lysistrata's method?" She replies: "It's one way. I don't know if it's the right one." She then imagines herself doing a striptease before the assembled journalists and before her husband and his two mistresses. She takes off her bra and flings it into her husband's face. The other women in the cast strip to their underwear. Zetterling suddenly cuts to a broad farcical male-against-female brawl in the play: "Get them, girls!" The twofold abruptness – from modern reality to modern fantasy and to ancient stage fantasy – speaks volumes. In the battle between the sexes, women's victory is assured, but not in reality. "Actors are always quoting lines, confusing theater and reality," one of the modern husbands later observes – before his wife imagines first him as a buffoon, then both of them in a contemporary *Taming of the Shrew* moment: He spanks her in public, and she enjoys it.

Liz soon imagines her own funeral, in which the Proboulos actor functions as a political demagogue and delivers a rousing sexist speech on this "joyful occasion." To thunderous applause he tells the assembled men that now, with her dead, they can do anything, even start wars: "You may kill, betray, cheat, exploit, and destroy! As much as you want!" (A case of *Get them, boys!*) In turn, Liz has a surrealist vision in which the three women address their listeners from City Hall, the equivalent of the Athenian women occupying the Acropolis in Aristophanes. One speaks through a bank of microphones from the balcony – no, not to the citizens but to a square filled with cars, their horns sounding in comment or protest. No drivers or passengers are visible. The second woman speaks through a megaphone on the building's steps, but only to a group of schoolgirls. Liz herself speaks quietly to a small number of middle-aged women, but this gives way to a general squabble, in which she is attacked. Things looked

[84] Quoted from Brison 2003: 197. The interview took place in 1976.

different in the play. Zetterling shows that women can win in ancient and modern fantasy but that reality is different.

In the course of the film we watch a number of scenes from *Lysistrata* being performed; the final one is the happy ending. The tour is now over, too, and the actresses are interviewed on television while the principal male actors, the Proboulos and a young Cinesias, react to their words being broadcast. This balances an early scene in which the actresses were interviewed while still in rehearsal and the same men commented as they do now. What have the men learned? The older one observes: "A man has a right to a life of his own. It's different for women." The younger one retorts: "They'll grow up one day, too." The other replies: "They haven't since Aristophanes' day. So why now?" At an elegant reception held in the cast's honor, the older actor compliments Liz on her interview: "You were fantastic on TV, darling." She returns: "I'm always fantastic." Her husband adds: "You should see her in bed – or in the kitchen." This exchange prompts Liz's final flight into imagination, on which the film ends. The images on the screen start as a realistic-looking fantasy (I use the paradoxical expression purposely) but then are progressively distorted until everything has become unrecognizable: not a happy ending at all. The second greatest sex is still the first sex.

With its high contrast, the film's exceptional black-and-white photography makes for a suitably somber atmosphere in which, again and again, reality and imagination are juxtaposed and the former turns seamlessly into the latter. Quotations from Aristophanes' play, laid over images of modern reality, diminish our sense of security aurally; some striking wide-angle shots distort our perspective visually. Together they make for an unsettling effect and a feeling of uncertainty, insecurity, or even alienation on the viewer's part. Zetterling's staging of the scene between Myrrhine and Cinesias in the play is a particularly clever example. She incorporates the modern husband and a modern setting into the original. Ancient costumes, modern dress, and modern surroundings are predominantly rendered in an exaggerated, even blinding, clinical white, with some black accents interspersed here and there.

That's why Aristophanes wrote this play: Scholars tell us differently. Aristophanes was not a social reformer, not a feminist, and certainly not a precursor of Carry Nation. But Zetterling's perspective is powerful and moving enough to make even the Athenian playwright agree, providing he could understand twentieth-century mentalities. My description here may have given readers who have not seen the film a false impression. *The Girls* is certainly committed and serious but also witty and funny. Although virtually no male cuts a wholly decent figure, the females come in for their share of criticism and satire as well.

In content and style and with its remarkable cast, *The Girls* is much indebted to the cinema of writer-director Ingmar Bergman, with whom Zetterling, her three principal actresses, and some of the men in the cast, primarily Gunnar Björnstrand as the Proboulos actor and Erland Josephson as Liz Lindstrand's husband, had all been closely associated. Bibi Andersson had appeared in Bergman's *Now About These Women* (1964; *All These Women* in the US) and, most memorably, in *Persona* (1966). Harriet Andersson became internationally famous in Bergman's *Summer with Monika* (1953; *Monika, the Story of a Bad Girl* in the US); the following year she was in his comedy *A Lesson in Love* and followed up with the part of a saucy maid in his erotic comedy *Smiles of a Summer Night* (1955). She, too, was in *Now About These Women*. Gunnel Lindblom gave extraordinary performances in *The Virgin Spring* (1960) and *The Silence* (1963). Bergman's entire body of work deals with love, marriage, and male-female relations, often as intense psychodrama but sometimes as comedy. *A Lesson in Love, Smiles of a Summer Night, The Devil's Eye* (1960), and *Now About These Women* are famous instances of the latter. Best known internationally among the former are *Cries and Whispers* (1972) and *Scenes from a Marriage* (1973), originally a five-hour television film. Robin Wood, one of Bergman's most perceptive critics, has observed:

One of the first things the outsider notices about Bergman's films is the remarkable strength, energy, and forcefulness of the women – both the characters and the actresses who play them: if there is a "weaker sex" in the film, it is clearly not the female.[85]

Wood was not thinking of Aristophanes or *Lysistrata*, but certain analogies suggest themselves.

Zetterling had first been associated with Bergman on Alf Sjöberg's *Torment* (1944; *Frenzy* in the UK), which Bergman had written, and first acted for him in *Night is My Future* (1948). She then appeared in international productions, especially in England and the US. Her writing-directing debut came in 1962 with *The War Game*, a short film co-written with David Hughes. In Zetterling's words:

The theme was to be one that I kept repeating in all my movies in one way or another, sometimes as a sub-plot: war, or rather anti-war. The work was also to be a condemnation of the stupidity which can lead to war.

---

[85] Wood 2013: 284–285, in chapter section titled "Bergman's Women . . . and His Men" (ellipsis in original).

Two boys, playing on a building site, become more and more engrossed in their game, until things begin to get nasty.[86]

The War Game is without dialogue, so its message is immediately clear. Following it, Zetterling and Hughes wrote, and she directed, *Loving Couples* (1964), which featured part of the same cast as *The Girls*. Zetterling describes the series of novels by "Swedish Proust" Agnes von Krusenstjerna, on one of which Zetterling's film was based, as "a severe, funny, often moving critique of family life and hypocrisy in human relationships. It was very Swedish, but had a universal theme." Her film is in elegant black-and-white and has an intricate flashback structure. Zetterling characterized it in words that foreshadow *The Girls*:

Loving Couples was a film about women and their deeper attitudes to the fundamentals of life: birth and marriage, sexual relations, human feelings, freedom. It explored the differences between their attitudes and those of men. The tragedy of women, Agnes von Krusenstjerna believed, was their natural loneliness, which only a child can fully assuage; a man is not enough. Women are imprisoned in a world that doesn't belong to them, whose language they don't speak. And yet, a woman's world without the rough texture of men is unhealthy.[87]

Zetterling's Bergmanesque *Night Games* (1966) and *Doctor Glas* (1968), the latter based on a novel by Hjalmar Söderberg and dealing with love and sexual obsession and with marriage, adultery, and murder, are little-known today. Zetterling was the only woman among the eight directors of *Visions of Eight* (1973), a film about the 1972 Summer Olympics in Munich. In 1982 she contributed three segments to the international anthology film *Love*. The following year she remade, as *Scrubbers* and from a female perspective, Alan Clarke's *Scum*, a 1979 exposé of the British borstal (youth prison) system. *Amorosa* (1986), about an intellectual couple's love and marriage and the incursion of mental illness, was her last feature-length work. As these short descriptions show, in spite of Bergman's influence *The Girls* is Zetterling's own.

The year after her death in 1994, the three actresses from *The Girls* met at Zetterling's house and reminisced about their film and their profession. The meeting was preserved in Christina Olofson's documentary *Lines from the Heart* (1996). In retrospect, their reactions to *The Girls* are rather mixed. Here are some of their comments:

I saw it as an ironic picture of the actress and the housewife. It didn't apply to me.

---

[86] Zetterling 1985: 181–182.   [87] Quotations from Zetterling 1985: 183.

I didn't like my character to have such an old man. Why did she choose an old married man and to have children [rather, one child] by him, too?
And I played the one who was always late and apologizing.

On their director:

She tried to combine extremes. It didn't really work.
I admire her for being so strong.
Was Mai political, or was she just an artist?
She probably wore people down and forced them to say yes.
She saw the reality. – I think she was wrong.

The penultimate quotation turns Zetterling into a kind of Lysistrata. But a woman who wanted to be an artistic and not a commercial filmmaker had no choice but to wear down her predominantly male opposition. The actresses are aware of this. In 1995 the women who in *The Girls* played women who were experiencing male power and playing women revolting against males still reveal a sense of frustration with balancing or combining work and family. At the end of Olofson's documentary we see Gunnel Lindblom in rehearsal for a stage production of Euripides' *Iphigenia in Aulis* and watch her, as Clytemnestra, pleading with her unyielding husband for the life of their daughter. Bibi Andersson, Zetterling's Liz and Lysistrata, became a political activist after visiting war-torn Sarajevo; she grew highly critical of politicians, whom she has compared to bad actors. Perhaps unintentionally, Olofson echoes the parallelism of fiction and reality in Zetterling's film: One of the actresses sees the reality and acts on it, the other enacts it on stage. Mai was both political and an artist. Even if she tried to combine extremes, *The Girls* did really work.

8   The Beeb Lurking in Pompeii

In 1969, inspired by the success of *A Funny Thing Happened on the Way to the Forum*, British producers David Croft and Sydney Lotterby, comic Frankie Howerd, who had played Pseudolus on the London stage, and writer Talbot Rothwell launched *Up Pompeii*, a series of half-hour episodes broadcast by "the Beeb," as comedian Peter Sellers had dubbed the venerable British Broadcasting Corporation on *The Goon Show* in the 1950s. *Up Pompeii* ended in 1970 after thirteen episodes, but it was briefly revived in 1975 and 1991. A feature film by the same title was released in

1971. After Howerd's death an updated stage play toured Britain in 2011. Rothwell was the principal screenwriter for a number of entries in the popular *Carry On* series, including *Carry On Cabby*. Writer-producer Croft is best known today for the classic television series *Dad's Army* (1968–1977), *Are You Being Served?* (1972–1985), and *'Allo 'Allo* (1982–1992).

Up Pompeii is a loud and broad farce set in the early Roman Empire – sort of, because historical anachronisms abound. The entire enterprise is more Plautine than Aristophanic. An Olympian Plautus – up in the clouds – appears briefly in the early episodes and dispenses, like a one-person Greek chorus, words of medium-funny wisdom about what is happening on earth. The episodes work chiefly through puns and naughty double entendres. Feminists and prudes need not tune in. Howerd plays a Pseudolus-like clever slave called Lurcio. (Helpful mini-parabatic aside: Pronounce this, dear reader, as *Lur-kee-o*.)[88] His owners are henpecked and senile senator Ludicrus Sextus ("all tuss and no sex"), Sextus' nymphomaniac wife Ammonia, and their teenage kids Erotica, a sexpot, and Nausius, a puerile twit of a wannabe romantic poet. In each episode Lurcio addresses the unseen studio audience as if he were an imitator of Lester's Pseudolus. The fourth wall, the illusion of a self-contained stage world, is intentionally broken. Classical and other scholars are fond of calling this aspect of dramatic performances meta-theatrical or self-referential.[89] Episodes begin with Lurcio's attempts to tell audiences a story, but he is invariably interrupted. His stories never get told.

Aristophanes provided *Up Pompeii* with its most inspired moments, which come in an episode called "The Peace Treaty." Two earlier episodes had, as it were, set the stage. In one, a wall poster announces the opening, at the Hippodrome of all places, of performances of three famous dramas. These are "OEDIPUS REX! MEDEA!! LYSISTRATA!!!" Lurcio confesses to us: "I'm a bit of a thespian myself, you know." He then professes his love for the stage: "All these Greek tragedies, like, you know, *Lysistrata* and *Oidipus* – *Eedipus* – and, eh, *Never on Sunday* . . . I like *anything* like that." At the beginning of a later episode Lurcio announces: "our story today concerns Lysistrata. Now you've heard of Lysistrata. Now her real name

---

[88] Howerd reincarnated, as it were, his Lurcio in two feature films: as Lurkalot, history's unknown twin brother of Richard Lionheart, in *Up the Chastity Belt* (1971) and as Lurk in the World War I farce *Up the Front* (1972).

[89] This trend in scholarship on classical comedy began (in earnest) with Slater 1985 and continued with Slater 2002. Dobrov 2001 deals with both comedy and tragedy. On tragedy see, e.g., Bierl 1991. We can easily imagine what fun Aristophanes could have had with their Thinkery-type terminology had he but known of it.

actually was Elizabeth Strata." Predictably, her story does not get told but has to wait until "The Peace Treaty." Here Peacenik Nausius is faced with imminent conscription into the Roman army. He embarks on a "peace movement" and composes an "Ode to Peace." His four-line "odes" are regular ingredients in the episodes and always work on the same principle. Lurcio reads them to the audience, with a strategic pause during the fourth line, for which studio and home audiences have to supply the final rhyme themselves. So it is here:

LURCIO [*reading*]: *Ode to Peace*
 O'er all their promises of peace
 [still] blows the martial trumpet. [*He looks into the camera to
 prime the off-screen audiences.*]
 But we don't want a peace of words;
 we want a peace – [*looking at the viewers again, he pauses to let
 the innuendo sink in, then continues over huge laughter*] of
 mind and body.
NAUSIUS [*as always*]: I was lost for a rhyme there; I'm sorry.
LURCIO: Yes, you will be more sorry if you didn't.
NAUSIUS: What we really need here is a Lysistrata.
LURCIO: That's ridiculous. You can't find *Lysistrata* to match with *trumpet*.
NAUSIUS: No, no, Lurcio. She was the famous Greek woman who stopped the
 men from going to war.
LURCIO [*somewhat surprised*]: Oh, oh.
NAUSIUS: Lysistrata!
LURCIO: *That* Lizzie; yes.

Lurcio apparently does not remember the time when he himself had been prepared to tell the story of that Lizzie. But consistency is the hobgoblin of unfunny minds. The dialogue continues:

NAUSIUS: You know how she did it?
LURCIO: Yes, everybody knows how she – [*interrupts himself*] – did what?
NAUSIUS: Well, she stopped the men from going to war by persuading their
 women to – [*he stops himself*]
LURCIO: Well?
NAUSIUS: Oh, well, by – not to.
LURCIO: Not to *what*?
NAUSIUS: You know, Lurcio: not to let their men – [*making stealthy sounds and
 gestures*] . . . Oh, Lurcio, I can't say it out loud!
LURCIO [*loudly*]: On *this* show? You can say anything! Now, come on; don't be
 shy. Go on a bash.
NAUSIUS: Well, not to – *cohabit*!

LURCIO: Cor, he *said* it! The dreaded seven-letter word: *cohabit.* Wasn't so bad,
     was it? I can't think what all the fuss has been about.
NAUSIUS: Oh well, we'll never find a Lysistrata here.
LURCIO: No, I don't think we ever will.

But of course they will; or, rather, Lurcio, smart slave that he is, will. Soon he,
too, gets served with his "call-up tablets" and begins to look for a way out:
"because then the men wouldn't go off fighting if they didn't get their bit of
cohabit first. And if *they* didn't go, *I* wouldn't have to go." He hits upon the
idea to "drag up," which he says is currently fashionable, and "pretend to be
Lysistrata." All excited, he addresses, in close-up, the unseen studio audience: "Let's try it out, shall I? Now, all you women in the audience: If I were
to preach *No cohabiting*, no cohabiting with men, would you support it?"
A resounding "Yes!" follows. Lurcio: "Yes, well, in that case none of you
need bother to come around to my dressing room after the show." Big
laughs all around.

   Lurcio drags up as Titicata, a name whose justification is obvious up
front from her pleasingly plump personality. Titicata organizes the women
of Pompeii in a strike, and placards proclaim their slogans: NO PIECE
WITHOUT PEACE! and BAN THE BANG BANG. Titicata is, well, the
man of the hour or, rather, of "D-Day" ("D for *Don't*"), and Nausius
promptly falls in love with her. So does Captain Bumptius, the local
recruiter:

BUMPTIUS [*amorously*]: My dear Titicata – may I just call you –
LURCIO: No, you *mayn't*! I ought to shorten *your* name, Bumptius!

The plot proceeds apace, but, given its raucous nature, details had better
remain undisclosed and undisclothed. The climax is a hilarious scene in
which lecherous but bumbling Bumptius attempts to seduce Titicata to
break the women's resistance through her. Titicata is having major mis-
haps with the front of her costume. For the sake of scholarly accuracy
(what else?) I add that these are not, strictly speaking, wardrobe malfunc-
tions in the current sense; rather, the falsie-fied contents of Titicata's
dress yield to the force of gravity at inopportune moments. The captain
gets his comedownance, and Titicata's strike is successful, but only for
a while. In a final twist it is the women who march off to war and on their
victorious return chase after the men, including Lurcio. None of this is
sophisticated, but Aristophanes might have been pleased by all the
bumptious rambunctiousness. This episode is the highlight of the entire
series.

9   Lysistrata Defies Greek Dictators and Helps Bring About Gay Lib

Aristophanes died around 386 B C. More than 2,300 years later his work was granted the ultimate proof that he had done exactly right by his Muse: "Right-wing governments from the 1950s through the 1970s felt [his] presence with such discomfort that they banned his comedies" in Greece.[90] Most infamous among these governments was the military dictatorship that ruled from 1967 to 1974. An exception (of sorts) to its ban of Aristophanes was *I gynaikokratia* ("The Rule of Women," 1973), a comedy-farce directed and co-written by Errikos Thalassinos. In this film a modern battle of the sexes parallels the story of *Lysistrata*. Scenes from the play appear in flashbacks. The ancient settings are appropriately inauthentic; the women's costumes are skimpy, loose, and revealing, especially when a convenient breeze lifts a skirt or two. Moments of male and female callipygia also appear. When the women swear an oath to go on their strike, their arm-and-hand gestures come close to, and in some cases are identical with, the modern Fascist Salute.[91] The plot is partly indebted to an actual Macedonian custom: One day each year women assume authority over men. One year, the leader of the women in a village, who is also the mayor's wife, decides not to hand power back to their husbands. These in turn decide to "refrain from loving" them until they return to their usual roles.[92]

One directly Aristophanic film could be made with official support. This is *Lysistrata* (*Lysistrati*, 1972), directed by Giorgos Zervoulakis and starring the husband-and-wife team of Jenny Karezi (or Kareze) as Lysistrata and Kostas Kazakos as Cinesias. Both were popular performers but also enemies of the junta; in 1973 they were imprisoned for several days because of a stage play they produced together. Kazakos became best known internationally for his tragic Agamemnon in Michael Cacoyannis's *Iphigenia* (1977).

Their *Lysistrata* is a high-spirited if occasionally labored musical-comedy-farce filmed in modern Athens.[93] Costumes, inventively silly for the men and daringly sexy for the women, and hearty overacting indicate the overall level of sophistication (low). Verbal humor, of course, is prominent. Lysistrata exhorts her women: "Let us raise the eternal flag of the

---

[90]   Van Steen 2000: 4.

[91]   Valverde García 2012: 96 briefly discusses this film. As mentioned, 1967 also saw the short film *Lysistrata '67*.

[92]   Koliodimos 1999: 594–595 (no. 2258).   [93]   On the film see Valverde García 2010.

Cretan-Mycenaean-Athenian super-civilization! Let us tear the paper tiger of male imperialism!" But there is a clear political purpose as well:

Kareze and Kazakos subordinated the forms and themes of Aristophanes' play to their modern historical and ideological conception. They incorporated . . . even parodies of contemporary political opposition . . . . Kareze . . . cast herself as a militant heroine of the Greek War of Independence [1821–1830], yet toyed with Western-style feminism and with controversial American music and flags. Against the main backdrop of the hippie and pop culture of the late sixties and early seventies, her women constantly intimidated the pathetic older men who represented the junta leadership. Explicit sex scenes expanding the movie beyond Aristophanes' text flouted the regime's . . . self-assigned mission to "save" Greece.[94]

The film's most explicit scene is the one in which Cinesias implores his wife Myrrhine to relieve his pent-up energies.[95] But its funniest is the one in which the women respond to Lysistrata's exhortation quoted above. From behind an entrance draped with the Stars and Stripes and to the tune of the US Marines' official hymn ("From the Halls of Montezuma / To the Shores of Tripoli"), a phalanx of women advance, not quite in lockstep, on the men ogling them. Marching in place and lifting their long skirts in close-up, the ladies, with come-hither smiles, expose their panties, decorated with peace symbols, to the panting paper tigers. Two especially bold belly dancers go further and lasciviously writhe in close-up to fake oriental music. The cowardly lions low-tail it out of there while being pelted from above with vegetables, cucumbers among them.

The peace panties of *Lysistrata* were so amazing that they featured prominently in a newspaper cartoon advertising the film. A word balloon reads *Molôn labai*, a misspelled version of Leonidas' famous *molôn labe* ("Come and get it") as a defiant sexual come-on spoken by one of the women, who is lifting her skirt: "The deliberate spelling mistakes . . . must have offended the establishment all the more for subverting heroic words of antiquity."[96] The visual gag is more daring than a later American equivalent. In Mel Brooks's *History of the World, Part I* (1981), Roman soldiers enter the private quarters of Empress Nympho – a spoof of Poppaea – who is in the company of several buxom Vestals. "All right, virgins! Put on your *No Entry* signs," commands the empress. The Vestals, played by *Playboy* playmates and wearing immaculately white if loosely

---

[94] Van Steen 2000: 206.
[95] After Aristophanes, *Lysistrata* 865–979. The scene does justice to Cinesias and his name, which Cartledge 1990: 39 aptly renders as "Roger Screw-ton of Bang-cock." Cinesiastic cinephiles may think of Rock Hardson or Rod le Rock (or le . . .).
[96] Van Steen 2000: 207, with reproduction of the cartoon.

flowing dresses (*Let joys be unconfined!*) protect their virtue with strategically placed traffic signs. No trafficking here!

In Aristophanes' day the Athenian Puritans, as we could call them *avant la lettre*, may have been shocked, *shocked*, by all the sexual humor and gender-bending that went on in *Lysistrata*. Since all parts were played by men, the implications for such a farce boggle, as they say, the mind.[97] Shocking the Puritans: that is what comedy and satire are all about. Ralf König, a homosexual German comic-book author, is a case in point.

König began publishing in underground and gay magazines and originally appealed only to homosexuals. Today he has fans among gays and straights alike. He is a bestselling artist published by well-known houses both in German and in translation, and some of his comic books have been filmed.[98] Although he seems to be an equal-opportunity offender, König is not lacking in seriousness. He has been especially concerned about questions of sexual freedom in the age of AIDS. In 2006 he took part in public debates about the freedom of the press in connection with Danish cartoons about the Prophet Muhammad. In 2008 he tackled religion in his books *Prototyp* (on Adam, Eve, and God) and *Archetyp* (both "Archetype" and "Ark Type," i.e. Noah).

König had once seen a school production of Aristophanes' *Lysistrata*: "I thought that Aristophanes had forgotten the gays and the lesbians, and I got the idea that this would make for a great comic . . . It was the first time that I took up someone else's idea in order simply to dust it off a little and to turn it into my own version."[99] His *Lysistrata* (1987), a hit as a comic book, was filmed in Spain as *Lisístrata* (2002) by Francesc Bellmunt. König did not believe that Aristophanes had any political or social changes in mind but wrote "just a comedy" despite its serious background. For that reason König sees "no point in adducing any political modern parallels," although the play "has a lot to say about relations between the sexes." By contrast, Bellmunt seemed more concerned with bringing out such parallels in his film, which he wrote and co-produced: "I remember the effect that Ralf's comic had on me when, in 2001, the US spread a worldwide atmosphere of

---

[97] Henderson 1987: xliv: "Female nakedness is represented by tights to which breasts and genitalia were attached." Cf. Henderson 1987: 195–196 on *Lysistrata* 1106–1127.

[98] *Der bewegte Mann* (1994; literally: "Man, Moved"; in English *Maybe . . . Maybe Not* or *Pretty Baby*), *Kondom des Grauens* (1996; literally, "Condom of Horror"; in English *Killer Condom*), *Wie die Karnickel* (2002; *Like Rabbits*).

[99] This and my following quotations from König and Bellmunt are taken from interviews with them included on the German DVD of the film. Quotations from the film's dialogue below are translated from the German-dubbed version, which König approved, unless otherwise indicated.

war, and realized that it [the comic] had a clear anti-war message. These ideas survived more than 2,000 years." Bellmunt wanted to make "an antiwar comedy in ancient dress, and that's what *Lisístrata* turned out to be." In preparation Bellmunt read Aristophanes and several works of scholarship on him and his time. He observes: "König has modernized Aristophanes' message perfectly. I would not, in principle, say that he treated the original text of *Lysistrata* ironically. He respects its humor and adds a modern perspective without losing the central thought."

Lisístrata is a very free version of Aristophanes, made as a full-fledged costume drama. It combines its Greek setting with obvious importations from Roman culture, familiar from numerous historical films. Lysistrata is played by Maribel Verdú, best known internationally from Fernando Trueba's *Belle époque* (1992) and Alfonso Cuarón's *Y tu mamá también* (2001). The year is 411 BC, but the war is said to have been going on for thirty years. Lysistrata and Lampito organize the wives' revolt even though both are lesbians. Their motto: "The power is with us – Women's Power!" For emphasis, the women cup their breasts with both hands when they utter this cry. Lysistrata, Lampito, and the others take over the Acropolis with its war chest, and the Spartan wives soon follow their example. The soldiers on both sides begin to suffer mightily from sexual frustration. It shows – protuberantly. They become so incapable of fighting that Hepatitos, the middle-aged transvestite leader of the effeminate Athenian gays, offers generals Inkognitos (who is secretly gay), Thermos, and Acapello (Camarero in Spanish), and all others a new alternative to deliver the straights from the dire straits of their pent-up tensions. The Proboulos – named Ajax in the Spanish but Oropax in the German version – imposes mandatory homosexual relief. The strategy works for a while, and the war begins to peter out. But now the wives become frustrated in their plan for peace because the Athenian and Spartan males have begun to fall in love with one another and, as one specific case demonstrates, cannot rise to their marital occasions. "His noodle was at best *al dente*," complains a newly married wife. So Ajax-Oropax and the Spartan leader Klinex (pronounce this the German way) make a peace treaty. At the end, the acceptance of love between man and woman and between man and man is about to be established. Hepatitos and Lysistrata together deserve credit for peace and equality of the sexes. He tells her: "For us [gays] the matter of peace was at least as important as for you [women]." Women's lib and gay lib go hand in hand, so to speak. This is in pointed contrast to Aristophanes' play, in which "extramarital outlets for husbands that in comedy and in a slave-owning society are normally available must be ignored in order to motivate the sexual tension on which the strike plot turns."[100]

Most of the film's humor is farcical and only intermittently sophisticated. Fake beards abound. The ancient bronze statuette of the ithyphallic dancing satyr that is on postcards for sale all over Greece is here a full-blown statue that decorates the entrance of Club Adonis, a gay disco.[101] We also meet the Spartan envoy Domestos, representative of the Radical Gay Front Spartacus, and a terminally infantile Oedipus who hates his father: "All the time he stands between me and my mommy. I could kill him!" Hepatitos, who exhibits a pronounced mothering streak, takes him under his wings while Oedipus' mother is on her sex strike. Oedipus' authoritarian father comes on to Hepatitos, and for the time being they live together as a happy family, sort of.

Bellmunt adhered closely to the comic, his source, but his ending is somewhat different from König's. While Athenians and Spartans are happy, Lysistrata and Lampito prepare to leave the Acropolis. Before the giant statue of Athena in the Parthenon, they decide not to return home and begin to question the wisdom of the gods, who have absolute power over humans. Why do they not bring about peace on earth? Lysistrata reminds Lampito that Zeus, "the father of all the gods," is "himself a guy." So men will always oppress women: "That is our fate," Lysistrata continues. But: "We women have the power to change the course of fate." Now Zeus himself intervenes. In storm and lightning the women hear a male voice above them, laughing contemptuously. In the German version it proclaims:

Right, Lysistrata – and what a guy good old Zeus is! You have really wonderful ideas. Do you want me to climb down from my Olympus and show you and your little girlfriend? After that you'll certainly won't be lesbians any more.

The voice recedes amid more laughter. In the Spanish version Zeus refers to himself as "the most masculine [*macho*] god in the universe." In both he more than implies a sexual threat. The ending thus sounds an almost incongruously serious note.

An alternate text given to Zeus is a little more upbeat and might have amused Aristophanes, although it does not remove all the gloom. Zeus tells Lysistrata: "Oh yes, Lysistrata. I *am* a guy." Then he informs her that all the

---

[100] Henderson 1987: xxxiii. König was aware of this circumstance.

[101] Allain Rochel's 2008 theatrical farce *Sissystrata* is set in West Hollywood's gay community in the year 2013: "a politically incorrect fantasy in which West Hollywood musclemen are called in to help the Iraq war effort, leaving their sissy boyfriends home to whine, bicker and complain – fabulously." The quotation is from Provenzano 2008.

Figure 4.9 Lysistrata and Lampito on the Acropolis in Francesc Bellmunt's *Lisístrata*.

goddesses have occupied Olympus and will no longer admit the males until they bring about peace on earth: "That's what we get from your ideas!" Zeus still threatens to come down and show the women what's what, thus ending lesbianism once and for all, but a soothing and effeminate Hermes prevents this.

Bellmunt's change to König's ending now follows. The two women have given up on Athenian and Spartan society, but they are not cowed by Zeus and regain their spirits (Figure 4.9). Where to go? "I know a small solitary island," Lysistrata informs Lampito in the German version. Classically trained viewers can easily supply the island's name. In the Spanish version Lysistrata utters it: "We'll still have the island of Lesbos." For these two, and presumably for all other lesbians, the only escape from male power is retreat to a *Women Only* paradise. Bellmunt has commented:

> The ending of Aristophanes' *Lysistrata* is very "positive" and König's ending terribly realistic. The true reality causes Lysistrata's plans to fail. Even Zeus, the father of the gods, is a chauvinist macho bastard! I respect this ending, but injected a little bit of *Casablanca* into Lysistrata's text. Still the ending appears to be very harsh and leads us to believe that there is no way out from patriarchy.

The archetypal prototype prevails.

10 *Katabasis*: Lysistrata in the Lower Depths

Neither König nor Bellmunt is likely to have known of an earlier Lysistrata who exhibited lesbian tendencies. (Ignorance sometimes *is* bliss.) In 1968, a sixty-five-minute pornographic *Lysistrata*, directed by one Jon Matt and produced by a company calling itself ModFilm, presented American viewers with this story:

Hippie model Lysistrata, raped or rejected by the men in Manhattan, has become a man-hater. She forms an all-women sex club, the members of which read Aristophanes' *Lysistrata* and vow their hatred. Their plan is to tease men beyond endurance and frustrate all their attempts at sexual satisfaction. The women satisfy themselves by engaging in autoeroticism and oral intercourse. Pamela comes under Lysistrata's spell and rejects her boyfriend, Fred. For revenge, Fred spies on the secret rites in which Lysistrata demands slavish sex worship. Lysistrata becomes jealous at an orgy, and she stabs each of her disciples. Aware of Lysistrata's crime, Fred blackmails her with torture, but before the whip can be administered, she stabs herself to death.[102]

A poster for the film juxtaposes Aubrey Beardsley's drawing of Lysistrata to some nude or near-nude actresses engaged in various acts of osculation that I ought not to specify here. The same poster proclaims the production to be "A MODFILM CLASSIC" that is "STRICTLY FOR ADULTS ONLY!" Its main tag boldly states: "3,000 YEAR OLD SEX CLASSIC GOES MOD!" The last word is printed extra-large and in the same screaming red as the film's title. If that is not enough to arouse passing males' curiosity, there is more: "A legend of erotic love! SEXCITING!" And: "SEE! sex-happy chicks!" And: "SEE! men frustrated beyond belief!" See this *Lysistrata* then? Better not. Alas, few classics are safe from such sexcessive sexploitation.

Lysistrata fared slightly better in the early 1970s. At this time in Germany, Italy, and elsewhere, then-racy sex comedies, shockers, and other kinds of soft-core "Euro trash" featured plenty of female nudity, displayed by shapely actresses in skimpy outfits. Director Bruno Corbucci, brother of better-known and better director Sergio Corbucci of *Django* fame, contributed a prehistoric Lysistrata to film history with his farcical *Quando gli uomini armarono la clava e . . . con le donne fecero din-don* (1971), released abroad as *When Men Carried Clubs and Women Played Ding-Dong*. (Brief parabasis: Do I really have to explain, dear reader, what playing ding-dong is? I thought not. Still, here is a hint to the innocent: English-language posters tell us that it is "a new name for an old game . . . " – still unclear? Then remember the second placard in *Up Pompeii!*)

Corbucci's film is a cheap rip-off of Don Chaffey's *One Million Years B. C.* (1966), Val Guest's *When Dinosaurs Ruled the Earth* (1970), and a few

---

[102] Quoted from http://www.tcm.com/tcmdb/title/739251/Lysistrata/full-synopsis.html.

antediluvian sex comedies made in Italy.[103] Chaffey's prehistoric adventure story had its greatest asset in curvaceous Raquel Welch; Corbucci's film displays the charms of Nadia Cassini, an actress not quite in the league of the superstars of comparable contemporary fare. Cassini plays luscious virgin Listra, whom tribal stud Ari (after *Aristophanes*???) wins as his wife in a pig-catching contest. But constant battles with a neighboring tribe prevent them from playing ding-dong. So Listra organizes a no-ding-dong strike among the women of both tribes to free their men for better pastimes. A gay caveman lusting after Ari has been thrown into the mix as well. The aptly named Lucretia Love, better known from Roger Corman and Steve Carver's *The Arena* (1974), here plays one Lella. Other ladies are called Lolo and Sissi. *Silly* might be a better term all around.

11   Lysistrata Flips the Script in the 'Hood and Moves into the House of Babes

Black American director Melvin James made *A Miami Tail* in 2003. It is set in the world of black and Latino teenagers and young adults.[104] Hip-hop star Trina plays Alicia Strada, Lysistrata's sista. Trina, of mixed black and Latina heritage, was controversial for her profane and sexually explicit lyrics. Her first hit was "Da Baddest Bitch." The modern equivalent of the Peloponnesian War is black and Latino gang violence in Miami's Liberty City, a neighborhood with a history of drug wars, where the film was shot and where Trina was living. The black gang lord is called Black Zeus, as in: "I think Black Zeus is gonna have to come down from Mount-motherfucking-Olympus and strike his Spic ass down with this" (i.e. his gun). The body part in question belongs to his rival boss.

Black Zeus, descending from his Olympus, almost runs down Alicia's little nephew. Fearless, she confronts him, running the risk of deadly gun violence. Alicia then initiates the sex strike: "We're fools for our men … We give them so much of ourselves. And for what? So they can abuse us and betray our trust? … I'm talking about the world we leave for our children, or should I say: this mess?" Reactions range from surprise to rejection to ridicule: "Oh, girl, lighten up. This one has a near-death experience, and all of a sudden she's Al Sharpton!" After further discussion Alicia

---

[103] I refrain from discussing these except to mention the following titles: *When Women Had Tails* (1970) and *When Women Lost Their Tails* (1972), both directed by Pasquale Festa Campanile and with Austrian actress Senta Berger heading notable casts. They deserved better.
[104] Cf. Wetmore 2014.

explains: "We gotta save our men from themselves . . . . there's only one way to stop the drugs, violence, and destruction: through total and complete abstinence from sex." The others eventually agree, and she declares: "Tomorrow, ladies, we hit 'em where it hurts." An advertising line for the film had already explained to prospective viewers what is at stake: "No peace in the streets means no piece between the sheets." Posters proclaimed: "In this battle of the sexes, these girls won't lay down!" The trailer concluded: "Until they lay down their guns, this gang ain't banging."[105]

Brooms and supplies in hand, the women march to the public playground-and-park, clean it up, put up tents, and lock themselves in: a clever update of the occupation of the Acropolis in Aristophanes. When the men appear and tell the women to open the gate, the following dialogue between Alicia and Black Zeus takes place:

ALICIA: We're flipping the script on your ass.
BLACK ZEUS: Is you stupid?
ALICIA: Yes, for letting you turn this neighborhood into a hellhole. But not any
        more . . . This the deal: We will no longer lay down and be your concubines,
        your bitches, hos, and tricks.
BLACK ZEUS: My concu – *what*?
ALICIA: Con-cu-*bines* . . . *No peace* means *no piece*! No coochie, no *chocha*, no
        cookie, no nookie, *no mas* until you and your dawgs lay down the guns once
        and for all.
BLACK ZEUS: You must be out your motherfucking mind.
ALICIA [*pushing him in the chest*]: Try me.

The black women's example catches on, and the Latinas join them. They all put their men on "pussy probation." Booty calls; but grrls rule, boys drool. A black reverend ruefully confesses to the other males when asked to help them out of this crisis: "I'm just a man of the cloth. And with my wife gone, I'm a man of the Kleenex, towel, Handi-Wipe, whatever I can put my hands on."

Although the dialogue is spicy and funny throughout, the film is visually surprisingly tame. Director James shows no full nudity, although the girls and women look titillating (and assillating in tight low pants that show their thongs). But his strategy works, for it enhances the women's erotic allure and explains their power over their macho men. A peace agreement follows (Figure 4.10). Alicia proclaims the happy ending: "Ladies and gentlemen, it is my extreme pleasure to announce: Y'all can have sex

---

[105] Parallel cases occurred in real life. In 2006, several wives went on a "strike of crossed legs" in Pereira, Columbia, a city with a devastating history of gang violence and murder. Comparable strikes for various political goals have been reported. For a more recent example see Karen Smith 2011.

Figure 4.10 Alicia Strada (ctr.) and rival gang bosses (extr. l. and r.) negotiating for peace in Melvin James's *A Miami Tail.*

again." General rejoicing over this tail peace ensues. Piece, brothers! *A Miami Tail* presents a refreshing contemporary take on an ancient tale and now makes for a witty counterpart to Zetterling's earnest approach. We have come a long way from Coontown suffragettes.

Writer-director Tara Judelle's *Manfast*, made the same year as *A Miami Tail* and also set in Florida, loosely reworks *Lysistrata* without ever referring to it. Four young women who are by no means averse to the opposite sex live together in the pink "House of Babes" (their term) and publish a "post-feminist response to their surroundings" (their phrase), the magazine *Biotch*. (Hint to the benighted: The meaning of the title is identical with one of the words in the magazine's motto: "all the bitch that's fit to print.") In order to help a girlfriend with her research project for a master's thesis in Women's Studies, for which she has received a $25,000 grant (yes, it's a fantasy!), the four agree to keep away from men: no talking, touching, flirting, and certainly no sex for a hundred days. They report on their progress in *Biotch*, and the media take notice. Eventually one of the women's fathers, a rich businessman, delivers a challenge on national television. He offers a million dollars to be paid to the first man who can break the manfast. Yes, one of the fathers! A lame explanation later reveals that he decided on this course of action as "a promotional gag for the 'zine." Hordes of men, more greedy than horny, now rise up and swing into action. A nationwide media circus is the result. "Can they make it without making it?" the film's advertising asked dramatically. At the end, of course, the sexes are reconciled, the strike has caused greater feminist awareness for the one or other of the women, and true love triumphs. Overall, *Manfast* is a good-hearted comedy, too cute and cuddly to qualify as Aristophanic. This is despite a few attempts to be outrageous and some satiric potshots at academia that are added into the pink mix. One *Biotch* article calls the Women's Studies department of the local university "about as cutting-edge as a post-modern feminist dialectic symposium led by Billy Graham and Pat Robertson." Nice try! *A Miami Tail* has much more bite.

12   *Lysistrata* Goes Global

The year in which Alicia Strada was flipping the script in the 'hood made evident that Aristophanes' *Lysistrata* was speaking to contemporary concerns, not only in the US. The Bush administration was waging wars in Afghanistan and Iraq and exploited an invented threat from weapons of mass destruction to persuade the world that the invasion of Iraq was legitimate.[106] A possible third war, an invasion of Iran, loomed on the horizon. In protest, professional, semi-professional, and amateur productions and readings of *Lysistrata* and of Euripides' *The Trojan Women*, a tragedy about the horrors of war and the suffering of the innocent, proliferated. Most remarkable was the Lysistrata Project, a worldwide event that took place on one specific day. It became the subject of *Operation Lysistrata* (2006), a documentary film directed by Michael Patrick Kelly, which won several international awards. The production company provides the following information:

In January 2003, Kathryn Blume and Sharron Bower, two actresses from New York City, thought to organize readings of the ancient Greek play by Aristophanes, *Lysistrata*, as a protest of the imminent preemptive war on Iraq. Originally conceived as a local event, over the course of several weeks word of the Project quickly gained momentum and became a worldwide happening for peace. On March 3, 2003, nearly 1,100 simultaneous productions of *Lysistrata* were performed in 59 countries around the globe. *Operation Lysistrata* illuminates the way in which two women transformed their individual aspirations for peace into a movement which allowed the global community to share in their vision, using grassroots activism, conflict resolution,

[106] Documentation of this and related matters is abundant. A good starting point is Rich 2006. On the Bush presidency see now Jean Edward Smith 2016.

community building, and the role of art in a functioning democracy. The organized readings of the ancient Greek play, all performed on March 3, 2003, was [*sic*] extraordinarily successful. Celebrities as well as small theatre companies world-wide turned out in force for this unique event. Tapes of readings poured in from England, Iceland, Japan, Singapore, Australia, Italy, Montreal, Nova Scotia, the U.S.A. From a Kurdish Refugee Camp in Northern Greece to Havana, Cuba, to Moscow, Idaho, all to document this once-in-a-lifetime and truly amazing experience.[107]

No classical author has ever reached as global an audience as Aristophanes did on 03/03/03.[108] Zetterling would have been pleased. One of the results of the project's impact was the stage play *A Peace of Women* by Egyptian playwright and screenwriter Lenin El Ramly (transliterations vary), produced in Cairo in late 2004.[109]

Two years earlier, the women of the remote Turkish mountain village of Sirt had gone on strike, not for martial but for hydraulic reasons. The only source of the village's water supply, an old pipeline, had fallen into disrepair, and the women had to fetch it from miles away. Eventually most of them had had enough. After about a month of enforced abstinence, their husbands went about repairing their damaged or disused pipes, even appealing for government support. The Sirt sex strike inspired German filmmaker Veit Helmer to make *Absurdistan* (2008). Helmer reports that he traveled to Sirt for initial script research: "The strike and the ensuing extensive worldwide news coverage had created deep rifts within the village community. I was only allowed to speak to the women when the Imam was present."[110] Then he was confronted with a variety of conflicting accounts,

---

[107] This description appears on the film's Internet site (http://aquapiofilms.com/lys01.html) and is here quoted with a few minor corrections of punctuation etc. The page contains a link to images about the Project. See further Hardwick 2010: 86–89; Kotzamani 2006a; Klein 2014: 108–126; Dutsch 2015.

[108] In this light the comment by Ewans and Phiddian 2012 that there were "119 performances worldwide in the years 1990–2010, according to the [Oxford University] Archive of Performances of Greek and Roman Drama" seems rather ill informed, especially since they also mention "dramatised readings" of the play. They focus mainly on their own experiences with performances of the play in Australia, beginning in 2005 and "with modern anti-war slogans (e.g. 'NO MORE BUSH WARS')." The archive summarily reports: "On this day more than one thousand readings of Lysistrata [*sic*] were held in 59 countries to protest against the rush towards a pre-emptive war against Iraq" (http://www.apgrd.ox.ac.uk/productions/pro duction/6279).

[109] On this see Kotzamani 2006b, especially 26–29, and Hardwick 2010: 86–89. The latter mistakenly calls the author a "film director" (86).

[110] This and the following quotations about this film are taken from its Internet site (http://www .veithelmer.com/absurdistan), which provides further details, a plot outline, and numerous illustrations.

even denials that there had been a strike: "Slowly it dawned on me that there were as many 'true' stories as there were people in the village. I decided to invent my own version of the strike – 'Absurdistan'!"

After four years of preparation, Helmer filmed in Azerbaijan, primarily in a village four thousand years old, and with a multinational cast. Dialogue, in Russian, is kept to a minimum. The story of the strike ("No water, no sex!") is cleverly connected with the romance of a couple whose wedding, the consummation of their lifelong devotion to each other from early youth, is on hold until the young man has seen to the repair of the water supply. *Absurdistan* is irresistibly charming, a gentle and whimsical comedy replete with a few touches of Magic Realism.

Helmer further reports: "By the end of each shooting day the crew was utterly fed up with the notion of sex strikes. 17 couples got together during filming, two have already got married and two children have been born!" Had Aristophanes only known! The Internet site of the film's American theatrical and video distributor rightly pointed to Aristophanes' *Lysistrata* as "Recommended Reading."[111]

The women's sex strike has even been projected into the future: *Lysistrata, 2411 A.D.* was an American stage musical from the 1980s.[112] Clearly the lady was far ahead of her time and ours. Samuel Fuller was already aware of this. But 2011 was especially notable for Lysistrata's return to stage and screen and into print. Meg Wolitzer's novel *The Uncoupling* deals with the staging of *Lysistrata* at an American high school, with partly predictable and partly unexpected results. The title part is played by a black student; the American war in Afghanistan is one of the issues the novel tackles. More surprisingly the French film *The Source* (*La source des femmes*; literally, "The Women's Spring"), directed by Roumanian Radu Mihaileanu, is based on the same event as Helmer's film of 2008. Here is a plot summary:

The location is a small remote village, somewhere between North Africa and the Middle East. Since the dawn of time, the women of this village have been forced to go and fetch water from a spring high in the mountains, under a blazing sun. But now they have decided to take a stand. Leila, a young bride, gathers the women of the village together and persuades them they should go on a love strike. They will deny their husbands their conjugal rights unless they agree to fetch the water in their place . . .[113]

---

[111] At http://firstrunfeatures.com/absurdistandvd.html.   [112] Coates and Calandra 1990.
[113] Quoted from http://filmsdefrance.com/FDF_La_Source_des_femmes_2011_rev.html. Further details are available at http://www.lasourcedesfemmes.com.

The political events in the Arab world early in the year, commonly called the "Arab Spring," appear to have provided the filmmakers with their impulse.

Another film released that year is equally noteworthy. Lebanese writer-director and actress Nadine Labaki conceived the idea for her film *Where Do We Go Now?* in 2008, when Lebanon appeared to be on the brink of civil war once again. Labaki was pregnant at the time and began to think about what kind of environment her child might be born into: "I don't think I would have written this film if I were not pregnant." Labaki's film is "a musical-comedy fable" set in a small mountain village in which Christians and Muslims have been living peacefully side by side.[114] Then their co-existence is threatened by a trivial accident:

Set against the backdrop of a war-torn country, "Et maintenant on va où?" [this is the film's French release title] tells the heart-warming tale of a group of women's determination to protect their isolated, mine-encircled, community from the pervasive and divisive outside forces that threaten to destroy it from within.

United by a common cause, the women's unwavering friendship transcends, against all the odds, the religious fault lines which crisscross their society and they hatch some extraordinarily inventive, and oftentimes comical, plans in order to distract the village's menfolk and defuse any sign of inter-religious tension.[115]

A series of chaotic incidents tests the women's ingenuity as they manage, with sass, successfully to stave off the fall-out from the distant war. But when events take a tragic turn, just how far will the women go in order to prevent bloodshed and turmoil?

Labaki's women use a variety of feminine wiles to keep their men's minds off war, but a sex strike is not one of their strategies. Nevertheless the film has reminded viewers and critics of Aristophanes' play. Labaki has said about her film:

what I'm talking about in the film is universal .... this conflict does not only happen in Lebanon. I see it everywhere ... We are scared of each other as human beings ... What's absurd is that anything can happen and we can become enemies ... That's what's absurd.

Labaki overcame various obstacles in getting her film made ("Everybody wanted this film to happen"), and it became an immediate success with audiences in the Arab world and beyond.[116] The fact that she used non-

---

[114] Both quotations are from Hornaday 2012.

[115] Quoted from the film's French distributor's Internet site at http://www.patheinternational .com/en/fiche.php?id_film=693#.

[116] Both quotations are from Hornaday 2012.

professionals in her cast whose own circumstances reflected those of the people in her fictional village may have increased her film's topical appeal.

Two films of 2011 called *Lysistrata* remained largely unknown. One is a Czech version by writer-director Jirí Suchý. The other is American. Its credits state: "Written by Aristophanes" and "Screenplay by Rodney Smith." It was directed by Stewart Goldstein and co-produced by one Don "Fruity" Pebbles. This *Lysistrata* is rated R. Tag lines proclaimed: "A delightful tale of men and women behaving ... badly!" (Ellipsis in original.) And: "The battle of the sexes has never been this much FUN!" The Lysistrata on the film's poster wears a fanciful pseudo-Grecian dress, and a NO ACCESS sign is strategically placed once again. An independent *Lysistrata Unleashed: The Love and Peace Film* (its subtitle varies) appears to have been in development in and around Santa Cruz, California, under the direction of one Phoenix Dr Now (aka Thaddeus P. Now), a "visionary artist, musician, magician, show producer, designer," as the film's Internet site modestly proclaims him to be. This version, should it ever get made, is said to be simultaneously indebted, of all things, to Marcel Camus' classic *Black Orpheus* (1959) and Charles Dickens. Its most obvious debt, to Zetterling's film, goes unacknowledged.[117]

Lysistrata conquered the theater as well. Theodora Skipitares staged an adaptation, written and directed by her, with life-sized puppets; this was a follow-up to three earlier plays, also with puppets, about the Trojan War that she had conceived of in response to the American war in Iraq (*Trilogy: Helen, Queen of Sparta; Odyssey: The Homecoming*, and *Iphigenia*; 2003–2005). Off-Broadway and then Broadway brought *Lysistrata Jones*, a teenage musical set mainly on a high-school basketball court. The show's Internet site proudly summarizes its plot as follows: "Lyssie J. and her girl-power posse [parabatic question: Is this a pun?] won't 'give it up' to their basketball playing boyfriends until they win a game – and ultimately find that abstinence truly does make the heart grow fonder!" One reviewer calls *Lysistrata Jones* "a bright and bouncy [ahem!] new musical that ... expertly delivers plenty of laughs, perky songs, sexy goings-on and a stage smoking

---

[117] The film's general URL is http://www.lysistrataunleashed.com, which contains the following capsule description: "We are making a movie about the ancient and modern message of peace, about the power of women to solve difficult social issues, and about the arts as a crucial inspirational factor in culture. Our vehicle is an ancient Greek comedy, Lysistrata. Our medium is the cutting-edge lifestyle and creativity of Santa Cruz, CA." Various other pages can be reached from the one mentioned here. A rather flamboyant synopsis, given at http://www .lysistrataunleashed.com/about.html, makes one suspect that this project is the last gasp of the Age of Aquarius.

with cute young hotties!"[118] We may suspect, though, that Alicia Strada would sleep through most of its innocuous plot turns. Lyssie's Americanization has a distinguished model in Carmen Jones, the titular heroine of Oscar Hammerstein II's adaptation of Bizet's opera *Carmen*, filmed by Otto Preminger in 1954.[119] So there is no danger that Aristophanes' amazing Athenian will ever fall out of favor.

In 2012 American graphic artist Valerie Schrag contributed a new Lysistrata to an anthology of visual retellings of world literature that includes, to mention only classical authors, Homer, Sappho, Euripides, Aristophanes, Plato, Lucretius, and Virgil.[120] Schrag's is an attractive if not outrageous adaptation, drawn in black and white. The book's editor, introducing her version, comments: "Valerie Schrag has given us a fully ribald, raunchy adaptation, exactly [!] as Aristophanes intended it." He also informs us that she used her own translation, "having been a classics major at the University of Chicago."[121] The exactitude may legitimately be doubted in such a brief retelling, but Schrag's titular heroine is cute, curvaceous, and young, and she wears a sexy dress revealing enough to chase off any philologists complaining about lack of accuracy.

One other twenty-first-century Lysistrata phenomenon, with its own filmic record, deserves mention although it was not inspired by Aristophanes' play. Leymah Gbowee's Liberian Mass Action for Peace, a coalition of Christian and Muslim women, was instrumental in overthrowing Charles Taylor,

[118] The quotations are taken from http://www.lysistratajones.com/about/synopsis and http://www.lysistratajones.com/reviews. On the production, and on Wolitzer's novel, see Klein 2014: 127–145.

[119] Lysistrata Jones is only one musical incarnation of Aristophanes' most famous female character on the stage. No less a composer than Franz Schubert had turned to her with *The Conspirators* (*Die Verschworenen*, 1823), his final opera. And in 1902 popular German composer Paul Lincke had scored the operetta *Lysistrata*, which contained the famous "Glühwürmchen-Idylle" ("Glow-worm Idyll") that became a perennial hit in the US after Johnny Mercer revised and expanded its original English lyrics for a 1952 hit recording by the Mills Brothers ("Shine, little glow-worm, glimmer, glimmer"). The little-known American musical *The Happiest Girl in the World* opened (and closed) on Broadway in 1961, with lyrics by E. Y. "Yip" Harburg; its score was adapted from works by Jacques Offenbach. Here Lysistrata is married to Cinesias, and the goddess Diana (not Artemis) begs Jupiter (not Zeus) to send her to earth as a peacemaker; Diana inspires Lysistrata with a certain idea. Pluto, the Underworld god, is the one who causes wars and worse. "Never Trust a Virgin!" he advises the women. Additional information and photographs can be found at http://www.masterworksbroadway.com/music/the-happiest-girl-in-the-world. In 2005 Mark Adamo composed, and wrote the libretto for, his opera *Lysistrata or The Nude Goddess*. On all this see Beta 2001, 2002, 2005, and 2010. Beta 2005: 185–188 and 2010: 251–252 discusses *Un trapezio per Lisistrata*, the stage version of Molinari's television film *Mai di sabato, signora Lisistrata*, mentioned above. See further Beta 2014; Kotzamani 2014; Iglesias Zoido 2010.

[120] Schrag 2012.   [121] Kick 2012: 82.

president of war-torn Liberia. Taylor was eventually found guilty of war crimes and crimes against humanity. In 2006 he was succeeded in office by Ellen Johnson Sirleaf, the first female head of state in all of Africa. The Liberian Mass Action for Peace included a sex strike. Gbowee reports in her memoirs:

What does it take to make those who fight listen to reason? What haven't we tried? One day, when Asatu [one of Gbowee's earliest Muslim associates] was talking to a journalist, she joked, "Maybe it will just get to the point where we deny men sex." Everyone laughed, but it was something to think about: as a woman, you have the power to deny a man something he wants until the other men stop what they are doing.

As Gbowee comments: "The strike lasted, on and off, for a few months. It had little or no practical effect, but it was extremely valuable in getting us media attention."[122] Fasting and prayers for peace, accompanied by the women's sexual abstention, seems to have been more effective and amounted to "a covert sex strike."[123] Gbowee adds, in retrospect: "Until today, nearly ten years later, whenever I talk about the Mass Action, 'What about the sex strike?' is the first question everyone asks."[124] The ghost of Aristophanes might be pleased. But when American television host and comedian Stephen Colbert asked her, in 2009, about the parallel to *Lysistrata*, Gbowee replied that she "had not read the Greek play" and "didn't have any idea of that play."[125]

The documentary film *Pray the Devil Back to Hell* (2008), directed by Gini Reticker, provides details of the women's campaigns; it has won numerous international awards and has been shown on virtually a global scale. Together with a woman from Yemen, Gbowee and Sirleaf were awarded the 2011 Nobel Peace Prize. The documentary film seems to have increased their chances for this award.

13   A Chicago Tail: *Chi-Raq*

In 2015 Lysistrata went global again. In the wake of increased homicides of black Americans by white police officers, the Black Lives Matter movement, several mass shootings, and continuing black-on-black gang violence, black writer-director Spike Lee released *Chi-Raq*. Screenwriter, director, actor, and film professor Kevin Willmott had written an adaptation of *Lysistrata* some years earlier; Willmott and Lee now updated it and

---

[122] Both quotations from Gbowee 2011: 147.   [123] Hilkovitz 2014: 126.
[124] Gbowee 2011: 147.
[125] Quoted from Hilkovitz 2014: 124, with source reference there in note 1.

set it in Chicago's South Side. Parts of the area are known as the Wild Hundreds and Terror Town. The film's title also contains a reminder of the American war in Iraq: Chicago as a war zone. The expression was coined, Lee has said, by "local Chicago rappers." It is also the street name of one of two gang bosses. Lee reports about the time he was filming: "We started shooting *Chi-Raq* June 1. We finished July 9. During that time, 331 people got wounded, 65 murdered. New York City has three times the population of Chicago; Chicago has more homicides than New York City." "THIS IS AN EMERGENCY" appears prominently at the beginning of the film. Lee calls black gang killings "self-inflicted genocide" and adds: "Cops ain't just killing us. We're killing ourselves, too." As a result, his purpose with *Chi-Raq* was primarily serious:

> This film is righteous. The No. 1 goal of anybody involved in this film – in front of the camera, behind the camera – was to save lives . . . Save lives. This film is about more than Chicago. This film is about the America we are living in today.[126]

Lee has been a socially and politically committed filmmaker throughout his career.[127] His third feature film, *Do the Right Thing* (1989), dealt with black-and-white tensions in a serio-comic manner and became immediately controversial. He has also been alert to issues of male-female relationship since *She's Gotta Have It* (1986), his first feature: "I'm just amazed at the things men tell women. And when you think about it, the only reason why they say that stuff is that it must work some of the time, because if it never worked, they wouldn't keep on saying that dumb stuff."[128] The main character of *She's Gotta Have It* strings along three lovers at the same time and eventually decides on abstinence, but to no avail: "That celibacy thing didn't last too long. Who was *I* fooling?" She concludes: "It's about control – *my* body, *my* mind. Who's gonna own it, them or me? I am not a one-man woman. So there you have it." We do; she will – 'cause she's gotta. But at the end of the film she is in bed alone. Lee once told an interviewer: "I'm married to a very intelligent woman . . . and since we've been married I've made a concerted effort to have a better understanding of female characters."[129] The subject of *Lysistrata* was thus almost a natural for him.

---

[126] All preceding quotations are from Bryan Smith 2015.

[127] Scholarship on Lee is extensive. Good first orientations are Hamlet and Coleman 2009, especially 271–341 (section titled "No, Baby, No: Sex, Sexuality, and Gender Roles"); Conard 2011, especially 73–183 (section titled "Race, Sexuality, and Community"); McGowan 2014.

[128] Glicksman 1986; quoted from Fuchs 2002: 11.

[129] Crowdus and Georgakas 2001; quoted from Fuchs 2002: 208.

Chi-Raq exhibits a number of similarities to *A Miami Tail*; both films are worth considering side by side. For example, the motto "No peace, no piece" recurs but is now a bit more explicit: "No peace, no pussy!" The women's strategy is clear: "Lock it up!" They mean this literally and wear modern chastity belts. Aristophanes' Myrrhine-Cinesias scene becomes a very brief reprise with three couples and is relegated to an outtake on home video. Greek drama was in verse (although without rhyme); dialogue in *Chi-Raq* is chiefly, but not exclusively, in loose and loosely rhyming couplets. These are rarely elegant or clever and may eventually get on viewers' nerves. A one-man chorus comments on the action throughout. This is Mr. Dolmedes. (Not Dolmades, thank the immortal gods!) He informs viewers about Aristophanes and introduces Lysistrata:

> In the year 411 BC . . .
> that's before
> baby Jesus, y'all,
> the Greek Aristophanes
> penned a play
> satirizing his day.
> And in the style of his time,
> 'Stophanes made that shit rhyme.
> Transplanted today,
> we retain his verse
> to show our love
> for the universe.
>   . . .
> They call her Lysistrata,
> a woman like no other.
> This chocolate-brown sister
> was finer than a motherfucker . . .
> With a mind like Einstein
> and a truly luscious behind,
> that gal put
> gap-goody hurting
> on all mankind.

At the end he sums up the story's moral:

> Lysistrata formed an army
> more powerful
> than the Roman Empire.
> Burned through the city

just like that Chicago fire.
So remember
queen prophet Lysistrata
and the lessons
that she taught you.
The only real security
is love, y'all.
L-O-V-E.

In spite of the badass language – or, rather, because of it – all this is
'Stophanic enough. So is the often-broad satire, not least of the local
power structure. The mayor of Chicago is an incompetent opportunist
with an ancient-Egypt sex fixation: "Imhotep arrives!" and "I will now
take my Chi-Town Cleopatra!" At one point he calls the Commissioner
of Public Safety, his second-in-command and the one who does his dirty
work, "a devious bastard," only to be told: "That's why I went into
public service, Your Honor." Mayor and commissioner function as
modern equivalents of Aristophanes' Proboulos. The women's occupation of the Eighth Regiment Armory, the country's first for black
soldiers, results in especially farcical satire of militarism in the person
of troglodytic General King Kong, a homage of sorts to Major "King"
Kong in Stanley Kubrick's *Dr. Strangelove* (1964). The dinosaurian
Knights of Euphrates, members of a black lodge, fare no better.
"Misogyny today, misogyny tomorrow, misogyny for goddam ever!" is
their unofficial motto. As with König and Bellmunt, here, too, there is
an Oedipus. When he is told "sometimes I think you married to your
damn mommy," his answer is of the expected kind: "Well, I love my
mother and my mommy loves me."

   In the age of instant worldwide communication, the sex strike of
Chicago, Killinois, goes global; there is even a brief moment in which
a television news report shows us women in Athens marching down the
street carrying signs that say OXI! Aristophanes has come home. So has
the element of exuberant fantasy to be found in his plays. For instance, at
the end all of the Fortune 500 companies offer the inner-city blacks good
jobs. *As if!* So Aristophanes' spirit is alive and well – or is it?[130] The most
jarring and also the most crucial deviation from his *Lysistrata* is that of
tone. Mr. Dolmedes had already told us at the beginning: "But warning! /

---

[130] A phrase of his is even quoted in medium close-up: "By words the mind is winged" (loosely
after *Birds* 1436–1439).

You gonna see some pain! / But that's only natural, / 'cause it involves the gangs." *Some* pain is an understatement.

Gang violence had been the real and serious starting point of *A Miami Tail*, but it was never shown realistically. Black Zeus narrowly missed running down Alicia's little nephew, but the child was unharmed. Equally, the dangerous confrontation between Alicia Strada and Black Zeus ended without violence. Reality did not bite. And that is why *A Miami Tail* remained a comedy. Like some comedies by Plautus and Shakespeare and, of course, Aristophanes, the film has its darker side, although it is not on the artistic level as the works by these dramatists. But *Chi-Raq* is something else. Early on, a little girl is killed by a stray bullet in a street shootout, and we see her mother's anguish. She even tries to clean her child's blood off the asphalt. All this is serious and tragic. So is the girl's funeral service, a long sequence that is even longer in an alternate version on home video. None of this is funny.

Lee has stated: "Some people are gonna twist it and think this is a comedy. *Chi-Raq* is not a comedy. *Chi-Raq* is a satire. And there's a difference between humor and comedy."[131] Despite its Aristophanic basis, then, the film is different. Is it a satire? In part, as we have seen, it is. At the beginning of Lee's film *Bamboozled* (2000), its main character, who is also its narrator, defines satire and irony to prepare viewers for his story. Satire is "a literary work in which human vice or folly is ridiculed or attacked scornfully." Irony is "derision or caustic wit, used to attack or expose folly, vice, or stupidity." *Bamboozled* is just such a film, but then it turns tragic. In a homage to Billy Wilder's *Sunset Boulevard* (1950), the narrator of *Bamboozled* turns out to have been dead all along. Lee has pointed out about *Bamboozled*:

Three-quarters of the way in, there was a tonal shift and it was deliberate. We ... wanted the laughs to stop and get serious . . . . I love films where you mix it up – where a film doesn't really even keep the same rhythm, the same tone all the way through. I mean, it's hard to do, but when it's successful I think it works very well.[132]

Lee is right. But the satire in *Chi-Raq* is canceled out by its tragedy even more than the ending of *Bamboozled* undermined that film's main plot. In *Bamboozled* the laughs did stop, and matters got entirely serious. In *Chi-Raq* the laughs are stopped by tragedy, then are restarted, then stopped again. The tone keeps shifting back and forth. It is this very to-ing

---

[131] Quoted from the short "The Making of *Chi-Raq*" on the film's home-video release.
[132] Sragow 2000; quoted from Fuchs 2002: 192.

and fro-ing that undoes the film. In this regard Lee's words about *Do the Right Thing* are to the point:

It is possible to address a very serious subject matter and still have humor. I've done it before. *Do the Right Thing* was serious as hell. It was so serious you can still show that film today – it's still contemporary. But *Do the Right Thing* was also funny as a motherfucker. Another example – one of my favorite films, one of my favorite filmmakers: Stanley Kubrick, *Dr. Strangelove*. What's more serious than the planet's destruction? But that movie was hilarious. There are many examples – music, plays, novels, movies – where humor has been injected into very serious subject matter.[133]

Here, too, Lee is right. His words show that *Chi-Raq* is not in the same league as *Sunset Boulevard* or *Dr. Strangelove*. Kubrick's film is hilarious and serious as hell *at every moment*. *Chi-Raq* is not. Serious drama and hilarious satire take turns but are kept separate. *When it's successful it works very well*: Lee is right about this. But it is not successful in *Chi-Raq*. Directors like Charles Chaplin, Howard Hawks, and John Ford, to name only three obvious American examples, handled such *palintonos harmônia*, as we might call it, much better: Chaplin in *Modern Times* (1940), Hawks in *The Big Sleep* (1946), Ford in *The Searchers* (1956).[134]

The rhyming dialogue in *Chi-Raq*, which appears equally in funny and serious scenes, may be considered a counter-argument: that drama and humor are *not* being kept apart. But that argument does not hold. In the serious scenes, which are presented visually with utter realism, the language's artificiality undermines the tragedy; it does not enhance it or throw it into greater relief. This is especially the case at the end, when the (predictable) identity of the little girl's killer becomes known alongside another horrendous revelation. Pathos turns into bathos – or at least comes perilously close to doing so. This is in noticeable contrast to the rhymes, both spoken and sung, in Schünzel's *Amphitryon – Happiness from the Clouds*. There they mostly work, especially in the songs. But *Amphitryon* is what Lee says *Chi-Raq* is not: a comedy.

From such a perspective, *Chi-Raq* is almost a failure. But if it is a failure, it is an honorable one. *Chi-Raq* and its world may be beyond comedy and satire. After all, what Shakespeare's Polonius had called "tragical-comical-historical-pastoral, scene individable," is extremely difficult to attain.[135]

---

[133] Quoted from Bryan Smith 2015.

[134] On *palintonos harmônia*, the harmonious and effective combination of opposites, see especially Seidensticker 1982. On the humor in *The Searchers* see Winkler 2001c: 144–145 note 60.

[135] Shakespeare, *Hamlet* 2.2.394–395; quoted from Jenkins 1982: 259.

For *pastoral* we should, of course, here substitute *urban*. *Chi-Raq* demonstrates beyond doubt how annihilating the level, extent, and nature of mindless violence in contemporary America has become. And not only there. "I'm a global citizen," Lee has said in connection with *Chi-Raq*.[136] He is; so, as it were, is his film. It is therefore entirely fitting that none other than Leymah Gbowee, who briefly appears in news footage, should become the direct inspiration for the sex strike in *Chi-Raq*. Lee's Lysistrata wants no less than world peace.

If Lysistrata had to descend to the lower depths on a few occasions, her latest incarnation may well prove to be the nadir. Writer-director Matt Cooper's *Is That a Gun in Your Pocket?* (2016) is a kind of modern Western and touches on several aspects of *A Miami Tail* and *Chi-Raq*, this time among whites in Texas. Lest I be considered prejudiced or overcritical – always a risk with some of my reviewers – I give the word to a professional, who sums up the matter as follows, if not without his own spelling error about our play:

There are bad movies, and then there are worse movies, and then there are full-bore misfires such as "Is That a Gun in Your Pocket?" Loosely based on Aristophanes' "Lysistrada" [*sic*] . . . writer-director Matt Cooper's smutty, smarmy farrago plays like the sort of wink-wink, nudge-nudge B-movie flotsam that might have amused habitués of Deep South drive-ins during the 1970s . . . Cooper evidences a colossal amount of tastelessness in launching his plot by having a grade-schooler swiping a handgun from his father's closet to impress a classmate, then inadvertently wounding a crosswalk guard. It's difficult to forget how many times such a tragedy has unfolded in real life, and pretty close to impossible not to feel uncomfortable as this misadventure is played for laughs.

When it isn't straining for cheap laughs with horny guys, alluring wives and girlfriends, stereotypically sex-obsessed Hispanics, and blustering gun-culture extremists . . ., "Is That a Gun in Your Pocket?" relies on veteran supporting players to make fools of themselves . . . To say anything else about this debacle, or the people for whom it provided an easy paycheck, would be needlessly unkind.[137]

Even so, I add two brief points. Jenna Keeley, the name of the Lysistrata character who organizes the sex strike after the gun incident, is not even close to any of the clever updates we have encountered before. This in itself may be a dead give-away. And the film's title is close to a disgrace for witty and sexy Mae West, who coined this immortal phrase. In another critic's words (at the very beginning of his review): "Everybody involved with [this] awful comedy . . . owes Aristophanes an apology."[138] 'Nuff said.

---

[136] Bryan Smith 2015.   [137] Leydon 2016.   [138] Genzlinger 2016.

14   *To kinêma Aristophanikon*

"How far it is possible deliberately to imitate Aristophanes in writing a comedy for the general public, either in the theatre or in the cinema," famous classicist Kenneth Dover mused decades ago, "is a difficult question." But he pointed to Jacques Feyder's *Carnival in Flanders* (*La kermesse héroïque*, 1935) as a work that "in our own time" exhibits "the Aristophanic spirit." He explained:

Feyder's film portrays an occasion on which a town in the Low Countries, in the early seventeenth century, is faced with the disagreeable prospect of a Spanish army staying the night. The town council being torn between helpless panic and a desire to close the gates and put up a heroic resistance, the burgomaster's wife organizes the women of the town, pretends to the Spaniards that her husband has just died, and sees to the entertainment of the army in such style that rape is unnecessary and drunkenness does not issue in resentful violence. The townswomen will keep the good-looking Spaniards in a secret and cherished corner of memory for a long time to come. Now, what gives this film its Aristophanic character is not simply the seizure of initiative by the women, nor even their uncomplicated sexuality, but the fact that the peril which the town council so vividly imagines, the spearing of babies on pikes, the roasting alive of old men, are [*sic*], at that time and place, part of the real world with which people have to come to terms; which does not prevent them from enjoying themselves and maintaining their preferred style of life in the intervals between perils.[139]

At a time when classical scholars still disdained "the movies" as a matter of course, this notice of a classic film by a Fellow of the British Academy (and later Sir Kenneth) was exceptional. Things have changed. A detailed scholarly approach to a modern film comedy, writer-director Colin Higgins's *9 to 5* (or *Nine to Five*, 1980), shows how convincing a thorough analysis of the persistence of classical archetypes in modern culture can be.[140] *9 to 5* fully exhibits the spirit of Aristophanes. Its four main characters, American office workers suffering under a sexist male boss, resemble Lysistrata,

---

[139] Dover 1972: 238–239.
[140] Baron 2001. Valverde García 2011 sees Aristophanic analogies in Michael Cacoyannis's anti-imperialist and environmental comedy *The Day the Fish Came Out* (1967). Palomar 2011 examines Aristophanes' *Birds* in connection with Pier Paolo Pasolini's film *The Hawks and the Sparrows* (1966). Decades earlier, an Italian film scholar had been struck by the similarity of Aristophanes, *Birds* 1131–1157, with the scene in Walt Disney's animated *Snow White and the Seven Dwarfs* (1937) in which a variety of birds and forest animals help the heroine clean the dwarfs' hut: Bonajuto 1940. On Aristophanic overtones in American television (e.g. *The Simpsons*) see Euben 2003: 64–84 and 182–187 (notes; chapter titled "Aristophanes in America"). The title of Euben's book alludes to that of Don DeLillo's novel *White Noise* (1985).

Myrrhine, Calonice, and Lampito, the last of these a double-barreled standout in the personification of buxom Dolly Parton. To ancient Athenians, Spartans were hicks from the sticks, and this Lampito's Texas accent sticks out among all the urban, if not necessarily urbane, big-city types. Higgins's film demonstrates how Aristophanic plotting can reappear in modern dress and how specific features of *Lysistrata* can be translated into a new medium. *9 to 5* may not be a milestone in the history of film comedy, but the study mentioned is certainly a milestone in the history of film interpretation based on principles of classical philology.

Any attempt at a comprehensive or systematic survey of the Aristophanic spirit in the cinema is to carry strikers to the Acropolis, but some outstanding examples should be mentioned. Concerning female-to-male gender-benders, the palm of victory goes to sophisticated Renate Müller as the titular cross-dressing heroine of Reinhold Schünzel's *Viktor und Viktoria* (Germany, 1933), remade under the same title by Karl Anton in 1957, as *First a Girl* (UK, 1935) by Victor Saville, and as *Victor Victoria* (US, 1982) by Blake Edwards. The male-to-female (and back to male) victory belongs to Billy Wilder's *Some Like It Hot* (US, 1959), with Jack Lemmon as Jerry ("I'm a girl!"), Daphne ("I'm a boy!"), and Jerry again ("*I'm a man!*") and with an immortal closing line. Richard Lester's *The Ritz* (1976) and some of the early films of John Waters (*Pink Flamingos*, 1972; *Female Trouble*, 1974) and Pedro Almodóvar (*Pepi, Luci, Bom and Other Girls Like Mom*, 1980; *Labyrinth of Passion*, 1982; *What Have I Done to Deserve This?* 1984) are still outrageous. Comedy and satire of mindless male militarism appears in Stanley Kubrick's *Dr. Strangelove* (UK, 1964) and Robert Altman's *MASH* (US, 1970). Wilder's *One, Two, Three* (1961), set in the divided city of Berlin, is a loud and unsubtle but clever comedy-satire on love and marriage, patriotism and militarism, Cold War ideology, and what at one point is called "Coca-Cola colonialism." Gluttony on a Heraclean scale, combined with sex and death, is the subject of Marco Ferreri's *La grande bouffe* (*Blow-Out* or *The Big Feast*, 1973). The absurdity of the American funeral industry is on view in Tony Richardson's *The Loved One* (US, 1965), adapted from Evelyn Waugh's novel and marketed as "The motion picture with something to offend everyone." That may no longer be true. A few years later Peter Medak's *The Ruling Class* (1972) tried again. In a category by themselves are films by Luis Buñuel, cinema's great surrealist: *L'age d'or* (1930, in collaboration with Salvador Dalí), *The Discreet Charme of the Bourgeoisie* (1970), *The Phantom of Liberty* (1972), and *That Obscure Object of Desire* (1974). So are the absurd grotesqueries of Lina Wertmüller, Federico Fellini's former assistant. *The Seduction of Mimi* (1972; Mimi is a male) and *Seven Beauties*

(1975) pose little men vis-à-vis physically imposing (to put it mildly) women and feature situations that must be seen to be believed or disbelieved. *My Friends* (1975) and *My Friends Part 2* (1982), episodic Italian comedies directed by Mario Monicelli, are funny send-ups of male friendship, the impossibility that middle-aged men might ever grow up, and their puerile behavior in general and toward women in particular. Once you have watched Monicelli's whirlwinds of hilarious inventiveness you will be unlikely ever again to stick your head out of your compartment window when your train is about to depart, and you will *never* leave your camera or now phone unguarded in an apparently cozy Italian *trattoria* for even one moment. (Mini-parabasis: Trust me!)

The failure of modern American masculinity before potential mates and in the face of an eccentric mother is satirized in Carl Reiner's *Where's Poppa?* (1970); Reiner later became more successful by playing it safer. During Hollywood's golden age the battle of the sexes reached its greatest height in Howard Hawks's *Twentieth Century* (1934), *Bringing Up Baby* (1940; this Baby is not a baby), and *His Girl Friday* (1940). These sophisticated comedies are marked by rapid-fire dialogue, in which sexy, sharp-witted, strong-willed, and independent-minded women are equal to or better than their men. Leo McCarey's *The Awful Truth* (1937) and Garson Kanin's *My Favorite Wife* (1940) are classic comedies about divorce or remarriage. A special case is that of the titular lady in Melvin Frank's *Buona Sera, Mrs. Campbell* (1968), co-written by British wit Dennis Norden, with its case of triply possible and possibly triply mistaken paternity.

Madcap characters are *de rigueur* for these and other Hollywood screwball comedies. Not a sane character is to be found in Joel and Ethan Coen's *The Big Lebowski* (1998), a pitch-black comedy with a clueless slob for its non-hero. This lone relic from the Age of Aquarius ("The Dude abides!") becomes entangled in a labyrinthine plot of hilarious, farcical, and nihilistic absurdity. Verbally it is the opposite of Hawks's films and their sparkling dialogue, for here the Maculate Muse of Aristophanic humor triumphs. She does so again in the raunchy teenage sex comedies that became popular around that time. As representative I mention only Greg Mottola's *Superbad* (2007), which is about the hormone-fueled attempts by three male potty-mouthed mega-nerds to get first soused and then laid. The film is irreverent of authority, very sexist, very tasteless – the Maculate Muse collects a Grand Prize – and super funny. Those for whom all this is too much can turn to the crowning glory of comedy that is Leo McCarey's *Duck Soup* (1933). This maddest of all Marx Brothers farces is bent on a free-wheeling slaughter of sacred American cows like patriotism and history, power and militarism, and matronly and nubile womanhood. Woody Allen, of course, deserves another mention here, too.[141] And we should not forget about the cartoon zanies at Warner Brothers, who were housed in what they called, first sarcastically and then affectionately, Termite Terrace and who gave the world of comedy such indelible characters as Daffy Duck, the archetypal embodiment of an unleashed Id – "There ought to be a law against crazy ducks," a helpless Porky Pig sighs in *Boobs in the Woods* (1950); of course there is none – and Bugs Bunny, to name only two of the greatest examples. That's *not* all, folks!

15 Coda: Tail End

In a chapter of *The Comic Mind* entitled "The Case for Comedy," Gerald Mast appropriately summarized our topic:

From the beginning, comedy has been bent on destruction – of objects, egos, social assumptions, society's leaders, and the goals of society itself. Aristophanes was a perfectionist of destruction. Similarly, the greatest comic artists in film – [Mack] Sennett, [Charles] Chaplin, [Buster] Keaton, [Ernst] Lubitsch, [Jean] Renoir, the Marx Brothers, [W. C.] Fields, [Jacques] Tati, [Preston] Sturges – are pure destroyers. They wreck the idol that society and men have built to, for, and of themselves, and they fail to build anything in its place.[142]

A few decades later we can considerably expand Mast's list. Aristophanes is alive and well on the screen. His unexpected appearances on screen, even if only as a marmoreal observer, tell us that his spirit hovers over more of the cinema than we might suspect. And whatever her European, American, or Eastern guise or disguise, his gal named Lysistrata is always fantastic.[143] Many classical scholars are still sadly unfamiliar with this pleasing fact. A recent introduction to Aristophanes, for instance, is innocent of words like *cinema, film,* or *movie* even in its final chapter, which is titled "Aristophanes in the Modern World."[144] *O cogitatorium, o mores!* Fortunately the Muse of Cinema ensures Aristophanes' survival. So lovers of film and fans of Aristophanes can only hope that Academy Award-winning animator Richard Williams will be able to make his adaptation of *Lysistrata*, for

---

[141] Cf. Andrisano 2014.   [142] Mast 1979: 338.

[143] Those who are not easily shocked, *shocked* can find a combination of Lysistrata, Messalina, and Elizabeth Taylor's Cleopatra at http://ancientsites.com/member/Terentius/Messalina/2634. Proceed at your own intellectual risk!

[144] Robson 2009. The situation is minimally improved in Philip Walsh 2016.

which his six-minute short *Prologue*, released in 2015, is a promising, well, prologue.

Liza McClure could give you all the data on the gal called Lysistrata. Your dedicated and occasionally pseudo-parabatic author, dear reader, confesses that he cannot quite match her, not even in regard to the gal's screen appearances. After all, we're not in Kansas anymore. But he hopes to have done justice to the striking and sexciting gal at least as she and her sisters and sistas have brightened our screens for a century. As Samuel Fuller could have told us, in *Lysistrata* Aristophanes showed us the battlefield of love's emotions. Those among my male readers who laugh at and with the characters of his play but also think about what they have seen and heard might adapt Bernard-Henri Lévy's words about *Pierrot le fou* to our context: *Lysistrata has taught us love. We love women more because of Aristophanes' play on our screens*. And thereby hangs a tale. And many a tail.

PART III

Non-elective Affinities

Plot and Theme

5 | "More Striking"
Aristotelian Poetics in Achilles Tatius, Heliodorus, and Alfred Hitchcock

Surviving ancient Greek and Roman novels are conspicuous for their high level of vividness (*enargeia*) and fully bear out Simonides' saying about painting and poetry – in modern terminology, literature. The conversation of Kalasiris and Knemon about the festival at Delphi in Book 3 of Heliodorus' *An Ethiopian Story* provides us with an explicit analogy between hearing and mentally visualizing a story: *sub oculos subiectio*. Even more remarkably, Heliodorus' opening scene is a virtual blueprint for a screenplay.[1]

This chapter illustrates the affinity between ancient novels and the cinema by examining the context and purpose of a specific narrative device, that of a character's unexpected death in a shocking plot turn. In spite of their complexities and individual differences, Achilles Tatius' *Leucippe and Clitophon*, Heliodorus' *An Ethiopian Story* (or *Aithiopika*, *Aethiopica*), and Alfred Hitchcock's *Psycho* (1960) adhere to formulaic ways of telling their romance-adventure-mystery plots. All three are driven primarily by narrative considerations and not by any nuanced presentation of their characters' psychology.[2] We may compare the observation that John Dickson Carr, one of the most famous and most formulaic of authors, gives Dr. Gideon Fell, his sleuth: "we're in a detective story, and we don't fool the reader by pretending we're not … Let's candidly glory in the noblest pursuits possible to characters in a book."[3]

As early as Aristotle, plots have been granted narrative primacy.[4] If pursuit of psychological depth makes for a narrative in which character is plot, as a common phrase has it, genre stories work in the opposite way. Plot determines and usually restricts characterization: "By giving narrative

---

[1] So shown in Winkler 2000–2001.

[2] On formulaic fiction and film see Cawelti 1976, especially 5–36 and 37–50 (chapters entitled "The Study of Literary Formulas" and "Notes toward a Typology of Literary Formulas").

[3] Quoted from Carr 1986: 159–160. Cf. Symons 1985: 110 on Carr: "Since the whole story is built around the puzzle there is no room for characterization…. what one remembers … is never the people, but only the puzzle."

[4] Aristotle, *Poetics* 1450a37–38 (plot as the "soul" of tragedy). Concerning modern literature cf., e.g., Brooks 2002.

emphasis to a constant flow of action, the writer avoids the necessity of exploring character with any degree of complexity."[5]

1   Aristotle and Mystery Plots

In his *Poetics* Aristotle defends the tragic poet's use of "the wondrous" (*to thaumaston*) and the epic poet's use of "the irrational" (*to alogon*), "on which the wondrous depends for its chief effects."[6] Storytellers in all genres of fiction rely on implausible or nearly impossible plot turns in order to ensure or deepen their audience's emotional involvement with the fate of their characters. In such cases Aristotle advises that an author "should prefer probable impossibilities [*adynata eikota*] to improbable possibilities [*dynata apithana*]."[7] This is because "what is possible [*to dynaton*] is credible [*pithanon*]: what has not happened we do not at once feel sure to be possible: but what has happened is manifestly possible: otherwise it would not have happened."[8] Elsewhere Aristotle states that what is credible is so because it is credible only specifically: to someone (*pithanon tini pithanon*).[9] A modern commentator observes about Aristotle's terms *adynaton* and *alogon*:

> The significance of the saying lies in the undoubted truth that a series of events containing no impossibility may strike an audience as much less convincing than one which maintains the sequence of cause and effect but requires suspension of disbelief on some incidental impossibility. Few coincidences are impossible; but a plot which turns on unlikely coincidences violates the feeling for logical coherence. It does not trouble a sophisticated audience that Medea [in Euripides' tragedy] murders her rival with a poison unknown to science, but the unmotivated arrival of Aegeus at a convenient moment causes dissatisfaction.[10]

Aristotle even goes so far as to admonish spectators and readers that, "once the irrational has been introduced and an air of likelihood imparted to it, we must accept it in spite of its absurdity . . . If he [an author] describes the impossible [*adynata*], he is guilty of an error; but the error may be justified,

---

[5] Quoted from Cawelti 1976: 19. The statement accurately describes the works of the Greek novelists. *Psycho* and most of Hitchcock's mature work, however, transcend mere formula while still adhering to, playing with, but never breaking the rules of the thriller genre.

[6] Aristotle, *Poetics* 1460a11–13; quoted from Butcher 1907: 95. While there exists extensive modern scholarship on the *Poetics*, this older work is highly valuable for the clarity of its explanations and the wide range of creative arts to which Aristotle's text is applied.

[7] Aristotle, *Poetics* 1460a26–27; Butcher 1907: 95.

[8] Aristotle, *Poetics* 1451b15–19; Butcher 1907: 37.   [9] Aristotle, *Rhetoric* 1356b28.

[10] D. W. Lucas 1968: 230 (on 1460a26). Canter 1930 and Dutoit 1936 are fundamental on *adynata*.

if . . . the effect of this or any other part of the poem [i.e. of any narrative] is thus rendered more striking [*ekplêktikôteron*]."[11] Here the wider context in which the irrational or impossible occurs is decisive, for it justifies an author's use of the impossible or incredible and prepares the way for its acceptance by an audience. Aristotle states: "in examining whether what has been said or done by someone is poetically right or not, we must not look merely to the particular act or saying, and ask whether it is poetically good or bad. We must also consider by whom it is said or done, to whom, when, by what means, or for what end." And: "The element of the irrational (*alogia*) and, similarly, depravity of character, are justly censured when there is no inner necessity for introducing them."[12] He concludes:

In general, the impossible [*to adynaton*] must be justified by reference to artistic requirements, or to the higher reality, or to received opinion. With respect to the requirements of art, a probable impossibility [*pithanon adynaton*] is to be preferred to a thing improbable and yet possible [*apithanon kai dynaton*] . . . To justify the irrational [*aloga*], we appeal to what is commonly said to be. In addition, we urge that the irrational sometimes does not violate reason.[13]

Credo quia absurdum: If it can be the case that the irrational does not violate the rational – that is, if a crucial moment in the development of a plot does not simply make us throw up our hands in frustration with the nonsense we are reading or watching – then a storyteller has succeeded in making us care, and we are willingly suspending our disbelief.[14] In Chapter 14 of his *Biographia Literaria* (1817), Samuel Taylor Coleridge describes the use of the supernatural in literature "so as to transfer from our inward nature a human interest and a semblance of truth sufficient to procure for these shadows of imagination that willing suspension of disbelief for the moment, which constitutes poetic faith."[15] As a modern scholar has put it: "Aristotle shows that an argument from probability can be drawn from the sheer improbability of a story: Some stories are so improbable that it is reasonable to believe them."[16]

[11] Aristotle, *Poetics* 1460b24–27; Butcher 1907: 99.
[12] Aristotle, *Poetics* 1461a4–8 and 1461b19–20. Both quotations are from Butcher 1907: 101 and 107.
[13] Aristotle, *Poetics* 1461b9–12 and 14–15; Butcher 1907: 105 and 107. Cf. D. W. Lucas 1968: 248 (on 1461b14): "If the odds are a hundred to one against something happening, it is still likely [i.e. not merely possible] that it will happen 'some time' in a hundred times."
[14] On *credo quia absurdum*, the common if not textually accurate version of Tertullian's most famous dictum, see Moffat 1916 and Sider 1980.
[15] Quoted from Engell and Bate 1983: 6. Their note on this passage cites additional statements by Coleridge on the matter.
[16] Sider 1980: 417–418.

Aristotle's term *ekplêktikôteron* ("more striking") fits all the ancient novels.[17] Apuleius' *Golden Ass*, for example, contains a direct, although brief, defense of this kind of tale, which the very novel itself exemplifies. The listener of a supernatural story that is equally grotesque, scary, and hilarious "at once and from the beginning rejected" the tale "with obstinate incredulity," saying: "Nothing is more fantastic than this story, nothing more absurd than that sort of lying tale!" The main narrator strongly disagrees. He believes nothing to be impossible, and "wondrous things that have practically never occurred" (*mira et paene infecta*) "may lose all credibility when told to a boor" (*ignaro relata fidem perdant*), but an elegant and charming story of this kind is just the thing for intelligent entertainment.[18]

Aristotle's perspective also fits any romantic-adventure fiction, including our suspense and detective stories, whether told in texts or in images. Modern mystery fiction has some precursors in the Greek and Roman novels.[19] Heliodorus' Kalasiris is the first private eye in Western literature; Sophocles' Oedipus is its first detective.[20] In escapist fiction the plausibilities of real life are set aside in favor of striking implausibilities. The same had been the case in fifth-century tragedy, Aristotle's subject in the surviving parts of the *Poetics*. The Athenian tragedians derived most of their plots from myths, which are by nature unrealistic and implausible to the rational and logic-minded because of their ubiquitous gods, monsters, and other manifestations of the supernatural. Aristotle gives the classic explanation of how the implausible functions and why it is an important, indeed crucial, aspect of narrative literature. During the Golden Age of the detective story Dorothy Sayers even advanced the thesis that Aristotle's *Poetics* could be regarded as a theory of mystery fiction: "Aristotle ... contrived to hammer out ... a theory of detective fiction so shrewd, all-embracing and practical that the *Poetics* remains the

---

[17] Butcher's translation of *ekplêktikôteron* is appropriate, but since the word derives from *ekplêttô* ("to scare away" [so already at Homer, *Odyssey* 18.231], "to scare out of one's mind"), the translation "more shocking" is also apt. Below, I consider *striking* to be synonymous with *shocking*. D. W. Lucas 1968: 227 (on 1460a12) translates the noun *ekplêxis* as "thrill."

[18] Apuleius, *The Golden Ass* 1.20; quotations at 1.20.1–2 and 4. The story in question is the tale of Aristomenes about the death of Socrates, a fictional character done in by witches (*The Golden Ass* 1.6–19).

[19] See especially John J. Winkler 1985. Cf. Haight 1950 and J. R. Morgan 1994. Papadimitropoulos 2012 has a number of good observations that can be directly applied to the present chapter, including on plot points examined here, and additional references to scholarship. On Aristotle and modern popular fiction, especially fiction that involves the supernatural (J. K. Rowling, Philip Pullman), see Jill Paton Walsh 2005.

[20] John J. Winkler 1982 links Heliodorus' novel to mystery fiction on several occasions.

finest guide to the writing of such fiction that could be put, at this day, into the hands of an aspiring author."[21]

Edgar Allan Poe, the father of the detective story, confirms Aristotle's and Sayers's perspectives in his Tales of Ratiocination, especially in "The Murders in the Rue Morgue" (1841; the first-ever locked-room mystery), "The Mystery of Marie Rogêt" (1842), and "The Purloined Letter" (1844). In the standard history of mystery fiction Julian Symons, himself an award-winning author of mysteries, comments on the last of these: "The story was the prototype of detective novels and short stories based on the idea that the most apparently unlikely solution is the correct one, with the ingenious addition in Poe's story that what seems most unlikely is really perfectly obvious."[22] What Poe termed the "Calculus of Probabilities" includes consideration of improbability and chance. The narrator of "The Mystery of Marie Rogêt" and companion of Auguste Dupin, Poe's famous sleuth, explains the Calculus at the beginning:

There are few persons, even among the calmest thinkers, who have not occasionally been startled into a vague yet thrilling half-credence in the supernatural, by *coincidences* of so seemingly marvellous a character that, as *mere* coincidences, the intellect has been unable to receive them. Such sentiments – for the half-credences of which I speak have never the full force of *thought* – are seldom thoroughly stifled unless by reference to the doctrine of chance, or, as it is technically termed, the Calculus of Probabilities. Now this Calculus is, in its essence, purely mathematical; and thus we have the anomaly of the most rigidly exact in science applied to the shadow and spirituality of the most intangible in speculation.

Dupin himself adds the following points:

I have before observed that it is by prominences above the plane of the ordinary, that reason feels her way, if at all, in her search for the true, and that the proper question in cases such as this, is not so much 'what has occurred?' as 'what has occurred that has never occurred before?' In the investigations [the police] were discouraged and confounded by that very *unusualness* which, to a properly regulated intellect, would have afforded the surest omen of success ... It is the malpractice of the courts to confine evidence and discussion to the bounds of apparent relevancy. Yet experience has shown, and a true philosophy will always show, that a vast, perhaps the larger portion of truth, arises from the seemingly irrelevant. It is through the spirit of this principle ... that modern science has resolved to *calculate upon the unforeseen. . . .* We make chance a matter of absolute calculation.

[21] Sayers 1947b: 223. Her essay originally appeared in 1935.
[22] Symons 1985: 37. Poe exerted a strong influence on Carr (Symons: 110).

We subject the unlooked for and unimagined to the mathematical *formulae* of the schools.[23]

We may adduce here another master of mystery from the Golden Age. Symons has observed about the early mysteries by Ellery Queen: "The ingenuity [rests] in a relentlessly analytical treatment of every possible clue and argument. In the early books a 'Challenge To The Reader' appears some three-quarters of the way through, in the form of a statement saying that the reader has now been presented with all the clues needed to solve the case, and that only one solution is possible. The rare distinction of the books is that this claim is accurate."[24]

The *adynata eikota* of Aristotle are essential to Poe's stories. As Dupin puts it in "The Murders in the Rue Morgue": "Fortunately, there is but one mode of reasoning upon the point, and that mode *must* lead us to a definite decision. . . . Now, brought to this conclusion in so unequivocal a manner as we are, it is not our part, as reasoners, to reject it on account of apparent impossibilities. It is only left for us to prove that these apparent 'impossibilities' are, in reality, not such."[25] Poe himself once characterized Eugène Sue's *The Mysteries of Paris* (1842–1843) in the following terms: "It has this point in common with all the 'convulsive' fictions – that the incidents are *consequential* from the premises, while the premises themselves are laughably incredible."[26]

The greatest affirmation of Aristotelian *adynata eikota* in mystery fiction appears in a lecture given by the master sleuth in John Dickson Carr's novel *The Hollow Man* (1935; US title: *The Three Coffins*). Carr was one of the most accomplished Golden-Age authors, unique in his designs of fiendishly intricate variations on one particular, and particularly unrealistic, plot element: murder in a locked room. Carr was the man who explained miracles.[27] Some paperback editions of his books feature a blurb by Agatha Christie: "Very few detective stories baffle me nowadays, but Mr. Carr's always do."

Dr. Gideon Fell's lecture is the pre-eminent defense of the Aristotelian *pithanon adynaton*. Fell first confesses to his own addiction to what he calls "sensational fiction." (Poe had called it "convulsive fiction.") Then he

---

[23] Poe 1984c: 506–507, 520, and 534. Cf. both the definition of the probable (*to eikos*) in Aristotle, *Rhetoric* 1357a34 and Halliwell 1998: 101–103.

[24] Symons 1985: 111.   [25] Quoted from Poe 1984b: 417.

[26] Quoted from Harrison 1902: 104. Poe's text first appeared in *Graham's Magazine* of November 1846.

[27] I allude to the subtitle of Douglas Greene 1995. On Carr see also Adey 1992: xxi–xxvii (section titled "The Maestro").

addresses the appeal of mystery fiction, the necessary precondition for Aristotle's *ekplêktikôteron*:

I like my murders to be frequent, gory, and grotesque. I like some vividness of colour and imagination flashing out of my plot, since I cannot find a story enthralling solely on the grounds that it sounds as though it might really have happened. All these things, I admit, are happy, cheerful, rational prejudices, and entail no criticism of more tepid (or more able) work.

Fell then draws attention to the "few people who do not like the slightly lurid" and who "use, as a stamp of condemnation, the word 'improbable',," which to them "simply means 'bad.'" But they are mistaken: "Now, it seems reasonable to point out that the word improbable is the very last which should ever be used to curse detective fiction in any case. A great part of our liking for detective fiction is *based* on a liking for improbability." After giving examples of standard improbabilities in such fiction, Fell continues:

In short, you come to a point where the word improbable grows meaningless as a jeer. There can be no such thing as any probability until the end of the story. And then, as you wish the murder to be fastened on an unlikely person . . ., you can hardly complain because he acted from motives less likely or necessarily less apparent than those of the person first suspected.

Concerning an apparently impossible situation, Fell concludes: "You see, the effect is so magical that we somehow expect the cause to be magical also. When we see that it isn't wizardry, we call it tomfoolery. Which is hardly fair play. The last thing we should complain about with regard to the murderer is his erratic conduct." He now comes to the heart of the matter:

The whole test is, *can* the thing be done? If so, the question of whether it *would* be done does not enter into it. A man escapes from a locked room – well? Since apparently he has violated the laws of nature for our entertainment, then heaven knows he is entitled to violate the laws of Probable Behaviour! . . . Bear that in mind, gents, when you judge. Call the result uninteresting, if you like, or anything else that is a matter of personal taste. But be very careful about making the nonsensical statement that it is improbable or far fetched.[28]

Symons has commented on Carr: "Often his postulates are improbable, but the reader rarely feels them to be impossible, and the deception [of the reader] is . . . at last revealed with staggering skill . . . His books are full of macabre events and possibilities."[29] This is true for Achilles Tatius and

---

[28] All quotations are from Carr 1986: 159–162. The book regularly ranks high or highest on lists of the best mystery fiction ever written.
[29] Symons 1985: 110.

Heliodorus, even if the ancient authors' plots are less intricate than the modern master's.

Can *the thing be done?* None other than Aristotle himself provides an answer. Aristotle does not speak for himself; rather, he quotes the words of Agathon, one of the greatest and most important of the classical Athenian dramatists. None of his plays survives, but we have about fifty lines and know the titles of a few of his tragedies. The prize Agathon won with his very first production occasioned the dinner party which is the setting for Plato's *Symposium*. A particular innovation that Agathon brought to dramatic art was duly noted by Aristotle. While other tragedies retold stories familiar from myth and, less frequently, from history, in at least one of his plays Agathon introduced an entirely fictitious plot with invented characters.[30] So we may not be wholly surprised when we hear what Agathon had to say about improbabilities: "'it is probable,' he says, 'that many things should happen contrary to probability.'"[31] The appearance of the improbable has become a function of its opposite, for the very concept of probability includes improbabilities. What greater authority besides Aristotle himself could one wish for in support of Carr's view?

Would *the thing be done?* A Roman maxim extends Agathon's, Aristotle's, and Carr's perspectives from fiction to real life: "What can happen to somebody can happen to anybody," as unique or far-fetched as that somebody's circumstances may be.[32] For readers and viewers who consider themselves firmly rooted in reality, this saying reinforces the universal appeal of fictional characters placed in unlikely surroundings or situations so extreme as rarely or never to find a counterpart in actual life: *There, but for the grace of God* [or *the gods*], *go I.* The universal appeal of the Oedipus myth may be the best example.

An influential literary scholar has supported the views of Dupin and Fell. Discussing verisimilitude in narrative literature, a concept akin to that of probability as outlined above, Tzvetan Todorov observes:

The law of reconstruction [of a fictional crime] is never the law of ordinary verisimilitude ... The guilty man in a murder mystery is the man who does not seem guilty. In his summing up, the detective will invoke a logic which links the hitherto scattered clues; but such logic derives from a scientific notion of possibility, not from one of verisimilitude. The revelation must obey these two imperatives: possibility and absence of verisimilitude.

[30] Aristotle, *Poetics* 1451b19–21.   [31] Aristotle, *Poetics* 1456a23–25; Butcher 1907: 69.
[32] Publilius Syrus, *Mimorum fragmenta* 119 (Ribbeck): *Cuivis potest accidere quod cuiquam potest.* The saying is quoted, with illustrative examples, by Seneca, *Consolation to Marcia* 9.5.

The revelation, that is, the truth, is incompatible with verisimilitude, as we know from a whole series of detective plots based on the tension between them.

Todorov concludes from this: "Verisimilitude is the theme of the murder mystery; its law is the antagonism between truth and verisimilitude ... By relying on antiverisimilitude, the murder mystery has come under the sway of another verisimilitude, that of its own genre." The author of mystery fiction "establishes a new verisimilitude, one linking his text to the genre to which it belongs."[33]

2   Achilles Tatius: Sudden Deaths

Leucippe and Clitophon is a prime example of an adventure plot thoroughly imbued with implausibilities of the kind that recur in modern mystery fiction: a story with a whole series of hair-raising twists and turns. Taking our cue from Aristotle, we might characterize such a plot as an *ekplêktikon*, something striking or shocking. The first unexpected instance occurs about a third into the novel. Clitophon, its hero and narrator, becomes a helpless eyewitness to the fate of Leucippe, his beloved, who has been kidnapped by a gang of outlaws. He recounts what he saw in harrowing detail (3.15):

We could in fact see brigands aplenty and fully armed ... They had improvised an altar of earth and near it a coffin. Two of them were leading a girl to the altar with her hands tied behind her back ... One of the attendants laid her on her back and tied her to stakes fixed in the ground ... He next raised a sword and plunged it into her heart and then sawed all the way down to her abdomen. Her viscera leaped out. The attendants pulled out her entrails and carried them in their hands over to the altar. When it was well done they carved the whole lot up, and all the bandits shared the meal.

As each of these acts was performed ... I, contrary to all reason, just sat there staring. It was sheer shock; I was simply thunderstruck by the enormity of the calamity ... When the [sacrificial] ceremony was concluded ... they placed her body in the coffin, covered it with a lid, razed the altar, and ran away without looking behind them.[34]

---

[33] Todorov 1978b: 85 and 86–87. This essay first appeared in 1967. Cf. Cawelti 1976: 9: "the audience's past experience with a formula gives it a sense of what to expect in new individual examples, thereby increasing its capacity for understanding and enjoying the details of a work." For classical Greek literature see Scodel 1999, with additional references.

[34] Achilles Tatius, *Leucippe and Clitophon*, tr. John J. Winkler, in Reardon 1989: 170–284 (with different transliterations of Greek names). Below, numbered references to books and chapters in the novel will be given parenthetically in my text; quotations from the translation will be identified according to the volume in which it appeared; here Reardon 1989: 216.

The murder of Leucippe is sufficiently gory and grotesque to satisfy Dr. Fell. But killing the heroine is a violation of the one plot element with which authors of romance-adventure fiction must never tamper: the happy ending. Is the bizarre manner of Leucippe's unexpected death in a perverted religious ritual that includes cannibalism "laughably incredible," as Poe had concluded about *The Mysteries of Paris*? Or is it made believable by its very absurdity, described in gruesome detail? Either way, the moment is a thrilling example of an *ekplêktikon*. The story appears to be irrevocably over, and Clitophon is about to kill himself over the loss of his beloved (3.16–17).

Readers are stunned. How can this story possibly continue? Fortunately we are in the hands of a master. In a twist that restarts the adventure and the protagonists' romance and that is equally *ekplêktikon* to Clitophon and to the readers, Achilles Tatius brings Leucippe back to life. Within the story this occurs on the following day; within the novel it occurs on the following page (in a modern edition) – that is to say, as soon as possible. If Leucippe's graphic death and disembowelment resemble comparable scenes in modern shockers like slasher films, her reappearance (3.17) is akin to the apparition of a living corpse in a horror film:

He [Clitophon's friend Menelaos] opened the coffin, and Leukippe rose up, a frightening (O gods!) and blood-chilling sight. The entire length of her stomach hung open, and the visceral cavity was hollow. She fell into my arms' embrace . . . and then we both collapsed . . . "And now," said Menelaos, "she will recover her innards, her frontal gash will grow together, and you will see her once more sound . . . ." Then, as he spoke, he removed a contraption from her stomach and restored her to her original condition.[35]

The explanation, as improbable as anything Dr. Fell could wish for, follows in minute detail (3.19–22). Menelaos' account makes what had happened not so much plausible as understandable or, in Fell's words, replete with the "vividness of colour and imagination flashing out" in sensational or convulsive fiction. Everything had been a fakery engineered to save Leucippe's life, a deception that Menelaos, a wily Egyptian, played on the outlaws by means of stage props borrowed from an actor who serendipitously happened to be on hand. The sword had a retractable blade – the direct ancestor of countless such props used in modern plays and films. A soft animal hide filled with animal entrails had been tied across Leucippe's stomach. *Credo qui absurdum*: We believe it because it is

[35] Reardon 1989: 217–218.

a perfect explanation, appealing in its ingenuity although nonsensical from a realistic point of view. Cleverness is all that counts, as we know from Dr. Fell: "The whole test is, *can* the thing be done? If so, the question of whether it *would* be done does not enter into it."

In convulsive fiction, then, the thing can be done and often is; in predictable and boring reality, it would not be done. A helpful comment on the matter occurs in Plutarch's essay on how to read poetry – i.e. fiction, as we would say:

> But when poetic art is divorced from the truth, then chiefly it employs variety and diversity. For it is the sudden changes that give to its stories the elements of the emotional, the surprising, and the unexpected, and these are attended by very great astonishment [*pleistê . . . ekplêxis*] and enjoyment; but sameness is unemotional and prosaic [*amouson*].[36]

Evidently Plutarch was on to something well before Achilles' time. The Greek text here translated has *amouson* ("Muse-less," i.e. *unrefined*), emended from *amython* ("mythless," i.e. *without mythic elements*). But since *mythos* is also the common term for "plot," we may be justified in understanding *amython* as "plotless": not, of course, in a literal sense but in that of pedestrian rather than clever storytelling.

So the novel is back on track: Hero and heroine are reunited, and a happy ending is possible again. But after we have read through another third of the novel, Achilles sets out to trick us again. In Book 5 he kills off Leucippe a second time, again in full view of a helpless Clitophon, only to resurrect her a second time. Experienced readers will mentally have fortified themselves against their author's trickery. At the end of Book 3 we can readily imagine their state of mind: *How dare he kill one of the two characters who must not be killed under any circumstances and then bring her back to life? Well, I fell for this, but I'm certainly not falling into the same trap again!* In order to pull off this second deception, Achilles must up the ante. Todorov explains why: "according to a general narrative law, temporal succession [of plot elements] corresponds to a gradation of intensity, so that the final episode is to be the most impressive one."[37] This narrative law applies not only to mystery fiction but also to action and adventure

---

[36] Plutarch, "How the Young Man Should Study Poetry" 25.7 (= *Moralia* 25d); quoted from Babbitt 1927: 133 and 135. *Ekplêxis* is the noun from which *ekplêktikon* is derived; Babbitt's translation of *pleistê . . . ekplêxis* does not do justice to the expression's full force. Whitmarsh 2011: 205 renders it as "maximum shock" and observes: "Plutarch sees these effects as wholly intrinsic to literary creation" (205–206).

[37] Todorov 1978b: 84.

stories. With its progression of bloody duels and slaughters, Homer's *Iliad* is the first example in Western literature.

How does this work in Achilles Tatius? The second murder and resurrection of Leucippe and the explanation to follow must be different from the first. And so they are. Clitophon reports (5.7) Leucippe kidnapped by pirates. Their pursuers were about to catch up:

> When the pirates saw our vessel closing in and us prepared to fight, they stood Leukippe on the top deck with her hands tied behind her, and one of them cried out in a loud voice, "Here's your prize!" and so saying, he cut off her head and toppled the rest of the body into the sea.[38]

The manner of Leucippe's murder is significant. As unlikely or antiverisimilitudinous (to coin a term following Todorov) as it may appear, trickery involving survival after disembowelment may just possibly be *tini pithanon* – credible to someone, in this case to readers of adventure fiction willing to suspend disbelief. But survival after decapitation? There is no possibility for Leucippe to be resurrected, or so it seems to us and to Clitophon. Achilles is careful to drive home this very point. First he has Clitophon report that Leucippe's head and torso are separated when the pirate throws her body (but not the head) into the sea. Shortly after, he has Clitophon reinforce the point in his lament, holding Leucippe's body (but not the head) in his arms: "This time, Leukippe, you are without doubt dead twice over, divided in death between land and sea. I hold a headless relic; I've lost the real you .... let me kiss your butchered neck."[39] Finally (5.8) Achilles has Clitophon bury the torso (but not the head).

To Clitophon the finality of Leucippe's death is beyond doubt. So, at this moment, it is to readers. Achilles even stops the narrative altogether by having Clitophon return to Alexandria, his home, and by jumping ahead in time ("Six months had now passed"). Clitophon begins to get over his loss: "Even extreme grief ... cools when it is overcome by the soothing passage of time" (5.8).[40] Achilles' technique anticipates the cinema's: In a film we would watch a fade-out in which this strand of the story comes to an end, albeit an unresolved one, followed by a fade-in which takes us to a different time and place. A narrative dead end has occurred again.

Leucippe's two deaths happen in full view of her lover Clitophon, from whose perspective we follow the entire story. Like Clitophon we are convinced that Leucippe is dead. After he has overcome his grief, we may even suspect a new romance for him when he meets Melite, an attractive young

---

[38] Reardon 1989: 236.   [39] Reardon 1989: 236–237.   [40] The quotations at Reardon 1989: 237.

widow who has eyes only for him (5.13). To us as to Clitophon, the second instance of Leucippe's death appears to be final: Because of her decapitation and burial (in two parts), her end must be irreversible. As we will find out, we have fallen into the same narrative trap a second time. Still, experienced readers suspect that Leucippe will come back, although Achilles does not let us off the hook as quickly as before. The explanation of Leucippe's first death had followed immediately; the one for her second death is delayed for as long as possible. It comes shortly before the novel's very end, at 8.16 – the book's last chapter is 8.19 – after we have seen her reappear in the story (5.17). Moreover, the explanation provided is more far-fetched than the first; in Aristotle's terms, it is more striking. Leucippe provides the solution to "the riddle of the severed head" (8.15) in her own account (8.16):

"The bandits deceived a woman," she said, "one of those unfortunate creatures who sell their favors for money … Removing that poor woman's ornaments and clothes, they dressed me as her and put my modest little shift on her. Stationing her on the stern, where you in pursuit would see her, they sliced off her head and hurled the body (as you saw) down into the sea, but the head, as it fell, they caught and kept on the ship. A little later they got rid of this too, tossing it overboard . . . . they slew her in my place to deceive their pursuers, thinking they would stand to gain more profit from my sale than from hers."[41]

So the decapitation was real enough. The victim was without doubt dead, as Clitophon had exclaimed. It was just not the person he and we had been led to believe it was. The introduction into the story of the unfortunate creature who has to serve as a substitute for Leucippe and her nearly simultaneous ejection from the story is a clear instance of an authorial sleight of hand that is necessary in a mystery incompatible with verisimilitude. As Poe had said about convulsive fiction, "the incidents are *consequential* from the premises, while the premises themselves are laughably incredible." Still, Achilles considerably increases the effect that the shocking and the apparently impossible can have on the reader. Not in spite of but by means of near-impossible implausibilities, and with an increasing level of *adynata eikota*, he makes his story *ekplêktikôteron* before eventually bringing hero and heroine to their expected and well-deserved happy ending. Readers who are committed to realism or plausibility are not the kind of readers Achilles wants.

Achilles has twice pulled off the trick of presenting his readers with a narrative *adynaton* – the impossibility of a happy ending required in an

---

[41] Quotations at Reardon 1989: 281–282.

adventure-romance plot – that additionally incorporates two instances of the *ekplêktikon*. Will he try for a third time? As befits the complexity and antiverisimilitude of his plot, the answer to this question is: Yes and no. Yes, there will be a third pretended death for Leucippe; but no, it is not part of the main narrative but only reported verbally. In Book 7 Clitophon is in prison awaiting trial, and his rival Thersandros is planning revenge. Under false pretenses Thersandros contrives a henchman of his to become Clitophon's cell mate (7.1): "The plan was that this man, on instructions from Thersandros, was very artfully to introduce the news that Leukippe had been killed ... This fiendishly clever strategy was devised by Thersandros to throw me into despair at the death of my beloved so that even if I was judged innocent at the trial, I would not set out to find her." The accomplice gives Clitophon a false eyewitness account of Leucippe's death (7.3–4). Clitophon, who might be expected to know better by now, immediately believes the lie (7.4–5) and yields to despair: "O my Leukippe, how many times have you died on me!" (7.5). His friend Kleinias tries to talk some sense into him (7.6): "Who knows whether she is alive this time too. Hasn't she died many times before? Hasn't she often been resurrected?"[42] *Many times*? *Often*? No, only twice. But to Clitophon, Kleinias, and readers it feels like a whole series. At the end of Book 7 the two lovers are reunited (7.16). Shortly before (7.10 and 13), readers have become familiar with what happened to Leucippe.

The difference between this episode and the two others involving Leucippe's death is instructive about Achilles' narrative strategy. Since he cannot expect to fool his readers a third time, he changes tactics. Death is only reported, not witnessed; in theater or film terminology, it happens off stage or off screen. The mystery is resolved soon after. So the episode barely qualifies as an *ekplêktikon*. Even so, it is not a miscalculation on Achilles' part because the change from deaths witnessed to death told still works. The effect on his readers that Achilles apparently aims for is more complex than the brief episode might make us think. We can imagine him saying: *If you think I cannot deceive you a third time with a false death as I have done before, you are right, but I can still turn the screw once more by changing the way in which I present you with her third death.* After the gruesome details given in the two eyewitness accounts, Achilles here completely withholds how the third murder of Leucippe was supposedly committed. Thersandros' accomplice only tells Clitophon (7.4): "All I heard from the murderer was that he had killed the girl. He didn't tell

---

[42] Quotations at Reardon 1989: 260 and 261.

me where or how!"[43] This third death is anticlimactic, as Achilles must himself have realized. The radical change of moving it off screen does not save it from being much less gripping than the other two. Only an author's joy at playing narrative games with his readers can justify its inclusion. Achilles does not really deceive his readers, but he does not give up the game of deception.

3 Heliodorus: Death in a Cave

Scholars date *Leucippe and Clitophon*, the second-longest and second-most-complex surviving Greek novel, to around A D 150–175. The longest and most complex is *An Ethiopian Story*, best dated to after A D 350. It represents the apex of extant Greek novels.[44] Heliodorus' narrative trickery is even greater than that of Achilles Tatius: "The *Aethiopica* sets up a dazzling play with the course of its own action."[45] What Todorov observes about the narrative law within an individual work applies to the mystery-adventure genre as a whole: Temporal succession demands a gradation of intensity. Readers always want to be surprised. We may compare the reaction of Carr's Superintendent Hadley, experienced in crime as he is, at Dr. Fell's explanation of the impossible-looking murders in *The Hollow Man*: "By God! It fulfills every condition of the facts, and yet I never thought of it."[46] Clever authors take readers' generic experiences into consideration while adhering to the formulaic demands of their genre. To make his plot *ekplêktikôteron* than all predecessors', Heliodorus uses an omniscient third-person narrator, whose story contains first-person narrators and narrators speaking within another narrator's account. Moreover, the novel's first half is told by means of an intricate non-linear structure. Heliodorus contrives a strikingly fake death for his heroine as well, one that outdoes *Leucippe and Clitophon*. This kind of plot twist, with or without faked deaths, occasionally occurs in modern mystery fiction as well. A clever example is *An Instance of the Fingerpost* (1997) by Iain Pears, a novel set in seventeenth-century Oxford and incorporating into the fate of its fictional heroine the actual execution of Anne Greene in 1650.[47]

---

[43] Reardon 1989: 261.
[44] The novel will be cited and quoted according to Heliodoros, *An Ethiopian Story*, tr. J. R. Morgan, in Reardon 1989: 349–588. References to the text will again be parenthetical, quotations from the translation according to the volume in which it appeared.
[45] So Grethlein 2016: 317. He gives extensive references to scholarship on the novel's complexity.
[46] Carr 1986: 209.
[47] On Anne Greene see Gowing 2004. On Pears's novel see my brief comments in Winkler 1999.

The lovers Theagenes and Charikleia, Heliodorus' hero and heroine, undergo all manner of dangerous plot twists until the inevitable happy ending. In Book 1 we also become familiar with Knemon and Thisbe, a secondary pair erotically linked but in a way radically different from the main couple's romance. In Egypt Theagenes and Charikleia are captured by Thyamis, the leader of a local gang of robbers. He sets Knemon, a young Athenian, to guard the two. Knemon tells them his story (1.9–17). As he reveals, Thisbe, a slave girl, was in cahoots with Knemon's stepmother Demainete in Athens; both women are clever and unscrupulous connivers. Knemon had to fend off the advances of Demainete but was seduced by Thisbe on the order of a vindictive Demainete. As a result of Demainete's plots against him, Knemon was exiled from Athens and left for Egypt. En route he heard that Demainete and Thisbe had started turning against each other. Demainete's machinations were exposed by Thisbe's own, and the former came to a well-deserved end. The Athenian part of the novel's plot is complete.

Thyamis has fallen in love with Charikleia and proposes to marry her (1.18–21). But the robbers are now being attacked by a large enemy force, and Thyamis orders Knemon to hide Charikleia in a cave. Knemon does as instructed (1.27–29). After a fierce battle Thyamis despairs of ever possessing Charikleia. In wrath and frustration he decides to kill her (1. 30–31). As the narrator tells it:

Once embarked on a course of action, the heart of a savage brooks no turning back. And when a barbarian loses all hope of his own preservation, he will usually kill everything he loves before he dies .... crazed with love and jealousy and anger, he went to the cave as fast as he could run and jumped down into it, shouting long and loud in the Egyptian tongue. Just by the entrance he came upon a woman who spoke to him in Greek. Guided to her by her voice, he seized her head in his left hand and drove his sword through her breast, close to the bosom. With a last, piteous cry, the poor creature fell dead.[48]

Readers have been informed about the presence of only one person in the cave. So it appears that, less than one tenth into the tale, its heroine is dead – a greater shock (*ekplêktikôteron*) than the stabbing of Leucippe in Achilles' novel because this death occurs extremely early. But the narrator does not actually name or otherwise identify the victim except to say that she is Greek. And this points us to the explanation. At the beginning of Book 2 the robbers have been routed. Theagenes, who does not know about the cave, presumes his beloved Charikleia dead and decides to commit

---

[48] Reardon 1989: 377.

suicide (2.1). Knemon, however, tells him that she is alive and leads him to the cave. We are told that "Theagenes' spirits revived," only to be immediately informed: "Little did he know what sorrow awaited him there!"[49] The narrator's comment conforms to what we know or assume we know: Charikleia is dead; Knemon is not aware of any death in the cave. Once they arrive, Theagenes and Knemon quickly find the corpse and believe it to be Charikleia. Theagenes is again ready to kill himself (2.3–5). But from deep inside the cave he is called by a voice which Knemon identifies as Charikleia's. He looks at the dead woman's face and recognizes Thisbe, who is carrying a writing tablet under her arm (2.5–6).

Stunning as the identification of the corpse must be to Knemon, it is an even greater surprise to readers: *What is Thisbe doing here? How did she, last left in Athens at the end of Knemon's story, get to Egypt and into this cave?* The revelation that Charikleia is not dead is no huge surprise to readers familiar with romance fiction; the reappearance of Thisbe, a character whose narrative function had supposedly been fulfilled before, may have struck ancient readers as nothing less than a shock, an *ekplêktikon*. Knemon himself functions as our mouthpiece when he exclaims (2.5): "What is this? O gods, you have brought about the impossible!" A little later he comments to Theagenes (2.7): "you found that the dead woman was who you least expected it to be." Half a page on, we read (2.8): "Charikleia was astounded. 'It is not possible, Knemon!' she said. 'How can someone suddenly be spirited away . . . out of the heart of Greece to the remotest parts of Egypt? . . .'"[50] Our question exactly.

Unlike Leucippe's deaths, Thisbe's is real. Thyamis could not have used a trick sword and had no reason to deceive anybody. So what led to Thisbe's presence in the cave? The explanation arrives soon enough. First Knemon continues his own story and reports that Thisbe had left Athens to escape punishment for the death of her mistress Demainete (2.8–9). Then Thisbe's tablet solves the main part of the riddle: She had been the robbers' captive for several days (2.10). Knemon has also recognized the murder weapon still protruding from the corpse as belonging to Thyamis (2.6 and 11). Everybody now knows the essentials. The only part still unclear is how Thisbe ended up in the cave (2.11). This last piece of the puzzle falls into place when the narrator tells us in a third-person flashback that Thyamis' second-in-command Thermouthis had secretly shut Thisbe in the cave near its entrance to keep her for himself (2.12). Thermouthis is just as surprised at discovering Thisbe dead as we were a little earlier.

---

[49] Reardon 1989: 380.   [50] Reardon 1989: 382 and 383.

Credo quia complexum: The apparent death of Charikleia is the real death of Thisbe and occurs as a result of the author's false pretenses and a character's mistaken identity. It is at first as sudden and *ekplêktikon* as it is mysterious, the more so because Thisbe is not the story's heroine and has already been dropped from the main narrative and the readers' awareness. Neither ancient nor modern readers are likely to have expected a secondary character to receive such prominence in the plot. How did this woman whom we had left in a far-away city end up in a different country, in an improbable place, and at a time when the heroine's life but not her own is in danger? The greater is the effect of the *ekplêktikon* at this point. It is evident that Heliodorus was counting on just this kind of readers' thinking to spring his narrative trap: the secure, although here false, sense that secondary characters play only minor parts. The extreme complexity of Heliodorus' plot and that of his presentation make the *ekplêktikon* possible. The death in the cave is one instance of an *apiston* that is fully integrated into a whole series of larger ones, all of them interconnected.

Through mysterious foreshadowing Heliodorus had thrown down a narrative gauntlet even before we learned of the existence of the cave, which is first mentioned at 1.28. At 1.18 Thyamis has a dream in which the goddess Isis delivers Charikleia to him: "you shall have her and not have her; you shall do wrong and slay her, but she shall not be slain." Ancient dream visions, oracles, and other prophecies routinely contained enough enigmas, illogicalities, and impossibilities to cause headaches in those blessed or cursed to receive them. So it is with Thyamis. His reaction to the dream is an apt summary of any mystery reader's absorption in a complex plot: "The dream caused him great perplexity, and he turned the vision over and over in his mind, wondering what it could mean. Eventually, in desperation he forced the interpretation to conform with his own desires."[51] Readers do the same thing: Perplexed, they force the kind of solution they wish to be true by trying to make sense of something that only the author, the man who explains miracles, can clear up. In *An Ethiopian Story* this process is pushed even further. At the beginning of its second half Knemon hears Thisbe's name mentioned again and assumes that she is still alive, although, as he remembers, "with my own eyes I saw and recognized her lifeless body, and with my own hands I buried her."[52] He then overhears a woman's lament, in which she refers to her narrow escape from violent death and calls herself Thisbe (5.2). The narrator at once provides the correct identification: "the woman he had heard

---

[51] Both quotations at Reardon 1989: 369.   [52] Reardon 1989: 446.

lamenting was not Thisbe, but Charikleia!" The next sentence brings the explanation in a flashback: "This is what had happened to her ..." (5.4).[53] Here is another *ekplêktikon*, made more effective by its reversal of identities: First Thisbe had been mistaken for Charikleia, now Charikleia has been mistaken for Thisbe. Why the latter should call herself by the name of the former is enough to make us react as Knemon does (5.2): "he racked his brains in bewilderment and despair to make sense of it."[54] The information that makes it all clear comes a little later (5.8). How does Dr. Fell put it? "A great part of our liking for detective fiction is *based* on a liking for improbability." Doubtless the good doctor and his creator would have enjoyed *An Ethiopian Story* had they known it.

To literate ancient readers, the kind Heliodorus is writing for, there will have been one other aspect in the story of Thisbe that made this part of the plot still more of an *ekplêktikon* than it may be to many modern readers. Death by the sword near, if not in, a cave had come to a more famous Thisbe as a result of a misunderstanding, not through mistaken identity but through incorrect interpretation of what had happened. In his *Metamorphoses* Ovid told the story of Pyramus and Thisbe, the star-crossed lovers of Babylon.[55] The tale is probably of Hellenistic Greek origin. Ovid's Thisbe sought refuge from a lion in a cave; Heliodorus' Thisbe was put in a cave for safekeeping. Ovid's Thisbe killed herself with Pyramus' sword when she found him dead – Pyramus had rashly assumed her killed by the lion and had carried out what Theagenes is prevented from doing; Heliodorus' Thisbe is killed by someone else. Thisbe's name practically preordains her fate. *Nomen est omen*: Beware of swords and caves if your name is Thisbe! Heliodorus cleverly plays with the earlier tale; he expects his readers to notice and to appreciate his deviations.[56] And his deviousness as author.

In retrospect we can apply Agatha Christie's praise of John Dickson Carr to our ancient authors: *Very few mystery stories baffle us nowadays, but Mr. Achilles Tatius' and Mr. Heliodorus' always do*. All three – and Dame Agatha as well – are masters of the *pithanon adynaton* and the *ekplêktikon*.

On March 1, 1909, Arthur Conan Doyle gave a speech at the Authors' Club in London, honoring the centenary of Poe's birth. He observed:

His tales were one of the great landmarks and starting points in the literature of the last century ... For those tales have been so pregnant with suggestion, so

---

[53] Reardon 1989: 448.   [54] Reardon 1989: 446.   [55] Ovid, *Metamorphoses* 4.55–166.
[56] On Heliodorus' narrative cleverness in the cave scene in regard to languages (Egyptian, Greek) see the clever comments by John J. Winkler 1982: 105.

stimulating to the minds of others, that it may be said of many of them that each is a root from which a whole literature has developed ... Where was the detective story until Poe breathed the breath of life into it?[57]

We can now answer the question, which was meant to be only rhetorical, in a way Conan Doyle was not thinking of. The detective story, at least in regard to certain archetypal plot turns, was alive and well in classical antiquity. Some of the ancient Greek novelists wrote stories pregnant with suggestions and stimulating to others' minds – or rather, they would have had a stimulating effect if their modern successors had known them. The roots from which the whole literature of mystery fiction was to develop reached back even deeper in time than the years between Poe and Conan Doyle.

4   Hitchcock: Sudden Death in the Shower

In the cinema there is one master of mystery who can claim to be the ancient Greeks' equal, even if he was unaware of their existence. His most profound work we might characterize as *ekplêktikôtaton* – "perhaps the most terrifying film ever made."[58]

   The most notorious sequence in *Psycho*, Alfred Hitchcock's most famous thriller, is the murder of Marion Crane in her shower, a little over halfway into the film. Marion's death is even more shocking to viewers than Leucippe's and Thisbe's ordeals can have been to readers. Marion is, ostensibly, the film's heroine, whose journey into crime we have been following. But a character as prominent as her should never be killed off. Experienced thriller producer-director William Castle, a filmmaker considerably below the artistic level of a Hitchcock but nevertheless knowledgeable about delivering the suspense and goose bumps audiences expect, stated this unwritten law of plot construction in "How to Plan a Movie Murder," a promotional short for his shocker *Strait-Jacket* (1964). *Strait-Jacket* was written by Robert Bloch, author of the novel on which *Psycho* had been based, and starred Joan Crawford as an axe murderess. No credits for this short film are provided, but it is most likely that it was Castle's own concoction, made after the feature film had already been shot. (Footage from *Strait-Jacket* appears in it.) Castle,

---

[57] Quoted from Conan Doyle 1967: 162–163 note 62; quotation at 163. In *A Study in Scarlet*, Holmes is as dismissive of Dupin as Conan Doyle was appreciative of Poe.

[58] The quotation is from Wood 2002: 142.

Bloch, and Crawford are discussing various aspects of a murder plot; their playfully gruesome dialogue, full of word plays and rather forced humor, has been scripted beforehand. Castle defines his kind of plot as "a story so full of unexpected thrills and shocks and suspense that the audience has no chance to catch its breath between gasps." After the three have chosen the location and weapon for their thriller, they turn to the question of the murder victim. "Who shall it be?" Castle asks. Bloch replies: "Would it be bad taste to head off with our star?" Castle's immediate answer: "Ridiculous! It's just not done." The three then pretend to consider some other candidates from their cast.

In principle, of course, Castle was right. It really *is* not done – except that Hitchcock had done it in *Psycho*, and the result was anything but ridiculous. But is Marion's murder plausible or verisimilitudinous? Before we turn to the shower sequence, we should be aware of the close analogy in the plots of novels and films in general and of mystery novels and films in particular. Four film scholars, writing collectively, provide us with a concise overview of the plausible in the cinema.

"The plausible," they explain, "is tied to the motivations of the actions undertaken within the story" and belongs to more than one story: "The plausible simultaneously involves the relationship between a text and commonly held opinion [an echo of Aristotle], its relation to other texts [an echo of Todorov; cf. below], and also the internal functioning of the story being told." It follows that "the plausible restrains the number of narrative possibilities and imaginable diegetic situations [i.e., situations within the world of the story being told], all in the name of preserving the rules." How do these rules work?

The plausible also consists of a certain number of rules that affect character actions in terms of the maxims by which those very actions may be conditioned. These rules, which are tacitly recognized by the public, yet never explained, are applied so well that the relationship between a story and the system of plausibility to which it submits is essentially a silent one . . . . whatever is foreseeable is considered to be plausible. By contrast, the implausible is judged to be that which the audience cannot possibly foresee, whether from the angle of the story or that of its maxims, and the implausible will suddenly appear as a show of force of the narrative instance trying to achieve its goals.

As a result, "the narrative is able to transform the artificial and arbitrary relations established by the narration into a plausible and natural relation-ship established by the diegetic facts . . . . the plausible becomes only one means of naturalizing the arbitrariness of the narrative and then realizing it (in the sense of making it pass for real)."[59]

Earlier I linked Todorov's general narrative law of the gradation of intensity within individual plots to the temporal succession within a genre. Our film scholars explain why such an approach is necessary:

> If the plausible is defined in relation to common opinions or maxims, it is also necessarily defined in relation to other texts to the extent that the latter always tend to disseminate a commonly held opinion by their very convergence. Thus, a film's plausibility owes much to previous, already produced films, since plausibility will be judged as that which has already been seen in a previous work ... One may argue, therefore, that the plausible is established not as a function of reality, but as a function of already established texts (or films) ...
>
> Consequently, it becomes clear that a work's content is decided much more in relation to previous works (whether to copy or oppose them) than in relation to any more detailed or more correct observation of reality. The plausible, therefore, must be understood as a form, which is to say an organization, of the standardized content of a string of texts. Its changes and its evolution then become functions of the earlier plausible's system. Within this evolution of the plausible, the new system only appears "real" because the old one is declared out of date and hence denounced as conventional, even though the new system is obviously just as conventional.[60]

Christian Metz, one of the most influential scholars of film semiotics, begins his discussion of the plausible with a brief reference to Aristotle.[61] Later, in passing, he mentions Alfred Hitchcock. Each of his films is "the product of a controlled genre intended to be viewed as a performance of

---

[59] Aumont et al. 1992: 115, 114, and 116 (from section "The Plausible" in a chapter titled "Realism in the Cinema"). The entire section is important. The authors, who provide a number of illuminating examples, are indebted to the detailed discussion of the plausible in Metz 1974: 236–251. Metz, 97–98 gives a definition of *diegesis* ("narration") in cinema as "the sum of a film's denotation: the narration itself, but also the fictional space and time dimensions implied in and by the narrative, and consequently the characters, the landscapes, the events, and other narrative elements" (98). On the plausible in the recognition scenes of Greek and Roman novels, also in connection with visual aspects, see Montiglio 2013, e.g. 4–6 and 122–123. On recognition in general, beginning with Aristotelian *anagnôrisis*, see Cave 1988.

[60] Aumont et al. 1992: 116–117. The immediately following section ("The Genre Effect") is important for our subject as well: "the plausible will ... be more solid within a long series of films that are closely related in their expression and their content" (117). In regard to *Psycho*, their point that the implausible and shocking easily becomes conventional is borne out by the ubiquity of graphic violence on screen in horror, slasher, and other such films. Hitchcock's film is not on the same low level as those of his imitators or epigones.

[61] Metz 1974: 238. At least in the English edition the Greek spelling of Aristotle's *to eikos* is incorrect. On Metz's original *le Vraisemblable* ("the Plausible"; cf. Todorov's "Verisimilitude") see the translator's note in Metz 1974: 250.

discourse in relation to the other works of the same 'genre'." Every such work *"rejects Plausibility . . .* since it renounces the attempt to *appear true."* This narrative perspective also applies to Achilles Tatius and Heliodorus, as we have seen. Metz continues, and again we should think of our Greek storytellers: "Works of this variety afford their spectators (who know the rules of the game) some of the most intense 'aesthetic' enjoyment there is: The enjoyment of complicity, or of competence, of microtechniques, and of comparisons within a closed field."[62]

A particular moment in Hitchcock's *Dial M for Murder* (1954) is both instructive for our topic and amusing in its straightforwardness and elegant irony. A writer of mystery fiction is explaining his theory of why and by whom the titular murder must have been committed to a Chief Inspector of Scotland Yard; he does so in the presence of the man whom he suspects and we already know to be guilty. The criminal, however, is not fazed: "If I'd told that story of his, would anyone believe me?" he asks the inspector. "No, not a chance," is the reply. On the face of it, the story is far too convoluted to be credible or even plausible. But *we* know it to be true. The inspector, who will soon catch the clever criminal, may already suspect or even know as much, too. Whether he does we do not know. Not a chance, however, that the fiendish plot twists will not be straightened out eventually. The very implausibility of the murder scheme and the unforeseen because accidental circumstances that derail it make this the classic suspense film it is. Astonishingly, it all works because at one crucial moment Hitchcock had withheld a tiny but decisive piece of information from us.

So we are justified to consider the striking plot turns in *Leucippe and Clitophon, An Ethiopian Story, Dial M for Murder,* and *Psycho* as high points in a long narrative tradition that uses plausible implausibilities and antiverisimilitudinous shocks as means to create thrilling stories that are unsurpassed for their vividness and effect.[63] How does Hitchcock accomplish this in *Psycho*? Why is Marion Crane's death still shocking after more than half a century of murder and mayhem on our screens, most of it far more explicit than anything Hitchcock could have believed possible or necessary?

The first thing to note is that Hitchcock takes care to adhere as closely as possible to one of the basic rules for gripping narratives as outlined by

---

[62] Metz 1974: 248; emphases in original. What Metz, 249 goes on to say about plausible works and their claims to be linked to reality is instructive.

[63] John J. Winkler 1982: 94 obliquely refers to the shower murder in *Psycho* in a discussion of surprise and suspense.

Aristotle: unity of action.[64] From the very beginning, when we are introduced to Marion Crane, we are drawn inexorably into her world, for until her death we never leave her.[65] Rarely does a film make a viewer's identification with a character more compelling: "So far in the film [i.e. up to her death] the spectator has shared Marion's consciousness almost exclusively."[66] Not only do we side with Marion emotionally from the start, but we also understand her when she embezzles a large sum of money and hope for her escape. By the time that a guilty Marion encounters a policeman, one of the most intense sequences in the film, we have completely committed ourselves to her. First, and in a reversal of the rule that crime must never pay, we want her to go scot-free. Later, Marion has a crucial conversation with Norman Bates, a nice young man whose hobby is taxidermy and who rents her a room in his motel. As a result Marion decides to face the consequences of her action, and we hope that her punishment will be lenient or suspended. We want Marion to live happily ever after with the man she loves. When she steps into her shower, we stay with her and see her in close-ups. By now we have become practically inseparable from her. Then the killer strikes. When Norman sinks Marion's car with her dead body in the trunk into a nearby swamp and the scene fades out, the film seems to be over: "the story has stopped dead."[67] We watch a fade-out in which Marion's story comes to an end, albeit an unresolved one, followed by a fade-in which shows us a different time and place and introduces new characters. This parallels what I discussed above concerning the apparent dead end in Book 5 of *Leucippe and Clitophon*.

Viewers are stunned. There is no clue why Marion was killed. The fact that Marion did not know why she had to die, either, only makes her death *ekplêktikôteron*. Our emotional bond with her had become so close that we are at a loss to understand how the story we have been following can possibly be continued: "The murder . . . constitutes an alienation effect so shattering that . . . we scarcely recover from it. Never . . . has identification been broken off so brutally . . . . we are left shocked, with nothing to cling to, the apparent center of the film entirely dissolved."[68] And: "it is a vital part of the design [of the film] that we should be cut adrift emotionally by

---

[64] On unity of action and the unities of time and place, usually considered together, see the sensible remarks by Butcher 1907: 274–301 (chapter titled "The Dramatic Unities"). Butcher, 289 calls the theory of the three unities a "famous literary superstition."

[65] I omit discussing the film's opening here; cf. my comments on it in connection with the opening of *An Ethiopian Story* in Winkler 2000–2001: 175–177. Wood 2002: 142 rightly observes about the beginning of *Psycho*: "this . . . could be *us*."

[66] Quoted from Perkins 1972: 108. On this see also Wood 2002: 144–145.

[67] Durgnat 2002: 122.   [68] Wood 2002: 146.

the shock removal of the picture's chief identification figure, heroine and star."[69] We also do not know yet what the film's title means. Only later will we find out that *Psycho* is not Marion's story after all – or rather, not *only* her story. The title hints at this. For all we know, no psychopath or psychologically unstable character has appeared so far. The fact that Janet Leigh, the most popular star of *Psycho* who was featured prominently in its advertising, does not receive first or second billing in the credits also gives us a clue. Hers is the last of six title cards naming the cast, although her importance is indicated by the same size of her name's letters as those of the three actors receiving top billing and by the addition of her character's name. The cinematic tradition of protagonists' deaths works like this:

such deaths were carefully prepared by moral-dramatic patterning: they follow some sin or tragic flaw, or they're morally affirmative or gloriously vitalist, or 'a good cry'. Here the death of Janet Leigh, normally a happy star, is carefully *not* prepared, and defies all standard dramatic protocol since Aristotle. It proclaims a state of chaos.[70]

As we have seen with Achilles Tatius and Heliodorus, however, Hitchcock is not quite as defiant of Aristotle or Greek literature as all that. Rather, in Hitchcock's own words: "The whole *point* is to kill off the star – that is what makes it so unexpected."[71] In Aristotle's word: *ekplêktikôteron*.

Ancient authors did not give interviews, keep diaries or other notes on their creative processes or intentions, or let their readers know what they had in mind. Today we are better off. Hitchcock repeatedly spoke about *Psycho* and its shower sequence. Considering that the two ancient novels and this film include scenes of sudden death to make each story *ekplêktikôteron*, Hitchcock's words about *Psycho* are instructive for our Greek novels, too. With some obvious adjustments, we could be hearing Achilles or Heliodorus.

Hitchcock said about the heart of the matter, the *ekplêktikon*: "I think that the thing that appealed to me and made me decide to do the picture was the suddenness of the murder in the shower, coming, as it were, out of the blue. That was about all."[72] The audience had to be deceived about what the story was going to be like:

---

[69] Perkins 1972: 108.

[70] Durgnat 2002: 111. Two of Leigh's earlier parts in *film noir* thrillers, however, were anything but happy. In Fred Zinnemann's *Act of Violence* (1948) she gets caught up in the guilty past of her husband; in Orson Welles's *Touch of Evil* (1958) she is terrorized in a seedy motel by a gang of sadistic hoodlums.

[71] Quoted from Bogdanovich 1997: 533.   [72] Quoted from Truffaut 1984: 268–269.

the first part of the story was a red herring. That was deliberate ... to detract the viewer's attention to heighten the murder ... You turn the viewer in one direction and then in another; you keep him as far as possible from what's actually going to happen. I purposely killed the star so as to make the killing even more unexpected .... that game with the audience was fascinating. I was directing the viewers.[73]

The shower murder "took us seven days to shoot ..., and there were seventy camera setups for forty-five seconds of footage ... Naturally, the knife never touched the body; it was all done in the montage."[74] But this is not quite the case: For a split second the knife does touch the body.[75] And yes, it was the kind of knife we encountered in Achilles Tatius: "Hitch used a retractable knife. In fact, he held the knife himself because he knew exactly where he wanted that to be for his camera."[76]

The extreme care that went into the filming revealed Hitchcock's enjoyment in telling such a gripping tale: "It was rather exciting to use the camera to deceive the audience .... I don't care about the subject matter ... but I do care about the pieces of film ... and all of the technical ingredients that make the audience scream ... They were aroused by pure film."[77] If they could, Achilles and Heliodorus would agree: *It was rather exciting to use the stylus to deceive the readers. We care about all the ingredients that make the audience react. They were aroused by pure text.* Hitchcock concludes about *Psycho* in particular and his kind of thriller in general: "It's an area of film-making in which it's more important for you to be pleased with the technique than with the content."[78] We can imagine our ancient novelists as well as Poe and Carr nodding their assent.[79]

Unlike Achilles' Leucippe but like Heliodorus' Thisbe, Hitchcock's Marion Crane is really dead. And again *nomen est omen*: If your last name

---

[73] Truffaut 1984: 269.

[74] Truffaut 1984: 277. Anobile 1974: 92–113 presents a still image of each shot in the sequence; his book reproduces the entire film in frame enlargements. On the shower sequence see Rothman 1982: 292–310, especially 302–307; Rebello 1990: 100–118; Leigh 1984: 254–259; Leigh 1995: 65–76; Durgnat 2002: 108–125; and Skerry 2009: 219–260 (this book's main title is unfortunate). The number of days devoted to filming the shower sequence may have been longer (Rebello 1990: 116), and there may have been as many as seventy-eight shots for the murder; so, e.g., Hitchcock himself in Gottlieb 2003: 99, 107, and 188. But cf. Skerry 2009: 215 and 242–252. Krohn 2000: 230 furnishes some additional details. See also Kolker 2004a and Smith III 2009.

[75] Kolker 2004b: 247–248 examines this moment (with frame enlargements). See also Durgnat 2002: 115–116 and Skerry 2009: 222–223, 225, and 250–251 (with frame enlargement).

[76] Janet Leigh, quoted in Rebello 1990: 112. Cf. Skerry 2009: 19 (quoting Leigh). A real knife appears in the other shots.

[77] Truffaut 1984: 277 and 283.   [78] Truffaut 1984: 283.

[79] On the affinities between Poe and Hitchcock cf. Perry 2003.

is Crane, beware of anyone who stuffs birds! Unlike the cases of Leucippe and Thisbe, however, the main reason for Marion's death is a plot development of such deviousness that viewers will be in for an even greater shock when they receive the explanation. Hitchcock, master creator of mystery and suspense and, as here, of shocking twists, is the modern heir to Achilles and Heliodorus. Hitchcock was not a reader of Aristotle or our two ancient novelists.[80] But he adhered to the theory of *adynata eikota* and the *ekplêktikôteron* as outlined by Aristotle and restated by Poe and Carr; he also applied this theory in the manner practiced by Achilles and Heliodorus. The similarities and the comparable plot functions of sudden murders justify juxtaposing the ancient authors and the modern director. What Robin Wood once wrote about Hitchcock's *The Birds* (1963) applies to our context as well: "whether or not Hitchcock consciously intended these interpretations [i.e., those Wood advances] is quite immaterial: the only question worth discussing is whether they are sufficiently *there*, in the film .... there is no need to suppose them consciously worked out."[81]

Like the Greek novelists, Hitchcock was aware of the gap between fiction grounded in realism and his own thrillers. He repeatedly made fun of critics who objected to improbabilities in his films and sarcastically dismissed them as "our friends, the plausibles and logicians."[82] "We should have total freedom to do as we like," was his artistic creed, "just so long as it's not dull. A critic who talks to me about plausibility is a dull fellow."[83] In other words: "Film should be stronger than reason."[84] Viewers who are committed to realism or plausibility are not the kind of viewers Hitchcock wants. Disarmingly, however, Hitchcock also said: "On the one hand I claim to dismiss the plausibles, and on the other I'm worried about them. After all, I'm only human!"[85] His plots are far too complicated to be tied down by pure realism, although they are not what Poe had called the convulsive kind that begins from laughably incredible premises. On the appearance of the local police official shortly after the second half of *Psycho* begins, Hitchcock observed:

---

[80] Or of Xenophon of Ephesus, who includes an embalmed corpse in *An Ephesian Tale*. The fisherman Aegialeus keeps his beloved wife Thelxinoe with him after she dies. He talks to her, eats with her, and even sleeps next to her (5.1). Hitchcock might have appreciated the macabre nature of this chaste necrophilia.

[81] Wood 2002: 171. [82] Quoted from Truffaut 1984: 151. [83] Quoted from Kapsis 1992: 81.

[84] Quoted from McGilligan 2003: 24. Amusingly but erroneously, McGilligan calls the plausibles "implausibles."

[85] Quoted from Truffaut 1984: 151.

The sheriff's intervention comes under the heading of . . . "Why don't they go to the police?" I've always replied, "They don't go to the police because it's dull." Here is a perfect example of what happens when they go to the police.[86]

The sheriff serves an obvious plot necessity, but Hitchcock's point is valid: This soon after the film's most shocking sequence – as Aristotle might have called it, the *ekplêktikôtaton* – the normal world comes as a disappointment. Even more disappointing to many, viewers and critics alike, has been the psychiatrist's explanation of Marion's killer's state of mind at the film's end. It has come in for extensive criticism from the plausibles as being unconvincing or superficial.[87] But what not even the logicians among the plausibles seem to have noticed is the contradiction between the explanation and what it is intended to explain. The doctor tells us that Norman, who ten years earlier had killed his widowed mother and her lover, "was simply doing everything possible to keep alive the illusion of his mother being alive." Mother takes over Norman's personality: "when reality came too close, when danger or desire threatened that illusion, he'd dress up . . . He'd walk about the house, sit in her chair, speak in her voice. He'd try to *be* his mother!" But the images on the screen have already undermined what the words now attempt to make plausible. On arriving at the Bates Motel, Marion and we, from her point of view, see the silhouette of an old woman through a window. This is the first moment that Hitchcock showed us Norman as Mother, although neither Marion nor we know this yet. If Mother takes over whenever reality comes too close, when danger or desire threatens – then *why is Mother already there* before she or Norman can have had the slightest inkling of Marion's presence? At that moment there had been no need for Norman to keep the illusion alive. A well-known film scholar has observed about the second time Mrs. Bates is being observed through her window early in *Psycho*: "Why, a plausible might ask, would Norman put her in the window, for all the world to see, when supposedly she's dead? Good question. Available answer: when Norman was in the motel, the sight of her in the window soothed his uneasy mind."[88] Good answer?

Is Hitchcock playing with us? Of course he is – for the sake of a more striking story. If all's fair in love and war, all's fair in the world of narrative as well. The *apiston* or *adynaton* has become the *pithanon*. As Aristotle had said: *pithanon tini pithanon* – what is credible is so because it is credible to someone. Hitchcock has made *Psycho* completely credible to us.

[86] Truffaut 1984: 269–270.
[87] Contrast the detailed examination of the psychiatrist's speech in Durgnat 2002: 208–216.
[88] Durgnat 2002: 216.

5 Aristotle Vindicated

As Dorothy Sayers pointed out, if Aristotle could have returned in the twentieth century, he could easily have included a consideration of modern mystery fiction in his *Poetics*. Could he also have added the cinema? The answer to this question, posed some years ago, now seems obvious.[89]

S. H. Butcher, one of the most perceptive commentators on the *Poetics*, concluded about Aristotle's discussion of possibilities and impossibilities: "These so-called *adynata* [impossibilities in reality] are the very *dynata* [possibilities] of art, the stuff and substance of which poetry [i.e. every story] is made … The *adynata*, things impossible in fact, become *pithana* [things credible or convincing in a narrative]."[90] His words apply to Achilles Tatius, Heliodorus, and Hitchcock in equal measure. They are also applicable to most, and probably all, fictional or creative narratives, especially action-driven ones. In the age of computer-generated images (CGI), which make viewers' willing suspension of disbelief even in the applicability of the laws of nature not only possible but also easy, we find ample confirmation. Here is just one example.

J. J. Abrams begins *Mission: Impossible III* (2006) with the hero at the mercy of the villain and pleading for the life of a woman who turns out to be his wife in an extended flashback. The villain shoots her point-blank before the hero's eyes. Can such a thing be? Not in genre fiction or films, as we now know. At the end, when the narrative circles back to this opening scene for its closure, we find out that the woman killed was, after all, someone else. Our hero will save his wife, and they will live happily ever after. As with the second death of Leucippe, we witnessed a real and sadistic death, just not of the person we and the hero were misled to believe it was. Plausibility is not the issue or, in Dr. Fell's words, does not enter into it. And just as in Achilles Tatius, the hero is at first deceived as well. The exact manner of deception involves a facial mask that disguises its wearer's identity. We have previously watched an elaborate sequence involving the hero wearing the villain's face. Now we accept the implausibility inherent in the revelation of the woman's identity more readily since we already saw an even more complicated assumption of false identity. In an additional plot twist, the hero himself dies momentarily but is resuscitated at the last moment by his wife. Presumably not even Achilles Tatius or Heliodorus would have twisted a plot toward this particular turn of events. And rightly so, for no one in the cinema would believe for even one moment

---

[89] I allude to the title of Barilli 2007.   [90] Quoted from Butcher 1907: 170–171 and 173.

in the death of such a hero. He is played by Tom Cruise, a star much more popular in his time than Janet Leigh had been in hers. In general, however, certain extreme plot contrivances firmly established in ancient fiction are alive and more than well in contemporary popular narratives, especially in blockbuster spectacles. To update Butler's words: The traditional *adynata* have become *pithana* on our CGI-saturated screens.

"What is drama after all, but life with the dull bits cut out."[91] This definition by Hitchcock fits all narrative literature from antiquity to today, from mysteries and adventure-romances to serious epics, dramas, and novels. It also applies to narratives in images.

In 1881 Thomas Hardy jotted down the following observations about the nature of fiction, possibly as notes for an article that was never written. His points pertain directly to our topic:

> The real, if unavowed, purpose of fiction is to give pleasure by gratifying the love of the uncommon in human experience mental or corporeal.
>
> This is done all the more perfectly in proportion as the reader is illuded to believe the personages true and real like himself.
>
> Solely to this latter end a work of fiction should be a precise transcript of ordinary life: but,
>
> The uncommon would be absent and the interest lost. Hence,
>
> The writer's problem is, how to strike the balance between the uncommon and the ordinary so as on the one hand to give interest, on the other to give reality.
>
> In working out this problem, human nature must never be made abnormal, which is introducing incredibility. The uncommonness must be in the events, not in the characters; and the writer's art lies in shaping that uncommonness while disguising its unlikelihood, if it be unlikely.[92]

Hardy's perceptive summation amounts to a classic definition of the purpose of fiction. It squarely puts him into the camp of Aristotle, of whom he must have known, and of Achilles Tatius and Heliodorus, of whom he probably did not know. And equally, although after his time, of Hitchcock.

Equally, Hitchcock's witty description of the differences between a cinema that adheres to drab reality and probability at any price and his own work that is exciting at the expense of verisimilitude may stand as a final comment on our topic: "Some directors film slices of life, I film slices of cake."[93] Aristotle, Achilles, Heliodorus, and Hardy would have no problem

---

[91] Quoted from Truffaut 1984: 103.

[92] Hardy 1989: 154. *The Mayor of Casterbridge* (1886) is just one example among Hardy's novels in which a complex plot hinges on an astonishing, even shocking, but verifiable implausibility.

[93] Quoted from Truffaut 1984: 339; cf. 103. This and Hitchcock's preceding aphorism are often quoted in slightly different wording.

understanding Hitchcock's meaning concerning the timeless pleasure of narrative, whether in word or image. From an Aristotelian perspective, one that Hardy's words only corroborate, even reinforce, the striking plot turns here examined confirm the modernity of Achilles Tatius and Heliodorus and the classical timelessness of Alfred Hitchcock (but not of J. J. Abrams). All three provide us with pleasurable and satisfying slices of cake that are also intellectually nourishing.

6 | John Ford, America's Virgil

John Ford, who directed his first film in 1917 and his last in 1966, is the only major American artist to recreate virtually the entire course of American history from the Revolutionary War (*Drums Along the Mohawk*, 1939) to contemporary politics (*The Last Hurrah*, 1958). While World Wars I and II, social problems like the plight of the Okies, and other aspects of twentieth-century history take up a large part in his extensive body of work, the portrayal of the history and myth of the American West in the 1800s is Ford's greatest and most famous legacy. "My name is John Ford; I am a Director of Westerns" – this is how he once defined himself on a memorable occasion.[1]

"Westward the Course of Empire Takes Its Way" – the title of Emanuel Leutze's painting of 1861, on display in the US Capitol and one of the best-known examples of Manifest Destiny, is perhaps the fundamental expression of the nature of American history both in fact and in the popular imagination about this history.[2] So it is in Ford, but with a complexity that is likely to surprise all those who consider the cinema to be merely "the movies" and Westerns to be no more than horse operas or shoot-'em-ups.

1 The Courses of Empire

A brief summary regarding empire may be instructive about the similarity between American and Roman foundation histories and the myths accompanying them.[3] In both, small but intrepid groups of emigrants are more or less forced to abandon their home (Troy, England) and, after a long and

---

[1] This was a meeting of the Screen Directors Guild on October 22, 1950, concerning a loyalty oath and the blacklist. Since there was only a stenographic record, Ford's words have been reported in different versions, and eyewitness accounts vary in a number of details. My quotation is from Brianton 2016: 67. This book now supersedes all earlier accounts and commentaries, which it lists in its bibliography. Ford speaks at length about himself in Bogdanovich 1978 and Peary 2001.

[2] The title of Leutze's painting is a quotation of line 21 in Bishop Berkeley's poem "On the Prospect of Planting Arts and Learning in America" (1752); an earlier version dates to 1726.

[3] Concerning Virgil see, e.g., Miles 1999, with brief comments on Roman and American parallels and on other ancient versions of Rome's foundation. On the wider context see Quint 1993; Waswo 1997, especially 308–324 (chapter titled "The Epic as History: John Ford's Westerns"). On the spellings *Virgil* and *Vergil* see the comments by Gransden 1996: xxxv.

dangerous sea voyage westward, land in a new world (Latium in Italy, America). They find a partly friendly and partly hostile reception among the aboriginal tribes. Against all odds they survive hardship, setbacks, and wars. To a certain extent they eventually merge with the native population, but the tribes are mostly conquered or destroyed and leave only minor traces in the new dominant culture. In retrospect the natives, nearly vanished, become highly romanticized by their conquerors. Their newly established society soon begins an expansion that will turn it into a global power. Its conquests are by force of arms. The Roman legions were a nearly invincible military machine in antiquity, and so was the American military-industrial complex during and after World War II.

The rise and eventual fall of Rome has provided Americans with much soul-searching about the rise and possible fall of their own superpower. Are they Rome?[4] Throughout their history Americans have considered themselves spiritual descendants of the ancient Romans. A revealing early illustration is the series of five paintings by Thomas Cole, collectively called *The Course of Empire* (1834–1836). The individual images are "The Savage State," "The Arcadian or Pastoral State," "The Consummation of Empire," "Destruction," and "Desolation." They chart a symbolic course of all empires. Cole gives his series the look of the Roman Empire, the archetypal or paradigmatic empire in Western history and imagination. All architecture in the series is Roman, rather bombastically so in the third and central painting, which is also the largest. The first painting, however, shows what appears like a small village of tents or tepees arranged in a semicircle. The point this makes is understated but obvious. What Virgil said about the Romans' course of empire in the proem of the *Aeneid*, Rome's national epic as it has sometimes been called, may be applied to the course of the American empire with a few adjustments of geographical terms, with emphasis less on one leader and more on his people, and with the omission of a Roman deity's name and involvement:

> Arms and the man I sing of Troy, who first from its seashores
> Italy-bound, fate's refugee, arrived at Lavinia's
> Coastlands. How he was battered about over land, over high deep
> Seas by the powers above! Savage Juno's anger remembered
> Him, and he suffered profoundly in war to establish a city,
> Settle his gods into Latium, making this land of the Latins
> Future home to the Elders of Alba and Rome's mighty ramparts.[5]

---

[4] I here refer to the title of Murphy 2007. Cf. also Williams 1980.
[5] Virgil, *Aeneid* 1.1–7; quoted from Ahl 2007: 3.

As from Troy to Rome, so from Plymouth to Plymouth Rock; as from Italy to east and west (and north and southeast), so from the New World's east coast to its west coast; as from the Tiber and all around the Mediterranean, so from sea to shining sea. At least if painted on a large enough canvas, history does repeat itself in certain of its aspects. Just as the ancient Roman prototype had been the *agricola militans*, the farmer-soldier, so the modern *homo Americanus* had begun as a farmer and Minuteman. Increases in power and advancing technologies in both societies then replaced the militiamen with standing armies and brought about large estates: *latifundia*, an early form of plantation economy, to the Romans; huge farms, plantations, and cattle empires to the Americans. The Roman quasi-ancestry of the Americans is evident in crucial ways. Among the most prominent examples are the Constitution and the government, replete with a senate, now fifty-one capitols, and an eagle as symbol of power, and the neoclassical architecture of Washington, DC, which is consciously modeled on that of ancient Rome.[6] Essayist, novelist, playwright, and screenwriter Gore Vidal, who grew up in Washington, once memorably observed:

I was steeped in Rome. I also lived in a city whose marble columns were a self-conscious duplicate of the old capital of the world. Of course Washington then lacked six of the seven hills and a contiguous world empire. Later, we got the empire but not the hills ... There was the temple [the Lincoln Memorial] ... at the heart of the city. Once I got interested in Rome and Greece, I used to haunt that part of Washington, imagining myself in ancient Rome.[7]

2 Frontiers

Conquest, with its subjugation of native peoples and its taming of the wilderness, is the precondition for new arrivals to establish a stable and enduring society. The frontier of imperial expansion is also a place of

---

[6] Work on the close analogies between American and Roman history and culture, especially in connection with the Founding Fathers, is extensive; I here list only a few noteworthy studies: Gummere 1963; Eadie 1976; Reinhold 1984; Wills 1984; McDonald 1985; Vance 1986; Wiltshire 1992; Richard 1994 and 2009; Bederman 2008. Adams 1931, a classic work, is silent on Rome.

[7] Vidal 1992: 51–52 and 67–68. Cf. Vidal 1993b: 1057–1060, especially 1059 ("an imperial Roman – literally, Roman – capital") and 1060 ("a capital that [had been] little more than a village down whose muddy main street ran a shallow creek that was known to some even then as – what else? – the Tiber"). This essay first appeared in 1982. Vidal's own works set in ancient Rome are *Romulus: A New Comedy, Adapted from a Play by Friedrich Dürrenmatt* (1962) and the novel *Julian* (1964). He was among the uncredited screenwriters on William Wyler's epic film *Ben-Hur: A Tale of the Christ* (1959). Cf. Tatum 1992, where correct "*Mons Capitolium*" (209) to *mons Capitolinus*.

conflict, where nature and culture, savagery and civilization meet and clash. The Americans' view of their frontiers in the nineteenth century is comparable to that of the Romans of theirs, as a modern historian of the Roman Empire makes evident:

Frontiers were always dividing lines between civilized and barbarian worlds . . . and it has been in this light that Roman frontiers have often been conceived . . . The opening up of the West in the United States was in many respects the closest parallels to the Roman experience of a moving frontier . . . Americans were preoccupied by frontiersmen and their influence on the ideals of American manhood, and less with the interaction of frontier communities and native populations. At root lies an inherent admiration for the pioneer ever pushing outwards and a distaste for static borders. That, too, has had its influence on historians of antiquity.[8]

The West, to Ford especially the mesas and buttes of the American Southwest, is the area that will change from a wilderness into a garden. In particular Monument Valley, which one Ford scholar has aptly called "his own moral universe," is the setting that witnesses the near-mythic conflict between *physis* and *nomos, chaos* and *kosmos*, to put the matter in classical terms.[9] The pictorial beauty of Monument Valley, simultaneously mysterious, seductive, and forbidding, lends itself particularly well to Ford's exquisite sense of visual poetry, both in black-and-white and in color.[10] To Ford and most Americans of his generation, an agrarian society, mainly consisting of farming and ranching, is the perfect beginning for the development of the American Adam. Infused with a manageable and non-threatening degree of industrialization, this kind of society will progress to an ideal state for twentieth-century Americans, joining together domestic stability and foreign power.[11] But the combination of agrarianism and benevolent industrialism is only an intermediate stage, one that will in turn be forced to yield to more advanced capitalism and technology. Ford, born in 1894, could witness this development during his lifetime. The populist American view of social and political development parallels traditional Roman views about the origin, progress, and decline of their own *imperium*.

---

[8] Quoted from Whittaker 2000: 293–294; footnotes omitted. He gives additional references.
[9] The quotation is from French 2005: 64. On Ford and Monument Valley see also McBride and Wilmington 1974: 36–37 ("Monument Valley is a moral battleground"); Leutrat and Liandrat-Guigues 1998; Hutson 2004.
[10] Cowie 2004 has an extensive collection of images in black-and-white and color.
[11] Marx 1964 is the classic work on the subject. On the American West see especially Henry Nash Smith 1950, another classic. See further Athearn 1986; Goetzmann 2009; Nash 2014.

Virgil had concluded at the end of the proem to the *Aeneid*: "Planting the Roman nation's roots was a task of immense scale" (*tantae molis erat Romanam condere gentem*).[12] This finds a modern parallel in Ford's body of work, especially his Westerns. With a slight if unmetrical change we could summarize the common theme of his Westerns in near-Virgilian terms: *tantae molis erat Americanam condere gentem*.

As the modern theory of the "two voices" in the *Aeneid* or "the other Virgil" indicates, Romans themselves were ambiguous about empire.[13] The historian quoted above comments: "Roman historiography contained a deeply pessimistic consciousness of the fragility of imperial rule, if allowed to outgrow its own resources."[14] Similarly we can observe two contrasting and perhaps conflicting voices in Ford: first an affirmation of civilizing and benign empire while the country was advancing to take its place on the world stage, then disillusionment with modern society and its military and political system once the US had become a superpower. Ford's portrayal of the Indians, controversial to many viewers, illustrates this point. His Westerns often require them to be the enemies of white culture, as in *The Iron Horse* (1924, an influential silent epic), *Stagecoach* (1939), *Fort Apache* (1948), *She Wore a Yellow Ribbon* (1949), *Rio Grande* (1950), or *The Searchers* (1956), to name only a few famous instances. But even then they are rarely unredeemable savages. The Apache chief in *Fort Apache*, modeled on the historical Cochise, is far nobler than the cavalry fort's commander, whose arrogance leads to his own and his men's death in a pointless battle that is patterned on the fate of George Armstrong Custer at the Little Bighorn. And Ford's last Western, the epic *Cheyenne Autumn* (1964), fully takes the Indians' side with a story reminiscent of the Cherokees' (and others') Trail of Tears in the 1830s. The theme of white captivity, a crucial aspect in American frontier history, is addressed most famously in *The Searchers*, in which a young girl is reintegrated into her society, but it finds an ironic counterpoint in *Two Rode Together* (1961), in which a young white boy who has been "liberated" from a life among the Indians after years of captivity is desperate to return to them. The Navajos, who regularly acted in Ford's films as Apaches, Comanches, Cheyennes, and others, made Ford an honorary member of their tribe, not least because on several occasions he was instrumental in rescuing them from economic hardship, even near-starvation. Ford, looking back, once said:

---

[12]   Virgil, *Aeneid* 1.33; Ahl 2007: 4.

[13]   On this see in particular Parry 1963; Johnson 1976; Lyne 1986; Clausen 1995; Kallendorf 2007. Stahl 2016 presents the opposite view. All have further references.

[14]   Whittaker 2000: 298.

"My sympathy was always with the Indians."[15] On another occasion he commented:

I've killed more Indians than Custer, Beecher and Chivington put together ... There are two sides to every story ... Let's face it, we've treated them very badly – it's a blot on our shield; we've cheated and robbed, killed, murdered, massacred and everything else, but they kill one white man and, God, out come the troops.[16]

Ford's attitude toward Indians conforms to white tradition, as two well-known nineteenth-century observations, among others, can tell us. Early in *A History of New York* (1809), the humorous account that Washington Irving wrote under the satirical persona of Diedrich Knickerbocker, we read:

Think you the first discoverers of this fair quarter of the globe, had nothing to do but go on shore and find a country ready laid out and cultivated like a garden, wherein they might revel at their ease? No such thing – they had forests to cut down, underwood to grub up, marshes to drain, and savages to exterminate.[17]

Irving's personal view was quite different. While traveling in the West, he wrote in a letter to his sister: "I find it extremely difficult, even when so near the seat of action, to get at the right story of these feuds between the white and the red men, and my sympathies go strongly with the latter."[18]

Alexis de Tocqueville commented on the treatment of Indians in the second volume of *Democracy in America* (1835) in terms both serious and sarcastic:

The Spaniards were unable to exterminate the Indian race by those unparalleled atrocities which brand them with indelible shame, nor did they even succeed in wholly depriving it of its rights; but the Americans of the United States have accomplished this twofold purpose with singular felicity; tranquilly, legally, philosophically, without shedding blood, and without violating a single great principle of morality in the eyes of the world. It is impossible to destroy men with more respect for the laws of humanity.

---

[15] Quoted from Gallagher 1986: 254.
[16] Quoted from Bogdanovich 1978: 104. Besides Custer, Ford refers to the 1864 Sand Creek Massacre and the 1868 Battle of Beecher Island. Nabokov 1999 is a useful starting point for information about the other side of history.
[17] Quoted from Irving 1983b: 404.
[18] Letter written in St. Louis on September 13, 1832, with addendum of September 16; quoted from Pierre M. Irving 1883: 166–167; quotation at 167.

Tocqueville's sympathies go strongly with the Indians, as his melancholic conclusion reveals: "The Indians will perish in the same isolated condition in which they have lived."[19]

3   Ford's Cavalry Trilogy

The increasing degree of ennoblement of the Indians in Ford's Western films has its inverse parallel in his disillusionment with white society – that is, with all of contemporary America – in his mature work made after 1945, when the US had become a world empire.[20] That year a tone of resignation even at a time of victory marked *They Were Expendable*, a film about the American defeat in the Philippines in the wake of Pearl Harbor that Ford made around the end of the war. One of its most poignant moments occurs when an American shipwright stoically awaits his impending death at the hands of the advancing Japanese. The nineteenth-century folk song "Red River Valley," heard in several other Ford films but most memorably in *The Grapes of Wrath* (1940), links the story of World War II to the American West. The actor who plays the shipwright in *They Were Expendable* had played Pa Joad in *The Grapes of Wrath*. He was also a regular member of Ford's unofficial "stock company" and frequently appeared in his Westerns. In this genre the turning point for Ford had come in what is unofficially known as his Cavalry Trilogy of 1948–1950, in which a strong sense of ambiguity about the role of the army in the settlement of the West becomes palpable.[21]

Fort Apache, first in the trilogy, shows the falsehood on which a myth about a famous hero is based and the silence of history about a genuine but unknown hero. The complex ending of this film, ostensibly an affirmation of a false legend or myth, is one of the most extensively debated issues in Ford scholarship. It is important for our context as well.[22]

---

[19]   Both quotations are taken from Tocqueville 1904: 380. This translation, the first into English, dates to ca. 1839.

[20]   On this see especially Wood 1971. "Shall We Gather at the River," quoted in the title of Wood's essay, is an 1864 hymn by American composer Robert Lowry. It is featured repeatedly in Ford's work and has become something of his signature tune. It is heard at the beginning of the church-dance sequence in *My Darling Clementine* and in *The Searchers*.

[21]   On Ford and the cavalry cf. now Cowie 2004: 72–119 and 215 (notes; chapter titled "The U.S. Cavalry and the Scars of War"); on the trilogy Matheson 2016: 143–199.

[22]   McBride 2001: 456–458 and Gallagher 2007: 314–317 account for the film's ending. On the subject see especially Poague 1988, with references to and discussions of earlier work on the film. Poague's essay elicited a reply from critic Robert Ray, on which Poague commented in turn (Ray and Poague 1988).

At Fort Apache on the Indian frontier and just before a new military campaign against the Apaches, several journalists are concluding an interview with Col. York, the cavalry regiment's commanding officer, about the heroism of his predecessor, Col. Thursday. Thursday, arrogant, bigoted, and eager for military glory, foolishly rejected the advice of York, an experienced officer, and caused an easily avoidable Indian war and the massacre of his men and himself. The journalists, however, do not know the truth. They report, mainly to us in the audience, that Thursday's Charge had brought glory to his regiment and that Thursday had become a national hero. "He must have been a great man, and a great soldier," one of them comments. York replies: "No man died more gallantly or won more honor for his regiment." Just as Custer's Last Stand was painted and widely published in newspapers and magazines, so a painting of Thursday's Charge is now on display in Washington. An excited reporter describes it, but the scene in that picture is pure fantasy. A stoic, almost brooding York affirms its accuracy, however, looking straight ahead in medium close-up as if seeing through the childish ignoramuses: "Correct in every detail."

When the deaths of Thursday's men are mentioned, one of the journalists observes: "We always remember the Thursdays, but the others are forgotten." York now launches into a brief speech of praise for these men who, he says, live on in the memory of the regiment: "They'll keep on living as long as the regiment lives." Then he adds: "They're better men than they used to be. Thursday did that. He made it a command to be proud of." Whereas we had previously seen York with his back turned to Thursday's portrait on the wall, he is now looking directly at it, as if in agreement with his own words. We know better. But then comes a surprise. Before riding out on patrol, York puts on his cap, which has a piece of cloth in the back to protect its wearer from the sun. It is identical to the one Thursday had worn – the only officer in the film previously to don such a cap. Is York a new Thursday? Is this why he has not corrected the journalists' affirmation of the legend? Is he, too, perpetuating the lie? Rather, as a critic observed, York is "a fervid opponent of the official line. Yet he does not once disobey a command, and the lineaments in Ford's world become clear. Insubordination is acceptable in [certain regards], but not in serious military affairs. York is the obedient rebel."[23] He is caught between opposing senses of duty and responsibility. The tragic nature of the film rests not so much on Thursday or on Thursday and the Apaches as on York. From this point of view it makes sense that John Wayne, who plays York, should

---

[23] The quotation is from Campbell 1971: 10–11.

get first billing over Henry Fonda, who plays Thursday, although Thursday is on screen much longer than York.

Here we have an anticipation of the famous "Print the legend" theme that will be crucial in one of Ford's last Westerns, discussed below. Ford detested Custer, the model for Thursday, but Ford himself affirmed the usefulness of myth in connection with the ending of *Fort Apache*: "It's good for the country to have heroes to look up to. Like Custer – a great hero. Well, he wasn't. Not that he was a stupid man – but he did a stupid job that day."[24] A scholar comments:

Army-post pictures had been common enough in Hollywood … What Ford brought new to the genre was more characters, more individualized, more differentiated, more interestingly interlinked, and thus a community richer in detail and mores. The land, its inhabitants red and white, their daily rituals and furnishings, the sight of a horse, all have "mythic" emotions [and] evoke in all of us not only life itself, and what matters, but [also] the sense of eternally repeating what every person has done. Myth rules us.[25]

Ford has shown us the exact truth, partly heroic, partly not, from which the myth derives, so the reason why York does not reveal what Thursday, who did a stupid job that day, had really been like is that the legend serves a necessary function. York lies when he affirms the correctness of the myth and only pretends to be a new Thursday even when he dons Thursday's cap, but he does so out of a sense of responsibility toward his men. Everything else he says about Thursday is not, strictly speaking, a lie, although it seems so. Thursday did die gallantly if, like Custer, foolishly and did, through his death, win honor or glory for his regiment. Thursday did make better men of the soldiers, if only indirectly by showing them how not to deal with the Indians. York has had to undo the damage Thursday had caused, presumably by providing more responsible leadership. Still, York may be skirting the truth when he says that his is a command to be proud of. On this frontier the *pax Americana* comes only after irresponsible behavior, death, and suppression of truth: *tantae molis erat Americanam condere gentem*.

The themes of *Fort Apache* are war and peace, honor and glory, responsibility, and, perhaps most of all, the price to be paid for all this. This thematic complexity finds its parallel in the film's style, a combination of documentary realism in its black-and-white photography with the poetic beauty of the Southwestern locations and of Ford's sense of elegance. One

[24] Quoted from Bogdanovich 1978: 86.   [25] Gallagher 2007: 308.

particular moment stands out. It may remind us of a line from the *Aeneid*
which occurs as Virgil's identical comment on two separate heroic deaths
which have just been told: "Life flutters off on a groan, under protest, down
among shadows."[26] The epitaph-like formula, highly stylized in its vocabulary, word order, and rhythm, expresses the finality of death and appeals
to our emotions. Both times the line closes the episode in which it occurs.
Its second appearance is the final line of the entire epic. In *Fort Apache*
Ford rises to a comparable visual height of emotional power and finality in
connection with the disastrous battle in which Thursday and his men
perish – but he does so before, not after the battle occurs. Thursday faces
an Indian army led by several war chiefs; their leader is Cochise. In the
company of his fellow chiefs, Cochise observes the approach of Thursday
and his men from a rocky ridge; Ford films them in medium long shot from
a low angle against a towering sky. As if in disbelief at and contempt for
Thursday's foolishness and in anger at the unnecessary doom Thursday is
about to mete out to his own soldiers, Cochise bends down and picks up
a handful of dust from the ground. Looking straight ahead, he tosses it
diagonally across his body into the ditch before him. Falling, the dust forms
a small cloud that is immediately dispersed: Symbolically, life flutters off
(Figure 6.1). Cochise turns and leaves. Well beyond illustrating the common *Dust to dust* sentiment, which it also contains, the gesture expresses by
anticipation the inevitability of what is to come and the futility and finality
of death: "the soldiers are already dead."[27] In this way Ford intensifies,
through visual poetry and without a single word being spoken, the emotional power of the battle sequence, the film's epic climax. Once we see the
dust scattering, we know what will happen. Virgil looks back on poignant
deaths, Ford looks ahead; both ways, one verbal, the other visual, are
unforgettable. What price heroism?

Ford's next film, however, *She Wore a Yellow Ribbon*, affirms a positive
view of the military, if without turning the Indians into mere fiends. Its closing
shot shows a cavalry patrol riding out into the wilderness yet again and facing
uncertainty and danger. The narrator comments:

So here they are, the dog-faced soldiers, the regulars, the fifty-cents-a-day professionals, riding the outposts of a nation. From Fort Reno to Fort Apache, from
Sheridan to Stockton, they were all the same: men in dirty-shirt blue and only

---

[26] Virgil, *Aeneid* 11.831 (on Camilla) and 12.952 (on Turnus): *vitaque cum gemitu fugit indignata
sub umbras*; Ahl 2007: 293 and 327. Virgil's model is Homer, *Iliad* 16.855–857 and 22.361–363,
on the deaths of Patroclus and Hector.
[27] Gallagher 2007: 312.

Figure 6.1 Cochise and the dust of doom in John Ford's *Fort Apache*.

a cold page in the history books to mark their passing. But wherever they rode, and whatever they fought for, that place became the United States.

This epilogue is a remarkable echo, if probably an unconscious one, of a brief characterization of the US army made by Theodore Roosevelt in *The Wilderness Hunter* less than two decades after the time portrayed in the film:

in campaign after campaign, always inconceivably wearing and harassing, and often very bloody in character, the scarred and tattered troops had broken and overthrown the most formidable among the Indian tribes. Faithful, uncomplaining, unflinching, the soldiers wearing the national uniform lived for many weary years at their lonely little posts, facing unending toil and danger with quiet endurance, surrounded by the desolation of vast solitudes, and menaced by the most merciless of foes.[28]

The affirmation of military heroism in *She Wore a Yellow Ribbon* is followed in *Rio Grande* with a tale that could have been called *What Price Glory* (1952), the title of one of Ford's lesser films, which is set in World War I. *Rio Grande* is the story of a cavalry raid of questionable legality into Mexico against Apaches. The screenplay was based on a story

[28] Roosevelt 1904: 22–23. *The Wilderness Hunter* was originally published in 1893.

called "Mission with No Record." Although telling an independent story, *Rio Grande* has several strong links to *Fort Apache* and *She Wore a Yellow Ribbon*, not least in the identical or near-identical names of some of its characters, played by the same actors. The two earlier films, the first shot in elegant black and white, the second in exquisite color, displayed a quintessentially Fordian visual beauty. By contrast, the realistic black-and-white look of the third film yields a much harsher portrayal of military service. The commanding officer of a desolate border outpost sums it up for his son, an inexperienced volunteer: "put out of your mind any romantic idea that it's a way of glory. It's a life of suffering and of hardship, an uncompromising devotion to your oath and your duty." Shortly before, he had told his new recruits:

I don't want you men to be fooled about what's coming up for you. Torture, at least that. The War Department promised me 180 men. They sent me eighteen, all told. You are the eighteen . . . so each one of you will have to do the work of ten men. If you fail, I'll have you spread-eagled on a wagon wheel. If you desert, you'll be found, tracked down, and broken into bits. That is all.

Danger, harsh and inglorious service, and personal sacrifice are this film's theme, although it does not lack the affectionate and humorous touches that make Ford's films memorable.

4 Ambiguity and the Price of Empire

The two films that are most significant for Ford's increasingly darkening vision of the past came in 1956 and 1961. *The Searchers* is his undisputed if to some still controversial masterpiece, in which the previously idealized cavalry is satirized for brutality, inefficiency, and stupidity. A scene with General Custer as a massacring incompetent was, however, deleted. *The Man Who Shot Liberty Valance* is an elegy for a violent but heroic, romantic, and inspiring West. Since I have addressed both epic and tragic aspects of *The Searchers* in considerable detail elsewhere, I will limit my discussion of this decisive and influential film to a few comments later on.[29]

In *The Man Who Shot Liberty Valance* the West is personified in two antagonists. One is the psychopathic and ironically named outlaw Liberty Valance. The other is Tom Doniphon, a gunman-rancher (a significant

---

[29] Winkler 2001c and 2004b. On classical themes in the American Western see Winkler 1985 and 1996.

combination) who realizes that the days of the old frontier are numbered. The wilderness has vanished – better: has been conquered – and has been turned into a garden. But was it worth it? The film evokes an almost unbearable sense of loss, for viewers feel that the dignity and quiet honor inherent in the mythical West are irrevocably gone. The often intentionally drab if still strangely attractive look of the film reinforces its theme visually. What price civilization? Unavoidably for the betterment of society, guns have had to yield to the book of law. But the transition from gun law to true law is in turn followed by an early-twentieth-century world characterized by advanced technology, by social incivility representing the loss of chivalry and good manners, and by political and mercantile careerism and cynicism. What on the surface appears as a nostalgic look back at the West, made at the beginning of the last decade in which the Western genre was still popular, is much more: "it's both the most romantic of Westerns and the greatest American political movie."[30]

The narrative arc of *The Man Who Shot Liberty Valance* is in strong contrast to the society-building process movingly described in *My Darling Clementine* (1946), especially in the earlier film's famous sequence of a Sunday dance on the floor of a church that is being built. The visual composition of one particular long shot, as impeccable in its framing as Ford's work invariably is, carries a powerful sense of symbolism. Two flagpoles with the Stars and Stripes screen right and near center balance the church's bell tower screen left, with the rocks of Monument Valley in the distance (Figure 6.2). We watch an emerging society founded on the desert wilderness, held together by religion and morality (the church) and by its secular institutions (the flag): one nation indivisible. A comparable moment had occurred more briefly in *Drums Along the Mohawk*. In hindsight, the film that immediately preceded *My Darling Clementine* already hinted at what was to follow in *The Man Who Shot Liberty Valance*, for the very title of *They Were Expendable* indicates that the price of empire is high, perhaps too high.

Ford has often been regarded as a political conservative, not least through his long association with right-wing actors John Wayne and Ward Bond, the latter an extremist. But Ford is not that easy to categorize politically: "In his heart, he would always remain nostalgic, romantic, and, socially speaking, innately conservative, which makes his lifelong adherence to liberal principles

---

[30] The quotation is from Brody 2009. Cf. Giddins 2010b: 47; he concludes: "he [Ford] mourns . . . the rise of a new nation that will be no less self-deceptive ('print the legend') and painfully remade than the old one."

Figure 6.2 The harmonious symmetry of nature and civilization in John Ford's
My Darling Clementine.

even more startling."[31] And it is generally forgotten today how politically
explosive Ford's film of *The Grapes of Wrath* was at the time of its release only
a few months after the publication of John Steinbeck's novel.[32] The enormous
pressure of social and political – or capitalist – forces on what to Ford was the
crucial unit in society, the family, is evident throughout *The Grapes of Wrath*.
Alfred Kazin once observed about Steinbeck: "Steinbeck's people are always
on the verge of becoming human, but never do. There is a persistent failure to
realize human life fully in his books."[33] Such a failure is absent from the
central characters in Ford's adaptation, which "was single-handedly to transform [Ford] from a storyteller of the screen to America's cinematic poet
laureate."[34]

---

[31] Eyman 1999: 19–20. The comments in Eyman: 135, 169, 186–188 (with 595), 199, 205, 225, 377,
386, 483, 497, and 511 enable us to trace the developments and variations of Ford's political
views. McBride 2001 discusses Ford's political views throughout. But see also Brianton 2016:
passim and 118–120 (concluding summary).

[32] On this film see Gallagher 1986: 175–181 (= 2007: 217–223); Eyman 1999: 214–226; McBride
2001: 308–316.

[33] Kazin 1995: 394. For another early assessment cf. Wilson 1950b, revised and expanded from
Wilson 1940.

[34] Sarris 1975: 90.

Only one year after *The Grapes of Wrath* the same theme appears again in *How Green Was My Valley*, an elegy set among a family of Welsh coal miners. Even as innocuous-looking a film as *Stagecoach* (1939), Ford's first Western filmed in Monument Valley and on the surface no more than a rousing adventure yarn, had exhibited darker tones throughout. So did several of Ford's films set in the twentieth century, such as *Dr. Bull* (1933), *Judge Priest* (1934), and the latter's remake *The Sun Shines Bright* (1953), one of Ford's own favorites. *Stagecoach* exposes the arrogance of class distinctions and hypocrisy. At the end Doc Boone comments when another outsider, the Ringo Kid, escapes to Mexico with the prostitute Dallas: "Well, they're safe from the blessings of civilization." The doctor had joined Dallas when she was being thrown out of town by the rather harpy-like ladies of the Law and Order League, one of Ford's most memorable indictments of "the foul disease of social prejudice," as Doc Boone calls it. Ford's final film, *7 Women* (1966), is set far from home in the China of 1935, but thematically it, too, is a Western – twilight's last gleaming.

In view of the preceding it is somewhat ironic that it was a Republican who awarded Ford the Presidential Medal of Freedom in 1973, when Ford received the inaugural Life Achievement Award from the American Film Institute. Ford died a few months later. He lived long enough to see two decisive American debacles, one foreign, Vietnam, and one domestic, Watergate, although he did not witness the disgrace of President Nixon. Even if the history of the decline of the American empire did not begin in the Nixon years, the decline of the country's political and moral authority under President George W. Bush about thirty years later had at least some of its roots in that era. The portrait of domestic turmoil in *The Prisoner of Shark Island* (1936), Ford's film about the aftermath of the Lincoln assassination, now sounds and looks all too familiar. A particular scene deserves close attention for its words and images.

Over an image of Lincoln and with the Battle Hymn of the Republic briefly heard on the soundtrack, an intertitle introduces the sequence of the military trial of those charged with conspiracy and murder. It informs us that "the innocent as well as the guilty faced an angry and heart-broken people." Then we see a lynch mob and its agitators, ready to pass summary judgment. Before the trial begins, the Assistant Secretary of War instructs the officers who will form the court in the proper attitude:

I suppose you all realize that as members of the court martial for the trial of the conspirators in the assassination of our beloved president you have on your souls a grave responsibility. The object of this trial is not to determine the guilt or innocence of a handful of rebels but to save this country from further bloodshed. The solemn truth, gentlemen, is that the federal union is on the verge of hysteria. That is why the trial of these conspirators has been placed in your hands rather than in a civil court, because men of the sword can be hard, and hardness is all that can save this country from riots, mob rule, even a resumption of the war itself.

He then offers two suggestions "to help you to be hard":

First, you must not allow your judgment and decision in this case to be troubled by any trifling technicalities of the law or any pedantic regard for the customary rules of evidence. Second, and most important, you must not allow yourself [*sic*] to be influenced by that obnoxious creation of legal nonsense: reasonable doubt. Is that clear?

It is. Noise from the outside mob is heard off screen. The Secretary continues, his index finger raised dramatically:

Briefly, the voice of this court has got to be the voice of the people. [*More noise from outside.*] Before you start, I want you to hear that voice. [*He and the others move toward the open window.*] Listen to it.

They and we see the mob, shouting and burning the dummy of a hanged man. In medium close-up the Secretary meaningfully looks at the members of the court while wiping his hands on a handkerchief as if he were an American Pontius Pilate. The implication of his gesture is evident.

Ford now dissolves to the courtroom, with the Assistant Secretary moving among the people and commanding: "Bring the prisoners!" Armed guards ("Prisoners to the bar!") then lead in the eight accused. They are in hand- and leg-irons, and their heads are covered by hoods (Figure 6.3). The accused stand behind the bar while the charge against them is pronounced; then they are identified by name, their hoods are removed, and they are roughly sat down. Most of them are guilty, but Ford's images do not condone the way they are being treated, as when a helpless-looking old man wipes his eyes after his hood has been removed. This is Edward Spangler, to be found guilty but released in 1869. Hoods covering the heads of guilty and innocent, along with far worse treatment than what we see in this scene, were in the news again about seventy years after *The Prisoner of Shark Island* was released. A modern historian has made the analogy explicit:

Almost every account of the trial has focused on the treatment of the prisoners . . . . this was a landmark event that spoke volumes about the times and – since September 2001 – about our own as well . . . It is not easy to put aside the

Figure 6.3 The accused in John Ford's *The Prisoner of Shark Island.*

barbarous image of people in hoods and chains. Prisoners had not been treated that way since 1696, and would not be again until 2001. But just as strange, in a way, was the fact that not all of the prisoners were forced to endure it . . . Still, the treatment was shocking, and after some of the commission members objected to it, the hoods were no longer worn in the courtroom.

This historian comments on the outpourings of popular grief and anger at Lincoln's assassination in terms that fit reactions to the terror attacks on September 11, 2001:

The prospect of further attacks kept the nation on edge, and every citizen was on the alert for any sign that terrorists were in their midst. Hundreds of suspects were rounded up on the vaguest suspicions, and some were arrested on looks alone. Of those, many were kept in isolation, bound and hooded, to await a trial by military tribunal. The reaction was unprecedented.

   Who did this, and why? How large a conspiracy was behind these attacks? Is this the end, or will more follow? How far can we bend the rule of law to find and punish the conspirators? These were the questions on everyone's lips.[35]

---

[35]   The two quotations are from Kauffman 2004: 354 and ix (beginning of "Introduction").
Secretary of War Edwin Stanton ordered prisoners held captive on warships to "have for better security against conversation a canvas bag put over the head of each and tied around the neck with a hole for proper breathing and eating but not seeing." Quoted from Kauffman, 330.

In the wake of 2001, the scene in Ford's film has been called "a prophetic brief on attitudes toward torture."[36] The condemnation and subsequent rehabilitation of Dr. Samuel Mudd, one of the eight and the man referred to in the title of Ford's film, is a clear, if somewhat romanticized, vindication of the necessity for customary rules of evidence.[37]

Ford poetically chronicled the history of his country. So did Virgil, the Roman author who is closest in spirit to Ford and perhaps to all of America. In 1930 John Erskine published a revealing article titled "Vergil, the Modern Poet," on the occasion of the bimillennium of Virgil's birth.[38] The reason for Virgil's modernity is his affinity with American history:

Most of the international accord we dream of today, Rome had achieved at least temporarily, and, so far as Vergil knew, permanently. The known world was obedient to central control. The League of Nations was working ... daily, from the last horizon, came reports and tributes to the government supreme on the seven hills, and over them in return Rome spread to the four quarters the arts, the sciences, the religions of mankind. Through Rome had arisen order, communication, peace. What more could one ask?

Well, Vergil asked what it cost. The question ... makes him seem today the most representative of modern poets.[39]

Later on, Erskine makes a specific analogy between Virgil's way of presenting the history of Rome and Carthage on the one hand and imperial wars in later history on the other:

Had the poet been the shallow kind of patriot, he would have boasted of this terrific victory [over Carthage in 146 BC]. He prefers rather to ask why the two empires might not have been friends, and whether Rome, which wiped out its rival, was necessarily a better empire. The question takes many forms ... Why should the coming of the white man to our land have meant the destruction of the Indian? Why should American civilization already [!] seem ominous to other

---

[36] Giddins 2010b: 51.

[37] Robert Redford's film *The Conspirator* (2011), about the trial of Mary Suratt, in whose boarding house in Washington, DC, part of the conspiracy to assassinate Lincoln was planned, also emphasizes the modern parallels (hoods, military tribunals) of her trial. Secretary Stanton is the precursor of the modern Secretary of Defense: actor Kevin Kline "only won the part, I imagine, because Redford couldn't get Donald Rumsfeld." Quoted from Lane 2011: 130. The remark's flippancy is not without point.

[38] Erskine 1930: 280–286; here quoted from its reprint in Erskine 1935a: 315–332. A shorter edition of this book had appeared in 1928. We have encountered Erskine and his book before.

[39] Erskine 1935a: 317. Erskine's essay is a sobering antidote to the contemporaneous ideological use and abuse of Virgil in Fascist Italy. On this subject, which has received extensive scholarly attention by now, see the summary in Nelis 2011: 86–96. His book contains an exhaustive bibliography on the Fascists' views of Roman culture and history.

nations? The poet has no answer more than we, but he expounds the question with unique generosity.[40]

After 2001, the following words by Erskine about Virgil acquire new urgency: "Now that we realize that ... our imperialism is only a development of the Roman and carries with it the same or greater cruelties, Vergil lives afresh as our poet."[41] So does Ford.

   In Book 6 of the *Aeneid* Anchises shows Aeneas the spirits of future but by Virgil's time past Romans, while the scenes on Aeneas' shield in Book 8 summarize Roman history.[42] In both passages the poetic effect is one of *chiaroscuro*. The Civil War is prominent in Book 6, and the shield displays villains like Mettius Fufetius and Catiline and shows the rape of the Sabine women, members of an indigenous Italic population. War, death, and suffering are the price to be paid for imperial power – this is the main theme especially of the second half of the *Aeneid*. It has its American counterpoint in one of the key moments of *The Searchers*. In *The Grapes of Wrath*, one of Ford's greatest films about twentieth-century America, Ma Joad had been the center of the family and the steady force that kept the Joads' exodus on track. We might say: "a bold coup, led by a woman" (*dux femina facti*).[43] Mrs. Jorgensen in *The Searchers* is a comparable figure for nineteenth-century America. She is an immigrant's wife whose son has been killed by Indians. In a crucial scene she voices what all of Ford's major work is about. Her husband yields to his grief over the loss of his son, killed by Indians: "this country ... it's this country killed my boy." His quiet despair is then contrasted with his wife's stoic acceptance. She characterizes the pioneers' life on the edge of civilization as being "way out on a limb, this year and next, maybe for a hundred more, but I don't think it'll be forever. Someday this country is gonna be a fine, good place to be. Maybe it needs our bones in the ground before that time can come." Awareness of the necessity for sacrifices gives Mrs. Jorgensen the strength to endure. Savagery and violence will eventually be overcome, and there is hope for peace in the future. Her words perfectly summarize the underlying theme of *The Searchers* and of most of Ford's other Westerns: the evolution from savagery to civilization, the change in the land from wilderness to garden. They point to her own generation's part in this process and to the knowledge that the settlers will not

[40] Erskine 1935a: 327.
[41] Erskine 1935a: 321. Virgil, too, has been given renewed scrutiny since 2001; cf. in particular Thomas 2015.
[42] Erskine 1935a: 331–332 has some pertinent remarks on Book 6 of the *Aeneid* in connection with American culture and society.
[43] Virgil, *Aeneid* 1.364; Ahl 2007: 15.

live to see the task completed. The setting of this short scene, memorable for its peace and quiet, is the Jorgensens' porch at evening. In a touch typical for his reversals from seriousness to humor or vice versa, Ford avoids any melodramatic emotionalism by having Mr. Jorgensen explain his wife's surprising eloquence: "She was a school teacher, you know."[44] Adapting Virgil, we might add: *dux femina verbi.*

5　Darkness Visible

Is Mrs. Jorgensen's speech a thematic summation of Manifest Destiny, the equivalent of Virgil's "Destiny's spindles" or of Jupiter's prophecy concerning the Romans' *imperium sine fine*, an empire without end?[45] Not quite, because the one man who is crucial in bringing about the goal described in *The Searchers* is Ford's most complex and darkest figure. Ethan Edwards is a heroic Westerner but also at moments a neurotic, racist, obsessed, and irrational killer (Figure 6.4). The price to be paid for future peace and stability, a goal not easily reached in Ford's work, is emphasized by the film's moving poetic ending, which shows us that the man of violence cannot even become part of an incipient civilization, "the fine, good place to be." Instead of entering the garden, he is condemned to return to the desert (Figure 6.5). Mrs. Jorgensen was right: It needs their bones in the ground before the time of fulfillment can come. So there is darkness visible in the light of the West. *Darkness Visible* is the title of a well-known book on the *Aeneid*, taken from one of the poetically and thematically most resonant lines in the entire epic. In the Underworld, Virgil writes, Aeneas and the Sibyl, his guide, walked in such darkness: "Moving, blocked from sight under night's isolation, through shadows" (*ibant obscuri sola sub nocte per umbram*).[46]

　　Three crucial moments in *The Man Who Shot Liberty Valance* are visual analogies to Virgil's line. In all of them Ford uses a highly expressive play of light and shadow. The first occurs when Tom Doniphon realizes that he cannot act otherwise than to save the man of law who is helpless against Liberty Valance, even if he does so at the cost of losing the woman he loves. The third is his destruction of his own home, an act of drunken despair by which he condemns himself to a life of loneliness and poverty. The most

---

[44]　The preceding is taken from Winkler 2001c: 145–146.

[45]　Virgil, *Aeneid* 1.22 (*sic volvere Parcas*; Ahl 2007: 3) and 1.279. On the context see Johnson 1976: 88–92.

[46]　Virgil, *Aeneid* 6.268; Ahl 2007: 136. The book: Johnson 1976.

Figure 6.4 The dark side of the antihero in John Ford's *The Searchers.*

Figure 6.5 The poetic ending of John Ford's *The Searchers.*

important moment, however, comes in between. A flashback within the film's main flashback finally reveals the identity of the man who shot Liberty Valance and the unheroic way in which this showdown had occurred. An introductory close-up of Tom Doniphon's face shows us a social pariah

Figure 6.6 The hero as social outcast in John Ford's *The Man Who Shot Liberty Valance*.

(Figure 6.6). It reminds us of a comparable close-up of Ethan Edwards in *The Searchers* (see Figure 6.4). The flashback itself begins with an image that expresses the character of Tom Doniphon in particularly stark terms. In close-up he emerges from darkness and pauses in the light while his hat casts a large shadow on the wall behind him (Figure 6.7). Then he moves back into the dark and commits what he himself will later describe thus: "Cold-blooded murder, but I can live with it." The man who shot, from a kind of ambush, the vicious outlaw out of personal compassion and for the sake of advancing peace and civilization killed his own peace of mind, ruined his personal happiness, and condemned himself to a life of despair. *Ibat obscurus*: moving, blocked from sight.

The darkness that surrounds Ethan Edwards and Tom Doniphon is some-times literal but more often figurative.[47] A scholar has put the case in terms that, with a few obvious changes, are applicable to Virgil nearly in their entirety, if without their modern references:

In his work, Ford's Irish melancholy manifested itself in a sense of loss – for a vanished innocence, for a lost love, for a community, for a home. Many of Ford's films are large-scale, even epic, yet they contain the same warmth, domestic detail, and intimacy of his small movies . . . Ford's deepest moments concern memory and loss . . . A good case can be made that America's sense of itself, as far as the movies are

---

[47] Eckstein 1998 traces the process by which the central character became Ford's own artistic creation far beyond what the novel's author and the film's screenwriter had conceived.

Figure 6.7 The *chiaroscuro* effect in John Ford's *The Man Who Shot Liberty Valance*.

concerned, derives from two people: Frank Capra and John Ford. Of these two men, it was John Ford who told the truth ... Ford's social vision was every bit as intense [as Capra's], but far more nuanced and mature. America's humane idealism gave him his themes, and his best films are energized by his recognition of his country's internal conflicts ... Although Ford had an affecting faith in both the idea and the people of America, he was never blind to the ongoing presence of bigotry and racism ... Ford's Westerns have the feeling of life as well as the aura of legend.[48]

Ethan Edwards and Tom Doniphon are mythic figures who may be even more ambiguous than Virgil's Aeneas is to many classicists. Ethan's confrontation with Chief Scar and Tom's with Liberty Valance are anything but the heroic climaxes of epic narratives, the showdowns that audiences expect from their Westerns, especially if the "hero" is played, as in these two films, by John Wayne. The protagonist of either film faces an enemy who is his own *alter ego*. But the showdowns are intended to subvert genre expectations. So did the climactic duel in the *Aeneid*, the showdown, as it were, between Aeneas and Turnus, chief of the Rutulians: "Aeneas' javelin pierces his [Turnus'] corslet, his shield, then his thigh. Turnus is not facing his foe (or does not have his shield in front of him) when the shaft hits, and he is struck from behind."[49]

Aeneas hits Turnus in the back, then kills a suppliant Turnus in a fit of Achillean anger. He becomes as questionable a hero as his Homeric model

[48] Eyman 1999: 21–22.   [49] Ahl 2007: 441, on *Aeneid* 12.924–925.

had been. In *The Searchers* Ethan Edwards shoots several people in the back and scalps the corpse of Scar, an act never condoned in the American Western film or novel and parallel to acts of mutilation of dead bodies in the *Iliad*.[50] If we regard Ethan as a kind of American Aeneas, then Scar becomes a kind of Turnus, and Ford's Apaches, Comanches, Sioux, Cheyennes, and all the other vanished Americans are the equivalent of Virgil's Rutulians, Etruscans, Latins, Volscans, and all the other vanished native tribes we encounter in the second half of the *Aeneid*.[51] In *The Searchers* we watch the native people's forced disappearance in images that evoke nineteenth-century documentary photographs, except for being in color. The aftermath of an Indian massacre by the US cavalry that appears in *The Searchers* will have reminded knowledgeable viewers of the 1890 massacre at Wounded Knee.[52]

Massacres occurred not only in wars or campaigns between the original settlers and the new intruders but also in battles between the latter, divided as they came to be into North and South. The American Civil War (1861–1865) is dealt with or alluded to in several of Ford's films and in his contribution to the gigantic widescreen and stereophonic epic *How the West Was Won* (1963). It was released by M-G-M and Cinerama and featured a host of popular stars, narration by a beloved actor (Spencer Tracy), extensive shooting on location, expensive sets, spectacular action sequences, a rousing musical theme, and a running time of two hours and forty-five minutes. Ford and two other directors famous for their Westerns, Henry Hathaway and George Marshall (whom we met in Chapter 4), shared the responsibilities of putting on this huge spectacle. The opening credits name Ford before the other two, although his segment, entitled "The Civil War," appears only after the film's intermission. This placement signals to viewers the special emphasis placed on Ford because of the prestige of his name. But Ford's portrayal does not fit the surrounding and nearly non-stop glorification of America all that well. It is only around twenty minutes long, and about half of it is shot on a sound stage. The segment incorporates footage from earlier films for its exteriors. And it is relentlessly dark, literally and figuratively. Just as the long and complex history of the settlement of the West is abbreviated even in this epic film, so Ford's Civil War sequence deals only with one episode – or rather, with its aftermath – which stands in for the war's entire blood-soaked history. This is the 1862 Battle of Shiloh, which had well over 23,000 casualties of men killed, wounded, missing, or captured on both sides. As such, it can hardly be expected to form

---

[50] Cf. on this my comments in Winkler 2004b: 155–156 and 166 (notes with references).
[51] On the wider context cf. Shields 2001.
[52] For comparison, see Jensen, Paul, and Carter 2011: 105–114 (photos 66–75). Jerome Greene 2014: 259 (ill. 37) provides an unusually intense photo, with illuminating caption.

the centerpiece of a triumphalist epic suitable for family viewing. A mass grave is being dug and then filled in; the water near the battlefield is red with blood, an unusual thing to be seen even in a more serious film than this. A Union army tent serves as a field doctor's makeshift place for surgery, chiefly amputations. It consists of a wooden table on which the dead and dying are roughly deposited after a bucket of water is poured over the blood left on it from a previous surgery. As often, Ford shows us the price of empire through the dissolution of a family: a father killed, two brothers separated, a mother dead from grief. A dissolve from a family cemetery to a young soldier, returned from war and sitting on the porch before leaving his home for good, makes him appear to be leaning against his mother's tombstone – a poignant moment. It may, however, not be by Ford.[53] The martial nobility sometimes found in the Civil War is completely missing. In *The Horse Soldiers* (1959), an earlier Civil War film, Ford had shown military chivalry to be futile and anachronistic in one of his most memorable poetic sequences. It shows the young cadets of a Southern military academy marching, with flags and fifes and drums, against a Northern contingent. "Nothing but children; they're schoolboys!" exclaims a Union officer. Ford commented later: "that happened several times."[54]

"Human events stir tears" (*Sunt lacrimae rerum*): Aeneas' mournfully resigned words, one of the most famous and often-quoted winged words of the *Aeneid*, are uttered retrospectively and introspectively when he sees images of the Trojan War on the temple being built in the new city of Carthage.[55] They point out the frailty of the human condition. Such a melancholic spirit also exists beneath the surface heroism in Ford. The poetic affinities of Virgil and Ford become evident in the following assessment of the latter. With some obvious modification, it also expresses the essence of Virgilian epic:

Ford was a defiantly consistent filmmaker. His perspective, however, is neither static nor predictable, and he specialized in presenting two opposing ideas simultaneously. A brass band blasts military tunes and our first impression is: Ford patriotic blarney. Yet his military films are among the most devastatingly critical

[53] In the words of Henry Hathaway, who directed most of *How the West Was Won*: "He [Ford] shot the whole sequence on a sound stage." Quoted from Behlmer 2001: 236. Director Richard Thorpe filmed transitional scenes without receiving credit.
[54] Quoted from Bogdanovich 1978: 97. On the historical background and Ford's use of Jefferson Military Academy for setting and uniforms see McBride 2001: 596.
[55] Virgil, *Aeneid* 1.462; Ahl 2007: 18.

portraits of wartime lunacy made in Hollywood. Few American artists have addressed the myths with which we justify ourselves to the gods and our children with more trenchant analysis.

Ford earns his patriotism by seeing through veils of vast sadness; he understood why America is worth dying for and even forgiving, which can be a tougher chore. Battle hymns and bugle calls cannot drown out the misery of the broken families, disappointed lives, abandoned women, and expendable men he documents . . . His films isolate the individual and mourn each individual loss.[56]

Ford is the pre-eminent popular American artist whose work first celebrates a past that was imperfect but that is worth believing in and remembering, then mourns its vanishing. A particular shot from *The Man Who Shot Liberty Valance* elegantly and eloquently conveys this point in purely visual terms (Figure 6.8). On the wall of a make-shift schoolroom, screen left, a reminder of the country's foundation; on the extreme right, and in the same building, the frontier town's newspaper office, representing freedom of expression and progress; on the wall in the center and dominating the composition the flag, flanked by two different Americans: the man of the law and the man of the gun. The moment is not meant to impose its meaning forcefully; rather, it is understated and integrated into the story being told. But its composition is highly significant. "Ford represents pure classicism of expression in which an economy of means yields a profusion of effects .... any of his compositions selected at random will reveal [his] attention to nuanced detail and overall design."[57] We may compare a particular late-ancient manuscript illustration of the *Aeneid*, which, in conjunction with the passage it illustrates, makes nearly the same point. It shows the embassy of the Trojans, new arrivals in a new land, to indigenous King Latinus before a magnificent palace-plus-temple, symbol of culture and civilization.[58] Its architecture is anachronistic, but this very circumstance refers us to what is to come as the culmination of a long and complex historical process: "Rome's mighty ramparts" (quoted above). Ford makes a similar point with the church in *My Darling Clementine*.

---

[56] Quoted from Giddins 2010b: 49.   [57] Quoted from Sarris 1975: 185.

[58] Virgil, *Aeneid* 7.170–193. Several details in this passage (e.g. *fasces, rostra*) indicate the Roman society to come. Wright 1993: 64–65 prints a full-sized color photograph of this illustration (folio 60 *verso* of Vat. lat. 3225), with annotation and Virgil's text in Latin and English. On the image see also de Wit 1959: 126–130 ("Pictura 41"). For the sake of greater visual impact, the illustrator moved Virgil's indoor scene to the outdoors.

Figure 6.8 A summation of American culture in John Ford's *The Man Who Shot Liberty Valance.*

6 History and Epic

Ford directed about 140 films, ranging from short one-reelers to at least one full-scale epic. Virgil wrote two shorter works, the pastoral *Eclogues* and the agricultural *Georgics*, before his mythic-historical epic. As dissimilar as the Roman and the American necessarily are across time and place, Ford and Virgil have one overarching artistic principle in common. Classical scholar Friedrich Klingner decades ago drew attention to the spiritual unity within Virgil's works.[59] One of the most important early critical studies of Ford points to the same phenomenon. Its chapter headings read as follows:

> Early Days
> 1930–1939: The Storyteller
> 1940–1947: The Poet Laureate
> 1948–1966: The Poet and Rememberer of Things Past[60]

What Klingner saw as fundamental to Virgil is fundamental to Ford as well:

the farmer's life does not only embody a general ideal, but it is [also] the original way of life in Italy. Rome's grandeur rests upon it. It is not only the ideal opposite of a devastated present [after civil war] but also a surviving remainder of one's own

---

[59] Klingner 1965b: 274. Klingner's essay was first published in 1930.
[60] Sarris 1975: 5 (table of contents).

purer origin and of a better past. The present is, on the whole, a decline from this right and appropriate way of life.[61]

Virgil's theme in the *Georgics* is, "more and more, the entire *res Romana*, of which the country life is an important part, and the decision of Roman destiny in the present."[62] The artistic result is again comparable to Ford and the *res Americana*, as we may call it:

In Virgil's mind there arose a great historical image encompassing the entire Roman past and present and interpreting this present. Italy is the land of Saturn; its original and genuine essence had been realized in the peaceful and just conditions of the Golden Age. The farmer's life is a remainder of this, having survived until the present, a present destroyed by guilt and suffering. It is the basis on which Rome's majesty and world empire were erected.[63]

In Virgil's case as well as in Ford's, the movements from early works preparing the way to large-scale mature achievements are clearly traceable and make for a strong cohesion overall. The separate developments of Virgil's and Ford's societies from agrarianism to world empire have certain implications in common. So do their artistic creations:

The art of [Virgil's] poetry ... contains within itself what moves and is of importance to all, the great common concerns of historical experience. But history changes and combines itself with the order of existence, in which the poet is at home, with myth. It does so in such a manner that the factual historicity of the present as it has been experienced is preserved but merges with myth, just as a park merges with a natural mountain landscape. The poet experiences history, but to such depths that he senses greater things permeating it – things that are beyond political and historical facts and even beyond ethical conditions, things that are more essential and encompass those facts and conditions.[64]

Ford's body of work comes closest to the *Aeneid* when it expresses greatness and sacrifice, affirmation and resignation – that is to say, a strong sense of ambiguity and what in retrospect we might call the spirit of the end. In this regard, Ford's twentieth-century portrayal of the indigenous peoples conquered, pushed aside, or annihilated echoes nineteenth-century sentiments about them. A telling passage in *Charlemont*, a novel by William Gilmore Simms published in 1856, is worth quoting at some

---

[61] Klingner 1965b: 284.
[62] Klingner 1965b: 287. The Latin expression implies the totality of Roman life, history, culture, etc.
[63] Klingner 1965b: 285.   [64] Klingner 1965c: 303. This essay was first published in 1943.

length because it is barely known today. Simms wrote about the Indians of Kentucky:

The "dark and bloody ground," by which mournful epithet Kentucky was origin-ally known to the Anglo-American, was dark and bloody no longer. The savage had disappeared from its green forests for ever, and no longer profaned with slaughter, and his unholy whoop of death, its broad and beautiful abodes. A newer race had succeeded; and the wilderness, fulfilling the better destinies of earth, had begun to blossom like the rose. Conquest had fenced in its sterile borders with a wall of fearless men, and peace slept everywhere in security among its green recesses. Stirring industry – the perpetual conqueror – made the woods resound with the echoes of his biting axe and ringing hammer. Smiling villages rose in cheerful white, in place of the crumbling and smoky cabins of the hunter. High and becoming purposes of social life and thoughtful enterprise superseded that eating and painful decay, which has terminated in the annihilation of the red man; and which, among every people, must always result from their refusal to exercise, according to the decree of experience, no less than Providence, their limbs and sinews in tasks of well-directed and continual labor.

   A great nation urging on a sleepless war against sloth and feebleness, is one of the noblest of human spectacles. This warfare was rapidly and hourly changing the monotony and dreary aspects of rock and forest. Under the creative hands of art, temples of magnificence rose where the pines had fallen. Long and lovely vistas were opened through the dark and hitherto impervious thickets. The city sprang up beside the river, while hamlets, filled with active hope and cheerful industry, crowded upon the verdant hill-side, and clustered among innumerable valleys. Grace began to seek out the homes of toil, and taste supplied their decorations. A purer form of religion hallowed the forest-homes of the red-man, while expelling for ever the rude divinities of his worship; and throughout the land, an advent of moral loveliness seemed approaching, not less grateful to the affections and the mind, than was the beauty of the infant April, to the eye and the heart of the wanderer ... Though the savage had for ever departed from its limits, the blessings of a perfect civilization were not yet secured to the new and flourishing regions of Kentucky.[65]

The vanished tribes of pre-Roman Italy, evoked in the second half of the *Aeneid*, are predecessors of the native tribes of Kentucky. The nineteenth-century novelist could still affirm the progress that comes with white settlement; the twentieth-century director, whose most profound restate-ment of the theme came exactly one century later, can no longer do quite the same thing. In different ways and from different perspectives, Ford's

---

[65] Quoted from Simms 1856: 14–15. The passage appears in the opening section of the novel's first chapter ("The Scene").

The Searchers and, more explicitly, *The Man Who Shot Liberty Valance* and
Cheyenne Autumn all echo Simms, who was a poet and historian as well as
a novelist. But Ford's vision in the late works mentioned became far darker
than Simms's had been. "Is our progress then genuine?" we might ask with
John Erskine. "Is the spread of civilization after all a good thing?"[66]

The fundamental implications in Ford are comparable to the last line
Virgil ever composed, provided we are willing to widen that line's meaning
and to apply it beyond its particular situation, as Virgil himself may have
intended.[67] This line, translated and discussed above, can serve as a fitting
epigraph for the fate of the Indians in *Cheyenne Autumn*, Ford's last
Western, and for his eventual disenchantment with the West: "Life flutters
off on a groan, under protest, down among shadows."

A country's greatness comes at a price. Virgil, "father of the West," as he
has been called, showed this in the *Aeneid*.[68] Ford, "the American cinema's
great poet of civilization," as he has been called, showed this in many of his
films, primarily his Westerns.[69] "This is the West, sir. When the facts become
legend, print the legend" – this famous pronouncement on history and myth
in *The Man Who Shot Liberty Valance* points to the close ties between
history and poetry (i.e. all literary fiction) that Aristotle addressed in his
Poetics. Aristotle valued literature more highly than historiography.[70]
Klingner concluded about Virgil's epic and Roman history:

Admittedly, this is not history as a historian sees it. Fundamentally it is something
quite plain and simple, something that exists before history in a narrower sense –
myth. And it is this: the capacity to sense the whole of a fateful development,
stretching from the distant past to a decisive present, to feel one with the past, to
hallow one's origins.[71]

This again fits Ford's portrayals of history. To epic literature on important
themes of the past we may now add historical epic cinema. As far as

[66] Erskine 1935a: 320 and 321.
[67] So, e.g., Quinn 1969: 276: "The relevance of the death scene [i.e. Turnus' death] to the events of
their own times can hardly have escaped Virgil's contemporaries."
[68] So the title of Haecker 1934. The German original appeared in 1931.
[69] The quotation is from Wood 1971: 12.   [70] Aristotle, *Poetics* 1451a37–b32.
[71] Klingner 1965c: 311. Even if the *Aeneid* is not a historian's work of history, Virgil's affinities
with Roman historiography, especially Livy's account of early Rome, is well-known: "Virgil
elsewhere [besides the historical events depicted on Aeneas' shield in Book 8] writes like an
historian . . . . it is tempting to believe . . . that in his description of Aeneas' shield Virgil is again
resorting to the historian's manner." Quoted from Woodman 1989: 134 (= 2012: 150);
additional references there in note 14. On the subject see further Feldherr 2014: 299–312, with
extensive references.

America is concerned, this means primarily the Western.[72] Within the Western it means primarily Ford. Unlike Virgil, whose *Aeneid* was immediately recognized as transcending even Homeric epic, the model it was built on, Ford, to a large extent, had to wait for due recognition. What one perceptive critic recognized early on about his last film, which had been widely dismissed as a failure upon its release, applies to Ford's work in general: "The beauties of *Seven Women* are for the ages, or at least for a later time when the personal poetry of film directors is better understood between the lines of genre conventions ... [Ford is] one of the cinema's greatest poets, though he would be the last to say so himself."[73]

An analogy between Ford and one of the greatest American poets may add another instance of proof to this proposition. In his collection *Drum-Taps* (1865), Walt Whitman included a poem entitled "Cavalry Crossing a Ford." Its text immediately conjures up parallel iconic moments in several Ford Westerns. The poem consists of only seven lines. But it is as evocative as Ford's cinematic images and sounds:

> A line in long array where they wind betwixt green islands,
> They take a serpentine course, their arms flash in the sun – hark to the
>   musical clank,
> Behold the silvery river, in it the splashing horses loitering stop to drink,
> Behold the brown-faced men, each group, each person a picture, the
>   negligent rest on the saddles,
> Some emerge on the opposite bank, others are just entering the ford –
>   while,
> Scarlet and blue and snowy white,
> The guidon flags flutter gaily in the wind.[74]

Each group, each person a picture: It is no overstatement to say that the majority of camera set-ups in Ford's Westerns are as pictorial as Whitman's poem and as the paintings of Frederic Remington, Charles M. Russell,

---

[72] Political overtones in the Western appear with expected frequency. As director Sam Peckinpah, who is best known for his Westerns (and sometimes considered to be either the legitimate or the illegitimate successor of Ford), once put it: "The Western is a universal frame within which it is possible to comment on today." Source of quotation: "Press Violent About Film's Violence, Prod Sam Peckinpah Following 'Bunch'"; quoted from Prince 1999: 212. The film in question is *The Wild Bunch*, to which I will briefly turn in Chapter 7.

[73] Sarris 1975: 185 and 188. With characteristic grumpiness, Ford always denied that he was a poet and maintained that he did not know what such an expression meant. Here is an example from 1973, when Ford could look back on his entire career: "I am not a poet .... I'm just a hard-nosed, hardworking, run-of-the-mill director." Quoted from Wagner 1975: 54; rpt. as Wagner 2001, with quotation at 159. Ford deceived few if any, perhaps not even himself.

[74] Quoted from Kaplan 1982: 435.

Charles Schreyvogel, and a few others. If we modify the opening of the *Aeneid* – *arma virumque·cano* ("Arms and the man I sing") – we might put the matter of Ford into these terms: *arma virosque canit* (arms and the men he sings with his epic-historical themes) but also *arma virosque pinxit* (arms and the men he painted – on the screen itself).

7   Remembrance of Things Past

In Book 1 of the *Aeneid*, Aeneas and some of his men barely survive a savage storm on the sea. Aeneas attempts to instill courage into them with a brief but justly famous speech. In its center Virgil places a sentiment that resonates across time: "Maybe the day'll come when even this will be joy to remember" (*forsan et haec olim meminisse iuvabit*).[75] Eventually even dire hardship may turn into a pleasant memory. The thought had been long familiar from Greek and earlier Roman literature but received its canonical form here. As has been well said, "it is authentic of human experience and resilient hope."[76] Ford's Mrs. Jorgensen implied much the same thing.

A particular film by Ford may be the best illustration of this Virgilian perspective ever put on the American screen: *How Green Was My Valley*, adapted from the 1939 novel by Richard Llewellyn. The harsh fate of a family of miners and that family's eventual dissolution is as poignant and heart-rending as anything Ford ever put into images. *How Green Was My Valley* presents, in a narrator's voice-over, the youthful memories of a young boy from a melancholic perspective of decades later. A biographer of Ford succinctly summarizes the film's greatness:

the characters are . . . bathed in the golden glow of an adult's remembrance of his childhood. And it is one of the most cogent statements of one of Ford's deepest themes: the way that time's flow destroys the old ways, which must die in order for the future to take hold.

He then refers to the "tenacity and universality" of the emotions portrayed in this film.[77] Thematic parallels to the *Aeneid* are self-evident. Black American writer Stanley Crouch provides us with corroboration. In an essay on Ford he wrote, more than fifty years after the film was released:

[75] Virgil, *Aeneid* 1.203; Ahl 2007: 10. Aeneas' speech is at lines 198–207.
[76] Austin 1971: 84. Austin: 83–84 (on line 203) gives parallel citations ranging from Homer to the younger Seneca.
[77] Both quotations are from Eyman 1999: 242.

I watched it whenever I could because there was something in the tale that spoke to the world surrounding me even though the people, superficially, were so different. The cinematic depth gave me one of my earliest experiences of the meaning of the universal achieved through aesthetic form . . . I am back there just as the boy was in *How Green Was My Valley*, and nothing is dead, nothing gone, all is made perpetual through the regeneration of memory.[78]

Most of this, too, fits Virgil. Everything that is superficially different and long gone is still here. The depth of artistic perception in epic and in the cinema virtually guarantees the eternity of the past in later memory: "All that is truly important is the flow of history, a new world being built on what has come before – on sacrifices made, loves lost, families broken, entire communities disintegrated." These words about Ford are an unwitting echo of Virgil's epic, for both are "connecting the past and the present in an eternal ribbon of remembrance."[79]

The emotional appeal of the past as it is presented by a great artist guarantees that artist his eternity: a remembrance of poets past. Like many influential artists, both Virgil and Ford came to acquire near-mythic status themselves. Their respective apotheoses occurred in two twentieth-century German novels: Hermann Broch's *The Death of Virgil* and Peter Handke's *Short Letter, Long Farewell.*[80] "That's the pathway to heaven" (*sic itur ad astra*): Virgil's now proverbial expression may serve as my epigraph to this consideration of him and Ford side by side.[81] But an observation about epic and film once made by Jorge Luis Borges is equally fitting: "I think nowadays, while literary men seem to have neglected their epic duties, the epic has been saved, strangely enough, by the Westerns."[82]

---

[78] Quoted from Crouch 1998b: 270 and 288. The essay was originally published in 1996 (Crouch 1998a: 323).

[79] Both quotations from Eyman 1999: 341, in connection with *Fort Apache* and *The Man Who Shot Liberty Valance.*

[80] Broch 1945, published simultaneously with the German original (*Der Tod des Vergil*); Handke 1974; the German original (*Der kurze Brief zum langen Abschied*) was first published in 1972. On the mythical Ford who appears at the end of Handke's partly autobiographical novel see my comments in Winkler 1988: 575.

[81] Virgil, *Aeneid* 9.641; Ahl 2007: 229.

[82] Christ 1967: 123; rpt. in *The* Paris Review *Interviews* 2006: 111–159; quotation at 118.

PART IV

Counter-Affinities

Ideological and Narrative Distortions of History

The Battle of Thermopylae of 480 B C has been refought on the cinema screen on two occasions. Rudolph Maté's *The 300 Spartans* (1962) was filmed in Greece, although not at or near the historical site.[1] Zack Snyder's *300* (2007) adapted and expanded Frank Miller and Lynn Varley's award-winning graphic novel of 1998.[2] As is often the case, the story told in either film overshadows history with inventive mythmaking. Such creative rewriting or re-imagining of the past occurred in antiquity as well, for to Greeks and Romans myth and history had originally been one and the same.[3] For historical cinema, this is a familiar phenomenon: "It is a truism that historical films are always about the time in which they are made and never about the time in which they are set."[4] Just as *The 300 Spartans* reflected the cultural, social, and political concerns and preoccupations of its era, so *300* dealt much less with history than with a free version of Spartan "Honor," "Duty," "Glory," "Combat," and "Victory," to quote the titles of the book's original five installments. Miller, who served as consultant and executive producer on Snyder's film, had been inspired by *The 300 Spartans* for his own vision of Thermopylae. *300*, the film more than the comic book, is instructive about the process of historical distortion by means of modern ideology to a greater degree than most of its

[1] Classical scholars have written about *300* from a variety of perspectives. Cyrino 2011 gives an introduction and further references. Murray 2007 argues for historical accuracy in *300* and has useful illustrations. See further Thomas Jenkins 2015: 113–119. On the earlier film see Levene 2007; Redonet 2008; Nikoloutsos 2013c. Basic modern accounts on the Persian Wars, including the battle, are Green 1996 and Rahe 2016. Rahe 2015 examines the structure of Spartan society in detail. All three works contain extensive references.

[2] In the US, *300* had been shown once on December 9, 2006, at the Butt-Numb-A-Thon [*sic*] in Austin, Texas, and went into general release on March 9, 2007. It premiered outside the US in Sparta, Greece, on March 7, 2007, with a general release in Greece a day later. For classicists' perspectives on Miller's graphic series *300* and *Sin City*, in which Thermopylae also appears, see Tomasso 2011 and Fairey 2011.

[3] On this aspect of the classical cultures see the brief but pertinent remarks by Catenacci 2009: 166. It is ironic that Catenacci: 167–168 should contradict his argument by criticizing Wolfgang Petersen's *Troy* (2004) for the kind of "fluidity" of myth he had just extolled.

[4] Richards 2008: 1. Examples illustrating this side of cinema may be found in Winkler 2001b: 8 note 7.

worldwide viewers have noticed. It provides us with an object lesson as fascinating as it is depressing.

One particular question should be addressed at the outset. Is not all the intellectual heavy weather concerning *300* that is about to be unleashed on readers of this long chapter merely a storm in a teacup? After all, *300* is just a cartoonish action flick made for teenagers, not a film for thinking adults worth taking seriously – or is it? As one reviewer put it quite concisely: "the movie's just too darned silly to withstand any ideological theorizing."[5] Much ado about very little, then? Not at all, as I hope to show. My thesis is that, unintentionally and unwittingly on the part of its makers, *300* is a kind of neo-fascist work of popular culture.[6] To make that case in a manner that can convince even skeptics, I begin with a modern last-stand battle and then outline the myth of Sparta in Nazi Germany. Afterwards I will adduce several other aspects to support my argument: historical, ideological, theoretical, cinematic.

1   Leonidas at Stalingrad but Not at Kolberg

On February 2, 1943, the German Sixth Army that had been encircled at Stalingrad surrendered after a five-month siege. Three days earlier, Nazi Germany had observed the tenth anniversary of January 30, 1933, the day Adolf Hitler came to power and a *Großdeutsches Reich*, a Greater German Empire, came into existence. Each year on this date the *Führer* would address his people in a speech that was broadcast across the country and to the armies beyond its borders. Nazi propaganda had styled Hitler the Greatest Strategist of All Time (*Größter Feldherr aller Zeiten*) after the German victories in the early years of the war. But in 1943, with the inevitable disaster of Stalingrad on the horizon, Hitler thought it prudent to delegate the task of delivering his anniversary oration to one of his minions, Imperial Marshal (*Reichsmarschall*) Hermann Göring. Göring's *Appell an die Wehrmacht* was delivered in the Honor Hall (*Ehrensaal*) of the Air Ministry (*Reichsluftfahrtministerium*) before select members of the German armed

---

[5] Seymour 2007. He immediately adds: "And 'silly' is invoked here, more or less, with affection."

[6] Scholars often distinguish between the historical *Fascism* of the 1920s to 1940s and subsequent *fascism*, the political, ideological, and cultural offshoots of Fascism. For more on this see Roger Griffin 1991; he uses the term "generic fascism" for the latter. He provides useful definitions of Fascism and fascism: a concise one in Roger Griffin 1991: 26 and a more detailed one in 2007: 181–182; see further 2003. Roger Griffin 1995 and 1998 are useful anthologies of key Fascist and fascist texts.

forces.[7] The speech was broadcast; it could be heard by the German soldiers at Stalingrad.

Göring referred to two parallel cases, one German and mythic, the other historic and classical, of last-stand heroism and refusal to surrender in the face of inevitable doom. At some length Göring dealt with the destruction of the Nibelungen in King Etzel's hall, the climactic moment of the *Nibelungenlied*, the medieval German epic that had been the basis for Fritz Lang's five-hour film adaptation *Die Nibelungen* of 1924. This film was quickly appropriated for purposes of Nazi ideology and shown repeatedly in German theaters during the 1930s. At greater length and with greater pathos, Göring also extolled the Battle of Thermopylae. He adapted Greek poet Simonides' epitaph on the Spartans in the classic German version by Friedrich Schiller, the great poet and playwright whom the Nazis, along with virtually all other important figures from the German past, had claimed for their own ideology. Schiller's version of Simonides' distich reads:

> Wanderer, kommst du nach Sparta, verkündige dorten, du habest
> uns hier liegen gesehn, wie das Gesetz es befahl.

In rough translation: "Traveler, when you come to Sparta tell them there that you saw us lying here as the law commanded."[8] Göring, slightly misquoting Schiller, substituted Germany for Sparta and Stalingrad for Thermopylae. Here is the relevant section, with Göring's quotation left in German:

My soldiers, most of you will have heard of a similar example in the great, stupendous history of Europe. Even though at that time the numbers were small, there is, in the final analysis, no difference at all in the deed as such. When you think of it: Millennia have passed, and before these millennia, there stood in a narrow pass in Greece an infinitely brave and bold man with three hundred of his men, there stood Leonidas with three hundred Spartans from a tribe known for its bravery and boldness; and an overwhelming majority attacked and attacked anew again and again. The sky darkened from the number of arrows that were shot. Back then, too, it was an onslaught from the Asiatic East, which here was broken by Nordic Man. [S]tupendous masses of fighters were available to Xerxes, but the

---

[7] The official title of the speech is difficult to translate. "Appeal to the Armed Forces" is its basic meaning. But *Appell* in military contexts can also mean, or at least imply, "roll-call, muster, inspection, parade."

[8] Simonides' text is preserved by Herodotus, *Histories* 7.228 (= *F.G.E.* XXII(b) Page). Ziogas 2014 offers a new interpretation and the most important references. Schiller's version was based on Cicero, *Tusculan Disputations* 1.101, and appeared in lines 97–98 of his poem "Der Spaziergang" ("The Stroll"). The poem's text is in Fricke and Göpfert 1965: 228–234; this passage at 231.

three hundred men did not yield and did not waver, they fought and fought a hopeless fight. Hopeless, but not meaningless! And then the last man fell. And in this narrow pass, there is now written a sentence: *Wanderer, kommst du nach Sparta, berichte, du habest uns hier liegen sehen, wie das Gesetz es befahl.* They were three hundred men, my comrades! Millennia have passed – and still today this holds true, this fight there, this sacrifice made there, so heroically, so great an example of the highest military tradition – and it will once be said: If you come to Germany, tell them that you saw us lying at Stalingrad as the law commanded, that is to say, the law of our people's security. And this law each of you carries within your breast, the law to die for Germany, for the life of Germany is the hope of all laws.[9]

A few further allusions to the law that has to be obeyed follow, but the preceding passage is sufficient to tell us what Göring had in mind. Especially revealing are his references to the Spartans as representatives of the Nordic master race and the one to what we today would call *national security* – a ready reason or excuse for virtually any kind of military undertaking.

The listeners' reactions varied according to the degree of their belief in the *Vaterland.* Historian Antony Beevor reports:

This speech was not well received in Stalingrad, where it was listened to on radios. The fact that it was Goering [*sic*], of all people, who was delivering 'our own funeral speech', heaped insult upon injury … Goering's voice was instantly recognized. 'Turn it up!' somebody shouted. 'Switch it off!' yelled others, cursing him.

As Beevor also reports: "Some officers joked bitterly that the 'suicide of the Jews' on the top of Masada might have been a more appropriate comparison than Thermopylae."[10] But the fate of the Spartans at Thermopylae was the right analogy for a propaganda machine that had, time and again, emphasized the close ties of Nazi Germany to classical Greece. On February 4, 1943, the *Völkischer Beobachter* announced the defeat and surrender in a headline ("They Died That Germany Might Live"), accompanied by the design for a typically bombastic memorial in stone. A warrior who evokes classical antiquity in his heroic nudity embodies a kind of Spartan indomitability. The memorial was to be called *Vergeltung* ("Vengeance");

---

[9]   The original text is in Krüger 1991: 151–190; quotation at 180–181. The speech was published in the Nazi party's news organ *Völkischer Beobachter* on January 3. Krüger: 170–187 provides a transcript of Göring's actual words, different in places from the version published, with introductory comments and notes. Krüger: 190 note 37 adds that after the words "[S]tupendous masses" (*[G]ewaltige Mengen*) extraneous sounds began to make Göring's voice nearly incomprehensible. On the speech see further Watt 1985. On Thermopylae after antiquity see Albertz 2006.

[10] Both quotations are from Beevor 1998: 380 (with 472 for source references).

Figure 7.1 The title page of *Völkischer Beobachter* announcing the defeat at Stalingrad.

another headline below it proclaimed, in bold type: "Our Oath: Vengeance!" (Figure 7.1). The sculpture was by Arno Breker, the most prominent and most highly favored sculptor in Nazi Germany. His works perfectly express the spirit of Nazi bombast and kitsch in their *faux*-classicism.

Göring's mention of Thermopylae caused Joseph Goebbels, the Nazi propaganda minister, to start an extensive propaganda campaign along the same lines:

For almost two weeks ... the German press duly developed and cultivated the desired image of Stalingrad as Nazi Germany's Thermopylae, regularly presenting the catastrophe as a carefully planned, self-sacrificially heroic defence intended to gain vital breathing space for Germany and the rest of Western Europe before the Russian masses moved against them.[11]

This is an example of what we today call *spin*. The facts of both ancient history (Thermopylae) and contemporary history (Stalingrad) are cynically perverted and forced into the service of political and military propaganda, those concerning the later event even more than those concerning the earlier one. To put the point anachronistically: We could imagine Leonidas' last words in *300*, addressed to the film's narrator and lone survivor of the Battle, coming from high-ranking Nazi functionaries in February, 1943, with only one change: "you will make every Greek [or: German] know what happened here. You'll have a grand tale to tell. A tale of victory."

Thermopylae was repeatedly invoked in Nazi Germany.[12] January 30, 1945, brought the twelfth and last anniversary of the Nazis' hoped-for Thousand-Year Empire, together with Hitler's final anniversary address. That day also saw the premiere of *Kolberg*, Nazi Germany's last completed film, directed and co-written by Veit Harlan, the era's pre-eminent filmmaker. Its subject was the successful resistance by the population of Kolberg, a city in Pomerania, to Napoleon's *Grande Armée* in 1807. This resistance was organized under the leadership of Major August Graf von Gneisenau, later a General Field Marshal and one of Prussia's greatest military heroes. Gneisenau rejected the French offer of honorable capitulation, and the destruction of the city seemed inevitable. But an unexpected peace treaty between France and Prussia led to a truce. The city was spared. Although heavily bombarded and damaged, it survived and remained Prussian. The siege and the resistance did not end in a military victory for either side, but this was certainly a remarkable outcome. In March 1945, the Red Army took Kolberg on its advance west.

Harlan's *Kolberg* premiered simultaneously in Berlin and in the fortress of La Rochelle in France, which was going through its own last stand at the time; this was the reason La Rochelle was chosen. The print to be screened had to be dropped by parachute from an airplane. *Kolberg* is commonly regarded as a *Durchhaltefilm* – roughly, a "Stick-It-Out" or "Never-Surrender" film. A historian of German cinema has called it "a megalomaniacal, death-hungry, fight-to-the-last-man production."[13] *Kolberg* had

---

[11] Quoted from Watt 1985: 874. Cf. also Watt: 872 on Goebbels.

[12] On the topic see further Rebenich 2002. Boedtger 2009 has excerpts from ancient sources, Göring's speech, and a major Nazi article on the topic.

[13] Kreimeier 1996: 276. Cf. also Schenk 1994: 90–93.

been the pet project of Joseph Goebbels, the head of Nazi propaganda and also of the German film industry. The expensive epic, filmed in color and with a huge cast, was meant to inspire the German people with the will to endure against overwhelming odds or at least to shore up a crumbling will at a time when any determination to stick it out had become suicidal. The project had come to Goebbels in the wake of the defeat at Stalingrad. On May 7, 1943, he wrote in his diary:

With this film Harlan is to show the example of manly courage and strength of resistance on the part of a citizenry even under desperate conditions. This film will teach a great lesson, especially in the regions of air war.

And on May 25:

I have extraordinarily high hopes for this film by Harlan. It fits exactly the political-military surroundings that in all probability we will have to take account of when this film will be released.

On June 1 Goebbels ordered Harlan in writing to make *Kolberg* a *Großfilm*, an epic spectacle: "This film is charged with demonstrating by the example of the titular city that a people [*Volk*], united at home [*Heimat*] and at the front, will overcome any enemy." *Kolberg*, he explained further, was being produced specifically under his order and would "serve the spiritual conduct of the war."[14] Five days later he added in his diary that in the foreseeable future a certain kind of film would be needed: those that "will cultivate and praise the toughness of our resistance."[15] Goebbels wanted Harlan to include a flashback to the story of Leonidas and the three hundred Spartans, but it was too late.[16] Harlan reported in his autobiography:

I remember exactly that during the film's production he [Goebbels] twice brought up the subject whether I could not include a "Leonidas scene" in the film. He put great value on such a scene "for symbolic reasons." He wanted it shown, "in the garb of the Battle of Kolberg" how back then the king had sacrificed himself and his army at Thermopylae before Sparta in order to make the final victory [*Endsieg*] possible later. I told Goebbels that practically all battle scenes had already been filmed and that the structure of my subject was outlined far too closely to make it possible for me to fulfill his wish in any specific way.[17]

[14] The passages are taken from Buchloh 2010: 134; source reference at 305 note 470.
[15] Buchloh 2010: 136; source reference at 306 note 478.
[16] Harlan 1966: 180–194 describes his involvement with *Kolberg*, including Goebbels's interference in the editing process. Goebbels had much of Harlan's horrifying footage showing casualties of war removed in order to emphasize martial glory and heroism.
[17] Harlan 1966: 190–191. *Endsieg* is a key Nazi term.

Goebbels wrote the diary entries quoted above within six months of the surrender at Stalingrad and clearly saw a direct connection with Thermopylae: from antiquity's heroic defeat to improbable if glorious survival during the Napoleonic era, on to heroic but immense defeat in the recent past, and now on to final victory.

2   Sparta and Nazism

The Nazis' pervasive interest in classical Greece is well known. To Hitler, the Greeks and not the ancient Germans were the true ancestors of the Aryan Master Race. The Spartans, antiquity's greatest military elite, came to be regarded as the most Nordic of all Greeks. They resisted miscegenation and avoided the racial impurities that weakened or destroyed those who did not guard against such degeneracy.[18] The Spartans were famous warriors, and at Thermopylae they achieved the most Wagnerian kind of *Götterdämmerung* in ancient history, although on a human level. As Göring's speech about Stalingrad makes evident, the Spartans were fully the equals of the Aryan Nibelungen. From the Nazi perspective, Spartans and Nibelungen succumbed, defiantly and in blazes of glory, to massed barbarian hordes from the East. Ancient Persians and medieval Huns parallel modern Communists and Bolsheviks. Such an idea of a clash of civilizations is simplistic but effective.[19] It is immediately understandable and attractive to the unthinking. A fervent belief in patriotic death without surrender, one that amounts to an obsession less with Freudian Eros and Thanatos and more with an imperialist Dynamis (Power) and Thanatos, is part of the essence of Fascism and Nazism. A Nazi hero did not achieve greatness by victory but by death. Albert Speer, one of Hitler's intimates, was aware of "Hitler's liking for failed heroes" like Siegfried, Cola di Rienzi, and the Flying Dutchman and later told historian Joachim Fest: "It became clear to me that, above all else, he recognized himself in these figures and perhaps even foresaw his own end in

---

[18]   On this and its wider ramifications see Rawson 1969: 306–343 (chapter titled "Sparta in Germany"); Losemann 2012, an indispensable critical survey with numerous references; Roche 2012b (the German phrase in her title is a remark by Goebbels on the occasion of his 1936 visit to Sparta); Chapoutot 2016, especially 214–226 and 442–443 (notes) on Sparta, and 373–376 and 469–470 (notes) on Thermopylae and Stalingrad.

[19]   Cf. Huntington 1993, expanded as Huntington 1996. Note the absence of the question mark in the title of the latter – as if certainty had now been attained. Huntington 1996: 162 declares modern Greece a "non-Western country" and elaborates as follows: "Greece is not part of Western civilization, but it was the home of Classical civilization which was an important source of Western civilization." Here there seems to be a clash of logic with ideology and a remaking of Western history.

them."[20] Fest reports on "Hitler's fondness for metaphors from the ancient world" and comments, specifically:

When the ring closed around Berlin in March-April 1945 he liked to refer to Leonidas and the Spartans (who also fought and held out in a desperate situation) or sometimes to the Ostrogoths at Vesuvius. Speer said that he called it 'auto-suggestion through myths'. And, along with all these classical models, Hitler could draw on Frederick the Great and especially Richard Wagner, with all his crew of heroes besotted with downfall [*Untergang*].[21]

Nazi cinema made such besottedness more evident than any other form of art or popular culture could have done. The work of director and frequent screenwriter (or at least co-writer) Harlan is a case in point, even when a film's story appears not to be overtly ideological. His film *The Great Sacrifice* (*Opfergang*) is an expensive and attractive-looking color melodrama about a love triangle involving a husband, his wife, and their neighbor, an independent-minded unmarried young woman. But more than this, it is primarily about death. The young woman has contracted some tropical malady, and an outbreak of typhoid fever (in modern Hamburg!) is rather clumsily brought into the plot. At the beginning, we are introduced to the upper-class family of the future husband's bride. Their entire environment seems obsessed with death, not least because, on a sunny Sunday morning, they keep their curtains closed while the father recites a poem by Nietzsche that expresses, he says, its author's "intimation of death" (*Todesahnung*). This is only the beginning. Before encountering the family on screen, we are informed that the father's favorite authors are Horace and Virgil and that the daughter's name is Octavia.

Later, Octavia's rival, outwardly a picture of health, has this to say about death: "Oh, old age is of no concern here. You are always close to him, to Death. And it is very well now and then to smile at him a little and to say: 'You are my friend. You will come when I cannot go on any longer.'" Since *death* is a masculine noun in German (*der Tod*), it is easy for the speaker to consider it as a close friend and constant companion. At film's end the young lady will receive one of the most kitschy and bizarre death scenes in cinema history. Swedish actress Kristina Söderbaum, who was also Mrs. Harlan, was given several death-as-sacrifice scenes in her husband's films, often ending up in a watery grave. Here, too, water imagery plays a major part. *The Great*

---

[20] Both quotations from Fest 2007: 41.

[21] Fest 2007: 61. The second historical reference is to the Battle of Vesuvius or Battle of Mons Lactarius in the middle of the sixth century A D. The English term *downfall* barely expresses the gloomy doom and finality implied in *Untergang*.

Sacrifice was released in December, 1944, about six months before the end of the Third Reich. In retrospect, the emotional atmosphere that pervades the film acquires a meaning that is as uncanny as it is revealing. Söderbaum, impeccably Nordic (and of course blond), was just the type to convey subliminal but morbid messages of fate and death to a war-weary public looking for escapism from actual death in on-screen romance and melo-drama. The Nazi cult of death, especially of dead heroes, goes back to the deaths of NSDAP members killed in the party's earliest phase, its *Kampfzeit* ("Time of Struggle"), in particular at the Munich Beer Hall Putsch of 1923. As Hitler said privately in 1941: "I dream of a state of affairs in which every man knows that he lives and dies for the preservation of the species."[22]

The affinity of this attitude to actual classical literature is astonishing. Early-twentieth-century historians of antiquity soon realized the similarities between Sparta and Nazi Germany. Two examples will suffice. In 1934, German ancient historian and classicist Victor Ehrenberg, who later immi-grated to England, gave a radio talk in German from Prague; it was entitled, in its eventual English-language version, "A Totalitarian State."[23] Ehrenberg concluded with this statement: "Sparta set up, not an example to be imitated, but a danger to be avoided." In 1936, French historian Henri Lichtenberger, professor of German literature at the Sorbonne and biographer of Goethe and Nietzsche, drew a surprisingly positive image of what he called *L'Allemagne nouvelle*, a book published the next year in English in an expanded edition as *The Third Reich*. It included a chapter titled "Spartanism."[24] The Spartanism Lichtenberger describes can be seen in the Nazis' military, paramilitary, and youth organizations.

One eyewitness account of the Nazi obsession with death is especially illuminating. American Gregor Ziemer, head of the American Colony School in Berlin and long-time resident in Germany, was granted unique access to the Nazi system of education and wrote about his observations and findings in 1941.[25] His conclusions are worth quoting at length, but I here limit myself to a few statements from Ziemer's prologue that are apposite for

---

[22] Chapoutot 2016: 306; source reference at 459 note 115. The species here mentioned is presumably of a particular and ideologically circumscribed kind.

[23] Ehrenberg 1946b. On this see Losemann 2012: 278 and 280.

[24] Lichtenberger 1936 and 1937. The chapter mentioned is in Lichtenberger 1937: 161–184. On Lichtenberger see Losemann 2012: 282–284.

[25] Ziemer 1941. The book, and a few related articles by Ziemer, led to the production of two rather different Hollywood propaganda films: the feature film *Hitler's Children* (1942), directed by Edward Dmytryk, and the animated Disney short *Education for Death* (1943). The latter is more effective and gripping. On the former see Slane 2001: 42–70 and 299–304 (notes; chapter titled "American Nationalist Melodrama: Tales of *Hitler's Children*"). On Sparta in Nazi education see Roche 2012a, 2012c, and 2013, all with further references. The term *Pimpf*, which

what *300* shows us about the *agôgê* that young Spartan boys underwent. Ziemer reports in some detail on the Nazi party's official education manual, issued under the auspices of Minister of Education Bernhard Rust. Ziemer states:

The Nazi schools are no place for weaklings ... Those who betray any weakness of body or have not the capacity for absolute obedience and submission must be expelled.

The keynote of the whole doctrine as expounded by Rust ... is bitterly simple. The aim of education is not culture; it is not spiritual freedom; it is not emancipation of the mind. Education is training for a life of Might.

Rust insists on a Spartan interpretation of life ... Discipline is to be rigorous.

Ziemer concludes his prologue with a vivid, indeed chilling, summary, borne out by the chapters that follow:

Hitler's schools do their jobs diabolically well ... They are educating boys and girls for death. They are preparing them as a sacrifice for Hitler, who hath said, "LET THE CHILDREN COME UNTO ME FOR THEY ARE MINE UNTO DEATH!"[26]

And, if Hitler had had his way, German children would have been his even before birth. A programmatic speech of his, delivered more than four years before he assumed power, makes this chillingly evident. This speech, presented as Hitler's "Appeal to German Strength" (*Appell an die deutsche Kraft*), was delivered on August 4, 1929, and closed the fourth NSDAP congress held in Nuremberg, the city in which the Nazis' racial laws were later passed. Its title translates as "The Sword Is Our Weight." Since it is little known today, I quote it at some length. Hitler is discussing Germany's population:

If Germany grew annually by a million children and was to do away with seven to eight hundred thousand of the weakest, then the final result might even be an increase in strength. The danger is that we ourselves cut off the natural process of selection and thus gradually deprive ourselves of the opportunity to obtain heads. It is not the first-born who are the talents or the strong people. The most evident racial state in history, Sparta, planned and then implemented such racial laws. [*Der klarste Rassenstaat der Geschichte, Sparta, hat diese Rassegesetze planmäßig durchgeführt.*] With us, the opposite happens according to plan. By means of our modern humane sentimentality [*Humanitätsduselei*] we strive to preserve the weak at the expense of the healthier ... In this way we gradually breed and raise the weak

---

appears in the title of Roche 2012c, was the official designation for the youngest age group of the Hitler Youth.

[26] Ziemer 1941: 15, 18, 21, and 23. Cf. Chapoutot 2016: 219–221 (section titled "Spartan Education: An *agôgê* for the New Man").

and kill off the strong … Among a people this leads to gruesome results. The most horrendous is the fact that we do not diminish its numbers but actually its value. We attempt to keep up the numbers with exaggerated care for the weak and sick. This destroys [*zersetzt*] all our thinking. This goes so far that the state spares a criminal without taking into consideration that it was unable to protect the victim. It feels pity only for what is mean, wretched, morally weak; that is what it guards and protects. The others it abandons indiscriminately in the name of humanitarianism.[27]

The German obsession with Spartans, however, predates the Nazis and is an integral part of German nationalism. The quasi-mythical (and mystical) Dorians, among whom the Spartans belonged, had come to be regarded as closer in spirit to Germans than any other Greek tribe. The tight military and social organization of Sparta provided a model for nineteenth- and twentieth-century Germany. In a classic account Beryl Rawson summarized the cultural climate prevalent in the German states of that time:

Sparta, *der Dorische Normalstaat*, and thus by implication the pattern state of all Greece, is above all representative of the Greek realization, claims [Karl Otfried] Müller, that the state is not merely an institution for the defence of persons and property, as the modern heresy holds, but a single moral agent created by its components' possession of the same opinions, principles, and aims; something possible only where natural affinity binds a *Volk* [people], or smaller *Stamm* [tribe], together.[28]

And:

Increased sympathy with Sparta was to come … chiefly from … those who combined a belief that Greeks and Germans were racially closely connected with a mystical idea of the virtue of the *Volk*, and the need for the individual to return from

[27] Hitler 1939: 114–115. The book lists no place or publisher but was probably printed at Nuremberg in 1939. A *bon mot*, if that is the right term, by Hitler from 1925 is reproduced below a photographic portrait of him in the front of the book: "Heaven gives the lazy no bread and the coward no freedom!" (*Der Himmel gibt dem Faulen kein Brot und dem Feigen keine Freiheit!*). The title of Hitler's speech may allude to a famous episode in early Roman history (*vae victis!*).

[28] Rawson 1969: 323. Rawson here refers to Müller 1824, a highly influential work. It appeared again posthumously in a revised and augmented edition of 1844. Cf. Losemann 1998 and, more briefly, Losemann 2012: 254–255 and passim. Von Vacano 1940 is just one Nazi-era publication that illustrates the ideological affinities between Spartans and Aryans and does so in full Nazi terminology. This short book was an assigned textbook (*Arbeitsheft*), the first in fact, for students attending the elite *Adolf-Hitler-Schulen*. An expanded edition, dated 1942 but not available until 1943, contained the passages about Thermopylae from Göring's Stalingrad speech under the headline "Stalingrad – Thermopylä." On this see Losemann 2012: 292–294 and the detailed analysis of the book and the schools in Roche 2012c. Roche: 322 lists the contents of the second edition of Vacano's book, rightly emphasizing (330) the prominence given to Schiller's version of Simonides.

his artificial, urban, existence to his roots, living in mysterious and reverent community with his landscape and his ancestors .... a remarkable identification of Sparta and
Germany might result ... It was natural that a family of peoples who could ... be made
entirely, or largely, responsible for the triumphs of classical antiquity as well as modern
western civilization ... should appear the salt of the earth.[29]

The overall result was predictable: "Sparta ... really seemed to fit the Aryan
theory, or some versions of it."[30]

In classical literature, a fragment by the seventh-century-BC Spartan
poet Tyrtaeus comes close to expressing an ideology that would have
resonated with die-hard Nazis:

> For it is fine to die in the front line,
> a brave man fighting for his fatherland ...
> So let us fight with spirit for our land,
> die for our sons, and spare our lives no more.
> You young men, keep together, hold the line,
> do not start panic or disgraceful rout.
> Keep grand and valiant spirits in your hearts,
> be not in love with life – the fight's with men!
>   ... But for the young man, still
> in glorious prime, [death in battle] is all beautiful:
> alive, he draws men's eyes and women's hearts;
> felled in the front line, he is lovely yet.
> Let every man then, feet set firm apart,
> bite on his lip and stand against the foe.[31]

Or compare, in the fifth century, Simonides' poem on Leonidas:

> When men die [for their country,]
> fame is their fortune, fair their fate,
> their tomb an altar; in the place of wailing
> there is remembrance, and their dirge is praise.
> This winding-sheet is such
> as neither mould nor Time that conquers all
> can fade; this sepulchre
> of fine men has adopted as its sacristan
> Greece's good name. Witness Leonidas,
> the king of Sparta: he has left
> a monument of valour, and perennial fame.[32]

[29] Rawson 1969: 332–333.   [30] Rawson 1969: 336. See further Rawson, 336–342.
[31] Tyrtaeus, Fragment 10.1–2, 13–18, and 27–32 (West); quoted from West 1993: 24. There is
evidence that three centuries later Tyrtaeus' poems were recited to Spartan armies (West: xii).
[32] Simonides, Fragment *P.M.G.* 531 (Page); quoted from West 1993: 163.

It is doubtful that most Nazis were familiar with Simonides' poetry except for his epitaph on the three hundred Spartans or with Tyrtaeus. But the warrior's honor demands that he remain faithful unto death, as the SS practically tells us if we combine their death's head insignia with their motto: "My Honor's Name Is Loyalty" (*Meine Ehre heißt Treue*).

The heroic sentiments which the Greek poets expressed would have sounded familiar in Nazi Germany. As early as 1933, Fritz Schachermeyr, ancient historian and professor at Jena University, published an article entitled "The Nordic Leader Personality in Antiquity." Schachermeyr maintained: "The wars against the Persians were a struggle for Greek freedom from the threat of enslavement of both their state [i.e. Athens] and their spirit by the East." Nazi textbooks declared that "the history of the Indo-Germanic peoples in their southern lebensraum [*sic*] was that of the conflict with foreign influences over their patrimony."[33] The people who represent such influences are the very opposite of handsome Aryans. Only the latter are presumably capable of exemplifying what Tyrtaeus had said: "felled in the front line, he is lovely yet." Such beauty, the kind Breker celebrated, is best achieved in a mystic union with, first, blood and soil (*Blut und Boden*) and, subsequently, death.

One of the most important eyewitnesses from Nazi Germany is Victor Klemperer, a Jewish professor of Romance languages and specialist in French literature, whom the Nazis removed from office in 1935. Klemperer's vivid and detailed diary had to be written in secret and kept hidden from the authorities. Almost miraculously, it survived and was published posthumously. What Klemperer reports throughout about the ruling ideology is pertinent for our topic, because the similarities of certain pronouncements on the part of the Nazi hierarchy to what we see on screen in *300* are astonishingly close. Here are a few telling examples. First, a brief restatement of the familiar Nazi obsession with ancient Greece. Klemperer reports about Hitler's speech of December 11, 1941, in which he announced Germany's declaration of war against the US: "In this speech Hitler develops the concept of *Europe*. For him, the beginning and *sole* basis is Greece, permeated by Nordic tribes. Jerusalem eliminated, Hellas Germanized!"[34] The following year, Klemperer comments on one of the regular *Wochensprüche der Nationalsozialistischen Deutschen Arbeiterpartei*, the NSDAP's weekly slogans published in newspapers, on posters, and elsewhere:

---

[33] Chapoutot 2016: 297; source references at 457 notes 55 and 54. *Lebensraum* ("living space") is another key Nazi term.

[34] Klemperer 1999a: 190 (entry for December 12, 1941); emphasis in original.

At the beginning of the week, the newspapers regularly publish a "Weekly Motto of the NSDAP" under a special headline. A quotation, usually a saying by Hitler, is put at the beginning and then briefly commented and sermonized upon. Today the headline is "Pitiless and tough." Hitler's saying is: "Just as we were pitiless and tough in our struggle for power, we will be equally pitiless and tough in the struggle for the preservation of our people." In the sermon, which makes heavy weather of the word "tough," it says: Because our outer and inner enemies were so "implacable and tough" towards us, "we had to, and have to, be even tougher, always, today, and in the future. Each and every stirring of pity, even the smallest, would only be interpreted as weakness on our part . . ."[35]

We may compare a particular weekly motto by Joseph Goebbels. Klemperer records it without further comment since it speaks for itself: "Only an iron generation will be able to prevail in the tempests of our time. It must possess guts of iron and a heart of steel."[36]

This, in turn, fits in with an article by Goebbels on the heroic war dead, titled "Die Vollendeten" and published in the Nazi journal *Das Reich* on December 27, 1942, when it was already evident that the catastrophe of Stalingrad was imminent. Klemperer partly quotes and partly summarizes this article.[37] Its title is nearly untranslatable; a paraphrase that attempts to include its various connotations might be "Those Who Accomplished a Perfect End." Klemperer reports that Goebbels prominently referred to antiquity, even adducing Horace's famous saying "It is sweet and fitting to die for your country," but with a twist: "It is not sweet but still honorable to die for one's country" (*Es ist nicht süß, aber doch ehrenvoll, für das Vaterland zu sterben*).[38] Goebbels spoke of the absolute value of the home country, which demands everyone to do his duty but does not grant any right to individuals when they are facing death to protect and preserve the nation. The living owe their heroes an almost religious duty, which, when paid, should increase the heroism of the fallen into a national myth.

3   The Body: Beauty, Heroism, Kitsch

A related perspective appeared on the Nazi screen in Leni Riefenstahl's *Olympia* (1938), her two-part epic film about the Olympic Summer Games

[35] Klemperer 1999b: 187 (in entry for July 27, 1942).
[36] Klemperer 1999d: 84–85; quotation at 85 (in entry for July 19, 1944).
[37] Klemperer 1999c: 9–11 (in entry for January 9, 1943).
[38] Horace, *Odes* 3.2.13: *dulce et decorum est pro patria mori*. On cinematic contexts of this line see Winkler 2009a: 154–209.

of 1936 in Berlin. Riefenstahl's artistic creed is instructive, even if it is not expressed with impeccable logic:

I can simply say that I feel spontaneously attracted by everything that is beautiful. Yes: beauty, harmony ... Whatever is purely realistic, slice-of-life, what is average, quotidian, doesn't interest me. Only the unusual, the specific, excites me. I am fascinated by what is beautiful, strong, healthy, but what is living. I seek harmony. When harmony is produced, I am happy.[39]

What she said about *Olympia*, her paean to the beautiful body, is equally revealing. According to her, the film illustrates "the complete domination of the body and the will."[40] The phrase may remind us of the title of her most infamous work, *Triumph of the Will* (1935), the propagandistic record of the Nazi party's rally of the year before. This film's title was chosen by Hitler himself. The prologue to *Olympia* was partly filmed at the ancient location in Greece; it also presented famous Greek statues. Myron's *Discus Thrower* comes to life, as it were, in the body of a modern athlete by means of a dissolve. A Doric column is prominently on view as well. *Olympia* has even been characterized as a "Dorian film."[41]

The beauty of the body, both male and female, the beauty of heroic death, and the fascination with both are among the chief ingredients of the power that Fascism and Nazism exerted, and not only over contemporaries. In her essay "Fascinating Fascism" Susan Sontag argued that fascist thinking and feeling continued to thrive in post-war Europe and the US.[42] The cult of the body, which is fundamental to fascist aesthetics, is Sontag's main focus. In Nazi art, especially sculpture, this cult found its most monstrous manifestation in a pompous monumentality, which is a clear indication of its inherent quality as kitsch. On this aspect Saul Friedlaender has observed: "Kitsch emotion represents a certain kind of simplified, degraded, insipid, but all the more insinuating romanticism." There exists "an aesthetic frisson, created by the opposition between the harmony of kitsch ... and the constant evocation of themes of death and destruction."[43]

---

[39] Quoted from Sarris 1967: 462. The interview with Riefenstahl (Sarris: 453–473) was originally published in French in 1965; Sarris: 453 (note) provides references.
[40] Quoted from Sarris 1967: 463.
[41] So Hinz 2003, in connection with German poet Gottfried Benn's views on Dorians and Nazism. Dowling 2012 is a useful introduction to the film. Dowling: 66–70 describes the prologue.
[42] Sontag 1980b. The article was originally written in 1974; an earlier version was published in 1975.
[43] Friedlaender 1984: 39 and 18. The classic essay by Greenberg 1939 (= Greenberg 1961: 3–21) defines kitsch as "mechanical" and formulaic; it is "vicarious experience and faked sensations." He observes: "Where there is an avant-garde, generally we also find a rear-guard." He also notes that "enormous profits" are to be had from kitsch. The quotations are from Greenberg 1961: 10,

Figure 7.2 The head of Arno Breker's *Bereitschaft* in the short film *Arno Breker*.

I will turn to death and destruction in due course. But first, the kitschy representation of the male and female body in Nazi art. One of Breker's most famous works, titled *Bereitschaft* ("Readiness" or "Preparedness," 1939), was a gigantic bronze statue of a heroic nude male, holding a sheathed sword in his left hand and drawing the blade with his right. The face elicited a pithy voice-over comment in *Arno Breker*, a thirteen-minute film about the sculptor from 1944 (Figure 7.2). It was directed by Hans Cürlis and Arnold Fanck, Riefenstahl's mentor. Cürlis and Riefenstahl were its producers. Cürlis also wrote the script and provided the voice-over.[44] I provide the original text because no translation can do justice to the stylistic pathos that is typical of Nazi rhetoric:

Hier kommt das zum Durchbruch, was das ganze Volk erschüttert, innerlich umbricht und neu schafft. Dieser Kopf erzählt nicht die Geschichte eines Einzelmenschen. Er spricht: "Ich bin die geballte Manneskraft. Ich bin der

---

9, and 11. Macdonald 1953 is another classic contribution to the debate. Today both essays may strike us as too conservative in part. Gurstein 2003 puts Greenberg's, Macdonald's, and others' perspectives in context and examines the subject down to her own time. Gurstein: 139–140 states that Greenberg wrote his essay "because of his fears for the avant-garde, whose very survival, he warned, was threatened by the ubiquity and rapaciousness of kitsch."

[44] The head and the text quoted reappear in chapter 6, titled "Der Körper" ("The Body"), of Marcel Schwierin's documentary film *Ewige Schönheit: Film und Todessehnsucht im Dritten Reich* (2003), a compilation of original footage of Nazi feature films, documentaries, newsreels, etc. The modern voice-over commentary wrongly identifies the head as that of Dionysus, here regarded as god of ecstasy – implied is the ecstasy of slaughter and death. Breker had sculpted a large Dionysus in 1936, but its head looks nothing like this.

Grimm gegen das Feige. Ich hasse den Feind meines Volkes. Du müßtest sein wie ich."

Here something achieves its breakthrough that deeply stirs the entire people, profoundly changes its inner being, and creates it anew. This head does not tell the story of an individual. It proclaims: "I am male power tightly wound. I am the wrath against everything cowardly. I hate the enemy of my people. You ought to be like me."

This is a clear example of "body Fascism."[45] The heroism implied in the words quoted is on view, although without anything wrathful, in the prologue to *Olympia*. Images of male athletes engaged in various disciplines are followed by those of female athletes. The humans in the prologue are seen against symbolic natural backgrounds: skies with dramatic clouds, water, and fields of grain. The women are completely nude, although nothing too private appears on screen; the men, by necessity, wear a tiny *cache-sexe*. (Ancient athletes did not.) All bodies in the prologue, male and female, are perfect.[46] A prominent feature of the female athletes are their erect nipples, which are so immediately noticeable that one may wonder whether they are not intended to attract the gaze of male viewers. We may compare the Oracle in *300*: a young woman writhing so ecstatically (and athletically) under flimsy billowing cloth that the latter serves more to accentuate than to hide the nudity underneath. This Oracle's breasts are like those of Riefenstahl's women. The Oracle's unrealistic motions make for a kind of eroticized super-kitsch, not least because these images are entirely superfluous for the plot. The lady utters her prophecy and, a few seconds later, is lying on the ground and being ogled and almost pawed by the grotesque aged males who in *300* pass for Spartan ephors. Spectators of *300*, at least male teenagers, ogle the Oracle just as these ephors do.

Soon we also get to watch Leonidas and his wife Gorgo engage in vigorous lovemaking, in which Gorgo is equally writhing. Like the Oracle's, her chest is mamillarily prominent. As far as the film's characterization of Leonidas as hero is concerned, the entire plot of *300*, if put in colloquial terms, amounts to this: First he gets laid; then he gets to kill and be killed. Quite an attractive fate for any committed Nazi and a *reductio ad absurdum* of the Freudian Eros and Thanatos drives. Too bad, however, that the film makes Leonidas lose that very cool for which he and the Spartans were famous. When, early on, an outraged Leonidas screams "This is

---

[45] Squire 2011: 16–21, with brief discussions of Nazi sculpture and *Olympia*.

[46] See on this Peucker 2004; Gordon 2002, especially 170 on nudity and 192–200 on the prologue to *Olympia*. See further Davidson 2006, especially 113 and 131 (on *Schönheitstanz* ["dance of beauty"] and *Olympia*).

Sparta!" prior to kicking a Persian ambassador down a well, *300* loses much of its historical credibility. That Leonidas' outburst became the most often quoted line from *300* is revealing. The film's chief appeal is to testosterone-driven teenagers.

The beautiful Spartan bodies of *300* contrast with the nondescript bodies of the Persians. Several of these are the merest grotesques: monstrous, deformed, in one exaggerated case even theriomorphic (part human, part animal). They are either a soulless horde or deviant and decadent individuals. The Greek traitor Ephialtes, who is a Spartan in *300* but who was not one in history, is another example of a hideously deformed body. Unsuitable to join the three hundred at Thermopylae, he fits right in with the Persians:

the once-ostracized Ephialtes is delighted by the lavish freak show that awaits him [in Xerxes' tent]. It's an orgy of the bizarre .... the tent provides Snyder an opportunity to showcase the opulent debauchery of Xerxes' court ... while under-scoring the potency of dark, basic desires.[47]

Note the purple-prose rhetoric that concludes this summary. A similar opposition between Aryan beauty and physical degeneracy was character-istic for Nazi propaganda against Jews. *The Eternal Jew* (*Der ewige Jude*, 1940) remains the most notorious and vicious anti-Semitic propaganda film ever made; it was marketed, of course, as a documentary. At one point, footage of Jews in Polish ghettoes is followed by images of rats scurrying about among sacks of grains in storage basements. In voice-over the narrator explains the analogy to his viewers:

They are perfidious, cowardly, and cruel and mostly appear in large hordes. Among the animals they represent the element of insidious underground destruc-tiveness, no different from Jews among humans.

These words closely fit the portrayal of the Persians in *300*, although Persian destructiveness is chiefly in the open since they are posing a gigantic military threat. But their insidiousness is evident from the character of the high-ranking treacherous Spartan who is in their pay and is secretly trying to undermine Sparta from within – just like a rat or, to Nazis, a Jew. Viewers of *The Eternal Jew* were also shown famous Greek statues. They include Athena, athletes, and a horseman from the Parthenon frieze. The narrator explains why:

The concept of beauty as Nordic Man understands it is incomprehensible to the Jew in his entire natural disposition and will eternally remain incomprehensible to him.

[47] Quoted from Allie and Moody 2007: 102. The author of the book's main text is Tara DiLullo.

As were Jews to Nazis, so the Persians in *300* are subhumans (*Untermenschen*) without a shred of culture or civilization. They are vicious animals in human shape. On storyboard images for the film some of the Persians are identified simply as "Primitives."[48]

4   *300*: An American *Bergfilm*?

After his bedchamber heroics Leonidas is understandably pensive. (This is probably *not* meant as an indirect homage to Aristotle.) Now Leonidas gets what may be the most kitschy individual shot in the entire film. In heroic nudity and with his back turned to the viewers, he contemplates the mountains outside.[49] These are being illuminated by an impossibly large and perfect moon (Figure 7.3). The dramatic and romantic background may remind us of German Romantic paintings, especially those by Caspar David Friedrich. Friedrich strongly influenced Nazi images of nature, especially of majestic mountains and skies that sometimes dwarf the human figures in his paintings.[50] And Friedrich is famous for his use of what art historians term the *Rückenbild*: a figure seen from the back for greater emotional effect. The following comment by Eric Rentschler on Riefenstahl's film *The Blue Light* (1932) applies almost entirely to the post-coital Leonidas of *300*:

As in Friedrich, we partake of figures that stand with their backs to the viewer and stare into the distance, small dots against vast expanses, characters who embody yearning, persons wishing to merge with the grandeur before them.[51]

The scene in which Leonidas says his farewell to his wife and son and, later, the one in which Gorgo receives the news of his heroic death are set in a wheat field that ancient Spartans but not modern Germans may have had a hard time recognizing. Americans, too, are familiar with such images of their own heartland with its amber waves of grain. In Steven Spielberg's World War II epic *Saving Private Ryan* (1997), for instance, Mrs. Ryan is surrounded by just such a setting when she is being informed about the

---

[48] Two such examples may be found in Allie and Moody 2007: 84.   [49] Cf. Turner 2009.

[50] Useful orientation in word and image may be found in Hofmann 2000; Koerner 2009; Grave 2012.

[51] Rentschler 2008: 173 note 42. This is a revised and updated version of a chapter on *The Blue Light* in Rentschler 1996: 27–51.

Figure 7.3 Leonidas and the nocturnal landscape in Zack Snyder's *300*.

deaths of her sons. In this context it is important for us to be aware of a feature of Nazi cinema often overlooked:

It is common to reduce all Nazi films to hate pamphlets, party hagiography, or mindless escapism, films with too much substance or none at all, either execrable or frivolous. In the process, the reliance of the era's cinema on classical Hollywood conventions goes unnoticed, as does the recourse of so many productions and so much of Nazi film culture to American techniques and popular genres … In its cynical belief that it offered people what they wanted, Nazi mass culture emulated and replicated American patterns of recognition. It produced an entertainment industry with secondhand popular fare.[52]

In *300*, ominous rocky mountains and swirling dark clouds are the main weather pattern at Thermopylae. This is in spite of the fact that the actual battle took place in August, even though a major storm had just destroyed part of the Persian fleet. The landscape in *300* is strongly reminiscent of the mystical atmosphere in the *Bergfilme* ("mountain films"), a particular genre of German cinema in the late 1920s and early 1930s, in which Riefenstahl absolved her cinematic apprenticeship. She had earlier studied painting and drawing. Her own film *The Blue Light* is a good example:

The Blue Light abounds with images reminiscent of [Caspar David] Friedrich, sweeping unpeopled mountainscapes in general, or compositions that explicitly defer to his work … *The Blue Light* infuses nature with an arousing power; like Friedrich, Riefenstahl transforms exterior landscapes into emotional spaces.

---

[52] Quoted from Rentschler 1996: 23 and 22.

The physical world becomes irreal and fantastic, molded by an imagination whose highest goal is to represent invisible and ineffable forces ... The film's romantic images hallow nature's mystery and impart to the elemental a stirring resonance ... Romantic images ... accentuate nature's irrational potential.[53]

Apparently mountains are good for the Fascist (and fascist) soul. *The Blue Light, Olympia*, and other films by Riefenstahl illustrate the "pan-eroticism and nature worship" that is characteristic of her work as a whole.[54]

Intellectual and political developments that began with Romanticism and continued toward patriotism and nationalism and, beyond this, toward right-wing ideologies, especially Fascism and Nazism, have been well documented. The work of Isaiah Berlin is particularly pertinent here. In an essay called "Nationalism" Berlin observed that "the romantic movement ... in Germany ... celebrated the collective will, untrammeled by rules which men could discover by rational methods, the spiritual life of the people in whose activity – or impersonal will – creative individuals could participate."[55] Earlier in the same essay Berlin had defined nationalism, especially of the kind prevalent in Italy and Germany, as "the elevation of the interests of the unity and self-determination of the nation to the status of the supreme value before which all other considerations must, if need be, yield at all times."[56] With minimal adjustments, we can apply these statements wholesale to the style and story of *300*. Its images of misty landscapes with their subdued and eerie atmosphere are a visual manifestation of the nebulous ideology that underlies its story.

5   The Fascist Nebula

The term "Ur-Fascism," coined by Umberto Eco, is crucial for my argument about *300*. The concept it expresses is of particular importance in our age, when image-saturated viewers watch something like *300* but do not recognize its affinities with fascist aesthetics. They are likely to protest that they are against Fascism, Nazism, and fascism and to maintain that *300* is only a cartoon movie or just an action flick, whose chief appeal is in its translation of Frank Miller's graphics to the screen. Such viewers would strongly disagree with anyone who might voice the suspicion that Miller or

---

[53] Quoted from Rentschler 2008: 156–157.
[54] Quoted from Elsaesser 1993a: 16. This article, minus most of its illustrations, is reprinted as Elsaesser 1993b, where the quotation is at 189. On Riefenstahl before Hitler cf. also Seeßlen 1994: 75–79.
[55] Berlin 2013b: 440.   [56] Berlin 2013b: 427; a longer definition appears at 431–436.

Snyder come close to expressing a fascist mentality. Doubtless Miller and Snyder would themselves deny any such affinity.[57] But if no one involved in making *300* is in actual fact a fascist, how then can I maintain that *300* expresses a fascist perspective? Before we turn to an answer to this question, it is worth remembering that the terms *fascism* and *fascist* are often used rather loosely:

do various contemporary (non-Nazi) phenomena that live off the same tension between reality and the imaginary and the real then qualify as fascist? [This question] is particularly disconcerting in its implicit suggestion that fascism, if understood in a structural sense, may be alive and well in American political discourse, which is increasingly determined by the dissemination of aestheticized images, and in many other phenomena in contemporary societies currently discussed as features of postmodern societies. Since 1945 the terms *Nazi* and *fascist* have been used so restrictively as to shed little light on nazism's [sic] success in evoking a collective identity in its constituents, or so loosely as to signify a historically useless catchword for whatever its user opposes.[58]

Eric Rentschler has made the following valuable points about Nazi cinema and its influence:

Nazi films circulated within a vast complex of orchestrated and high-tech efforts to control thought and meaning. The Third Reich constituted the first full-blown media dictatorship, a political order that sought to occupy and administer all sectors of perceptual possibility, to dominate the human subject's every waking and sleeping moment ... The unprecedented historical example of the Nazi media dictatorship lingers as a very disturbing prospect, especially now, as sophisticated and pervasive technologies for the transmission and manipulation of audiovisual materials increasingly define who we are and how we exist. We refer to Hitler and Goebbels as madmen and demons, consigning them to the shadows. No matter how studiously we cloak these figures in darkness, however, they are clearly more than just ghouls or phantoms. Indeed, one might speak of Nazi Germany's irrepressible imagemakers as postmodernity's secret sharers, as grasping entrepreneurs who profited from the industrialized means of enchantment, as master showmen who staged extravagant spectacles as the ultimate political manifestations.[59]

With this in mind, let us now examine Eco's conception of Ur-Fascism. Eco grew up in Mussolini's Italy and made a convincing case for the

[57] Counter-arguments: Moore 2007; Stevens 2007; Moody 2011.
[58] Schulte-Sasse 1991, here quoted from its reprint in Murray and Wickham 1992: 140–166, at 141.
[59] Quoted from Rentschler 1996: 217 and 223. Cf. further Seeßlen 1996. Both Seeßlen 1994 and 1996 deal with the persistence of Nazi cinema in post-1945 Germany.

persistence of Fascism. He devised an intriguing diagram representing "a series of political groups":

1	2	3	4
abc	bcd	cde	def

He explains this as follows:

Group 1 is characterized by the aspects *abc*, group 2 by *bcd*, and so on. Group 2 is similar to 1 insofar as they have two aspects in common. Group 3 is similar to 2 and 4 is similar to 3 for the same reason. Note that 3 is also similar to 1 (they share the aspect *c*). The most curious case is that of 4, obviously similar to 3 and 2 but without any characteristic in common with 1. Nevertheless, because of the uninterrupted series of decreasing similarities between 1 and 4, there remains, by virtue of a sort of illusory transitiveness, a sense of kinship between 4 and 1.[60]

Eco's diagram shows why certain works of art or popular culture can be non-fascist on a conscious level and still exhibit fascist characteristics. As Eco says:

behind a regime and its ideology there is always a way of thinking and feeling, a series of cultural habits, a nebula of obscure instincts and unfathomable drives .... on an emotional level it [Fascism] was firmly anchored to certain archetypes.[61]

Equally, and in analogy to Eco's diagram, ideologies or creative works that came after the Fascist era adhered to earlier archetypes. Eco even speaks of "eternal Fascism," considering the expression synonymous with "Ur-Fascism." The Italian title of Eco's essay was "Totalitarismo *fuzzy* e Ur-Fascismo" – clearly the English adjective is *le mot juste*. The very fuzziness of Fascism points to the intellectual and philosophical shallowness of this ideology but also to its ramifications, which can be difficult to see or grasp.

For this reason it is pointless to advance an argument based on intention: that someone who is not a fascist and does not consciously adhere to this ideology does not or cannot produce fascist-type works. Rather, the decisive question to ask is this: Does a creative artist's work exhibit fascist features, whether intentionally and consciously or not, or does it not? From this point of view it can reasonably be argued that *300* indeed represents an instance of Ur-Fascism. In *300*, Fascist archetypes are quite obvious.

Eco provides a list of fourteen typical Fascist characteristics.[62] They pertain to history and political ideology, but not all are applicable to

[60] Eco 2001b: 76 and 76–77; diagram at 77.   [61] Eco 2001b: 70 and 76.
[62] Eco 2001b: 78–86. This is the heart of Eco's essay.

works of art. Still, as Eco maintains, "all you need is one of them to be present, and a fascist nebula will begin to coagulate."[63] *Nota bene:* just one! I will therefore discuss just one of the characteristics that Eco adduces in regard to *300*, although several others could be applied to the film as well.

6   CGI Modernity and Fascist Traditionalism in *300*

On the cult of tradition, and especially Fascist traditionalism, Eco observes: "although Nazism was proud of its industrial successes, its praise of modernity was only the superficial aspect of an ideology based on 'blood and soil' (*Blut and Boden*)."[64] Eco has earlier referred to Italian Futurism, a form of art that developed from 1909 to 1916. It had been founded by Filippo Tommaso Marinetti (1876–1944). Futurism was artistically advanced and forward-looking but politically deeply nationalistic. For the latter reason many of the Futurists became Fascists in the 1920s. In 1918 Marinetti had founded the *Partito Politico Futurista*, the Futurist Political Party. It was absorbed into Mussolini's *Fasci di Combattimento* the following year, and Marinetti became one of the earliest members of the *Partito Nazionale Fascista*, the National Fascist Party. Although he broke with the party in 1920, Marinetti supported Fascism until his death. The early Futurists, writes Eco, "backed Italy's entry into the First World War" and "celebrated speed, violence, and risk," aspects that "seemed close to the Fascist cult of youth."[65] Umberto Boccioni's collage *The Cavalry Charge* or *Lancers' Charge* (*Carica di lancieri*, 1915) illustrates this circumstance particularly well. It shows a traditional form of martial heroism that is re-imagined in hyper-modernist style.[66]

Some of Eco's observations about Futurism enable us to find certain parallels in *300*. The "blood and soil" traditionalism and nationalism is an integral part of its plot, and so is the youth cult, as I show below. Industrial success and modernity, the celebration of speed, violence, and risk that Eco points to – these are most clearly and effectively seen in the visual style of *300* with its extensive, indeed nearly ubiquitous, use of computer-generated images (CGI), especially in combat scenes. The emotional impact of such combat is heightened when state-of-the-art computer graphics are combined with a few old-fashioned film tricks: slow motion,

---

[63] Eco 2001b: 78.   [64] Eco 2001b: 79.

[65] Eco 2001b: 74. The English translation has the spelling *futurism*, not *Futurism*. On the wider context, including Futurism, see especially Roger Griffin 2007. Cf. further Settembrini 2003.

[66] A color image with explanatory text may be found, e.g., in Coen 1988: 190–191 (ill. 81).

sped-up motion, zooms. A signature moment, little more than a minute in
duration, occurs early in the fighting at Thermopylae. Leonidas and the
Spartans have just broken through the Persian front line and begin slaugh-
tering their enemy; emphasis is on individual combat, especially by
Leonidas, before the Spartans drive a number of Persians over a cliff.[67]
This brief scene within the larger combat sequence combines all aspects of
cinematic technology just mentioned to telling and weirdly fascinating
effect, enhanced by the kind of exotic vocals on the soundtrack that have
become nearly obligatory in films with ancient settings. But at the same
time the abrupt changes from accelerated motion by Leonidas and others
about to strike to extremely slow motion just before they plunge their
weapons deep into their enemy's bodies – or the other way around: from
slow to fast motion – will look familiar to sports fans who watch instant
replays of critical moments. The Battle of Thermopylae has been turned
into a mass-media sports event.

In this and in comparable scenes we can observe the rejection of modernity – not in a technological sense, given the advanced computer graphics,
but in the sense that what we get to watch is old and old-fashioned. Indeed, it
is outdated and questionable, for it is as cheap a glorification of martial
heroism as may be found anywhere. It is cheap because the Spartans of *300*
are soulless automatons of killing, just as the Persians are soulless automatons to be killed. For this very reason the extreme care and ingenuity of the
actual moments of killing do not deliver what they were intended to deliver:
viewers' emotional involvement. The following background information is
instructive since it amounts to a kind of creed, from a technical point of view,
concerning the loving portrayals of death in *300*. An analogy to Nazi or
Fascist obsession with death is not far-fetched:

Scenes that feature prominent, close-up shots of death … dictated their own
specific visual effects rules. Called "Hero Kills" by Production, they required
a slightly different approach in terms of focus and detail. To address this, the
visual effects team came up with the following approach: "… Hero Kills are where
the main focus of the shot is the act of violence, be it a spear, a sword strike, or
a punch. These are the shots where we also linger on the aftermath of the act, rather
than the simple moment of impact. Often some sort of time effect is applied to
these shots as well, e.g., ramping into slow-mo. In these situations, there needs to
be thought and design put into the depiction of the blood."[68]

---

[67] This occurs at 48:03–49:16 (end of chapter 14 on the Limited Collector's Edition of the film on
DVD, US release).
[68] Quoted from Allie and Moody 2007: 78.

Compare with this Marinetti's own words, both theoretical (about Futurism) and practical (as a remembrance of an incident in the Italian-Turkish war on October 26, 1911):

WE ARE ABOLISHING THE AGE-OLD VALUES (romantic, sentimental, and Christian) OF NARRATIVE, by virtue of which the importance of a wound, sustained in battle, was greatly exaggerated in comparison with the weapons of destruction, strategic positions, and atmospheric conditions . . . Indeed, I observed . . . how the bright, insistent volley of a cannon, made red-hot by the sun and by an increased rate of firing, makes the spectacle of mangled, dying human flesh almost negligible.[69]

Except for the momentary spurts of CGI blood, the Hero Kills in *300* equally emphasize the Spartans' weapons in comparison with the Persians' wounds. Marinetti's point about narrative is apropos as well, for the plot of this nearly two-hour film is linear and predictable.

One scene among all the depictions of slaughter in *300* is meant to stand out. A Spartan warrior's son is decapitated and his torso collapses in slow motion. But even this horrific moment is apt to leave viewers emotionally cold. Later, the father confesses that the one thing he regrets never having told his son is that he loved him. But this rings hollow because it flies in the face of everything we have already been told, in word and image, about the Spartans' toughness in battle. Here is how the narrator explained it to us when he commented on Leonidas taking his last farewell from Gorgo: "'Goodbye, my love.' He doesn't say it. There's no room for softness – not in Sparta. No room for weakness. Only the hard and strong may call themselves Spartan. Only the hard. Only the strong." This is another example of pseudo-Spartan garrulity.

Spartan fathers' toughness toward their children had been crammed down our throats in the film's travesty of the historical Spartan boys' *agôgê*.[70] Spartan education as shown in *300* borders on child abuse. If a seven-year old cannot, for example, survive a wolf's attack, too bad – or so *300* would have us believe. Spartan *agôgê* has long been regarded as an analogy to Nazi eugenics and euthanasia, the destruction of "life unworthy to live" (*lebensunwertes Leben*): "Her laws concerning marriage and children seemed to reveal a striking interest in eugenics – rashly supposed to amount to a conscious desire for racial purity . . . . eugenic theory condemned pity and aid for the

---

[69] Marinetti 2006: 136–137. The words capitalized appear in boldface as well.

[70] The chief ancient source is Xenophon, *The Spartan Constitution* 2.1–4.7. It is easily accessible in Lipka 2002. Lipka: 115 (on 2.1) observes that "Spartan education was not genuinely different from other educational systems" in Greece although it was still tough enough. Kennell 1995 and Ducat 2006 present detailed analyses from different perspectives.

weak as disastrous folly."[71] The Spartans of *300* are pitiless killers themselves, so what does the father expect from the enemy? His grief is wholly unconvincing. His words are neither in the spirit of Spartan imperturbability, amply attested in the historical record, nor do they conform to the nature of the Spartans with whom we are dealing in *300*.

By contrast, we are called upon to cheer the graphic presentation of slaughter with which we are bombarded, especially in the combination of on-screen mayhem with cranked-up sound effects, all reinforced by accelerated or slowed-down motion, zooms, and other tricks of the trade. The reaction that the filmmakers wish to evoke in us with such a barrage, however, is neither based on careful plot construction, of which there is very little, nor on the delineation of characters to whom we can relate or for whom we can root. Instead, Snyder relies exclusively on technical wizardry, which is considerable. The predictable reaction of male teenagers, the film's chief target audience, might be summarized as follows: *Wow! How, like, awesome is that?* This is a central part of the "cult of youth," to quote Eco, and it is the sort of thing that *300* depends upon and caters to. Celebration of speed and violence, of risk and killing as the ultimate adrenaline rush and vicarious death trip, all done so cleverly that perhaps even staid souls get sucked into its vortex of violence – how much more Ur-Fascist can it get? And it can fully be so even if no one involved in making *300* ever thought of Nazis and the Nazi death cult, even if Nazi-style *Heldentod*, the heroic death for the *Vaterland*, is the very plot impulse that seems to justify the film's eroticized presentation of the bloody deaths of beautiful youths and the equally gory if apparently deserved destruction of *Untermenschen*. The overall effect is a strong visceral arousal within the unresisting, an arousal that neutralizes any intellectual distance from or reservation about this repellent orgy of kitsch and death. We may be reminded of Nazi exploitation cinema, which combines, often grotesquely, sex, sadism, violence, and huge doses of kitsch.[72]

300 is a prime example of how the repulsive becomes attractive; that is to say, of how *fascination* works. We may know rationally that we dislike or disapprove of something, but we cannot take our eyes off it. Riefenstahl's

---

[71] Rawson 1969: 336; cf. 336–342. See further Vernant 1991b.

[72] Here are examples from international, especially Italian, cinema, which I mention without any further description; the curious are on their own: *Salon Kitty; Ilsa, She-Wolf of the SS; Elsa Fraulein* [sic] *SS, Love Camp 7* (after Billy Wilder's *Stalag 7*), *Nazi Love Camp, SS Girls, Last Orgy of the Third Reich* (*La ultima orgia de la Gestapo*), *Nathalie: Escape from Hell, The Black Gestapo*. There is no dearth of others. Occasionally this sort of thing even appears in art cinema, as with Luchino Visconti's *The Damned* (1969) or Liliana Cavani's *The Night Porter* (1974). On the topic see Hunter 2010. This book's subtitle (*Nazi Exploitation SSinema*) is wholly appropriate.

Triumph of the Will works in a similar way, except that its intended audiences were watching something they considered not ugly or evil but attractive and ennobling. By the same token, Miller and Snyder probably did not believe that *300* was showing viewers anything ugly (or worse). To return to Eco's point: In *300* the artistic impulse, technological artistry, provides the pretext and the format for a reactionary storyline. Worship of technology is wedded to traditionalist thought, if *thought* is the right word here. More directly, and again in Eco's terms, praise of modernity – *Just look how amazing and cool this is!* – is only the superficial aspect of an ideology based on blood and soil.

The death of Leonidas, the inevitable climax of the film, is revealing as well. Our last view of him lying dead on the battlefield is intended to elicit sympathy for the brave warrior-leader who took on an enemy of infinitely superior numbers, who made a heroic last stand and might have prevailed had he not been betrayed, and who nobly fell in the thick of missiles among his men, whose honor's name was loyalty. The camera slowly zooms out from a medium close-up of his body to a bird's-eye long shot of him and the Spartans, and a version of Simonides' epitaph is heard on the soundtrack: "Go tell the Spartans, passer-by, that here, by Spartan law, we lie." We are now also meant to feel hatred and contempt for the cowardly Persians, who relied more on long-distance warfare – their arrows – than on manly single combat the way the Spartans had done. More to the point, we see Leonidas lying on his back in a pose that instantly reminds us of a crucifixion (Figure 7.4). Leonidas is like Jesus: dead but immortal as savior of the West. Accordingly, the victory of the Spartans and their allies over the Persians at Plataea the following year is the logical next step in the presentation of history according to *300*. The Persian conquest of Greece after Thermopylae and before Plataea is left out. Leonidas died for the insufficiently martial and patriotic Greeks' sins. What Tyrtaeus said about the dead hero fully applies to him: "felled in the front line, he is lovely yet." Snyder and his special-effects team made sure that no arrow disfigures their handsome hero's face, something that seems to be of no interest to them as far as other Spartans are concerned.[73] The unlovely fate of the historical Leonidas' body, which does not fit this perspective, is therefore simply omitted.[74] The final image of Leonidas in *300* is another instance of utter kitsch.

---

[73] The large still image of Leonidas and his men on the battlefield in Allie and Moody 2007: 125 is instructive in this regard. The Spartan warrior closest to Leonidas on the lower right seems to have an arrow stuck in or near the bridge of his nose.

[74] Herodotus, *Histories* 7.238, reports that Xerxes had Leonidas' body decapitated. Xerxes does this himself in the sequel to *300*. On Xerxes see now Bridges 2015. Bridges: 193–199 examines the two *300* films.

Figure 7.4 Leonidas' dead body in Zack Snyder's *300*.

To those of my readers who think that I am here engaging in special pleading (*Old-fogey type prof hates* 300 *'cause he's uncool and totally out of it*), I propose a cinematic experiment. Watch *300* in conjunction with Sam Peckinpah's *The Wild Bunch* (1969), another famous film about the last stand of violent hero-killers. *The Wild Bunch* has two extremely intense and extended massacre sequences. The emotional power on viewers of the violence in Peckinpah's film, which was made long before CGI, has two main sources: its Eisensteinian montage, which includes slow motion (but not sped-up motion), and, even more importantly, the careful characterization of the outlaws who die in the final shootout. Unlike the nearly incessant slaughter in *300*, the two gun battles in *The Wild Bunch* serve to frame, and to put into greater relief, a heroic tale that is largely non-violent. The violence of *The Wild Bunch* is wholly different from that in *300*:

> *The Wild Bunch* achieves its wonder by its form. There is violence that is gripping not because of graphic images but because it touches fear and sacrifice and because it is filmed to show its pain and its amoral beauty. We see its attraction and we see its destruction . . . There is ambiguity that comes from the obvious savagery of the gang and the equally obvious qualities of courage, guilt, and loyalty they possess and are possessed by.
>
> The battles are stunning . . . because . . . carefully choreographed and shot, and because each one . . . has internal developments that bring out or resolve tensions in the characters . . . *The Wild Bunch* [is] an unusually powerful, unusually complex statement of ambiguity and of honor won in the face of ambiguity.

The battles in *The Wild Bunch* "became as intense [to viewers] . . . as they were because they were about more than themselves."[75]

In this context, Eco is again to the point: "Irrationalism," he states, "depends on the cult of *action for action's sake*. Action is beautiful in itself, and therefore must be implemented before any form of reflection. Thinking is a form of emasculation."[76] This fully applies to *300* but not at all to *The Wild Bunch*. As Peckinpah has said about the Bunch in connection with the film's most lyrical sequence, the gang's balladesque farewell from a Mexican village: "If you can ride out with them there and feel it, you can die with them and feel it" at the end.[77] Would anyone say about Miller and Snyder's Spartans: *If you can march out with them and feel it, you can die with them and feel it*? Peckinpah and Snyder tell stories about very different killer elites, and they do so in radically different ways. If, at the end of the experiment I suggested, readers are convinced that what Peckinpah said about the Bunch applies to Snyder's Spartans, then I have indeed done nothing but special pleading. But I doubt that anyone will reach such a conclusion.

7 Contemporary Rhetoric

Numerous reviewers and critics have commented on the contemporary context of *300*; that is to say, as an expression of the political and military climate during the presidency of George W. Bush. Image manipulation through which Snyder's Leonidas received Bush's face could be seen on the Internet soon after the film's release. Much more to the point is the speech that Gorgo, holding up the home front while Leonidas and the three hundred are at Thermopylae, addresses to the Spartan council. This is pure fiction. No Spartan women, not even queens, would have had such access to the assembly. But no matter; what counts is what Gorgo actually says.[78] At least part of this speech could come straight out of President Bush's or any neoconservative's mouths. Here are some excerpts:

---

[75] The preceding quotations are from Strug 2008: 21–22 and 25. The text of this slim volume was written in the year given in its title. Scholarship on *The Wild Bunch* is extensive. Bliss 1994 and Prince 1999 are useful overviews. On the wider context see Prince 1998, especially 47–101 and 259–261 (notes; chapter titled "Aestheticizing Violence"), and Prince 2000b. On explicit violence as depicted in ancient texts and images see Muth 2008 and Zimmermann 2009, both with extensive references.

[76] Eco 2001b: 80.   [77] Quoted from Seydor 1997: 198 note.

[78] Readers curious about actual Spartan women might wish to consult, as useful starting points, Hodkinson 2004 and Powell 2004, both with additional references. On Gorgo in *300* see now Tomasso 2013 and Nikoloutsos 2013b. Snyder and Miller were apparently unaware of the fact that Spartans had not one but two kings and presumably two queens as well.

Three hundred families ... bleed for our rights and for the very principles this room [the assembly hall] was built upon. We're at war, gentlemen. We must send the entire Spartan army to aid our king in the preservation of not just ourselves, but of our children. Send the army for the preservation of liberty. Send it for justice. Send it for law and order. Send it for reason. But most importantly, send our army for hope. Hope that a king and his men have not been wasted to the pages of history. That *their* courage bonds us together. That we are made stronger by their actions and that your choices today reflect their bravery ... The Persians will *not* stop until the only shelter we will find is rubble and chaos.

Gorgo's speech and Leonidas' death in battle exemplify a standard feature in Fascist and Nazi culture and cinema. As a German film and cultural scholar has put it:

In Fascist and post-Fascist films it is, in every case, a woman's *beautiful* pain to lose husband or son "on the battlefield," whose sacrifice in turn makes him immortal. By the way, never [does he die] during a heroic deed of rescuing others or in a fair fight man against man, but again and again by means of merely vanishing in the thick of battle, by [plane] crash or explosion, by sinking or drowning and in a fade-out: the hero of Fascist films of self-sacrifice apparently does not know what pain is.[79]

Gorgo elsewhere says: "Freedom isn't free at all." She quotes a familiar American saying. *Freedom is not free* appears, for example, on the Korean War Memorial in Washington, DC. The motto was frequently revived in the Bush years. But it has always been a handy slogan to patriots, right-wingers, and similar ideologues. Harlan's *Kolberg* presents us with an example worth considering side by side with *300*. Major von Gneisenau is addressing the assembled citizens before the arrival of the French army. With only a few obvious adjustments, what he says may remind us of Gorgo's speech, although the style of delivery is radically different in the two films. Gneisenau is exhorting his listeners:

Prussians! Germans! A heavy fate burdens your city and our unhappy home country [*Vaterland*]. Stronger than fate is the courage which bears it. If you had not dared defiantly to resist the foreign conqueror, I would not be here today. *That* is what forges us together. No love is holier than the love for one's country [*Vaterland*]; no joy is sweeter than the joy of freedom. But you know what is in store for us if we do not honorably win this fight. For this reason, whatever sacrifices may be demanded of each, they do not outweigh the sacred values for which we must fight and win unless we want to cease being Prussians and Germans.

[79] Quoted from Seeßlen 1994: 65.

If we substitute Spartans for Prussians and Greeks for Germans, we can imagine such a speech in *300*, for instance by a Spartan leader in the assembly or by Leonidas before his men. In *Kolberg*, Gneisenau's hectoring and almost snide tone was modeled on Hitler's harangues. Gneisenau's vocabulary is highly Nazi-like. On this sort of thing, Eco again has a pertinent observation:

> Ur-Fascism springs from individual or social frustration, which explains why one of the characteristics typical of historic Fascist movements was *the appeal to the frustrated middle classes*, disquieted by some economic crisis or political humiliation ... To those with no social identity at all, Ur-Fascism says that their only privilege is the most common privilege of all, that of being born in the same country ... Moreover, the only ones who can provide the nation with an identity are the enemy.[80]

Sloganeering, especially of a patriotic kind, is a substitute for thinking. As Eco says about Italian Fascism: "Mussolini had no philosophy: all he had was rhetoric." The same can be applied to Hitler and his cinematic mouthpiece in *Kolberg* and to Bush and his cinematic mouthpiece in *300*. Eco poignantly adds: "freedom of speech means freedom from rhetoric."[81]

  Patriotic rhetoric, Eco observes, manifests a "preaching [of] 'popular elitism'," in which one basic tenet is this: "Every individual belongs to the best people in the world."[82] So "everyone is trained to become a hero. In every mythology the hero is an exceptional being, but in the Ur-Fascist ideology heroism is the norm. This cult of heroism is closely connected to the *cult of death*: ... the Ur-Fascist hero aspires to death, hailed as the finest reward for a heroic life."[83] Compare what German philosopher Theodor Adorno once wrote about fascist propaganda:

> It may well be the secret of fascist propaganda that it simply takes men for what they are: the true children of today's standardized mass culture, largely robbed of autonomy and spontaneity, instead of setting goals the realization of which would transcend the psychological *status quo* no less than the social one. Fascist propaganda has only to *reproduce* the existent mentality for its own purposes; – it need not induce a change – and the compulsive repetition which is one of its foremost characteristics will be at one with the necessity for this continuous reproduction.[84]

---

[80] Eco 2001b: 81, from two of his fourteen characteristics.   [81] Eco 2001b: 71 and 66.

[82] Eco 2001b: 83.   [83] Eco 2001b: 84. We encountered this sort of thing on earlier pages.

[84] T. W. Adorno, "Freudian Theory and the Pattern of Fascist Propaganda," in Arato and Gebhardt 1978: 134; quoted from Rentschler 1996: 387–388 note 17. On the "continuous reproduction" of Nazi ideology in the ostensibly democratic society of the Federal Republic of Germany and in the unified country from the early 1950s to the mid-1990s see the sobering, although too little-known, analyses of popular media in Seeßlen 1994 and 1996.

Much more in Eco's essay is pertinent to my topic. Even the occasion for which Eco wrote it is worth mentioning. It was "conceived for an audience of American students" at Columbia University in 1995 and delivered orally "in the days when America was still shaken by outrage over the Oklahoma city [*sic*] bombing and by the discovery of the fact (by no means a secret) that extreme right-wing military organizations existed in America." Eco's "historical observations were intended to stimulate reflection on current problems in various countries."[85]

8 Political Paranoia and Ordinary American Fascism

The political rhetoric in the US during the Bush era exemplified Samuel Huntington's perspective on the clash of East-West civilizations and world order. "New World Order" had been a well-known slogan during the Gulf War under President George H. W. Bush. Such terminology, with all it implies, has been a regular element in the entire history of American political discourse, although appearing in various guises and disguises and used by various, often right-wing, factions or parties. The classic account is Richard Hofstadter's essay "The Paranoid Style in American Politics."[86] Hofstadter defined the paranoid style as deriving from a combination of "heated exaggeration, suspiciousness, and conspiratorial fantasy" and observed: "It is the use of paranoid modes of expression by more or less normal people that makes the phenomenon significant."[87] The "spokesman" of this style has convinced himself that "a nation, a culture, a way of life" are threatened and that "his political passions are unselfish and patriotic." He evinces a "feeling of righteousness" and "moral indignation."[88] The most obvious modern case, Hofstadter reported, is that of Fascist Germany – "though it [the paranoid style] appeals to many who are hardly fascists."[89] This is a crucial observation.

Hofstadter goes on to describe the elements of the paranoid style in considerable detail. The following points can be read with *300* directly in mind. A "vast and sinister conspiracy" (the Persians and the influential Spartan whom Gorgo exposes as a traitor in Xerxes' pay) leads the paranoid

---

[85] Eco, "Introduction" in Eco 2001a: ix–xii; quotations at xi.
[86] Hofstadter 1965b. The entire essay is highly pertinent. It was first delivered orally in 1963 and published in an abridged version the following year. Hofstadter 1965a contains his definitive text. Reading this book alongside Seeßlen 1994 and 1996 is extremely instructive.
[87] Hofstadter 1965b: 3 and 4.   [88] The quotations are from Hofstadter 1965b: 4.
[89] Hofstadter 1965b: 7.

(practically all Spartans in *300*) to see everything "in apocalyptic terms" and as "the birth and death of whole worlds, whole political orders, whole systems of human values" (East vs. West, the Persians' absolute monarchy and enslavement of others vs. Spartan and Greek freedom and self-government).[90] This is the result: "He [the paranoid spokesman] is always manning the barricades of civilization. He constantly lives at a turning point: it is now or never in organizing resistance to conspiracy."[91]

This fits *300* rather closely, except that the most outspoken individual is a woman (Gorgo), but one who voices what Leonidas might have said, if not in such detail. Cinematic warrior heroes act; they should not speechify. And the organization of resistance is more to an invasion than to a conspiracy. Even more to the point, however, is this:

Since what is at stake is always a conflict between absolute good and absolute evil, the quality needed is ... the will to fight things out to a finish. Nothing but complete victory will do. Since the enemy is thought of as totally evil and totally unappeasable, he must be totally eliminated ... This enemy is clearly delineated: he is a perfect model of malice, a kind of amoral superman: sinister, ubiquitous, powerful, cruel, sensual, luxury-loving ... He is a free, active, demonic agent.[92]

This wholly fits *300*. Specific details about the enemy's sexuality – or rather, inventive sexual decadence – which Hofstadter adduces appear in the film:

The sexual freedom often attributed to him, his lack of moral inhibition, his possession of especially effective techniques for fulfilling his desires, give exponents of the paranoid style an opportunity to project and freely express unacceptable aspects of their own minds.[93]

It seems self-evident that all this describes the minds behind *300*. A related perspective from the same year in which Hofstadter's essay was published in its final version reinforces his argument.

In 1965 Russian film director Mikhail Romm finished making an extraordinary historical film. It was called *Ordinary Fascism*. Romm had had access to large amounts of Nazi film footage and photographs. Some, previously undiscovered or rarely seen, came from Goebbels's Ministry of Propaganda and Hitler's private photo archives. Others had been taken by SS officers. Romm combined selections from these sources with other images, such as Nazi newsreels and footage of concentration camp horrors, into a kind of documentary and personal essay. Romm himself provided a voice-over commentary. Romm and his screenwriters sought, as he said

---

[90] Hofstadter 1965b: 29.   [91] Hofstadter 1965b: 29–30.   [92] Hofstadter 1965b: 31–32.
[93] Hofstadter 1965b: 34.

later, "to examine the psychological perspective of the average little man who becomes a Fascist," for German Fascism could become effective only "when millions of simple people felt the need for this demagoguery in order that the matter could become habitual to them." Romm followed this statement with one that applies to Eco's concept of Ur-Fascism and to our examination of *300*: "Fascism had to turn into their everyday routine; it was no longer even noticed as such."[94]

In a brief introduction to the East German release version Romm said, on screen, that this was a film "for reflection." Romm attempted an explanation, by means of the Nazis' own images, why and how common and originally decent people could have come under the spell of a totalitarian military ideology. In 1967 Romm commented:

> Fascism is a terrible and at the same time astonishing phenomenon. It shook up and aroused mankind not only by its brutality and its organization but also by the seductive power of its insidious propaganda ... Even more astonishing is the fact that Fascism continues to exist even though it had been smashed in World War II.[95]

As Eco has shown us, the survival of Fascism today is not as astonishing as it was only twenty years after its apparent demise. The fascist mind is alive and well. As the title of Romm's film tells us, Fascism – and fascism – is an everyday phenomenon.

Given all this, it is instructive to juxtapose *300* to a particular American film made close to the end of World War II for purposes of propaganda and morale-enhancement. In Raoul Walsh's *Objective, Burma!* a small troop of Americans is pitched against a much larger force of an Eastern enemy, the Japanese.[96] Like *300, Objective, Burma!* is primarily an action-adventure story. But one notorious scene stands out. A small group of GIs come to a village in which they find the result of atrocities perpetrated on some American soldiers by the Japanese. One of the most striking images in *300* shows the Spartans in a comparable scene, which culminates when they, and we, see a tree laden with corpses. This Persian barbarity is

---

[94] This comes from the abbreviated reprint of a discussion of two German film critics with Romm ("Ein Gespräch zwischen dem Regisseur Michail Romm und den Kritikern Hermann Herlinghaus und Friedrich Hitzer") in Beilenhoff and Hänsgen 2009: 268–274; quotations at 270 and 271. The full text of the conversation had first appeared in *Film*, 5 (1966): 49–56. The German title of Romm's film is *Der gewöhnliche Faschismus*. The book here referred to contains a complete reproduction of the film's original version in still images, Romm's commentary (in German), and valuable other background material.

[95] The quotation is taken from the leaflet accompanying the German DVD of the film.

[96] The film's title is often given without either or both of its punctuation marks. Except in quotations, I adopt the version that appears on the film's title card.

comparable to that by the Japanese in *Objective, Burma!* But Walsh handles the subject differently from Snyder by not showing us *any* atrocities. He creates great empathy among viewers by keeping a dying American lieutenant who is begging for death completely out of sight except for his lower legs and boots. A strong close-up on the face of the captain who is in command of the American soldiers, looking at the dying man off screen, reinforces the emotional power of the scene. Our imagination makes evident to us what Snyder crams down our throats. Then an American newspaper correspondent, who is accompanying the small troop and who has overheard the dying man, is given a verbal reaction. It is quite in the spirit of *300*:

I – I've been a newspaperman for thirty years. I thought I'd seen and read about everything that one man can do to another, from the torture chambers of the Middle Ages to the gang wars and the lynchings of today. But this, this is different. This was done in cold blood. They're people who claim to be civilized. *Civilized* – they're degenerate moral idiots, stinking little savages. Wipe 'em out, I say. *Wipe 'em out!* Wipe 'em off the face of the earth! [*Sobs.*] *Wipe 'em off the face of the earth!*

This speech was highly controversial at the time. It had not been in the original screenplay, whose writers protested to the film's producer that it was "very dangerous." Originally the captain, who says nothing in the release version, had answered the reporter: "There's nothing especially Japanese about this . . . You'll find it wherever you find fascists. There are even people who call themselves American who'd do it, too." The producer cut this response. One of the screenwriters told him: "You are falling into the enemy's trap. Wiping people off the face of the earth is a private idea – and policy – of fascists."[97] Obviously, in 1945 Walsh could never have put anything of what the American soldiers and the correspondent see onto the screen, but he did not have to. Viewers get the point, and the speech is out of place and out of tone with the rest of the film. Evidently and regrettably, we seem to have come quite a ways – down – in the sixty years between *Objective, Burma!* and *300*, both produced at Warner Brothers.

Still, remaining similarities between these two films in their notably different portrayals of superior enemy forces should not surprise us. What a film scholar has written about the Japanese in *Objective, Burma!* reminds us of the Persians in *300*:

The enemy of *Objective, Burma* is presented in a most prejudicial manner. Their faces in close-up are used to frighten a viewer with the sense of alien, unsmiling

---

[97] The three quotations are taken from Koppes and Black 2000: 263.

beings. The narrative suggests a group of truly barbaric men who torture and mutilate . . . They have . . . seemingly unlimited forces . . . . they advance in endless hordes . . . [98]

In this context, and in view of my earlier mention of *The Eternal Jew*, the following observations by Adorno on an American war documentary are enlightening. He wrote in 1944:

Cinema newsreel: the invasion of the Marianas, including Guam. The impression is not of battles, but of civil engineering and blasting operations undertaken with immeasurably intensified vehemence, also of 'fumigation', insect-extermination on a terrestrial scale. Works are put in hand, until no grass grows. The enemy acts as patient and corpse. Like the Jews under Fascism, he features now as merely the object of technical and administrative measures, and should he defend himself, his own action immediately takes on the same character. Satanically, indeed, more initiative is in a sense demanded here than in old-style war: it seems to cost the subject his whole energy to achieve subjectlessness. Consummate inhumanity is the realization of Edward Grey's humane dream, war without hatred.[99]

Americans are hardly immune to fascist leanings. In his anti-Fascist novel *It Can't Happen Here* (1935), Sinclair Lewis had already made the case, although in a satiric vein. Hollywood, a cultural and social seismograph of its country, on several occasions dealt with latent or not so latent fascist tendencies in the US: *Legion of Terror* (1936), *Black Legion* (1937), and *Storm Warning* (1951) take on the Ku Klux Klan and similar secret organizations under the influence of contemporary or recent European history. Earlier, the unusual political fantasy *Gabriel Over the White House* (1933) reveals such sympathy for Fascist or Nazi ideology that the review published in the left-leaning weekly *The Nation* was headed "Fascism Over Hollywood."[100] But most telling is *Keeper of the Flame* (1943), directed for M-G-M by George Cukor as a *noir*-ish if still glossy political warning at the height of Nazism. The sudden death of a popular and rising politician, a former war hero, causes nationwide mourning; eventually it turns out that he was not at all what he had appeared to be. His widow, who was implicated in his death, explains everything at the end. Here the film loses much of its earlier impact through preachy speechifying. But what she says is important. She admits to her prior weakness for a political strongman-type elite:

---

[98] Basinger 2003: 124–125.

[99] Adorno 1974b: 56. This passage is quoted, appropriately, by Rentschler 1996: 388 note 18; he adds: "These are chilling words; in the light of American media coverage of the Persian Gulf War, they have become even more chilling." Still more so after 2001.

[100] Troy 1933. On the film see especially McConnell 1976.

"I believed in a few people. Leaders, rulers." Her husband was one such. But then she learned about his true nature: "I saw the face of Fascism in my own home." He was ready to make deals with racists, including white suprema-cists like the Ku Klux Klan and anti-Semites: "Of course they didn't call it Fascism. They painted it red, white, and blue and called it Americanism." What the widow calls "America's first Storm Troopers," a boys' army with characteristics of the Hitler Youth, already exists. And the potential Leader was or might have been a conqueror as well. Earlier in the film he was compared to Alexander the Great. His youthful heroism in World War I led to a newspaper reporter's encomium that sounds rather Nazi-like in its rhetorical bombast: "That tattered scarecrow youth standing in a sort of ecstasy of faith against all the blazing powers of hell." As director Cukor later observed: "We made this picture during a period of undercover Fascism in this country . . . Certain things were in the air but hadn't come out into the open."[101]

With its anti-Fascist warning to Americans, *Keeper of the Flame* may well be the best indication that, even if full-blown Nazism can't happen here, the Fascist nebula of which Eco speaks certainly can. It was to return with a vengeance in *300*. That ordinary fascism, or at least something not far removed from it, has long been prevalent in American society is best seen in popular culture, especially with the caped crusaders of comic books or in vigilante cinema.[102] Heroic or tough loners usually bend right to their superior might, justifying the end they envision as good, with law and order restored. But their means are often quite bad. Due process of law, for instance, is easily set aside. The hero's death wish – I am alluding to a whole series of vigilante films – is focused on his enemy, the scum of the earth, who must be annihilated. Yes, it *can* happen here. Less than three weeks before *300* was released, a political analysis of contemporary politics pointedly referred to Sinclair Lewis's title: *It Can Happen Here: Authoritarian Peril in the Age of Bush*.[103]

9   Ideological Myopia

Classical scholars and historians of ancient Greece have repeatedly com-mented on *300* but evince a startling kind of ideological myopia concerning

---

[101] Quoted from Lambert 2000: 130.
[102] A connection of the cult of the body in fantasy fiction and Fascism exists as well. On the subject see, e.g., the brief but revealing comments by Seeßlen 1994: 130–132.
[103] Conason 2007; cf. Conason 2003.

the film's Ur-Fascist nature.[104] We can even find a hyperbolic assessment such as this: *300* is "the most authentic rendering of an ancient culture's *mores* yet achieved by a Hollywood director."[105] One especially telling case is that of classical scholar and historian Victor Davis Hanson, apologist of all things Greek, neoconservative pundit, and promoter of right-wing militarism in the Bush era. He is the author of a number of books on ancient agrarianism and warfare, separately and in combination, and on surveys of warfare from antiquity to today. Hanson shot to prominence as co-author of a screed about the decline of classical education.[106] He eventually became nearly ubiquitous as a political commentator and journalist. But what has he got to do with *300*? As it turns out, a lot.

In one of their interviews about the film Miller and Snyder referred to a book published to coincide with the film's release and then came to Hanson. Their view of him is worth quoting at some length, grammatical and typographical warts and all. Snyder begins: "In the Making Of book there's a guy named Victor Davis Hanson who is a . . . " Miller interrupts: "We're his fan club." Snyder then continues:

He's a frickin genius. He's a Greek historian and we showed him the movie because I wanted him to write a forward [*sic*] to the Making Of book. I was a little nervous to be honest, because I wasn't sure how he'd react. And Kurt Johnstad who he and I worked on the screenplay together, he actually also is a huge fan of Victor Davis Hanson. He went up to show him the movie at his house. And . . . at the end of the movie he . . . says that, 'Look, if you have a problem with distilling the Battle of Thermopylae down to freedom versus tyranny, you need to read Herodotus because he's the one. It's his fault, not modern culture's fault. He did it.' He references a lot of things like that because he feels like the spirit of the book and of the movie are very close to the Spartan aesthetic. That's really kind of what he feels.[107]

---

[104] The closest a classicist has come appears to be this: "*300* was . . . a *Triumph of the Will* for the twenty-first century." Quoted from Nisbet 2008: 141–142. Rather amusing is the tone adopted by Lauwers, Dhont, and Huybrecht 2013, who declare about negative critics: "Others vituperate the movie for supposed fascist ideals, pointing out uncanny parallels between the Spartan society and the 'Third Reich' . . . In response to these ready-made and superficial [!] criticisms, we aim to take the discussion to a deeper level" (79–80). Aim they do. They also seem shocked that "[e]ven Susan Sontag's terminology of 'fascist art' is used to categorize this movie" (80 note 4). Mendelsohn 2007 regrettably has nothing to say on this side of the film.

[105] Holland 2007: 181. Apparently he has never heard of Anthony Mann.

[106] Hanson and Heath 1998. Their titular question is best answered with "Nobody."

[107] Quoted from Rebecca Miller. The passages appear on page 3 (online) of this interview. Frank Miller was a fan of Hanson's even before Snyder's film was made, as is evident from his listing Hanson's book *The Western Way of War* (= Hanson 2000; originally 1989) as recommended reading at the end of his graphic novel, right after Herodotus.

Hanson came through with his foreword, which deserves a close look.[108] That he writes from a *parti pris* perspective is evident from an expression such as "Xerxes' horde" for the Persian army.[109] Hanson also reviewed the film in print, concluding that "the impressionism of *300* is Hellenic in spirit" and "the Spartans' mood of defiance is chilling."[110] In the review's most important paragraph Hanson elaborates on this:

> The movie does demonstrate real affinity with Herodotus in two areas. First, it captures the martial ethos of the Spartan state, the notion that the sum total of a man's life, the ultimate arbiter of all success or failure, is how well he fought on the battlefield, especially when it becomes clear at last that bravery cannot prevent defeat. And second, the Greeks, if we can believe Simonides, Aeschylus, and Herodotus, saw Thermopylae as a "clash of civilizations" that set Eastern central-ism and collective serfdom against the idea of the free citizen of an autonomous polis. That comes through in the movie, especially in the fine performances of [Gerard] Butler [as Leonidas] and Lena Headey (Gorgo). If the Spartans seem too cocky and self-assured in their belief that they are the more effective warriors of a superior culture, blame Herodotus, not Zack Snyder.

Hanson naturally considers any parallels between *300* and President Bush's concurrent wars to be "silly." Even if we agree with Hanson on this point, it is difficult to agree with his *Blame Herodotus* attitude, which is nonsensical. But Hanson had already said the same thing in his "Foreword" to the promotional book: "If critics think that *300* reduces and simplifies the meaning of Thermopylae into freedom vs. tyranny, they should carefully reread ancient accounts and then blame Herodotus, Plutarch, and Diodorus."[111]

Perhaps it is Hanson himself who should carefully reread Herodotus; that is to say, without ideological bias. In that case even he might reach a different conclusion. The following assessment by three historians writing together is closer to the truth:

---

[108] Hanson 2007a (in Allie and Moody 2007). The book's title page provides this information: "a Zack Snyder film" and, in smaller type: "Text by Tara DiLullo" and "Foreword by Dr. Victor Davis Hanson" (both in equal size). Hanson's name also appears on a "Special Thanks" page (126).

[109] Hanson 2007a: 5. The misspelling of British poet and classical scholar A. E. Housman's name as "Houseman" (6) may not be Hanson's responsibility.

[110] This and the following quotations are taken from Hanson 2007b. The review's main title continued with this subtitle: "Zack Snyder's *300*: A Spirited Take on a Clash of Civilizations." Hanson was one of the contributing editors of the online journal that published his review.

[111] Hanson 2007a: 6. Plutarch on several occasions describes Leonidas and Gorgo and collects famous sayings by Spartans and by Spartan women in his *Moralia* ("Moral Essays"). In the first century BC, Diodorus Siculus reported on the Battle in Book 11 of his *Historical Library*.

If one were to form an opinion about Herodotus the historian on the basis of *300*, one would likely conclude that Herodotus presents a prime example of the prejudiced mind ... Herodotus' *History* resists simple value-laden dichotomies and facile binary oppositions. It is truly a historical account for our times, since throughout it exhibits a wide-eyed, open-minded, and curious receptivity to foreign cultural practices. In today's familiar language, we can legitimately say that a world-view of multiculturalism, diversity, and pluralism characterizes Herodotus' writing ... For anyone to think, from an impression gained from a viewing of *300*, that Herodotus rather wrote a jingoistic, ethnocentric, triumphalist manifesto of Greek superiority over non-Greek, barbarian inferiors would be great pity, indeed.[112]

This assessment is as eloquent as it is accurate. It refutes Hanson's shallow understanding of Herodotus. Similar things may be said about Hanson's view of Aeschylus. His play *The Persians*, to which Hanson refers without naming it, is anything but a simplistic tale about good Greeks vs. evil Persians. The central function of the dead Persian king Darius, who had undertaken the first invasion of Greece ten years before his son Xerxes, is perhaps the clearest evidence. The spirit of Darius rises up and admonishes Xerxes about his folly. Aeschylus' Darius does so in purely Greek terms, emphasizing fate, hubris, and related concepts. One might have expected a philologically trained scholar like Hanson to be able to notice nuances and subtleties. Neither Aeschylus nor Herodotus or any classical author achieved canonical status by simple-mindedness.

But Hanson, like his Spartans, is not to be deterred. He returned to the defense of *300* in a contribution titled "The 300 – Fact or Fiction?" to the film's home video editions. There he says:

this film adaptation is consistent with a long line of interpretation, whether it's novelists in the nineteenth century or whether it's poets in the seventeenth or sixteenth or twelfth century or whether it's vase painters in the fourth or Herodotus in the fifth [centuries BC] – each person is trying to convey this wonderful event, a story of a few men who were willing to risk all for a larger Western concept of freedom and liberty ... Here's what Herodotus said happened, and here's Frank Miller's adaptation in modern context, and then here's the movie of Frank Miller's novel, derived from Herodotus derived from Thermopylae.

Hanson draws a direct line of influence from history to ancient historiography and on to Miller and Snyder. Neither of the latter is Herodotus' equal in intellect or humanity. The same goes for Hanson. His statement

[112] Quoted from Basu, Champion, and Lasch-Quinn 2007: 31. Their earlier summary (28) of "Orientalist discourse" about Thermopylae is worth keeping in mind as well.

that "the Spartans' mood of defiance is chilling" thus acquires an ulterior meaning. What is chilling is Miller's, Snyder's, and Hanson's Ur-Fascist conception of the Spartans. Hanson is right in pointing to a long line of interpretation, just not the correct one. *300* is consistent with a long line of German nationalist and National-Socialist interpretations of the Spartans.

Hanson's scholarship has come under critical scrutiny a number of times. Two European scholars writing together provide us with a useful summary. After a detailed examination of Hanson's origins in agricultural California, his intellectual debt to conservative Greek historian Donald Kagan, and Hanson's publications, they reach this verdict:

> we are facing an author who writes against history . . . because in his work he distorts the facts completely. He uses history as a mere vehicle for the transmission of certain values and with a political agenda in its most simple and straightforward form. It is precisely this lack of respect for [the historian's craft] which makes his books vulgarizing propaganda for the neoconservative right in the United States.[113]

We could add: not only his books.

On behalf of the National Endowment for the Humanities, an agency of the federal government, President George W. Bush awarded Hanson the National Humanities Medal in 2007, the year of *300*.

10   Return of the Fuzzy

Various other aspects connect *300* with Ur-Fascism. One is its portrayal of the Persians as *Untermenschen* characterized by barbarism and decadence. Another lies in the overtones of earlier American cinema, such as the red capes worn by Superman and the Spartans. Superman and various other caped or masked crusaders come suspiciously close to the Fascist fantasy of the insuperable and providential strongman who alone can save a helpless or cowardly people from destruction, who tirelessly and selflessly works on their behalf, and who is never wrong and is questioned only by quislings or bad guys. The people in general blindly revere and obey such a hero in variations on the Nazi slogan "Leader, command; we obey" (*Führer, befiehl; wir folgen*). It is then telling that Frank Miller, in his first sole directorial debut in 2008, should have turned to an adaptation of Will Eisner's comic-book series *The Spirit*. The film combines a neo-*noir* look with supernaturalism, fake-classical mythology (the

---

[113] González García and López Barja de Quiroga 2012: 148 and 149.

blood of Heracles can turn the super-villain into a god), and extreme Nazi Kitsch. The sequence in which the black villain and his female sidekick prepare to torture the hero while being dressed up in SS uniforms is especially grotesque (and embarrassing). The villain even gives the Nazi Salute; a huge photograph of Hitler appears in the background. In 2013 Snyder's own Superman epic, *Man of Steel*, was released; it was followed in 2016 by *Batman v Superman: Dawn of Justice*. Additional installments are said to be in the works.

Similarities between *300* and the *Star Wars* films are obvious, too, as with the facial masks worn by imperial Storm Troopers and Persian Immortals or the human-animal monster in *300*, a kind of ancient Jabba the Hutt. And the voice of Xerxes sounds not at all unlike that of Darth Vader. Here is Rentschler's assessment:

George Lucas restaged the closing scene from *Triumph of the Will* in the finale of *Star Wars*; a . . . rock video by Michael Jackson likewise unabashedly recycles Riefenstahl's images of soldier males paying deference to their master. American artists pilfer the Nazi legacy with relish . . . If Nazi horrors continue to repulse, the shapes of fascism continue to fascinate.[114]

Moreover, at least some of the Persians and their oversized fighting animals seem patterned on various Orcs and other monstrosities in the battle sequences of *The Return of the King*, the final installment of *The Lord of the Rings* film trilogy. Equally obvious is the debt of *300* to the cinema of Quentin Tarantino and to Japanese horror and violence films. Frank Miller's death-and-slaughter comic *Sin City* and the 2005 film, co-directed by Miller, Robert Rodriguez, and Tarantino, derive from it. But Snyder's film *Watchmen* (2009), also based on a graphic novel and featuring a caped superhero-crusader with as prominent a codpiece as the Spartans wore in *300*, is worth closer consideration. A contemporary reviewer concluded:

Snyder . . . is so insanely aroused by the look of vengeance, and by the stylized application of physical power, that the film ends up twice as fascistic as the forces [of evil] it wishes to lampoon . . . . nobody over twenty-five could take any joy from the savagery that is fleshed out onscreen, just as nobody under eighteen should be allowed to witness it.[115]

---

[114] Rentschler 1996: 6. He was not the first to notice these analogies. For more on this in the cinema see Winkler 1998 and 2009b; Pomeroy 2004.

[115] Lane 2009: 83.

This may remind us of the susceptibility to fascist ideology of the kind Eco describes. *Watchmen* and *300* exemplify what has been called "the hyper-trophy of male adolescence" in Fascism.[116] No wonder that the computer game *Spartan Total Warrior* does not miss out on this appeal. Its back cover tells us that this is about "the greatest battle ever seen on console." And who is fighting? "On one side the might of Rome, on the other the fury of the Spartans. And you, the Spartans' greatest hero, must lead the charge." Every teenage gamer his own Leonidas! Like Snyder's Spartans, these, too, are furious and not a bit cool.

300 was an instant target of satire, if on rather a puerile level. But the cheaply made *Meet the Spartans* (2008) got the point of Snyder's preten-tious epic: *300* is more about contemporary America than ancient culture and history. Various characters in *Meet the Spartans* are look-alikes of pop-culture celebrities; one of them is President Bush's near double.[117] Even an intellectual with a penchant for pop culture like playwright and filmmaker David Mamet went back to the Spartan archetype in one of his lesser films, called, simply, *Spartan* (2004). It tells the story of a Delta Force loner who singlehandedly ("One riot, one Ranger") rescues the daughter of the American president from Arab white slavers and takes on high-government corruption into the bargain. Mamet later revealed his right-wing leanings in a book of reactionary musings.[118]

One earlier American film, made by a Dutch director with a successful if checkered career in Hollywood, is also worth considering. Paul Verhoeven's *Starship Troopers* (1997), based on a 1959 novel by science-fiction author Robert Heinlein, describes what its producer once called "a fascist utopia" on the background of an American setting.[119] Verhoeven, born in 1938, grew up under the German occupation of his country. His film, he has said, was "reflecting a little bit the situation in the second World War, when the Americans were fighting the Japanese and the Germans. Basically, the enemy *was* evil and had to be destroyed. Nobody had time or even could bring himself to [face] the fact that these were also human beings, motivated by other thoughts, but as human as ourselves." He continued:

certainly the film is saying, "Every militaristic society has the possibility to grow into a fascistic one, if they take over too much." Because the military is

---

[116] Hesse 1990. Hesse illustrates this appeal by examining certain articles from the popular magazine *Am deutschen Herd: Das Blatt der Familie*, published in Berlin in 1933.

[117] On this film and related aspects see Poole 2013, especially 100–115.   [118] Mamet 2011.

[119] This and the following quotations about *Starship Troopers* are taken from McBride (n. d.).

authoritarian, and an authoritarian attitude is measured highly on the fascist scale … It's also a little bit looking at the fascist possibility even of American society … Our focus group in the movie is much more what you would call human, and not really, in my opinion, fascistic. That's the interesting thing – these [aspects] are correlated. And basically that's what I think about big societies like the American society. Look at the McCarthy period; that's a kind of a fascistic statement that was put forward, isn't it?

Verhoeven concludes about his teenage audiences: "I don't have the feeling that they would see it as a stimulation of fascistic feelings." The interviewer, however, is more skeptical: "whether his target audience of young movie-goers will draw such distinctions while watching this kinetic display of ultra-violence is a troubling question." The film was a big financial success and led to two sequels, a television series, a video game, and an animated feature. Whichever way adult audiences, especially those with a certain level of historical and ideological awareness, may answer the troubling question, *Starship Troopers* is as good an example as *300* to prompt reflection about the presence or absence of fascist tendencies in popular culture.

I return to Thermopylae and Stalingrad and their connections to *300*. As late as February 6, 1945, Hitler, the Greatest Strategist of All Time, told Martin Bormann, his deputy, the following about the Nazis' "Strategy of Grandiose Downfall" (*Strategie des grandiosen Untergangs*):

A desperate fight keeps its eternal value as an exemplar. Think of Leonidas and his three hundred Spartans. In any case, it does not fit our style to let ourselves be slaughtered like sheep. One may exterminate us, but one will not be able to lead us to the slaughter.[120]

Such pithy defiance in the face of the inevitable is worthy of the Leonidas in *300*. Göring might have said something very similar almost exactly two years earlier.

About six months after the premiere of *300*, a video titled "300 vs. Hermann Göring" appeared on YouTube.[121] The excerpts about Thermopylae in his speech on Stalingrad accompany the images of most of the official trailer of *300*. This clever if rather tasteless update makes the case for Sontag's and Eco's theses about Fascism. So we can on the whole agree with a British film

[120] Fest 2002a: 1022 (in chapter titled "Götterdämmerung" ["Twilight of the Gods"]). Losemann 2012: 294 provides some background information and a different English translation; source references at Losemann: 305 note 191 (with listing of the first [1973] edition of Fest's book).
[121] It is available at http://www.youtube.com/watch?v=zSt8Chn2nUk, http://holocaust-news.com/media/video/54, and doubtless elsewhere.

scholar's verdict on *300*, even though he slightly overstates matters since he is probably unfamiliar with actual Spartan military culture:

The film *300* (2007) is probably the most Fascistic film to come out in cinemas since the fall of the Third Reich . . . . this is a comprehensive celebration of Fascist ideology. It exalts a Sparta where weak and blemished children are hurled to their deaths on a heap of skulls, a policy emulated by Hitler with his programme for the elimination of the mentally and physically unfit in Nazi Germany. In Sparta, boys are taken from their families at seven and trained for war, like the Hitler Youth . . . . the Spartans resemble the naked Aryan supermen sculpted for the Reich by Hitler's favourite sculptor Arno Breker or the naked athletes celebrated in the eulogy to Ancient Greece that forms the prologue to Leni Riefenstahl's *Olympia* . . . Their "ho-ho" chant is delivered as if it were *Sieg Heil*. The last stand of the Spartans at Thermopylae becomes the ultimate "triumph of the will", the death Hitler ordered for his besieged army in Stalingrad.[122]

I juxtapose this quotation with a telling American comment, which appeared in a double review of *300* and Antoine Fuqua's *Shooter*, a thriller about a lone hero, appropriately named Bob Lee Swagger. The reviewer characterized *300* as "a porno-military curiosity – a muscle-magazine fantasy crossed with a video game and an army-recruiting film." He concluded: "Made in a time of frustration, when Americans are fighting a war that they can neither win nor abandon, '300' and 'Shooter' feel like the products of a culture slowly and painfully going mad."[123] Comparable phenomena occurred in Nazi propaganda films. Their "protagonists . . . unwaveringly and in full realization of the danger that threatens them persist in the conduct of their political activities, put their lives at risk, and so can plainly be regarded as political martyrs." The main purpose of such films is "the propagation of a fundamental attitude that is as ruthless and reckless towards oneself as it is against others."[124]

A sequel to *300* was released in 2014: Noam Murro's *300: Rise of an Empire*, co-written by Snyder and based on Miller's unpublished graphic novel *Xerxes*. This time it is the Athenian Themistocles who takes on the Persians, notwithstanding Leonidas' dismissive characterization of the Athenians in *300* as "those philosophers and boy-lovers." Translation: *Those cultural sophisticates are all talk and no action, and they are sissies to boot, not real men like us Spartans.* Leonidas and his screenwriters were forgetting that pederasty was an integral part of Spartan culture. It has been

---

[122] Richards 2008: 184–185. Cf. Stevens 2007: "If *300* . . . had been made in Germany in the mid-1930s, it would be studied today alongside *The Eternal Jew* as a textbook example of how race-baiting fantasy and nationalist myth can serve as an incitement to total war."

[123] Denby 2007: 89.   [124] The two quotations are taken from Loiperdinger 1991b: 159.

credited as a Dorian and Spartan import into Greek civilization since the nineteenth century.[125] But why worry about illogic or inconsistency when big box-office bucks are the only thing that count?

We can now revisit the question I raised earlier: Is *300* worth such a lengthy analysis as "a megalomaniacal, death-hungry, fight-to-the-last-man production," to quote the verdict about *Kolberg* already adduced? Here is one kind of answer, provided by Zack Snyder himself:

> You know, when ... I see someone use words like "neocon," "homophobic," "homoerotic" or "racist" in their review, I kind of just think they don't get the movie and don't understand. It's a graphic novel movie about a bunch of guys that are stomping the snot out of each other. As soon as you start to frame it like that, it becomes clear that you've missed the point entirely.[126]

Have we? If we remember Eco's reason for speaking about Ur-Fascism to American teenagers and Romm's words about the seductive power of Fascism long after its political-historical demise, as witnessed by neo-Nazis, Skinheads, and various others, most of them teenagers, then the answer is obvious – not least when an academically credentialed authority on Greek history and culture exemplifies what Eco and Romm had in mind. Fascinating Fascism and fuzzy Ur-Fascism seem to be ineradicable, even though the narrator proclaims near the end of *300*: "This day we rescue a world from mysticism and tyranny and usher in a future brighter than anything we can imagine." (He is not thinking of *Watchmen*, is he?) Rescue from mysticism? Hardly.

But enough of my stomping the snot out of *300*. I give the last word to William Faulkner. *Requiem for a Nun* (1950) contains one of the most famous lines in American literature. It is this: "The past is never dead. It's not even past."[127]

---

[125] Bethe 1907 is a classic statement. See further Dover 1989: 185–196.
[126] Quoted from Weiland 2007.   [127] Quoted from Faulkner 1994: 535.

8 | Good Nero; or, The Best Intentions

Julius Caesar may be the most famous Roman, but who might be the most infamous? One Roman emperor will probably come to most people's minds immediately: Nero! Even more than Caligula or Commodus, Nero is the baddest of them all. Everybody knows that he set fire to his city, fiddled while Rome burned, and then persecuted the innocent Christians as scapegoats. He was a sexual deviant and mad megalomaniac who deserved to be overthrown. So, at least, one might summarize Nero's reputation. But was he really that bad?

Late Roman historians mentioned, rather vaguely, that Nero had begun as a good emperor and had had a period of five years, a *quinquennium*, of good rule, presumably under the guidance of his tutor, the philosopher-statesman Seneca. Emperor Trajan was supposed to have considered the young emperor the equal of Augustus during that period. But whether there was such a continuous *quinquennium* and, if so, when it occurred are unanswered questions.[1] We may safely assume that this nebulous or legendary period never happened. But it tells us that occasionally, and since antiquity, Nero could be regarded as a good guy, at least in part. Then, in the sixteenth century, there came something else.

In 1562 the Italian physician, mathematician, and philosopher (among other things) Girolamo Cardano published his *Encomium Neronis*, a speech in defense of Nero as if delivered during a court trial of the emperor. Cardano dismisses the familiar charges against Nero as baseless and argues for his "client's" innocence on all counts. Was Cardano serious? False, because ironic, encomia have a long tradition in humanist and Renaissance literature, including, most famously before Cardano, Erasmus' *The Praise of Folly* (*Encomium Moriae* or *Laus Stultitiae*) and, after Cardano, Daniel Heinsius' encomia to the flea and to the ass (*Laus Pediculi, Laus Asini*).

---

[1] On the *quinquennium* see Aurelius Victor, *Liber de Caesaribus* ("Book on the Caesars") 5. 1–2, and the anonymous *Epitome de Caesaribus* ("Epitome on the Caesars") 5.1–3; translated in Barrett, Fantham, and Yardley 2016: 23–24. Both works are from the fourth century. Barrett, Fantham, and Yardley: 289 list the relevant scholarship on the elusive *quinquennium*.

The Praise of Folly, the greatest of these, can be read on two levels: Folly, personified, gives a speech in her own defense and makes many obviously correct points in her favor while simultaneously being exposed as wrong overall. May the same be said about Cardano's encomium to Nero?[2] Readers may have to decide for themselves.

1   In Praise of Nero

Cardano's astonishing instance of counter-historiography, as we may call it, has left various traces in the story and history of Nero's reputation across the centuries. As late as 1975, for instance, Louis Alexis, a teacher at the Sevenoaks School, Kent, self-published a volume of commentaries on selected passages of Silius Italicus, Statius, and Valerius Flaccus, epic poets writing under the Flavian emperors who followed on the Julio-Claudian dynasty after the Civil War of AD 68–69. Alexis's book, which comprises a little over a hundred pages, is titled *School of Nero* to indicate the literary and cultural origins of his authors. This seems innocuous enough; the beginning of the book's explanatory subtitle, however, is something entirely different: *Europe's first Christian ruler identified.*[3] Is Alexis implying or, rather, stating directly that Nero became a Christian – that, like Saul turning into Paul, the persecutor of Christians became their follower and patron? So he is. A contemporary reviewer of Alexis's book helpfully – and vividly – explains how this astonishing circumstance is supposed to have come about:

Using such 'evidence' as the Palermo mosaic to 'prove' that Nero delighted in St. Paul's teaching (and therefore St. Paul converted Nero to Christianity), A. [Alexis] goes on to believe that the *aurea domus* [Nero's palace, the Golden House] was the first Christian Church of Rome, that Nero died A.D. 110 – his death A.D. 68 is 'patently transferred material from his stage-life, or perhaps a Mithraic ordeal' – that Tac. *Ann.* 14.22 describes Nero's baptism ... [and] that Statius 'owed to Nero his secret conversion to Christianity'.[4]

---

[2] Eberl 1994 and Cardano 1998 are modern editions, with translation and commentary.
[3] Alexis 1975.
[4] Usher 1977: 281. A line drawing of the twelfth-century mosaic in the Capella Palatina, Palermo, showing St. Paul, St. Peter, and Simon Magus before Nero appears in Alexis's book. Tacitus, *Annals* 14.22.4, reports that Nero once went swimming in the basin of the Aqua Marcia and fell ill as a result of defiling and drinking from the sacred waters. – If Alexis's view of Nero beggars belief, other statements, e.g. on Hannibal and Oedipus, are even more "far out," as we might say colloquially; in the case of Statius' Tisiphone literally so! See the summary by Usher: 281 (beginning of paragraph quoted here).

Small wonder that Alexis begins his "Introduction," after a quotation from
Calpurnius Siculus as epigraph, with one from Cardano on Nero as "the
best of princes." The introduction carries the title "Saint Nero."[5] This is
a nod to the 1962 book of the same title, in French, by Jean-Charles Pichon,
from which Alexis appears to have taken his inspiration.[6] Pious Christians
could eventually turn even Pontius Pilate, Roman Christ killer *extraordi-
naire*, into a Christian saint.[7] Why, then, should we not have a St. Nero?
We may wonder if Alexis, and before him Pichon, did not fall victim to the
mindset summarized in Tertullian's well-known phrase *credo quia absurdum*, which can be paraphrased thus: *I believe it for the very reason that it
makes no sense whatever.*[8]

The preceding is intended to put my discussion of a particular, and
particularly remarkable, film about Nero in a wider perspective. This film
is by no means a milestone in the history of cinema or, rather, of
television. But it is noteworthy for its plot strategy to make Nero an
appealing character, although director and screenwriters do not go quite
as far as Cardano, Pichon, or Alexis. They do, however, go as far as is
possible in a modern mass medium to absolve Nero from blame for
various murders, the fire of Rome, and the persecution of Christians.
Their chief impulse seems to have been the realization that, to interest
viewers in what has by now become a hoary topic familiar from various
famous big-screen epics about this emperor, they have to present him
from an unexpected point of view. Their maxim: Make it new! In this
they were far from the first. Two remarkable television films about the
life of Jesus may have shown them the way: Franco Rossi's Italian
A Child Called Jesus (1987) and, in the US, Kevin Connor's *Mary,
Mother of Jesus* (1999). The titles of these films reveal their narrative
strategies: The miracles and passion of Jesus are presented from his
own perspective as a little boy and from his mother's. Neither the
young Jesus nor Mary, of course, are the focus of the films' plots.
Their main emphasis is exactly on what we expect to see in any story
or film about Jesus.

---

[5] Alexis 1975: 1–8 ("Introduction: Saint Nero"); quotations at 1. See further Alexis: 106 and 112
("Addenda, Corrigenda") and 107 ("Parerga and Paralipomena") concerning the introduction.
Alexis's translations of Calpurnius and Cardano are rather free.

[6] Pichon 1962; rev. ed. (cited by Alexis: 107): Pichon 1971.

[7] On Pilate see, e.g., Bond 1998 and Wroe 1999 (rev. ed. 2001). The title of Wroe's Chapter 3
("God's Secret Agent") and her book's alternate title (*Pontius Pilate: The Biography of an
Invented Man*) are telling.

[8] We have encountered this saying in Chapter 5.

2 Good Boy!

Imperium, a series of British-Italian television epics, began to be shown in 2003. Its first installment was a film about Augustus. Later additions were *St. Peter* (2005), *Pompeii* (2006), and *Augustine: The Decline of the Roman Empire* (2010). The second installment was *Nero* (2004). *Nero* was produced in Italy and filmed in Tunisia. Its British director, Paul Marcus, had been a director and producer on the highly regarded crime series *Prime Suspect* (1991–1996) and would later return to ancient Rome in the juvenile-adventure series *Roman Mysteries* (2007–2008). One of his two screenwriters on *Nero* had worked on *Prime Suspect*, the other was an Italian television writer. Scottish actor Hans Matheson was Nero; he would later have smaller parts in *Clash of the Titans* (2010) and *300: Rise of an Empire* (2014). Experienced German actor Matthias Habich played Nero's tutor, the Stoic philosopher Seneca. Most felicitously, Italian Laura Morante was Nero's mother Agrippina.

Like all *Imperium* films, *Nero* was intended for an international European and American market. As such, it fits in with what audiences of historical or biblical spectacles expect, but with a twist. The film presents once again the tired stereotypes that everybody mistakes for historical fact: the Manichaean opposition of, on the one hand, evil pagan Romans and their mad and bad emperors, in this case Caligula, and, on the other hand, the noble and long-suffering minority of the early Christians, who could redeem a world sunk into a morass of sex, violence, and vice if only that world would let them. Eventually, as we know from the common stereotypes about Roman and later European history, triumphant Christianity will do just that.

Readers of Cardano, Pichon, and Alexis will not be overly surprised at the portrayal of Nero in this film. There is even a precursor in modern fiction – an originally good Nero who turns monstrous – in Ernst Eckstein's *Nero: A Romance* of 1889 (German original of the same year: *Nero: Ein Roman*). As a revival of the rhetorical and ideological perspectives that Cardano and the others exemplify, the film's Nero is worth our attention. Once again, very little history makes it into the brazen fantasy that is this *Nero*.[9] The arc of the

---

[9] To avoid clutter, I will refrain from citing, every time, the ancient sources from which the film deviates. The chief authors and passages on Nero are these: Tacitus, *Annals* 12–16; Suetonius, *Nero*; Dio Cassius, *Epitome of Roman History* 61–63. Nero in ancient Christian texts is another matter. The following are among the most useful examples of standard modern scholarship in English, all with extensive references: Warmington 1969; Miriam T. Griffin 2001; Champlin 2003; Buckley and Dinter 2013. Miriam Griffin 2013 surveys Nero's rehabilitation in recent scholarship. Barrett, Fantham, and Yardley 2016 collect and comment on the ancient source texts (in translation). A good starting point concerning Nero's "afterlife" is Elsner and Masters 1994.

film's plot is constructed with the tight logic of almost eschatological fervor and precision. In any such endeavor, of course, facts that are inconvenient to the film's narrative strategy have to be distorted or omitted.

It all begins when a seven- or eight-year-old Nero is an eyewitness to the brutal assassination of his father (not so) by mad emperor Caligula's hench-man whom we will later recognize as Tigellinus (not so). Sadistic Caligula even threatens to kill young Nero before his mother Agrippina's eyes (not so). For ten years Nero grows up in low-class but idyllic surroundings. His tutor Apollonius and Apollonius' daughter Acte (not so), both slaves, have Christian leanings; Acte becomes Nero's one and only true love (not so).[10] Nero can quote Homer and learns to play the lyre. He also protects the poor. Although he cannot understand Apollonius' attitude of Christian charity and equal rights, Nero is already on the right path to potential greatness: "All men must be treated with respect." In good modern fashion he is also aware of human freedom, the social injustices resulting from class distinctions, and the plight of the poor. "The world is what Rome makes it, what the emperor makes it," Nero tells Acte. Recalled to court after Caligula's assassination and Claudius' ascension to the throne, Nero gives up his dream of traveling around Greece with Acte as a performing artist. He intends to follow his social conscience and to protect Agrippina, who, recalled from exile as well, is beginning to play a dangerous game in court. During her exile Agrippina has received a vision about Nero becoming emperor, but at a price: "My life? Is that all?" Her question about who her killer will be remains unanswered. This is loosely patterned on Tacitus' report that Chaldaean soothsayers had once given Agrippina such a prophecy but had added that it would be Nero himself who would kill her. Her defiant reply had been: "Let him kill me as long as he becomes emperor."[11]

Accordingly, Agrippina is now scheming to put Nero on the throne. She engages Seneca as Nero's tutor to "create the ideal emperor," as Seneca himself puts it. In history and in this film, Nero is a most promising pupil: "If there is a way to create an empire that is just and merciful, I want to play my part," he vows. Still, he is willing to give up everything just to be with

[10] Acte, freedwoman of Claudius and lover of Nero, has exercised the imagination through tantalizingly brief and erotically charged (Agrippina, Poppaea) mentions in ancient sources, mainly Tacitus, *Annals* 13.12.1–13.2 and 46, 14.2.1 and 63.3; Suetonius, *Nero* 28.1 and 50; Dio Cassius, *Epitome of Roman History* 61.7.1. On her see Mastino and Ruggeri 1995. Notable appearances of Acte in modern fiction are in Sienkiewicz's *Quo Vadis?* (1896) and Eckstein's *Nero*, Alexandre Dumas's *Acte* (1838), and Hugh Westbury's *Acte* (1896).

[11] Tacitus, *Annals* 14.9.3; her pithy words in Latin: *occidat dum imperet*. On Agrippina the Younger, as she is generally called, see Barrett 1996a (= 1996b) and Ginsburg 2006. See further McHugh 2013.

Acte, whom he has promised to marry. Agrippina contrives to separate them.

Agrippina betrays Claudius' wife Messalina to her husband (not so), who finds her (not so) in the process of marrying her lover Silius and has them both assassinated by Tigellinus (not so). Agrippina can then marry Claudius herself and become empress. That Agrippina was married to Passienus Crispus is conveniently passed over. Agrippina has Claudius adopt Nero as his son. During her wedding, Claudius' own son Britannicus, who is here several years older than the historical Britannicus, mysteriously collapses. This is an echo of Tacitus' report that Agrippina was trying to pass Britannicus off as epileptic, mentally retarded, and thus unsuitable for empire.[12]

3 Not Wisely and Not Too Well

In his first speech before Claudius and the senate, Nero calls for tax reform and refers to Troy, Aeneas, and Julius Caesar. "It's a magnificent beginning," observes Seneca, who seems to be easily impressed. Agrippina meanwhile becomes ever bolder. To her, power means safety. She wants Nero to marry Octavia, the daughter of Claudius and Messalina. Octavia is as sweet and innocent as Acte and even resembles her physically. Out of concern for his mother, Nero obeys. "When it's safe, I'll repudiate her," he tells Acte, to whom he explains his marriage on his wedding night. Octavia, Nero, and Acte all remain virginal. In view of the film's highly Christian message, the absence of virtually all nudity and sex is unremarkable. Only a very brief moment later will show us, most discreetly, Nero and Acte making love. Nothing racy, of course, is on display. Although pre- or extra-marital sex is not condoned in Christian ethics, we are encouraged to regard the couple's sex as an expression of their true love. We also know that the lovers are already planning to get married. Acte, of course, does not become pregnant.

Agrippina has coins struck with her profile on them (not so). The purpose of her outrageous action, she explains to Claudius, who has returned from campaigning in Britain, is to give the Romans "someone to hate" and to deflect popular dissatisfaction from him: "Dear old Claudius, at least he's not as bad as that witch," she says, assuming to speak with the *vox populi*, the voice of the people. The noun that viewers

[12] Tacitus, *Annals* 12.26.2 and 13.16.3.

may have expected from her mouth instead of the last one quoted was apparently deemed unsuitable for family audiences. Claudius is impressed and a bit intimidated by her but informs her that he has designated Britannicus, not Nero, to succeed him (not so). Claudius promptly dies of mushroom poisoning, and Seneca announces Nero's accession before the senate and people (not so).

The three-hour film is now almost exactly half over. So far we have seen virtually nothing about Nero that is bad. We have followed his development from traumatized but promising youngster to noble senator and on to emperor-designate with the best intentions. *Optimus princeps* – what Pliny the Younger was famously to call Emperor Trajan in the second century and what Cardano would call Nero in the sixteenth seems to lie ahead for the film's Nero in its second half: the "best of emperors" bringing about a perfect Rome. But that is not quite what is in store, for the film cannot simply ignore all of Nero's bad deeds or turn them into their opposite. Still, this Nero remains as virtuous as one could reasonably pass him off to the unsuspecting who have not read their Tacitus or Suetonius or who do not remember the history lessons of their school days. How then do writers and director proceed?

Nero tells Octavia, who sincerely loves him, that he does not love her. Out of concern for her, Nero has their marriage annulled. Octavia, who has never slept with Nero (not so), publicly states (not so) that she is infertile and agrees to be out of the picture. Tacitus reports that Octavia's infertility was Nero's own charge to dismiss her and to marry Poppaea.[13] The latter has not yet made any important contribution to the film's plot. Nero publicly proclaims his future wedding to Acte at the conclusion of the first Neronia. The historical Nero instituted this festival only in A D 60 after six years' rule; the poet Lucan won a prize for an encomium of the emperor, the *Laudes Neronis*. During the games held at the festival Nero, abhorring bloodshed, saves the lives of defeated gladiators and determines that the Neronia will consist of artistic contests and bloodless games only.

Agrippina is not amused, chiefly about Nero and Acte. But then Nero repeats his call for fair taxation in the senate. Now, for the first time, he shows a negative side to his character, albeit in a good cause. When his proposal fails to carry, Nero imposes his will by fiat and threatens to expose corruption in the senate. Here viewers steeped in Hollywood populism may be reminded of the cinema of Frank Capra. Just as Mr. Smith comes to Washington and deals with a corrupt senate, so here Mr. Nero comes to

[13] Tacitus, *Annals* 14.60.1.

Rome and takes on a comparable kind of political machine. But Nero is too
clueless to forestall or even to foresee the senators' next move. A conspiracy
is brewing. Agrippina is a smarter politician than Nero and finds out.
"The emperor has no spies – I do," she tells two of the main conspirators,
who are understandably taken by surprise when they see her barge in on
their secret meeting. Tigellinus is present, too. He informs Nero that his
mother had met with the conspirators, and Nero banishes her from his
court (not so). This is not what a good son should do to his mother,
especially if we remember how concerned Nero has always been about
her. So Acte is made to justify Agrippina's exile to us. "You had to do it; you
had no choice," she consoles Nero, who still cares about his mom.

Agrippina now turns ferocious: "I have no son." Her trump card is
Claudius' last will, in which he declared Britannicus his heir over Nero
and which Agrippina had spirited away without revealing its contents.
(Not so, as we already know.) She informs Seneca, who in turn tells Nero
about the threat Britannicus poses to his rule. Nero, quoting lines from
Homer about the wrath of Achilles, becomes angry: "That witch! . . . Is she
insane?" This outburst is intended to prepare the way for Nero's turn to
evil – sort of. Britannicus is in bad health and, Seneca says, may die soon
"before he can harm us." In this way it is Seneca, not Nero, who brings up the
subject of Britannicus' death. "So I, the son of the divine Claudius, can
presume to assist the gods?" Nero asks, immediately grasping the implication. Now comes the turning point in the development of Nero's character.
"As a politician I can see no other way," Seneca says. The screen image,
usually rock-steady, begins to wobble as the consequences of Seneca's words
begin to sink in. These shots were done with a hand-held camera. "As a man
I could never do it," Seneca adds, a little too piously. An anguished Nero
asks: "So, to save my title, I must murder my brother?" Nero's sole purpose
has been to create a just and fair world for everybody. Here is a clear case of
an end being passed off as justifying the means: One life – Britannicus' – is to
be sacrificed to save many lives by preventing the senatorial conspiracy from
succeeding. "Is that it?" Nero adds. It is. Alone, Nero takes refuge to his lyre.

Octavia, reading an evil-intentioned and well-timed letter from Agrippina
about Nero's new wedding plans, commits suicide. Not so, but in this way
Nero remains entirely innocent of her death. Tacitus leaves little to the
imagination in his detailed and impassioned account of her harrowing
fate, and we can readily understand why Octavia's death had to be completely rewritten.[14] Even a toned-down version would make Nero a monster.

---

[14] Tacitus, *Annals* 14.59.3–64.

Ironically, no screenwriter looking for a blood-and-thunder episode about Roman decadence could possibly have invented what Tacitus reports as fact. The circumstances of Octavia's death have never been fully depicted on screen because they are too sordid and too violent. In the twenty-first century, when presumably such an atrocity could be shown, it was not – another irony.

Anguished over his sister's death, Britannicus publicly blames and insults Acte and wishes her and Nero dead (not so). This seals his fate. He dies in front of Nero and the assembled senators (not so). Neither those present nor the viewers yet know the reason. Britannicus' grandmother Domitia publicly blames Nero, and Acte demands the truth from him. Nero first swears that he did not know anything but then adds: "I didn't mean to. Everything I have done I have done for us." The truth is about to come out. Acte is horrified: "Don't put blood on my hands. How can I love an assassin? How can I love a liar?" These are the first strongly negative terms in which anyone has so far spoken of Nero. Shattered, Acte runs away and takes refuge among the Christians. Agrippina immediately avails herself of the opportune moment. She asks her son, rhetorically: "How could you believe I would ever really hurt you? You had to learn what it means to be an emperor ... Now you're ready – my son." She embraces him a little too passionately. An extreme close-up on their faces in profile, together with subdued lighting, makes them appear like lovers during an intimate moment (Figure 8.1). This alludes visually to the story of mother-son incest reported by Tacitus and Suetonius.[15] It could, of course, not have been made explicit. At the same time Agrippina dominates the screen, with Nero's face taking up only a quarter of the image, just as she has dominated him all along.

Nero soon realizes what is going on: "She suffocates me," he tells Seneca. American cinephiles may be reminded of other power-driven or over-powering mothers. The one who puts her son on a career path in politics in both versions of *The Manchurian Candidate* (1962, directed by John Frankenheimer; 2004, directed by Jonathan Demme) may come closest. In both films, remarkable actresses portrayed Mother (Angela Lansbury, Meryl Streep); in both, mother and son have comparable moments of intimacy, also in close-up (Figures 8.2 and 8.3). "When you smile, that's what I live for," mother tells son in the remake. Two other quotations from this version are apropos in our context: "'What happened?' – 'Mother

---

[15] Tacitus, *Annals* 14.2.3; Suetonius, *Nero* 28.

Figure 8.1 Nero and Agrippina in Paul Marcus's *Nero*.

Figure 8.2 Mother and son in John Frankenheimer's *The Manchurian Candidate*.

happened.'" And: "It's not your fault. It's your mother." Sometimes a boy's best fiend is his mother (Figures 8.2 and 8.3).

"You must endure ills which have no remedy," Seneca next observes. He is, after all, a Stoic. No remedy? One is within reach to someone who is already

Figure 8.3 Mother and son in Jonathan Demme's *The Manchurian Candidate*.

on the slippery slope of assassination. "And *work* to fulfill your destiny," Seneca closes. We begin to understand better than Seneca or Tigellinus, who is also present (he has just that knack), what work lies ahead. But for the moment Nero is still dejected, seeing his chief obstacle in Agrippina: "How can we rebuild the empire with a harpy tearing at our backs?" He realizes that Agrippina is after absolute power: "as long as my mother draws breath, how can we aspire to anything? I wish she was dead!" The smirk on Tigellinus' face tells us that he understands only too well. Except for the very end, when he turns traitor to Nero, Tigellinus is nothing but the faithful henchman obeying his master's – any master's – voice. He leaves immediately and kills Agrippina (not so). Seneca, preserving an appearance of morality, urges Nero to call Tigellinus back, but Nero hesitates. His sin of matricide becomes a lesser evil: one of omission (to prevent it), not of commission (to order it). In this manner the death of Agrippina is more Tigellinus' than Nero's responsibility. The historical circumstances of her murder, like those of Octavia's, are such that no one could invent them without the risk of losing an audience's suspension of disbelief. They are also too gruesome not to turn anybody against Nero, so something far more mundane has to be invented instead.

The words Nero is given to utter make evident, not for the first time, that we are to anticipate Agrippina's fate and that she will get what she deserves. The screenwriters' invention of Agrippina's earlier vision about the future will now pay off. She had been shown her own violent death but without knowing who would be responsible for it. Now the imminent matricide is being presented as a necessity for reason of state. It is a variant on Britannicus' death, although a more justifiable one because Britannicus had been neither evil nor scheming. An Agrippina in ultimate power, we are led to believe, would never bring about the ideal world on which Nero is fixated. There is, however, another clever twist in all this. *I wish she was dead*: Is this meant seriously, or is it only an indication of momentary anger and frustration? Does Nero mean what he is saying? We may be reminded of King Henry II's apocryphal exclamation concerning Thomas Beckett: *Will no one rid me of this meddlesome* (or *turbulent*) *priest?* Did Henry mean it, or was it only a moment of exasperation? No one will ever know whether the four knights who murdered Beckett were reading the king's mind correctly or not, so Henry has to be given the benefit of the doubt. Much the same may be said about our Nero. In this way he does not plot against Agrippina and does not send a killer detail to finish her off when the plot fails. Tigellinus alone kills her, just as he had killed Nero's father, her first husband. Agrippina orders Tigellinus: "Strike the womb that bore him!" This detail comes from Tacitus.[16]

Nero is at first remorseful. When Acte refuses to leave the Christians and to return to him, Nero becomes lonely and isolated. "Nero is falling into darkness," comments Paul of Tarsus. As if to prove him right, Nero gives up on seeing Acte again and falls for sultry and sexy Poppaea. He orders the senate to participate in his wedding to Poppaea by engaging in mock-gladiatorial combat, only to alienate the senators even more. Seneca is not adroit enough to avoid being caught in the middle. Tigellinus denounces the most prominent senators and Seneca to Nero. Nero manages to find Acte and asks her for help. She tells him to give up his power if he wants to live with her: "You must abandon everything bought with death . . . Leave Nero behind." She has been calling him by his first name, Lucius. The word is related to the Latin root of the word for light and is meant to indicate the contrast between light and darkness, good and evil. But it is too late. While Nero marries Poppaea, Tigellinus and the Praetorians kill off the senatorial opposition. The massacre and the marriage ceremony are intercut in a faint echo of the famous slaughter-during-baptism sequence in Francis Ford Coppola's *The Godfather* (1972). Afterwards Nero threatens Seneca with death: "Why did you betray me?" "Why did you betray our work?" Seneca asks in return. He remembers their earlier noble intentions. Now comes

---

[16] Tacitus, *Annals* 14.3–8, provides a vivid account of the deteriorating relationship between Nero and Agrippina and the circumstances of her death. He reports that she called out to the centurion who was about to kill her: *ventrem feri* ("Strike my belly").

another crucial moment. "*Our* work," Nero replies emphatically, "is at an end. *Mine* is just beginning." He has irrevocably gone over to the dark side. About thirty minutes are left in the film. Nero must finally turn bad, but for two and a half hours we have observed him being mostly good.

Nero hands Seneca a dagger (not so) as a parting gift: "Resolve to die a Stoic." Seneca commits suicide, but not in the manner that has become famous. We see him slumped on the floor of the room where his last conversation with Nero had taken place. Apparently he had thrust Nero's dagger into his chest below his ribs. Again the film absolves Nero from guilt, since he leaves the decision to Seneca and offers him a noble way out rather than having him killed like the senators.

Soon Rome is burning, but the script offers no explanation for the fire, so Nero is not implicated at all. Nor does he look out over the burning city or play his beloved lyre while reciting Homer or his own verse. Such a moment is usually featured in Nero films to emphasize his insanity. Afterwards Nero announces his grandiose plans for the city: "Rome must be rebuilt to reflect its true glory." He reveals a wooden model to the senate: "And at the heart of it all, the *domus aurea*." In this way Nero's megalomania remains strictly architectural and subservient to a good cause, for, he adds, "Rome will be perfect." Now comes the necessary plot twist that sets up Nero's eventual downfall and his bad reputation ever after. He is advised that such an ambitious project may easily lead to rumors that will blame him for the fire. Ruthless Tigellinus proposes the clever strategy of launching a pre-emptive counter-rumor: "Fight fire with fire." The brazen imagery is intentional. This may be the verbally smartest moment in the screenplay. Poppaea adds a helpful suggestion: "Some people mistrust the Christians." Their persecution begins. But again Nero is absolved from responsibility since it was all someone else's fault. Once again he is guilty of omission (to prevent the Christians' fate) but not of commission (to order it).

Nero has his own head put on the statue of the sun god and gives a public performance – all in accord with the historical record because it is harmless. Poppaea, now pregnant, crowns him with a golden wreath and suddenly collapses. No, Nero has not kicked her in the stomach. Paul of Tarsus has the reputation of bringing the dead back to life; we have seen his prayer to save a little girl being answered just after the fire. Paul is summoned but tells Nero that only God has power over life and death. Nero promises to worship Paul's god if Poppaea survives but threatens the Christians if their god does not intervene: "There will be suffering beyond your imagination." This may strike us as extreme, but it is also meant to be understandable since these words are coming from someone in utter anguish over the lives of his wife and unborn child. Now Paul, a former persecutor of Christians himself, realizes, somewhat implausibly, that divine Providence may be at work here: "It was *you* the Lord sent me to save," he tells Nero. If so, the Lord moves in mysterious ways, for Paul and the Christians are condemned to death. With one brief exception, none of their agonies are shown on screen. Had they been, Nero could no longer remain fundamentally good to modern viewers. This is in strong contrast to such classic films as Cecil B. DeMille's *The Sign of the Cross* (1932) and Mervyn LeRoy's *Quo Vadis* (1951), both of which contained extensive sequences of the Christian martyrs' suffering and death. The arena scene in *The Sign of the Cross* is unsurpassed in its gruesomeness even today.

4   Christian Forgiveness

Nero, seated on his golden throne and playing his golden lyre, receives a surprise visit from Acte, whom Paul had baptized a little earlier. She pleads for the lives of the Christians: "You can begin again. No one is beyond redemption. No one." Obvious foreshadowing is intentional. But Nero baulks ("You would betray me again") and sentences her "to freedom and to life" rather than to the arena. True love triumphs, sort of. Evidently Nero is still not wholly bad; at least up to a point, he is Acte's Lucius even now. That his judgment on her is meant to be understood as an indication of inherent goodness becomes clear a moment later. He takes up the lyre again but, unable to play, smashes it. By this time, we understand, his artistic career is over.

The end follows quickly. Acte sees the cross-shaped torches of the dying Christians from afar. Then a text on the screen tells us that it is four years later. A revolt against Nero apparently has been growing, and Tigellinus, finally turned traitor, hands over the city of Rome to General Galba (not so). Tigellinus then comes for Nero as he had come for Nero's father and mother, but Nero is wandering around the Subura. The people pelt him with vegetables. Out in the country Nero throws his crown into a river, presumably the Tiber, and sits down at its edge. He cuts his wrists. This kind of suicide is in obvious contradiction to all our sources. But it is necessary for the fiction we have been following. Nero, it appears, is redeeming himself. The manner of his death here is a vague echo of the way the historical Seneca killed himself. So, dying almost like his former friend and tutor, Nero atones for whatever evil he may have caused. We are to feel sorry for him. Acte promptly finds him. "Acte, forgive me," Nero begs her. Of course she does: "We are all forgiven." Christian charity triumphs. This Nero is anything but a monster, much less the Antichrist that the prologue to *Quo Vadis* had called him. And, no longer an artist, Nero is not allowed his famous last words, which might have sounded strange or ridiculous to modern audiences and certainly to viewers of this film.

Acte has lit a simple pyre on which Nero's body is cremated and, in voice-over, tells us the film's overall message: "Nero had a dream of Rome. A dream of a better world. He did not start the fire, but the fire in his soul consumed him. Let us forgive him as we hope to be forgiven." The film's very last shot is a close-up on the setting sun. Fade-out; end credits.

This ending is rather facile, saccharinely pious, and quite bathetic. At the same time it is effective for all those viewers who understand that this film tells a tragic tale: that of star-crossed lovers or of a man who loved not wisely but too well – or rather, whom circumstances (beginning with Caligula) and evil schemers (Agrippina, Tigellinus) prevented from realizing his innate nobility. Unless we know our history much better, we will forgive Nero his trespasses just as we hope to be forgiven our own. This is why Acte plays such a major part in this film. She is mentioned in historical sources only in passing as a discarded mistress of Nero. She may have been a Christian, but there is no evidence. The Acte of *Quo Vadis* was an abandoned lover of Nero's and a Christian and remained dedicated to him in rather a masochistic manner. She even assisted him in his suicide. All that was invention. But the Acte of *Quo Vadis* did not come close to having the importance that Acte has in our film. Here she is intended to be the bridge between the pagan past and the Christian present. For this reason we see much of Nero's story as if with her eyes. German actress Rike Schmid is as cute and pure as such women must be, even if she is not in the same league as other incarnations of Christianity like Elissa Landi's Mercia in *The Sign of the Cross* or Deborah Kerr's Lygia in *Quo Vadis*.

To understand, with Acte, all about *this* Nero is to forgive all. Moreover, it is to forget all of what we have previously heard, read, seen, or been told about Nero. It is unlikely that the screenwriters of our film consulted Cardano or any other apologists of Nero when they concocted their plot. First viewers do not anticipate the twists by which a well-known monster is being turned into a saint – almost. But Cardano's perspective in his *Elogium Neronis* fits this *elogium Neronis cinematographicum*. Here is one representative passage from early in the work:

It is not appropriate that we should condemn Nero for his savagery, for the fact that he killed many, but only if he killed them unjustly or without cause. There is no clearer case of mere slander than when someone is charged with a deed by itself but when its circumstances are not being considered. He may have killed his father, mother, sons, brothers, wife – you are simply not making a case because you are not showing that he killed without cause. He could have killed without intending to, or forced by a just cause, or having been deceived: none of these situations should condemn him.[17]

Extenuating circumstances: If you can explain Nero's crimes and vices to your satisfaction, you can reach a better understanding of what he did. You can even turn a notorious bad guy's reputation around by presenting his life as a romantic-tragic melodrama of a perfect love that was not to be. O cruel Fates! Nero's fault, dear viewers, is in his stars, not in himself. This *Nero* is almost a "weepie," with the added advantage that it parades plenty of bad characters before us – just not the titular one – and sells us edifying pieties and platitudes. The latter circumstance explains why the film is far too talky to succeed as a visual or action spectacle.

There is, of course, no moral imperative for novelists, filmmakers, or any creative artists to adhere to historical facts; these can be ignored or changed at will. *Nero* may well be one of the prime examples in all of screen history of how this sort of thing can work. But in principle this is nothing new. It was not even new in Roman history. Ancient sources tell us that some years after Nero's death in AD 68 no fewer than three false Neros appeared on the scene and even found a measure of popularity among those willing to believe in the emperor's return.[18] Still, it is astonishing that two of the four historical advisors named in our film's final credits are respected and widely published scholars at major Italian universities. One of them, named first, is Andrea Giardina, co-author of a useful book on myths about Rome, including cinematic myths.[19] Presumably the two shared the common fate of such advisors: that their information went largely unheeded.[20]

---

[17] The text is taken from a posthumous edition: *Hier. Cardani Neronis Encomium* (Amsterdam, 1640): 5.

[18] Tacitus, *Histories* 2.8; Suetonius, *Nero* 57; Dio Cassius, *Epitome of Roman History* 64.7.3 and 66.19.3.

[19] Giardina and Vauchez 2000.

[20] This is a familiar phenomenon. Two well-known instances involve Ridley Scott's *Gladiator* (2000) and the television series *Rome* (2005, 2007). On these see the reports by Coleman 2004 and Milnor 2008.

PART V

Aesthetic Affinities

Portraits of Ladies

Italian writer-director Franco Rossi (1919–2000) adapted two of the three most influential classical epics, the *Odyssey* and the *Aeneid*, to the screen. Both films are little known internationally, but they provide us with unforgettable portrayals of some of the most fascinating women to be encountered in ancient epic.

  Rossi's career had an auspicious beginning in the 1950s but declined to such an extent that his name tends to be neglected even in detailed histories of Italian cinema. Rossi eventually divided his time between the silver screen, for which he made a number of mainly commercial films, and the small screen of television. With the latter Rossi came into his artistic own. Between 1968 and 1987 he directed and co-wrote for Italy's public television network four epic films set in antiquity. The first was an *Odissea* ("Odyssey"), a nearly perfect adaptation of Homer.[1] He followed it with an *Eneide* ("Aeneid," 1971). In 1910, Italian director Luigi Maggi had based *Dido Forsaken by Aeneas* (*Didone abbandonata*) on the most famous part of the *Aeneid*.[2] Decades later, American bodybuilder-turned-actor Steve Reeves had played Aeneas in two Italian epics in 1961 and 1962: Giorgio Ferroni's *La guerra di Troia* – variously called in English *The Trojan Horse*, *The Wooden Horse of Troy*, and *The Trojan War* – and Giorgio Rivalta's *La leggenda di Enea* (*The Avenger* or *War of the Trojans*). Neither of the latter films qualifies as Virgilian in any meaningful sense of the term.[3] Nor does the young Aeneas who unexpectedly appears at the end of Wolfgang Petersen's *Troy* (2004). Lina Mangiacapre's film *Didone non è morta*

---

[1] I provide an initial appreciation of this film in Winkler 2010 and discuss its ending in Winkler 2009a: 295–296. See further Bozzato 2005 and Pomeroy 2008: 67–72. Rossi's film is discussed at length, with illustrations, in Tim Lucas 2007: 762–775. Mario Bava, the subject of Lucas's book, directed the Polyphemus episode and did the optical tricks. Lucas's appreciation of the film is marred by elementary but easily detectable mistakes concerning antiquity.

[2] Aubert 2009: 230–231 has filmographic details. See further Antonucci 1984 on this and other silent films, primarily taken from Dante's *Divine Comedy* and showing Virgil as Dante's guide. Brief comments also in Eloy 1990.

[3] On these and a few other films that take up themes or characters from the *Aeneid*, including Maggi's and Rossi's, see Redonet 2003. Andrianova 2015 examines the Ukrainian burlesque *Eneïda* by Ivan Kotliarevskyi (1798, published 1842) and its animated film version (1991) by Volodymyr Dakhno – Virgil twice and thrice removed.

("Dido Is Not Dead," 1985) is a feminist retelling of Dido's story in combination with a modern one: Dido returns in the twentieth century.[4] Rossi's *Eneide* is therefore the only screen version of Virgil's epic ever made.[5] In 1985 Rossi directed the longest version of *Quo Vadis?* This by then hoary stalwart about pagan Rome and the first persecution of Christians under Nero had been filmed several times before.[6] The last of Rossi's ancient films was *A Child Called Jesus*. With the exception of this one, which runs to about three hours, Rossi's classical films are each about six hours long. Especially in the case of the first two, such length is the precondition for their artistic success, for adherence to the spirit of the original works requires a certain epic length, breadth, and depth, not least when the budget for the spectacular settings and large-scale action of the kind seen in gigantic Hollywood epics is outside a filmmaker's reach. Rather than turning the ancient epics into standard mythological cinema, which had been the case with, for instance, Mario Camerini's *Ulysses* (1954), Rossi and his screenwriters took pains to render Homer and Virgil in a way that does justice to the ancient works, if with some unavoidable differences and omissions. At least in their *Odissea*, these changes are rarely for the worse.

Homer's *Odyssey* is remarkable for its unforgettable gallery of women who, in different ways, interact with Odysseus. These include his divine protector Athena, who engineers his return home in the face of overwhelming odds. Below her in rank there are the immortal nymph Calypso, who loves Odysseus and offers him immortality, and the bewitching sorceress Circe, who also becomes his lover and gives him information crucial for his return. On the human level Odysseus' steadfast wife Penelope is the crowning glory among women. Other important mortals appear more briefly but are noteworthy as well. The most beautiful of them all, Helen, receives Odysseus' son Telemachus with her husband Menelaus in Sparta. On Scheria, the island of the Phaeacians, princess Nausicaa finds Odysseus on the beach and takes him to her parents' palace, where he receives help and hospitality. Nausicaa's mother, Queen Arete, is a formidable personage in her own right. And in a moving scene Odysseus encounters the shade of his mother in the Underworld. Any visual adaptation ought at least to attempt to do a measure of justice to this side of the *Odyssey*. Rossi's does. The most fascinating character portrayals in his film are presented on the following

---

[4] A plot summary and further information are available at http://www.queendido.org/malina.htm.

[5] For a charming curiosum see C. K. 1921. The initials stand for Charles Knapp, the editor of the *Classical Weekly*.

[6] Scodel and Bettenworth 2009 is a survey of the different versions.

pages, in ascending order of complexity. The final section of this chapter then turns to the most haunting female figure in Virgil's *Aeneid*. Rossi's characterization of Dido, queen of Carthage, deserves close attention, and not only because it is virtually unknown.

1 Romantic Nausicaa

As was Homer's, Rossi's Nausicaa is a fascinating embodiment of any young girl's experience with her first attraction to a man while she is about to change from a state of virginal innocence to that of adulthood. Nausicaa, the Homeric narrator reports, is shy even to broach the subject of marriage to her father.[7] To do justice to such a gently drawn character requires great sensitivity on a director's part and from the actress who performs this part. Nausicaa should be played as someone who is not wholly naïve or vulnerable, someone who is romantically inclined but not forward and certainly not eager to act on the longings whose beginnings may be stirring within her. Instead, a delicate balance between innocence and incipient experience is called for. Odysseus' gentlemanly treatment of her in the *Odyssey* evinces just such an awareness on his part. An actress and her director have to rise to a considerable challenge if they want to portray Homer's young princess, "a model of decorum and courtesy," in a convincing manner.[8] Rossi, it turns out, was up to the task. So was his actress.[9]

Nausicaa's first appearance is a telling instance of Rossi's visual sophistication and the irresistible attraction that Rossi manages to exert on the mind and senses of attentive viewers throughout most of his long film. In Book 6 of the *Odyssey*, a huge storm has driven Odysseus to the shore of an unknown island. He has barely saved his skin and is in dire need of help. Athena engineers Nausicaa's discovery of him in order to ensure him a hospitable reception at the Phaeacians' court. Athena appears to Nausicaa in a dream. She urges her to do her wash on the beach the next morning. There Nausicaa is to discover Odysseus. This is the divine plan, and here is how Athena sets it in motion:

---

[7] Homer, *Odyssey* 6.66–67.   [8] Quoted from Hainsworth 1988: 291 (in Introduction to Book 6).

[9] Two years before she took on the title part in Robert Wise's *Helen of Troy* (1956), young Italian actress Rossana Podestà had been Nausicaa in Camerini's colorful spectacle. Podestà acquitted herself well enough, but her part was rather one-dimensional. And she was overshadowed – no fault of hers – by Silvana Mangano, who played both Circe the temptress and faithful Penelope. We will meet Podestà as Helen in Chapter 10.

> It was to his [King Alcinous'] house that the grey-eyed goddess Athene
> went, devising the homecoming of great-hearted Odysseus,
> and she went into the ornate chamber, in which a girl
> was sleeping, like the immortal goddesses for stature and beauty,
> Nausikaa . . .
> She drifted in like a breath of wind to where the girl slept,
> and came and stood above her head and spoke a word to her,
> likening herself to the daughter of Dymas, famed for seafaring,
> a girl of the same age, in whom her fancy delighted.[10]

Athena's supernatural epiphany receives one of the most memorable translations of a text passage into images. While the epic narrator, who guides us through Rossi's film, introduces the young girl, the camera conveys to us the manner in which Athena infuses herself into Nausicaa's subconscious. It seems to descend, godlike, from on high into Nausicaa's bedchamber, coming to rest on a close-up of her face. A long shot then shows us a sleeping Nausicaa from outside a diaphanous curtain that surrounds her bed. A lateral camera movement appears to express the divine visitor's stately walk around that bed. Another long shot reveals this visitor's human shape. We hear Athena's message in voice-over and see her silhouette as if from Nausicaa's perspective, for the camera is now on the inside of the curtain. Athena keeps walking outside. The camera and Athena, in profile, at first both circle Nausicaa's bed in tandem, with the girl's upper body predominating in the foreground. The effect is such that, intriguingly, the curtain appears to follow the goddess's movements. Very soon, even Nausicaa's bedstead seems to be moving as if animated. We are observing two visual planes in the image, a mortal and a supernatural dimension, that are kept separate but still express a spiritual harmony between them. Then, near the end of Athena's message, this visual synchronicity is abandoned, as if the goddess were distancing herself from the girl. Without a cut the camera moves into an extreme close-up on Nausicaa's face, which then virtually fills the screen. This movement tells us that Athena's words have reached the girl's unconscious mind.

   The scene, which lasts for no more than a minute and a half, is extraordinary. Its nocturnal lighting and the music, at first slightly eerie but then gentle and dreamy, convey a mysterious aura throughout. Nausicaa's dream state is conveyed by the apparent movement of her bed when the camera follows Athena. Rossi's camera movements look simple but are

---

[10] Homer, *Odyssey* 6.13–17 and 20–23; quoted from Lattimore 1967: 102. The Homeric narrator also mentions two other young women sleeping in the room.

quite intricate; it seems likely, or at least possible, that he used a rotating platform on his set. The *mise-en-scène* that we watch evidently required careful planning. It is one of many that evince what we may call Rossi's will to style, the most characteristic feature of all his films set in antiquity.

Homer's Nausicaa is clearly attracted to the handsome stranger she has brought home. Even when they are still on the beach she realizes his divinely enhanced handsomeness: "Athene gilded with grace his head and his shoulders" and made him appear "radiant in grace and good looks; and the girl admired him."[11] Later, after a bath in the palace, Odysseus joins the Phaeacians in the hall and again impresses her: Nausicaa "gazed upon Odysseus with all her eyes and admired him."[12] Rossi and his screenwriters took these descriptions as a cue for the way in which to show Nausicaa's first romantic attraction. As is appropriate for an unmarried young girl, the Homeric Nausicaa is not present when Odysseus tells his hosts about his perilous journey; she takes her farewell of him before he begins. Rossi's Nausicaa stays. On several occasions during Odysseus' tale, which we see in a series of flashbacks interrupted by interludes that return us to the Phaeacians' palace, Rossi shows Nausicaa looking directly at Odysseus, but from a distance. Her reason is obvious. Whereas Homer's Odysseus tells everything in the banquet hall, Rossi's is, on occasion, outside and alone with Nausicaa. For a while she becomes his sole listener. When he tells her about Calypso, he does not hide that he had an affair with her. This is not entirely in the spirit of Homer or his ancient listeners and readers, but it is fully in the modern spirit of an effective visual retelling. Nausicaa's infatuation with Odysseus becomes palpable when we see both of them in close proximity and in close-ups, as when a dreamy Nausicaa lowers her head on her arms while gazing up at Odysseus (Figure 9.1). She is enchanted and beguiled, just as Shakespeare's Desdemona would be by Othello's stories. As Othello puts it: "She loved me for the dangers I had passed." Although their respective stories diverge, Desdemona and Nausicaa are at least comparable in their initial virginal stage. What Brabantio says about Desdemona applies almost entirely to Nausicaa: "A maiden never bold, / Of spirit so still and quiet that her motion / Blushed at herself."[13] Rossi's Nausicaa is never bold, even when she briefly and gently touches Odysseus' hand with hers. At the end of this scene the camera slowly moves into a lingering close-up on her face. Her mien is one of melancholia, even sadness, and frustrated

---

[11] Homer, *Odyssey* 6.235 and 237; Lattimore 1967: 108.
[12] Homer, *Odyssey* 8.459; Lattimore 1967: 133 – a felicitous translation.
[13] William Shakespeare, *Othello* 1.3.168 and 95–97; quoted from Honigmann 2016: 149 and 145.

Figure 9.1 Odysseus and a romantically spellbound Nausicaa in Franco Rossi's *Odissea.*

hope. Nothing like this occurs in the *Odyssey*, but the scene well matches the character of Homer's Nausicaa.

American-born actress and fashion model Barbara Goldbach, billed as Barbara Gregorini after she married an Italian, was about twenty when she played Nausicaa. She comes closest to embodying Homer's *euôpis kourê*, "with the gods' loveliness on her."[14] This was her first screen appearance. As Barbara Bach she was to become internationally famous in 1977, when she was a Bond girl opposite Roger Moore in *The Spy Who Loved Me*. A few years later she became Mrs. Ringo Starr and an international celebrity and sex symbol. She even made it into, and onto the cover of, *Playboy* magazine. *Habent sua fata puellae Homericae cinematographicae.*[15]

---

[14] So Homer, *Odyssey* 6.113 and 142: "the well-favored young girl" or "the well-favored girl" (Lattimore 1967: 105 and 106) and 8.457 (Lattimore: 133). The adjective-noun combination from Book 6 occurs nowhere else in the *Odyssey*.

[15] Nausicaa's mother deserves an honorable mention, too. Rossi's Queen Arete was played by an elegant Marina Berti, better known internationally as Eunice, the beautiful slave girl passionately in love with her owner Petronius, in Mervyn LeRoy's *Quo Vadis* (1951). She later appeared, very briefly, as the hero's Roman girlfriend in William Wyler's *Ben-Hur: A Tale of the Christ* (1959). She had a number of leading roles and was equally at home in historical and biblical spectacles and other genres. Berti always added something by her very presence.

2   Baleful Helen

In Book 4 of the *Odyssey* Telemachus and Nestor's son Pisistratus visit
Menelaus in Sparta in search of information about Odysseus. They arrive
during a double wedding and receive Menelaus' generous hospitality.
Helen is first mentioned after Menelaus has summarized to Telemachus
his own sufferings in the wake of Troy's fall. He concludes:

> I wish I lived in my house with only a third part of all
> these goods, and that the men were alive who died in those days
> in wide Troy land far away from horse-pasturing Argos.
> Still and again lamenting all these men and sorrowing
> many a time when I am sitting here in our palace
> I will indulge my heart in sorrow, and then another time
> give over, for surfeit of gloomy lamentation comes quickly.
> But for none of all these, sorry as I am, do I grieve so much
> as for one, who makes hateful for me my food and my sleep, when I
> remember, since no one of the Achaians labored as much
> as Odysseus labored and achieved, and for him the end was
> grief for him, and for me sorrow that is never forgotten
> for his sake, how he is gone so long, and we knew nothing
> of whether he is alive or dead.[16]

Telemachus begins to weep and hides his face at the mention of his father.
Now Helen appears in the banquet hall, accompanied by her maidservants.
She recognizes Telemachus' similarity to Odysseus, and so does Menelaus.
Further remembrances of Odysseus and his uncertain fate cause everybody
to mourn and weep. Menelaus eventually exhorts all to rejoice again in
their meal, and Helen offers them wine mixed with a drug that temporarily
cures their cares and afflictions.

  In Rossi's adaptation of Book 4, an aura of suffering and death replaces
Homer's wedding festivities, which are entirely absent. Rossi and his
writers shift the focus from Menelaus to Helen, whom we see even before
we meet her husband. Somewhat unrealistically, Helen meets Telemachus
and Pisistratus upon their arrival outside Sparta, welcomes them, and takes
them to the royal palace. Before they reach the city, they speak of Odysseus.
The subdued atmosphere that characterizes the visitors' arrival outside
Sparta is reinforced by a funereal interior of the royal palace. Menelaus'
residence is nothing like his splendid palace in Homer but resembles
a tomb. The set is modeled on the inside of the Bronze-Age *tholos* at

---

[16] Homer, *Odyssey* 4.97–110; Lattimore 1967: 67–68.

Mycenae, often called the Treasury of Atreus or the Tomb of Agamemnon. In this chamber Menelaus is having his death mask modeled on his face, a visual reference to the famous Mask of Agamemnon that Heinrich Schliemann had discovered at Mycenae. Appropriately, dead Agamemnon's armor is visible in the background and will soon be called to Telemachus' and the viewers' attention. Although nobody weeps, a kind of behavior that ill suits modern sensibilities, Rossi still conveys to us with great empathy the somber nature of the aftermath of a war whose wounds have not healed. To prepare us for this sequence, the narrator had introduced Helen as *la donna funesta* ("the baleful [literally, 'funereal'] woman") when we first saw her. Presumably to underscore this side of her, this Helen is raven-haired, although the Helen of Greek myth was a blonde, and she is wearing a blood-red dress. Then, in the palace, Helen tells Telemachus about Odysseus' secret meeting with her in Troy, as she does in Homer. In a flashback to Troy, we see a much younger but already regal Helen, a woman who can hold her own even against the central hero in whose epic she appears.

In the flashback, too, the atmosphere is dark and stark. Young Helen is very beautiful. So she must be in order to be credible as the cause of the Trojan War. Even jaded viewers can believe that countless men had gone to death and slaughter over her. Both as younger and older woman Helen wears striking eye makeup. The Spartan Helen, with her hair pulled straight back behind her head, resembles female faces and heads in ancient Egyptian art (Figure 9.2). This makes for a startling appearance, one that fits the Egyptian background of Book 4 extremely well. Its longest section is Menelaus' account of his sojourn in Egypt on his return from Troy. Unlike the Helen in the *Iliad*, the one in the *Odyssey* had been to Egypt. Some of the objects brought into the banquet hall by Helen's maids are said to come from there, and so does the herb that Helen mixes into the wine.[17] The film's narrator specifically mentions this fact. Unobtrusively, Rossi alludes to the wider Homeric context of the scene here discussed.

In Rossi's *Odissea* we encounter a unique twentieth-century incarnation of Helen. She is played by Italian actress Scilla Gabel (originally Gianfranca Gabellini), then about thirty. (Cf. also Chapter 10.) She had for years appeared in a number of costume adventures with ancient and other set-tings. Only with her Helen did she finally come into her own as a serious actress. Since 1968, the year she played the part, she has been married to director Piero Schivazappa, who was Rossi's co-director on one of the eight

---

[17] Homer, *Odyssey* 4.125–135 and 227–232.

Figure 9.2 Helen in Franco Rossi's *Odissea*.

installments of the *Odissea*. Can it be that romance and marriage blossomed on the set?

3   Proud Penelope

Irene Papas has long been one of the foremost Greek stars of stage and screen, dedicated to preserving the legacy of ancient culture. In Andrey Konchalovsky's American television *Odyssey* (1997) Papas played Odysseus' mother Anticleia, but almost thirty years earlier she had been the screen's greatest Penelope in Rossi's *Odissea*. At that time Papas was in her early forties. Although about a decade older than the Odysseus of Yugoslav actor Bekim Fehmiu, she was exactly right to portray as complex a character as Penelope: a faithful and loving wife, a woman of mature sexuality, a caring mother, and a commanding if sorely beleaguered queen.

The two plot strands of the *Odyssey*, that of Odysseus' journey and that of Penelope's plight on Ithaca during his absence, converge after the hero's return and end with the reunion of husband and wife, the poem's emotional climax. Crucial for their reunion is Penelope's proud affirmation of her rank and dignity as Odysseus' wife and as queen of Ithaca. This occurs in Books 19 and 23 of the *Odyssey* and is maintained in Rossi's *Odissea*. The film's dialogue and Rossi's staging render Penelope's recognition and acknowledgment of Odysseus as two separate moments. In both Homer and Rossi the first private conversation between husband and wife after a separation of twenty years takes place in the presence of Odysseus' nurse Eurycleia, who will soon recognize him by his scar. Since Odysseus is disguised as a beggar and does not reveal his true identity to Penelope, Homer's listeners or readers may well have asked themselves: Does she or does she not recognize him? The Homeric text, while not obviously ambiguous, invites and has received intense speculation about the answer to this question. A scholar explains:

> Underlying our inherited *Odyssey* there were perhaps versions of the tale in which ... Penelope recognized Odysseus much earlier, perhaps by his scar, and in which husband and wife conspired together in the destruction of the suitors. Such alternative versions of the epics are often hypothesized by modern readers puzzled by an apparently awkward turn of the plot, an inconsistency in detail, or some other inconcinnity that is the natural result of the conflation, so common in truly oral traditions, of disparate tales.[18]

Today we should judge and interpret the *Odyssey* primarily in the form in which it has come down to us: as an independent and artistically coherent work of literary art.

In the wake of feminism, some scholars have argued that Penelope knows who the unidentified beggar is but does not reveal her knowledge.[19] Since Odysseus does not acknowledge his identity to her even after more than sufficient evidence that she has been completely faithful to him throughout his absence, she is equally justified not to come clean about recognizing him: "the text does not give us full access to Penelope's thoughts and feelings."[20] The husband-and-wife conversation in Book 19, then, is one of the most tantalizing passages in the history of classical literature: "a sequence of complex and puzzling statements and responses."[21] Two scholars writing together have proposed to distinguish between recognition and acknowledgment in both Odysseus' and Penelope's words:

> She almost certainly figures out who he is well before she actually acknowledges him ... The difficulty is that scholars incline to assume that recognition and

---

[18] Reece 1994: 157. See further Ready 2014.

[19] Scholarship on this matter is extensive; Russo 1992: 7–12 gives a sensible overview, with additional references. Heitman 2005: 87 goes as far as to wonder: "Could she even be preparing some deception of her own?" Perhaps not.

[20] Foley 1995: 97.   [21] Russo 1992: 7.

acknowledgement occur simultaneously: if not, then recognition has not occurred ... Characters in the *Odyssey*, as in real life, rarely reveal everything they know.[22]

Another scholar has suggested, ingeniously, that Homer is "deliberately avoiding too close a look at what Penelope might be thinking and scheming" and that Penelope is fully as clever as Odysseus. In this way she can convince Odysseus as well as Homer's listeners and readers that she is "the best wife for the best husband."[23]

Is then Penelope's announcement to the beggar that the very next day she will choose the winner in an archery contest as her new husband a sign of her suspicion, confidence, conviction, or knowledge that he is Odysseus? Why else would she end her delaying tactics *now*?[24] What does Penelope know, and how can readers be sure to know what she does or does not know? A modern commentator summarizes the scholarly debates:

Some modern interpreters of the *Odyssey* have found Penelope's behaviour in this book [Book 19] so hard to comprehend that they have adopted the daring hypothesis that she does in some sense recognise her husband here, contrary to the surface meaning of the text ... Critics differ on the question of how conscious this recognition is: according to some, she is fully aware of her husband's identity,

[22] Ahl and Roisman 1996: 37, 156, and 209; cf. 152–157, 224–228, and 234.
[23] John J. Winkler 1990: 129–161; quotations at 130 and 161. Cf. also John Winkler: 143 and 160–161.
[24] Ahl and Roisman 1996: 237: "After years of waiting, her haste now is puzzling. She is, in effect, forcing Odysseus' hand." Cf. Russo 1992: 7: "Penelope's decision to accept a likely remarriage in one day, after successfully stalling the suitors for so long, and while still having no clear evidence that her husband has returned or is about to, is without evident motivation in our text and has never been successfully explained ... Since Penelope's decision represents the key turning-point in the plot, the obscurity of its motivation deserves our full attention." Russo: 104–105 (on 19.572–581) surveys the main scholarly attempts at explanation. Russo: 7 firmly denies that Penelope recognizes Odysseus (a "dubious theory") and observes that "it is thoroughly alien to Homeric narrative habit to allow an event of this magnitude to pass without comment." But even Russo acknowledges that Penelope comes close to recognition, emotionally and intellectually: "it is her attraction to the stranger and her intuitive sense of his latent power that move her now to act in a way that accords perfectly with his prediction [of Odysseus' imminent return], even as her words say the opposite" (11). Compare – or contrast – Rutherford 1992: 33–38, with references at 34–35 notes 27 and 29. Rutherford rejects any possibility that Penelope recognizes the beggar although she becomes "steadily more open with him" (33) during their solitary colloquy. Cf. Steiner 2010: 35: "Where earlier readings faulted the queen for her inconsistency, her obtuseness and seemingly irrational behaviour (so like a woman ...), contemporary Penelopes range from a canny plotter, hoodwinker of those around her, to an unconscious puppet, the instrument of the divine and human figures who orchestrate her moves" (ellipsis in original). Steiner: 37 note 73 lists additional scholarly references on "Penelope's 'intuitive' recognition of Odysseus." Edith Hall 2013 examines feminist approaches to the *Odyssey*.

and matches his cleverness with a sophisticated game of double-bluff; others see her intuition as vaguer, even subconscious; she suspects, but is not yet certain.[25]

Viewers of Rossi's film who are familiar with Homeric scholarship may find to their surprise that Rossi and his writers anticipated the question of Penelope's knowledge well before feminist classicists turned to it.[26] During Odysseus and Penelope's encounter the night before the contest of the bow, Rossi's Penelope is probing deeply into the identity of the beggar hiding in the shadows (Figure 9.3). Rossi at first keeps the two firmly separated. For example, he puts one in the foreground and in the light, dim as it is, while keeping the other in the background and in darkness. He may show one in focus and the other as a blurred silhouette when they are both on screen. Or he keeps one off screen. Early, a right-to-left panning shot across the hall emphasizes the distance between Penelope and Odysseus. Later, close-ups predominate. As in Homer, the stranger reports that he knew Odysseus shortly before and during the war at Troy, and Penelope demands proof. He tells her about Odysseus' purple cloak, which she immediately recognizes. Now Odysseus' tale triggers an unexpected reaction in Penelope, which Rossi emphasizes through a startling zoom into an extreme close-up of her face. Zoom lenses had a much more powerful effect on viewers in the 1960s than they do now. The zoom also bridges the spatial distance between the two and diminishes their emotional distance, but only on Penelope's part. "Stranger, how do you know all this?" Penelope now asks and approaches him. She is almost certain about the beggar's identity: "But you are -" He interrupts her, lying about his identity. "But you are – Odysseus," she repeats, more hesitatingly. He lies again. While he tells her about his invented ancestry, she gently strokes his cheek. All the while

[25] Rutherford 1992: 34. He rightly dismisses the possibility of other (earlier, oral) versions of the story in which there *was* a recognition and subsequent collusion between Odysseus and Penelope about getting rid of her suitors: "if Odysseus does not reveal himself to his wife in our *Odyssey*, this is a part of our poem's coherent design" (35). And: "Despite the genuine difficulties of these lines, this interpretation should be vigorously rejected; it is a flagrant example of the critical tendency to assume that something more devious, ambiguous or disreputable must be more interesting and make better poetry than what is morally and poetically direct and simple" (37).

[26] The more regrettable it is, then, that Edith Hall 2013 has nothing at all to say about Rossi's Penelope. She is right to observe (170): "There are major flaws ... in the argument that the inbuilt sexism of the *Odyssey* gives the modern writer [and screenwriter] no choice but to make Penelope feeble." The complete absence of Rossi's *Odissea* and of any awareness about Irene Papas's performance as Penelope from the volume in which Hall's chapter appeared (Nikoloutsos 2013a) leaves a large gap, the more noticeable in that Papas's screen portrayals of Electra, Helen, Clytemnestra, and Anticleia are included. The book's dust jacket shows Papas as Clytemnestra with Clytemnestra's daughter Iphigenia in Michael Cacoyannis's *Iphigenia* (1977).

Figure 9.3 A probing Penelope in Franco Rossi's *Odissea*.

Odysseus stonily lies to her face, quite literally since she is directly in front of him, and denies the truth. "If you are Odysseus," she asks, "why do you lie to me like this?"

His cunning and coying to be strange will soon come to haunt him. He tells her evasively: "Your reputation, queen, is that you are a very strong and brave woman" (*una donna molto forte*). Penelope keeps her doubts about his statements, which we know to be false. She is left hurt and anguished, disappointed and sad, but also angry and proud, as another close-up on her almost defiant face from a slightly low angle reveals. She calls Eurycleia to Odysseus, looking at him from the background of the screen, and Odysseus, foreground left, turns his head away as if he could not bear to look her in the face. This shot reveals his uneasy conscience and his awareness that he is making her suffer. The effect is that viewers feel with her, even if the Homeric simile, which the film's narrator recounts, had at the beginning made clear Odysseus' own pain at deceiving her. He acts in a manner consistent with his characteristic, if not ubiquitous, circumspection. This quality justifies his most famous epithet *polytropos* ("of many turns," i.e. "clever"), which had described him in the very first line of the *Odyssey*. Moreover, Odysseus is heeding Agamemnon's warning, received in the Underworld, not to trust even his own wife and Athena's exhortation to test Penelope before trusting her – that is to say, not to reveal who he is until the exactly right moment has come – although Athena also assures Odysseus that Penelope is and has been faithful to him.[27] But to modern readers of Homer and to viewers of Rossi's film alike, Odysseus' caution appears excessive and unjustified, indeed mean-spirited. It shows Odysseus in anything but a heroic light, let alone as a loving husband: "Homer is in danger of making Odysseus seem inhumanly callous."[28] Rossi makes Odysseus feel guilty. So, we concur, he deserves to feel.

Rossi drives home the importance of his remarkable zoom shot a little later. Odysseus, now alone, wonders whether Penelope has recognized him. He relives that very moment in his mind, for in an unexpected and very fast flashback Rossi shows us the zoom again. His handling of Book 19 bears out the verdict that the *Odyssey* "is as much Penelope's epic as it is Odysseus's."[29] Rossi's Penelope challenges Odysseus to show himself when she compels him to come into the open – literally, out of the shadows; figuratively, to reveal his identity. She also forces him into action by announcing to him that she will choose a new husband without waiting any longer. This crucial sequence exerts great emotional power over viewers and is among the most haunting in Rossi's film. Great care and thought must have been expended on its writing and staging. Script and direction would have been in vain, however, had not Fehmiu and Papas risen to the occasion.

Their encounter in the dark colors how Rossi stages Penelope's public announcement of the contest of the bow and her reunion with Odysseus after the deaths of the suitors. In the film perhaps even more than in Homer, the scenes comment on each other.

Penelope and her maids fetch Odysseus' bow, and she appears in the hall in all her undaunted courage. Odysseus, sitting, looks up to her; she, standing tall at the top of a flight of steps, looks directly at him, even down on him. There may be a hint of contempt in her expression. Penelope turns while he looks after her and walks over to Odysseus' throne, beside which she sits down. This is a subtle touch: She does not in any way interfere with the rightful king's authority. She announces the contest of the bow. When Odysseus requests his turn, Antinous, chief among the

---

[27] Agamemnon: *Odyssey* 11.441–456; Athena: 13.335–338, and cf. her words at 397–403. Athena even goes so far as to tell Telemachus that women cannot be trusted (15.20–23).

[28] Rutherford 1992: 166–167, on line 210. This is the case despite the Homeric narrator's comment that in his heart Odysseus felt pity for Penelope, which, like his (presumably, inner) tears, he hid behind eyes appearing as if made of horn or iron (19.210–212). Rutherford closes his note on line 210, which is worth reading in its entirety, with this statement: "The poet of the *Odyssey* is fascinated by the themes of concealment and partial knowledge, trust and failure to believe, appearance and reality" (167).

[29] Ahl and Roisman 1996: 206. Cf. Steiner 2010: 25: "For many readers, much of the richness of the poem's Ithacan books depends on the focal position of Penelope, a figure drawn in such subtle fashion that her character and motivation remain a source of debate." Cf. Foley 1995: 93: "The central moral decision on which the plot of the *Odyssey* turns is Penelope's."

suitors, threatens the old beggar with death, but Penelope reprimands him – in extreme close-up, her mien angry and her face veiled: a powerful moment – and commands Eumaeus to hand the bow to Odysseus: "Until tomorrow, *I* give the orders in this house!" The next day, she implies, she will defer to her husband, whichever it may be, as befits a dutiful wife, but not yet. A close-up on Odysseus' profile as he is contemplating the bow while Penelope, almost a silhouette, is barely discernible in the far background is followed by the same close-up on Penelope's face. He knows, as we do, who is in charge. Rossi reinforces the point by an extraordinary shot in which Odysseus, still in profile, turns his head in her direction. In extreme foreground screen left, his head goes out of focus; his and our full-length view of Penelope, who appears in the background but is fully in focus, reveals her predominance. Strikingly, Rossi frames her between Odysseus and the bow, also out of focus. Its string, also out of focus and barely visible, almost bisects Penelope's body vertically. Penelope rises and proudly walks away; Odysseus looks after her: *una donna molto forte.* Even before Odysseus the beggar reaches his home, Rossi had taken care to make this very point, for the narrator described Penelope in these words: "More beautiful had the goddess [Athena] made her, greater, and whiter than sawn [i.e. carved] ivory." He even repeats these words, now replacing "greater" with "more majestic to behold."[30]

Before the couple's reunion, powerful close-ups on Odysseus and on Penelope tell us that there still exists considerable tension between them, especially on her part. In the *Odyssey* he still has his beggar's appearance when they meet after the slaughter, and Penelope is unsure if he is really Odysseus. Only after his bath will he look regal and even divine. In Rossi this is condensed. Odysseus is no longer in his beggar's disguise.

As soon as she appears in the hall, Penelope rushes – no, not over to her husband, as we expect, but to her son. She pointedly ignores Odysseus, and Telemachus has to draw her attention to him. His words, though, are considerably toned down from their model.[31] Homer's Penelope replies to Telemachus, somewhat defensively:

> My child, the spirit that is in me is full of wonderment,
> and I cannot find anything to say to him, nor question him,
> nor look him straight in the face. But if he is truly Odysseus,
> and he has come home, then we shall find other ways, and better,
> to recognize each other, for we have signs that we know of
> between the two of us only, but they are secret from others.[32]

[30] His words are directly taken from Homer, *Odyssey* 18.195–196.
[31] Homer, *Odyssey* 23.96–103.   [32] Homer, *Odyssey* 23.105–110; Lattimore 1967: 338.

Rossi's Penelope refuses to deal with Odysseus. "I don't know this man," she informs Telemachus. She explains that, the day before, she thought that the beggar was Odysseus but that he told her "he was Aethon from Crete." He lied to her, she continues, as if he had no confidence in her: "as if I could have betrayed him; I, I, who am his wife. Why? Why?" The verbal repetitions underscore her anguish, but it is an anguish with an undercurrent of anger. Then she throws Odysseus' own words back at him: "The wife of Odysseus must be a strong and brave woman [*una donna forte*] . . . What do you want from me? Some proof that I haven't changed? . . . But now it is I who want proof. And the proof I want is something that concerns only him and me." While uttering these words, Penelope dominates the screen. Odysseus, his face out of focus, is relegated to the background. Her challenge to him is to prove that he, too, has not changed but that he remembers the short period of happiness they had had together, when Odysseus did not doubt her ability to stand by his side. Odysseus, now in close-up, listens. He is still being kept at a distance from her.

Homer's Odysseus chides Penelope for her iron heart, which kept her away from her husband. He commands Eurycleia to prepare a bed for him in the hall, but Penelope orders Odysseus' own bed to be brought. The Homeric narrator immediately identifies this command as a test. In response to Penelope, Odysseus, angry and insulted, now provides the proof of his identity. He tells her the story of their immovable marriage bed, built by himself into the trunk of an olive tree. Penelope rushes to embrace him and defends herself against his charge; both break into tears.

Rossi films this climactic moment with great psychological insight into Homer's characters while also taking modern sensibilities into account. From the same close-up camera angle on his face just mentioned, Odysseus asks Penelope to have a bed prepared for him and emphatically adds: "*My* bed." She commands: "Prepare the bed of Odysseus and bring it here." Odysseus interrupts. Addressing Telemachus, he tells the story of the marriage bed while Penelope, at a distance, keeps her back to him as she hears his words. He then approaches her while she is still turned away and continues his account. Their reunion begins when she acknowledges him in an intimate moment of subdued eroticism. Both are facing screen-right in a tight close-up; Penelope bends back her head toward him while closing her eyes and emitting a slight moan. "Then we were young," Odysseus adds and embraces her. "You were not yet born," he says to Telemachus. Penelope turns and puts her arms around his neck. The atmosphere is intense, but without any sentimentality. Odysseus does not weep, but in a particular moment evoking Homer's Andromache we see Penelope smiling through

Figure 9.4 Odysseus and Penelope's reunion in Franco Rossi's *Odissea*.

her tears.[33] The bittersweet memory of a young couple's happiness over-
comes the sorrow of the older couple's long separation and suffering; it leads
to a mutual reaffirmation of marital devotion and family (Figure 9.4). Rossi
preserves the simile that closes the scene in Homer.[34] But he goes beyond
Homer. His integration of Telemachus, who is not as important for his
parents' reunion in the *Odyssey*, is an instance of successful dramatic liberty
taken with a famous source. It increases the scene's appeal to modern
audiences. Rossi also counts on the memory of attentive viewers during
Penelope's test of Odysseus, for he had shown the immovable olive-tree bed
on several earlier occasions, if without drawing any specific attention to its
uniqueness.

To sympathetic spectators, the reunion of Odysseus and Penelope will be
unforgettable; some may even prefer it to its model. Classicists viewing
Rossi's film may in this context have thought of Aeneas' comforting words
to his men, weeping as he utters them: "Maybe the day'll come when even
this will be joy to remember."[35] The Virgilian line echoes the words of
Eumaeus to Odysseus: "afterwards a man who has suffered / much and

[33] Homer, *Iliad* 6.484.   [34] Homer, *Odyssey* 23.233–239.
[35] Virgil, *Aeneid* 1.203: *Forsan et haec olim meminisse iuvabit*; quoted from Ahl 2007: 10.

wandered much has pleasure out of his sorrows."[36] Both quotations fit the subdued emotionalism in Rossi's scene, with Odysseus and Penelope acquiescing to earlier loss and suffering.

Carlo Rustichelli's extraordinary score for the *Odissea* deserves to be acknowledged in this context. His haunting theme for Penelope, especially while she is waiting for Odysseus' return, beautifully captures her inner disquiet, hidden under a calm appearance. Elsewhere, eerie-sounding strings express a supernatural atmosphere, as when Odysseus is washed ashore on the Phaeacians' island. The score is a perfect aural complement to the cinematography of Aldo Giordani, whose often muted colors are another strong asset.

4 Doomed Dido

Rossi's film of the *Aeneid* is not quite as accomplished as his *Odissea*. In part, this is the result of too much condensation of the second half of Virgil's epic, some unusual costuming choices, and a cast not as uniformly distinguished as that of his *Odissea*. Although he looks handsome and heroic enough, Giulio Brogi as Aeneas is not the equal of Bekim Fehmiu. Still, the elegant photography of Vittorio Storaro and an unforgettable musical score by Mario Nascimbene are major assets. Even so, Rossi was able to maintain a high standard with his portrayal of Dido, the former Phoenician queen. He had shown Helen and Penelope less as opposites – the one a sexy adulteress, the other a faithful wife – than as complements. Both were strong women who exerted power over their husbands while at the same time dealing with the aftermath of a devastating war. Dido's situation is comparable in that she, too, has experienced a personal tragedy (the murder of her beloved husband) and its political ramifications (her and her people's exodus). She resembles Penelope more than Helen in her dedication and steadfastness. Like the queen of Ithaca, the queen of Carthage is a *donna molto forte*. It was therefore an appropriate decision on the part of Rossi and his screenwriters to make Aeneas' encounter with Dido in Carthage the heart of their film.[37]

---

[36] Homer, *Odyssey* 15.400–401; Lattimore 1967: 235.

[37] The assertion by Aziza 2009: 30 that the film gave "une toute petite place au personnage de Didon" can only result from ignorance. Could he have confused Dido with Helen of Troy, played by Annabella Incontrera, who indeed, although appropriately, receives only very little screen time in the *Eneide*?

Rossi shows us the primeval dawn of two future societies. One is imperial Rome as prophesied by Jupiter in Book 1 of the *Aeneid* and revealed to Aeneas in Book 6. The other is Rome's enemy, Carthage, now being born in the wilderness. Accordingly, Rossi avoided most of the visual stereotypes associated with films and paintings set in antiquity and took a radically different approach. His model may have been two recent films by Pier Paolo Pasolini, *Oedipus Rex* (1967) and *Medea* (1969), in which Morocco stood in for mythical Corinth and Thebes and Cappadocia for Colchis. Pasolini and Rossi made pre-classical history and myth fundamentally alien to their viewers in order to point out the archaic nature of societies in the making and the violent struggles that are necessary for the establishment of order: in ancient myth, the development from *chaos* to *kosmos*; in ancient history, that aspect of the foundation of a civilization or empire which can be summarized by Virgil's famous phrase, the conclusion of the proem to his epic: "Planting the Roman nation's roots was a task of immense scale."[38] For this reason the untouched beauty of pre-Roman Latium in Rossi's *Eneide*, filmed on pristine Italian locations, contrasts with the non-Western setting of Carthage, filmed in Afghanistan. Rossi's Carthage is Bamiyan, best known today for the two gigantic statues of the Buddha that were destroyed by the Taliban in 2001.[39] They can be seen in several shots.

When Aeneas silently prays to his mother, the goddess Venus, an unknown woman appears. She informs the "stranger," as she calls him, where he is and whom he is about to meet, and then leads him to Carthage. Now we get our first glimpse of a world that is as unfamiliar and strange to Rossi's audience as Africa must have been to Virgil's hero. The woman, clad in black, does not reveal her identity to Aeneas, but later we will see that she is Dido's sister Anna. This is a memorable change from Virgil, in which a local girl gives Aeneas the necessary information about his whereabouts and finally reveals herself as his mother. Rossi's Anna is also Venus, for we hear, in voice-over, Venus' own words addressed to Aeneas although only Anna is visible on screen. The close association of Anna and Venus will turn out to be crucial later.

The center of the Carthaginians' world is their temple-plus-palace, carved into the rock at the feet of one of the Buddha statues. This is an impressive stand-in for the Carthaginian temple that is being built in the *Aeneid*. The statue in Rossi and the temple in Virgil tell Aeneas that not

---

[38] Virgil, *Aeneid* 1.33: *tantae molis erat Romanam condere gentem*; Ahl 2007: 4.
[39] On these see Llewelyn Morgan 2012.

savages but a civilized if still archaic people are living here. Rossi's Carthaginians look exotic in their striking costumes, which seem to have been based on actual regional dress, but they have a familiar social organization, a monarchy. Their main characteristics are *religio* and *pietas*; the latter of these Latin terms expresses a sense of duty and mutual responsibility. Aeneas' first meeting with Dido occurs just after the narrator has recited Jupiter's prophecy to Venus concerning Aeneas' safety and the future greatness of Rome, if without any mention of an empire without end. Aeneas, a beggar nearly as lowly as Rossi's Odysseus had been, is sitting in a corner by the entrance to the temple and looking at a procession of Carthaginian elders, which includes Dido. She has just presided over a wedding ceremony, a foreshadowing of her later aspirations regarding Aeneas. Dido notices the stranger and speaks to him about an ideal but unidentified country, peaceful and hospitable. Surprisingly, she is quoting Aeneas' own words to Creusa back in Troy, then asks who Creusa is. Her question prompts Aeneas to think back to the fall of Troy, which we see in a flashback. Dido explains that sometimes she can hear the words spoken by absent people or know other people's thoughts. The effect is rather eerie, but it works on several levels. It reinforces the power of the supernatural in human affairs, already established in the appearance of Anna-Venus. It also indicates that Aeneas' affair with Dido will almost be a love triangle even after the death of his wife Creusa and that the Trojans' past and their future will come between Aeneas and Dido. Lastly, it prepares viewers for the fact that a majestic woman is about to eclipse the hero in this part of his story, as was already the case in Virgil. A key aspect in all this is Dido's musical theme, which dominates the soundtrack.

Anna tells Aeneas part of Dido's story – about Pygmalion, Sychaeus, and her flight – and calls her Elissa. In Virgil, Venus tells Aeneas all this in the scene mentioned earlier. According to the Greek historian Timaeus and the fourth-century *Aeneid* commentary by Servius, the queen's Phoenician name was Elissa, but the Carthaginians named her Dido (in Greek, *Deidô*) for her many wanderings.[40] Rossi's queen explains to Aeneas the meaning of her name Elissa as "the Fugitive." The name immediately links Dido to Aeneas. Both are or have been fugitive wanderers. The one is an epic hero; the other, like Rossi's Penelope, is *una donna molto forte*.

Dido herself continues Anna's report of her past to Aeneas. Dido speaks as ruler, as shots of the rocks and the Buddha accompanying her words tell

---

[40] FGrH 566 F 82 (Timaeus); *Servius auctus* (*Servius Danielis*) on *Aeneid* 1.340. Pease 1935: 16–17 collects the ancient texts on Dido's name.

us. This may be a visual equivalent of Venus' famous description of her to Aeneas – "a bold coup, led by a woman" – and of Venus' earlier statement: "Dido's the ruler in charge."[41] In a noteworthy deviation from Virgil, Dido tells Aeneas that Carthage, carved into living rock, had been inhabited but abandoned earlier and that the giant figure represents a god. She and her people had found the site in its current state. This is an elegant explanation of a non-classical setting and its remarkable sculptures in a classical context. Although she foresees Carthage's future greatness and fame, Dido has also made a pact with the gods to give shelter to all fugitives from injustice. She includes Aeneas, whose name she already knows, and the Trojans among those for whom Carthage is to be a refuge. Her observance of the concept of hospitality, one of the cardinal virtues of Greco-Roman culture, marks her as civilized. The *pietas* that in Virgil is Aeneas' chief characteristic – *pius Aeneas* is Virgil's formulation of this idea, recurring throughout the *Aeneid* – is also evident in Rossi's *pia Dido*, as we might call her.

By the end of the banquet during which Aeneas has told the Carthaginians about the fall of Troy and the Trojans' wanderings, Dido has fallen in love with him. Rossi shows this by drawing attention to her while she is listening with his close-ups, focus changes, and non-realistic lighting. The latter tells us that what appears to be the interior of the Bamiyan rock was actually filmed in a studio. Rossi expresses Dido's progress from compassion to fascination and finally to love through camera movements between her and Aeneas and through close-ups which bridge the space that separates the two when they appear in long shots. Like Rossi's Nausicaa, his Dido falls in love with the handsome stranger's tales. This is a realistic psychological change from Virgil and makes the supernatural reason for Dido's love in the *Aeneid* – Amor's kisses – superfluous.

In emphatic close-ups, Dido several times appears in profile (Figure 9.5). A juxtaposition of her profile with those of women in numerous Greek vase paintings is revealing. The similarities are so close that they may be regarded as intentional. Once again Rossi has an exceptional actress to play the central female character in his film. Greek actress and singer Olga Karlatou, as she is billed in Greece, or Karlatos, as she is billed internationally, was about twenty-three years old. She had her greatest part as Dido at an early stage in her career, but she was relegated to a series of generally undistinguished commercial cinema and television films. She had only brief parts in two famous films, Mario Monicelli's comedy *My Friends* (1975) and Sergio Leone's *Once Upon a Time in America* (1984). The latter will come as

---

[41] Virgil, *Aeneid* 1.364 (*dux femina facti*) and 340 (*imperium Dido . . . regit*); Ahl 2007: 15 and 14.

Figure 9.5 Dido in Franco Rossi's *Eneide.*

a surprise, even shock, to those who recognize her. Rossi then gave her a small role in *Quo Vadis?* as Epicharis, a conspirator against Nero, before she retired from the screen the year after. This is a pity, for she deserved much better. Her Dido, like Virgil's, is fully believable as a public figure, a queen whose authority even men, accustomed as they are to other males as power brokers, can willingly accept, and as a private figure, a loving woman with profound emotions. Rossi's sensitive staging of her scenes marks both sides of her character. Even so, his Dido would not have been as haunting a figure had it not been for the actress's beauty and aristocratic bearing. Or her voice.

The *Canto di Didone* ("Dido's Chant"), a simple but haunting melody, is the leitmotif of Nascimbene's score, repeatedly heard both instrumentally and as a vocalise sung by Karlatos. Dido's Theme, as we may call it, harks back to Dido's aria "When I Am Laid in Earth" and commonly called "Dido's Lament" in Henry Purcell's opera *Dido and Aeneas*, which was first performed in 1689. The tradition of visual and aural representations of Dido and her tragedy in the history of Western art here finds a worthy culmination on the screen. The somber atmosphere of Rossi's retelling of Dido and Aeneas' love has a haunting aural counterpart in Nascimbene's *Canto di Didone*. In retrospect or on a second viewing of the film, its plangent instrumental version that we hear as Dido approaches Aeneas for the first time becomes heartbreaking. The music already tells us how this part of the *Eneide* will end.

Rossi handles the fateful encounter in the cave when Dido and Aeneas become lovers with great tenderness. In an almost disquieting shot, Juno and Venus, both haughty and aloof – Rossi films them from a low angle – are standing outside the cave above the lovers. They appear to be eavesdropping on them or, worse, as if they were rejoicing in Dido's helplessness as victim of their plot. Dido's undoing is caused by the ruthless conniving of the two goddesses. In Virgil, Juno's words spell out what is at stake: "Thanks to a ruse, two gods tally up one woman defeated."[42] From the very beginning Rossi has been carefully reinforcing an atmosphere of insecurity and precariousness that pervades his entire Carthage sequence.

While he could not put Dido and Aeneas' lovemaking on the screen, Rossi later shows them in moments of intimacy in Dido's bedchamber, discreetly in extreme close-ups and in a mirror reflection as they lie down on her bed. Even now Dido's Theme hints at future tragedy. A flame that is briefly visible is a token of passion – the fire of love – and of doom: Dido's body burning on a pyre. Rossi presents the lovers' last time together as a mournful occasion that is quite different from Virgil. Individual close-ups when only one of them is on screen emphasize the lovers' intense emotions but keep them separate until one moment of great tenderness (to be discussed below). Aeneas, in Tyrian purple, explains to Dido that his descendants are fated to rule; Dido asks if she will be the mother of this new people after having a son by him. This is an allusion to her wish in the *Aeneid* for a little Aeneas.[43] Aeneas gives her no direct answer but tells her that he has to decide between her and his own people. He asks her whether she would decide in favor of him if she were in his situation. In close-up, Dido slowly lowers her head onto her bed. With this reaction Rossi communicates to us Dido's defeat as a woman in love, for she now knows that he will leave. But it also expresses her royal side. In his place, we realize, she would leave just as Aeneas must do.

Rossi then cuts to the beach from Aeneas' point of view, and the shell of a Trojan ship appears as if it were waiting to be repaired or finished, a powerful visual reminder of the urgency of the lovers' situation. While Aeneas is at the window looking outside, Dido has risen and is looking at him from her bed. Their faces are on screen together. Then she stands

---

[42] Virgil, *Aeneid* 4.95: *una dolo divum . . . femina victa duorum est*; Ahl 2007: 80. On deceit, both human and divine, in the early books of the *Aeneid* see now Bednarowski 2015, with extensive references.

[43] Virgil, *Aeneid* 4.328–329: *parvulus Aeneas*.

behind him and tells him the story of Orpheus and Eurydice, one of the greatest myths about loss caused by too much love. They do not look at each other, just as Orpheus could not look at Eurydice. Rossi has Dido and Aeneas re-enact, as it were, the Greek couple's precarious situation, but they are fated to lose each other regardless of either one's look. After this, the final extreme close-up on their faces, close together but worlds apart and gazing in separate directions, is wrenching. "Orpheus, I am leaving; I may not go to the light, Hades devours me," Dido quotes Eurydice, foreshadowing her own fate and indicating to literate viewers why the screenwriters imported this myth from Virgil's *Georgics*.[44] Dido already seems to have made the decision to die, although later she will be torn between hope and despair. During all of this Aeneas says nothing. He can neither defend nor explain himself; he can only leave. When he is gone, Dido has one more close-up, with a flame as a hint at what will come.

Then a distraught Dido no longer wants Aeneas to stay forever but only to delay his departure. With Dido alone on screen, the narrator quotes Aeneas quoting Anchises on the Trojans' new home and his – Aeneas' – own responsibility toward Ascanius, his son and heir. Dido, we realize, is hearing Aeneas' voice in her mind, a convincing illustration of the familiar phenomenon that we often relive and work through moments of great emotional stress. Dido now reacts with anger: "Then go!" The scene is adapted from Dido's confrontation with Aeneas in the *Aeneid*, but with this change Rossi keeps the two even further apart than did Virgil.

At the tragic climax of this sequence we observe Dido in her loneliness and despair (Figure 9.6). She looks directly into the camera while addressing an absent Aeneas. The *Canto di Didone*, sung by Karlatos, is heard softly on the soundtrack. The effect is nearly overwhelming – as if Dido's very soul were being exposed to us in its turmoil. Over her soliloquy, Rossi cuts to extreme and long close-ups of Aeneas as he is sailing away, thus creating the viewer's impression that Aeneas can hear Dido's words or at least imagine her reaction to his desertion. Rossi makes us realize that Aeneas feels guilty and torn over leaving Dido, for he does love her. At this stage the *Canto di Didone* is silenced when Aeneas is on screen, as if to indicate that he cannot fully fathom her love and despair. Rossi cuts back to a deserted Dido lying on her bed, with flames in the foreground more prominent than before. Then we see Dido at her house altar and in the temple: She has decided to kill herself. Anna comes to her and, over the

---

[44] Virgil, *Georgics* 4.453–527. The myth also appears in Ovid, *Metamorphoses* 10.1–85 and 11.1–66. Rossi later briefly incorporated the Dido and Aeneas story into his version of *Quo Vadis?*

Figure 9.6 Dido, doomed and defeated, in Franco Rossi's *Eneide*.

Canto di Didone rising on the soundtrack, tells Dido that the Trojans are gone. Dido wonders if she should follow Aeneas; in this way the Trojans would have to offer refuge and shelter to *her*, just as she had provided hospitality to them. Anna blames herself for causing Dido's misery, and Dido now realizes the truth. "It was a divine deception," she says, expressing the content of Juno's words quoted above. Immediately Rossi cuts to a close-up of a dagger. "Now go. Let me be alone," Dido tells Anna.

It is the following morning. Rossi cuts to a close-up of Aeneas on board his ship and back to Dido alone in the temple. Her great love and the cruelty of fate, necessitated by the divine master plan for the Trojans, are Dido's ruin. Although composed and calm in her resolve to die, she curses Aeneas and his descendants, as she does in Virgil. Over images of the fleet sailing and another close-up of Aeneas we hear in voice-over, as does he, Dido's hopeless wish, addressed to him, for a child, now with a quotation from Virgil: *parvulus Aeneas*. Dido invokes all the gods and calls for hatred and revenge. She is already enveloped by darkness. Rossi cuts to close-ups of Aeneas and to long shots of the Trojans on board their ships over part of her curse.

Readers and classical scholars are in agreement about Virgil's nuanced portrait of Dido as a tragic figure, someone who has been callously tricked into loving Aeneas. But scholars are divided about the nature of Aeneas as epic hero and, consequently, about the meaning of the *Aeneid* as a whole. Rossi, while emphasizing Dido's tragedy and ensuring that his viewers are emotionally on Dido's side, still takes pains to show that Aeneas sincerely loves her and that he, too, has to pay a high price for the gods' plan.

Traditionally classical scholars have taken it for granted that Aeneas sincerely loves Dido, if not in the same passionate way; only few have wondered about or questioned the nature or depth of his feelings for her.[45] Rossi follows the standard view.

To viewers, Aeneas' love for Dido becomes most obvious during the scene in her bedroom mentioned earlier. When Dido has lowered her head on her bed in a gesture of despair and defeat and in extreme close-up, Aeneas' hand gently stroking her hair appears at the top of the screen. Dido's Theme is on the soundtrack. The camera then slightly recedes, and we see that his face is just above hers. He, too, is defeated. He continues to stroke her hair, tenderly and comfortingly. The moment is neither senti-mental nor stereotypical. Rossi turns the conclusion of Virgil's proem about the immense task of planting the Romans' roots – *tantae molis erat Romanam condere gentem* – into a statement about the incompatibility of personal love and happiness with political and imperial power. The *Canto di Didone*, chanted over the closing credits of the film's individual episodes even after Dido's death, is the key to Rossi's *Eneide*. It serves as a constant reminder of the price for power and empire, the most important strand of meaning in the *Aeneid*.

Rossi could not have turned his Homeric and Virgilian heroines into such unforgettable figures on the screen if it had not been for the extra-ordinary women who played them. Rossi himself rarely had the chance to direct feature films that did justice to his talents. But his first two television films set in antiquity are labors of love and reveal a deep sense of affinity for their models. His films of Homer and Virgil are notable achievements, even milestones, in the history of screen adaptations of classical literature. His *Odissea* can take its place not beside but above all better-known film versions of the *Odyssey*. For everybody who values the survival of antiquity in modern media, Rossi's adaptations of Homer and Virgil are required viewing.

---

[45] The arguments pro and con are well summarized in D. H. Berry 2014, who concludes, convincingly but sadly for many, that Aeneas does not love her.

10 | Helen of Troy
Is This the Face That Launched a Thousand Films?

Aphrodite, Helen, and Cleopatra are probably the three women of classical myth and history who are most renowned for their beauty. The story of the Judgment of Paris closely associates the two mythical ladies with each other. Aphrodite wins the divine beauty contest when she promises Paris the most beautiful mortal woman: her bribe and his bride. *Cherchez les femmes:* Female beauty is the direct cause of antiquity's biggest myth. *Hinc illae lacrimae belli Troiani.*

Praise of Helen's beauty was an integral part of Greek and Roman letters. This beauty received its ultimate tribute in a composition by the Greek rhetorician Isocrates, a disciple of the Sophist Gorgias. Isocrates' Tenth Oration is the *Encomium to Helen*, which responds to Gorgias' own *En-comium to Helen*, which in turn was a reply to Stesichorus' *Palinode*.[1] Isocrates attributes to Helen the greatest beauty, which is the most divine quality of all and made Helen herself immortal. Even as a young girl and before reaching the full bloom of her beauty, Isocrates says, Helen already surpassed all other women. She even bewitched the great hero Theseus, himself a model of handsomeness.[2] Isocrates reports that sometimes Helen was credited with having been at Homer's side as he was composing his epics and so made the *Iliad* and the *Odyssey* the surpassing works they are. How then could we not honor Helen, Isocrates exclaims rhetorically. Philosophers and the educated are duty-bound to praise Helen in homage to her beauty.[3] The cinema has eagerly heeded Isocrates' call, even if his has never been a household name in Hollywood or elsewhere. "'What a Goddess!' raved the Poets, when they sang of famous Helen of Troy ....

---

[1] On this, and on portrayals of Helen in some American films, see Winkler 2009a: 210–250. See further the brief overview by Rodrigues 2012. On Helen in ancient visual arts see *Lexicon Iconographicum Mythologiae Classicae*, 4 (1988), 498–572 (s. vv. *Helene* and *Elina*); for the wider context (classical and later art) see Scherer 1964, especially 10–23, 28–39, and 115–123. Snell 1973 summarizes ancient views of Helen. See further Homeyer 1977; Blondell 2013; Edmunds 2016. On the subject of classical beauty see in particular Konstan 2014.

[2] Plutarch, *Theseus* 31; Hyginus, *Fabulae* 79; Apollodorus, *Library*, Epit. 1.23, are among the chief sources for this part of Theseus' and Helen's myths. Theseus was so deeply smitten with Helen that he kidnapped her. On this see Edmunds 2016: 66–102 (chapter titled "Dioscuri").

[3] See Isocrates, *Encomium to Helen* 18, 38, 54–55, 60–61, 65–66, and 69 (Isocrates' encouragement to others to follow his example).

she put the 'Hist!' in History, with a scandal the world has never stopped talking about!" Thus proclaimed, a little breathlessly, a full-page ad in 1927 for Alexander Korda's *The Private Life of Helen of Troy*, a comedy-romance about "this ravishing royal renegade."[4]

1 Art, Beauty, and a Little Sex

INTERIOR. DAY. A studio projection room. A director who has just pre-viewed his new film for his bosses enthusiastically explains its meaning and purpose: "You see? . . . It teaches a lesson, a moral lesson, it has social significance. I want this picture to be a commentary on modern conditions, stark realism, the problems that confront the average man."

The bosses have other things in mind. One of them immediately comes to the point: "But with a little sex." The director continues pontificating: "I want this picture to be a document. I want to hold a mirror up to life. I want this to be a picture of dignity, a true canvas of the suffering of humanity." Again he meets with the same objection: "But with a little sex in it." Resigned, he agrees: "With a little sex in it."

This opening scene of Preston Sturges's *Sullivan's Travels* (1941) cle-verly, poignantly, and humorously points us to the quandary that the cinema has always found itself in: the quarrel of art with commerce. "I wanted to make . . . something that would realize the potentialities of film as the sociological and artistic medium that it is," the director will soon add. But since *Sullivan's Travels* is a comedy, the scene ends on the side not of social significance but of the cinema's eternal appeal: with a little sex in it.

Films have always hyped the sex appeal of beautiful actresses and promoted female beauty whenever, wherever, and however possible. A minor but still amusing example occurred in 1942 with a Sweater Girl Contest designed to attract audiences to a musical-comedy film that was also a murder mystery. It was called – what else? – *Sweater Girl*. (No, it did not star Lana Turner.) Its trailer whetted prospective viewers' appetites by asking them about history's most outstanding women: "Venus de Milo, Helen of Troy, Cleopatra, Anne Boleyn, Lillian Russell, Madame DuBarry. Who are these ladies? They are the famous Sweater Girls of history."[5] Classical scholars would rather call the first three of these ladies *peplos*

---

[4] The ad appeared in *Photoplay Magazine*, 33 no. 1 (December 1927): 17.

[5] My information and the quotations are taken from "Fabian Sweater Girl Contest Scores a Hit" 1942, with illustrations (of course).

girls. But only Beckmessers will grumble at this homage to classical curves and culture.

2   Fade-In: From Mythical to Real Beauty

INTERIOR. DAY. A bedroom. We are observing a married couple in an intimate moment. The wife, unclothed, is lying on her stomach; her husband is playing with her blond hair. Over romantic strings surging on the soundtrack she begins to ask him a series of questions. Does he find her feet, ankles, knees and thighs, her derrière, her breasts and nipples, her shoulders and arms, her face with its mouth, eyes, and nose, her ears beautiful? Each time he answers in the affirmative. Meanwhile the camera is gliding along her body in a kind of visual caress. "Yes, everything," he replies at the end. "Then you love me completely," she concludes. He agrees: "Yes. I love you totally, tenderly, tragically." He cannot know how right he will turn out to be about that last word.

No husband in his right mind would say anything different in reply to a wife's questions such as these, but we believe that this husband is sincere. So does his wife – for now. Male viewers in particular will fully agree with the husband because his wife is being played by Brigitte Bardot. The scene here summarized occurs after the opening credits of Jean-Luc Godard's *Contempt* (1963). It was added as an afterthought when the film's producers wanted to capitalize on the body of their star, who had already become a screen sensation and international sex symbol. The wife in *Contempt* is not Helen, but she will later leave her husband for another man. The film's plot, adapted from a novel by Alberto Moravia, involves the production of an epic film. It is to be called *Odysseus* and is based on Homer's *Odyssey*.

Bardot, pre-stardom, had had a supporting part in Robert Wise's *Helen of Troy*, in which she played Helen's handmaid Andraste. The name, as Adreste, occurs in a single line of the *Odyssey*.[6] In retrospect, this piece of casting seems ironic, a missed opportunity. Might not B. B. have been the ultimate Helen of Troy? Her beauty and famous pout could have given Helen her cinematic apotheosis. *Hélas pour nous*, it was not to be. Still, enough beauties have embodied Helen on the screen to make an appreciation worth our while.

The following pages and images will provide a brief survey of the cinema's tributes to Helen's beauty. I limit myself to the most familiar

---

[6] Homer, *Odyssey* 4.123.

examples and to a few others that deserve a rediscovery. Naturally I include what I consider to be her most ravishing incarnations. But there is an immediate problem, even if actresses famous for their beauty portray her. Beauty, as the saying goes, is in the eye of the beholder. Then does not every film run the unavoidable risk of featuring an actress who may leave viewers cold or at least unimpressed? *I don't think this one is beautiful enough for Helen*, some may think. Even worse, male viewers might conclude: *This Helen is not my type, so I don't see why anybody should make such a fuss about her, much less get involved in a horrible war over her.* Indeed there is such a risk, as there is for screen portrayals of any of the sweater girls already mentioned. (There are, of course, yet others.) Operas and other stage plays can be in a comparable bind. No such problem applies to novels because their authors cannot show us what their beautiful heroines or seductresses actually look like. Christopher Marlowe's Doctor Faustus famously asked about Helen: "Was this the face that launched a thousand ships / And burnt the topless towers of Ilium?"[7] His question has been endlessly quoted, usually with the first verb in the present tense. Nowadays, when real women play Helen, the question may be worth pondering more than at Marlowe's time, when a boy actor embodied her.

3   Beauty Parade: The Main Attractions

Notwithstanding this drawback, let us now begin our stroll, in chronological order, through a highly selective gallery of cinematic beauties and pay tribute to the efforts of producers, directors, screenwriters, actresses, and the latters' makeup and costume designers to give us not only the faces but also the bodies that launched a thousand films. This number is rhetorical hyperbole, but it is intended as a tribute to Marlowe.

Classical and biblical antiquity provided the new medium of moving images with a vast treasury for stories from its earliest time. It took the cinema about a decade after its birth in 1895 to become sophisticated enough for epics or mini-epics, as we might call them in retrospect. (We could consider them modern *epyllia*.) But technical and aesthetic developments had reached astonishing heights before the mid-1910s. Our first three films are representative of this development in silent

[7] This and my later quotations from Scene 13 of *Dr. Faustus* (or *The Tragicall History of the Life and Death of Doctor Faustus*) are according to Marlowe 2003: 390. The complicated textual history of the play, published in 1604 (the A text) and 1616 (the B text), need not concern us here.

cinema. Three years after the earliest of them, its co-director Giovanni Pastrone made history with his colossal super-production *Cabiria*, which influenced the entire course of epic filmmaking in Europe and the US.

La caduta di Troia
(*The Fall of Troy*, 1911)

Giovanni Pastrone and Luigi Romano Borgnetto directed this half-hour silent epic, which must have looked spectacular at its time even though the Trojan War myth is rigorously abbreviated. The film combines outdoor scenes with large and impressive sets. During the opportune absence of her husband Menelaus from Sparta, Paris begins wooing Helen in her sumptuous palace garden, which is real except for its painted backdrop (Figure 10.1). Soon he will succeed with the help of Aphrodite, whose divine nature is indicated by a double exposure that makes her appear almost diaphanous. Helen is played by a Mme. Davesnes, now virtually unknown. As was the case with several famous actresses of that time, she is rather too voluminous to be regarded as a great beauty today.

Figure 10.1 Detail of Helen and Paris in Giovanni Pastrone and Luigi Romano Borgnetto's *La caduta di Troia*.

Helena: Der Untergang Trojas
("Helen: The Fall of Troy," 1924)

Now largely unknown and overshadowed in its own time by more prestigious UFA productions, this German epic with a total running time of three and a half hours awaits rediscovery. Sometimes called simply *Helena* (US title: *Helen of Troy*), it was directed by Manfred Noa on Bavarian locations and huge sets and starred Italian-born Edy Darclea as Helen. The film is a free rendition of Homer's *Iliad*, telling the myth of the Trojan War in two parts: *Der Raub der Helena* ("The Abduction of Helen") and *Die Zerstörung Trojas* ("The Destruction of Troy"). The story gets under way on the island of Cythera, sacred to Aphrodite. Helen has been chosen as queen of the goddess's festival and holds in her hands a dove, a symbol of Aphrodite and her power, which is not always as harmless as the cute little bird might mislead us into thinking (Figure 10.2). Helen will shortly meet Achilles, who immediately becomes enamored of her.

The Private Life of Helen of Troy (1927)

John Erskine's 1925 novel by this title, set in Sparta after the Trojan War, began with this "Note" by the author: "After Troy, Helen reestablished

Figure 10.2 Helen in Manfred Noa's *Helena: Der Untergang Trojas*.

herself in the home. It will be seen that apart from her divine beauty and entire frankness she was a conventional woman."

Well, not quite, for this Helen is no cricket on the hearth but rather an emancipated (*avant la lettre*) and independent-minded wife. As the advertising copy for a 1942 reprint informed readers: "Mr. Erskine takes one of the most beautiful women of all time, and makes her breathe and live. . . . Mr. Erskine has adapted the story from Greek legend and fact [!] with brilliant wit and spirit, giving it the actual feeling of modern times and conditions."[8] Dr. Erskine, Professor of English at Columbia University and the inspiration for the Great Books initiative, has indeed done just this. His paperback publishers, however, tended to add a little more sex with their covers. One is known to connoisseurs as "that naughty nipple cover."[9]

Erskine's novel was combined with parts of Robert Sherwood's play *The Road to Rome* (!) for this film by expatriate Hungarian Alexander Korda, who was at this time in Hollywood. He himself directed; his wife Maria Corda was Helen.[10] (The different spelling of their last names is intentional.) Perky starlet Alice White was Adraste [*sic*]. Impeccable Art-Deco sets and costumes gave the film much of its visual appeal. The effusive contemporary ad mentioned earlier went so far as to make Corda's Helen a double delight: "The Most Dangerous Blonde in History! . . . All dressed up in her long red hair." Other ad copy promised viewers: "You'll learn about 'IT' from HER." Glamor shots of Corda show her in different poses and moods, ranging from romantic cutie (Figure 10.3) to Jazz Age flapper to regal fashion plate, as this book's cover image illustrates. But the arrival of sound doomed her career. Korda's lavish romance-comedy-epic survives today only in fragments. Korda would, however, have a lasting impact on British cinema a few years later, beginning with *The Private Life of Henry VIII* (1933).

Almost three decades were to elapse before another retelling of the Trojan War as costume epic appeared on international screens. In between, however, came an overlooked little gem.

Sköna Helena (1951)

Whether she is called, as here, "Beautiful Helen" or, as this film's English-language release was titled, "Helen of Troy," the lady is always attractive, and never more so than when Eva Dahlbeck played her in this free Swedish adaptation of *La belle Hélène*, the popular *opera buffa* with music by

---

[8] Quoted from the inside front flap of the dust cover for Erskine 1942. The text below the cover image of this edition asks, rhetorically: "What kind of woman was the beautiful and unfaithful Greek wife whose face launched a thousand ships and destroyed a nation?"

[9] The editions in question are Erskine 1956 and 1947 (2nd ed., 1948 [no. 147]).

[10] See Coelho 2013b, with several illustrations.

Figure 10.3 Helen in Alexander Korda's *The Private Life of Helen of Troy*.

Jacques Offenbach. (Figure 10.4 shows a Swedish poster.) Gustav Ed-gren's film was not received too well by critics, partly because of its contemporary political overtones, but its titular lady makes it worth a look. Eva Dahlbeck would soon make her mark in film history with several romantic comedies or comedy-dramas written and directed by Ingmar Bergman: *Waiting Women* (1952), *A Lesson in Love* (1954), *All These Women* (1964), and the classic *Smiles of a Summer Night* (1955).

Offenbach's Helen even traveled to the wild American West in George Cukor's not-funny-enough comedy *Heller in Pink Tights* (1960), based on Louis L'Amour's 1955 novel *Heller with a Gun*. Sophia Loren plays an actress in a run-down traveling theater troupe, which is putting on *La belle Hélène* but runs into trouble with the puritan mayor of Cheyenne.

Figure 10.4 Swedish poster for Gustav Edgren's *Sköna Helena*.

What – a story about adultery? Not in *his* town! At least the film gives viewers the rare opportunity to watch a blond Sophia. The pesudo-Grecian dress she wears as Helen shows off her assets to good effect (Figure 10.5).

With the introduction in the early 1950s of extreme widescreen cinematography, enhanced by color and stereophonic sound, film epics entered their most glorious phase, which lasted for a little over a decade. Ancient subjects – Greek myth, Roman history, tales from the Bible – almost dominated Euro-pean and American screens. The Trojan War was back, too.

Helen of Troy (1956)

With *Ulysses* (1954) starring Kirk Douglas, Mario Camerini was the first director to turn to Homeric myth in the sound, color, and widescreen era.

Figure 10.5 Studio publicity for George Cukor's *Heller in Pink Tights*.

His Italian-American coproduction was soon followed by another one, Robert Wise's lushly romantic epic about Helen.[11] *Helen of Troy* had a star-studded international cast and an appealing, if archaeologically fanciful, recreation of Minoan Knossos for the city of Troy. Its intelligent script made free with Homer and myth but presented a coherent retelling of the Trojan War. A young and very beautiful Rossana Podestà played Helen

---

[11] Glücklich 2000: 97–108, especially 105–108, explains the film's romanticism as deriving from Ovid's *Heroides* 17, a fictive letter from Helen to Paris.

Figure 10.6 Studio publicity of Helen for Robert Wise's *Helen of Troy*.

under a large blond wig (Figure 10.6). She had been a brunette Nausicaa in Camerini's film and had made a strong impression in Valerio Zurlini's *The Girls of San Frediano* (1955).[12] As already mentioned, Helen's hand-maid Andraste was Brigitte Bardot, who here is a brunette. Frenchman Jacques Sernas, billed as "Jack" in American ads, was Paris. The parallel scenes in which Podestà finds a handsome stranger on the shore, first as Nausicaa and then as Helen, are textbook cases of cinematic intertextuality, as academics call this sort of thing. Podestà acted in several other epic films with ancient or biblical settings but never had the career as a serious actress that she deserved. *Peccato.*

La guerra di Troia
(*The Wooden Horse of Troy, The Trojan Horse*; 1961)

Giorgio Ferroni's underrated spectacle is yet another free reimagining. This time viewers are meant to be on the side of the Trojans. After Hector's death it is Aeneas, played, as mentioned, by Steve Reeves, who

---

[12] Nikoloutsos 2015: 81–87 examines Podestà and her Helen in detail. His misidentification of American starlet Marla English as Podestà (85 fig. 3) negates his argument about the latter at 83.

Figure 10.7 Lobby card of Helen in Giorgio Ferroni's *La guerra di Troia*.

is the Trojans' greatest hero. Paris is a cowardly villain scheming for power. At this stage, Helen has nothing but contempt for him. She would much rather seduce Aeneas, who, however, is a faithful husband to Creusa and, as Troy's last hope, a responsible public figure. A very blond Hedy (elsewhere Edy) Vessel in colorful costumes makes for a great-looking Helen who can also act the aloof sexpot (Figure 10.7). Helen remains supremely unconcerned when Menelaus revenges himself on Paris by first demeaning him in his masculinity and then stabbing him before her very eyes. In 1963 Vessel was one of the many (and better-known) actresses in Federico Fellini's *8½*.

Il leone di Tebe
(*The Lion of Thebes*, 1964)

Giorgio Ferroni revisited the Trojan War, or rather its aftermath, with this somewhat inferior film. Greek myth and literature knew of two major versions concerning Helen's whereabouts during the war. She was either in Troy, as in Homer's and most later accounts, including Euripides'

Figure 10.8 Helen (l.) and her Egyptian rival in Giorgio Ferroni's *The Lion of Thebes*.

The Trojan Women. Or she was in Egypt, as in Euripides' play *Helen*, while only a phantom of her stayed in Troy. Ferroni here follows the Helen-in-Egypt topic, of course not faithfully. Ravishing French redhead Yvonne Furneaux is Helen. The French release title of Ferroni's film even made her the queen of Troy: *Hélène, reine de Troie*. Only in the cinema! Helen has an invented muscleman for her protector and bodyguard. After the fall of Troy she is stranded in Egypt, where the titular city is located. The pharaoh, target of a court intrigue, offers Helen hospitality and promptly falls for her charms, thus rousing the wrath of his bride, played by sexy Rosalba Neri (Figure 10.8). When Ramses is assassinated, Helen is blamed. Although there is no tragic ending, there is no really happy ending, either. This rather melancholic Helen regrets her beauty, which has caused so much suffering. Furneaux frequently starred in commercial films like Ferroni's but also worked for such directors as Michelangelo Antonioni (*Le amiche*, 1955), Federico Fellini (*La dolce vita*, 1960), and Roman Polanski (*Repulsion*, 1965).

In the wake of the decline of gargantuan spectacles, smaller-scale art films and television productions became prominent. Often the latter were multipart mini-series. The three films listed next are above-average examples of this development.

Doctor Faustus (1967)

This adaptation of Christopher Marlowe's play as a full-fledged costume drama was a dual labor of love for Richard Burton. As an actor, Burton preferred the theater to the cinema. But the cinema made possible his greatest love affair (and marriage) when he and Elizabeth Taylor madly and scandalously fell for each other during the production of Joseph L. Mankiewicz's *Cleopatra*, released in 1963. Co-directing *Doctor Faustus* with Oxford English professor Nevil Coghill, Burton, playing the title role, naturally cast Taylor as his Helen (Figure 10.9). The brief encounter between Faustus and a raven-haired "Helen of Greece," who does not speak a single line, is charged with palpable eroticism. When Mephistopheles conjures up "the admirablest lady that ever lived," an eerie but alluring and wholly supernatural musical theme with a prominent soprano vocalise announces "that peerless dame of

Figure 10.9 Studio publicity of Helen in Richard Burton and Nevil Coghill's *Doctor Faustus*.

Greece," who appears in silhouette. Close-ups of Faustus-Burton and Helen-Taylor, hers slightly larger than his, reveal the "queen, whose heavenly beauty passeth all compare." Faustus then approaches to embrace her, but her phantom vanishes. Clearly smitten, Faustus asks Mephistopheles to call her back. When she returns, with the same vocalise on the soundtrack, Faustus manages to caress her face as she smiles at him mysteriously in extreme close-up. He then delivers the famous line about the thousand ships and continues: "Come, Helen, make me immortal with a kiss." While they exchange a lingering kiss, the vocalise yields to romantic strings. A second kiss ("give me my soul again") while she is sitting on his lap is even more passionate. "Heaven is in these lips, and all is dross that is not Helena," Faustus declares – or is it Burton? Male viewers are likely to concur. The two kiss again. "None but thou shalt be my paramour," Faustus says as, with another kiss, their faces sink below the frame for an erotic encounter. Close attention to the words spoken reveals that minuscule changes from Marlowe's wordings appear to have been introduced for modern viewers' easier comprehension. The darkness that has surrounded the lovers in both of Helen's scenes only enhances their intimacy. Taylor appears for no more than about five minutes but leaves a lasting impression. She is the only great actress ever to have played the two most famous human beauties of antiquity on our screens.

Odissea
("Odyssey," 1968)

We encountered Franco Rossi's extraordinary film and its equally extraordinary Helen, played by Scilla Gabel, in Chapter 9. In Sparta, Helen takes Telemachus to Menelaus and recounts to Telemachus her encounter with Odysseus in Troy, seen in flashback. Unlike Homer's, this Helen is more important for the story and more in charge of her home than Menelaus. Gabel's appearance is highly unusual. Except in the flashback, her black hair is tightly pulled back into a large bun; the pronounced black makeup around her eyes makes her look Egyptian. Gabel's is the most eerily beautiful Helen of all (Figure 10.10). As mentioned in Chapter 9, Rossi had Annabella Incontrera as another noteworthy Helen in his *Eneide*.

In 1959 Gabel had doubled Sophia Loren in *Boy on a Dolphin*, a contemporary fiction about the discovery of an ancient Greek bronze sculpture. Gabel later appeared in several Greco-Roman costume dramas and in Giorgio Ferroni's gothic cult shocker *Mill of the Stone Women*

Figure 10.10 Helen, once more, in Franco Rossi's *Odissea*.

(1960). Given her striking looks, it is not surprising that she also became a celebrity as a pin-up and beauty icon. But Helen is her screen apotheosis. She deserves a higher reputation and greater appreciation than she has been accorded.

The Trojan Women (1971)

Michael Cacoyannis wrote and directed three films of Euripidean drama, which all featured Irene Papas in major parts. She played the title character in *Electra* (1961) and Electra's mother Clytemnestra in *Iphigenia* (1977); in between came her Helen in *The Trojan Women*. This film is remarkable for its all-star female cast, which includes Katharine Hepburn as Trojan queen Hecuba, Vanessa Redgrave as Hector's widow Andromache, and Geneviève Bujold as Hecuba's daughter Cassandra.

The chorus of Aeschylus' *Agamemnon* characterizes Helen as a cute and playful lion cub that, once grown, causes a bloodbath among those who reared it in their home.[13] Cacoyannis, too, resorts to animal imagery when he introduces his Helen to viewers. Held captive by the victorious Greeks after the fall of Troy, Helen looks out from behind the wooden planks of

---

[13] Aeschylus, *Agamemnon* 717–736.

Figure 10.11 Menelaus (l.), Helen (ctr.), and Hecuba (r.) in Michael Cacoyannis's
The Trojan Women.

a dark shed. At first we only see her brooding eyes in an extreme close-up.
Cacoyannis has not yet informed us of this woman's identity, but it does
not take us long to realize who she is and why she is a prisoner. We also find
out that she is completely naked: Defiantly and in full view of the outraged
Trojan women, she uses a bowl of precious water for a quick bath. She is
preparing herself for her first encounter with Menelaus after ten years.
Later, dressed in a magnificent robe that keeps her back uncovered, she
succeeds in wrapping Menelaus around her little finger. He was intent on
killing her here and now, as Hecuba urged him to do, but he changes his
mind and takes her back home with him (Figure 10.11).

Papas projects a mature and smoldering, although controlled, eroticism.
This and the manner of her delivery of Euripides' lines (in English translation) make Helen's rhetorical victory over Menelaus and Hecuba entirely
convincing to modern audiences. This Helen is fully conscious of her
power over men and rejoices, not without arrogance, in surpassing all
other women in her irresistible allure. Viewers understand why this magnificent female animal has made so many men lose their heads and lives.
The dress, of course, helps. Helen makes sure that its effect is not lost on
Menelaus, and Cacoyannis at one point has his camera glide up Helen's
bare back in extreme close-up. The dress is anachronistic but functions as
the equivalent of something that Helen did with her clothing as reported in
ancient sources but that Cacoyannis could never have put on the screen.

When Menelaus finds her in Troy and is about to kill her, she bares her chest to accept his sword thrust. He throws his weapon away.

Papas had played the title part in Giorgos Tsavellas's *Antigone* (1961) and had been a memorable Penelope in Franco Rossi's *Odissea*. Eventually she was Odysseus' mother in Andrey Konchalovsky's American television film *The Odyssey* (1997). Her three greatest achievements in films of Greek myth were for Rossi and Cacoyannis: a proud and smart Penelope, a magnificent Helen, and an unforgettable Clytemnestra.

Over three decades, from the mid-1960s to 2000, had to pass before the silver screen returned to classical antiquity – with a vengeance. The unexpected global success of Ridley Scott's *Gladiator* revived a film genre long written off as outdated. Advanced computerized special effects could now show viewers the distant past in ways it had never been seen before. The year 2004 brought not one but two giant epics on classical Greek subjects, one from history (Oliver Stone's *Alexander*), the other from myth. The latter even had its own small-screen precursor.

Helen of Troy (2003)

Presumably in anticipation of the big-screen release of *Troy*, John Kent Harrison directed this three-hour television film from a feminist script by Ronni Kern. Its heroine, played by former British model Sienna Guillory, starts out as a strong-willed tomboy. After Theseus kidnaps her – Harrison's is the only film to include this part of Helen's backstory – she begs him to end her virginity; surprisingly he demurs. Her foster father Tyndareus wants to get rid of Helen by marrying her off as soon as possible (Figure 10.12). Aphrodite engineers her marriage to Menelaus. But Helen has already fallen in love with someone unknown whom she had seen in a vision. Agamemnon has fallen in lust with Helen at first sight and contrives to have her displayed nude to the assembled Greek kings. As in Wise's *Helen of Troy*, Paris arrives as a Trojan ambassador. He sees Helen naked; she recognizes the man in her vision. Helen saves Paris' life and, unlike Wise's Helen, impulsively leaves with him. When Troy falls, a helpless Menelaus must watch Helen being publicly raped by Agamemnon. Menelaus has devotedly loved her all these years and takes her back home. He knows that she does not and will not love him.

Guillory's Helen is not a stereotypical bland blond beauty but has more *élan* and vitality than most other actresses bring to the part. Her physical charms are repeatedly on view, perhaps to a degree unexpected in a film made for television. Connoisseurs and philosophers of posterior analytics will readily appreciate Helen's *kallipygia*. Her chest is usually covered by a loose and

Figure 10.12 Tyndareus and Helen in John Kent Harrison's *Helen of Troy.*

occasionally diaphanous garment, which serves to accentuate rather than to hide her well-rounded and freedom-loving personality. The message seems to be that, in a society whose patriarchal power structure is never seriously threatened, a spunky woman can preserve her spiritual and emotional independence even if she has to suffer public humiliation, kidnapping, and rape. Helen's Lib precedes Women's Lib. The shade of John Erskine might not have been terribly surprised.

Troy (2004)

Director Wolfgang Petersen had read parts of Homer's *Iliad* in Greek in high school in Germany and had made waves with *Das Boot* (1981), his epic about doomed heroism set in World War II. So he was just right for this large-scale Homeric film. *Troy* was extensively criticized for changing ancient myth and the plot of the *Iliad* in unexpected ways, but this sort of thing is attested for ancient authors as well, to say nothing of filmmakers even before Pastrone. In 2007 Petersen released a Director's Cut, which significantly improves on his original.[14] There is a new opening scene and an expanded ending. The new version also contains more graphic violence and additional nudity.

As Helen, Petersen cast former German fashion model Diane Kruger, who is pretty, blond, and curvaceous enough for the part. Like Sienna Guillory, Kruger can be seen wearing gold jewelry on her head that appears

---

[14] On the film see Winkler 2006a and 2015b.

Figure 10.13 Helen in Wolfgang Petersen's *Troy*.

patterned on pieces discovered by Heinrich Schliemann at the site of Hisarlik (Figure 10.13).[15] Like Robert Wise's Helen, this one is married to a brutish Menelaus. Hector is leading a Trojan peace mission; his brother Paris, played by handsome and rather boyish Orlando Bloom, has other interests. Helen's elopement with Paris is presented as an escape from a Hades on earth and so becomes wholly forgivable. Kruger once said about Helen:

> What I really tried to do with Helen was make her show this sad side of her. She was married off at sixteen, was so young and living in this castle that she can't leave because of how she looks, and married to a man she hates and three times her age. Her beauty didn't do her any good, and she couldn't use it in any positive way or manipulative way.

Paris survives the Trojan War and leaves the burning city of Troy with his sweetheart. Menelaus and Agamemnon are by now dead.

Petersen's epic does not give Helen as much screen time as she had had in Wise's and Harrison's versions. Her affair with Paris is juxtaposed to that of Achilles with Briseis – Achilles finds new meaning for his largely empty existence as a fighting machine, despite his greed for heroic glory – and to the perfect marital love between Hector and Andromache. Helen and Paris' affair is an enduring romance, but with more than a little sex in it. A comparison of the first scene between the lovers in Helen's bedroom in Sparta as presented in the two versions is instructive. While Kruger gets to

[15] That Helen's natural beauty was enhanced by attractive clothing and jewelry is frequently attested in ancient sources. A particular poignant example in its context is Virgil, *Aeneid* 1.648–652 (Helen's cloak). For images, many in color, of the objects discovered by Schliemann see Tolstikov and Treister 1996.

show off her *kallipygia* in both, Petersen reveals more of her frontal physique in the Director's Cut than in the original release. By contrast, another intimate but non-sexual scene of the original version is now missing. After Hector has killed Menelaus to save a cowardly Paris, Helen tends his wounds and his ego, saying: "Menelaus ... lived for fighting. And every day I was with him, I wanted to walk into the sea and drown. ... I don't want a hero, my love. I want a man I can grow old with." This excision was a sensible choice on Petersen's part, for Helen's words had drawn large amounts of ridicule.

Petersen's Helen is not among the most memorable. Still, Kruger manages to convey at least some of what she saw in Helen. A comparison with her 2012 performance as another doomed queen is telling. The Marie Antoinette she played in Benoît Jacquot's *Farewell, My Queen* shows her considerably matured – to advantage.

The visual appeal and commercial success of CGI-based epic films about ancient history and myth inevitably led to the production of films that were all spectacle and action but had little to offer in terms of compelling stories or characters whom viewers could care about. Perhaps our last-to-date film is a reaction to the overwhelming but empty special effects unleashed on the big screen: a long, good-looking, and character-driven retelling of the *Odyssey* on television, but with a twist. The two-season television series *Rome* (2005, 2007) may conceivably have inspired, if that is the right word, the production of this one.

Odysseus (2013)

This twelve-part French series with a running time of about ten hours was created by Frédéric Azémar, its chief writer, and directed by Stéphane Giusti for broadcast over the prestigious French-German culture channel ARTE. It is what we could call a counter-Homeric version of the *Odyssey*. Greek myth and literature have been changed into something completely different and with a lot more than just a little sex in it. (Warning to all traditionalists, Homer aficionados, and classical scholars: Watch this at your own risk!) The film's main character is Penelope, who has her hands full not only with the suitors but also with Telemachus and, worst of all, with Odysseus himself after his return. Viewers may be forgiven if they cannot decide whether this Odysseus is a war veteran suffering from post-traumatic stress disorder or simply a jerk, despite his originally passionate reunion with his faithful wife.[16] There is also

---

[16] Classical portrayals of Odysseus as villain, especially on the tragic stage, may come to mind here. On the subject see Stanford 1954.

Figure 10.14 Helen in Frédéric Azémar and Stéphane Giusti's *Odysseus*.

a blind youngster called Homer, who records for posterity what happens by dictating his verse to a scribe.

Petersen's Agamemnon had pursued ruthless imperialist dreams and come to a sticky end. This time it is Menelaus' turn. He intends to take military advantage of the power vacuum on Ithaca while Odysseus is absent. Menelaus visits Ithaca in the company of his wife. Helen is wearing a flowing white robe that also covers her head and keeps her face hidden. When she removes her veil we see a subdued and melancholic Helen (Figure 10.14). She says that, even if she had not gone with Paris, the Greeks would still have attacked Troy. This is a cliché found earlier in Wise's, Cacoyannis's, and Petersen's films. "I'd passionately loved Paris; I didn't know that this passion would lead to a bloodbath," Helen confides in a Trojan princess who is now Penelope's slave and whose daughter is Telemachus' lover. This Helen makes no more than a cameo appearance, but she contrasts with virtually all others ever put on screen. She is mostly surrounded by half-light and half-darkness, a symbolic *chiaroscuro* that is meant to tell us about her sad fate. Penelope discovers marks of physical abuse on Helen's body. Helen explains: "Every day Menelaus makes me pay for his degradation. He wants me to carry my crime on my body in order to be sure that I'll never forget it." Penelope chides her for causing immense suffering, but Helen pleads youthful innocence and adds that she did not want to call the gods' revenge upon herself. "Revenge of men," not of gods, Penelope retorts, "has punished you." "I am paying for *all* women," Helen says.

The minor part of Helen in *Odysseus* might be negligible if it were not for actress Julie Gayet, who manages to infuse a certain *tristesse* into the few moments she has. But there is a kind of extratextual twist, if it may be called that. Tabloid headlines in 2014 charged Gayet with being the mistress of French President François Hollande, who was at that time engaged in an affair with another woman. Gayet denied all allegations.

4   Fade-Out: Hedy's Helen and the Eternal Woman

We have now come to the end of our appreciation of Hellenic (and Helenic) beauty. Our short survey of Helen as damned damsel (for adultery and for causing a huge war) and blessed damozel (for her beauty), as seductive siren and *femme fatale* is woefully incomplete. Let us therefore pay a final tribute to the bevy of beauteous bodies by remembering just one other Helen. Austrian Hedy Lamarr had caused a scandal and launched her international career in 1933 with a brief nude scene in *Ecstasy*. Arrived in Hollywood, she was the titular seductress in Cecil B. DeMille's *Samson and Delilah* (1949). In 1954 she played Helen of Troy in the segment "The Face That Launched a Thousand Ships" in the ill-fated and now seldom seen *Loves of Three Queens*. Massimo Serato, who would later fall in love with Helen as the pharaoh in *The Lion of Thebes*, here was her Paris (Figure 10.15). Lamarr also played Empress Josephine and Geneviève of Brabant. The project had a complicated production history.[17] Its director was Edgar G. Ulmer. As had happened before, director and star could not agree. Ulmer was replaced by French director Marc Allegret. The film's original three-hour version, titled *L'eterna femmina* ("The Eternal Woman"), was never released. This title and that of Lamarr's final film (*The Female Animal*, 1958) tell us all we need to know about Hedy and Helen. *Vive la beauté des femmes – au bonheur ou malheur des hommes!*

"Sweet Helen, make me immortal with a kiss," Marlowe's Faustus continued immediately after posing his immortal question about her face. Robert Wise's screenwriters had King Priam quote part of this question upon first seeing Helen in Troy: "The face that launched a thousand ships," he muses. They also provided Paris with a nearly verbatim

---

[17] An outline appears in Nikoloutsos 2015: 74–81, with additional references. Accounts by participants and scholars tend to vary in details. The film, however, is not "the first of the sound era that draws on Greek antiquity" (Nikoloutsos, 72).

Figure 10.15 Detail of Italian poster for Marc Allegret's *Loves of Three Queens.*

restatement to Helen of what Faustus said next: "Make me immortal with your kiss." Apparently studio publicists were so much smitten with this osculatory attraction that they displayed it prominently in one of their advertising slogans during the film's premiere in Los Angeles but misattributed its source: "The Kiss Immortal from the famed 'Iliad' of Homer!"

The cinema is the best medium for such an apotheosis, especially one with a kiss immortal or with a little (or more) sex in it. As long as we watch films and remember their stories, we preserve their characters' immortality. Wise's writers knew this as well. They had Helen tell Paris: "What is remembered is forever young." This may sound like a saccharine cliché, but it is true nevertheless. Before THE END appears on screen, Wise's Helen remembers an exchange she had with Paris, who had been killed by Menelaus during Troy's fall. We hear it in voice-over:

HELEN: What has been lived and shared is never lost.
PARIS: Never, Helen
HELEN: Then this is not good-bye. You shall always be with me.
PARIS: And you with me.

And we with them. THE END is not the end, for the cinema has launched, and doubtless will continue to launch, if not a thousand then a sufficiently large number of films to keep Helen's memory alive. Why the cinema more than any other modern medium? The end of the opening-credit sequence of Godard's *Contempt* provides an answer. Only a few seconds before the scene described above, Godard has his narrator quote a statement attributed to influential film scholar André Bazin: "'The cinema,' said André Bazin, 'affords to our gaze an alternate world that conforms to our desires.'"[18] So it does, with a little sex in it. Herein lies its limitless appeal, not least when applied – retroactively, as it were – to stories and characters from myth or legend that have proven their fascination over millennia. Godard's narrator adds that *Contempt* will be the story of this alternate world. As mentioned, that story involves Homer and the *Odyssey*. And the *Odyssey* prominently features Helen in Book 4.

Who, we may ask, and not merely rhetorically, has been more appealing than Helen? A famous verdict about another ancient lover and seductress, albeit a historical and not a mythical one, applies here. This brief encomium comes from Marlowe's greatest rival. Here it is in a non-metrical variation adapted to our topic:

> Films cannot wither her, nor custom stale
> her beauty's infinite variety on our screens.

[18] More on this saying in Chapter 2, especially note 39.

Bibliography

Adams, James Truslow. 1931. *The Epic of America*. Rpt. New Brunswick: Transaction, 2012.

Adey, Robert. 1992. *Locked Room Murders and Other Impossible Crimes: A Comprehensive Bibliography*. 2nd ed. Minneapolis: Crossover Press.

Adorno, Theodor W. 1974a. *Minima Moralia: Reflections from Damaged Life*. Tr. E. F. N. Jephcott. Rpt. London: Verso, 1978. Several rpts.

   1974b. "Out of the Firing-Line." In Adorno 1974a: 53–56.

   1991a. *The Culture Industry: Selected Essays on Mass Culture*. Ed. J. M. Bernstein. London: Routledge. Rpt. 2001.

   1991b. "Freudian Theory and the Pattern of Fascist Propaganda." In Adorno 1991a: 132–157.

Adrianova, Anastassiya. 2015. "Aeneas Among the Cossacks: *Eneïda* in Modern Ukraine." In Goldwyn 2015: 91–110.

Ahl, Frederick (tr.). 2007. *Virgil: Aeneid*. Oxford: Oxford University Press. Rpt. 2008.

Ahl, Frederick, and Hanna M. Roisman. 1996. *The* Odyssey *Re-Formed*. Ithaca: Cornell University Press.

Albertz, Anuschka. 2006. *Exemplarisches Heldentum: Die Rezeptionsgeschichte der Schlacht an den Thermopylen von der Antike bis zur Gegenwart*. Munich: Oldenbourg.

Alexander, L. A. 2013. *Fictional Worlds: Traditions in Narrative and the Age of Visual Culture*. Brooklyn: Storytelling on Screen.

Alexis, Louis E. M. 1975. *School of Nero: Europe's First Christian Ruler Identified and Excerpts Edited from His Literary Heirs: Silius Italicus, Papinius Statius, Valerius Flaccus*. Sevenoaks School, Kent: The Author.

Allie, Scott, and Katie Moody (eds.). 2007. *300: The Art of the Film*. Milwaukie, Oregon: Dark Horse Books.

Anan, Nobuko. 2006. "*Medea*." *Asian Theatre Journal*, 23: 407–411.

Andreotti, Roberto (ed.). 2009. *Resistenza del Classico*. Milan: BUR Rizzoli.

Andrew, Dudley. 1984. *Concepts in Film Theory*. New York: Oxford University Press.

Andrisano, Angela Maria. 2014. "Aristofane a Manhattan: *Mighty Aphrodite* di Woody Allen." *Dionysus ex machina* [electronic journal], 5: 350–377.

Anobile, Richard J. (ed.). 1974. *Alfred Hitchcock's* Psycho. New York: Universe Books.

Antonucci, Giovanni. 1984. "Cinema." *Enciclopedia virgiliana*. Vol. 1: *A-Da*. 784–785.

Arato, Andrew, and Eike Gebhardt (eds.). 1978. *The Essential Frankfurt School Reader*. New York: Urizen.

Arieti, James A., and John M. Crossett (trs.). 1985. *Longinus: On the Sublime*. New York: Mellen.

Athearn, Robert G. 1986. *The Mythic West in Twentieth-Century America*. Lawrence: University Press of Kansas.

Aubert, Natacha. 2009. *Un cinéma d'après l'antique: Du culte de l'Antiquité au nationalisme italien*. Paris: L'Harmattan.

Aumont, Jacques, Alain Begala, Michel Marie, and Marc Vernet. 1992. *Aesthetics of Film*. Tr. and rev. Richard Neupert. Austin: University of Texas Press.

Austin, R. G. 1971 (comm.). *P. Vergili Maronis Aeneidos liber primvs*. Oxford: Clarendon Press. Several rpts.

Aziza, Claude. 2009. *Le péplum, un mauvais genre*. Paris: Klincksieck.

Babbitt, Frank Cole (ed. and tr.). 1928. *Plutarch's Moralia*. Vol. 1: *1A–86A*. London: Heinemann / New York: Putnam's. Several rpts.

   (ed. and tr.). 1936. *Plutarch's Moralia*. Vol. 4: *263D–351B*. London: Heinemann / Cambridge: Harvard University Press. Several rpts.

Badley, Linda. 2010. *Lars von Trier*. Urbana: University of Illinois Press.

Baertschi, Annette M. 2013. "Rebel and Martyr: The *Medea* of Lars von Trier." In Nikoloutsos 2013a: 117–136.

Bainbridge, Caroline. 2007. *The Cinema of Lars von Trier: Authenticity and Artifice*. London: Wallflower Press.

Bakker, Egbert J. 2005. *Pointing at the Past: From Formula to Performance in Homeric Poetics*. Washington, DC: Center for Hellenic Studies / Cambridge: Harvard University Press. Rpt. 2006.

Bakogiannis, Anastasia (ed.). 2013. *Dialogues with the Past*. Vol. 2: *Classical Reception Theory and Practice*. London: Institute of Classical Studies.

Barilli, Renato. 2007. "Un Aristotele redivivo avrebbe inserito il cinema nella sua *Poetica*?" In Biasin, Bursi, and Quaresima 2007: 23–27.

Barnes, Jonathan. 1982. *The Presocratic Philosophers*. 2nd ed. London: Routledge & Kegan Paul. Several rpts.

Barolsky, Paul. 2009. "Homer and the Poetic Origins of Art History." *Arion*, 3rd ser., 16 no. 3: 13–44.

Baron, James R. 2001. "Tricksters and Typists: *9 to 5* as Aristophanic Comedy." In Winkler 2001: 172–192.

Barrett, Anthony [or Anthony A.]. 1996a. *Agrippina: Mother of Nero*. London: Batsford.

   1996b. *Agrippina: Sex, Power, and Politics in the Early Empire*. New Haven: Yale University Press. Rpt. 1999.

Barrett, Anthony, Elaine Fantham, and John C. Yardley (eds.). 2016. *The Emperor Nero: A Guide to the Ancient Sources*. Princeton: Princeton University Press.

Bartels, Heike, and Anne Simon (eds.). 2010. *Unbinding Medea: Interdisciplinary Approaches to a Classical Myth from Antiquity to the 21st Century.* London: Legenda.

Bartsch, Shadi, and Thomas Bartscherer (eds.). 2005. *Erotikon: Essays on Eros, Ancient and Modern.* Chicago: University of Chicago Press.

Bartsch, Shadi, and Alessandro Schiesaro (eds.). 2015. *The Cambridge Companion to Seneca.* Cambridge: Cambridge University Press.

Bartz, Christina, and Jens Ruchatz (eds.). 2006. *Mit Telemann durch die deutsche Fernsehgeschichte: Kommentare und Glossen des Fernsehkritikers Martin Morlock.* Bielefeld: Transcript.

Basinger, Jeanine. 2003. *The World War II Combat Film: Anatomy of a Genre.* Updated ed. Middletown: Wesleyan University Press.

Basu, Subho, Craige Champion, and Elisabeth Lasch-Quinn. 2007. "*300*: The Use and Abuse of History." *Classical Outlook*, 85 no. 1: 28–32.

Baumann, Mario. 2011. *Bilder schreiben: Virtuose Ekphrasis in Philostrats 'Eikones.'* Berlin: De Gruyter.

Bazin, André. 1982. *The Cinema of Cruelty: From Buñuel to Hitchcock.* Ed. François Truffaut; tr. Sabine d'Estrée with Tiffany Fliss. New York: Seaver Books.

　1997a. *Bazin at Work: Major Essays and Reviews from the Forties and Fifties.* Ed. Bert Cardullo; tr. Alain Piette and Bert Cardullo. New York and London: Routledge.

　1997b. "The Technique of *Citizen Kane*." In Bazin 1997a: 231–239.

　2014a. *André Bazin's New Media.* Ed. and tr. Dudley Andrew. Berkeley: University of California Press.

　2014b. "The 3D Revolution Did Not Take Place." In Bazin 2014a: 258–268.

Bederman, David J. 2008. *The Classical Foundations of the American Constitution: Prevailing Wisdom.* Cambridge: Cambridge University Press.

Bednarowski, K. Paul. 2015. "Dido and the Motif of Deception in *Aeneid* 2 and 3." *Transactions of the American Philological Association*, 145: 135–172.

Beevor, Anthony. 1998. *Stalingrad.* New York: Viking.

Beilenhoff, Wolfgang, and Sabine Hänsgen (eds.). 2009. *Der gewöhnliche Faschismus: Ein Werkbuch zum Film von Michail Romm.* Berlin: Vorwerk 8.

Berger, John. *Ways of Seeing.* 1972. London: BBC / New York: Penguin. Rpt. 2008.

Bergson, Henri. 1913. *Laughter: An Essay on the Meaning of the Comic.* Tr. Cloudesley Brereton and Fred Rothwell. London: Macmillan.

Berlin, Isaiah. 2013a. *Against the Current.* Ed. Henry Hardy. 2nd ed. Princeton: Princeton University Press.

　2013b. "Nationalism: Past Neglect and Present Power." In Berlin 2013a: 420–448.

Bermel, Albert. 1982. *Farce: A History from Aristophanes to Woody Allen.* Rpt. Carbondale: Southern Illinois University Press, 1990.

Bernardini, Aldo, Vittorio Martinelli, and Matilde Tortora. 2005. *Enrico Guazzoni: regista pittore.* Doria (Cosenza): La Mongolfiera.

Berry, D. H. 2014. "Did Aeneas Love Dido?" *Proceedings of the Virgil Society*, 28: 197–217.

Berry, David M., et al. 2012. *New Aesthetics, New Anxieties.* E-book. http://v2.nl /files/2012/publishing/new-aesthetic-new-anxieties-pdf/view.

Bertazzoli, Raffaella (ed.). 2009. *Percorsi: Miti senza frontiere.* Brescia: Morcelliana. Vol. 5.1 of Gibellini (gen. ed.), *Il mito nella letteratura italiana.*

Berthelius, Marie, and Roger Narbonne. 2003. "*A Conversation with Lars von Trier.*" In Lumholdt 2003: 47–58.

Berti, Irene, and Marta García Morcillo (eds.). 2008. *Hellas on Screen.* Wiesbaden: Steiner.

Beta, Simone. 2001. "Aristofane a Vienna: *Le congiurate* di Franz Schubert." *Quaderni Urbinati di cultura classica*, n. s. 67: 143–159.

   2002. "Aristofane a Berlino: La Lysistrata di Paul Lincke." *Quaderni Urbinati di cultura classica*, n. s. 72: 141–162.

   2005. "Aristofane e il musical: Le molte facce della *Lisistrata.*" *Dioniso*, 4: 184–195.

   2010. "The Metamorphosis of a Greek Comedy and Its Protagonist: Some Musical Versions of Aristophanes' *Lysistrata.*" In Brown and Ograjensek 2010: 240–257.

   2014. "'Attend, O Muse, Our Holy Dances and Come to Rejoice in Our Songs': The Reception of Aristophanes in the Modern Musical Theater." In Olson 2014: 824–848.

Behlmer, Rudy (ed.). 2001. *Henry Hathaway: A Directors Guild of America Oral History.* Lanham: Scarecrow Press.

Bethe, E. 1907. "Die dorische Knabenliebe: Ihre Ethik und ihre Idee." *Rheinisches Museum für Philologie*, 62: 438–475.

Biasin, Enrico, Giulio Bursi, and Leonardo Quaresima (eds.). 2007. *Lo stilo cine-matografico / Film Style.* Udine: Forum.

Bierl, Anton. 1991. *Dionysos und die griechische Tragödie: Politische und 'metathea-tralische' Aspekte im Text.* Tübingen: Narr.

Bierl, Anton, Arbogast Schmitt, and Andreas Willi (eds.). 2004. *Antike Literatur in neuer Deutung.* Munich: Saur.

Björkman, Stig (ed.). 2003. *Trier on von Trier.* Tr. Neil Smith. London: Faber & Faber.

Bliss, Michael (ed.). 1994. *Doing It Right: The Best Criticism on Sam Peckinpah's The Wild Bunch.* Carbondale: Southern Illinois University Press.

Blondell, Ruby. 2013. *Helen of Troy: Beauty, Myth, Devastation.* New York: Oxford University Press.

Bloom, Harold. 1997. *The Anxiety of Influence: A Theory of Poetry.* 2nd ed. New York: Oxford University Press.

Bock, Hans-Michael. 2009. "Fritz Kortner." In Bock and Bergfelder 2009: 256–257.

Bock, Hans-Michael, and Tim Bergfelder (eds.). 2009. *The Concise Cinegraph: Encyclopaedia of German Cinema*. New York: Berghahn.

Boedtger, Christian. 2009. "Thermopylae und das Opfer der 300 – Antikenrezeption und nationaler Opfermythos." In Krüger and Lindner 2009: 98–110.

Bogdanovich, Peter. 1978. *John Ford*. Rev. ed. Berkeley: University of California Press.

    1998. *Who the Devil Made It: Conversations with Legendary Film Directors*. New York: Ballantine. Originally 1997.

Bogle, Donald. 2001. *Toms, Coons, Mulattoes, Mammies, and Bucks: An Interpretive History of Blacks in American Films*. 4th ed. New York: Continuum. Rpt. 2006.

Bonajuto, Vincenzo. 1940. "'Gli ucelli' di Aristofane e Disney." *Bianco e Nero*, 4 no. 4. Rpt. in Verdone and Autera 1964: 372–376.

Bond, Helen K. 1998. *Pontius Pilate in History and Interpretation*. Cambridge: Cambridge University Press. Rpt. 2004.

Booth, Wayne C. 1983. *The Rhetoric of Fiction*. 2nd ed. Chicago: University of Chicago Press.

Bordwell, David. 1989. *Making Meaning: Inference and Rhetoric in the Interpretation of Cinema*. Cambridge: Harvard University Press. Rpt. 1996.

Bordwell, David, and Noël Carroll (eds.). 1996. *Post-Theory: Reconstructing Film Studies*. Madison: University of Wisconsin Press.

Bosher, Kathryn, Fiona Mackintosh, Justine McConnell, and Patrice Rankine (eds.). 2015. *The Oxford Handbook of Greek Drama in the Americas*. Oxford: Oxford University Press.

Bowman, Alan K., Peter Garnsey, and Dominic Rathbone (eds.). 2000. *The Cambridge Ancient History*. 2nd ed. Vol. 11: *The High Empire, A. D. 70–192*. Cambridge: Cambridge University Press.

Boyle, A. J. (ed.). 2012. *Roman Medea*. *Ramus*, 41 no. 1–2.

    (ed., tr., and comm.). 2014. *Seneca: Medea*. Oxford: Oxford University Press.

Bozzato, Alessandro. 2005. "L'occhio del Ciclope: Momenti di cinema nell'*Odissea* di Franco Rossi." In Cavallini 2005: 27–39.

Bradford, Ernle. 1980a. *The Battle for the West: Thermopylae*. New York: McGraw-Hill.

    1980b. *The Year of Thermopylae*. London: Macmillan.

    1993. *Thermopylae: The Battle for the West*. New York: Da Capo. Rpt. 2004.

Braund, Susanna Morton, and Christopher Gill (eds.). 1997. *The Passions in Roman Thought and Literature*. Cambridge: Cambridge University Press. Rpt. 2007.

Brianton, Kevin. 2016. *Hollywood Divided: The 1950 Screen Directors Guild Meeting and the Impact of the Blacklist*. Lexington: University Press of Kentucky.

Bridges, Emma, Edith Hall, and P. J. Rhodes (eds.). 2007. *Cultural Responses to the Persian Wars: Antiquity to the Third Millennium*. Oxford: Oxford University Press.

Brink, C. O. 1982. *Horace on Poetry*. Vol. 3: Epistles *Book II: The Letters to Augustus and Florus*. Cambridge: Cambridge University Press. Rpt. 2011.

Brison, Susan J. 2003. "Beauvoir and Feminism: Interview and Reflections." In Card 2003: 189–207.

Brisson, Luc. 1976. *Le mythe de Tirésias: Essai d'analyse structurale*. Leiden: Brill.

Broch, Hermann. 1945. *The Death of Virgil*. Tr. Jean Starr Untermeyer. New York: Pantheon.

Brody, Richard. 2008. *Everything is Cinema: The Working Life of Jean-Luc Godard*. Rpt. New York: Picador, 2009.

   2009. "*The Man Who Shot Liberty Valance.*" *The New Yorker*: The Front Row (October 21). http://www.newyorker.com/online/blogs/movies/2009/10/2.html.

Brooks, Peter. 1984. *Reading for the Plot: Design and Intention in Narrative*. Rpt. Cambridge: Harvard University Press, 2002.

Brown, Peter, and Suzana Ograjensek (eds.). 2010. *Ancient Drama in Music for the Modern Stage*. Oxford: Oxford University Press.

Buchanan, Sophie. 2012. "Representing Medea on Roman Sarcophagi: Contemplating a Paradox." In Boyle 2012: 144–160.

Buchloh, Ingrid. 2010. *Veit Harlan: Goebbels' Starregisseur*. Paderborn: Schöningh.

Buckley, Emma, and Martin T. Dinter (eds.). 2013. *A Companion to the Neronian Age*. Malden: Wiley-Blackwell.

Burgoyne, Robert (ed.). 2011. *The Epic Film in World Culture*. New York: Routledge.

Burlingame, Anne Elizabeth. 1920. *The Battle of the Books in Its Historical Setting*. Rpt. New York: Biblo and Tannen, 1969.

Burney, Charles. 1969. *Music, Men and Manners in France and Italy 1770*. Ed. H. Edmund Poole. Rpt. London: Eulenburg, 1974.

Buruma, Ian. 2006a. *Murder in Amsterdam: The Death of Theo van Gogh and the Limits of Tolerance*. London: Atlantic Books.

   2006b. *Murder in Amsterdam: Liberal Europe, Islam and the Limits of Tolerance*. New York: Penguin. Rpt. 2007.

Buscombe, Edward, and Roberta E. Pearson (eds.). 1998. *Back in the Saddle Again: New Essays on the Western*. London: British Film Institute.

Bussels, Stijn. 2013. *The Animated Image: Roman Theory on Naturalism, Vividness and Divine Power*. Berlin: Akademie Verlag / Leiden: Leiden University Press.

Butcher, S. H. 1907. *Aristotle's Theory of Poetry and Fine Arts, with a Critical Text and Translation of* The Poetics. 4th ed. Rpt. New York: Dover, 1951. Several rpts.

Butt, John (gen. ed.). 1961. *The Twickenham Edition of the Poems of Alexander Pope*. Vol. 1: *Pastoral Poetry and An Essay on Criticism*. Ed. E. Audra and Aubrey Williams. London: Methuen / New Haven: Yale University Press.

C. K. [i.e. Charles Knapp]. 1921. "Aeneid VI in the 'Movies'." *The Classical Weekly*, 14 no. 10 (January 3): 79–80.

Cadau, Cosetta. 2015. *Studies in Colluthus' Abduction of Helen.* Leiden: Brill.

Cairns, Francis, and Malcolm Heath (eds.). 1990. *Papers of the Leeds International Latin Seminar.* Vol. 6: *Roman Poetry and Drama; Greek Epic, Comedy, Rhetoric.* Leeds: Cairns.

Calder III, W. M., and Renate Schlesier (eds.). 1998. *Zwischen Rationalismus und Romantik: Karl Otfried Müller und die antike Kultur.* Hildesheim: Olms.

Cameron, Ian, and Elisabeth. 1969. *Dames.* New York: Praeger.

Campbell, Russell. 1971. "*Fort Apache.*" *The Velvet Light Trap*, 2: 8–12.

Campi, Alessandro (ed.). 2003. *Che cos'è il fascismo? Interpretazioni e prospettive di ricerca.* Rome: Ideazione Editrice.

Canter, H. V. 1930. "The Figure AΔYNATON in Greek and Latin Poetry." *American Journal of Philology*, 51: 32–41.

Card, Claudia (ed.). 2003. *The Cambridge Companion to Simone de Beauvoir.* Cambridge: Cambridge University Press.

Cardano, Girolamo. 1998. *Elogio di Nerone.* Ed. Marcello Dell'Utri and Piero Cigada. Milan: Gallone.

Carne-Ross, D. S. 1969. "Scenario for a New Year." *Arion*, 8: 171–260 and 262–287.

Carr, John Dickson. 1986. *The Three Coffins.* New York: International Polygonics.

Carroll, Noël. 2013. *Minerva's Night Out: Philosophy, Pop Culture, and Moving Pictures.* Malden: Wiley-Blackwell.

Cartledge, Paul. 1990. *Aristophanes and His Theatre of the Absurd.* London: Bristol Classical Press.

    2006. *Thermopylae: The Battle That Changed the World.* London: Macmillan. Several British and American rpts.

Catenacci, Carmine. 2009. "Le Termopili, i '300' e l'archeologia dell'immaginario." In Andreotti 2009: 160–172.

Caughie, John (ed.). 1981. *Theories of Authorship: A Reader.* London: Routledge.

Cavallini, Eleonora (ed.). 2005. *I Greci al cinema: Dal peplum 'd'autore' alla grafica computerizzata.* Bologna: d.u.press.

    (ed.). 2010. *Omero mediatico: Aspetti della ricezione omerica nella civiltà contemporanea.* 2nd ed. Bologna: d.u.press.

Cave, Terence. 1988. *Recognitions: A Study in Poetics.* Oxford: Clarendon Press.

Cawelti, John G. 1976. *Adventure, Mystery, and Romance: Formula Stories as Art and Popular Culture.* Chicago: University of Chicago Press.

Champlin, Edward. 2003. *Nero.* Cambridge: Harvard University Press / Belknap Press. Rpt. 2005.

Chapoutot, Johann. 2016. *Greeks, Romans, Germans: How the Nazis Usurped Europe's Classical Past.* Tr. Richard R. Nybakken. Berkeley: University of California Press.

Chapuy, Arnaud. 2001. *Martine Carol filmée par Christian-Jaque: Un phénomène du cinéma populaire.* Paris: L'Harmattan.

Christ, Ronald. 1967. "Jorge Luis Borges: An Interview." *Paris Review*, 40: 116–164. Rpt. in *The* Paris Review *Interviews*. Vol. 1: 111–159.

Christie, Ian. 2000. "Between Magic and Realism: Medea in Film." In Hall, Macintosh, and Taplin 2000: 144–165.

Cistaro, Maria. 2009. *Sotto il velo di Pantea:* Imagines *e* Pro imaginibus *di Luciano*. Messina: Dipartimento di Scienze dell'Antichità – Università degli Studi di Messina.

Clausen, W. V. 1995. "Appendix: The 'Harvard School'." In Horsfall 1995: 313–314.

Clauss, James J., and Sarah Iles Johnston (eds.). 1997. *Medea: Essays on Medea in Myth, Literature, Philosophy, and Art*. Princeton: Princeton University Press.

Clergue, Lucien. 2001. *Jean Cocteau and The Testament of Orpheus: The Photographs*. New York: Viking Studio.

   2003. *Phénixologie: Photographies de Lucien Clergue: Tournage du film* Le Testament d'Orphée *de Jean Cocteau*. Arles: Actes Sud.

Coates, Donald, and Dale Calandra. 1990. *Lysistrata, 2411 A.D.* Rev. ed. Garden City: Fireside Theater.

Coelho, Maria Cecília de Miranda Nogueira. 2008. "Who's Afraid of Lysistrata?" Unpublished.

   2013a. "Five Medeas: Euripides in Brazil." In Bakogiannis 2013: 359–380.

   2013b. "*A vida privada de Helena de Tróia* nos loucos anos 20 em Hollywood." *Classica*, 26: 191–223.

Coen, Ester. 1988. *Umberto Boccioni*. Tr. Robert Eric Wolf. New York: Metropolitan Museum of Art / Abrams.

Cohen, Beth (ed.). 1995. *The Distaff Side: Representing the Female in Homer's* Odyssey. New York: Oxford University Press.

Coleman, Kathleen M. 2004. "The Pedant Goes to Hollywood: The Role of the Academic Consultant." In Winkler 2004a: 45–52.

Collins, Christopher. 1991. *The Poetics of the Mind's Eye: Literature and the Psychology of Imagination*. Philadelphia: University of Pennsylvania Press.

Comte de Caylus, Anne Claude Philippe. 1756. *Recueil d'Antiquités egyptiennes, etrusques, grecques et romaines*. Vol. 2. Paris: Duchesne.

Conan Doyle, Sir Arthur. 1967. *The Annotated Sherlock Holmes*. Ed. William S. Baring-Gould. Vol. 1. New York: Potter.

Conard, Mark T. (ed.). 2011. *The Philosophy of Spike Lee*. Lexington: University Press of Kentucky.

Conason, Joe. 2003. *Big Lies: The Right-Wing Propaganda Machine and How It Distorts the Truth*. New York: St. Martin's. Rpt. 2004.

   2007. *It Can Happen Here: Authoritarian Peril in the Age of Bush*. New York: St. Martin's. Rpt. 2008.

Conrad, Joseph. 1979. *The Nigger of the "Narcissus": An Authoritative Text, Background and Sources, Reviews and Criticism*. Ed. Robert Kimbrough. New York: Norton.

Conte, Gian Bagio. 1994. *Latin Literature: A History*. Tr. Joseph B. Solodow; rev. Don Fowler and Glenn W. Most. Baltimore: Johns Hopkins University Press. Rpt. 1999.

Cook, Pam, and Philip Dodd (eds.). 1993. *Women and Film: A* Sight and Sound *Reader*. London: Scarlet Press / Philadelphia: Temple University Press.

Corliss, Richard. 1974. *Talking Pictures: Screenwriters in the American Cinema*. Woodstock: Overlook Press. Rpt. 1985.

Corti, Lillian. 1998. *The Myth of Medea and the Murder of Children*. Westport: Greenwood Press.

Cowie, Peter. 2004. *John Ford and the American West*. New York: Abrams.

Craik, T. W. (ed.). 1995. *The Arden Shakespeare: King Henry V*. London: Routledge. Several rpts.

Crouch, Stanley. 1998a. *Always in Pursuit: Fresh American Perspectives, 1995–1997*. Rpt. New York: Vintage, 1999.

   1998b. "Bull Feeney Plays the Blues: John Ford and the Meaning of Democracy." In Crouch 1998a: 268–288.

Crowdus, Gary, and Dan Georgakas. 2001. "Thinking about the Power of Images: An Interview with Spike Lee." *Cineaste*, 26 no. 2: 4–9. Rpt. in Fuchs 2002: 202–217.

Cueva, Edmund, and Shannon Byrne (eds.). 2014. *A Companion to the Ancient Novel*. Malden: Wiley-Blackwell.

Currie, Gregory. 1995. *Image and Mind: Film, Philosophy and Cognitive Science*. Cambridge: Cambridge University Press. Rpt. 2008.

   2010. *Narratives and Narrators: A Philosophy of Stories*. Oxford: Oxford University Press. Rpt. 2012.

Currie, Gregory, and Ian Ravenscroft. 2004. *Recreative Minds: Imagination in Philosophy and Psychology*. Oxford: Clarendon Press. Rpt. 2011.

Cyrino, Monica S. [or Silveira] (ed.). 2008. *Rome Season One: History Makes Television*. Oxford: Blackwell.

   2011. "'This is Sparta!' The Reinvention of the Epic in Zack Snyder's *300*." In Burgoyne 2011: 19–38.

   (ed.). 2013. *Screening Love and Sex in the Ancient World*. New York: Palgrave Macmillan.

Cyrino, Monica S., and Meredith E. Safran (eds.). 2015. *Classical Myth on Screen*. New York: Palgrave Macmillan.

Danese, Roberto M. 2013. "La *Medea* di Seneca di fronte allo specchio cinematografico: *Así es la vida* di Arturo Ripstein." In Moore and Polleichtner 2013: 131–162.

D'Antonio, Joanne. 1991. *Andrew Marton*. Metuchen: Directors Guild of America / Scarecrow Press.

Davidson, John E. 2006. "Cleavage: Sex in the Total Cinema of the Third Reich." *New German Critique*, 98 (= vol. 33.2): 101–133.

Davies, Malcolm. 2014. "Oedipus and the Riddle of the Sphinx." *Trends in Classics*, 6: 431–436.

De Baecque, Antoine. 2003. *La cinéphilie: Invention d'un regard, historie d'une culture, 1944–1968*. Paris: Fayard. Rpt. 2013.

De la Mora, Sergio. 1999. "A Career in Perspective: An Interview with Arturo Ripstein." *Film Quarterly*, 52 no. 4: 2–11.

De Oliveira, Francisco (ed.). 2003. *Penélope e Ulisses*. Coimbra: Associação Portuguesa de Estudos Clássicos.

De Tocqueville, Alexis. 1904. *Democracy in America*. Tr. Henry Reeve. Vol. 1. New York: Appleton.

De Wit, Johannes. 1959. *Die Miniaturen des Vergilius Vaticanus*. Amsterdam: Swets & Zeitlinger.

Deleuze, Gilles, and Félix Guattari. 1977. *Anti-Oedipus: Capitalism and Schizophrenia*. Tr. Robert Hurley, Mark Seem, and Helen R. Lane. Rpt. London: Bloomsbury, 2013.

Denby, David. 2007. "Men Gone Wild." *The New Yorker* (April 2): 88–89.

Dickie, Matthew. 1990. "Talos Bewitched: Magic, Atomic Theory and Paradoxography in Apollonius' *Argonautica* 4.1638–88." In Cairns and Heath 1990: 267–296.

Diggle, James, John Barrie Hall, and H. D. Jocelyn (eds.). 1989. *Studies in Latin Literature and Its Tradition in Honour of C. O. Brink*. Proceedings of the Cambridge Philological Society, suppl. 15. Cambridge: Cambridge Philological Society.

Dobrov, Gregory. 2001. *Figures of Play: Greek Drama and Metafictional Poetics*. Oxford: Oxford University Press.

Dombrowski, Lisa. 2008. *The Films of Samuel Fuller: If You Die, I'll Kill You!* Middletown: Wesleyan University Press.

Dover, Kenneth [or K. J.]. 1972. *Aristophanic Comedy*. Berkeley: University of California Press.

 1989. *Greek Homosexuality*. Rev. ed. Rpt. London: Bloomsbury Academic, 2016.

 (ed.). 1993. *Aristophanes: Frogs*. Oxford: Clarendon Press. Rpt. 2002.

Dowling, Taylor. 2012. *Olympia*. 2nd ed. Basingstoke: Palgrave Macmillan.

Duarte, Adriane da Silva. 2011. "O Destino de Lisístrata: Uma Adaptação para o Cinema da Comédia de Aristófanes." *Archai*, 7 no. 2: 123–129.

Ducat, Jean. 2006. *Spartan Education: Youth and Society in the Classical Period*. Tr. Emma Stafford, P.-J. Shaw, and Anton Powell. Swansea: Classical Press of Wales.

Duckworth, George E. 1992. *The Nature of Roman Comedy: A Study in Popular Entertainment*. 2nd ed. Norman: University of Oklahoma Press.

Dumont, Hervé. 2009. *L'Antiquité au cinéma: Vérités, légendes et manipulations*. Paris: Nouveau Monde editions / Lausanne: Cinémathèque suisse.

Durgnat, Raymond. 2002. *A Long Hard Look at "Psycho."* London: British Film Institute.

Dutoit, Ernest. 1936. *Le thème de l'adynaton dans la poésie antique.* Paris: Les Belles Lettres.

Dutsch, Dorota. 2015. "*Democratic Appropriations:* Lysistrata *and Political Activism.*" In Bosher, Mackintosh, McConnell, and Rankine 2015: 575–594.

Eadie, John W. (ed.). 1976. *Classical Traditions in Early America: Essays.* Ann Arbor: University of Michigan Press.

Eagleton, Terry. 2003. *Sweet Violence: The Idea of the Tragic.* Oxford: Blackwell.

Eberl, Nikolaus. 1994. *Cardanos Encomium Neronis: Edition, Übersetzung und Kommentar.* Frankfurt: Lang.

Eckstein, Arthur M. 1998. "Darkening *Ethan:* John Ford's *The Searchers* from Novel to Screenplay to Screen." *Cinema Journal*, 21: 3–24.

Eckstein, Arthur M., and Peter Lehman (eds.). 2004. The Searchers: *Essays and Reflections on John Ford's Classic Western.* Detroit: Wayne State University Press.

Eco, Umberto. 2001a. *Five Moral Pieces.* Tr. Alastair McEwen. New York: Harcourt. Rpt. 2002.

    2001b. "Ur-Fascism." In Eco 2001a: 65–88.

Edmunds, Lowell. 1995. "The Sphinx in the Oedipus Legend." In Edmunds and Dundes 1995: 147–173.

    2016. *Stealing Helen: The Myth of the Abducted Wife in Comparative Perspective.* Princeton: Princeton University Press.

Edmunds, Lowell, and Alan Dundes (eds.). 1995. *Oedipus: A Folklore Casebook.* Rpt. of 1984 ed. with bibliographical addendum. Madison: University of Wisconsin Press.

Ehrenberg, Victor. 1946a. *Aspects of the Ancient World: Essays and Reviews.* Oxford: Blackwell.

    1946b. "A Totalitarian State." In Ehrenberg 1946a: 94–105.

Eisenstein, Sergei M. 1988. "Cinema and the Classics." In Taylor 1988: 276.

Eliot, T. S. 1950a. *The Sacred Wood: Essays on Poetry and Criticism.* 7th ed. Rpt. London: Routledge, 1989.

    1950b. "Tradition and the Individual Talent." In Eliot 1950a: 47–59.

Elliott, Andrew B. R. (ed.). 2014. *The Return of the Epic Film: Genre, Aesthetics and History in the Twenty-First Century.* Edinburgh: Edinburgh University Press.

Eloy, Michel. 1990. "Énée et Didon à l'écran et dans la bande dessiné des années 50 et 60." In René Martin 1990: 289–297.

Elsaesser, Thomas. 1993a. "Portrait of the Artist as a Young Woman." *Sight and Sound*, 3 no. 2: 14–18.

    1993b. "Leni Riefenstahl: The Body Beautiful, Art Cinema and Fascist Aesthetics." In Cook and Dodd 1993: 186–197.

Elsner, Jaś, and Jamie Masters (eds.). 1994. *Reflections of Nero: Culture, History, and Representation.* London: Duckworth.

Elsner, Jaś, and Michel Meyer (eds.). 2014. *Art and Rhetoric in Roman Culture.* Cambridge: Cambridge University Press.

Enders, Jody. 1999. *The Medieval Theater of Cruelty: Rhetoric, Memory, Violence.* Ithaca: Cornell University Press.

Engell, James, and W. Jackson Bate (eds). 1983. *The Collected Works of Samuel Taylor Coleridge.* Pt. 7: *Biographia Literaria.* Vol. 2. London: Routledge & Kegan Paul / Princeton: Princeton University Press.

Erskine, John. 1930. "Vergil, the Modern Poet." *Harper's Magazine* (August): 280–286. Rpt. in Erskine 1935a: 315–332.

1935a. *The Delight of Great Books.* Indianapolis: Bobbs-Merrill.

1935b. "On Reading Great Books." In Erskine 1935a: 11–29.

1942. *The Private Life of Helen of Troy.* New York: Sun Dial Press / Center Books.

1947. *The Private Life of Helen of Troy.* New York: Popular Library. 2nd ed., 1948 (no. 147).

1956. *The Private Life of Helen of Troy.* New York: Graphic Books (Graphic Giant G-216).

Esrock, Ellen J. 1994. *The Reader's Eye: Visual Imaging as Reader Response.* Baltimore: Johns Hopkins University Press.

Euben, J. Peter. 2003. *Platonic Noise.* Princeton: Princeton University Press.

Ewans, Michael, and Robert Phiddian. 2012. "Risk-Taking and Transgression: Aristophanes' *Lysistrata* Today." *Didaskalia* [electronic journal], 9 no. 1.

Eyman, Scott. 1999. *Print the Legend: The Life and Times of John Ford.* Rpt. Baltimore: Johns Hopkins University Press, 2000.

"Fabian Sweater Girl Contest Scores a Hit." 1942. *Showmen's Trade Review*, 37 no. 8 (September 12): 20–21.

Fainaru, Dan (ed.). 2001. *Theo Angelopoulos: Interviews.* Jackson: University Press of Mississippi.

Fairey, Emily. 2011. "Persians in Frank Miller's *300* and Greek Vase Painting." In Kovacs and Marshall 2011: 159–172.

Faulkner, William. 1994. *Novels 1942–1954.* Ed. Joseph Blotner and Noel Polk. New York: Library of America / Penguin.

Feldherr, Andrew. 2014. "Viewing Myth and History on the Shield of Aeneas." *Classical Antiquity*, 33: 281–318.

Fest, Joachim. 2002a. *Hitler: Eine Biographie.* New ed. Berlin: Ullstein. Rpt. 2010.

2002b. *Der Untergang: Hitler und das Ende des Dritten Reiches: Eine historische Skizze.* Rpt. Hamburg: Rowohlt, 2003. Several rpts.

2004. *Inside Hitler's Bunker: The Last Days of the Third Reich.* Tr. Margot Bettauer Dembo. Rpt. New York: Picador, 2005.

2007. *Albert Speer: Conversations with Hitler's Architect.* Tr. Patrick Camiller. Cambridge: Polity Press.

Fest, Joachim, and Bernd Eichinger. 2004. *Der Untergang: Das Filmbuch.* Hamburg: Rowohlt.

Figueira, Thomas J. (ed.). 2004. *Spartan Society.* Swansea: Classical Press of Wales.

Fikes, Robert Jr., 2002. "It Was Never Greek to Them: Black Affinity for Ancient Greek and Roman Culture." *Negro Educational Review*, 53: 3–12.

Fitzgerald, Allan D. (ed.). 1999. *Augustine through the Ages: An Encyclopedia.* Grand Rapids: Eerdmans. Rpt. 2009.

Foley, Helene P. 1995. "Penelope as Moral Agent." In Cohen 1995: 93–115.

Frazer, Sir James George (ed. and tr.). 1921. *Apollodorus: The Library.* Vol. 1. Cambridge: Harvard University Press / London: Heinemann. Numerous rpts.

French, Philip. 2005. *Westerns: Aspects of a Movie Genre* and *Westerns Revisited.* Manchester: Carcanet.

Fricke, Gerhard, and Herbert G. Göpfert (eds.). 1965. *Friedrich Schiller: Sämtliche Werke: Gedichte / Dramen I.* Vol. 1. 4th ed. Munich: Hanser. Rpt. 1967.

Friedlaender, Saul. 1984. *Reflections of Nazism: An Essay on Kitsch and Death.* Tr. Thomas Weyr. Rpt. Bloomington: Indiana University Press, 1993.

Frye, Northrop. 1957. *Anatomy of Criticism: Four Essays.* Princeton: Princeton University Press. Rpt. 1971.

Fuchs, Cynthia (ed.). 2002. *Spike Lee: Interviews.* Jackson: University Press of Mississippi.

Fuller, Samuel, with Christa Lang Fuller and Jerome Henry Rudes. 2002. *A Third Face: My Tale of Writing, Fighting, and Filmmaking.* New York: Knopf.

Fumaroli, Marc. 1980. *L'âge de l'éloquence: Rhétorique et 'res literaria' de la Renaissance au seuil de l'époque classique.* Geneva: Droz. Rpt. 2002.

    2001. "Les abeilles et les araignées." In Lecoq 2001: 7–218.

Galasso, Silvia. 2013. "Pittura vascolare, mito e teatro: l'immagine di Medea tra VII e IV secolo a. C.: Saggio e galleria." *Engramma* [electronic journal], 107 (June).

Gallagher, Tag. 1986. *John Ford: The Man and His Films.* Berkeley: University of California Press. Rpt. 1988.

    2007. *John Ford: The Man and His Films.* Electronic update of Gallagher 1986. http://rapidshare.com/files/61830908/ford_tag3.pdf.zip.

Gambetti, Giacomo. 1991. "Maria Callas: Sono per una Medea non aggressiva." In Pasolini 1991: 463–476.

Gamel, Mary-Kay. 2007. "Sondheim Floats *Frogs.*" In Hall and Wrigley 2007: 209–230.

Garber, Marjorie. 2000. *Bisexuality and the Eroticism of Everyday Life.* New York: Routledge. Rpt. 2009.

    1995. *Vice Versa: Bisexuality and the Eroticism of Everyday Life.* New York: Simon & Schuster.

Garcia, Lorenzo F., Jr. 2015. "John Cameron Mitchell's Aristophanic Cinema: *Hedwig and the Angry Inch.*" In Cyrino and Safran 2015: 173–182.

Gbowee, Leymah, with Carol Mithers. 2011. *Mighty Be Our Powers: How Sisterhood, Prayer, and Sex Changed a Nation at War: A Memoir.* New York: Beast Books. Rpt. 2013.

Genzlinger, Neil. 2016. "Review: A Sex-or-Guns Comedy That Might Make Aristophanes Wince." *The New York Times* (September 16, 2016): C5. Online at http://www.nytimes.com/2016/09/16/movies/is-that-a-gun-in-your-pocket-review.html?referrer=google_kp&_r=0.

Georgakas, Dan, and Petros Anastasopoulos. 1978. "'A Dream of Passion': An Interview with Jules Dassin." *Cineaste*, 9 no. 1: 20–24.

Gerber, Douglas E. 1978. "The Female Breast in Greek Erotic Literature." *Arethusa*, 11: 203–212.

Giardina, Andrea, and André Vauchez. 2000. *Il mito di Roma: Da Carlo Magno a Mussolini*. Rome and Bari: Laterza.

Gibellini, Pietro (gen. ed.). 2009. *Il mito nella letteratura italiana*. Vol. 5.1: *Percorsi: Miti senza frontiere*. Ed. Raffaella Bertazzoli. Brescia: Morcelliana.

Giddins, Gary. 2010a. *Warning Shadows: Home Alone with Classic Cinema*. New York: Norton.

  2010b. "The John Ford Code." In Giddins 2010a: 43–51.

Gill, Christopher. 1996. *Personality in Greek Epic, Tragedy, and Philosophy: The Self in Dialogue*. Oxford: Clarendon Press. Rpt. 2002.

Gilmartin, Kristine. 1975. "A Rhetorical Figure in Latin Historical Style: The Imaginary Second Person Singular." *Transactions of the American Philological Association*, 105: 99–121.

Ginsburg, Judith. 2006. *Representing Agrippina: Constructions of Female Power in the Early Roman Empire*. Oxford: Oxford University Press.

Giuliani, Luca. 2013. *Image and Myth: A History of Pictorial Narration in Greek Art*. Tr. Joseph O'Donnell. Chicago: University of Chicago Press.

Given, John. 2011. "Creating the Outsider's Political Identity: Nathan Lane's Dionysus." *Helios*, 38: 221–236.

Glicksman, Marlaine. 1986. "Lee Way." *Film Comment*, 22 (September–October): 46–49. Rpt. in Fuchs 2002: 3–12.

Glücklich, Hans-Joachim. 2000. *Die schöne Helena: Von Sparta über Troja nach Europa und Amerika*. Göttingen: Vandenhoeck & Ruprecht.

Goetzmann, William H., and William N. 2009. *The West of the Imagination*. 2nd ed. Norman: University of Oklahoma Press.

Goldwyn, Adam J. (ed.). 2015. *The Trojan Wars and the Making of the Modern World*. Uppsala: Uppsala Universitet.

González García, Francisco Javier, and Pedro López Barja de Quiroga. 2012. "Neocon Greece: V. D. Hanson's War on History." *International Journal of the Classical Tradition*, 19: 129–151.

Gordon, Terri J. 2002. "Fascism and the Female Form: Performance Art in the Third Reich." *Journal of the History of Sexuality*, 11: 164–200.

Gottlieb, Sidney (ed.). 2003. *Alfred Hitchcock: Interviews*. Jackson: University Press of Mississippi.

Gow, Gordon. 1970. "Style and Instinct." Pt. 2. *Films and Filming*, 16 no. 6: 66–70.

Gowing, Laura. 2004. "Greene, Anne (c. 1628–1659)." *Oxford Dictionary of National Biography*. Vol. 23: *Goss-Griffiths*. Oxford: Oxford University Press. http://www.oxforddnb.com/view/article/11413.

Gransden, K. W. (ed.). 1996. *Virgil in English*. London: Penguin.

Grave, Johannes. 2012. *Caspar David Friedrich*. Tr. Fiona Elliott. New York: Prestel.

Green, Peter. 1996. *The Greco-Persian Wars*. Berkeley: University of California Press. Rpt. 1998.

Greenberg, Clement. 1939. "Avant-Garde and Kitsch." *Partisan Review*, 6 no. 5: 34–49. Rpt. in Greenberg 1961: 3–21.

   1961. *Art and Culture: Critical Essays*. Boston: Beacon Press. Rpt. 1989.

Greene, Douglas G. 1995. *John Dickson Carr: The Man Who Explained Miracles*. New York: Penzler.

Greene, Jerome A. 2014. *American Carnage: Wounded Knee, 1890*. Norman: University of Oklahoma Press.

Greer, Germaine. 2000. *Lysistrata—The Sex Strike: After Aristophanes*. London: Aurora Metro Press.

Grethlein, Jonas. 2013. *Experience and Teleology in Ancient Historiography: "Futures Past" from Herodotus to Augustine*. Cambridge: Cambridge University Press.

   2016. "Minding the Middle in Heliodorus' *Aethiopica*: False Closure, Triangular Foils and Self-Reflection." *The Classical Quarterly*, 66: 316–335.

Griffin, Miriam T. [or Miriam]. 2001. *Nero: The End of a Dynasty*. New ed. London: Routledge.

   2013. "*Nachwort*: Nero from Zero to Hero." In Buckley and Dinter 2013: 467–480.

Griffin, Roger. 1991. *The Nature of Fascism*. London and New York: Routledge. Rpt. 1993.

   (ed.). 1995. *Fascism*. Oxford: Oxford University Press.

   (ed.). 1998. *International Fascism: Theories, Causes and the New Consensus*. London: Arnold / New York: Oxford University Press.

   2003. "Il nucleo palingenetico dell'ideologia del 'fascismo generico'." Tr. Alessandro Campi and Barbara Mennitti. In Campi 2003: 95–122.

   2007. *Modernism and Fascism: The Sense of a Beginning Under Mussolini and Hitler*. Basingstoke and New York: Palgrave Macmillan. Rpt. 2010.

Griffith, R. Drew. 2015. "The Aristophanic Slapstick (*Nub.* 537–44)." *The Classical Quarterly*, 65: 530–533.

Guazzoni, Enrico. 1918. "Mi confesserò." *In Penombra*, 1 no. 2 (July): 55–57.

Günther, H.-C. (ed.). 2015. *Virgilian Studies: A Miscellany Dedicated to the Memory of Mario Geymonat (26.1.1941 – 17.2.2012)*. Nordhausen: Bautz.

Guiraud, Hélène. 1996. "La figure de Médée sur les vases grecs." *Pallas*, 45: 207–218.

Gummere, Richard M. 1963. *The American Colonial Mind and the Classical Tradition: Essays in Comparative Culture*. Rpt. Westport: Greenwood Press, 1985.

Gunning, Tom. 2005. "The Desire and Pursuit of the Hole [*sic*]: Cinema's Obscure Object of Desire." In Bartsch and Bartscherer 2005: 261–277.

Günther, H.-C. (ed.). 2015. *Virgilian Studies: A Miscellany Dedicated to the Memory of Mario Geymonat (26.1.1941 – 17.2.2012)*. Nordhausen: Bautz.

Gurstein, Rochelle. 2003. "Avant-garde and Kitsch Revisited." *Raritan*, 22 no. 3: 136–158.

Haecker, Theodor. 1934. *Virgil: Father of the West*. Tr. A. W. Wheen. New York: Sheed and Ward. Rpt. 1975.

Haight, Elizabeth Hazelton. 1950. "Ancient Greek Romances and Modern Mystery Stories." *Classical Journal*, 46: 5–10 and 45.

Hainsworth, J. B. 1988. "Books V-VIII." In Heubeck, West, and Hainsworth 1988: 247–385.

Haley, Shelley P. 1995. "Self-Definition, Community and Resistance: Euripides' *Medea* and Toni Morrison's *Beloved*." *Thamyris*, 2: 177–206.

Hall, Edith. 2013. "Why Is Penelope Still Weaving? The Missing Feminist Reappraisal of the *Odyssey* in Cinema, 1963–2007." In Nikoloutsos 2013a: 163–185.

Hall, Edith, and Amanda Wrigley (eds.). 2007. *Aristophanes in Performance, 421 BC-AD 2007: Peace, Birds, and* Frogs. London: Maney / Legenda.

Hall, Edith, Fiona Macintosh, and Oliver Taplin (eds.). 2000. *Medea in Performance 1500–2000*. London: Legenda. Rpt. 2013.

Hall, Jon. 2014. *Cicero's Use of Judicial Theater*. Ann Arbor: University of Michigan Press.

Halliwell, Stephen. 1998. *Aristotle's Poetics*. 2nd ed. University of Chicago Press.

Hamlet, Janice D., and Robin R. Means Coleman (eds.). 2009. *Fight the Power! The Spike Lee Reader*. New York: Lang.

Handke, Peter. 1974. *Short Letter, Long Farewell*. Tr. Ralph Manheim. Rpt. New York: New York Review Books, 2009.

Hanson, Victor Davis. 2000. *The Western Way of War: Infantry Battle in Classical Greece*. 2nd ed. Berkeley: University of California Press. Rpt. 2009.

　2007a. "Foreword: History and the Three Hundred." In Allie and Moody 2007: 5–6.

　2007b. "With Your Shield or On It." *City Journal* (March 7). http://www.city-journal.org/html/rev2007-03-07vdh.html.

Hanson, Victor Davis, and John Heath. 1998. *Who Killed Homer? The Demise of Classical Education and the Recovery of Greek Wisdom*. New York: Free Press.

Hardie, Alex. 2016. "The Camenae in Cult, History, and Song." *Classical Antiquity*, 35: 45–85.

Hardie, Philip (ed.). 1999. *Virgil: Critical Assessments*. Vol. 4: *The* Aeneid *(Continued)*. London: Routledge.

Hardwick, Lorna. 2010. "*Lysistratas* [sic] on the Modern Stage." In Stuttard 2010: 80–89.

Hardy, Thomas. 1989. *The Life and Work of Thomas Hardy*. Ed. Michael Millgate. Corrected rpt. Basingstoke and London: Macmillan.

Harlan, Veit. 1966. *Im Schatten meiner Filme: Selbstbiographie*. Ed. H. C. Oppermann. Gütersloh: Mohn.

Harrison, James A. (ed.). 1902. *The Complete Works of Edgar Allen Poe*. Vol. 16: *Marginalia – Eureka*. Rpt. New York: AMS Press, 1965.

Harty, Kevin J. 2014. "The Decline and Fall of the Roman Empire and America Since the Second World War: Some Cinematic Parallels." In Elliott 2014: 36–56.

Heavey, Katherine. 2015. *The Early Modern Medea: Medea in English Literature, 1558–1688.* Basingstoke and New York: Palgrave Macmillan.

Heinzle, Joachim, and Anneliese Waldschmidt (eds.). 1991. *Die Nibelungen: Ein deutscher Wahn, ein deutscher Albtraum: Studien und Dokumente zur Rezeption des Nibelungenstoffs im 19. und 20. Jahrhundert.* Frankfurt: Suhrkamp.

Heitman, Richard. 2005. *Taking Her Seriously: Penelope and the Plot of Homer's Odyssey.* Ann Arbor: University of Michigan Press.

Hembus, Joe. 1995. *Das Western-Lexikon: 1567 Filme von 1894 bis heute.* 3rd ed. Ed. Benjamin Hembus. Munich: Heyne.

Henderson, Jeffrey. 1980. "*Lysistrate*: The Play and Its Themes." *Yale Classical Studies,* 26: 153–218.

    (ed.). 1987. *Aristophanes: Lysistrata.* Oxford: Clarendon Press. Rpt. 1990.

    1991. *The Maculate Muse: Obscene Language in Attic Comedy.* 2nd ed. Oxford: Oxford University Press.

    (ed.). 1998. *Aristophanes.* Vol. 2: *Clouds, Wasps, Peace.* Cambridge: Harvard University Press.

    (ed.). 2000. *Aristophanes.* Vol. 3: *Birds, Lysistrata, Women at the Thesmophoria.* Cambridge: Harvard University Press.

Heslin, Peter. 2015. *The Museum of Augustus: The Temple of Apollo in Pompeii, the Portico of Philippus in Rome, and Latin Poetry.* Los Angeles: Getty Museum.

Hesse, Silke. 1990. "Fascism and the Hypertrophy of Male Adolescence." In Milfull 1990: 157–175.

Heubeck, Alfred, and Arie Hoekstra. 1989. *A Commentary on Homer's Odysssey.* Vol. 2: *Books IX–XVI.* Oxford: Clarendon Press. Rpt. 1990.

Heubeck, Alfred, Stephanie West, and J. B. Hainsworth. 1988. *A Commentary on Homer's Odyssey.* Vol. 1: *Introduction and Books I–VIII.* Oxford: Clarendon Press. Rpt. 1990.

Highsmith, Patricia. 1966. *Plotting and Writing Suspense Fiction.* Boston: The Writer. Several rpts.

Hilkovitz Andrea. 2014. "Beyond Sex Strikes: Women's Movements, Peace Building, and Negotiation in *Lysistrata* and *Pray the Devil Back to Hell.*" *Journal for the Study of Peace and Conflict:* 124–134.

Hinz, Thorsten. 2003. "Dorischer Film." *Benn-Jahrbuch,* 1: 193–212.

Hitler, Adolf. 1939. "Das Schwert ist unser Gewicht." In Preiß 1939: 111–121.

Hochberg, Julian, and Virginia Brooks. 1996. "Movies in the Mind's Eye." In Bordwell and Carroll 1996: 368–387.

Hodkinson, Stephen. 2004. "Female Property Ownership and Empowerment in Classical and Hellenistic Sparta." In Figueira 2004: 103–136.

Hodkinson, Stephen, and Ian Macgregor Morris (eds.). 2012. *Sparta in Modern Thought: Politics, History and Culture.* Swansea: Classical Press of Wales.

Hofmann, Werner. 2000. *Caspar David Friedrich*. Tr. Mary Whittall. London: Thames & Hudson. Rpt. 2005.

Hofstadter, Richard. 1965a. *The Paranoid Style in American Politics and Other Essays*. Rpt. New York: Vintage, 1967. Rpt. 2008.

1965b. "The Paranoid Style in American Politics." In Hofstadter 1965a: 3–40.

Holland, Tom. 2007. "Mirage in the Movie House." *Arion*, 3rd ser., 15 no. 1: 173–181.

Homeyer, Helene. 1977. *Die spartanische Helena und der Trojanische Krieg: Wandlungen und Wanderungen eines Sagenkreises vom Altertum bis zur Gegenwart*. Wiesbaden: Steiner.

Honigmann, E. A. J. (ed.). 2016. *The Arden Shakespeare: Othello*. Rev. ed. London: Bloomsbury.

Horan, Geraldine, Felicity Rash, and Daniel Wildmann (eds.). 2012. *English and German Nationalist and Anti-Semitic Discourse, 1871–1945*. Oxford: Lang.

Hornaday, Ann. 2012. "Nadine Labaki on 'Where Do We Go Now?' and the Absurdity of War." *The Washington Post* (May 11). http://www.washington post.com/lifestyle/style/nadine-labaki-on-where-do-we-go-now-and-the-abs urdity-of-war/2012/05/10/gIQA66rGIU_story.html.

Horsfall, Nicholas (ed.). 1995. *A Companion to the Study of Virgil*. Leiden: Brill.

Horton, Andrew. 1984. "Jules Dassin: A Multi-National Filmmaker Considered." *Film Criticism*, 8 no. 3: 21–35.

(ed.). 1991a. *Comedy/Cinema/Theory*. Berkeley: University of California Press.

1991b. "Introduction." In Horton 1991a: 1–21.

2001. "National Culture and Individual Vision." In Fainaru 2001: 83–88.

2016. Review of Alexander 2013. *Film and History*, 46 no. 1: 62–63.

Hubbard, Thomas K. 1991. *The Mask of Comedy: Aristophanes and the Intertextual Parabasis*. Ithaca: Cornell University Press.

Hüppauf, Bernd-Rüdiger, and Dolf Sternberger (eds.). 1973. *Über Literatur und Geschichte*. Frankfurt: Athenäum.

Hunter, Jack. 2010. *Sex, Death, Swastikas: Nazi Exploitation SSinema*. London: Creation Books.

Huntington, Samuel P. 1993. "The Clash of Civilizations?" *Foreign Affairs*, 72 no. 3: 22–49.

1996. *The Clash of Civilizations and the Remaking of World Order*. New York: Simon & Schuster. Rpt. 1997.

Hurley, Donna W. 2013. "Biographies of Nero." In Buckley and Dinter 2013: 29–44.

Hutson, Richard. 2004. "Sermons in Stone: Monument Valley in *The Searchers*." In Eckstein and Lehman 2004: 93–108.

Iampolski, Mikhail. 1998. *The Memory of Tiresias: Intertextuality and Film*. Tr. Harsha Ram. Berkeley: University of California Press.

Iglesias Zoido, Juan Carlos. 2010. "Los múltiples rostros de Lisístrata: Tradición e influencia de la *Lisístrata* de Aristófanes." *Cuadernos de Filología Clásica: Estudios griegos e indoeuropeos*, 20: 95–114.

Innocenti, Beth. 1994. "Towards a Theory of Vivid Description as Practiced in Cicero's Verrine Orations." *Rhetorica*, 12: 355–381.

Irving, Pierre M. (ed.). 1883. *The Life and Letters of Washington Irving*. Vol. 2. New York: Putnam.

Irving, Washington. 1983a. *History, Tales and Sketches*. New York: Library of America / Viking.

   1983b. *A History of New York, From the Beginning of the World to the End of the Dutch Dynasty: By Diedrich Knickerbocker*. In Irving 1983a: 363–729.

Jacobs, Lewis. 1939. *The Rise of the American Film: A Critical History*. New York: Harcourt, Brace. Several rpts.

James, Nick. 2010. "Print the Legend." *Sight and Sound*, 20 no. 6: 16–20, 22–24, and 26–28.

Jenkins, Harold (ed.). 1982. *The Arden Shakespeare: Hamlet*. London: Methuen. Several rpts.

Jenkins, Thomas E. 2015. *Antiquity Now: The Classical World in the Contemporary American Imagination*. Cambridge: Cambridge University Press.

Jensen, Richard E., R. Eli Paul, and John E. Carter. 2011. *Eyewitness at Wounded Knee*. New ed. Lincoln: University of Nebraska Press.

Johnson, W. R. 1976. *Darkness Visible: A Study of Vergil's* Aeneid. Berkeley: University of California Press. Rpt. 1979.

Jones, Richard Foster. 1936. *Ancients and Moderns: A Study of the Background of The Battle of the Books*. St. Louis: Washington University.

Jordan, Jessica Hope. 2009. *Sex Goddesses in American Film 1930–1965: Jean Harlow, Mae West, Lana Turner, and Jayne Mansfield*. Amherst: Cambria Press.

Jorgens, Jack J. 1977. *Shakespeare on Film*. Rpt. Lanham: University Press of America, 1991.

Joshel, Sandra R., Margaret Malamud, and Donald T. McGuire, Jr. (eds.). 2001. *Imperial Projections: Ancient Rome in Modern Popular Culture*. Baltimore: Johns Hopkins University Press. Rpt. 2005.

Junge, Traudl. 2011. *Hitler's Last Secretary: A Firsthand Account of Life with Hitler*. Ed. Melissa Müller; tr. Anthea Bell. New York: Arcade.

   with Melissa Müller. 2002. *Bis zur letzten Stunde: Hitlers Sekretärin erzählt ihr Leben*. Rpt. Munich: List, 2003. Several rpts.

Kallendorf, Craig. 2007. *The Other Virgil: Pessimistic Readings of the* Aeneid *in Early Modern Culture*. Oxford: Oxford University Press.

Kaplan, Justin (ed.). 1982. *Walt Whitman: Complete Poetry and Collected Prose*. New York: Library of America / Viking.

Kapsis, Robert E. 1992. *Hitchcock: The Making of a Reputation*. Chicago: University of Chicago Press.

Kauffman, Michael W. 2004. *American Brutus: John Wilkes Booth and the Lincoln Conspiracies*. New York: Random House. Rpt. 2005.

Kazin, Alfred. 1995. *On Native Grounds: An Interpretation of Modern American Prose Literature.* Fiftieth anniversary ed. New York: Harcourt.

Keaney, J. J., and Robert Lamberton (eds. and trs.). 1996. *[Plutarch] Essay on the Life and Poetry of Homer.* Atlanta: Scholars Press.

Kennell, Nigel. 1995. *The Gymnasium of Virtue: Education and Culture in Ancient Sparta.* Chapel Hill: University of North Carolina Press.

Kerényi, Karl. 1944. *Töchter der Sonne: Betrachtungen über griechische Gottheiten.* Zurich: Rascher.

Kick, Russ (ed.). 2012. *The Graphic Canon.* Vol. 1: *From* The Epic of Gilgamesh *to* Dangerous Liaisons. New York: Seven Stories Press.

Klein, Emily B. 2014. *Sex and War on the American Stage:* Lysistrata *in Performance 1930–2012.* London and New York: Routledge.

Klemperer, Victor. 1999a. *Tagebücher 1940–1941.* Ed. Walter Nowojski. Berlin: Aufbau Taschenbuch Verlag. Rev. ed.

    1999b. *Tagebücher 1942.* Ed. Walter Nowojski. Berlin: Aufbau Taschenbuch Verlag. Rev. ed.

    1999c. *Tagebücher 1943.* Ed. Walter Nowojski. Berlin: Aufbau Taschenbuch Verlag. Rev. ed.

    1999d. *Tagebücher 1944.* Ed. Walter Nowojski. Berlin: Aufbau Taschenbuch Verlag. Rev. ed.

Klingner, Friedrich. 1965a. *Römische Geisteswelt: Essays zur lateinischen Literatur.* Ed. Karl Büchner. 5th ed. Rpt. Stuttgart: Reclam, 1984.

    1965b. "Die Einheit des virgilischen Lebenswerkes." In Klingner 1965a: 274–292.

    1965c. "Virgil und die geschichtliche Welt." In Klingner 1965a: 293–311.

Kniebe, Tobias. 2004. "Homer ist, wenn man trotzdem lacht: 'Troja'-Regisseur Wolfgang Petersen über die mythischen Wurzeln des Erzählens und den Achilles in uns allen." *Süddeutsche Zeitung* (May 11). http://www.sued deutsche.de/kultur/petersen-interview-homer-ist-wenn-man-trotzdem-lacht -1.429599. No longer freely accessible.

Koerner, Joseph Leo. 2009. *Caspar David Friedrich and the Subject of Landscape.* 2nd ed. London: Reaktion Books.

Koliodimos, Dimitris. 1999. *The Greek Filmography, 1914 Through 1996.* Jefferson: McFarland.

Kolker, Robert (ed.). 2004a. *Alfred Hitchcock's* Psycho: *A Casebook.* New York: Oxford University Press.

    2004b. "The Form, Structure, and Influence of *Psycho.*" In Kolker 2004a: 206–255.

Konstan, David. 2007. "Rhetoric and Emotion." In Worthington 2007: 411–425.

    2014. *Beauty: The Fortunes of an Ancient Greek Idea.* New York: Oxford University Press.

Koppes, Clayton R., and Gregory D. Black. 2000. *Hollywood Goes to War: Patriotism, Movies and the Second World War from* Ninotchka *to* Mrs Miniver. London: Tauris Parke. Originally *Hollywood Goes to War: How Politics, Profits and Propaganda Shaped World War II Movies.* 1987.

Kortner, Fritz. 1961. *Die Sendung der Lysistrata.* Munich: Kindler.

   1969. *Aller Tage Abend.* Rpt. Munich: Deutscher Taschenbuch Verlag. Rpt. 1976. Originally 1959.

   1971. *Letzten Endes: Fragmente.* Munich: Kindler.

"Kortner: Na sowas." 1961. *Der Spiegel,* no. 5: 50–61.

Kotzamani, Marina. 2006a. "Artist Citizens in the Age of the Web: The Lysistrata Project (2003–Present)." *Theater,* 36 no. 2: 103–110.

   2006b. "Lysistrata on the Arabic Stage." *PAJ: A Journal of Performance and Art,* 28 no. 2: 13–41.

   2014. "Lysistrata on Broadway." In Olson 2014: 807–823.

Kovacs, George, and C. W. Marshall (eds.). 2011. *Classics and Comics.* New York: Oxford University Press.

Kramer, Steven Philip, and James Michael Welsh. 1974. "Film as Incantation: An Interview with Abel Gance." *Film Comment,* 10 no. 2: 18–22.

   1978. *Abel Gance.* Boston: Twayne.

Kreimeier, Klaus. 1996. *The Ufa Story: A History of Germany's Greatest Film Company, 1918–1945.* Tr. Robert and Rita Kimber. Rpt. Berkeley: University of California Press, 1999.

Krohn, Bill. 2000. *Hitchcock at Work.* London: Phaidon.

Krüger, Christine G., and Martin Lindner (eds.). 2009. *Nationalismus und Antiken-rezeption.* Oldenburg: BIS-Verlag.

Krüger, Peter. 1991. "Etzels Halle und Stalingrad: Die Rede Görings vom 30.1.1943." In Heinzle and Waldschmidt 1991: 151–190.

Kühnel, Jürgen, et al. (eds.) 1988. *Mittelalter-Rezeption III: Mittelalter, Massenmedien, Neue Mythen.* Göppingen: Kümmerle.

Kvistad, Ivar. 2010. "Cultural Imperialism and Infanticide in Pasolini's *Medea.*" In Bartels and Simon 2010: 224–237.

Kyriakos, Konstantinos. 2013. "Ancient Greek Myth and Drama in Greek Cinema (1930–2012): An Overall Approach." *Logeion* [electronic journal], 3: 191–232.

Lacour, Léopold. 1903. "Maurice Donnay." *La revue de Paris,* 10 no. 1–2: 379–400.

Lambert, Gavin. 2000. *On Cukor.* Rev. ed. Ed. Robert Trachtenberg. New York: Rizzoli.

Lane, Anthony. 2009. "Dark Visions." *The New Yorker* (March 9): 82–83.

   2011. "Casualties of War." *The New Yorker* (April 18): 130–131.

Lattimore, Richmond (tr.). 1967. *The Odyssey of Homer.* Rev. ed. Rpt. New York: HarperCollins, 2007.

Lausberg, Heinrich. 2008. *Handbuch der literarischen Rhetorik: Eine Grundlegung der Literaturwissenschaft.* 4th ed. Stuttgart: Steiner.

Lauwers, Jeroen, Marieke Dhont, and Xanne Huybrecht. 2013. "'This Is Sparta!' Discourse, Gender, and the Orient in Zack Snyder's *300.*" In Renger and Solomon 2013: 79–94.

Law, Vivien. 1989. "Learning to Read with the *oculi mentis:* Virgilius Maro Grammaticus." *Journal of Literature and Theology,* 3: 159–172.

Lecoq, Anne-Marie (ed.). 2001. *La Querelle des Anciens et des Modernes: XVIIe-XVIIIe siècles*. Paris: Gallimard. Rpt. 2005.

Leigh, Janet. 1984. *There Really Was a Hollywood*. Garden City: Doubleday.
  with Christopher Nickens. 1995. Psycho: *Behind the Scenes of the Classic Thriller*. New York: Harmony Books.

Leutrat, Jean-Louis, and Suzanne Liandrat-Guigues. 1998. "John Ford and Monument Valley." In Buscombe and Pearson 1998: 160–169.

Levaniouk, Olga. 2010. *Eve of the Festival: Making Myth in* Odyssey *19*. Washington, DC: Center for Hellenic Studies / Cambridge: Harvard University Press. Rpt. 2011.

Levene, D. S. 2007. "Xerxes Goes to Hollywood." In Bridges, Hall, and Rhodes 2007: 383–403.

Levine, Joseph M. 1991. *The Battle of the Books: History and Literature in the Augustan Age*. Ithaca: Cornell University Press.
  1999. *Between the Ancients and the Moderns: Baroque Culture in Restoration England*. New Haven: Yale University Press.

Leydon, Joe. 2016. "Film Review: 'Is That a Gun in Your Pocket?'" *Variety* (September 14). http://variety.com/2016/film/reviews/is-that-a-gun-in-your-pocket-review-1201861096/.

Lichtenberger, Henri. 1936. *L'Allemagne nouvelle*. Paris: Flammarion.
  1937. *The Third Reich*. Tr. and ed. Koppel S. Pinson. New York: Greystone Press.

Lipka, Michael. 2002. *Xenophon's* Spartan Constitution: *Introduction, Text, Commentary*. Berlin: De Gruyter.

Loiperdinger, Martin (ed.). 1991a. *Märtyrerlegenden im NS-Film*. Opladen: Leske + Budrich.
  1991b. "Zur filmischen Rhetorik faschistischer Märtyrerlegenden." In Loiperdinger 1991a: 159–172.

Losemann, Volker. 1998. "Die Dorier im Deutschland der dreißiger und vierziger Jahre." In Calder and Schlesier 1998: 313–348.
  2012. "The Spartan Tradition in Germany, 1870–1945." In Hodkinson and Morris 2012: 253–314.

Lovatt, Helen. 2013. *The Epic Gaze: Vision, Gender and Narrative in Ancient Epic*. Cambridge: Cambridge University Press.

Lovatt, Helen, and Caroline Vout (eds.). 2013. *Epic Visions: Visuality in Greek and Latin Epic and Its Reception*. Cambridge: Cambridge University Press.

Lowe, Barry. 2008. *Atomic Blonde: The Films of Mamie Van Doren*. Jefferson: McFarland.

Lowe, Dunstan, and Kim Shahabudin (eds.). 2009. *Classics for All: Reworking Antiquity in Mass Culture*. Newcastle Upon Tyne: Cambridge Scholars Publishing.

Lucas, D. W. (ed. and comm.). 1968. *Aristotle: Poetics*. Oxford: Clarendon Press. Rpt. 2002.

Lucas, Tim. 2007. *Mario Bava: All the Colors of the Dark*. Cincinnati: Video Watchdog.

Lumholdt, Jan (ed.). 2003. *Lars von Trier: Interviews*. Jackson: University Press of Mississippi.

Lyne, R. O. A. M. 1986. *Further Voices in Vergil's* Aeneid. Oxford: Clarendon Press. Rpt. 1992.

"*Lysistrata*: Ehestreik gegen Atomtod." 1960. *Der Spiegel*, no. 51: 83–84.

"*Lysistrata*: Südlich der Gürtellinie." 1961. *Der Spiegel*, no. 4: 57–59.

MacCabe, Colin, Kathleen Murray, and Rick Warner (eds.). 2011. *True to the Spirit: Film Adaptation and the Question of Fidelity*. New York: Oxford University Press.

Macdonald, Dwight. 1953. "A Theory of Mass Culture." *Diogenes*, 1 no. 3: 1–17.

MacKinnon, Kenneth. 1986. *Greek Tragedy into Film*. Rpt. London: Routledge, 2013.

    2016. "Filmed Tragedy." In van Zyl Smit: 2016: 486–505.

Mamet, David. 2011. *The Secret Knowledge: On the Dismantling of American Culture*. New York: Sentinel. Rpt. 2012.

Marinetti, Filippo Tommaso. 2006. *Critical Writings*. Ed. Günter Berghaus; tr. Doug Thompson. New York: Farrar, Straus, and Giroux.

Marlowe, Christopher. 2003. *The Complete Plays*. Ed. Frank Romany and Robert Lindsey. London: Penguin.

Marquardt, Patricia. 1985. "Penelope ΠΟΛΥΤΡΟΠΟΣ." *American Journal of Philology*, 106: 32–48.

Martin, Adrian. 2008. Review of Verevis 2006. *The Velvet Light Trap*, 61: 60–62.

Martin, René (ed.). 1990. *Énée et Didon: Naissance, fonctionnement et survie d'un mythe*. Paris: Éditions du Centre Nationale de la Recherche Scientifique.

Marx, Leo. 1964. *The Machine in the Garden: Technology and the Pastoral Ideal in America*. New York: Oxford University Press. Rpt. 2000.

Mast, Gerald. 1979. *The Comic Mind: Comedy and the Movies*. 2nd ed. Chicago: University of Chicago Press.

Mastino, Attilio, and Paola Ruggeri. 1995. "*Claudia Augusti liberta Acte*, la liberta amata da Nerone ad Olbia." *Latomus*, 54: 513–544.

Mastronarde, Donald J. (ed. and comm.). 2002. *Euripides: Medea*. Cambridge: Cambridge University Press.

Matheson, Sue. 2016. *The Westerns and War Films of John Ford*. Lanham: Rowman & Littlefield.

Mavromoustakos, Platon. 2000. "Medea in Greece." In Hall, Macintosh, and Taplin 2000: 166–179.

McBride, Joseph [n. d.]. "Big Bugs! Big Bucks! Director Paul Verhoeven Rides 'B-Movie' *Starship Troopers* to a Timely Comeback." http://industrycentral.net/director_interviews/PV01.HTM.

    2001. *Searching for John Ford: A Life*. New York: St. Martin's. Rpt. 2003.

McBride, Joseph, and Michael Wilmington. 1974. *John Ford*. Rpt. New York: Da Capo, 1988.

McConnell, Robert L. 1976. "The Genesis and Ideology of *Gabriel over the White House*." *Cinema Journal*, 15 no. 2: 7–26.

McDonald, Forrest. 1985. *Novus Ordo Seclorum: The Intellectual Origins of the Constitution*. Lawrence: University Press of Kansas.

McDonald, Marianne, and Martin M. Winkler. 2001. "Michael Cacoyannis and Irene Papas on Greek Tragedy." In Winkler 2001a: 72–89.

McFarlane, Brian. 1996. *Novel to Film: An Introduction to the Theory of Adaptation*. Oxford: Clarendon Press.

McGilligan, Patrick. 2003. *Alfred Hitchcock: A Life in Darkness and Light*. New York: HarperCollins / Regan Books. Rpt. 2004.

McGinn, Colin. 2005. *The Power of Movies: How Screen and Mind Interact*. Rpt. New York: Vintage, 2007.

McGowan, Todd. 2014. *Spike Lee*. Urbana: University of Illinois Press.

McHugh, Mary R. 2013. "*Constantia memoriae*: The Reputation of Agrippina the Younger." In Morcillo and Knippschild 2013: 225–242.

Mendelsohn, Daniel. 2007. "Duty." *The New York Review of Books* (May 31): 37–39. Rpt. in Mendelsohn 2008: 138–149.

   2008. *How Beautiful It Is and How Easily It Can Be Broken: Essays*. New York: Harper. Rpt. 2009.

Mercouri, Melina. 1971. *I Was Born Greek*. Garden City: Doubleday.

Metelmann, Jörg (ed.). 2005. *Porno-Pop: Sex in der Oberflächenwelt*. Würzburg: Königshausen & Neumann.

Metz, Christian. 1974. *Film Language: A Semiotics of the Cinema*. Tr. Michael Taylor. Rpt. Chicago: University of Chicago Press, 1991.

Michelakis, Pantelis. 2013. *Greek Tragedy on Screen*. Oxford: Oxford University Press.

Miles, Gary B. 1999. "The *Aeneid* as Foundation Story." In Perkell 1999: 231–250 and 331–333.

Milfull, John (ed.). 1990. *The Attractions of Fascism: Social Psychology and Aesthetics of the "Triumph of the Right"*. New York: Berg.

Miller, Rebecca [n. d.]. "Zack Snyder and Frank Miller Talk About '300'." *About. com: Hollywood Movies*. http://movies.about.com/od/300/a/300movie 111506_3.htm.

Milnor, Kristina. 2008. "What I Learned as an Historical Consultant for *Rome*." In Cyrino 2008: 42–48.

Mimoso-Ruiz, Duarte-Nuno. 1981. "La *Medea* de Dreyer (Sur un manuscrit pour un film non realisé de 1965)." *Orbis Litterarum*, 36: 332–342.

   1996. "Le mythe de Médée au cinéma: L'incandescence de la violence à l'image." *Pallas*, 45: 251–268.

Moffat, Paul. 1916. "Aristotle and Tertullian." *Journal of Theological Studies*, 17: 170–171.

Montiglio, Silvia. 2013. *Love and Providence: Recognition in the Ancient Novel*. New York: Oxford University Press.

Moody, Rick. 2011. "Frank Miller and the Rise of Cryptofascist Hollywood." *The Guardian* (November 24). http://www.guardian.co.uk/culture/2011/nov/24/frank-miller-hollywood-fascism.

Moore, Roger. 2007. "*300* as Fascist Art." *Orlando Sentinel* (blog; March 7). http://web.archive.org/web/20070321024222/http://blogs.orlandosentinel.com/entertainment_movies_blog/2007/03/300_as_fascist_.html.

Moore, Timothy J., and Wolfgang Polleichtner (eds.). 2013. *Form und Bedeutung im lateinischen Drama / Form and Meaning in Latin Drama*. Trier: Wissenschaftlicher Verlag.

Morcillo, Marta García, and Silke Knippschild (eds.). 2013. *Seduction and Power: Antiquity in the Visual and Performing Arts*. London: Bloomsbury.

Morgan, J. R. 1994. "The *Aithiopika* of Heliodorus: Narrative as Riddle." In Morgan and Stoneman 1994: 97–113.

Morgan, J. R., and Richard Stoneman (eds.). 1994. *Greek Fiction: The Greek Novel in Context*. London: Routledge.

Morgan, Llewelyn. 2012. *The Buddhas of Bamiyan*. Rpt. Cambridge: Harvard University Press, 2015.

Morse, Ruth. 1996. *The Medieval Medea*. Cambridge and Rochester: Brewer. Rpt. 1998.

Most, Glenn W. (ed. and tr.). 2007. *Hesiod: The Shield, Catalogue of Women, Other Fragments*. Cambridge: Harvard University Press.

Mourlet, Michel. 1959. "Sur un art ignoré." *Cahiers du cinéma*, 98 (August): 23–37.

Müller, Karl Otfried. 1824. *Geschichten hellenischer Stämme und Städte*. Vols. 2–3: *Die Dorier*. Breslau: Max. 2nd ed., 1844.

Murphy, Cullen. 2007. *Are We Rome? The Fall of an Empire and the Fate of America*. Rpt. New York: Mariner Books, 2008.

Murray, Bruce Arthur, and Chris Wickham (eds.). 1992. *Framing the Past: The Historiography of German Cinema and Television*. Carbondale: Southern Illinois University Press.

Murray, G. N. 2007. "Zack Snyder, Frank Miller and Herodotus: Three Takes on the 300 Spartans." *Akroterion*, 52: 11–35.

Muth, Susanne. 2008. *Gewalt im Bild: Das Phänomen der medialen Gewalt im Athen des 6. und 5. Jahrhunderts v. Chr.* Berlin: De Gruyter.

Myrsiades, Kostas (ed.). 2011. *Early Recognition in Homer's* Odyssey. *College Literature*, 38 no. 2.

Nabokov, Peter (ed.). 1999. *Native American Testimony: A Chronicle of Indian-White Relations from Prophecy to the Present, 1942–2000*. Rev. ed. New York: Viking-Penguin.

Nash, Roderick Frazier. 2014. *Wilderness and the American Mind*. 5th ed. New Haven: Yale University Press.

Neill, Alex. 1996. "Empathy and (Film) Fiction." In Bordwell and Carroll 1996: 175–194.

Nelis, Jan. 2011. *From Ancient to Modern: The Myth of* romanità *During the* ventennio *fascista: The Written Imprint of Mussolini's Cult of the 'Third Rome'*. Brussels: Belgian Historical Institute at Rome.

Nikoloutsos, Konstantinos P. (ed.) 2013a. *Ancient Greek Women in Film*. Oxford: Oxford University Press.

　　2013b. "Between Family and the Nation: Gorgo in the Cinema." In Nikoloutsos 2013a: 255–278.

　　2013c. "Reviving the Past: Cinematic History and Popular Memory in *The 300 Spartans* (1962)." *Classical World*, 106 no. 2: 261–283.

　　2015. "From Text to Screen: Celluloid Helens and Female Stardom in the 1950s." *Cambridge Classical Journal*, 61: 70–90.

Nisbet, Gideon. 2008. *Ancient Greece in Film and Popular Culture*. 2nd ed. Exeter: Bristol Phoenix Press.

Norman, Larry F. 2011. *The Shock of the Ancient: Literature and History in Early Modern France*. Chicago: University of Chicago Press.

O'Grady, Gerald. 2001. "Angelopoulos's Philosophy of Film." In Fainaru 2001: 66–74.

Olson, S. Douglas (ed.). 2014. *Ancient Comedy and Reception: Essays in Honor of Jeffrey Henderson*. Berlin: De Gruyter.

Otto, Nina. 2009. Enargeia: *Untersuchung zur Charakteristik alexandrinischer Dichtung*. Wiesbaden: Steiner.

Page, Denys L. (ed. and comm.). 1938. *Euripides: Medea*. Oxford: Clarendon Press. Several corrected rpts.

Pages, Neil Christian, Mary Riehl, and Ingeborg Majer-O'Sickey (eds.). 2008. *Riefenstahl Screened: An Anthology of New Criticism*. New York: Continuum.

Paige, Nicholas. 2004. "Bardot and Godard in 1963 (Historicizing the Postmodern Image)." *Representations*, 88 no. 1: 1–25.

Palomar, Natalia. 2011. "*Uccellacci e uccellini*: Un doble giro coral más allá de Aristófanes." *Dionysus ex Machina* [electronic journal], 2: 537–563.

Papadimitropoulos, Loukas. 2012. "Suspense and Surprise in Achilles Tatius' *Leucippe and Clitophon*." *Classica et Mediaevalia*, 63: 161–187.

Parini, Jay (ed.). 1992. *Gore Vidal: Writer Against the Grain*. New York: Columbia University Press.

Paris Review Interviews, The. 2006. Vol. 1. New York: Picador.

Parry, Adam. 1963. "The Two Voices of Virgil's *Aeneid*." *Arion*, 2 no. 4: 66–80. Rpt. in Philip Hardie 1999: 49–64.

Pasolini, Pier Paolo. 1991. *Il vangelo secondo Matteo, Edipo re, Medea*. Milan: Garzanti.

Paul, William. 1991. "Charles Chaplin and the Annals of Anality." In Horton 1991: 109–130.

Peary, Gerald (ed.). 2001. *John Ford: Interviews*. Jackson: University Press of Mississippi.

Pease, A. S. (ed.). 1935. *Publi Vergili Maronis Aeneidos liber quartus*. Cambridge: Harvard University Press. Rpt. Darmstadt: Wissenschaftliche Buchgesellschaft, 1967.

Perkell, Christine (ed.). 1999. *Reading Vergil's* Aeneid: *An Interpretive Guide*. Norman: University of Oklahoma Press.

Perkins, V. F. 1972. *Film as Film: Understanding and Judging Movies*. Rpt. New York: Da Capo, 1993.

Perrault, Charles. 1692. *Parallèle des Anciens et des Modernes, en ce qui regarde les Arts et les Sciences: Dialogues: Avec le Poëme du Siecle de Louis le Grand, et une Epistre en Vers sur le Génie*. 2nd ed. Vol. 1. Paris: Coignard. One-volume rpt. of original four vols. (1692–1697): Geneva: Slatkine Reprints, 1971.

Perry, Dennis R. 2003. *Hitchcock and Poe: The Legacy of Delight and Terror*. Lanham: Scarecrow Press.

Petrain, David. 2014. *Homer in Stone: The* Tabulae Iliacae *in Their Roman Context*. Cambridge: Cambridge University Press.

Peucker, Brigitte. 2004. "The Fascist Choreography: Riefenstahl's Tableaux." *MODERNISM/modernity*, 11 no. 2: 279–297.

Phelan, James. 1996. *Narrative as Rhetoric: Technique, Audiences, Ethics, Technology*. Columbus: Ohio State University Press.

Pichon, Jean-Charles. 1962. *Saint Néron*. Paris: Laffont.

   1971. *Néron et le mystère des origines chrétiennes*. Paris: Laffont. Rev. ed. of Pichon 1962.

Plantinga, Carl [or Carl. R.]. 1997. *Rhetoric and Representation in Nonfiction Film*. Cambridge: Cambridge University Press. Rpt. 1999.

   2009. *Moving Viewers: American Film and the Spectator's Experience*. Berkeley: University of California Press.

Plantinga, Carl, and Greg M. Smith (eds.). 1999. *Passionate Views: Film, Cognition, and Emotion*. Baltimore: Johns Hopkins University Press.

Plett, Heinrich F. 2012. *Enargeia in Classical Antiquity and the Early Modern Age: The Aesthetics of Evidence*. Leiden: Brill.

Poague, Leland. 1988. "'All I Can See Is the Flags': *Fort Apache* and the Visibility of History." *Cinema Journal*, 27 no. 2: 8–26.

Poe, Edgar Allen. 1984a. *Poetry and Tales*. Ed. Patrick F. Quinn. New York: Viking / Library of America.

   1984b. "The Murders in the Rue Morgue." In Poe 1984a: 397–431.

   1984c. "The Mystery of Marie Rogêt." In Poe 1984a: 506–554.

Pollitt, J. J. 1974. *The Ancient View of Greek Art: Criticism, History, and Terminology*. New Haven: Yale University Press.

Pomeroy, Arthur J. 2004. "The Vision of a Fascist Rome in *Gladiator*." In Winkler 2004a: 111–123.

   2008. *'Then It Was Destroyed by the Volcano': The Ancient World in Film and on Television*. London: Duckworth.

Poole, Ralph J. 2013. "'Everybody Loves a Muscle Boi [*sic*]': Homos, Heroes, and Foes in Post-0/11 Spoofs of the 300 Spartans." In Renger and Solomon 2013: 95–121.

Powell, Anton. 2004. "The Women of Sparta – and of Other Greek Cities – at War." In Figueira 2004: 137–150.

Powell, Anton, and Stephen Hodkinson (eds.). 2002. *Sparta: Beyond the Mirage*. London: Classical Press of Wales / Duckworth.

Preiß, Heinz (ed.). 1939. *Adolf Hitler in Franken: Reden aus der Kampfzeit*. [Nuremberg].

"Press Violent About Film's Violence, Prod Sam Peckinpah Following 'Bunch'." 1969. *Variety* (July 2): 15. Rpt. in Prince 1999: 209–212.

Prieto, Alberto. 2003. "Penélope en el cine." In de Oliveira 2003: 411–421.

Prince, Stephen. 1998. *Savage Cinema: Sam Peckinpah and the Rise of Ultraviolent Movies*. Austin: University of Texas Press.

  (ed.). 1999. *Sam Peckinpah's* The Wild Bunch. Cambridge: Cambridge University Press.

  (ed.). 2000a. *Screening Violence*. New Brunswick: Rutgers University Press.

  2000b. "Graphic Violence in the Cinema: Origins, Aesthetic Design, and Social Effects." In Prince 2000a: 1–44.

Prolo, Maria Adriana. 1951. *Storia del cinema muto italiano*. Vol. 1. Milan: Poligono.

Provenzano, Tom. 2008. "Sissystrata." *L. A. Weekly* (August 28). http://www.la weekly.com/2008–08-28/calendar/sissystrata.

Pucci, Pietro. 1980. *The Violence of Pity in Euripides'* Medea. Ithaca: Cornell University Press.

Pundt, Christian. 2002. "Konflikte um die Selbstbeschreibung der Gesellschaft: Der Diskurs über Privatheit im Fernsehen." In Weiß and Gröbel 2002: 247–414.

  2005. "Spot an, Lust aus: Wie der Sex ins Fernsehen kam und darin verschwand." In Metelmann 2005: 167–182.

Quinn, Kenneth. 1969. *Virgil's* Aeneid: *A Critical Description*. 2nd ed. Ann Arbor: University of Michigan Press.

Quint, David. 1993. *Epic and Empire: Politics and Generic Form from Virgil to Milton*. Princeton: Princeton University Press.

Rackham, H. (tr.). 1942. *Cicero*. Vol. 4: De oratore *Book III*, De fato, Paradoxa Stoicorum, De partitione oratoria. Cambridge: Harvard University Press / London: Heinemann. Several rpts.

Rahe, Paul A. 2015. *The Grand Strategy of Classical Sparta: The Persian Challenge*. New Haven: Yale University Press. Rpt. 2017.

  2016. *The Spartan Regime: Its Character, Origins and Grand Strategy*. New Haven: Yale University Press.

Rainey, Lawrence (ed.). 2005. *The Annotated Waste Land with Eliot's Contemporary Prose*. New Haven: Yale University Press.

Rawson, Elizabeth. 1969. *The Spartan Tradition in European Thought.* Oxford: Clarendon Press.

Ray, Robert, and Leland Poague. 1988. "Dialogue: Robert Ray Responds to Leland Poague's "'All I Can See Is the Flags": *Fort Apache* and the Visibility of History' (*Cinema Journal*, Winter 1988)." *Cinema Journal*, 27 no. 3: 45–50.

Ready, Jonathan L. 2014. "ATU 974 *The Homecoming Husband*, the Returns of Odysseus, and the End of *Odyssey* 21.'" *Arethusa*, 47: 265–285.

Reardon, B. P. (ed.). 1989. *Collected Ancient Greek Novels.* Berkeley: University of California Press. Rpt. 2007.

Rebello, Stephen. 1990. *Alfred Hitchcock and the Making of* Psycho. Rpt. New York: St. Martin's, 1998.

Rebenich, Stefan. 2002. "From Thermopylae to Stalingrad: The Myth of Leonidas in German Historiography." In Powell and Hodkinson 2002: 323–349.

Redonet, Fernando Lillo. 2003. "Virgilio y Catulo en el cine y la television." *Cuadernos de Filologia Clásica – Estudios Latinos*, 23: 437–452.

  2008. "Sparta and Ancient Greece in *The 300 Spartans*." In Berti and García Morcillo 2008: 117–130.

Reece, Steve. 1994. "The Cretan Odyssey: A Lie Truer Than Truth." *American Journal of Philology*, 115: 157–173.

Reinhold, Meyer. 1984. *Classica Americana: The Greek and Roman Heritage in the United States.* Detroit: Wayne State University Press.

Renger, Almut-Barbara, and Jon Solomon (eds.). 2013. *Ancient Worlds in Film and Television: Gender and Politics.* Leiden: Brill.

Rentschler, Eric. 1996. *The Ministry of Illusion: Nazi Cinema and Its Afterlife.* Cambridge: Harvard University Press.

  2008. "A Founding Myth and a Master Text: *The Blue Light* (1932)." In Pages, Riehl, and Majer-O'Sickey 2008: 151–178.

Revermann, Martin. 2010. "On Misunderstanding the *Lysistrata*, Productively." In Stuttard 2010: 70–79.

Rich, Frank. 2006. *The Greatest Story Ever Sold: The Decline and Fall of Truth in Bush's America.* New York: Penguin Press. Rpt. 2007.

Richard, Carl J. 1994. *The Founders and the Classics: Greece, Rome, and the American Enlightenment.* Cambridge: Harvard University Press. Rpt. 1996.

  2009. *The Golden Age of the Classics in America: Greece, Rome, and the Antebellum United States.* Cambridge: Harvard University Press.

Richards, Jeffrey. 2008. *Hollywood's Ancient Worlds.* London: Continuum, 2008.

  2014. "Sir Ridley Scott and the Rebirth of the Historical Epic." In Elliott 2014: 19–35.

Richardson, Nicholas. 1993. *The Iliad: A Commentary.* Vol. 6: *Books 21–24.* Cambridge: Cambridge University Press. Rpt. 2000.

Robson, James. 2006. *Humour, Obscenity and Aristophanes.* Tübingen: Narr.

  2009. *Aristophanes: An Introduction.* London: Duckworth.

Roche, Helen. 2012a. "'Go, Tell the Prussians': The Spartan Paradigm in Prussian Military Thought During the Long Nineteenth Century." *New Voices in Classical Reception Studies* [electronic journal], 7: 25–39.

2012b. "'In Sparta fühlte ich mich wie in einer deutschen Stadt' (Goebbels): The Leaders of the Third Reich and the Spartan Nationalist Paradigm." In Horan, Rash, and Wildmann 2012: 91–114.

2012c. "*Spartanische Pimpfe*: The Importance of Sparta in the Educational Ideology of the Adolf Hitler Schools." In Hodkinson and Morris 2012: 315–342.

2013. *Sparta's German Children: The Ideal of Ancient Sparta in the Royal Prussian Cadet-Corps, 1818–1920, and in National Socialist Elite Schools (the Napolas), 1933–1945.* Swansea: Classical Press of Wales.

Rodighiero, Andrea. 2003. "'*Ne pueros coram populo Medea trucidet*': Alcuni modi dell'infanticidio." In Vox 2003: 115–159.

2009. "Cinema e mito classico." In Gibellini (gen. ed.) 2009: 563–599.

Rodrigues, Nuno Simões. 2012. "Helena de Troya en el séptimo arte." *Ámbitos*, 2nd ser., 27: 27–37.

Roosevelt, Theodore. 1904. *The Wilderness Hunter*. New York: The Review of Reviews Co. (Statesman Edition).

Rosen, Marjorie. 1973. *Popcorn Venus: Women, Movies, and the American Dream*. New York: Coward, McCann, and Geoghegan.

Rothman, William. 1982. *Hitchcock – The Murderous Gaze*. Cambridge: Harvard University Press. Rpt. 2002.

Russell, Donald A. (ed. and tr.). 2001. *Quintilian: The Orator's Education*. Vol. 3: *Books 6–8*. Cambridge: Harvard University Press.

Russo, Joseph. 1992. "Books XVII-XX." In Russo, Fernández-Galiano, and Heubeck 1992: 3–127.

Russo, Joseph, Manuel Fernández-Galiano, and Alfred Heubeck. 1992. *A Commentary on Homer's Odyssey*. Vol. 3: *Books XVII–XXIV*. Oxford: Clarendon Press.

Rutherford R. B. (ed.). 1992. *Homer: Odyssey Books XIX and XX*. Cambridge: Cambridge University Press.

2015. "*Lysistrata* and Female Song." *The Classical Quarterly*, 65: 60–68.

Ryan, Marie-Laure (ed.). 2004. *Narrative Across Media: The Languages of Storytelling*. Lincoln: University of Nebraska Press.

Ryan, Marie-Laure, and Jan-Noël Thon (eds.). 2014. *Storyworlds Across Media: Toward a Media-Conscious Narratology*. Lincoln: University of Nebraska Press.

Sarris, Andrew (ed.). 1967. *Interviews with Film Directors*. Rpt. New York: Avon, 1972.

1975. *The John Ford Movie Mystery*. Bloomington: Indiana University Press.

Sayers, Dorothy L. 1947a. *Unpopular Opinions: Twenty-One Essays*. New York: Harcourt, Brace.

Sayers, Dorothy L. 1947b. "Aristotle on Detective Fiction." In Sayers 1947a: 222–236.

Schechter, Joel. 1994. *Satiric Impersonations: From Aristophanes to the Guerilla Girls*. Carbondale: Southern Illinois University Press.

Schefold, Karl. 1997. *Die Bildnisse der antiken Dichter, Redner und Denker*. 2nd ed. Basel: Schwab.

Schenk, Irmbert. 1994. "Geschichte im NS-Film: Kritische Anmerkungen zur film-wissenschaftlichen Suggestion der Identität von Propaganda und Wirkung." *montage/av*, 3 no. 2: 73–98.

Scherer, Margaret R. 1964. *The Legends of Troy in Art and Literature*. New York and London: Phaidon Press / Metropolitan Museum of Art.

Schierl, Petra. 2006. *Die Tragödien des Pacuvius*. Berlin: De Gruyter.

Scholes, Robert, and Robert Kellogg. 1966. *The Nature of Narrative*. New York: Oxford University Press.

Scholes, Robert, James Phelan, and Robert Kellogg. 2006. *The Nature of Narrative*. New York: Oxford University Press.

Schrag, Valerie. 2012. *Aristophanes: Lysistrata*. In Kick 2012: 83–96.

Schulte-Sasse, Linda. 1991. "Leni Riefenstahl's Feature Films and the Question of a Fascist Aesthetic." *Cultural Critique*, 19: 123–148. Rpt. in Murray and Wickham 1992: 140–166.

Schwartz, Barth David. 1992. *Pasolini Requiem*. Rpt. New York: Vintage, 1995.

Schwinge, Ernst-Richard. 2004. "Wer tötete Medeas Kinder? Einige Bemerkungen zu Euripides, Kreophon und Christa Wolf." In Bierl, Schmitt, and Willi 2004: 203–211.

Scodel, Ruth. 1999. *Credible Impossibilities: Conventions and Strategies of Verisimilitude in Homer and Greek Tragedy*. Stuttgart: Teubner.

Scodel, Ruth, and Anja Bettenworth. 2009. *Whither* Quo Vadis? *Sienkiewicz's Novel in Film and Television*. Malden: Wiley-Blackwell.

Seeßlen, Georg. 1994. *Tanz den Adolf Hitler: Faschismus in der populären Kultur*. Berlin: Edition TIAMAT.

  1996. *Natural Born Nazis* [var.: *Nazi*]: *Faschismus in der populären Kultur*. Berlin: Edition TIAMAT.

Seidensticker, Bernd. 1982. *Palintonos Harmonia: Studien zu komischen Elementen in der griechischen Tragödie*. Göttingen: Vandenhoeck & Ruprecht.

Seidensticker, Bernd, and Martin Vöhler (eds.). 2006. *Gewalt und Ästhetik: Zur Gewalt und ihrer Darstellung in der griechischen Klassik*. Berlin: De Gruyter.

Segal, Charles P. 1962. "Gorgias and the Psychology of the Logos." *Harvard Studies in Classical Philology*, 66: 99–155.

Serafim, Andreas. 2015. "Making the Audience: Ekphrasis and Rhetorical Strategy in Demosthenes 18 and 19." *The Classical Quarterly*, 65: 96–108.

Server, Lee. 1994. *Sam Fuller: Film Is a Battleground: A Critical Study, with Interviews, a Filmography and a Bibliography*. Jefferson: McFarland.

Settembrini, Domenico. 2003. "Fascismo e modernità." In Campi 2003: 373–406.

Seydor, Paul. 1997. *Peckinpah: The Western Films: A Reconsideration*. Urbana: University of Illinois Press. Rpt. 1999.

Seymour, Gene. 2007. "On the Field of This Battle, War Is Swell." *Newsday* (March 9): B 08.

Shapiro, Susan O. 2013. "Pasolini's *Medea*: A Twentieth-Century Tragedy." In Nikoloutsos 2013a: 95–116.

Shelley, Peter. 2011. *Jules Dassin: The Life and Films*. Jefferson: McFarland.

Sheppard, Anne. 2014. *The Poetics of Phantasia: Imagination in Ancient Aesthetics*. London: Bloomsbury.

Shields, John C. 2001. *The American Aeneas: Classical Origins of the American Self*. Knoxville: University of Tennessee Press.

Sider, David. 1980. "*Credo quia absurdum?*" *Classical World*, 73: 417–419.

Sidney, Sir Philip. 2002. *An Apology for Poetry* or *The Defense of Poesy*. Ed. Geoffrey Shepherd. 3rd ed. Ed. R. W. Maslen. Manchester: Manchester University Press.

Sidwell, Keith. 2009. *Aristophanes the Democrat: The Politics of Satirical Comedy during the Peloponnesian War*. Cambridge: Cambridge University Press.

Simkin, Stevie. 2006. *Early Modern Tragedy and the Cinema of Violence*. Basingstoke and New York: Palgrave Macmillan.

Simms, W. Gilmore. 1856. *Charlemont; or The Pride of the Village: A Tale of Kentucky*. New York: Redfield.

Skerry, Philip J. 2009. *Psycho in the Shower: The History of Cinema's Most Famous Scene*. New York: Continuum.

Slane, Andrea. 2001. *A Not So Foreign Affair: Fascism, Sexuality, and the Cultural Rhetoric of American Democracy*. Durham: Duke University Press.

Slater, Niall W. 1985. *Plautus in Performance: The Theatre of the Mind*. Princeton: Princeton University Press. Rpt. 1987.

   2002. *Spectator Politics: Metatheatre and Performance in Aristophanes*. Philadelphia: University of Pennsylvania Press.

Sloan, Jane. 2008. "Making the Scene Together: Mai Zetterling's *Flikorna* [*sic*] / *The Girls* (1968) and Aristophanes' *Lysistrata*." *Quarterly Review of Film and Video*, 25: 97–106.

Smethurst, Mae J. 2014. "Interview with Miyagi Satoshi." *Publications of the Modern Language Association*, 129: 843–846.

Smith, Bryan. 2015. "Spike Lee Sounds Off on *Chi-Raq*, Gun Violence, and Rahm." *Chicago Magazine* (October 22). http://www.chicagomag.com/Chicago-Magazine/December-2015/Spike-Lee-Chiraq/.

Smith, Henry Nash. 1950. *Virgin Land: The American West as Symbol and Myth*. Cambridge: Harvard University Press. Rpt. 1994.

Smith, Jean Edward. 2016. *Bush*. New York: Simon & Schuster.

Smith, Karen. 2011. "Sex Strike Brings Peace to Filipino Village" (CNN report; September 19). http://www.cnn.com/2011/WORLD/asiapcf/09/19/philippines.sex.strike/.

Smith III, Joseph W. 2009. *The* Psycho *File: A Comprehensive Guide to Hitchcock's Classic Shocker*. Jefferson: McFarland.

Snell, Bruno. 1973. "Was die Alten von der schönen Helena dachten." In Hüppauf and Sternberger 1973: 5–22.

Solomon, Jon. 2015. "'Oedipus . . . The Structure of Funny': Allusions to Greek Tragedy in Contemporary Cinema." *Illinois Classical Studies*, 40: 373–389.

Sondheim, Stephen. 2010. *Finishing the Hat: Collected Lyrics (1954–1981) with Attendant Comments, Principles, Heresies, Grudges, Whines and Anecdotes*. New York: Knopf.

Sontag, Susan. 1980a. *Under the Sign of Saturn*. Rpt. New York: Picador, 2002.
    1980b. "Fascinating Fascism." In Sontag 1980a: 73–105.

Spina, Luigi. 2005. "L'*enárgheia* prima del cinema: Parole per vedere." *Dionysus*, 4: 196–209.

Squire, Michael. 2011a. *The Art of the Body: Antiquity and Its Legacy*. London: Tauris / New York: Oxford University Press.
    2011b. *The* Iliad *in a Nutshell: Visualizing Epic on the* Tabulae Iliacae. Oxford: Oxford University Press. Rpt. 2016.
    (ed.). 2016. *Sight and the Ancient Senses*. London and New York: Routledge.

Sragow, Michael. 2000. "Black Like Spike." *Salon* [electronic magazine]: October 26. Rpt. in Fuchs 2002: 189–198.

Stack, Oswald. 1970. *Pasolini on Pasolini*. Bloomington: Indiana University Press.

Stahl, Hans-Peter. 2016. *Poetry Underpinning Power: Vergil's* Aeneid: *The Epic for Emperor Augustus*. Swansea: Classical Press of Wales.

Stam, Robert. 2005. *Literature Through Film: Realism, Magic, and the Art of Adaptation*. Oxford: Blackwell.

Stanford, W. B. 1954. *The Ulysses Theme: A Study in the Adaptability of a Traditional Hero*. Oxford: Blackwell. Several rpts.

Stehlíková, Eva. 2012. "Jules Dassin Meets Greek Tragedy." *Eirene*, 48: 143–146.

Steiner, Deborah (ed.). 2010. *Homer: Odyssey Books XVII and XVIII*. Cambridge: Cambridge University Press.

Stephan, Inge. 2006. *Medea: Multimediale Karriere einer mythologischen Figur*. Cologne: Böhlau.

Stephens, Susan A. (ed., tr., and comm.). 2015. *Callimachus: The Hymns*. New York: Oxford University Press.

Stevens, Dana. 2007. "A Movie Only a Spartan Could Love: The Battle Epic *300*." *Slate* [electronic magazine]: March 8. http://web.archive.org/web/200703150 93130/http://www.slate.com/id/2161 450/.

Stöckl, Ula. 1985. "The Medea Myth in Contemporary Cinema." *Film Criticism*, 10 no. 1: 47–51.

Strasberg, Lee. 1987. *A Dream of Passion: The Development of the Method*. Ed. Evangeline Morphos. Boston: Little, Brown. Several rpts.

Strug, Cordell. 2008. *Lament of an Audience on the Death of an Artist (1985)*. St. Paul: Ytterli Press.

Studlar, Gaylin, and Matthew Bernstein (eds.). 2001. *John Ford Made Westerns: Filming the Legend in the Sound Era.* Bloomington: Indiana University Press.

Stuttard, David (ed.). 2010. *Looking at Lysistrata: Eight Essays and a New Version of Aristophanes' Provocative Comedy.* London: Bristol Classical Press.

Symons, Julian. 1985. *Bloody Murder: From the Detective Story to the Crime Novel.* 2nd ed. New York: Viking.

Taaffe, Lauren K. 1993. *Aristophanes and Women.* London: Routledge.

Tapper, Michael. 2003. "A Romance in Decomposition." In Lumholdt 2003: 71–80.

Tatum, James. 1992. "The *Romanitas* of Gore Vidal." In Parini 1992: 199–220.

Taylor, Richard (ed. and tr.). 1988. *S. M. Eisenstein: Selected Works.* Vol. 1: *Writings, 1922–34.* Rpt. London: Tauris, 2010.

Tedeschi, Gennaro. 2010. *Commento alla* Medea *di Euripide.* Trieste: Edizioni Università di Trieste. http://hdl.handle.net/10077/5147.

Telemann [pseudonym]. 1960. "Verpulvert." *Der Spiegel*, no. 51: 84.

    1961. "Münster aus Stein." *Der Spiegel*, no. 5: 52.

Thomas, Richard F. 2015. "Aeneas in Baghdad." In Günther 2015: 453–473.

Thomsen, Christian Braad. 2003. "Control and Chaos." In Lumholdt 2003: 106–116.

Todini, Umberto. 1985. "Pasolini and the Afro-Greeks." *Stanford Italian Review*, 5 no. 2: 219–222.

Todorov, Tzvetan. 1978a. *The Poetics of Prose.* Tr. Richard Howard. Ithaca: Cornell University Press. Rpt. 1992.

    1978b. "An Introduction to Verisimilitude." In Todorov 1978a: 81–88.

Tolstikov, Vladimir, and Mikhail Treister. 1996. *The Gold of Troy: Searching for Homer's Fabled City.* Tr. Christina Sever and Mila Bonnichsen. New York: Abrams.

Tomasso, Vincent. 2011. "Hard-Boiled Hot Gates: Making the Classical Past Other in Frank Miller's *Sin City*." In Kovacs and Marshall 2011: 145–158.

    2013. "Gorgo at the Limits of Liberation in Zack Snyder's *300* (2007)." In Cyrino 2013: 113–126.

Torrance, Isabelle. 2010. "Retrospectively Medea: The Infanticidal Mother in Alejandro Amenábar's Film *The Others*." In Bartels and Simon 2010: 124–134.

Torres, José. 2014. "Teiresias, the Theban Seer." *Trends in Classics*, 6: 339–356.

Toubiana, Serge, and Frédéric Strauss. 2001. "Landscape in the Mist." In Fainaru 2001: 60–65.

Tovar Paz, Francisco Javier. 2002. "Medea de Séneca en *Así es la vida* (2000), filme de Arturo Ripstein." *Revista de Estudios Latinos*, 2: 169–195.

Trapp, M. B. 1997. *Maximus of Tyre: The Philosophical Orations.* Oxford: Clarendon Press.

Troy, William. 1933. "Fascism over Hollywood." *The Nation*, 136: 482–483.

Truffaut, François, with Helen G. Scott. 1984. *Hitchcock.* Rev. ed. New York: Simon & Schuster.

Turner, Susanne. 2009. "'Only Spartan Women Give Birth to Real Men': Zack Snyder's *300* and the Male Nude." In Lowe and Shahabudin 2009: 128–149.

Usher, H. J. K. 1977. Review of Alexis 1975. *Classical Review*, n. s. 27: 279–281.

Valverde García, Alejandro. 2010. "'Lisístrata' (1972) de Yorgos Dservulakos, una denuncia política con humor, sexo y budsuki." *Estudios neogriegos*, 13: 189–201.

2011. "Elementos aristofánicos in *The Day the Fish Came Out:* La ciudad del futuro y el fin del mundo según Michael Cacoyannis." In Ventura 2011: 241–254.

2012. "Grecia antigua en el cine griego." *Thamyris*, n. s. 3: 81–101.

Van Fleteren, Frederick. 1999. "*Acies mentis* (Gaze of the Mind)." In Fitzgerald 1999: 5–6.

Van Hoorn, Willem. 1972. *As Images Unwind: Ancient and Modern Theories of Visual Perception*. Amsterdam: University Press Amsterdam.

Van Steen, Gonda A. H. 2000. *Venom in Verse: Aristophanes in Modern Greece*. Princeton: Princeton University Press.

Van Zyl Smit, Betine (ed.). 2016. *A Handbook to the Reception of Greek Drama*. Malden: Wiley-Blackwell.

Vance, William L. 1986. *America's Rome*. Vol. 1: *Classical Rome*. New Haven: Yale University Press. Rpt. 1989.

Ventura, Francisco Salvador (ed.). 2011. *Cine y ciudades*. Santa Cruz de Tenerife: Intramar Ediciones.

Verdone, Mario, and Leonardo Autera (eds.). 1964. Antologia di *Bianco e Nero*. Vol. 3. Ed. Leonardo Autera: *Scritti storici e critici*. Pt. 1. Rome: Edizioni di Bianco e Nero.

Verevis, Constantine. 2006. *Film Remakes*. Edinburgh: Edinburgh University Press.

Vernant, Jean-Pierre. 1991a. *Mortals and Immortals: Collected Essays*. Ed. Froma I. Zeitlin. Princeton: Princeton University Press. Rpt. 1992.

1991b. "Between Shame and Glory: The Identity of the Young Spartan Warrior." Tr. Deborah Lyons. In Vernant 1991a: 220–243.

1991c. "The Birth of Images." Tr. Froma I. Zeitlin. In Vernant 1991a: 164–185.

Vidal, Gore. 1992. *Screening History*. Cambridge: Harvard University Press.

1993a. *United States: Essays 1952–1992*. New York: Random House. Rpt. 1994.

1993b. "At Home in Washington, D.C." In Vidal 1993a: 1057–1060.

Vita, Antonio Aguilera. 2011. "Las dos Medeas de Arturo Ripstein." *Metakinema* [electronic journal], 9. http://www.metakinema.es/metakineman9s3a1_Antonio_Aguilera_Vita_Medea_Ripstein.html.

Von Vacano, Otto Wilhelm (ed.). 1940. *Sparta: Der Lebenskampf einer nordischen Herrenschicht*. Kempten: Allgäuer Druck- und Verlagsanstalt.

Vout, Caroline. 2012. "Unfinished Business: Re-Viewing Medea in Roman Painting." In Boyle 2012: 119–143.

Vox, Onofrio (ed.). 2003. *Ricerche euripidee*. Lecce: Pensa multimedia.

Wagner, Walter. 1975. *You Must Remember This*. New York: Putnam.

2001. "One More Hurrah." In Peary 2001: 151–159.

Walker, Andrew D. 1993. "*Enargeia* and the Spectator in Greek Historiography." *Transactions of the American Philological Association*, 123: 353–377.

Walsh, Jill Paton. 2005. "*The Poetics* of Aristotle as a Practical Guide." *The Lion and the Unicorn*, 29: 211–221.

Walsh, Philip (ed.). 2016. *Brill's Companion to the Reception of Aristophanes*. Leiden: Brill.

Warmington, B. H. 1969. *Nero: Reality and Legend*. London: Chatto & Windus / New York: Norton. Rpt. 1981.

Waswo, Richard. 1997. *The Founding Legend of Western Civilization: From Virgil to Vietnam*. Hanover: University Press of New England / Wesleyan University Press.

Watt, Roderick H. 1985. "'Wanderer, kommst du nach Sparta': History Through Propaganda into Literary Commonplace." *Modern Language Review*, 80: 871–883.

Webb, Ruth. 1997. "Imagination and the Arousal of the Emotions in Greco-Roman Rhetoric." In Braund and Gill 1997: 112–127.

  2016a. "Sight and Insight: Theorizing Vision, Emotion and Imagination in Ancient Rhetoric." In Squire 2016: 205–219.

  2016b. *Ekphrasis, Imagination and Persuasion in Ancient Rhetorical Theory and Practice*. New York: Routledge. Originally 2009.

Weiland, Jonah. 2007. "'300' Post-Game: One on One with Zack Snyder." *Comic Book Resources* [electronic journal]: March 14. http://www.comicbookresour ces.com/?page=article&old=1&id=9982.

Weiß, Ralph, and Jo Gröbel (eds.). 2002. *Privatheit im öffentlichen Raum: Medienhandeln zwischen Individualisierung und Entgrenzung*. Opladen: Leske + Budrich.

Weisser, Thomas. 1992. *Spaghetti Westerns: The Good, the Bad and the Violent: A Comprehensive, Illustrated Filmography of 558 Eurowesterns and Their Personnel, 1961–1977*. Jefferson: McFarland. Rpt. 2005.

Weitz, Eric. 2009. *The Cambridge Introduction to Comedy*. Cambridge: Cambridge University Press.

West, M. L. (tr.). 1993. *Greek Lyric Poetry*. Oxford: Oxford University Press. Rpt. 1994.

Wetmore, Kevin J. 2013. *Black Medea: Adaptations for Modern Plays*. Amherst: Cambria Press.

  2014. "She (Don't) Gotta Have It: African-American Reception of *Lysistrata*." In Olson 2014: 786–796.

Whitmarsh, Tim. 2011. *Narrative and Identity in the Ancient Greek Novel: Returning Romance*. Cambridge: Cambridge University Press.

Whittaker, C. R. 2000. "Frontiers." In Bowman, Garnsey, and Rathbone 2000: 293–319.

Williams, William Appleman. 1980. *Empire as a Way of Life: An Essay on the Causes and Character of America's Present Predicament, Along with a Few Thoughts About an Alternative.* Oxford: Oxford University Press. Rpt. 1982.

Wills, Garry. 1984. *Cincinnatus: George Washington and the Enlightenment.* Garden City: Doubleday.

Wilson, Edmund. 1940. "The Californians: Storm and Steinbeck." *The New Republic,* 103 no. 24 (December 9): 784–787.

  1950a. *Classics and Commercials: A Literary Chronicle of the Forties.* New York: Farrar, Straus.

  1950b. "The Boys in the Back Room: John Steinbeck." In Wilson 1950a: 35–45.

Wiltshire, Susan Ford. 1992. *Greece, Rome, and the Bill of Rights.* Norman: University of Oklahoma Press.

Winkler, John J. 1982. "The Mendacity of Calasiris and the Narrative Strategy of Heliodorus' *Aithiopika.*" In Winkler, John J., and Williams 1982: 93–158.

  1985. *Auctor & Actor: A Narratological Reading of Apuleius's* The Golden Ass. Berkeley: University of California Press. Rpt. 1991.

  1990. *The Constraints of Desire: The Anthropology of Sex and Desire in Ancient Greece.* New York and London: Routledge.

Winkler, John J., and Gordon Williams (eds.). 1982. *Yale Classical Studies.* Vol. 27: *Later Greek Literature.* Cambridge: Cambridge University Press.

Winkler, Martin M. 1985. "Classical Mythology and the Western Film." *Comparative Literature Studies,* 22: 516–540.

  1988. "Mythologische Motive im amerikanischen Western-Film." In Kühnel et al. 1988: 563–578.

  1996. "Homeric *kleos* and the Western Film." *Syllecta Classica,* 7: 43–54.

  1998. "The Roman Empire in American Cinema After 1945." *Classical Journal,* 93: 167–196. Rev. in Joshel, Malamud, and McGuire, Jr. 2001: 50–76.

  1999. "Achilles Tatius and Heliodorus: Some 1998 Parallels." *Petronian Society Newsletter,* 29 no. 1–2: 6–7.

  2000–2001. "The Cinematic Nature of the Opening Scene of Heliodorus' *Ai-thi-o-pi-ka.*" *Ancient Narrative,* 1: 161–184.

  (ed.). 2001a. *Classical Myth and Culture in the Cinema.* New York: Oxford University Press.

  2001b. "Introduction." In Winkler 2001a: 3–22.

  2001c. "Tragic Features in John Ford's *The Searchers.*" In Winkler 2001a: 118–147.

  (ed.). 2004a. Gladiator: *Film and History.* Oxford: Blackwell.

  2004b. "Homer's *Iliad* and John Ford's *The Searchers.*" In Eckstein and Lehman 2004: 145–170.

  (ed.). 2006a. Troy: *From Homer's* Iliad *to Hollywood Epic.* Oxford: Blackwell.

  2006b. "The *Iliad* and the Cinema." In Winkler 2006a: 43–67.

  2009a. *Cinema and Classical Texts: Apollo's New Light.* Cambridge: Cambridge University Press. Rpt. 2012.

2009b. *The Roman Salute: Cinema, History, Ideology.* Columbus: Ohio State University Press.

2010. "Leaves of Homeric Storytelling: Wolfgang Petersen's *Troy* and Franco Rossi's *Odissea*" / "Foglie di narrazione omerica: *Troy* di Wolfgang Petersen e l'*Odissea* di Franco Rossi." In Cavallini 2010: 153–177.

2013. "Three Queens: Helen, Penelope, and Dido in Franco Rossi's *Odissea* and *Eneide.*" In Morcillo and Knippschild 2013: 133–153.

2014a. "Achilles Tatius and Heliodorus: Between Aristotle and Hitchcock." In Cueva and Byrne 2014: 570–583.

2014b. "Aristophanes in the Cinema; or, The Metamorphoses of *Lysistrata.*" In Olson 2014: 894–944.

2015a. "Cinemetamorphosis: Toward a Cinematic Theory of Classical Narrative." *Dionysus ex Machina* [electronic journal], 6: 216–238.

(ed.). 2015b. *Return to* Troy: *New Essays on the Hollywood Epic.* Leiden: Brill.

2015c. "Introduction: *Troy* Revisited." In Winkler 2015b: 1–15.

2015d. "*Troy* and the Cinematic Afterlife of Homeric Gods." In Winkler 2015b: 108–164.

2016. "*Helenê kinêmatographikê*; or, Is This the Face That Launched a Thousand Films?" *Nuntius Antiquus*, 12 no. 1: 215–257.

Wood, Robin. 1971. "Shall We Gather at the River? The Late Films of John Ford." *Film Comment*, 7: 8–17. Rpt. in Caughie 1981: 83–101, Studlar and Bernstein 2001: 23–41.

2002. *Hitchcock's Films Revisited.* Rev. ed. New York: Columbia University Press.

2013. *Ingmar Bergman.* New ed. Ed. Barry Keith Grant. Detroit: Wayne State University Press.

Woodman, A. J. 1989. "Virgil the Historian: *Aeneid* 8.626–62 and Livy." In Diggle, Hall, and Jocelyn: 132–145. Rpt. in Woodman 2012: 147–161.

2012. *From Poetry to History: Selected Papers.* Oxford: Oxford University Press.

Worthington, Ian (ed.). 2007. *A Companion to Greek Rhetoric.* Malden: Wiley-Blackwell. Rpt. 2010.

Wright, David H. 1993. *The Vatican Vergil: A Masterpiece of Late Antique Art.* Berkeley: University of California Press.

Wroe, Ann. 1999. *Pontius Pilate.* London: Cape / New York: Random House. Rev. ed. 2001.

Yanal, Robert J. 2005. *Hitchcock as Philosopher.* Jefferson: McFarland.

Zanker, G. 1981. "Enargeia in the Ancient Criticism of Poetry." *Rheinisches Museum für Philologie*, 124: 297–311.

Zanker, Paul. 1995. *The Mask of Socrates: The Image of the Intellectual in Antiquity.* Tr. Alan Shapiro. Berkeley: University of California Press.

Zetterling, Mai. 1985. *All Those Tomorrows.* London: Cape.

Ziemer, Gregor. 1941. *Education for Death: The Making of the Nazi.* London: Oxford University Press.

Zimmermann, Martin (ed.). 2009. *Extreme Formen von Gewalt in Bild und Text des Altertums.* Munich: Utz.

Ziogas, Ioannis. 2014. "Sparse Spartan Verse: Filling Gaps in the Thermopylae Epigram." *Ramus,* 43: 115–133.

Index

CPSIA information can be obtained
at www.ICGtesting.com
Printed in the USA
LVHW101837290119
605669LV00016B/354/P